WORLD
CIVILIZATIONS

W·W·NORTON & COMPANY · NEW YORK · LONDON

EDWARD MCNALL BURNS

PHILIP LEE RALPH

ROBERT E. LERNER

STANDISH MEACHAM

WORLD CIVILIZATIONS

Their History and Their Culture

VOLUME I   SIXTH EDITION

To our students

W. W. Norton & Company, Inc. 500 Fifth Avenue, New York, N.Y. 10110
W. W. Norton & Company Ltd. 37 Great Russell Street, London WC1B 3NU

ISBN 0 393 95083 2

1 2 3 4 5 6 7 8 9 0

CONTENTS

Part Two   THE WORLD IN THE CLASSICAL ERA

Part Three   THE WORLD IN THE MIDDLE
AGES

MAPS

PREFACE

Edward McNall Burns observed in an earlier preface:

"The time has long since passed when modern man could think of the world as consisting of Europe and the United States. Western culture is, of course, primarily a product of European origins. But it has never been that exclusively. Its original foundations were in Southwestern Asia and North Africa. These were supplemented by influences seeping in from India and eventually from China. From India and the Far East the West derived its knowledge of the zero, the compass, gunpowder, silk, cotton, and probably a large number of religious and philosophical concepts. Especially in recent times the East has increased in importance. The exhaustion of Europe by two World Wars, the revolt of the colored races against Caucasian domination, and the struggle for the world between the Communist powers and the United States have made every part of the earth of vital importance to every other. If peace is indivisible, so are prosperity, justice, and freedom; so, in fact, is civilization itself.

"The purpose of this work is to present a compact survey of man's struggle for civilization from early times to the present. No major area or country of the globe has been omitted. Europe, the Commonwealth of Nations, the Middle East, Southeast Asia, Africa, India, China, Japan, and North, Central, and South America have all received appropriate emphasis. Obviously, the history of none of them could be covered in full detail. The authors believe, however, that a broad view of the world as a whole is necessary to understand the basic problems of any of its parts. This thesis acquires additional validity as the nations increase in interdependence. Perspective in history becomes more and more urgent as the momentous problems of our own generation press for solution. If there is any basic philosophical interpretation underlying the narrative, it is the conviction that most of human progress thus far has resulted from the growth of intelligence and respect for the rights of man, and that therein lies the chief hope for a better world in the future."

As its title indicates, this work is not exclusively or even primarily a political history. Political events are recognized as important, but they are not the whole substance of history. In the main, the facts of political history are subordinated to the development of institutions and ideas or are presented as the groundwork of cultural, social, and economic movements. The authors consider the effects of the Industrial Revolutions to be no less important than the Napoleonic Wars. They believe it is of greater value to understand the significance of Buddha, Confucius, Newton, Darwin, and Einstein than it is to be able to name the kings of France. In accordance with this broader conception of history, more space has been given to the teachings of John Locke, Karl Marx, and John Stuart Mill, of Mahatma Gandhi, Mao Tse-tung, and Julius Nyerere than to the military exploits of Gustavus Adolphus or the Duke of Wellington.

The first edition of *World Civilizations* was published in 1955, the second in 1958, the third in 1964, the fourth in 1969, and the fifth in 1974. Each edition has included the whole of Edward McNall Burns' *Western Civilizations,* except for sections on the non-Western world, which are more fully covered in this work. The sixth edition of *World Civilizations* incorporates Burns' *Western Civilizations* as revised for its ninth edition by Robert E. Lerner of Northwestern University and Standish Meacham of the University of Texas at Austin. The qualities that have made the Burns text a leader during the past thirty years have been preserved, while at the same time Professors Lerner and Meacham, utilizing the results of recent scholarship, have sharpened the focus on areas of greatest concern for today's students. The authors' considerable reorganization of the chapters dealing with the Western world has enabled them to give fuller treatment to the Middle Ages and to the nineteenth century, to living conditions during the successive stages of Western development, and to the status of women and minority groups.

In addition to the extensive changes in the chapters on Western history, those devoted to the non-Western and third world have been thoroughly revised. They contain much new material, designed not merely to supply up-to-date information on the course of events but also to take account of new interpretations and to provide a clearer perspective on the character, competing forces, and problems of the troubled era into which contemporary societies have been propelled. In accord with this objective, more space has been allotted to Latin America and to the Middle East than in the previous edition. This edition, like its immediate predecessor, benefits substantially from the contribution of Professor Richard Hull of New York University, who has revised, updated, and expanded the sections on Africa in Chapters 12, 17, 23, 32, and 38. His narrative provides a compact and enlightening account of the peoples and the major civilizations of the African continent and of their present state. For all chapters, the accompanying reading lists have been revised.

The sixth edition of *World Civilizations* has been redesigned for easier reading and to accommodate literally hundreds of new illustrations from Western and non-Western archives. Virtually 50 percent of the 950 illustrations are new to this edition. The text was the first to include color illustrations and continues to include far more color plates than any other book in the field. Most of the 65 maps are either new or thoroughly amended. The new edition is published in both a one-volume and a two-volume format. Available for use with either is a new Teacher's Manual and a thoroughly revised Study Guide, which, as its most distinctive feature, includes numerous extracts from original sources.

In preparing this revision the authors have profited from the assistance and counsel of many individuals whose services no words of appreciation can adequately measure. The list would include not only various specialists but also teachers and students who have used the text in their courses. The authors owe a debt of gratitude to demanding but kindly editors who have worked with them over the years. For this edition, as for the preceding one, Robert E. Kehoe of W. W. Norton & Company has been an indispensable adviser and co-worker. The authors are continually indebted to their wives for often unacknowledged assistance and, even more, for their forbearance, patience, and understanding.

Philip Lee Ralph

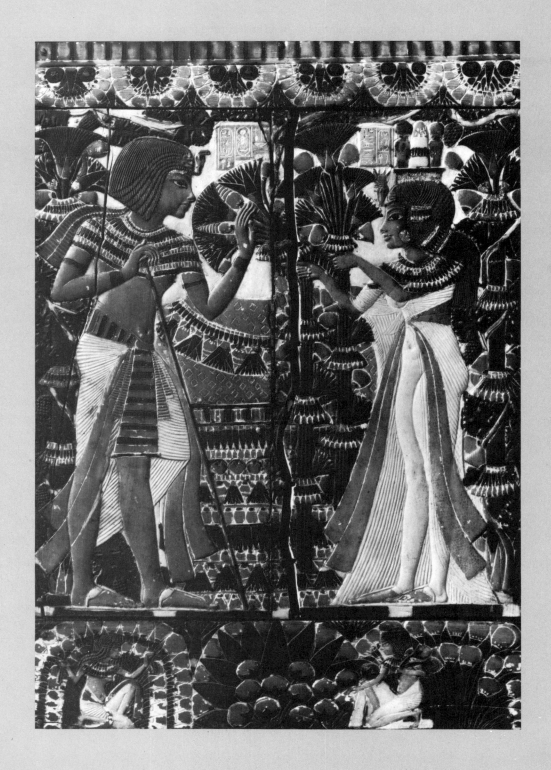

Part One

THE DAWN OF HISTORY

No one knows the place of origin of the human species. There is evidence, however, that it may have been south-central Africa or possibly central or south-central Asia. Here climatic conditions were such as to favor the evolution of a variety of human types from primate ancestors. From their place or places of origin members of the human species wandered to southeastern and eastern Asia, northern Africa, Europe, and eventually, to America. For hundreds of centuries they remained primitive, leading a life which was at first barely more advanced than that of the higher animals. About 3500 B.C., a few of them, enjoying special advantages of location and climate, slowly developed superior civilizations. These civilizations, which attained knowledge of writing and considerable advancement in the arts and sciences and in social organization, began in that part of the world known as the Near East. This region extends from modern-day Iran to the Mediterranean Sea and to the farther bank of the Nile. Here flourished, at different periods between 3000 and 300 B.C., the mighty empires of the Egyptians, the Babylonians, the Assyrians, the Chaldeans, and the Persians, together with the smaller states of such peoples as the Hittites, the Phoenicians, and the Hebrews. The only other very early civilization existed in India in the area of the Indus valley from about 2500 to 1500 B.C. The earliest signs of civilization in China date from about 1800 B.C., and the earliest civilizations in Europe—on the island of Crete and mainland Greece—similarly date from around that time.

The Earliest Development of Humanity

	CULTURE PERIOD	TYPE OF HUMAN	CHARACTERISTIC ACHIEVEMENTS
2 million years ago	Earlier Paleolithic (Early Old Stone Age)	*Homo habilis*	Walking erect; use of objects taken from nature as tools; hunting
500,000 years ago		Java Man; Peking Man	Larger brains: greater intelligence
50,000 years ago		Neanderthal Man: first *Homo sapiens*	Speech; ability to think in the abstract; earliest tool-making
20,000 years ago	Later Paleolithic (Late Old Stone Age)	Cro-Magnon Man	Variety of tools and weapons made from stone and bone; cooked food; cave-painting
12,000 years ago	Mezolithic (Middle Stone Age)	Modern physical types	More settled living conditions; earliest transition from food-gathering to food-raising
7,000 years ago	Neolithic (New Stone Age)		Agriculture; domestication of animals; pottery; earliest village life; origin of states
5,500 years ago	Bronze Age		Earliest civilizations in Egypt and Mesopotamia; writing; bronze metallurgy; developed political, social, and economic institutions

Chapter 1

THE EARLIEST BEGINNINGS

As we turn to the past itself . . . we might well begin with a pious tribute to our nameless [preliterate] ancestors, who by inconceivably arduous and ingenious effort succeeded in establishing a human race. They made the crucial discoveries and inventions, such as the tool, the seed, and the domesticated animal; their development of agriculture, the "neolithic revolution" that introduced a settled economy, was perhaps the greatest stride forward that man has ever taken. They created the marvelous instrument of language, which enabled man to discover his humanity, and eventually to disguise it. They laid the foundations of civilization: its economic, political, and social life, and its artistic, ethical, and religious traditions. Indeed, our "savage" ancestors are still very near to us, and not merely in our capacity for savagery.

—Herbert J. Muller, *The Uses of the Past*

1. THE NATURE OF HISTORY

Catherine Morland, the heroine of Jane Austen's novel *Northanger Abbey,* complained that history "tells me nothing that does not either vex or weary me. The quarrels of popes and kings, with wars or pestilences in every page; the men all so good for nothing, and hardly any women at all, it is very tiresome." Although Jane Austen's heroine said this around 1800, she might have lodged the same complaint until quite recently, for until deep into the twentieth century most historians considered history to be little more than "past politics"—and a dry chronicle of past politics at that. The content of history was restricted primarily to battles and treaties, the personalities and politics of statesmen, the laws and decrees of rulers. But important as such data are, they by no means constitute the whole substance of history. Especially within the last few decades historians have come to recognize that history comprises a record of past human activities in every sphere—not just political developments, but also social, economic, and intellectual ones. Women as well as men, the ruled as well as the rulers, the poor as well as the rich, are part of his-

History more than battles and treaties

tory. So too are the social and economic institutions that men and women have created and that in turn have shaped their lives: family and social class; manorialism and city life; capitalism and industrialism. Ideas and attitudes too, not just of intellectuals but also of men and women whose lives may have been virtually untouched by "great books," are all part of the historian's concern. And, most important, history includes an inquiry into the causes of events and patterns of human organization and ideas—a search for the forces that impelled humanity toward its great undertakings, and the reasons for its successes and failures.

As historians have extended the compass of their work, they have also equipped themselves with new methods and tools, the better to *New historical methods* practice their craft. No longer do historians merely pore over the same old chronicles and documents to ask whether Charles the Fat was at Ingelheim or Lustnau on July 1, 887. To introduce the evidence of statistics they learn the methods of the computer scientist. To interpret the effect of a rise in the cost of living, they study economics. To deduce marriage patterns or evaluate the effect upon an entire population of wars and plagues, they master the skills of the demographer. To explore the phenomena of cave-dwelling or modern urbanization, they become archeologists, studying fossil remains, fragments of pots, or modern city landscapes. To understand the motives of the men and women who have made history, they draw on the insights of social psychologists and cultural anthropologists. To illuminate the lives of the poor and of those who have left few written records, they look for other cultural remains—folk songs, for example, and the traditions embodied in oral history.

Perhaps the most important lesson historians have learned is that they must no longer condescend to the past, no longer assume that *Necessity for studying past* their civilization is worthier than those that have come before. History *on its own terms* is primarily the study of change over time, but that does not mean that it is a tale of uninterrupted progress from past to present or that all change was ordained to produce our own modern world. Those who write history and those who study it must look to see how one event led to another and how the entire past is prologue to the present, but they must also appreciate the past on its own terms, examining it, so far as possible, through the eyes and with the minds of those who lived it.

2. HISTORY AND PREHISTORY

It is the custom among many historians to distinguish between historic and prehistoric periods in the evolution of human society. By the *The so-called prehistoric* former they mean history based upon written records. By the latter *era* they mean the record of human achievement before the invention of writing. But this distinction is not altogether satisfactory. It suggests that human accomplishments before they were recorded in characters or symbols representing words or concepts were not important. Nothing could be farther from the truth. The foundations, at least, of many of the great accomplishments of modern technology, and even of social and political systems, were laid before human beings could write a word. It is preferable, therefore, that the whole period of human life on earth be regarded as historic, and that the era before the invention of writing be designated by a term such as "preliterate." The records of preliterate societies are, of course, not books and documents, but tools, weapons, fossils, utensils, carvings, paintings, and fragments of jewelry and ornamentation. These, commonly known as "artifacts," are often almost as valuable as the written word in providing knowledge of a people's deeds and modes of living.

The entire span of human history can be divided roughly into two periods, the Age of Stone and the Age of Metals. The former is roughly coterminous with the Preliterate Age, or the period before the invention of writing. The latter coincides roughly with the period of history based upon written records. The Preliterate Age covered all but the smallest fraction of humanity's existence and did not come to an end until about 3500 B.C., although some Stone Age cultures persisted after that time and a few tribes still exist in remote areas. The Age of Metals practically coincides with the history of civilized nations. The Age of Stone is subdivided into the Paleolithic, or Old Stone Age, and the Neolithic, or New Stone Age. Each takes its name from the type of stone tools and weapons characteristically manufactured during the period. Thus during the greater part of the Paleolithic Age implements were commonly made by chipping pieces off a large stone or flint and using the core that remained as a hand ax or "fist hatchet." Toward the end of the period the chips themselves were used as knives or spearheads, and the core thrown away. The Neolithic Age witnessed the supplanting of chipped stone tools by implements made by grinding and polishing stone.

Fist Hatchet

3. THE CULTURE OF THE EARLIER PALEOLITHIC PEOPLES

The Paleolithic period can be dated from roughly 2,000,000 B.C. to 10,000 B.C. It is commonly divided into two stages, an earlier and a later one. The earlier Paleolithic period was vastly the longer of the two, covering about 99 percent of the entire Old Stone Age. During this time at least four species of humanlike creatures inhabited the earth. Momentous discoveries pertaining to the earliest of these have been made very recently by scientific teams working in East Africa. In 1961, the anthropologist Jonathan Leakey uncovered in Tanzania parts

Homo habilis

The Skull (left) *of a Young Woman of the Species Homo habilis,* believed to have lived in Tanzania, East Africa, about 1,750,000 years ago. On the right is the skull of a present-day African. Though *Homo habilis* was smaller than a pygmy, the brain casing was shaped like that of modern humans.

of a skull that was about 1.8 million years old, far older than any humanlike skull previously known. (Chemical tests such as the carbon-14 method or the potassium-argon method are used in determining the age of the geological strata in which bones are found and sometimes the age of the bones themselves.) Then, in 1972, a team led by Jonathan's brother Richard discovered in Kenya a similar and nearly complete skull that was more than 2 million years old. The species which left behind these remains has been named *Homo habilis,* or "man having ability." *Homo habilis* may be counted as a true ancestor of modern man because he walked erect, possessed a brain that was larger than that of any apes, and was intelligent enough to use tools. Of course, his tools were extremely primitive. For the most part they consisted of objects taken from nature: bones of animals, limbs from trees, and chunks of stone, perhaps broken or crudely chipped. But they allowed *Homo habilis* to survive in times of food shortage as a hunter rather than as a food gatherer or forager. It must not be thought that reliance on hunting led these earliest ancestors to kill each other. Quite to the contrary, their survival depended upon cooperation. Most likely only after the development of agriculture and herding—more than a million years later—did humans start warring with each other for the possession of territory. The cooperation necessary in hunting made *Homo habilis* the first truly social creature and led toward the use of language. *Homo habilis* was, therefore, clearly in the vanguard of the human race.

Java Man

Two subsequent inhabitants of the earlier Paleolithic period were Java man and Peking man. Java man was long thought to be the oldest of humanlike creatures, but it is now generally agreed that the date of his origin was about 500,000 B.C. His skeletal remains were found on the island of Java in 1891. The remains of Peking man were found in China, about twenty-five miles southwest of Peking between 1926 and 1930. Since the latter date, fragments of no fewer than thirty-two skeletons of the Peking type have been located, making possible a complete reconstruction of at least the head of this ancient species. Anthropologists generally agree that Peking man and Java man are of approximately the same antiquity, and that both probably descended from the same ancestral type.

Neanderthal Man

During the last 25,000 years of the earlier Paleolithic period a fourth species of ancient man made an appearance. He was Neanderthal man, famous as an early caveman. Although first discovered a few years earlier at Gibraltar, Neanderthal man is named after a find of skeletal fragments in 1856 in the valley of the Neander, near Düsseldorf, in northwestern Germany. Since then numerous other discoveries have been made, in some cases complete skeletons, in such widely separated regions as Belgium, Spain, Italy, Yugoslavia, Russia, and Israel. So closely did Neanderthal man resemble modern man that he is classified as a member of the same species, *Homo sapiens*. The resemblance, however, was by no means perfect. Neanderthalers, on the average, were only about five feet, four inches in height. They had receding chins and heavy eyebrow ridges. Although their foreheads sloped back and their brain cases were low-vaulted, their average cranial capacity was slightly greater than that of modern Caucasians. What this may have signified with respect to their intelligence cannot be determined.

Peking Man

The knowledge we possess of the culture of earlier Paleolithic peoples is scanty. The skills they achieved and the learning they acquired must have been pitiful in quantity even when compared with the accomplishments of modern primitive groups. Yet Neanderthal man and his successors were not mere apes, forgetting in a moment the chance triumphs they had made. They undoubtedly had the capacity for speech, which enabled them to communicate with their fellows and to pass on what they had learned to succeeding generations. The Neanderthalers had some ability to think in the abstract, as evidenced by their burial of their dead with objects intended for use in an afterlife. They also progressed beyond *Homo habilis* by fashioning their own tools instead of just using the ones they found. They discovered that stones could be chipped in such a way as to give them cutting edges. Thus were developed spearheads, borers, and much superior knives and scrapers. Indications have been found also of a degree of advancement in nonmaterial culture. In the entrances to caves where Neanderthalers lived, or at least took refuge, evidence has been discovered of flint-working floors and stone hearths where huge fires ap-

*Accomplishments of earlier
Paleolithic peoples*

Cro-Magnon Man

Later Paleolithic Fishhook

pear to have been made. These would suggest the origins of cooperative group life and possibly the crude beginnings of social institutions.

4. LATER PALEOLITHIC CULTURE

About 30,000 B.C. the culture of the Old Stone Age passed to the later Paleolithic stage. This period lasted for only about two hundred centuries, or from 30,000 to 10,000 B.C. A new and superior type of human being dominated the earth in this time. Biologically these peoples were closely related to modern humans. Their foremost predecessors, Neanderthal men, had ceased to exist as a distinct variety. What became of the Neanderthalers is not known.

The name used to designate the prevailing breed of later Paleolithic humans is Cro-Magnon, from the Cro-Magnon cave in southern France where some of the most typical remains were discovered. These people lived by hunting reindeer, bison, and mammoths, which freely roamed through southern Europe and Asia because the climate, dominated by glaciers, was very cold. The Cro-Magnon people were tall, broad-shouldered, and walked erect, the males averaging over six feet. They had high foreheads, well-developed chins, and a cranial capacity about equal to the modern average. The heavy eyebrows so typical of earlier species were absent. Whether Cro-Magnon men left any survivors is a debatable question. They do not seem to have been exterminated but appear to have been driven into mountainous regions and to have been ultimately absorbed into other breeds.

Later Paleolithic culture was markedly more advanced than that which had gone before. Not only were tools and implements better made, they existed in greater variety. They were not fashioned merely from flakes of stone and an occasional shaft of bone; other materials were used in abundance, particularly reindeer horn and ivory. Examples of the more complicated tools included the fishhook, the harpoon, the dart-thrower, and, at the very end, the bow and arrow. That later Paleolithic people wore clothing is indicated by the fact that they invented the needle (made out of bone). They did not know how to weave cloth, but animal skins sewn together proved a satisfactory substitute. It is certain that they cooked their food, for enormous hearths, evidently used for roasting meat, have been discovered. In the vicinity of one at Solutré, in southern France, was a mass of charred bones, estimated to contain the remains of a hundred thousand large animals. Although Cro-Magnon people built no houses, except a few simple huts in regions where natural shelters did not abound, their life was not wholly nomadic. Evidence found in caves that served as homes indicate that they must have been used, seasonally at least, for years at a time.

With respect to nonmaterial elements there are also indications that later Paleolithic culture represented a marked advancement. Group life was now more highly organized than ever before. The profusion of charred bones at Solutré and elsewhere probably indicates cooperative enterprise in the hunt and sharing of the results in community feasts. The amazing workmanship displayed in tools and weapons and highly developed techniques in the arts could scarcely have been achieved without some division of labor. It appears certain, therefore, that later Paleolithic communities included professional artists and skilled craftsmen. In order to acquire such talents, certain members of the communities must have gone through long periods of training and given all their time to the practice of their specialties.

Substantial proof exists that the Cro-Magnons had highly developed notions of a world with supernatural aspects. They bestowed more care upon the bodies of the dead than did the Neanderthalers, painting the corpses, folding the arms over the heart, and depositing pendants, necklaces, and richly carved weapons in the graves. The Cro-Magnons also formulated an elaborate system of sympathetic magic designed to increase their food supply. Sympathetic magic is based upon the principle that imitating a desired result will bring about that result. Applying this principle, Cro-Magnon people

Sympathetic magic

Later Paleolithic Engraving and Sculpture. The two objects at the top and upper right are dart-throwers. At the lower right is the famous Venus of Willendorf.

The Venus of Laussel

painted murals on the walls of their caves depicting, for example, the capture of reindeer in the hunt. At other times they fashioned clay models of the bison or mammoth and mutilated them with dart thrusts. The purpose of such representation was probably to facilitate the results portrayed and thereby to increase the hunter's success and make easier the struggle for existence. Possibly incantations or cere-monies accompanied the making of these pictures or images, and it is likely that the work of producing them was carried on while the actual hunt was in progress.

In fact, the supreme achievement of the Cro-Magnon people was their art—an achievement so original and resplendent that it ought to be counted among the Seven Wonders of the World. Nothing else il-lustrates so well the great gulf between their culture and that of their predecessors. Later Paleolithic art included nearly every branch that the material culture of the time made possible. Sculpture, painting, and carving were all represented. The ceramic arts and architecture were lacking; pottery had not yet been invented; and the only build-ings erected were of simple design. The Cro-Magnon art par ex-cellence was cave painting. On cave walls were exhibited the greatest number and variety of their talents—their discrimination in the use of color, their meticulous attention to detail, their capacity for the em-ployment of scale in depicting a group, and above all, their genius for imitating natural detail. Especially noteworthy was their skill in repre-senting movement. Almost all of the murals depict animals run-ning, leaping, chewing their cud, or facing the hunter at bay. Ingen-ious devices were often employed to give the impression of motion. Chief among them was the drawing or painting of additional outlines to indicate the areas in which the legs or the head of the animal had moved. The scheme was so shrewdly executed that no appearance whatever of artificiality resulted.

Cave painting throws a flood of light on many problems relating to primitive mentality and folkways. To a certain extent it was undoubt-edly an expression of a true aesthetic sense. Cro-Magnon people did obviously take some delight in a graceful line or symmetrical pattern or brilliant color. The fact that they painted and tattooed their bodies and wore ornaments gives evidence of this. But their chief works of art can scarcely have been produced for the sake of creating beautiful objects. Such a possibility must be excluded for several reasons. To begin with, the best of the paintings and drawings are usually to be found on the walls and ceilings of the darkest and most inaccessible parts of the caves. The gallery of paintings at Niaux, for instance, is more than half a mile from the entrance of the cave. No one could see the artists' creations except in the imperfect light of torches or primi-tive lamps, which must have smoked and sputtered badly, for the only illuminating fluid available was animal fat. Furthermore, there is evi-dence that Cro-Magnon people were largely indifferent to their

Cave Drawings at Lascaux, France. On the left are characteristic examples of the realism of Cro-Magnon art. On the right, a view of the entrance to the caves.

murals after they were finished. Numerous examples have been found of paintings or drawings superimposed upon earlier ones of the same or of different types. Evidently the important thing was not the finished work itself, but the act of making it.

The real purpose of nearly all of later Paleolithic art was apparently not to delight the senses but to increase the supply of animals useful for food. The artist was not an aesthete but a magician, and art was a form of magic designed to promote the hunter's success. In this purpose lay its chief significance and the foundation of most of its special qualities. It suggests, for example, the real reason why game animals were almost the exclusive subjects of the great murals and why plant life and inanimate objects were seldom represented. It aids us in understanding the Cro-Magnons' neglect of finished paintings and the predominant interest in the process of making them. The placing of the art in the most inaccessible part of the cave is further proof of a religious motivation on the part of the artist—the art then becomes secreted in a sacred place.

Later Paleolithic culture ended around 10,000 B.C. because of a disappearance of the food supply. As the last glacier retreated farther and farther north, the climate of southern Europe became too warm for the reindeer, and they gradually migrated to the shores of the Baltic.

Art an aid in the struggle for existence

The end of later Paleolithic culture

The mammoth, whether for the same or for different reasons, became extinct. Cro-Magnon peoples probably followed the reindeer northward, but any later cultural achievements remain unknown to us.

5. NEOLITHIC CULTURE

From roughly 10,000 B.C. to roughly 5000 B.C., varying very much according to location, ensued the Mesolithic, or Middle Stone Age. This was a transitional period in which peoples became more sedentary and found new sources of food, such as shellfish and edible grasses, now that most of the world was freed from ice. The Mesolithic stage was succeeded by the Neolithic, or New Stone Age. This name is applied because stone weapons and tools were now generally made by grinding and polishing instead of by chipping or fracturing as in the preceding periods. The bearers of Neolithic culture were new varieties of modern peoples who poured into Africa and southern Europe from western Asia. Since no evidence exists of their later extermination or wholesale migration, they must be regarded as the immediate ancestors of most of the peoples now living in Europe.

The meaning of the term Neolithic

It is impossible to fix exact dates for the Neolithic period because different peoples passed through the Neolithic stage of development at different rates in different areas. Exciting recent archeological discoveries on the west bank of the Jordan River give evidence of Neolithic settlements in their earliest forms around 7500 B.C. Fully developed Neolithic culture existed in Mesopotamia and Egypt by 5000 B.C., but the culture was not well established in Europe until about 3000 B.C. There is also variation in the dates of its ending. It was superseded in Mesopotamia and Egypt by the first literate civilizations around 3500 B.C., but except on the island of Crete it did not come to an end anywhere in Europe before 2000, and in northern Europe much later still. In a few regions of the world it has not terminated yet. The peoples of some islands of the Pacific, the Arctic regions of North America, and the jungles of Brazil are still in the Neolithic culture stage except for a few customs acquired from explorers and missionaries.

The varying dates of the Neolithic stage

In many respects the New Stone Age was the most significant in the history of the world thus far. The level of material progress rose to new heights. Neolithic peoples had a better mastery of their environment than any of their predecessors. They were less likely to perish from a shift in climatic conditions or from the failure of some part of their food supply. This decided advantage was the result primarily of the development of agriculture and the domestication of animals. Whereas all of the peoples who had lived heretofore were mere food-gatherers, Neolithic peoples were *food-producers*. Tilling the soil and keeping flocks and herds provided them with much more dependable food resources and at times even yielded them a surplus. The develop-

The Neolithic revolution

ment of agriculture, one of the most important of all transitions in human history, promoted a settled existence and made possible an increase in population. Such were the elements of a great social and economic revolution whose importance it would be impossible to exaggerate.

The new culture also derives significance from the fact that it was the first to be distributed over the *entire* world. Although some earlier cultures, especially those of the Neanderthalers and Cro-Magnons, were widely dispersed, they were confined chiefly to the accessible mainland areas of the Old World. Neolithic culture penetrated into every habitable area of the earth's surface—from Arctic wastes to the jungles of the tropics. Neolithic peoples apparently made their way from a number of centers of origin to every nook and cranny of both hemispheres. They traveled enormous distances by water as well as by land, and eventually occupied every major island of the oceans, no matter how remote.

Migration over long distances was not the only example of Neolithic achievements. Neolithic peoples developed the arts of knitting and weaving. They made the first pottery and knew how to produce fire by friction. They built houses of wood and sun-dried mud. Toward the end of the period they discovered the possibilities of metals, and a few implements of copper and gold were added to their stock. Since nothing was yet known of the arts of smelting and refining, the use of metals was limited to the more malleable ones occasionally found in the pure state in the form of nuggets.

Activities Around a Neolithic Dwelling. This model represents part of a Neolithic village that was located at Troldebjerg, Denmark, about 2700 B.C. Note the hunters, the wood-gatherer, the potter, the weaver, the grain-grinder, and the carver.

Neolithic Flint Sickles

But the real foundations of Neolithic culture were the domestication of animals and the development of agriculture. Without these it is inconceivable that the culture would have attained the complexity it did. More than anything else they made possible a settled mode of existence and the growth of villages and social institutions. The first animal to be domesticated is generally thought to have been the dog, on the assumption that he would be continually hanging around the hunter's camp to pick up bones and scraps of meat. Eventually it would be discovered that he could be put to use in hunting, or possibly in guarding the camp. After achieving success in domesticating the dog, Neolithic peoples would logically turn their attention to other animals, especially those used for food. Before the period ended, at least five species—the cow, the dog, the goat, the sheep, and the pig— had been made to serve their needs.

The exact spot where agriculture originated has never been determined. All we know is that wild grasses which were probably the ancestors of the cereal grains have been found in a number of places. Types of wheat grow wild in the Near East and southern Russia. Wild ancestors of barley have been reported in North Africa, the Near East, and central Asia. Though it is probable that these were the first crops of Neolithic agriculture, they were by no means the only ones. Millet, vegetables, and numerous fruits were also grown. Flax was cultivated in the Eastern Hemisphere for its textile fiber, and in some localities the growing of the poppy for opium had already begun. In the Western Hemisphere maize (Indian corn) was the only cereal, but the American Indians cultivated numerous other crops, including tobacco, beans, squashes, tomatoes, and potatoes.

The most important consequence of Neolithic settled life was the development of lasting institutions. An institution may be defined as a combination of group beliefs and activities organized in a relatively permanent fashion for the purpose of fulfilling some group need. It ordinarily includes a body of customs and traditions, a code of rules and standards, and physical extensions such as buildings, punitive devices, and facilities for communication and indoctrination. Since humans are social beings, some of these elements probably existed from earliest times, but institutions in their fully developed form seem to have been an achievement of the Neolithic Age.

One of the most ancient of human institutions is the family. Sociologists do not agree upon how it should be defined. Historically, however, the family has always meant a more or less permanent unit composed of parents and their offspring, which serves the purposes of care of the young, division of labor, acquisition and transmission of property, and preservation and transmission of beliefs and customs. The family is not now, and never has been, exclusively biological in character. Like most institutions, it has evolved through a long period of changing conventions which have given it a variety of functions and forms. No doubt there were primitive families in Paleolithic times, but we know practically nothing about them and they probably were not very stable. In Neolithic times the family clearly emerges and appears to have been dominated by the male patriarch who had one or more wives depending upon region.

A second institution known earlier but developed in more complex form by Neolithic peoples was religion. On account of its infinite variations, it is hard to define, but perhaps the following would be accepted as an accurate definition of the institution in at least its basic character: "Religion is everywhere an expression in one form or another of a sense of dependence on a power outside ourselves, a power which we may speak of as a spiritual or moral power."[1] Modern anthropologists emphasize the fact that early religion was not so much a matter of belief as a matter of rites. For the most part, the rites came first; the myths, dogmas, and theologies were later rationalizations. Primitive people were universally dependent upon nature—on the regular succession of the seasons, on the rain falling when it should, on the growth of plants and the reproduction of animals. Unless they performed sacrifices and rites these natural phenomena, according to this notion, would not occur. For this reason they developed rainmaking ceremonies in which water was sprinkled on ears of corn to imitate the falling of the rain. The members of a whole village or even a whole tribe would attire themselves in animal skins and mimic the habits and activities of some species they depended upon for food. They apparently had an idea that by imitating the life pattern of the species they were helping to guarantee its continuance.

The nature of primitive religion; rites and ceremonies

Still another of the great institutions to be developed by Neolithic peoples was the state. This may be defined as an organized society occupying a specific territory and possessing an authoritative government independent of external control. The essence of the state is the power to make and administer laws and to preserve social order by punishing people for infractions of those laws. Except in time of crisis the state does not exist in a very large proportion of preliterate societies—a fact which probably indicates that it originated rather late in the Neolithic culture stage.

The state: definition

The major explanation for the development of states in the Neolithic period lies in the development of agriculture. In areas such as the Nile valley, where a large population lived by cultivating intensively a limited area of fertile soil, a high degree of social organization was absolutely essential. Ancient customs would not suffice for the definition of rights and duties in such a society, with its high standard of living, its unequal distribution of wealth, and its wide scope for the clash of personal interests. New measures of social control would become necessary, which could scarcely be achieved in any other way than by set-

Role of agriculture in the origin of states

[1] A. R. Radcliffe-Brown, *Structure and Function in Primitive Society*, p. 157.

ting up a government of sovereign authority and submitting to it; in other words, by establishing a state.

Other causes

As important as the emergence of agriculture was in the origin of states, it was not the only cause. In some areas where there was no settled agriculture, states evidently were founded as a result of military activities. That is, they emerged for the purposes of conquest, for defense against invasion, or to make possible the expulsion of an invader from the country. The Hebrew monarchy seems to have been a product of the first of these reasons. With the war for the conquest of the Holy Land none too successful, the Hebrew people petitioned their leader Samuel to give them a king, that they might be "like all the nations" with a powerful ruler to keep them in order and to lead them to victory in battle. One has only to observe the effects of modern warfare, both offensive and defensive, in enlarging the powers of government to see how similar influences might have operated to bring the state into existence in the first place.

6. FACTORS RESPONSIBLE FOR THE ORIGIN AND GROWTH OF CIVILIZATIONS

The meaning of civilization

Some time around 3500 B.C. the earliest *civilizations* emerged out of Neolithic culture. We may say that civilization is a stage in human historical development when writing is used to a considerable extent; some progress has been made in the arts and sciences; and political, social, and economic institutions have developed sufficiently to conquer at least some of the problems of order, security, and efficiency in a complex society. What causes contributed to the rise of civilizations? What factors account for their growth? Why do some civilizations reach much higher levels of development than others? Inquiry into these questions is one of the chief pursuits of historians and social scientists. Some decide that factors of geography are most important. Others stress economic resources, food supply, contact with older civilizations, and so on. Usually a variety of causes is acknowledged, but one is commonly singled out by historians as deserving special emphasis.

Geographic theories: the climatic hypothesis

Probably the most popular of the theories accounting for the rise of advanced cultures are those which come under the heading of geography. Prominent among them is the hypothesis of climate. The climatic theory, advocated by such philosophers as Aristotle and Montesquieu, received its most eloquent exposition in the writings of an American geographer, Ellsworth Huntington. Huntington acknowledged the importance of other factors, but he insisted that no nation, ancient or modern, rose to the highest cultural status except under the influence of a climatic stimulus. He described the ideal climate as one in which the mean temperature seldom falls below 38 degrees or rises above 64 degrees Fahrenheit. But temperature is not alone important. Moisture is also essential, and the humidity should average about 75 percent. Finally, the weather must not be uniform: cyclonic storms, or ordinary storms resulting in weather changes from day to day, must have sufficient frequency and intensity to clear the atmosphere every once in a while and produce those sudden variations in temperature which seem to be necessary to exhilarate and revitalize human beings.[2]

Much can be said in favor of the climatic hypothesis. Certainly some parts of the earth's surface, under existing atmospheric conditions, could never give rise to a superior culture. They are either too hot, too humid, too cold, or too dry. Such is the case in regions beyond the Arctic Circle, the larger desert areas, and the rainforests of India, Central America, and Brazil. Evidence is available, moreover, to show that some of these places have not always existed under climate so adverse as that now prevalent. Desolate sections of Asia, Africa, and America contain unmistakable traces of better days in the past. Here and there are the ruins of towns and cities where now the supply of water is totally inadequate, or which are entrapped by growths of dense foliage. Roads traverse deserts which at present are impassable, or come to an end at the mouth of a jungle.

Evidence in favor of the climatic hypothesis

The best-known evidences of the cultural importance of climatic change are those pertaining to the civilization of the Mayas. Mayan civilization flourished in Guatemala, Honduras, and on the peninsula of Yucatan in Mexico from about 400 to 1500 A.D. Numbered among its achievements were the making of paper, the invention of the zero, the perfection of a solar calendar, and the development of a system of writing partly phonetic. Great cities were built; marked progress was made in astronomy; and sculpture and architecture reached advanced levels. At present most of the civilization is in ruins. No doubt many factors conspired to produce its end, including deadly wars between tribes, but climatic change was also probably involved. The remains of most of the great Mayan cities are now surrounded by jungles, where malaria is prevalent and agriculture difficult. That the Mayan civilization or any other could have grown to maturity under present-day conditions is hard to believe.

The Mayan civilization

Related to the climatic hypothesis is the soil-exhaustion theory. A group of modern conservationists has hit upon this theory as the sole explanation of the decay and collapse of the great empires of the past and as a universal threat to the nations of the present and future. At best it is only a partial hypothesis, since it offers no theory of the birth or growth of civilizations. But its proponents seem to think that almost any environment not ruined by humans is capable of nourishing a superior culture. The great deserts and barren areas of the earth, they maintain, are not natural but artificial, created by bad grazing and

The soil-exhaustion theory

[2] Ellsworth Huntington, *Civilization and Climate*, 3d ed., pp. 220–23.

farming practices. Ecologists discover innumerable evidences of waste and neglect that have wrought havoc in such areas as Mesopotamia, Palestine, Greece, Italy, China, and Mexico. The mighty civilizations that once flourished in these countries were ultimately doomed by the fact that their soil would no longer provide sufficient food for the population. As a consequence, the more intelligent and enterprising citizens migrated elsewhere and left others to sink slowly into stagnation and apathy. But the fate that overtook the latter was not of their making alone. The whole nation had been guilty of plundering the forests, mining the soil, and pasturing flocks on the land until the grass was eaten down to the very roots. Among the tragic results were floods alternating with droughts, since there were no longer any forests to regulate the run-off of rain or snow. At the same time, much of the top soil on the close-cropped or excessively cultivated hillsides was blown away or washed into the rivers to be carried eventually down to the sea. The damage done was irreparable, since about three hundred years are required to produce a single inch of topsoil.

A recent hypothesis of the origin of civilizations is the British historian Arnold J. Toynbee's adversity theory. According to this theory, conditions of hardship or adversity are the real causes which have brought superior cultures into existence. Such conditions constitute a *challenge* which not only stimulates humans to try to overcome it but generates additional energy for new achievements. The challenge may take the form of a desert, a jungle area, rugged topography, or a grudging soil. The Hebrews and Arabs were challenged by the first, the Indians of the Andes by the last. The challenge may also take the form of defeat in war or even enslavement. Thus the Carthaginians, as a result of defeat in the First Punic War, were stimulated to conquer a new empire in Spain. In general it is true that the greater the challenge, the greater the achievement; nevertheless, there are limits. The challenge must not be too severe, else it will deal a crushing blow to all who attempt to meet it.

7. WHY THE EARLIEST CIVILIZATIONS BEGAN WHERE THEY DID

Which of the great civilizations of antiquity was the oldest is still a sharply debated question. The judgment of some scholars inclines toward the Egyptian, though a larger body of authority supports the claims of the Tigris-Euphrates valley. These two areas were geographically the most favored sections in the Near East. In both, larger numbers of artifacts of undoubted antiquity have been found than in any other regions. Furthermore, progress in the arts and sciences had reached unparalleled heights in both of these areas as early as 3000 B.C., when most of the rest of the world was backward in the extreme. If the foundations of this progress were really laid elsewhere, it seems strange that they should have disappeared, although of course there is no telling what archeologists may uncover in the future.

Of the several causes responsible for the earliest rise of civilizations in the Nile and Tigris-Euphrates valleys, geographic factors would seem to have been the most important. Both regions had the notable advantage of a limited area of exceedingly fertile soil. Although it extended for a distance of 750 miles, the valley of the Nile was not more than 10 miles wide in some places, and its maximum width was 31 miles. The total area was less than 10,000 square miles, or roughly the equivalent of Maryland. Through countless centuries the river had carved a vast canyon or trench, bounded on either side by cliffs ranging in height from a few hundred to a thousand feet. The floor of the canyon was covered with a rich alluvial deposit, which in places reached a depth in excess of thirty feet. The soil was of such amazing productivity that as many as three crops per year could be raised on the same land. This broad and fertile canyon constituted the arable land of ancient Egypt. Here several million people were concentrated. In Roman times the population of the valley approximated seven million, and probably it was not much smaller in the days of the pharaohs. Beyond the cliffs there was nothing but desert—the Libyan desert on the west and the Arabian on the east.

A limited area of fertile soil in the Nile valley

See color map facing page 96

In the Tigris-Euphrates valley—a part of the region known as the Fertile Crescent—similar conditions prevailed. As in Egypt, the rivers provided excellent facilities for inland transportation and were alive with fish and waterfowl for a plentiful supply of protein. The distance between the Tigris and Euphrates rivers at one point was less than twenty miles, and nowhere in the lower valley did it exceed forty-five miles. Since the surrounding country was desert, the people were kept from scattering over too great an expanse of territory. The result, as in Egypt, was the welding of the inhabitants into a compact society, under conditions that facilitated a ready interchange of ideas and discoveries. As the population increased, the need for agencies of social control became ever more urgent. Numbered among such agencies were government, schools, legal and moral codes, and institutions for the production and distribution of wealth. At the same time conditions of living became more complex and artificial and necessitated the keeping of records of things accomplished and the perfection of new techniques. Among the consequences were the invention of writing, the practice of smelting metals, the performance of mathematical operations, and the development of astronomy and the rudiments of physics. With these achievements the first great ordeal of civilization was passed.

A similar condition in Mesopotamia

Climatic influences also played their part in both regions. The atmosphere of Egypt is dry and invigorating. Even the hottest days produce none of the oppressive discomfort which is often experienced during the summer seasons in more northern countries. The mean temperature in winter varies from 56 degrees Fahrenheit in the Nile

Climatic advantages in Egypt

Delta to 66 degrees in the valley above. The summer mean is 83 degrees and an occasional maximum of 122 is reached, but the nights are always cool and the humidity is extremely low. Except in the Delta, rainfall occurs in negligible quantities, but the deficiency of moisture is counteracted by the annual floods of the Nile from July to October. Also very significant from the historical standpoint is the total absence of malaria in Upper Egypt, while even in the coastal region it is practically unknown. The direction of the prevailing winds is likewise a favorable factor of more than trivial importance. For more than three-quarters of the year the wind comes from the north, blowing in opposition to the force of the Nile current. The effect of this is to simplify immensely the problem of transportation. Upstream traffic, with the propulsion of the wind to counteract the force of the river, presents no greater difficulty than downstream traffic. This factor in ancient times must have been of enormous advantage in promoting communication among a numerous people, some of whom were separated by hundreds of miles.

Climatic influences in Mesopotamia

Climatic conditions in Mesopotamia do not seem to have been quite so favorable as in Egypt. The summer heat is more relentless; the humidity is somewhat higher; and tropical diseases take their toll. Nevertheless, the torrid winds from the Indian Ocean, while enervating to human beings, blow over the valley at just the right season to bring the fruit of the date palm to a full ripeness. More than anything else the excellent yield of dates, the dietary staple of the Near East, encouraged the settlement of large numbers of people in the valley of the two rivers. Finally, the melting of the snows in the mountains of the north produced an annual flooding of the Babylonian plain similar to that in Egypt. The effect was to enrich the soil with moisture and to cover it over with a layer of mud of unusual fertility. At the same time, it should be noted that water conditions in Mesopotamia were less dependable than in Egypt. Floods were sometimes catastrophic, a factor which left its mark on the development of culture.

The importance of scanty rainfall as a spur to initiative

Most significant of all of the geographic influences, however, was the fact that the scanty rainfall in both regions provided a spur to initiative and inventive skill. In spite of the yearly floods of the rivers there was insufficient moisture left in the soil to produce abundant harvests. A few weeks after the waters had receded, the earth was baked to a stony hardness. Irrigation was accordingly necessary if full advantage was to be taken of the richness of the soil. As a result, in both Egypt and Mesopotamia elaborate systems of dams and irrigation canals were constructed as long as five thousand years ago. The mathematical skill, engineering ability, and social cooperation necessary for the development of these projects were available for other uses and so fostered the achievement of civilization.

Which of the two civilizations, the Egyptian or the Mesopotamian, was the older? Until recently most historians appeared to take it for granted that the Egyptian was the older. They based their assumption upon the conclusions of two of the world's most renowned Egyptologists, James H. Breasted and Alexandre Moret. Between the two world wars of the twentieth century, however, facts were unearthed which seemed to prove a substantial Mesopotamian influence in the Nile valley as early as 3500 B.C. This influence was exemplified by the use of cylinder seals, methods of building construction, art motifs, and elements of a system of writing of undoubted Mesopotamian origin. That such achievements could have radiated into Egypt from the Tigris-Euphrates valley at so early a date indicated beyond doubt that the Mesopotamian civilization was one of vast antiquity. It did not necessarily prove, though, that it was older than the Egyptian. For the achievements mentioned were not taken over and copied slavishly. Instead, the Egyptians modified them radically to suit their own culture pattern. On the basis of this evidence, it would seem that the only conclusion which can be safely drawn is that both civilizations were very old, and that to a large extent they developed concurrently. With them both we begin the story of the history of Western civilizations.

Uncertainty as to which civilization was older

SELECTED READINGS

• Items so designated are available in paperback editions.
• Ashley Montague, M. F., ed., *Culture and the Evolution of Man,* New York, 1962.
• Boas, Franz, *The Mind of Primitive Man,* New York, 1927. A very influential and thought-provoking older work.
• Childe, V. Gordon, *Man Makes Himself,* London, 1936.
• ———, *What Happened in History?* New York, 1943. Emphasizes materialistic explanations for the emergence of the earliest civilizations. A modern classic.
  Clark, Grahame, *World Prehistory in New Perspective: An Illustrated Third Edition,* New York, 1978. Highly recommended.
  Hawkes, Jacquetta, *Prehistory,* New York, 1965. A thorough, up-to-date introduction.
  Leakey, Richard E., and R. Lewin, *People of the Lake,* New York, 1978. A recent popular account of Leakey's discoveries pertaining to *Homo habilis* and their significance.
  Linton, Ralph, *The Tree of Culture,* New York, 1955.
• Malinowski, B., *Magic, Science and Religion,* New York, 1954. Essays by one of the founders of modern anthropology.
• Piggott, Stuart, *Approach to Archaeology,* New York, 1965. An excellent introduction to the whole field of archeological studies.
• Radcliffe-Brown, A. R., *Structure and Function in Primitive Society,* Glencoe, Ill., 1952.
• Sandars, N. K., *Prehistoric Art in Europe,* Baltimore, 1968.
  Vlahos, Olivia, *Human Beginnings,* New York, 1966. A brisk, informal account of human origins up through the invention of writing and the emergence of civilizations.

Ancient Civilizations of the East and West

	POLITICAL	ECONOMIC

3000
B.C.
	Old Kingdom in Egypt, c. 3100–c. 2200
	
	Supremacy of Sumerian cities in Mesopotamia,
	   c. 2800–c. 2340
	Indus Valley civilization, c. 2500–1500
	Dominance of Akkadian Empire in Mesopotamia,
	   2334–c. 2200
		Development of irrigation and large-scale farming
		   in Egypt and Mesopotamia, c. 3500–c. 2500

2000
B.C.
	Sumerian revival, c. 2200–c. 2000
	Middle Kingdom in Egypt, 2050–1786
	Old Babylonian Empire in Mesopotamia, c. 2000–
	   c. 1550
	Height of Minoan civilization under leadership of
	   Knossos and Phaistos, c. 2000–c. 1500
	Hyksos conquer Egypt, 1786–1575
	Shang Dynasty in China, c. 1766–1027
	
	Mycenaean civilization on mainland Greece,
	   c. 1600–c. 1200
	Hittite Empire in Asia Minor, c. 1600–c. 1200
	The Empire in Egypt, 1575–1087
	Kassites overthrow Babylonians, c. 1550
		Extended commerce in Egypt and Crete, c. 2000
		
		Slavery in Egypt, c. 1575

1500
B.C.
	Mycenaean dominance on Crete, c. 1500–c. 1400
	Destruction of Knossos and end of Minoan
	   civilization, c. 1400
	Hebrew occupation of Canaan, c. 1300–c. 1025
	
	Trojan War, c. 1250
	Mycenaeans succumb to Dorians in Greece,
	   c. 1200–c. 1100
	Chou Dynasty in China, 1100–256
	Unified Hebrew monarchy under Saul, David, and
	   Solomon, c. 1025–922
		Use of iron by Hittites, c. 1500

1000 **B.C.**	Height of Phoenician civilization, c. 1000–c. 700 Kingdom of Israel, 922–722 Kingdom of Judah, 922–586 Feudalism in China, 800–250 Height of Assyrian Empire, c. 750–612 Chaldean Empire, 612–539 Nebuchadnezzar conquers Jerusalem, 586 Persian Empire, 559–330 Height of Lydia under Croesus, c. 550	Mediterranean trade of Phoenicians, c. 1000–c. 700 Invention of coinage by Lydians, c. 625
500 **B.C.**	Persian conquest of Egypt, 525 Darius the Great, height of Persia, 522–486	Royal Road of Persians, c. 500

CULTURAL	RELIGIOUS	
Egyptian hieroglyphic writing, c. 3100	Egyptian sun worship, c. 3000	**3000** **B.C.**
Sumerian cunieform writing, c. 3000		
Construction of great pyramids in Egypt, c. 2700		
Development of Indus Valley writing, c. 2500	Egyptian belief in personal immortality, c. 2500	
Sumerian legal codes, c. 2100		
Gilgamesh epic, c. 2000		**2000** **B.C.**
Code of Hammurabi, c. 1790	Ethical religion in Egypt, c. 1800	
Egyptian diagnostic medicine, c. 1700		
Development of ideographic writing in China, c. 1700		
Egyptian temple architecture, c. 1580–c. 1090		
Development of alphabet by Phoenicians, c. 1500		**1500** **B.C.**
Naturalistic art in Egypt under Ikhnaton, c. 1375	Religious revolution of Ikhnaton, c. 1375	
	Hebrew worship of Yahweh, c. 1000	**1000** **B.C.**
Realistic sculpture of Assyrians, c. 750	Hebrew prophetic revolution, c. 750–c. 600	
	Astral religion of Chaldeans, c. 600–c. 500	
Deuteronomic code, c. 600	Zoroaster, c. 600	
		500 **B.C.**
Book of Job, c. 400		

Chapter 2

THE EGYPTIAN CIVILIZATION

Thou makest the Nile in the Nether World,
Thou bringest it as thou desirest,
To preserve alive the people of Egypt.
For thou hast made them for thyself,
Thou lord of them all, who weariest thyself for them;
Thou sun of day, great in glory. . . .

—Hymn to Aton, from reign of the Pharaoh Ikhnaton

Modern crowds that flood museums to view fabled treasures of Egyptian art are still caught by the spell of one of the oldest and most fascinating civilizations in history. Although the Egyptian civilization was not necessarily the oldest in the ancient world, it was certainly of great antiquity; its origins date from about 3500 B.C. We may consider it here first because somewhat more is known about its accomplishments than about those of most other early peoples. It should be borne in mind while reading this chapter, however, that Mesopotamian and, later, other civilizations were developing simultaneously and sometimes influenced Egyptian developments.

Chronological primacy of Egypt and Mesopotamia

The hallmark of Egyptian civilization was the sense of stability offered by the Nile valley. The fact that the Nile flooded regularly year after year gave Egyptians a feeling that nature was predictable and benign. Moreover, the fertility of the soil in the valley provided for great agricultural wealth, and the fact that the valley was surrounded by deserts and the sea meant that Egypt was comparatively free from threats of foreign invasion. For all these reasons Egyptian civilization was both very advanced and remarkably peaceful. The Greek historian Herodotus was undoubtedly correct when he referred to Egypt as "the gift of the Nile."

Favorable conditions for the development of Egyptian civilization

1. POLITICAL HISTORY UNDER THE PHARAOHS

The ancient history of Egypt is usually divided into three periods: the Old Kingdom, the Middle Kingdom, and the Empire. Even before the Old Kingdom some cultural achievements had been attained. The Egyptians had begun their earliest attempts at irrigation and drainage. They had also learned to use copper tools in place of stone ones, thereby benefiting from the advantages that copper outlasted stone and that copper could be easily sharpened or recast when blunted. Above all, they had developed a system of laws based upon customs and had worked out the initial stage of a system of writing.

The Old Kingdom

About 3100 B.C. Egypt was united into a single unit known as the Old Kingdom. From 3100 B.C. to 2200 B.C. six dynasties ruled the country. Each was headed by a line of "pharaohs," from the Egyptian *per-o,* meaning "great house" or "royal house." The pharaoh was considered to be the son of the sun god and was forbidden to marry anyone other than one of his own sisters lest the divine blood be contaminated. Limitation of rule to the members of a single family also meant that there could be fewer claimants to the throne, and hence less chance of revolution. The authority of the pharaoh was limited to the ancient law: he was not above the law but subject to it. No separation of religious and political life existed. The pharaoh's chief subordinates were priests, and he himself was the chief priest.

The nonmilitaristic character of the Old Kingdom

The government of the Old Kingdom was founded upon a policy of peace and nonaggression. In this respect it was virtually unique among ancient states. The pharaoh had no standing army, nor was there anything that could be called a national militia. Each local area had its own militia, but militias were commanded by civil officials, and when called into active service generally devoted their energies to labor on the public works. In case of a threat of invasion the various local units were assembled at the call of the pharaoh and placed under the command of one of his civil subordinates. At no other time did the head of the government have a military force at his disposal. The Egyptians of the Old Kingdom were content for the most part to work out their own destinies and to let other nations alone. The reasons for this attitude are to be found in the protected position of their country, in their possession of land of inexhaustible fertility, and in the fact that their state was a product of cooperative need instead of being grounded in exploitation.

End of the Old Kingdom

After roughly a millennium of peace and relative prosperity the Old Kingdom came to an end about 2200 B.C. Several causes were responsible. Governmental revenues became exhausted because the pharaohs invested heavily in such grandiose projects as pyramid-building. These enterprises also placed great burdens upon Egyptian subjects who were pressed into forced labor and helped to impoverish and demoralize them. In the meantime provincial nobles usurped more and

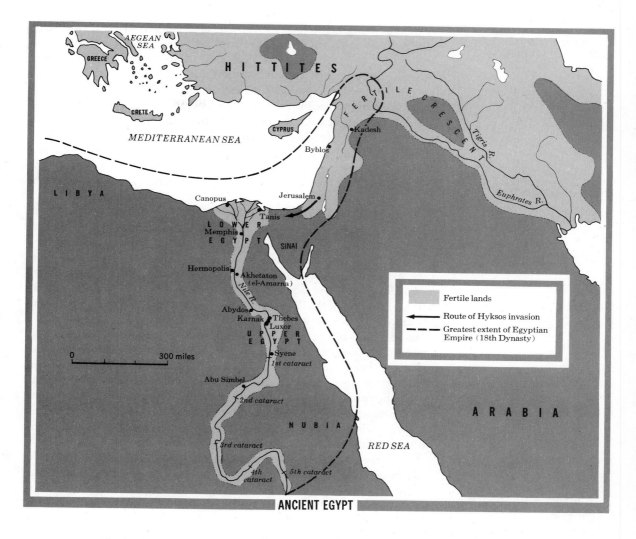

ANCIENT EGYPT

more power until central authority virtually disappeared. The period which followed is called the First Intermediate Age. Anarchy now prevailed. The nobles created their own rival principalities, and political chaos was aggravated by internal brigandage and invasion by desert tribes. The Intermediate Age did not end until the rise of the Eleventh Dynasty which restored centralized rule around 2050 B.C. The next great stage of Egyptian history, known as the Middle Kingdom, ensued.

Throughout most of its life the government of the Middle Kingdom was more socially responsible than that of the Old Kingdom. The Eleventh Dynasty could not withstand the power of the nobles, but the Twelfth, which followed around 1990 and lasted until 1786 B.C., ruled strongly by means of an alliance with a middle class com-

The Middle Kingdom

posed of officials, merchants, artisans, and farmers. This alliance kept the nobility in check and laid the foundations for unprecedented prosperity. During the rule of the Twelfth Dynasty there were advances in social justice and much intellectual achievement. Public works that benefited the whole population, such as extensive drainage and irrigation projects, replaced the building of pyramids, which had no practical use. There was also a democratization of religion which extended to common people a hope for salvation that they had not been granted before. Religion now emphasized proper moral conduct instead of ritual dependent on wealth. For all these reasons the reign of the Twelfth Dynasty is commonly considered to be Egypt's classical or golden age.

The invasion of the Hyksos

Immediately afterwards, however, Egypt entered its Second Intermediate Era. This was another period of internal chaos and foreign invasion which lasted for more than two centuries, or from 1786 to 1575 B.C. The contemporary records are scanty, but they seem to show that the internal disorder was the result of a counterrevolt of the nobles. The pharaohs were again reduced to impotence, and much of the social progress of the Twelfth Dynasty was destroyed. About 1750 the land was invaded by the Hyksos, or "Rulers of Foreign Lands," a mixed horde originating in western Asia. Their military prowess is commonly ascribed to the fact that they possessed horses and war chariots, but their victory was certainly made easier by the dissension among the Egyptians themselves. Their rule had profound effects upon Egyptian history. Not only did they familiarize the Egyptians with new methods of warfare, but by providing them with a common grievance in the face of foreign tyranny they also enabled them to forget their differences and unite in a common cause.

Near the end of the seventeenth century B.C. the rulers of northern Egypt launched a revolt against the Hyksos, a movement which was eventually joined by most of the Egyptians of the south. By 1575 all of the conquerors who had not been killed or enslaved had been driven from the country. The hero of this victory, Ahmose, founder of the Eighteenth Dynasty, now made himself master of Egypt. The regime he established was much more highly consolidated than any that had hitherto existed. In the great resurgence of nationalism which had accompanied the struggle against the Hyksos, local loyalties were reduced, and with it the power of the nobles.

The period which followed the accession of Ahmose is called the period of the Empire. It lasted from 1575 to 1087 B.C., during which time the country was ruled by three dynasties of pharaohs in succession: the Eighteenth, Nineteenth, and Twentieth. No longer was the prevailing state policy pacific and isolationist; a spirit of aggressive imperialism rapidly pervaded the nation. The causes of this change are not far to seek. The military ardor generated by the successful war against the Hyksos whetted an appetite for further victories. A vast

Ramses II (XIXth Dynasty)

military machine had been created to expel the invader, which proved to be too valuable an adjunct to the pharaoh's power to be discarded immediately.

The first steps in the direction of the new policy were taken by the immediate successors of Ahmose in making extensive raids into Palestine and claiming sovereignty over Syria. With one of the most formidable armies of ancient times the new pharaohs speedily annihilated all opposition in Syria and eventually made themselves masters of a vast domain extending from the Euphrates to the farther cataracts of the Nile. But they never succeeded in welding the conquered peoples into loyal subjects, and weakness was the signal for widespread revolt in Syria. Their successors suppressed the uprising and managed to hold the Empire together for some time, but ultimate disaster could not be averted. More territory had been annexed than could be managed successfully. The influx of wealth into Egypt weakened the national fiber by fostering corruption and luxury, and the constant revolts of the vanquished eventually sapped the strength of the state beyond all hope of recovery. By the twelfth century most of the conquered provinces had been permanently lost.

Failures of the Empire

The government of the Empire resembled that of the Old Kingdom, except for the fact that it was more absolute. Military power was now the basis of the pharaoh's rule. A professional army was always available with which to overawe his subjects. Most of the former nobles now became courtiers or members of the royal bureaucracy under the complete domination of the king.

The government of the Empire

The last of the great pharaohs was Ramses III, who ruled from 1182 to 1151 B.C. He was succeeded by a long line of nonentities who inherited his name but not his ability. By the middle of the twelfth century Egypt had fallen prey to numerous ills of invasion and social decadence. Libyans and Nubians were swarming over the country and gradually debasing cultural standards. About the same time the Egyptians themselves appear to have lost their creative talent. To win immortality by magic devices was now the commanding interest of people of every class. The process of decline was hastened also by the growing power of the priests, who finally usurped the royal prerogatives and dictated the pharaoh's decrees.

The last of the pharaohs

From the middle of the tenth century to nearly the end of the eighth a dynasty of Libyans occupied the throne of the pharaohs. The Libyans were followed by a line of Nubians, who came in from the desert regions west of the Upper Nile. Nubia, though flourishing throughout most of its history in the shadow of Egypt, enjoyed a rich civilization as early as 3500 B.C. with cultural traditions of its own. By 2000 B.C. their sophisticated civilization radiated from the city of Kerma, some one thousand miles south of Aswan in what is today the Sudan Republic. Ancient Nubians were noted for their delicate polychrome pottery, far more sophisticated than anything produced else-

The downfall of Egypt

where along the Nile Valley at that time, and their steep-sided pyramids, bearing strong Egyptian influence. By 750 B.C. the black-skinned Nubians had formed a unified kingdom, making it the oldest truly Negro nation. In 670 Egypt was conquered by the Assyrians, who succeeded in maintaining their supremacy for only eight years. After the collapse of Assyrian rule in 662 the Egyptians regained their independence, and a brilliant renaissance of culture ensued. It was doomed to an untimely end, however, for in 525 B.C. the country was conquered by the Persians. The ancient civilization was never again revived.

2. EGYPTIAN RELIGION

The importance of religion in Egypt

Religion played a dominant role in the life of the ancient Egyptians, leaving its impress upon almost everything. The art was an expression of religious symbolism. The literature and philosophy were suffused with religious teachings. The government of the Old Kingdom was to a large extent a theocracy, and even the military pharaohs of the Empire professed to rule in the name of the gods. Material resources in considerable amounts were expended in providing elaborate tombs and in supporting priests.

The early religious evolution

The religion of the ancient Egyptians went through various stages: from simple polytheism to the earliest known expression of monotheism, and then back to polytheism. In the beginning each city or district appears to have had its local deities, who were guardian gods of the locality or personifications of nature powers. The unification of the country under the Old Kingdom resulted not only in a consolidation of territory but in a fusion of divinities as well. All of the guardian deities were merged into the great sun god Re. Under the Middle Kingdom, with the establishment of Theban dynasties in control of the government, this deity was commonly called Amon or Amon-Re from the name of the chief god of Thebes. The gods who personified the vegetative powers of nature were fused into a deity called Osiris, who was also the god of the Nile. Throughout Egyptian history these two great powers who ruled the universe, Amon and Osiris, vied with each other for supremacy. Other deities, as we shall see, were recognized also, but they occupied a distinctly subordinate place.

The solar faith

During the period of the Old Kingdom the solar faith, embodied in the worship of Re, was the dominant system of belief. It served as an official religion whose chief function was to give immortality to the state and to the people collectively. The pharaoh was the living representative of this faith on earth; through his rule the rule of the god was maintained. But Re was not only a guardian deity. He was in addition the god of righteousness, justice, and truth, and the upholder of the moral order of the universe. He offered no spiritual blessings or even material rewards to people as individuals. The solar faith was not a religion for the masses as such, except insofar as their welfare coincided with that of the state.

The cult of Osiris, as we have already observed, began its existence as a nature religion. The god personified the growth of vegetation and the life-giving powers of the Nile. The career of Osiris was wrapped about with an elaborate legend. In the remote past, according to belief, he had been a benevolent ruler, who taught his people agriculture and other practical arts and gave them laws. After a time he was treacherously slain by his wicked brother Set, and his body cut into pieces. His wife Isis, who was also his sister, went in search of the pieces, put them together, and miraculously restored his body to life. The risen god regained his kingdom and continued his beneficent rule for a time, but eventually descended to the nether world to serve as judge of the dead. Horus, his posthumous son, finally grew to manhood and avenged his father's death by killing Set.

The Osiris cult

Originally this legend seems to have been little more than a nature myth. The death and resurrection of Osiris symbolized the recession of the Nile in the autumn and the coming of the flood in the spring. But in time the Osiris legend began to take on a deeper significance. The human qualities of the deities concerned—the paternal solicitude of Osiris for his subjects, the faithful devotion of his wife and son— appealed to the emotions of average Egyptians, who were now able to see their own tribulations and triumphs mirrored in the lives of the gods. More important still, the death and resurrection of Osiris came to be regarded as conveying a promise of personal immortality. As the

Significance of the Osiris legend

Funerary Papyrus. The scene shows the heart of a princess of the XXIst Dynasty being weighed in a balance before the god Osiris. On the other side of the balance are the symbols for life and truth.

*Ikhnaton and His Wife Nefertiti
Making Offerings to Aton.* A stele
from the XVIIIth Dynasty.
Aton is symbolized as the sun.

god had triumphed over death and the grave, so might also the individual who followed him faithfully inherit everlasting life. Finally, the victory of Horus over Set appeared to foreshadow the ultimate ascendancy of good over evil.

Egyptian ideas of the hereafter attained their full development in the later history of the Middle Kingdom. For this reason elaborate preparations had to be made to prevent the extinction of one's earthly remains. Not only were bodies mummified but wealthy men left munificent endowments to provide their mummies with food and other essentials. As the religion advanced toward maturity, however, a less naive conception of the afterlife was adopted. The dead were now believed to appear before Osiris to be judged according to their deeds on earth.

All of the departed who met the tests included in this system of judgment entered a celestial realm of physical delights and simple pleasures. Here in marshes of lilies and lotus-flowers they would hunt wild geese and quail with never-ending success. Or they might build houses in the midst of orchards with luscious fruits of unfailing yield. They would find lily-lakes on which to sail, pools of sparkling water in which to bathe, and shady groves inhabited by singing birds and every manner of gentle creature. The unfortunate victims whose hearts revealed their vicious lives were utterly destroyed.

The Egyptian religion attained its highest perfection about the end of the Middle Kingdom. By this time the solar faith and the cult of Osiris had been merged in such a way as to preserve the best features of both. The province of Amon as the god of the living, as the champion of good in this world, was accorded almost equal importance with the functions of Osiris as the giver of personal immortality and the judge of the dead. The religion was now quite clearly an ethical one. People repeatedly avowed their desire to do justice because such conduct was pleasing to the great sun god.

Soon after the establishment of the Empire the religion which has just been described underwent a serious debasement. Its ethical significance was largely destroyed, and superstition and magic gained the ascendancy. The chief cause seems to have been that the long and bitter war for the expulsion of the Hyksos fostered the growth of irrational attitudes and correspondingly depreciated the intellect. The result was a marked increase in the power of the priests, who preyed upon the fears of the masses to promote their own advantage. They inaugurated the practice of selling magical charms, which were supposed to have the effect of preventing the heart of the deceased from betraying his or her real character. They also sold formulas which, inscribed on rolls of papyrus and placed in the tomb, were alleged to be effective in facilitating the passage of the dead to the celestial realm. The aggregate of these formulas constituted what is referred to as the Book of the Dead.

Contrary to the general impression, it was not an Egyptian Bible, but merely a collection of mortuary inscriptions.

This degradation of the religion at the hands of the priests into a system of magical practices finally resulted in a great religious upheaval. The leader of this movement was the Pharaoh Amenhotep IV, who began his reign about 1375 B.C. and died or was murdered about fifteen years later. After some fruitless attempts to correct the most flagrant abuses, he resolved to crush the system entirely. He drove the priests from the temples, hacked the names of the traditional deities from the public monuments, and initiated the worship of a new god whom he called "Aton," an ancient designation for the physical sun. He changed his own name from Amenhotep ("Amon rests") to Ikhnaton, which meant "Aton is satisfied." His wife Nefertiti became Nefer-nefru-aton: "Beautiful is the beauty of Aton." In keeping with his desire to begin entirely anew, Ikhnaton built a new capital, El-Amarna, which he dedicated to the worship of the new deity.

More important than these physical changes was the new set of doctrines enunciated by the reforming pharaoh. He taught first of all a religion of qualified monotheism. Aton and Ikhnaton himself were the only gods in existence. Like none of the gods before him, Aton had no human or animal shape but was to be conceived in terms of the life-giving, warming rays of the sun. He was the creator of all, and thus god not merely of Egypt but of the whole universe. Ikhnaton deemed himself to be Aton's heir and co-regent; while the pharaoh and his wife worshiped Aton, others were to worship Ikhnaton as a living deity. Aside from this important qualification Ikhnaton restored the ethical quality of Egyptian religion at its best by insisting that Aton was the author of the moral order of the world and the rewarder of mankind for integrity and purity of heart. He envisaged the new god as the sustainer of all that is of benefit to humanity, and as a heavenly father who watches with benevolent care over all his creatures. Conceptions like these of the unity, righteousness, and benevolence of God were not attained again until the time of the Hebrew prophets some 600 years later.

Despite the energy with which Ikhnaton pursued his religious revolution it was still a failure. The religion of Aton gained little popular following because the masses remained devoted to their old gods. The new religion was too strange for them and was lacking in the greatest attraction of the older faith: the promise of an afterlife. Moreover, the pharaohs who followed Ikhnaton were allied with the priests of Amon and accordingly restored the older modes of worship. Ikhnaton's successor, the pharaoh whom we refer to as "King Tut," changed his name from Tutankhaton to Tutankhamen, abandoned El-Amarna for the old capital of Thebes, and presided over a return to all the old ways. His own burial was a lavish demonstration of commitment to

Monotheism under Ikhnaton

Tutankhamen or "King Tut." This solid gold coffin weighs 2,500 pounds.

the old rituals and belief in life after death. Thereafter Egyptian religion was characterized by growing faith in ritualism and magic. Priests sold formulas and charms which were supposed to trick the gods into granting salvation: thus even the cult of Osiris lost most of its elevated moral quality.

3. EGYPTIAN INTELLECTUAL ACHIEVEMENTS

The philosophy of ancient Egypt was chiefly ethical and political, although traces of broader philosophic conceptions are occasionally to be found. The idea that the universe is controlled by mind or intelligence, for example, is a notion that appeared from time to time in the writings of priests. Other philosophic ideas of the ancient Egyptians included the conception of an eternal universe, the notion of constantly recurring cycles of events, and the doctrine of natural cause and effect. No Egyptian writers could be classified as "pure" philosophers. They were concerned primarily with religion and with questions of individual conduct and social justice.

The earliest examples of Egyptian ethical philosophy were maxims similar to those of the Book of Proverbs in the Old Testament. They went little beyond practical wisdom, but occasionally they enjoined tolerance, moderation, and justice.

As political philosophers the Egyptians developed a concept of the state as a welfare institution presided over by a benevolent ruler. This concept was embodied especially in the *Plea of the Eloquent Peasant,* written about 2050 B.C. It sets forth the idea of a ruler committed to benevolence and justice for the good of his subjects. He is urged to act as the father of the orphan, the husband of the widow, and the brother of the forsaken. He is supposed to judge impartially and to execute punishment upon whom it is due; and to promote such an order of harmony and prosperity that no one will be deprived of basic human necessities.

The branches of science which most absorbed the attention of the Egyptians were astronomy, mathematics, and medicine. All were developed for practical ends—astronomy primarily to compute the time of the Nile floods, mathematics for building purposes, and medicine for healing. The Egyptians were by no means pure scientists. They had little interest in the nature of the universe as such, a fact which probably accounts for their failure to advance very far in the science of astronomy. Nonetheless they did perfect a calendar based on the annual appearance of Sirius, the brightest star in the sky, whose yearly rising invariably preceded the overflowing of the Nile. In addition they worked out a lunar calendar to mark the succession of religious rites.

Mathematics was more highly developed. The Egyptians laid the foundations for arithmetic and geometry. They devised the arithmetical operations of addition, subtraction, and division, but never discovered how to multiply except through a series of additions. They invented the decimal system, but had no symbol for zero. Fractions caused them some difficulty: all those with a numerator greater than one had to be broken down into a series, each with *one* as the numerator, before they could be used in mathematical calculations. The only exception was the fraction two-thirds, which the scribes had learned to use as it stood. The Egyptians also achieved a surprising degree of skill in the mathematics of measurement, computing with accuracy the areas of triangles, rectangles, and hexagons. The ratio of the circumference of a circle to its diameter they calculated to be 3.16, thereby coming very close to the modern calculation of 3.14. They learned how to compute the volume of the pyramid, the cylinder, and the hemisphere.

The Egyptians also did some remarkable work in medicine. Early medical practice was conservative and profusely corrupted by superstition, but a document dating from about 1700 B.C. reveals a fairly adequate conception of scientific diagnosis and treatment. Egyptian physicians were frequently specialists: some were oculists, others were dentists, surgeons, specialists in diseases of the stomach, and so on. In the course of their work they made many discoveries of lasting value. They recognized the importance of the heart and had some appreciation of the significance of the pulse. They acquired a degree of skill in the treatment of fractures and performed simple operations. Unlike some peoples of later date they ascribed disease to natural causes. They discovered the value of cathartics, noted the curative properties of numerous drugs, and compiled the first *materia medica,* or catalogue of medicines. Many of their remedies were later carried into Europe by the Greeks and are still employed by the peasantry of isolated regions.

In other scientific fields the Egyptians contributed less. Although they achieved great building feats, they possessed but the scantiest knowledge of physics. They knew the principle of the inclined plane, which they applied to the building of pyramids, but they were ignorant of the pulley. To their credit, on the other hand, must be assigned considerable progress in metallurgy, the invention of the sundial, and the making of papyrus and glass. With all their deficiencies as pure scientists, they equaled or surpassed in actual accomplishment most of the other peoples of the ancient Near East.

The Egyptians developed their first form of writing during the predynastic period. This system, known as the *hieroglyphic,* from the Greek words meaning sacred carving, was originally composed of pictographic signs denoting concrete objects. Gradually, certain of these signs were conventionalized and used to represent abstract concepts. Other characters were introduced to designate separate syllables which could be combined to form words. Finally, twenty-four symbols, each representing a single consonant sound of the human voice, were added early in the Old Kingdom. Thus the hieroglyphic system of writing had come to include at an early date three separate types of characters, the pictographic, syllabic, and alphabetic.

The ultimate step in this evolution of writing would have been the complete separation of the alphabetic from the nonalphabetic characters and the exclusive use of the former in written communication. But the Egyptians, although they made frequent use of the consonant signs, did not commonly employ them as an independent system of writing. It was left for the Phoenicians to do this some 1,500 years later. Nevertheless, the Egyptians must be credited with the invention of the principle of the alphabet. It was they who first perceived the value of single symbols for the individual sounds of the human voice. The Phoenicians merely copied this principle, based their own system of writing on it, and diffused the idea among neighboring nations. In the final analysis it is therefore true that the Egyptian alphabet was the parent of every other that has ever been used in the Western world.

4. THE MEANING OF EGYPTIAN ART

No single interpretation will suffice to explain the meaning of Egyptian art. In general, it expressed the aspirations of a collectivized national life. It was not art for art's sake, nor did it serve to convey the individual's reactions to the problems of his or her personal world. Yet there were times when the conventions of a communal society were broken down, and the supremacy was accorded to a spontaneous individual art that expressed the beauty of a flower or caught the radiant idealism of a youthful face. Seldom was the Egyptian genius for faithful reproduction of nature entirely suppressed. Even the rigid formalism of official architecture was commonly relieved by touches of naturalism—columns in imitation of palm trunks, lotus-blossom capitals, and occasional statues of pharaohs that were not stylized types but true individual portraits.

See color plates following page 96

In most civilizations where the interests of society are exalted above those of individuals, architecture tends to be the most typical and the most highly developed of the arts. Egypt was no exception. Whether in the Old Kingdom, Middle Kingdom, or Empire it was the problems of building construction that absorbed the talent of the artist. Although sculpture and painting were by no means primitive, they nevertheless had as their primary function the embellishment of temples. Only at times did they rise to the status of independent arts.

The characteristic examples of Old Kingdom architecture were the pyramids, the first of which were built at least as early as 2700 B.C. An amazing amount of labor and skill were expended in their construction. The Greek historian Herodotus estimated that 100,000 workers

The Pyramids of Gizeh with the Sphinx in the Foreground

must have been employed for twenty years to complete the single pyramid of Khufu (or Cheops) at Gizeh. Its height was 481 feet, and the more than 2 million limestone blocks it contains are fitted together with a precision which few modern masons could duplicate. Each of the blocks weighs between 2.5 and 15 tons. They were evidently hewn out of rock cliffs with drills and wedges and then dragged by gangs of workers without the aid of wheeled vehicles (as yet unknown) up earthen ramps and fitted into place.

Several theories have been advanced to explain the building of the pyramids. They may have been intended for the economic purpose of providing employment opportunities. This explanation would assume that the population had increased to overcrowding, and that the resources of agriculture, mining, industry, and commerce were no longer adequate to provide a livelihood for all the people. There may be some validity to this theory, but it is certain that the pyramids had primarily religious significance for those who ordered them built. The pyramids were unquestionably meant to be the tombs of the divine pharaohs: the mightier the pharaoh, the larger his resting place was supposed to be. Since the pharaoh stood for the state the pyramids probably also took on political significance. Not only did they glorify the rulers but they may have helped to enhance the idea that the might of the Egyptian state was indestructible.

During the Middle Kingdom and the Empire, when concern for personal salvation became predominant, the temple displaced the pyr-

Significance of the pyramids

The temples

Egyptian sculpture

amid as the leading architectural form. The most noted examples were the great temples at Karnak and Luxor, built during the period of the Empire. Many of their gigantic, richly carved columns still stand as silent witnesses of a splendid architectural talent. Egyptian temples were characterized by massive size. The temple at Karnak, with a length of about 1,300 feet, covered the largest area of any religious edifice ever built. Its central hall alone could contain almost any of the Gothic cathedrals of Europe. The columns used in the temples had stupendous proportions. The largest of them were seventy feet high, with diameters in excess of twenty feet. It has been estimated that the capitals which surmounted them could furnish standing room for a hundred men.

As already mentioned, Egyptian sculpture and painting served primarily as adjuncts to architecture. The former was heavily laden with conventions that governed its style and meaning. Statues of pharaohs were commonly of colossal size. Those produced during the Empire ranged in height from seventy-five to ninety feet. Some of them were colored to enhance the portrait, and the eyes were frequently inlaid with rock crystal. The figures were nearly always rigid, with the arms folded across the chest or fixed to the sides of the body and with the eyes staring straight ahead. Countenances were generally represented as impassive, utterly devoid of emotional expression. Anatomical distortion was frequently practiced: the natural length of the thighs might be increased, the squareness of the shoulders accentuated, or all of the fingers of the hand made equal in length. A familiar example of nonnaturalistic sculpture was the Sphinx, of which there were thousands in Egypt; the best-known example was the Great Sphinx at Gizeh. This represented the head of a pharaoh on the body of a lion. The purpose was probably to symbolize the notion that the pharaoh possessed the lion's qualities of strength and courage. The figures of

The Temple at Karnak. Most of this building has collapsed or been carried away, but the huge pylons and statues give an idea of the massiveness of Egyptian temples.

sculpture in relief were even less in conformity with nature. The head was presented in profile, with the eye full-face; the torso was shown in the frontal position, while the legs were rendered in profile.

The meaning of Egyptian sculpture is not hard to perceive. The colossal size of the statues of pharaohs was doubtless intended to symbolize their power and the power of the state they represented. It is significant that the size of these statues increased as the empire expanded and the government became more absolute. The conventions of rigidity and impassiveness were meant to express the timelessness and stability of the national life. Here was a nation which, according to the ideal, was not to be torn loose from its moorings by the uncertain mutations of fortune but was to remain fixed and imperturbable. The portraits of its chief men consequently must betray no anxiety, fear, or triumph, but an unvarying calmness throughout the ages. In similar fashion, the anatomical distortion can probably be interpreted as a deliberate attempt to express some national ideal.

An intriguing exception to the mainstream of Egyptian artistic development is the art produced during the reign of Ikhnaton. Because the pharaoh wished to break with all manifestations of the ancient Egyptian religion, including its artistic conventions, he presided over an artistic revolution. The new style he patronized was naturalistic because his new religion reverenced nature as the handiwork of Aton. Accordingly portrait busts of the pharaoh himself and his queen Nefertiti abandoned the earlier grandiloquent impassivity and distortion in favor of more realistic detail. A surviving bust of Nefertiti which reveals her slightly quizzical and haunting femininity is one of the greatest monuments in the history of art. For the same reasons painting under the patronage of Ikhnaton also emerged as a highly expressive art form. Murals of this period display the world of experience above all in terms of movement. They catch the instant action of the wild bull leaping in the swamp, the headlong flight of the frightened stag, and the effortless swimming of ducks in a pond. But just as Ikhnaton's religious reform was not lasting, neither was the more naturalistic art of his reign.

5. SOCIAL AND ECONOMIC LIFE

During the greater part of the history of Egypt the population was divided into five classes: the royal family; the priests; the nobles; the middle class of scribes, merchants, artisans, and wealthy farmers; and the peasants, who comprised by far the bulk of the population. During the Empire a sixth class, the professional soldiers, was added, ranking immediately below the nobles. Thousands of slaves were also captured in this period, and for a time these formed a seventh class. Despised by all, they were forced to labor in the government quarries and on the temple estates. Gradually, however, they were allowed to enlist in the army and even in the personal service of the pharaoh.

Pharaoh Mycerinus and His Queen. Sculpture from the IVth Dynasty, c. 2590 B.C.—an example of the impassive, grandiloquent style.

Nefertiti. The famous portrait bust executed in Ikhnaton's studios at El-Amarna.

Fishing and Fowling: Wall Painting, Thebes, XVIIIth Dynasty. Most of the women appear to belong to the prosperous classes, while the simple garb and insignificant size of the men indicates that they are probably slaves.

The principal classes of Egyptian society

With these developments they ceased to constitute a separate class. The position of the various ranks of society shifted from time to time. In the Old Kingdom the nobles and priests among all of the pharaoh's subjects held the supremacy. During the Middle Kingdom the classes of commoners came into their own. Merchants, artisans, and farmers gained concessions from the government. Particularly impressive is the dominant role played by the merchants and manufacturers in this period. The establishment of the Empire, accompanied as it was by the extension of government functions, resulted in the ascendancy of a new nobility, made up primarily of officials. The priests also gained more power with the growth of magic and ritualism.

The gulf between rich and poor

The gulf that separated the standards of living of the upper and lower classes of Egypt was perhaps even wider than it is today in Europe and America. The wealthy nobles lived in splendid villas that opened into fragrant gardens and shady groves. Their food had all the richness and variety of sundry kinds of meat, poultry, cakes, fruit, wine, and sweets. They ate from vessels of alabaster, gold, and silver, and adorned their persons with expensive fabrics and costly jewels. By contrast, the life of the poor was wretched indeed. The laborers in the towns inhabited congested quarters composed of mud-brick hovels with roofs of thatch. Their only furnishings were stools and boxes and a few crude pottery jars. The peasants on the great estates enjoyed a less crowded but no more abundant life.

Although polygamy was permitted, normally the basic social unit was the monogamous family. Even the pharaoh, who could keep a

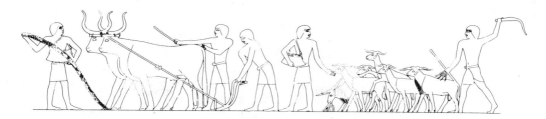

Sowing Seed and Working It into the Soil. From a bag which he wears over his left shoulder, the sower casts seed under the feet of cattle yoked to a plow. The plow is here used to harrow the soil. While one laborer guides the cows with a stick, another guides the plow straight and keeps the plowshare in the ground by bearing down on the handles. Sheep are then driven across the field to trample in the seed. From wall paintings at Sheikh Saîd, about 2700 B.C.

harem of secondary wives and concubines, had a chief wife. Concubinage, however, was a socially reputable institution. Yet compared to women in most other ancient societies, Egyptian women were not entirely subordinated to men. Wives were not totally secluded; women could own and inherit property and engage in business. Almost alone among ancient peoples the Egyptians late in their history permitted women to succeed to the throne.

Egyptian women

The Egyptian economic system rested primarily upon an agrarian basis. Agriculture was diversified and highly developed, and the soil yielded excellent crops of wheat, barley, millet, vegetables, fruits, flax, and cotton. Theoretically the land was the property of the pharaoh, but in the earlier periods he granted most of it to his subjects, so that in actual practice it was largely in the possession of individuals.

Agriculture, trade, and industry

Ikhnaton's son, "King Tut," and His Queen. The child-rulers in their garden are portrayed in the more naturalistic style held over from Ikhnaton's reign.

Commerce did not amount to much before 2000 B.C., but after that date it grew rapidly to a position of first-rate importance. A flourishing trade was carried on with the island of Crete, with Phoenicia, Palestine, and Syria. Gold mines in Libya controlled by Egypt were an important source of wealth. The chief articles of export consisted of gold, wheat, linen fabrics, and fine pottery. Imports were confined largely to silver, ivory, and lumber. Of no less significance than commerce was manufacturing. As early as 3000 B.C. large numbers of people were already engaged in industrial pursuits, mostly in separate crafts. In later times factories were established, employing twenty or more persons under one roof, and with some degree of division of labor. The leading industries were quarrying, shipbuilding, and the manufacture of pottery, glass, and textiles.

The development of instruments of business

From an early date the Egyptians made progress in the perfection of instruments of business. They knew the elements of accounting and bookkeeping. Their merchants issued orders and receipts for goods. They invented deeds for property, written contracts, and wills. While they had no system of coinage, they had nevertheless attained a money economy. Rings of copper or gold of definite weight circulated as media of exchange. This Egyptian ring-money is apparently the oldest currency in the history of civilizations. Probably it was not used except for larger transactions. The simple dealings of the peasants and poorer townsfolk doubtless continued on a basis of barter.

Economic collectivism

The Egyptian economic system was always collective. From the very beginning the energies of the people had been drawn into socialized channels. The interests of the individual and the interests of society were conceived as identical. The productive activities of the entire nation revolved around huge state enterprises, and the government remained by far the largest employer of labor. But this collectivism was not all-inclusive; a considerable sphere was left for private initia-

Left: *Making Sun-dried Bricks*. Nile mud (generally mixed with chaff or straw) is being worked with a hoe, carried away in buckets and dumped in a pile. Lying on the ground in a row are three bricks, from the last of which a wooden mold, used in shaping them, is being lifted. An overseer with a stick is seated close by. The finished bricks are carried off by means of a yoke across the shoulders. From a wall-painting at Thebes about 1500 B.C. Right: *Stonecutters Dressing Blocks*. Men with mallets and chisels are dressing down blocks to true surfaces. Below, two of them test the accuracy of the dressed surface. After two edges of the block are determined, a cord is stretched between two pegs to help gauge how much remains to be chiseled away.

 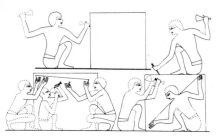

Sculptors at Work. From a tomb of the VIth Dynasty, c. 2300 B.C.

tive. Merchants conducted their own businesses; many of the craftsmen had their own shops; and as time went on, larger and larger numbers of peasants gained the status of independent farmers. The government continued to operate the quarries and mines, to build pyramids and temples, and to farm the royal estates.

The extreme development of state control came with the founding of the Empire. The growth of a military absolutism and the increasing frequency of wars of conquest augmented the need for revenue and for unlimited production of goods. To fulfill this need the government extended its control over economic life. The services of craftsmen were conscripted for the erection of magnificent temples and for the manufacture of implements of war, while foreign trade became a state monopoly. As the Empire staggered toward its downfall, the government absorbed more and more of the economic activities of the people.

The extreme development of state control under the Empire

6. THE EGYPTIAN ACHIEVEMENT

Few civilizations of ancient times surpassed the Egyptian in impressive accomplishments. Important elements of mathematics and science had their beginnings in the Nile valley. The Egyptians also perfected techniques of irrigation, engineering, and the making of pottery and glass. They were one of the first peoples to have any clear conception of art for other than utilitarian purposes, and they originated architectural principles that were destined for extensive use in subsequent ages.

Egyptian contributions: (1) intellectual and artistic

Equally noteworthy were Egyptian religious and ethical ideas. Aside from the Persians, the dwellers on the banks of the Nile were the only peoples of the ancient world to build a national religion around the doctrine of personal immortality and the idea of rewards and punishments after death. Beyond that, Ikhnaton's experiment in the cult of Aton was the first example in history of a religion of universal monotheism. Egyptian ethical prescriptions, moreover, were remarkably advanced in embracing not only the ordinary prohibitions of lying, theft, and murder, but in including exalted ideals of justice, benevolence, and equal rights. Egyptian thought had little direct influence on subsequent formulations because the Egyptian language and writing was hardly understood by others, but all told the Egyptian civilization stands as a remarkable and ever-fascinating monument of human accomplishments at the dawn of recorded time.

7. KUSHITIC CIVILIZATION

Egyptian splendor rested in large measure on vast human and physical resources lying beyond its southern periphery. Successive Egyptian dynasties drew heavily on the area known today as the Sudan Republic for laborers and soldiers as well as for precious stones and exotic woods used in the crafting of jewelry and fine furniture. The contributions of these darker-skinned neighbors are vividly recorded in scenes etched on objets d'art found in the tombs of Egypt's pharaohs.

The origin of the Negroid southerners, long shrouded in mystery, is beginning to come to light through recent archeological discoveries. We are now fairly certain that from at least 2200 B.C. food-producing Neolithic groups from the ecologically-deteriorating southern Sahara were dispersing to more fertile parts of Africa. Some migrated to the Lower Nile where they joined peoples of Mediterranean and Asian stock in laying the foundations of the so-called New Kingdom of Egypt. Others wandered southward to the Upper Nile in a region

Foundation of the Kingdom of Kush

Egyptian Tomb Art. Egypt's Sundanic neighbors were frequently portrayed in Egyptian art.

later known to the Egyptians as "Kush." By 1500 B.C. these black-complexioned Kushites, showing remarkable cultural affinities to late predynastic Egypt, had established their own kingdom. Indeed, this Kingdom of Kush became the first highly advanced, essentially Negroid, civilization in Africa. Its vigorous inhabitants traded actively with Egypt and borrowed extensively from their culture. Within four centuries, the capital at Napata, just south of the Fourth Cataract, had flowered into a major religious center for the worship of the Egyptian god Amon-Re.

Under their king, Kashta, the Kushites began to take advantage of Egypt's decaying social fabric. In about 750 B.C. Kashta's armies swept into the temple city of Thebes, capital of Upper Egypt. Kashta's son, Piankhy, went on to capture Memphis and to extend Kushitic dominion over Lower Egypt as well. With the entire country in hand, Piankhy assumed the title of pharaoh and established Egypt's Twenty-fifth Dynasty

Kushitic invasion of Egypt

The rule of the Kushites was short-lived. Their genius at governance was no match for the Iron Age Assyrians who burst into Egypt in 670 B.C. The Kushites quickly retreated to their former homelands along the far reaches of the Upper Nile. A new Kushitic power base was established at Meroë, some 120 miles north of modern Khartoum, in the fertile pastures between the river Atbara and the Blue Nile. They may have acquired from the Assyrians the technique of iron-smelting, for Meroë soon became the major iron-working center of ancient Africa and the first black industrial city south of the Sahara.

Meroë: black Africa's first industrial city

The Kushites made an indelible imprint on numerous Mediterranean civilizations. By the fifth century B.C. their likeness appeared on vases, wall murals, and statues from Cyprus in the eastern Mediterranean to ancient Etruria on the Italian peninsula. They were variously depicted as athletes, dancers, court attendants, and warriors. Greek merchants, active in Egyptian markets, called the Kushites "Ethiopians" meaning "men with burnt faces."

Kushitic impact on Mediterranean civilizations

In 322 B.C. Egypt was conquered by Alexander the Great and became a Greek-ruled kingdom. Thenceforth, via Hellenized Egypt, Kushitic exposure to Mediterranean civilizations increased. A brisk trade with the Greeks and Hellenized Egyptians brought prosperity to Kush and enabled its people to develop distinctive architectural and artistic traditions. Unique stone pyramids cast haunting shadows across the Nile at Meroë; and Meroitic pottery, decorated with incised geometric designs, could compare favorably to the finest produced in the ancient world at that time. Kush reached its zenith between 250 B.C. and 200 A.D. By that time Meroitic hieroglyphs had even begun to replace Egyptian as the literary language.

The flowering of Kushitic civilization 250 B.C.–200 A.D.

The Kushitic window on the non-African world opened still further between 13 A.D. and the third century, when Egypt was under Roman rule. After that, Nile valley trade quickly declined and with it Kushitic civilization. For centuries, the Nile's treacherous cataracts had shielded Kush from northern invasions and permitted its inhabitants to adopt only those aspects of Egyptian, Greek, and Roman culture they found desirable. But with the Nile valley connection weakened, Kush suffered economically and fell vulnerable to desert infiltrators from the west. This made it rather easy in the mid-fourth century for Meroë to be overrun by the armies of neighboring Axum, a rising kingdom in the southeast.

Tantalizing legends suggest that Meroë's royal family migrated to West Africa where they may have contributed to the evolution of new political and cultural institutions. West Africans were less advanced politically and economically even though their trans-Saharan links with North Africa and the Nile extend far into antiquity. Since at least 130 B.C. West Africans supplied the north with gold, slaves, precious stones, and wild animals for sports arenas. An ancient chariot route extended from the Punic settlements on the North African coast through the oases of the Fezzan to the Chad Basin. The Kushitic refugees may have followed an even more ancient trail connecting the Nile with the Niger river by way of Fezzan.

8. THE CHRISTIAN KINGDOM OF ETHIOPIA

Unlike landlocked Kush, Axum to the southeast could profit from a fast moving trade with Ptolemaic Egypt via the Red Sea. Axumite seaports were busy entrepôts for interior goods destined for the Mediterranean world, the Persian Gulf, India, and beyond. Egyptian Greek middlemen provided Axumites a window on the eastern Mediterranean while their Arabian counterparts exposed them to the outlets of the Orient.

The Axumites as a people were the product of peaceful mingling of African and Semitic Arabians. The latter had been migrating in small bands toward the rugged Ethiopian highlands since 1000 B.C. With intermarriage came cultural enrichment, so superbly reflected in giant religious obelisks, cut with incredible precision from single blocks of stone. Great strides were also made in agricultural productivity through the introduction of the plow and the art of stone terracing and irrigation.

In the mid-fourth century King Ezana converted to Christianity and declared it the official state religion. Christianity became an effective instrument for the cultural and political unification of the various Axumite chieftaincies into a centralized kingdom called Ethiopia. Monasteries took root in Ethiopia and served as vital centers of learning and cultural transmission. Ethiopian monks translated the Bible into Ge'ez, the indigenous language. In time, the monasteries became economically powerful, as successive emperors endowed them with huge tracts of land. Monasticism as a way of life spread quickly to neighboring Nubian kingdoms, before it had appeared in Christian western Europe.

Ethiopia, centered in mountainous and almost inaccessible highlands, became a natural citadel. In relative seclusion, its inhabitants forged a powerfully stable monarchy and a distinctive Christian culture. Representing one of the world's most stable and enduring civilizations, Ethiopia continued into the twentieth century under essentially the same time-honored institutions and the same royal family.

An enduring kingdom

SELECTED READINGS

• *Items so designated are available in paperback editions.*

   Aldred, Cyril, *The Egyptians,* New York, 1963. A short but reliable account covering culture as well as political history.

   Bibby, Geoffrey, *Four Thousand Years Ago,* Baltimore, 1961. Egyptian developments from 2000 to 1000 B.C. seen from the perspective of contemporary events elsewhere.

• Breasted, James H., *The Development of Religion and Thought in Ancient Egypt,* New York, 1912. Stimulating, but exaggerated in its claims for the work of Ikhnaton; should be read in conjunction with Wilson.

   ———, *History of Egypt,* New York, 1912. The standard older work by America's first great Egyptologist. Full of valuable information but now somewhat out of date in its extreme claims for Egyptian originality and influence.

• Childe, V. Gordon, *New Light on the Most Ancient East,* 4th ed., New York, 1957. Covers origins of civilization not just in Egypt but also in Mesopotamia and India.

   Cottrell, Leonard, *Life under the Pharaohs,* New York, 1960. Fascinating account of life during the period of the Empire.

   Desroches-Noblecourt, C., *Egyptian Wall Paintings,* New York, 1962.

• Edwards, I. E. S., *The Pyramids of Egypt,* Baltimore, 1961. Traces evolution of the form and speculates on the meaning of the pyramids.

   Emery, Walter, *Archaic Egypt,* Baltimore, 1961. Controversial account of the earliest period.

• Frankfort, Henri, *Ancient Egyptian Religion: An Interpretation,* New York, 1948. A penetrating, profound study.

• Mertz, B., *Temples, Tombs and Hieroglyphs,* New York, 1965. Intriguing approach by means of archeological discoveries.

   Smith, W. S., *Art and Architecture of Ancient Egypt,* Baltimore, 1958.

• Steindorff, G., and K. C. Seele, *When Egypt Ruled the East,* Chicago, 1963. Best account of political history of the Empire.

• Wilson, John H., *The Burden of Egypt,* Chicago, 1951. (Paperback edition under the title, *The Culture of Ancient Egypt.*) In a class by itself as the one book to read on Egypt if the student only wishes to read one book. Scintillating and masterful.

SOURCE MATERIALS

Grayson, A. Kirk, and D. B. Redford, eds., *Papyrus and Tablet,* Englewood Cliffs, N.J., 1973. Sources from both ancient Egypt and Mesopotamia. The best short collection for the beginner.

• Pritchard, James B., *The Ancient Near East: An Anthology of Texts and Pictures,* Princeton, N.J., 1965. Also covers both Egypt and Mesopotamia. An excellent selection.

Chapter 3

THE MESOPOTAMIAN AND PERSIAN CIVILIZATIONS

If a son strike his father, they shall cut off his fingers.
If a man destroy the eye of another man, they shall destroy his eye.
If one break a man's bone, they shall break his bone.
If one destroy the eye of a freeman or break the bone of a freeman, he shall
    pay one mina of silver.
If one destroy the eye of a man's slave or break a bone of a man's slave he
    shall pay one-half his price.

             —The Code of Hammurabi, lines 195–199

The other of the most ancient civilizations was that which began in the Tigris-Euphrates valley at least as early as 3500 B.C. This civilization was formerly called the Babylonian or Babylonian-Assyrian civilization. It is now known, however, that the civilization was not founded by either the Babylonians or the Assyrians but by an earlier people called the Sumerians. It seems better, therefore, to use the name Mesopotamian to cover the whole civilization, even though Mesopotamia is sometimes applied only to the northern portion of the land between the two rivers.

Origin of the Mesopotamian civilization

The Mesopotamian civilization differed from the Egyptian in many fundamental respects. Because the Tigris and Euphrates rivers—unlike the Nile—flooded irregularly, and sometimes disastrously, the Mesopotamians, unlike the Egyptians, could not take nature for granted. Furthermore the Mesopotamians were not naturally protected, as the Egyptians were, from foreign incursions. In general, therefore, life in the Tigris-Euphrates regions was far more of a struggle. The results of this can be seen in both political and cultural history. The political history of the Mesopotamian area was marked by much sharper interruptions than transpired in Egypt, as the dominance of one people succeeded that of another. Mesopotamian culture too was more warlike and far more gloomy and pessimistic than the Egyptian.

Comparisons with Egypt

Moreover, whereas the native of Egypt believed in immortality and dedicated a large part of his energy to preparing for the life to come, his Mesopotamian counterpart lived in the present and cherished few hopes regarding human fate beyond the grave. Further religious differences were that the Mesopotamians never advanced as far as the Egyptians did toward monotheism and conceived of their divinities more in terms of fear than of love. Finally, Mesopotamian art was fiercer and less personal than the Egyptian.

Similarities

But there were also important similarities between the two. Both civilizations made progress in ethical theory and in concepts of social justice. Both had their evils of slavery and imperialism, of oppressive kings and priests. Both had common problems of irrigation and land boundaries; and, as a result, both made notable progress in the sciences, especially in mathematics. Finally, rivalry among small states led eventually to consolidation and to the growth of mighty empires, especially in the case of Mesopotamia.

1. FROM THE SUMERIAN TO THE PERSIAN CONQUEST

The Sumerians

The pioneers in the development of the Mesopotamian civilization were the people known as Sumerians, who settled in the lower Tigris-Euphrates valley around 3500 B.C. Their exact place of origin is obscure, but it seems likely that they came from the plateau of central Asia. They spoke a language unrelated to any now known, although their culture bore a certain resemblance to the earliest civilization of India. By a process of peaceful interaction they gradually began to guide the natives hitherto living in the lower valley, a mysterious people who were already advancing well beyond the Neolithic cultural stage. From around 2800 to 2340 B.C. a number of independent Sumerian city-states, the most important of which were Ur and Lagash, flourished in Lower Mesopotamia. Then, however, the period of Sumerian predominance was interrupted by a successful invasion from the north of Mesopotamia led by the mighty Sargon of Akkad (c. 2334–2279).[1] The Akkadians were Semites, a large grouping of peoples of the Near East who spoke related languages (the leading Semitic peoples today are Arabs and Jews). Under Sargon's leadership the Akkadians established the first extensive military empire in Mesopotamia, but this declined around 2200 B.C. and was supplanted by a Sumerian revival led by the city of Ur.

See color map following page 96

The period of Sumerian revival did not last long. Around 2000 B.C. the Amorites, another tribe of Semites, advanced from the west, conquered the Sumerian cities, and established a new empire in the Meso-

---

[1]Here, as elsewhere, dates following a ruler's name refer to dates of reign.

potamian region. Since the Amorites made the village of Babylon the capital of their empire they are commonly called the Babylonians, or the Old Babylonians, to distinguish them from the Neo-Babylonians or Chaldeans, who occupied the Tigris-Euphrates valley much later. The rise of the Old Babylonians inaugurated the second important stage of Mesopotamian civilization after the Sumerian stage. Although most of the Sumerian culture survived, Sumerian dominance was now at an end. The Babylonians established an autocratic state and during the reign of their most famous king, Hammurabi (c. 1792–1750 B.C.), extended their dominion north to Assyria. But after his time their empire gradually declined until it was finally overthrown by the Kassites about 1550 B.C.

With the downfall of Old Babylonia a period of retrogression set in which lasted for 600 years. The Kassites were barbarians with no interest in the cultural achievements of their predecessors. Their lone contribution was the introduction of the horse into the Tigris-Euphrates valley. The old culture would have died out entirely had it not been for its partial adoption by another Semitic people who, as early as 3000 B.C., had founded a tiny kingdom on the plateau of Assur some 500 miles up the Tigris River. These people came to be called the Assyrians, and their ultimate rise to power marked the beginning of the third stage in the development of the Mesopotamian civilization. They began to expand about 1300 B.C. and soon afterward made themselves masters of the whole northern valley. In the tenth century they overturned what was left of Kassite power in Babylonia. Their empire reached its height in the eighth and seventh centuries under Sargon II (722–705 B.C.) and Sennacherib (705–681), who built Nineveh, a magnificent new capital on the Tigris. The Assyrian Empire had now come to include nearly all of the Near East, since the Assyrians had conquered, one after another, Syria, Phoenicia, the Kingdom of Israel, and Egypt. Only the little Kingdom of Judah was able to withstand the Assyrian hosts, probably because of an outbreak of pestilence in the ranks of Sennacherib's army, alluded to in the Old Testament (II Kings 19: 35) as a deathly visit by an angel of the Lord.

Brilliant though the successes of the Assyrians were, they did not endure. So rapidly were new territories annexed that the empire soon reached an unmanageable size. The Assyrians' genius for government was far inferior to their appetite for conquest. Subjugated nations chafed under the despotism that had been forced upon them and, as the empire gave signs of cracking from within, determined to regain their freedom. The death blow was delivered by the Chaldeans (pronounced Kaldeans), a nation of Semites who had settled southeast of the valley of the two rivers. Under the leadership of Nabopolassar, who had served the Assyrian emperors in the capacity of a provincial governor, they organized a revolt and finally captured Nineveh in 612 B.C. The most famous of the Chaldeans was Nebuchadnezzar

The rise and fall of the Old Babylonians

The Kassites and the Assyrians

Assyrians Storming an Enemy City

(605–562 B.C.), who conquered Judah and made his capital of Babylon the leading city of the Near East.

In 539 B.C. the empire of the Chaldeans fell, after an existence of less than a century. It was overthrown by Cyrus the Persian, as he himself declared, "without a battle and without fighting." The easy victory appears to have been made possible by assistance from the Jews, who were being held captive in Babylon, and by a conspiracy of the priests of Babylon to deliver the city to Cyrus as an act of vengeance against the Chaldean king, whose policies they did not like. Members of other influential classes appear also to have looked upon the Persians as deliverers.

Although the Persian state incorporated all of the territories that had once been embraced by the Mesopotamian empires, it included many other provinces besides. It was the vehicle, moreover, of a new and different culture. The downfall of Chaldea must therefore be taken as marking the end of Mesopotamian political history.

2. SUMERIAN ORIGINS OF MESOPOTAMIAN CIVILIZATION

More than to any other people, the Mesopotamian civilization owed its character to the Sumerians. Much of what used to be ascribed to the Babylonians and Assyrians is now known to have been developed by the nation that preceded them. The system of writing was of Sumerian origin; likewise the religion, the laws, and a great deal of the science and commercial practice. Only in the evolution of government and military tactics and in the development of the arts was the originating talent of the later conquerors particularly manifest.

Through the greater part of their history the Sumerians lived in a loose confederation of city-states, united only for military purposes. At the head of each was a *patesi,* who combined the functions of chief priest, commander of the army, and superintendent of the irrigation system. Occasionally one of the more ambitious of these rulers would extend his power over a number of cities and assume the title of king, but no true empire was ever created like those of the Akkadians, or subsequent Babylonians, Assyrians, or Chaldeans.

The Sumerian economic pattern was relatively simple and permitted a wider scope for individual enterprise than was generally allowed in Egypt. The land was never the exclusive property of the ruler either in theory or in practice. Neither was trade or industry a monopoly of the government. The temples, however, seem to have fulfilled many of the functions of a collectivist state. They owned a large portion of the land and operated business enterprises. Because the priests alone had the technical knowledge to calculate the coming of the seasons and lay out canals, they controlled the irrigation system. The masses of the

Diorama of a Part of Ur about 2000 B.C. *A modern archeologist's conception. Walls are omitted to show interiors at left.*

people had little they could call their own. Many of them were serfs, but even those who were technically free were little better off, forced as they were to pay high rents and to labor on public works. Slavery in the strict sense of the word was not an important institution.

Agriculture was the chief economic pursuit of most of the citizens, and the Sumerians were excellent farmers. By virtue of their knowledge of irrigation they produced large crops of cereal grains and subtropical fruits. Since most of the land was divided into large estates held by the rulers, the priests, and the army officers, the average rural citizen was either a tenant farmer or a serf. Commerce was the second most important source of Sumerian wealth. A flourishing trade was established with all of the surrounding areas, revolving around the exchange of metals and timber from the north and west for agricultural products and handicrafted goods from the lower valley. Nearly all of the familiar adjuncts of business were highly developed; bills, receipts, notes, and letters of credit were regularly used.

Agriculture

The most distinctive achievement of the Sumerians was their system of law. It was the product of a gradual evolution of local usage merging together with ideas absorbed from neighboring Semitic peoples. Only a few fragments of this law have survived in their original form, but the famous Code of Hammurabi, the Babylonian king, is now recognized to have been little more than a revision of the code of the Sumerians. Ultimately this code became the basis of the laws of nearly all of the Semites—Babylonians, Assyrians, Chaldeans, and Hebrews.

Sumerian law

The following may be regarded as the essential features of the Sumerian law:

(1) The *lex talionis,* or law of retaliation in kind—"an eye for an eye, a tooth for a tooth, a limb for a limb." This fundamental concept was one that the Sumerians learned from the Semites.

Essential features of Sumerian law

(2) Semiprivate administration of justice. It was incumbent upon the victim or his family to bring the offender to justice. The court served principally as an umpire in the dispute between the plaintiff and defendant, not as an agency of the state to maintain public security, although constables attached to the court might assist in the execution of the sentence.

(3) Inequality before the law. The code divided the population into three classes: patricians or aristocrats; burghers or commoners; serfs and slaves. Penalties were graded according to the rank of the victim, but also in some cases according to the rank of the offender. The killing or maiming of a patrician was a much more serious offense than a similar crime committed against a burgher or a slave. On the other hand, when a patrician was the offender he was punished *more severely* than a person of inferior status would be for the same crime. The origin of this curious rule was probably to be found in considerations of military discipline. Since the patricians were army officers and therefore the chief defenders of the state, they could not be permitted to give vent to their passions or to indulge in riotous conduct.

(4) Inadequate distinction between accidental and intentional homicide. A person responsible for killing another accidentally did not escape penalty, as under modern law, but had to pay a fine to the family of the victim, apparently on the theory that children were the property of their fathers and wives the property of their husbands.

Quite as much as their law, the religion of the Sumerians illuminates their social attitudes and the character of their culture. They did not succeed in developing a very exalted religion; yet it occupied an important place in their lives. To begin with, it was polytheistic and anthropomorphic. They believed in a number of gods and goddesses, each a distinct personality with human attributes. Shamash, the sun god; Enlil, the lord of the rain and wind; and Ishtar, the goddess of the generative powers of nature, were only a few of them. All of these numerous deities were thought to be capable of performing both good and evil.

The Sumerian religion was a religion for this world exclusively; it offered no hope for a blissful, eternal afterlife. The afterlife was a mere temporary existence in a dreary, shadowy place which later came to be called Sheol. Here the ghosts of the dead lingered for a time, perhaps a generation or so, and then disappeared. No one could look forward to resurrection in another world and a joyous external existence as a recompense for the evils of this life; the victory of the grave was complete. In accordance with these beliefs the Sumerians bestowed only limited care upon the bodies of their dead. No mummification was practiced, and no elaborate tombs were built. Corpses were commonly interred beneath the floor of the house without a coffin and with comparatively few articles for the use of the ghost.

There was little spiritual content in Sumerian religion. As we have seen, the gods were not spiritual beings but creatures cast in the

Male Votive Figure, Sumer. This statue of white gypsum colored with bitumen shows the huge staring eyes characteristic of Mesopotamian art.

human mold, with most of the weaknesses and passions of mortals. Nor were the purposes of the religion any more spiritual. It provided no blessings in the form of solace, uplift of the soul, or oneness with God. If it benefited humanity at all, it did so chiefly in the form of material gain—abundant harvests and prosperity in business. The religion did have some ethical content. All the major deities in the Sumerian pantheon were extolled in hymns as lovers of truth, goodness, and justice. The goddess Nanshe, for example, was said "to comfort the orphan, to make disappear the widow, to set up a place of destruction for the mighty." Yet the same deities who personified these noble ideals created such evils as falsehood and strife, and endowed every human being with a sinful nature. "Never," it was said, "has a sinless child been born to its mother."

In the field of intellectual endeavor the Sumerians achieved no small distinction. They produced a system of writing which was destined to be used for a thousand years after the downfall of their nation. This was the celebrated *cuneiform* writing, consisting of wedge-shaped characters (*cuneus* is Latin for wedge) imprinted on clay tablets with a square-tipped reed. At first a pictographic system, it was gradually transformed into an aggregate of syllabic and phonetic signs, some 350 in number. No alphabet was ever developed out of it, but cuneiform nonetheless became the standard medium for commercial transactions throughout most of the Near East (often including Egypt) from about 3000 to about 500 B.C. The Sumerians wrote nothing that could be called philosophy, but they did make some notable beginnings in science. In mathematics, for example, they surpassed the Egyptians in every field except geometry. They discovered the processes of multiplication and division and even the extraction of square and cube root. Their systems of numeration and of weights and measures were duodecimal, with the number sixty as the most common unit. They invented the water clock and the lunar calendar, the latter an inaccurate division of the year into months based upon cycles of the moon. In order to bring it into harmony with the solar year, an extra month had to be added from time to time. The Sumerians were the first known peoples to believe in astrology—the belief that that human fates are determined by the courses of the stars—and this interest led them to pioneer in astronomical observations and predictions of planetary movements. Their medicine was a curious compound of herbalism and magic. The repertory of the physician consisted primarily of charms to exorcise the evil spirits which were believed to be the cause of the disease.

Gudea of Lugash. A black diorite statue of the late Sumerian ruler.

As artists, the Sumerians excelled in metalwork, gem carving, and sculpture. They produced some remarkable specimens of naturalistic art in their weapons, vessels, jewelry, and animal representations, which revealed alike a technical skill and a gift of imagination. Evidently religious conventions had not yet imposed any paralyzing influence, and consequently the artist was still free to follow his own im-

The Great Ziggurat, or Flat-topped Temple, at Ur

See color plates following page 96

pulses. Architecture, on the other hand, was distinctly inferior, probably because of the limitations enforced by the scarcity of good building materials. Since there was no stone in the valley, the architect had to depend upon sun-dried brick. The characteristic Sumerian edifice, extensively copied by their Semitic successors, was the *ziggurat,* a terraced tower set on a platform and surmounted by a shrine. Its construction was massive, its lines were monotonous, and little architectural ingenuity was exhibited in it. The royal tombs and private houses showed more originality. It was in them that the Sumerian inventions of the arch, the vault, and the dome were regularly employed, and the column was used occasionally.

3. OLD BABYLONIAN DEVELOPMENTS

The shortcomings of the Old Babylonians

Although the Old Babylonians were an alien nation, they had lived long enough in close contact with the Sumerians to be influenced profoundly by them. They had little culture of their own when they came into the valley, and in general they only appropriated and modified what the Sumerians had already developed. Thus the changes in Mesopotamian culture during the Old Babylonian period were essentially variations on Sumerian themes.

First among the alterations which the Old Babylonians made in their inheritance may be mentioned the political and legal. As military conquerors holding in subjection numerous vanquished nations, they found it necessary to establish a consolidated state. Vestiges of the old system of local autonomy were swept away, and the power of the king of Babylon was made supreme. Kings became gods, or at least claimed divine origin. A system of royal taxation was adopted as well as compulsory military service. The system of law was also changed to conform to the new condition of centralized despotism. The list of crimes against the state was enlarged, and the king's officers assumed a more active role in apprehending and punishing offenders, although it was still impossible for any criminal to be pardoned without the consent of the victim or the victim's family. The severity of penalties was decidedly increased, particularly for crimes involving any suggestion of treason or sedition. Such apparently trivial offenses as "gadding about" and "disorderly conduct at a tavern" were made punishable by death, probably on the assumption that they would be likely to foster disloyal activities. Whereas under the Sumerian law the harboring of fugitive slaves was punishable merely by a fine, the Babylonian law made it a capital crime. According to the Sumerian code, the slave who disputed his master's rights over him was to be sold; the Code of Hammurabi prescribed that he should have his ear cut off. Adultery was also made a capital offense, whereas under the Sumerian law it did not even necessarily result in divorce. In a few particulars the new system of law revealed some improvement. Wives and children sold for debt could not be held in bondage for longer than four years, and a female slave who had borne her master a child could not be sold at all.

The Old Babylonian laws also reflect a more extensive development of business than that which existed in the preceding culture. That an influential merchant class traded for profit and enjoyed a privileged position in society is evidenced by the fact that the commercial provisions of Hammurabi's code were based upon the principle of "Let the buyer beware." The Babylonian rulers did not believe in a regime of free competition, however. Trade and industry were subject to elaborate regulation by the state. There were laws regarding partnership, storage, and agency; laws respecting deeds, wills, and the taking of interest on money; and a host of others. For a deal to be negotiated without a written contract or without witnesses was punishable by death. Agriculture, which was still the occupation of a majority of the citizens, did not escape regulation. The code provided penalties for failure to cultivate a field and for neglect of dikes and canals. Both government ownership and private tenure of land were permitted; but, regardless of the status of the owner, the tenant farmer was required to pay two-thirds of all he produced as rent.

Religion under the Old Babylonians underwent only superficial changes. Deities that had been venerated by the Sumerians were now neglected and new ones exalted in their stead. Above all, a new god, Marduk, was imported to head the Mesopotamian pantheon. He and the other new deities carried no spiritual significance, however, conveying no promise of resurrection from the dead or of personal im-

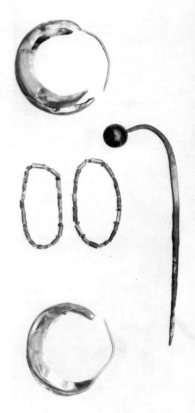

Gold Jewelry from Ur, c. 3500–2800 B.C.

Changes in religion

Panel of Glazed Brick, Babylon, Sixth Century B.C. An ornamental relief on a background of earth brown. The lion is in blue, white, and yellow glazes.

Scenes from the Epic of Gilgamash. A Sumerian inlaid shell panel.

mortality. The Old Babylonians were no more otherworldly in their outlook than the Sumerians. The religions of both peoples were fundamentally materialistic.

Although there was some decline in artistic accomplishments during the period of Babylonian rule, this was by no means true of developments in literature. Building upon legends and myths already evolving under the Sumerians, the Babylonians contributed to world literature one of the greatest epics of all time, the epic of *Gilgamesh*. This long poem, comparable in sweep and power to the Greek *Iliad* and *Odyssey,* is a compilation of stories that were told and re-told over many generations. Its hero, Gilgamesh, is a Mesopotamian king who experiences many adventures. In one he seeks the secret of immortality from an old man and his wife who had been saved when the gods had decided to destroy the world by a flood. Many of the elements of this story are strikingly similar to the Old Testament story of Noah, including the details that the couple had survived the flood by floating in an ark. But the message is rather different, for the Babylonian hero learns only resignation from the old couple: the gods will preserve those that they please and there is nothing mankind can do to understand divine decisions. Gilgamesh does learn from the old pair of a plant that will at least bring back his youth, but after gaining it with great effort from the floor of the sea he leaves it unguarded while asleep, and a snake eats it instead. According to the epic, this is why snakes gain new life every year when they shed their skins. But the human hero is finally forced to recognize that he himself can never transcend old age and death. As the epic states in resigned summary: "When the gods created man, they let death be his share, and life they kept in their own hands."

4. THE METAMORPHOSIS UNDER ASSYRIA

Of all the peoples of the Mesopotamian area after the time of the
Sumerians, the Assyrians went through the most completely independent evolution. For several centuries they had lived a comparatively
isolated existence on top of their small plateau in the upper valley of
the Tigris. Eventually they came under the influence of the Babylonians, but not until after the course of their own history had been partially fixed. As a consequence, the period of Assyrian supremacy
(from about 1300 B.C. to 612 B.C.) had a more peculiar character than
any other era of Mesopotamian history.

*The evolution of Assyrian
supremacy*

The Assyrians were preeminently a nation of warriors because of
the special conditions of their own environment. The limited resources of their original home and the constant danger of attack from
hostile nations around them forced the development of warlike habits
and imperial ambitions. It is therefore not strange that their hunger for
territory should have known no limits. The more they conquered, the
more they felt they had to conquer, in order to protect what they had
already gained. Every success excited ambition and riveted the chains
of militarism more firmly than ever. Disaster was inevitable.

A nation of warriors

The exigencies of war determined the whole character of the Assyrian system. The state was a great military machine. The army commanders were at once the richest and the most powerful class in the
country. Not only did they share in the plunder of war, but they were
frequently granted huge estates as rewards for victory. At least one of

*Features of Assyrian
militarism*

Assyrian Winged Human-Headed Bull.
This relief was found in the palace of
King Sargon II (722–705 B.C.). It measures 16 feet wide by 16 feet high and
weighs approximately 40 tons.

them, Sargon II, dared to usurp the throne. The military establishment itself represented the last word in preparedness. The standing army greatly exceeded in size that of any other nation of the Near East. New and improved armaments and techniques of fighting gave to the Assyrian soldiers unparalleled advantages. Iron swords, heavy bows, long lances, battering rams, fortresses on wheels, and metal breastplates, shields, and helmets were only a few examples of their superior equipment.

Frightfulness

But swords and spears and engines of war were not their only instruments of combat. As much as anything else the Assyrians depended upon frightfulness as a means of overcoming their enemies. Upon soldiers captured in battle, and sometimes upon noncombatants as well, they inflicted unspeakable cruelties—skinning them alive, impaling them on stakes, cutting off ears, noses, and sex organs, and then exhibiting the mutilated victims in cages for the benefit of cities that had not yet surrendered. Accounts of these cruelties are not taken from atrocity stories circulated by their enemies; they come from the records of the Assyrians themselves. Their chroniclers boasted of them as evidences of valor, and the people believed in them as guaranties of security and power. It is clear why the Assyrians were the most hated of all the nations of antiquity.

The tragedy of Assyrian militarism

Seldom has the decline of an empire been so complete as was that of Assyria. In spite of its magnificent armaments and its wholesale destruction of its foes, Assyria's period of imperial splendor lasted little more than a century. Nation after nation conspired against the Assyrians and finally accomplished their downfall. Their enemies took frightful vengeance. The whole land was so thoroughly sacked and the people so completely enslaved or exterminated that it has been difficult to trace any subsequent Assyrian influence upon history. The power and security which military strength was supposed to provide proved a mockery in the end. If Assyria had been utterly defenseless, its fate could hardly have been worse.

Assyrian economic life

With so complete an absorption in military pursuits, it was inevitable that the Assyrians should have neglected in some measure the arts of peace. Industry and commerce appear to have declined under the regime of the Assyrians; for such pursuits were generally scorned as beneath the dignity of a soldierly people. The minimum of manufacturing and trade which had to be carried on was left quite largely to the Arameans, a people closely related to the Phoenicians and the Hebrews. The Assyrians themselves preferred to derive their living from agriculture. The land system included both public and private holdings. The temples held the largest share of the landed wealth. Although the estates of the crown were likewise extensive, they were constantly being diminished by grants to army officers.

Neither the economic nor the social order was sound. The frequent military campaigns depleted the energies and resources of the nation. In the course of time the army officers became a pampered aristocracy, delegating their duties to their subordinates and devoting themselves to luxurious pleasures. The stabilizing influence of a prosperous and intelligent merchant class was precluded by the rule that only foreigners and slaves could engage in commercial activities. Yet more serious was the treatment accorded to the lower classes, the serfs and the slaves. The former comprised the bulk of the rural population. Some of them cultivated definite portions of their master's estates and retained a part of what they produced for themselves. Others were "empty" men, without even a plot to cultivate and dependent on the need for seasonal labor to provide for their means of subsistence. All were extremely poor and were subject to the additional hardships of labor on public works and compulsory military service. The slaves, who were chiefly an urban working class, were of two different types: the domestic slaves, who performed household duties and sometimes engaged in business for their masters; and the war captives. The former were not numerous and were allowed a great deal of freedom, even to the extent of owning property. The latter suffered much greater miseries. Bound by heavy shackles, they were compelled to labor to the point of exhaustion in building roads, canals, and palaces.

Whether the Assyrians adopted the law of the Old Babylonians has never been settled. Undoubtedly they were influenced by it, but several of the features of Hammurabi's code are entirely absent. Notable among these are the *lex talionis* and the system of gradation of penalties according to the rank of the victim and the offender. Whereas the Babylonians prescribed the most drastic punishments for crimes suggestive of treason or sedition, the Assyrians reserved theirs for such offenses as abortion and homosexuality, probably for the military reason of preventing a decline in the birthrate. Another contrast is the more complete subjection of Assyrian women. Wives were treated as chattels of their husbands, the right of divorce was placed entirely in the hands of the male, a plurality of wives was permitted, and all married women were forbidden to appear in public with their faces unveiled.

That a military nation like the Assyrians should not have taken first rank in intellectual achievement is easily understandable. The atmosphere of a military campaign is not favorable to reflection or disinterested research. Yet the demands of successful campaigning may lead to a certain accumulation of knowledge, for practical problems have to be solved. Under such circumstances the Assyrians accomplished some measure of scientific progress. They appear to have divided the circle into 360 degrees and to have estimated locations on the surface of the earth in something resembling latitude and longitude. They recognized and named five planets and achieved some success in predicting eclipses. Since the health of armies is important, medicine received considerable attention. More than five hundred drugs, both vegetable and mineral, were catalogued and their uses indicated. Symptoms of various diseases were described and were generally in-

Assyrian Relief Sculpture. This panel depicts the Emperor Assurbanipal (668–626 B.C.) hunting lions.

terpreted as due to natural causes, although incantations and the prescription of disgusting compounds to drive out demons were still commonly employed as methods of treatment.

The excellence of Assyrian art

In the domain of art the Assyrians surpassed the Old Babylonians and at least equaled the work of the Sumerians, although in different form. Sculpture was the art most highly developed, particularly in the low reliefs. These portrayed dramatic incidents of war and the hunt with the utmost fidelity to nature and a vivid description of movement. The Assyrians delighted in depicting the cool bravery of the hunter in the face of terrific danger, the ferocity of lions at bay, and the death agonies of wounded beasts. Unfortunately this art was limited almost entirely to the two themes of war and sport. Its purpose was to glorify the exploits of the ruling class. Architecture ranked second to sculpture from the standpoint of artistic excellence. Assyrian palaces and temples were built of stone, obtained from the mountainous areas of the north, instead of the mud brick of former times. Their principal features were the arch and the dome. The column was also used but never very successfully. The chief demerit of this architecture was its hugeness, which the Assyrians appeared to regard as synonymous with beauty.

See color plates following page 96

5. THE CHALDEAN RENASCENCE

The Chaldean or final stage in Mesopotamian civilization

The Mesopotamian civilization entered its final stage with the overthrow of Assyria and the establishment of Chaldean supremacy. This stage is often called the Neo-Babylonian, because Nebuchadnezzar and his followers restored the capital at Babylon and attempted to revive the culture of Hammurabi's time. As might have been expected, their attempt was not wholly successful. The Assyrian metamorphosis had altered that culture in various profound and ineffaceable ways. Besides, the Chaldeans themselves had a history of their own which they could not entirely escape. Nevertheless, they did manage to revive certain of the old institutions and ideals. They restored the ancient law and literature, the essentials of the Old Babylonian form of government, and the economic system of earlier times with its dominance of industry and trade. Farther than this they were unable to go.

It was in religion that the failure of the Chaldean renascence was most conspicuous. Although Marduk was restored to his traditional place at the head of the pantheon, the system of belief was little more than superficially Babylonian. What the Chaldeans really did was to develop an astral religion. The gods were divested of their human qualities and exalted into transcendent, omnipotent beings. They were actually identified with the planets themselves. Though still not entirely aloof from humans, they certainly lost their character as beings who could be cajoled and threatened and coerced by magic. They ruled the universe almost mechanically. While their immediate intentions were sometimes discernible, their ultimate purposes were inscrutable.

The astral religion of the Chaldeans

Two significant results flowed from these conceptions. The first was an even greater attitude of fatalism than before. Since the ways of the gods were past finding out, all that humans could do was to resign themselves to their fate. It behooved them therefore to submit absolutely to the gods, to trust in them implicitly, in the vague hope that the results in the end would be good. Thus arose for the first time in history the concept of piety as submission—a concept which was adopted in several other religions, as we shall see in succeeding chapters. For the Chaldeans it implied no otherwordly significance; one did not resign oneself to calamities in this life in order to be justified in the next. The Chaldeans had no interest in a life to come. Submission might bring certain earthly rewards, but in the main, as they conceived it, it was not a means to an end at all. It was rather the expression of an attitude of despair, of humility in the face of mysteries that could not be fathomed.

The growth of fatalism

The second great result which came from the growth of an astral religion was the development of a stronger spiritual consciousness. This is revealed in the penitential hymns of unknown authors and in the prayers which were ascribed to Nebuchadnezzar and other kings as the spokesmen for the nation. In most of them the gods are addressed as exalted beings who are concerned with justice and righteous conduct on the part of humanity, although the distinction between ceremonial and genuine morality is not always sharply drawn. It has been asserted by one scholar that these hymns could have been used by the Hebrews with little modification except for the substitution of the name of Yahweh for that of the Chaldean god.

The development of a spiritual consciousness

With the gods promoted to so lofty a plane, it was perhaps inevitable that human beings should have been abased. Creatures possessed of mortal bodies could not be compared with the transcendent, passionless beings who dwelt in the stars and guided the destinies of the earth. Humans were lowly creatures, sunk in iniquity and vileness, and hardly even worthy of approaching the gods. The consciousness of sin already present in the Babylonian and Assyrian religions now reached a stage of almost pathological intensity. In the hymns people are compared to prisoners, bound hand and foot, languishing in darkness. Their transgressions are "seven times seven." Their misery is increased by the fact that their evil nature has prompted them to sin unwittingly. Never before had humans been regarded as so hopelessly depraved, nor had religion been fraught with so gloomy a view of life.

Curiously enough, the pessimism of the Chaldeans does not appear to have affected their morality very much. So far as the evidence reveals, they indulged in no rigors of asceticism. They did not mortify the flesh, nor did they even practice self-denial. Apparently they took it for granted that humans could not avoid sinning, no matter how hard they tried. They seem to have been just as deeply engrossed in the material interests of life and in the pursuit of the pleasures of the senses as any of the earlier nations. Occasional references were made in their prayers and hymns to reverence, kindness, and purity of heart as virtues, and to oppression, slander, and anger as vices, but these were intermingled with ritualistic conceptions of cleanness and uncleanness and with expressions of desire for physical satisfactions. When the Chaldeans prayed, it was not always that their gods would make them good, but more often that they would grant long years, abundant offspring, and luxurious living.

Aside from religion, the Chaldean culture differed from that of the Sumerians, Babylonians, and Assyrians chiefly in regard to scientific achievements. Without doubt the Chaldeans were the most capable scientists in all of Mesopotamian history, although their accomplishments were limited primarily to astronomy. They worked out the most elaborate system for recording the passage of time that had yet been devised, with their invention of the seven-day week and their division of the day into twelve double-hours of 120 minutes each. They kept accurate records of their observation of eclipses and other celestial occurrences for more than 350 years—until long after the downfall of their empire. The motivating force behind Chaldean astronomy was religion. The chief purpose of mapping the heavens and collecting astronomical data was to discover the future the gods had prepared for mankind. Since the planets were gods themselves, that future could best be divined in the movements of the heavenly bodies. Astronomy was therefore primarily astrology.

Sciences other than astronomy continued in a backward state. Medicine showed little advance beyond the stage it had reached under the Assyrians. The same was true of the remaining aspects of Chaldean culture. Art differed only in its greater magnificence. Literature, dominated by the antiquarian spirit, revealed a lack of originality. The writings of the Old Babylonians were extensively copied and reedited, but they were supplemented by little that was new.

6. THE PERSIAN EMPIRE AND ITS HISTORY

Comparatively little is known of the Persians before the sixth century B.C. Up to that time they appear to have led an obscure and peaceful existence on the eastern shore of the Persian Gulf. They were not Semites but spoke an Indo-European language, that is, one of a group that includes Sanskrit (the language of ancient India), Greek, Latin, and most of the modern European tongues. Their homeland afforded only modest advantages. On the east it was hemmed in by high mountains, and its coastline was destitute of harbors. The fertile valleys of the interior, however, were capable of providing a generous subsistence for a limited population. Save for the development of an elaborate religion, the people had made little progress. At the dawn of their history they were not independent but were vassals of the Medes, a kindred people who ruled over a great empire north and east of the Tigris River.

The Persian background

In 559 B.C. a prince by the name of Cyrus became king of a southern Persian tribe. About five years later he made himself ruler of all the Persians, overthrew the domination of the Medes, and then began to conquer neighboring areas. As Cyrus the Great he has gone down in history as one of the most sensational conquerors of all time. Within the short space of twenty years he founded a vast empire, larger than any that had previously existed.

The rise of Cyrus

The first of the conquests of Cyrus was the kingdom of Lydia, which occupied the western half of Asia Minor and was separated from the lands of the Medes by the Halys River, in what is now northern Turkey. Perceiving the ambitions of the Persians, Croesus, the fabulously rich Lydian king, decided to wage a preventive war to preserve his own nation from conquest. According to the Greek historian Herodotus, Croesus consulted the oracle at Delphi as to the advisability of an immediate attack and gained the reply that if he would cross the Halys and assume the offensive he would destroy a great nation. He did, but that nation was his own. His forces were completely overwhelmed, and his prosperous realm was annexed as a province of the Persian state. Seven years later, in 539 B.C., Cyrus took advantage of discontent and conspiracies in the Chaldean Empire to capture the city of Babylon. His victory was an easy one, for he had the assistance of the Jews within the city and of the Chaldean priests, who were dissatisfied with the policies of their king. The conquest of the Chaldean capital made possible the rapid extension of control over the whole empire and thereby added the Fertile Crescent to the domains of Cyrus.

The conquests of Cyrus

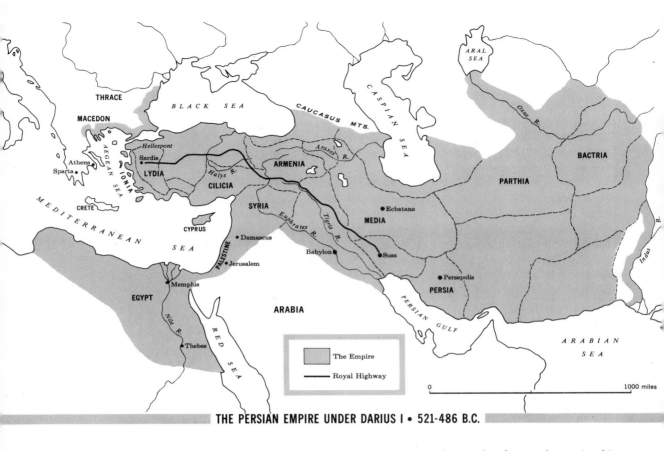

The successors of Cyrus

Cyrus the Great died in 529 B.C., as the result of wounds received in a war with barbarian tribes. Soon afterward a succession of troubles overtook the state he had founded. Like so many other empire-builders both before and since, he had devoted too much energy to conquest and not enough to internal development. He was succeeded by his son Cambyses, who conquered Egypt in 525 B.C. During the new king's absence revolt spread throughout his Asiatic possessions. Chaldeans and Medes strove to regain their independence. The chief minister of the realm, abetted by the priests, organized a movement to gain possession of the throne for a pretender who was one of their puppets. Upon learning of conditions at home, Cambyses set out from Egypt with his most dependable troops, but he was murdered on the way. The most serious of the revolts was finally crushed by Darius, a powerful noble, who killed the pretender and seized the throne for himself.

Darius the Great

Darius I, or the Great, as he is often called, ruled the empire from 522 to 486 B.C. The early years of his reign were occupied in suppressing the revolts of subject peoples and in improving the administrative organization of the state. He completed the division of the empire into satrapies, or provinces, and fixed the annual tribute due from each province. He standardized the currency and weights and measures. He repaired and completed a primitive canal from the Nile to the Red Sea. He followed the example of Cyrus in tolerating and protecting the institutions of subject peoples. Not only did he restore ancient temples and foster local cults, but he ordered his satrap of Egypt to codify the Egyptian laws in consultation with the native priests. But in some of his military exploits Darius overreached himself. In order to check the incursions of the Scythians, who lived on the European shore of the Black Sea, he crossed the Hellespont and conquered a large part of the Thracian coast. In addition, he increased the oppression of the Greeks on the shore of Asia Minor, who had fallen under Persian domination with the conquest of Lydia. He collected heavier tribute from them, and forced them to serve in his armies. The immediate result was a revolt of the Greek cities with the assistance of Athens. And when Darius attempted to punish the Athenians for their part in the rebellion, he found that they offered stiff resistance.

Darius the Great died before the war with Athens and allied Greek cities had come to an end. The struggle was prosecuted vigorously but ineffectively by his successor, Xerxes I. By 479 B.C. the Persians had been driven from all of Greece. Though they recovered temporarily possession of the Ionian islands and continued to hold sway as a major power in Asia, their attempt to extend their dominion into Europe was thwarted. The last century and a half of the empire's existence was marked by frequent assassinations, revolts of provincial governors, and barbarian invasions, until finally, in 330 B.C., its independence was annihilated by the armies of Alexander the Great.

The end of the Persian Empire

Although the Persian government had its defects, it was certainly superior to most of the others that had existed in the Near East. The Persian kings did not imitate the terrorism of the Assyrians. They levied tribute upon conquered peoples, but they generally allowed them to keep their own customs, religions, and laws. Indeed, it may be said that the chief significance of the Persian Empire lay in the fact that it resulted in a synthesis of Near-Eastern cultures, including those of Persia itself, Mesopotamia, Asia Minor, the Syria-Palestine coast, and Egypt.

Significance of the Persian Empire

The Persian kings built excellent roads to help hold their empire together. Most famous was the Royal Road, some 1,600 miles in length. It extended from Susa near the Persian Gulf to Sardis near the western coast of Asia Minor. So well kept was this highway that the king's messengers, traveling day and night, could cover its entire length in less than a week. Other roads linked the various provinces with one or another of the four leading Persian cities: Susa, Persepolis, Babylon, and Ecbatana. Although they naturally contributed to ease of trade, the highways were all built primarily to facilitate control over the outlying sections of the empire.

Persian roadways

*The eclectic culture of
Persia*

7. PERSIAN CULTURE

The culture of the Persians, in the narrower sense of intellectual and artistic achievements, was largely derived from that of previous civilizations. Much of it came from Mesopotamia, but a great deal of it from Egypt, and some from Lydia and northern Palestine. Their system of writing was originally the cuneiform, but in time they devised an alphabet of thirty-nine letters, based upon the alphabet of the Arameans who traded within their borders. In science they accomplished nothing, except to adopt with some slight modifications the solar calendar of the Egyptians and to encourage exploration as an aid to commerce. They deserve credit also for diffusing a knowledge of the Lydian coinage throughout many parts of western Asia.

*The eclectic character of
Persian architecture*

It was the architecture of the Persians which gave the most positive expression of the eclectic character of their culture. They copied the raised platform and the terraced building style that had been so common in Babylonia and Assyria. They imitated also the winged bulls, the brilliantly colored glazed bricks, and other decorative motifs of Mesopotamian architecture. But at least two of the leading features of Mesopotamian construction were not used by the Persians at all—the arch and the vault. In place of them they adopted the column and the colonnade from Egypt. Such matters as interior arrangement and the use of palm and lotus designs at the base of columns also point very distinctly toward Egyptian influence. On the other hand, the fluting of the columns and the volutes or scrolls beneath the capitals were not Egyptian but Greek, adopted not from the mainland of Greece itself but from the Ionian cities of Asia Minor. If there was anything unique about Persian architecture, it was the fact that it was purely secular.

The Great Palace of Darius and Xerxes at Persepolis. Persian architecture made use of fluted columns, probably copied from the Greeks, and reliefs resembling those of the Assyrians.

Two Reliefs from the Staircase of the Great Palace at Persepolis

The great Persian structures were not temples but palaces. They served to glorify not gods, but the "King of Kings." The most famous were the magnificent residences of Darius and Xerxes at Persepolis. The latter, built in imitation of the temple at Karnak, had an enormous central audience-hall containing a hundred columns and surrounded by innumerable rooms which served as offices and as quarters for the eunuchs and members of the royal harem.

8. THE ZOROASTRIAN RELIGION

By far the most enduring influence left by the ancient Persians was that of their religion. Their system of faith was of ancient origin. It was already highly developed when they began their conquests. So strong was its appeal, and so ripe were the conditions for its acceptance, that it spread through most of western Asia. Its doctrines turned other religions inside out, displacing beliefs which had been held for ages.

The religion of the Persians

Although the roots of this religion can be traced as far back as the fifteenth century B.C., its real founder was Zoroaster (the Greek form of the Persian name Zarathustra), who appears to have lived shortly before 600 B.C. From him the religion derives its name of Zoroastrianism. Zoroaster was probably the first real theologian in history, the first known person to devise a completely developed system of religious belief. He seems to have conceived it to be his mission to purify the traditional customs of his people—to eradicate polytheism, animal sacrifice, and magic—and to establish their worship on a more spiritual and ethical plane. But in spite of his reforming efforts many of the old superstitions survived and were gradually fused with the new ideals.

The founding of Zoroastrianism

Zoroastrianism had a character unique among the religions of the world up to that time. It was dualistic—not monistic like the Sumerian and Babylonian religions, in which the same gods were capable of both good and evil; but it did not go as far in the direction of monotheism as did the religion of the Hebrews. According to Zoroaster, two spiritual principles ruled the universe: one, Ahura-Mazda, supremely good and incapable of any wickedness, embodied the principles of light, truth, and righteousness; the other, Ahriman, treacherous and malignant, presided over the forces of darkness and evil. The two were engaged in a desperate struggle for supremacy. Although they were about evenly matched in strength, the god of light would eventually triumph, and the world would be saved from the powers of darkness. On the last great day Ahura-Mazda would overpower Ahriman and cast him down into the abyss. The dead would then be raised from their graves to be judged according to their deserts. The righteous would enter into immediate bliss, while the wicked would be sentenced to the flames of hell. Ultimately, though, all would be saved; for the Persian hell, unlike the Christian, did not last forever.

The Zoroastrian religion was definitely an ethical one. Although it contained suggestions of predestination, of the election of some from all eternity to be saved, in the main it rested upon the assumption that humans possessed free will, that they were free to sin or not to sin, and that they would be rewarded or punished in the afterlife in accordance with their conduct on earth. Ahura-Mazda commanded that men should be truthful, that they should love and help one another to the best of their power, that they should befriend the poor and practice hospitality. The essence of these broader virtues was perhaps expressed in another of the god's decrees: "Whosoever shall give meat to one of the faithful . . . he shall go to Paradise." The forms of conduct forbidden were sufficiently numerous and varied to cover the whole list of the Seven Cardinal Sins of medieval Christianity and a great many more. Pride, gluttony, sloth, covetousness, wrathfulness, lust, adultery, abortion, slander, and waste were among the more typical. The taking of interest on loans to others of the same faith was described as the "worst of sins," and the accumulation of riches was strongly discountenanced. The restraints which believers were to practice included also a kind of negative Golden Rule: "That nature alone is good which shall not do unto another whatever is not good for its own self."

9. THE MYSTICAL AND OTHERWORLDLY HERITAGE FROM PERSIA

The religion of the Persians as taught by Zoroaster did not long continue in its original state. It was corrupted, first of all, by the persistence of primitive superstitions, of magic and priestcraft. The farther the religion spread, the more of these relics of barbarism were engrafted upon it. As the years passed, additional modification resulted from the influence of alien faiths, particularly that of the Chaldeans. The outcome was the growth of a powerful synthesis in which the dualism of the Persians was combined with the pessimism and fatalism of the Chaldeans.

Out of this synthesis gradually emerged a profusion of cults, alike in their basic dogmas but according them different emphases. The oldest of these cults was Mithraism, deriving its name from Mithras, the chief lieutenant of Ahura-Mazda in the struggle against the powers of evil. At first only a minor deity in the religion of Zoroastrianism, Mithras finally won recognition by many of the Persians as the god most deserving of worship. The reason for this change was probably the emotional appeal made by the incidents of his career. He was believed to have lived an earthly existence involving great suffering and sacrifice. He performed miracles giving bread and wine to man and ending a drought and also a disastrous flood. Finally, he created much of the ritual of Zoroastrianism, proclaiming Sunday as the most sacred day of the week and the twenty-fifth of December as the most sacred day of the year. Since the sun was the giver of light and the faithful ally of Mithras, his day was naturally the most sacred. The twenty-fifth of December also possessed its solar significance: as the approximate date of the winter solstice it marked the return of the sun from its long journey south of the Equator. It was in a sense the "birthday" of the sun, since it connoted the revival of its life-giving powers for the benefit of humanity.

Mithraism

Exactly when the worship of Mithras became a definite cult is unknown, but it was certainly not later than the fourth century B.C. Its spread thereafter was rapid. In the last century B.C. it was introduced into Rome, although it was of little importance in Italy itself until after 100 A.D. It drew its converts especially from the lower classes, from the ranks of soldiers, foreigners, and slaves. Ultimately it rose to the status of one of the most popular religions of the empire, the chief competitor of Christianity and of old Roman paganism itself. After 275, however, its strength rapidly waned. How much influence this astonishing cult exerted is impossible to say. Its superficial resemblance to Christianity is certainly not hard to perceive, but this does not mean, of course, that the two were identical, or that one was an offshoot of the other. Nevertheless, it is probably true that Christianity as the younger of the two rivals borrowed a good many of its externals from Mithraism, at the same time preserving its own philosophy essentially untouched.

The spread and influence of Mithraism

One of the principal successors of Mithraism in transmitting the legacy from Persia was Manicheism, founded around 250 A.D. by Mani, a high-born priest of Ecbatana. Like Zoroaster he conceived it to be his mission to reform the prevailing religion, but he received scant

Manicheism

sympathy in his own country and had to be content with missionary ventures in India and western China. About 276 A.D. he was condemned and executed by his Persian opponents. Following his death his teachings were carried by his disciples into practically every country of western Asia and finally into Italy about 330 A.D.

Of all the Zoroastrian teachings, the one that made the deepest impression upon the mind of Mani was dualism. But Mani gave to this doctrine a broader interpretation than it had ever received in the earlier religion. He conceived not merely of two deities engaged in a relentless struggle for supremacy, but of a whole universe divided into two kingdoms, each the antithesis of the other. The first was the kingdom of spirit ruled over by a God eternally good. The second was the kingdom of matter under the dominion of Satan. Only "spiritual" substances such as fire, light, and the souls of human beings were created by God. Darkness, sin, desire, and all things bodily and material owed their origin to Satan.

The moral implications of this rigorous dualism were readily apparent. Since everything connected with sensation or desire was the work of Satan, humanity should strive to free itself as completely as possible from enslavement to physical needs. Humans should refrain from all forms of sensual enjoyment, the eating of meat, the drinking of wine, the gratification of sexual desire. Even marriage was prohibited, for this would result in the begetting of more physical bodies to people the kingdom of Satan. In addition, humans should subdue the flesh by prolonged fasting and infliction of pain. Recognizing that this program of austerities would be too difficult for ordinary mortals, Mani divided the human race into the "perfect" and the "hearers." Only the former would be obliged to adhere to the full program as the ideal of what all should hope to attain. To aid humanity in its struggle against the powers of darkness, God had sent prophets and redeemers from time to time to give comfort and inspiration. Noah, Abraham, Zoroaster, Jesus, and Paul were numbered among these divine emissaries; but the last and greatest of them was Mani. Since Mani called himself "the apostle of Jesus Christ," many Manicheans in the West, including the great St. Augustine during his early career, considered themselves to be radical Christians. The faith had many followers in the Roman Empire around 400, but it died out thereafter as a result of persecution.

The third most important cult which developed as an element in the Persian heritage was Gnosticism (from the Greek *gnosis*, meaning knowledge). It had no single founder but evolved out of Persian and Greek religious ideas and came to be fully formed around the first century A.D. It reached the height of its popularity in the latter half of the second century. Although it gained some followers in Italy, its influence was confined primarily to the Near East.

The feature which most sharply distinguished this cult from the others was mysticism. The Gnostics denied that the truths of religion could be discovered by reason or could even be made intelligble. They regarded themselves as the exclusive possessors of a secret spiritual knowledge revealed to them directly by God. This knowledge was alone important as a guide to faith and conduct.

The combined influence of these several Persian-derived religions was enormous. Most of them were launched at a time when political and social conditions were particularly conducive to their spread. The breakup of Alexander the Great's empire about 300 B.C. inaugurated a peculiar period in the history of the ancient world. International barriers were broken down; there was an extensive migration and intermingling of peoples; and the collapse of the old social order gave rise to profound disillusionment and a vague yearning for individual salvation. People's attentions were centered as never before upon compensations in a life to come. Under such circumstances religions of the kind described were bound to flourish like the green bay tree. Otherwordly and mystical, they offered the very escape that people were seeking from a world of anxiety and confusion.

The combined influence of the several off-shoots of Zoroastrianism

Although not exclusively religious, the heritage left by the Persians contained few elements of a secular nature. Their form of government was adopted by the later Roman monarchs, not in its purely political aspect, but in its character of a divine-right despotism. When such emperors as Diocletian and Constantine I invoked divine authority as a basis for their absolutism and required their subjects to prostrate themselves in their presence, they were really following patterns laid down by the Persians. At the same time the Romans were impressed by the Persian idea of a world empire. Darius and his successors conceived of themselves as the rulers of the whole civilized world, with a mission to reduce it to unity and, under Ahura-Mazda, to govern it justly. For this reason they generally conducted their wars with a minimum of savagery and treated conquered peoples humanely. Their ideal was a kind of prototype of the Roman peace. Traces of Persian influence upon certain Hellenistic philosophies are also discernible; but here again it was essentially religious, for it was confined almost entirely to spiritual and mystical theories.

Persian legacy

SELECTED READINGS

- *Items so designated are available in paperback editions.*
- Chiera, Edward, *They Wrote on Clay,* Chicago, 1956. An engrossing account of the discovery and decipherment of cuneiform tablets.
  Contenau, G., *Everyday Life in Babylonia and Assyria,* New York, 1954. Based on archeological evidence and well illustrated.
- Frankfort, H., *The Art and Architecture of the Ancient Orient,* rev. ed., Baltimore, 1971.

————, *The Birth of Civilization in the Near East,* Bloomington, Ind., 1951. Brief but useful.

• ————, et al., *The Intellectual Adventure of Ancient Man,* Chicago, 1946. Essays by leading experts on ancient myths; see that by T. Jakobsen on Mesopotamia.

Frye, R. N., *The Heritage of Persia,* New York, 1963. A fascinating history of Persia from earliest times to the triumph of Islam in the seventh century A.D.

• Ghirshman, R., *Iran,* Baltimore, 1954.

• Hallo, W. W., and W. K. Simpson, *The Ancient Near East: A History,* New York, 1971. An authoritative survey.

• Kramer, S. N., *History Begins at Sumer,* New York, 1959.

• ————, *Sumerian Mythology,* New York, 1961. Develops different point of view about early myth than that found in Frankfort, et al., *Intellectual Adventure.*

• ————, *The Sumerians, Their History, Culture, and Character,* Chicago, 1963. Best general treatment of Sumerian civilization.

Lloyd, Seton, *Foundations in the Dust,* Baltimore, 1955. Describes the development and accomplishments of Mesopotamian archeology.

• Moscati, S., *The Face of the Ancient Orient,* New York, 1962. Deals with Assyrians and Chaldeans.

Neugebauer, Otto, *The Exact Sciences in Antiquity,* Princeton, 1952. Excellent on Mesopotamian mathematical accomplishments.

• Olmstead, A. T., *History of the Persian Empire,* Chicago, 1948. Detailed but somewhat uncritical.

• Oppenheim, A. Leo, *Ancient Mesopotamia,* Chicago, 1964. Concentrates on Babylonian and Assyrian culture.

• Roux, G., *Ancient Iraq,* London, 1964.

Russell, Jeffrey B., *The Devil: Perceptions of Evil from Antiquity to Primitive Christianity,* Ithaca, N.Y., 1977. Particularly strong on the religious revolution accomplished by Zoroaster.

• Saggs, H. W. F., *The Greatness That Was Babylon,* London, 1962.

Widengren, G., *Mani and Manicheism,* London, 1965.

• Woolley, C. L., *The Sumerians,* New York, 1928. A pioneer work, brief and interestingly written.

Zaehner, R. C., *The Dawn and Twilight of Zoroastrianism,* New York, 1961. The standard treatment.

SOURCE MATERIALS

• *Epic of Gilgamesh,* tr. N. Sandars, Baltimore, 1960.

Grayson, A. K., and D. B. Redford, *Papyrus and Tablet,* Englewood Cliffs, N.J., 1973.

Herodotus, *The Persian Wars,* tr. A. de Sélincourt, Baltimore, 1954.

Luckenbill, D. D., *Ancient Records of Assyria and Babylonia,* Chicago, 1926, 2 vols.

Pritchard, James B., *Ancient Near Eastern Texts Relating to the Old Testament,* Princeton, N.J., 1965.

Chapter 4

THE HEBREW CIVILIZATION

I am the Lord thy God, which brought thee out of the land of Egypt from
   the house of bondage.
Thou shalt have none other Gods before me.
Thou shalt not make thee any graven image, or any likeness of any thing
   that is in heaven above, or that is in the earth beneath, or that is in the
   waters beneath the earth . . .
Thou shalt not take the name of the Lord thy God in vain.

                         —Deuteronomy 5: 6–11

O f all the peoples of the ancient Near East, none has been of
greater importance to the modern world than the Hebrews.
It was the Hebrews, of course, who provided much of the
background of the Christian religion—its Commandments, its stories
of the Creation and the Flood, its concept of a single, transcendent
God as law-giver and judge, and more than two-thirds of its Bible.
Hebrew conceptions of morality and political theory have also profoundly influenced modern nations. For these reasons we tend today
to think of the Hebrew accomplishment as unique, and there is much
truth in that assumption. But although Hebrew culture gradually
came to differ greatly from that of neighboring Egypt and Mesopotamia it is necessary to remember that the Hebrews did not develop
their culture in a vacuum. No more than any other people were they
able to escape the influence of nations around them.

*Importance of the Hebrew
civilization*

1. HEBREW ORIGINS AND RELATIONS WITH OTHER PEOPLES

The origin of the Hebrews is still a puzzling problem. Certainly they
did not have any physical characteristics sufficient to distinguish them
clearly from their neighbors, and their language belonged to the Near-

Eastern Semitic family. Most scholars agree that the original home of the Hebrews was the Arabian Desert. The first definite appearance of the founders of the nation of Israel, however, was in northwestern Mesopotamia. Apparently as early as 1800 B.C. a group of Hebrews under the leadership of Abraham had settled there. Later Abraham's grandson Jacob led a migration westward and began the occupation of Palestine. It was from Jacob, subsequently called Israel, that the Israelites derived their name. Sometime after 1600 B.C. certain tribes of Israelites, together with other Hebrews, went down into Egypt to escape the consequences of famine. They appear to have settled in the Nile delta and to have been enslaved by the pharaoh's government. Around 1300–1250 B.C. their descendants found a new leader in the indomitable Moses, who freed them from bondage, led them to the Sinai peninsula, and persuaded them to become worshipers of Yahweh, a god whose name was much later written erroneously as Jehovah. Hitherto Yahweh had been the deity of Hebrew shepherd folk in the general locality of Sinai. Making use of a Yahwist cult as a nucleus, Moses welded the various tribes of his followers into a confederation. It was this confederation which played the dominant role in the occupation of Palestine, or the land of Canaan.

With its scanty rainfall and rugged terrain, Palestine was a barren and inhospitable place. But compared with the arid wastes of Arabia it was a veritable paradise, and it is not surprising that the leaders should have pictured it as a "land flowing with milk and honey." Most of it was already occupied by the Canaanites, another people of Semitic speech who had lived there for centuries. Through contact with the Babylonians, Hittites, and Egyptians they had built up a culture which was no longer primitive. They practiced agriculture and carried on trade. They knew the art of writing, and they had adapted the laws of Hammurabi's code to the needs of their simpler existence. Their religion, which was also derived in large part from Babylonia, was cruel and sensual, including human sacrifice and temple prostitution.

The Hebrew occupation of the land of Canaan was a slow and difficult process. Seldom did the tribes unite in a combined attack, and even when they did, the enemy cities were well enough fortified to resist capture. After several generations of sporadic fighting the Hebrews had succeeded in taking only the limestone hills and a few of the less fertile valleys. In the intervals between wars they mingled freely with the Canaanites and adopted no small amount of their culture. Before they had a chance to complete the conquest, they found themselves confronted by a new and more formidable enemy, the Philistines, who had come into Palestine from Asia Minor and from the islands of the Aegean Sea. Stronger than either the Hebrews or Canaanites, especially because they used iron weapons while the others used bronze, the new invaders rapidly overran the country and forced the Hebrews to surrender much of the territory they had already gained. It is from the Philistines that Palestine derives its name.

2. THE RECORD OF POLITICAL HOPES AND FRUSTRATIONS

The crisis produced by the Philistine conquests served not to discourage the Hebrews but to unite them and to intensify their ardor for battle. Moreover, it led directly to the founding of the Hebrew monarchy about 1025 B.C. Up to this time the nation had been ruled by "judges," who possessed little more than the authority of religious leaders over twelve independent Hebrew tribes. But now with a greater need for organization and discipline, the people demanded a king to rule them and lead them in war. The man selected as the first incumbent of the office was Saul, a member of the tribe of Benjamin, who at first gained considerable success.

The founding of the Hebrew monarchy

But the reign of King Saul ultimately was not a happy one, either for the nation or for the ruler himself. Only a few suggestions of the reasons are given in the Old Testament account. Evidently Saul incurred the displeasure of Samuel, the last of the great judges, who had expected to remain the power behind the throne. Before long there appeared on the scene the ambitious David, who, with the encouragement of Samuel, carried on skillful maneuvers to draw popular support from the king. Waging his own military campaigns, he achieved one bloody triumph after another. By contrast, the armies of Saul met disastrous reverses. Finally the king, being critically wounded, requested his armor-bearer to kill him. When the latter would not, Saul drew his own sword, fell upon it, and died.

The reign of King Saul

David now became king and ruled for forty years. His reign was one of the most glorious periods in Hebrew history. He smote the Philistines hip and thigh and reduced their territory to a narrow strip of coast in the south. He united the twelve tribes into a consolidated state under an absolute monarch, and he began the construction of a magnificent capital at Jerusalem. But strong government, military glory, and material splendor were not unmixed blessings for the people. Their inevitable accompaniments were high taxation and conscription. As a consequence, before David died, rumblings of discontent were plainly to be heard in certain parts of his kingdom.

The mighty David

David was succeeded by his son Solomon, the last of the kings of the united monarchy. As a result of the nationalist aspirations of later times, Solomon has been pictured in Hebrew lore as one of the wisest and most enlightened rulers in all history. The facts of his career furnish little support for such a belief. About all that can be said in his favor is that he was a shrewd diplomat and an active patron of trade. Most of his policies were oppressive, although of course not deliberately so. Ambitious to copy the luxury and magnificence of other Oriental despots, he established a harem of 700 wives and 300 concubines and completed the construction of sumptuous palaces, stables for 4,000 horses, and a costly temple in Jerusalem. Since Palestine was

Solomon aspires to Oriental magnificence

Model of King Solomon's Temple. Significant details are: A, royal gates; B, treasury; C, royal palace; D, people's gate; E, western (wailing) wall; F, priests' quarters; G, courthouse; H, Solomon's porch.

poor in resources, most of the materials for the building projects had to be imported. Gold, silver, bronze, and cedar were brought in in such quantities that the revenues from taxation and from the tolls levied upon trade were insufficient to pay for them. To make up the deficit Solomon ceded twenty towns and resorted to a system of conscripting labor. Every three months 30,000 Hebrews were drafted and sent into Phoenicia to work in the forests and mines of King Hiram of Tyre, from whom the most expensive materials had been purchased.

The secession of the Ten Tribes

Solomon's extravagance and oppression produced acute discontent among his subjects. His death in 922 B.C. was the signal for open revolt. The ten northern tribes, refusing to submit to his son Rehoboam, seceded and set up their own kingdom. Sectional differences played their part also in the disruption of the nation. The northern Hebrews were sophisticated and accustomed to urban living. They benefited from their location at the crossroads of Near-Eastern trade. While this factor increased their prosperity, it also caused them to be steeped in foreign influences. By contrast, the two southern tribes were composed very largely of pastoral and agricultural folk, loyal to the religion of their fathers, and hating the ways of the foreigner. Perhaps these differences alone would have been sufficient in time to break the nation asunder.

Roman Coin Celebrating the Destruction of Jerusalem. This coin, struck about 70 A.D., bears the inscription "IVDAEA CAPTA" (Captive Judea), and shows a female personification of the Jews propping her head in an attitude of dejection.

The northern kingdom came to be known as the Kingdom of Israel, having its capital in Samaria, while the two southern tribes comprised the Kingdom of Judah, which continued to have its capital in Jerusalem. For more than two centuries the two little states maintained their separate existences. But in 722 B.C. the Kingdom of Israel was conquered by the Assyrians. Its inhabitants were scattered throughout the vast empire of their conquerors and were eventually absorbed by the more numerous population around them. They have ever since been referred to as the Ten Lost Tribes of Israel. The Kingdom of Judah managed to survive for more than a hundred years longer, successfully outlasting the Assyrian menace. But in 586 B.C. it was

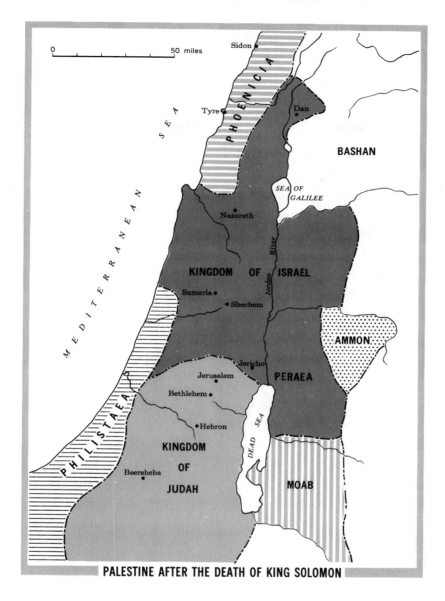

PALESTINE AFTER THE DEATH OF KING SOLOMON

overthrown by the Chaldeans under Nebuchadnezzar. Jerusalem was plundered and burned, and its leading citizens were carried off into captivity in Babylon. When Cyrus the Persian conquered the Chaldeans, he freed the Jews and permitted them to return to their native land. Few were willing to go, and considerable time elapsed before it was possible to rebuild the temple. From 539 to 332 B.C. Palestine was a vassal state of Persia. In 332 B.C. it was conquered by Alexander the Great and after his death was placed under the rule of Egypt. In 63 B.C. it became a Roman protectorate. Its political history as a Jewish commonwealth was ended in 70 A.D. after a desperate revolt which the

Masada. This ancient mountaintop fortress, which towers above the western shore of the Dead Sea in Israel, was the final outpost of the Jews in their war against Roman domination. The fortress, occupied by 1,000 men, women, and children, was besieged by the Roman army for two years before it fell in 73 A.D. Defiant to the end, almost all of the Jewish defenders killed themselves rather than be captured and enslaved by the Romans.

Romans punished by destroying Jerusalem and annexing the country as a province. The inhabitants were gradually diffused through other parts of the Roman Empire.

The Diaspora

The destruction of Jerusalem and annexation of the country by the Romans were the principal factors in the so-called Diaspora, or dispersion of the Jews from Palestine. Even earlier large numbers of them had fled into various parts of the Greco-Roman world on account of difficulties in their homeland. In their new environment they rapidly succumbed to foreign influences, a fact which was of tremendous importance in promoting a fusion of Greek and Oriental ideas. It was a Hellenized Jew, St. Paul, who was mainly responsible for remolding Christianity in accordance with Greek philosophical doctrines.

3. THE HEBREW RELIGIOUS EVOLUTION

Few peoples in history have gone through a religious evolution comparable to that of the Hebrews. Its cycle of development ranged all the way from the crudest superstitions to the loftiest spiritual and ethical conceptions. Part of the explanation is doubtless to be found in the peculiar geographic position occupied by the Hebrew people. Located as they were after their conquest of Canaan on the highroad between Egypt and the major civilizations of Asia, they were bound to be affected by an extraordinary variety of influences.

Reasons for the varied evolution of Hebrew religion

At least four different stages can be distinguished in the growth of the Hebrew religion. The first we can call the pre-Mosaic stage, from the earliest beginnings of the people to approximately 1250 B.C. This stage was characterized at first by animism, the worship of spirits that dwelt in trees, mountains, sacred wells and springs, and even in stones of peculiar shape. Diverse forms of magic were practiced also at this time—necromancy, imitative magic, scapegoat sacrifices, and so on. Numerous relics of these early beliefs and practices are preserved in the Old Testament.

The pre-Mosaic stage

Gradually animism gave way to anthropomorphic gods. How this transition occurred cannot be determined. Perhaps it was related to the fact that Hebrew society had become patriarchal, that is, the father exercised absolute authority over the family and descent was traced through the male line. The gods may have been thought to occupy a similar position in the clan or tribe. Apparently few of the new deities were as yet given names; each was usually referred to merely by the generic name of "El," that is, "God." They were guardian deities of particular places and probably of separate tribes. No *national* worship of Yahweh was known at this time.

Anthropomorphic gods

The second stage, which lasted from the thirteenth century B.C. to the ninth, is frequently designated the stage of national monolatry. The term may be defined as the exclusive worship of one god but without any denial that other gods exist. Due chiefly to the influence of Moses, the Hebrews gradually adopted as their national deity during this period a god whose name appears to have been written "Yhwh." How it was pronounced no one knows, but scholars generally agree that it was probably uttered as if spelled "Yahweh." The meaning is also a mystery. When Moses inquired of Yahweh what he should tell the people when they demanded to know what god had sent him, Yahweh replied: "I AM THAT I AM: and he said, Thus shalt thou say unto the children of Israel, I AM hath sent me unto you" (Exodus 3: 13–14).

The stage of national monolatry

During the time of Moses and for two or three centuries thereafter Yahweh was a somewhat peculiar deity. He was conceived almost exclusively in anthropomorphic terms. He possessed a physical body and the emotional qualities of men. He was capricious on occasions, and somewhat irascible—as capable of evil and wrathful judgments as he was of good. His decrees were often quite arbitrary, and he would punish someone who sinned unwittingly just about as readily as one whose guilt was real. By way of illustration, Yahweh reportedly struck Uzza dead merely because that unfortunate individual placed his hand upon the Ark of the Covenant to steady it while it was being transported to Jerusalem (I Chronicles 13: 9–10). Omnipotence was scarcely an attribute that Yahweh could claim, for his power was limited to the territory occupied by the Hebrews themselves. Nonetheless, some of the most important Hebrew contributions to subsequent Western thought were first formulated during this time. It was during this period that the Hebrews came to believe that God was not part of nature but entirely outside of it, and that humans, while part of na-

Characteristics of Yahweh

ture, became the rulers of nature by divine dispensation. This "transcendent" theology meant that God could gradually be understood in purely intellectual or abstract terms, and that humanity could be regarded as having the potential for altering nature as it pleased.

The religion of this stage was neither primarily ethical nor profoundly spiritual. Yahweh was revered as a supreme law-giver and as the stern upholder of the moral order of the universe. According to the Biblical account, he issued the Ten Commandments to Moses on top of Mount Sinai. Old Testament scholars, however, do not generally accept this tradition. They admit that a primitive set of commandments may have existed in Mosaic times, but they doubt that the Ten Commandments in the form in which they are preserved in the Book of Exodus go back any farther than the seventh century. In any event, it is clear that Moses's God was interested just about as much in sacrifice and in ritualistic observances as he was in good conduct or in purity of heart. Moreover, the religion was not vitally concerned with spiritual matters. It offered nothing but material rewards in this life and none at all in a life to come. Finally, the belief in monolatry was corrupted by certain elements of fetishism, magic, and even grosser superstitions that lingered from more primitive times or that were gradually acquired from neighboring peoples. These varied all the way from serpent worship to bloody sacrifices and fertility orgies.

The really important work of religious reform was accomplished by the great prophets—Amos, Hosea, Isaiah,[1] and Micah. And their achievements represented the third stage in the development of the Hebrew religion, the stage of the prophetic revolution, which occupied the eighth and seventh centuries B.C. The great prophets were men of broader vision than any of their forerunners. Three basic doctrines made up the substance of their teachings: (1) rudimentary monotheism—Yahweh is the ruler of the universe; He even makes use of nations other than the Hebrews to accomplish His purposes; the gods of other peoples are false gods and should not be worshiped for any reason; (2) Yahweh is a god of righteousness exclusively; He is not really omnipotent, but His power is limited by justice and goodness; the evil in the world comes from humanity not from God; (3) the purposes of religion are chiefly ethical; Yahweh cares nothing for ritual and sacrifice, but that His followers should "seek justice, relieve the oppressed, judge the fatherless, plead for the widow." Or as Micah expressed it: "What doth the Lord require of thee, but to do justly, and to love mercy, and to walk humbly with thy God?" (Micah 6: 8).

These doctrines contained a definite repudiation of nearly every-

---

[1] Most Old Testament authorities consider the Book of Isaiah the work of three authors. They ascribe the first part to Isaiah, the second part from chapters 40 to 55 to Deutero-Isaiah, or the second Isaiah, and the end to someone who wrote after the return to Jerusalem. The second Isaiah was more emphatic than the first in denying the existence of the gods of other peoples.

Remains of an Ancient Synagogue at Capernaum. Capernaum was supposed to have been the scene of many of the miracles attributed to Jesus. Here also he called out Peter, Andrew, and Matthew to be his disciples.

thing that the older religion had stood for. Such, however, was apparently not the intention of the prophets. They conceived it rather as their mission to restore the religion to its ancient purity. The crudities within it they regarded as foreign corruptions. But like many such leaders, they built better than they knew. Their actual accomplishments went so far beyond their original objectives that they amounted to a religious revolution. To a considerable extent this revolution also had its social and political aspects. Wealth had become concentrated in the hands of a few. Thousands of small farmers had lost their freedom and had passed under subjection to rich proprietors. If we can believe the testimony of Amos, bribery was so rife in the law courts that the plaintiff in a suit for debt had merely to give the judge a pair of shoes and the defendant would be handed over as a slave (Amos 2: 6). Overshadowing all was the threat of Assyrian domination. To enable the nation to cope with that threat, the prophets believed that social abuses should be stamped out and the people united under a religion purged of its alien corruptions.

Contrasts with the older religion; political and social aspects

The results of this revolution must not be misinterpreted. It did eradicate some of the most flagrant forms of oppression, and it rooted out permanently most of the barbarities that had crept into the religion from foreign sources. But the Hebrew faith did not yet bear much resemblance to modern orthodox Judaism. It contained little of a spiritual character. Instead of being otherwordly, it was oriented toward this life. Its purposes were social and ethical—to promote a just and harmonious society and to abate man's inhumanity to man—not to confer individual salvation in an afterlife. As yet there was no belief in heaven and hell or in Satan as a powerful opponent of God. The shades of the dead went down into Sheol to linger there for a time in the dust and gloom and then disappear.

The religion not yet otherworldly or mystical

The final significant stage in Hebrew religious evolution was the post-Exilic stage or the period of Persian influence. This period may be considered to have covered the years from 539 to about 300 B.C. Perhaps enough has been said already to indicate the character of the influence from Persia. It will be recalled from the preceding chapter that Zoroastrianism was a dualistic, messianic, otherwordly, and esoteric religion. In the period following the exile in Babylon these ideas gained wide acceptance among the Jews. They adopted a belief in Satan as the Great Adversary and the author of evil. They developed an eschatology (a set of doctrines concerning the end of the world) which included such notions as the coming of a spiritual savior, the resurrection of the dead, and a last judgment. They turned their attention to salvation in an afterworld as more important than enjoyment of this life. Lastly, they embraced the conception of a revealed religion, that is, they regarded the books of their Bible as having been directly inspired by God Himself.

4. HEBREW CULTURE

In certain respects the Hebrew genius was inferior to that of some other great nations of antiquity. In the first place, it revealed no talent for science. Not a single important discovery in any scientific field has ever been traced to the ancient Hebrews. Nor were they particularly adept in appropriating the knowledge of others. They could not build a bridge or a tunnel except of the crudest sort. Whether it was from lack of interest in these things or whether it was because of too deep an absorption in religious affairs is not clear. In the second place, they seem to have been almost entirely devoid of artistic skill. In part because of religious prohibitions concerning "graven images" they had no sculpture, but they also had no architecture or painting worthy of mention. The famous temple at Jerusalem was not a Hebrew building at all but a product of Phoenician skill, for Solomon imported artisans from Tyre to finish the more complicated tasks.

It was rather in law, literature, and philosophy that the Hebrew genius was most perfectly expressed. Although all of these subjects were closely allied with religion, they did have their secular aspects. The finest example of Jewish law was the Deuteronomic Code, which forms the core of the Book of Deuteronomy. Despite claims of its great antiquity, it was probably an outgrowth of the prophetic revolution. It was based in part upon an older Code of the Covenant, which was derived in considerable measure from the laws of the Canaanites and the Old Babylonians. In general, its provisions were more enlightened than those of Hammurabi's code. One of them enjoined liberality to the poor and to the stranger. Another commanded that the Hebrew slave who had served six years should be freed, and insisted that he must not be sent away empty. A third provided that judges and other officers should be chosen by the people and forbade them to accept gifts or to show partiality in any form. A fourth condemned witchcraft, divination, and necromancy. A fifth denounced the punishment of children for the guilt of their fathers and affirmed the principle of individual responsibility for sin. A sixth prohibited the taking of interest on any kind of loan made by one Jew to another. A seventh required that at the end of every seven years there should be a "release" of debts. "Every creditor that lendeth aught unto his neighbour shall release it; he shall not exact it of his neighbour, or of his brother . . . save when there shall be no poor among you" (Deuteronomy 15: 1–4).

The literature of the Hebrews was the best that the ancient Near East produced. Nearly all of it now extant is preserved in the Old Testament and in the books of the Apocrypha (ancient Hebrew works not recognized as scriptural because of doubtful religious authority). Except for a few fragments like the Song of Deborah in Judges 5, it is not really so old as is commonly supposed. Scholars now recognize that the Old Testament was built up mainly through a series of collections and revisions in which the old and new fragments were merged and generally assigned to an ancient author—Moses, for example. But the oldest of these revisions was not prepared any earlier than 850 B.C. The majority of the books of the Old Testament were of even more recent origin, with the exception, of course, of certain of the chronicles. As one would logically expect, the philosophical books were of later authorship. Although the bulk of the Psalms were ascribed to King David, a good many of them actually refer to events of the Babylonian Captivity. It seems certain that the collection as a whole was the work of several centuries. Most recent of all were the books of Ecclesiastes, Esther, and Daniel, composed no earlier than the third century B.C. Likewise, the Apocryphal books did not see the light of day until Hebrew civilization was almost extinct. Some, like Maccabees I and II, relate events of the second century B.C. Others, including the Wisdom of Solomon and the Book of Enoch, were written under the influence of Greco-Oriental philosophy.

Hebrew literature

Not all of the writings of the Hebrews had high literary merit. A considerable number were dull, repetitious chronicles. Nevertheless, many, whether in the form of battle song, prophecy, love lyric, or drama, were rich in rhythm, concrete images, and emotional vigor. Few passages in any language can surpass the scornful indictment of social abuses voiced by the prophet Amos:

Amos's indictment of social abuses

Hear this, O ye that swallow up the needy, even to make the
  poor of the land to fail,
Saying, when will the new moon be gone, that we may sell
  corn?

King David as a Musician. A much later conception of David from the eighth century A.D. shows the Hebrew king playing his lyre and charming animals. According to tradition, David was the author of the Psalms, which he sung to his lyre (also known as a *psaltery*).

And the sabbath that we may set forth wheat,
Making the ephah small, and the shekel great,
And falsifying the balances by deceit?
That we may buy the poor for silver, and the need for a pair
   of shoes;
Yea, and sell the refuse of the wheat?

The Song of Songs   The most beautiful of Hebrew love lyrics was the Song of Songs, or the Song of Solomon. Its theme was probably derived from an old Canaanite hymn of spring, celebrating the passionate affection of the Shulamith or fertility goddess for her lover, but it had long since lost its original meaning. The following verses are typical of its sensuous beauty:

I am the rose of Sharon
and the lily of the valleys.
As the lily among thorns,
so is my love among the daughters.

.   .   .   .

My beloved is white and ruddy,
the chiefest among ten thousand.
His head is as the most fine gold;
his locks are bushy and black as a raven:
His eyes are as the eyes of doves by the rivers of waters,
washed with milk and fitly set.

His cheeks are as a bed of spices, as sweet flowers;
his lips like lilies, dropping sweet smelling myrrh.

. . . .

How beautiful are thy feet with shoes, O prince's daughter!
The joints of thy thighs are like jewels,
the work of the hands of a cunning workman.

One other of the supreme Hebrew literary achievements was the Book of Job, written sometime between 500 and 300 B.C. In form the work is a drama of the tragic struggle between man and fate. Its central theme is the problem of evil: how it can be that the righteous suffer while the wicked prosper. The story was an old one, adapted very probably from an Old Babylonian writing of similar content. But the Hebrews introduced into it a much deeper realization of philosophical possibilities. The main character, Job, a man of unimpeachable virtue, is suddenly overtaken by a series of disasters: he is despoiled of his property, his children are killed, and his body is afflicted with a painful disease. His attitude at first is one of stoic resignation; the evil must be accepted along with the good. But as his sufferings increase he is plunged into despair. He curses the day of his birth and praises death, where "the wicked cease from troubling and the weary be at rest."

The Book of Job

Then follows a lengthy debate between Job and his friends over the meaning of evil. The latter take the traditional Hebraic view that all suffering is a punishment for sin, and that those who repent are forgiven and strengthened in character. But Job is not satisfied with any of their arguments. Torn between hope and despair, he strives to review the problem from every angle. He even considers the possibility that death may not be the end, that there may be some adjustment of the balance hereafter. But the mood of despair returns, and he decides that God is an omnipotent demon, destroying without mercy wherever His caprice or anger directs. Finally, in his anguish he appeals to the Almighty to reveal Himself and make known His ways to him. God answers him out of the whirlwind with a magnificent exposition of the tremendous works of nature. Convinced of his own insignificance and of the unutterable majesty of God, Job despises himself and repents in dust and ashes. In the end no solution is given of the problem of individual suffering. No promise is made of recompense in a life hereafter, nor does God make any effort to refute the hopeless pessimism of Job. Humans must take comfort in the philosophic reflection that the universe is greater than themselves, and that God in the pursuit of His sublime purposes cannot really be limited by human standards of equity and goodness.

The problem of evil

As philosophers the Hebrews surpassed every other people before the Greeks, including the Egyptians. Although they were not brilliant metaphysicians and constructed no great theories of the universe, they did concern themselves with most of the problems relating to human life and destiny. Their thought was essentially personal rather than ab-

Hebrew philosophy: early examples

stract. Probably the earliest of their writings of a distinctly philosophical character were the Book of Proverbs and the Book of Ecclesiasticus. In their final form both were of late composition, but much of the material they contain was doubtless quite ancient. Not all of it was original, for a considerable portion had been taken from Egyptian sources as early as 1000 B.C. The books have as their essential teaching: be temperate, diligent, wise, and honest, and you will surely be rewarded with prosperity, long life, and a good reputation. Only in such isolated passages as the following is any recognition given to higher motives of sympathy or respect for the rights of others: "Whoso mocketh the poor reproacheth his Maker; and he that is glad at calamities shall not be unpunished" (Proverbs 17: 5).

Ecclesiastes

A much more profound and critical philosophy is contained in Ecclesiastes, an Old Testament book, not to be confused with the Ecclesiasticus mentioned above. The author of Ecclesiastes is unknown. In some way it came to be attributed to Solomon, but he certainly did not write it, for it includes doctrines and forms of expression unknown to the Hebrews for hundreds of years after his death. Modern critics date it no earlier than the third century B.C. The basic ideas of its philosophy may be summarized as follows:

(1) Mechanism. The universe is a machine that rolls on forever without evidence of any purpose or goal. Sunrise and sunset, birth and death are but phases of constantly recurring cycles and "there is nothing new under the sun."

(2) Fatalism. Humans are victims of the whims of fate. There is no necessary relation between effort and success. "The race is not to the swift, nor the battle to the strong, neither yet bread to the wise . . . but time and chance happeneth to them all."

(3) Pessimism. "All is vanity and vexation of spirit." Fame, riches, extravagant pleasure are snares and delusions in the end. Although wisdom is better than folly, even it is not a sure key to happiness, for an increase in knowledge brings a keener awareness of suffering.

(4) Moderation. Extremes of asceticism and extremes of indulgence are both to be avoided. "Be not righteous over much . . . be not over much wicked: why shouldest thou die before thy time?"

5. THE MAGNITUDE OF THE HEBREW INFLUENCE

The nature of the Hebrew influence

The influence of the Hebrews, like that of most other Near-Eastern peoples, has been chiefly religious and ethical. While it is true that the Old Testament has served as a source of inspiration for some of the literature and art of medieval and early modern civilizations, this has resulted largely because the Bible was already familiar material as a part of the religious heritage. The same explanation can be applied to the use of the Old Testament as a source of law and political theory by the Calvinists in the sixteenth century, and by many other Christians both before and since.

But these facts do not mean that the Hebrew influence has been slight. On the contrary, the history of nearly every Western civilization during the past two thousand years would have been radically different without the heritage from Israel. For it must be remembered that the Hebrews developed the first sustained monotheism known to mankind and that Hebrew beliefs were among the principal foundations of Christianity. The relationship between the two religions is frequently misunderstood. The movement inaugurated by Jesus of Nazareth is commonly represented as a revolt against Judaism; but such was only partly the case. On the eve of the Christian era the Jewish nation had come to be divided into several different religious parties, including a majority group of Pharisees, and minority groups of Sadducees and Essenes. The Pharisees represented the middle classes and some of the better educated common folk. They believed in the resurrection, in rewards and punishments after death, and in the coming of a political messiah. Intensely nationalistic, they advocated participation in government and faithful observance of the ancient ritual. They regarded all parts of the law as of virtually equal importance, whether they applied to matters of ceremony or to obligations of social ethics. Their concern for the law was so great that they debated such questions as whether one could eat an egg laid on the Sabbath.

Hebrew foundations of Christianity: the beliefs of the Pharisees

Representing altogether different strata of society, the minority parties disagreed with the Pharisees on both religious and political issues. The Sadducees, including the priests and the wealthier classes, were most famous for their denial of the resurrection and of rewards and punishments in an afterlife. Although they favored the temporary acceptance of Roman rule, their attitude toward the ancient law was even more inflexible than that of the Pharisees. The Essenes, who were not even a unified party but consisted of various similar but separate communities, drew their members from the lower classes, practiced asceticism and preached otherworldliness as means of protest against the wealth and power of priests and rulers. They ate and drank only enough to keep themselves alive, held all their goods in common, and looked upon marriage as a necessary evil. Far from being fanatical patriots, they regarded government with indifference and refused to take oaths under any conditions. They emphasized the spiritual aspects of religion rather than the ceremonial, and stressed particularly the immortality of the soul, the coming of a religious messiah, and the early destruction of the world.

The Sadducees and the Essenes

Until recently scholars were dependent for their knowledge of the Essenes almost entirely upon secondary sources. But in 1947 an Arab shepherd unwittingly opened the way to one of the most spectacular discoveries of documentary evidence in world history. Searching for a lost sheep on the western shore of the Dead Sea, he threw a stone that

The Dead Sea scrolls

The Dead Sea Scrolls. Now on display in an underground vault at the Hebrew University in Jerusalem. The oldest extant examples of Hebrew religious literature, they furnish us with evidence of the activities of the Essenes and mystical and other worldly sects about the beginning of the Christian era.

entered a hole in the rocks and made such a peculiar noise that he ran away in fright. He returned, however, with a friend to investigate and discovered a cave in which were stored about fifty cylindrical earthen jars stuffed with writings on leather scrolls. Studied by scholars, the scrolls revealed the existence of a monastic community which flourished from about 130 B.C. to 67 A.D. Its members lived a life of humility and self-denial, holding their goods in common, and devoting their time to prayer and sacraments and to studying and copying Biblical texts. They looked forward confidently to the coming of a messiah, the overthrow of evil, and the establishment of God's kingdom on earth. That they belonged to the same general movement that fostered the growth of the Essenes seems beyond question.

Hebrew influence upon Christianity

All branches of Judaism except the Sadducees strongly influenced the development of Christianity. From Jewish sources Christianity obtained its cosmogony, or theory of the origin of the universe; the Ten Commandments; and a large portion of its theology, including the "transcendent" view of God as outside of nature and humanity as master of nature. Jesus himself, although he condemned the Pharisees for their legalism and hypocrisy, did not repudiate all of their tenets. Instead of abolishing the ancient law, as he is popularly supposed to have done, he demanded its fulfillment, insisting, however, that it should not be made the essential part of religion. In the first flush of enthusiasm at the discovery of the Dead Sea Scrolls it seemed as if Christianity might have been most directly influenced by the Essenes. Scholars now, however, speak less of direct influences than of similarities, for early Christians, like the Essenes, practiced asceticism, regarded government with indifference and the Roman Empire with hostility, held their goods in common, and believed in the imminent end of the world. These parallels do not mean, of course, that Christianity was a mere adaptation of beliefs and practices emanating from Judaism. There was much in it that was unique; but that is a subject which can be discussed more conveniently later on.[2]

The ethical and political influence of the Hebrews has also been substantial. Their moral conceptions have been a leading factor in the development of the negative approach toward ethics which has prevailed for so long in Western countries. For the early Hebrews, "righteousness" consisted primarily in the observance of taboos or prohibitions. "Thou shalt not . . ." is a major theme of many parts of the Old Testament. But a positive morality of charity and social justice made rapid headway during the time of the prophets and has had its great influence as well. With respect to political thought, Hebrew ideals of the sovereignty of law, and regard for the dignity and worth of the individual have been among the major formative influences which have shaped the growth of modern democracy. It is now almost universally recognized that the traditions of Judaism contributed equally with the influence of Christianity and Stoic philosophy in fostering recognition of human rights and in promoting the development of free society.

Ethical and political influence of the Hebrews

SELECTED READINGS

• *Items so designated are available in paperback editions.*
   Albright, W. F., *The Archaeology of Palestine*, Baltimore, 1949. The best survey by the master of American archeologists of the Holy Land.
•   ———, *From the Stone Age to Christianity*, New York, 1957. Emphasizes the development of Hebrew monotheism.
   Baron, Salo W., *A Social and Religious History of the Jews*, 3 vols., New York, 1937. A modern classic.
• Bickermann, E., *From Ezra to the Last of the Maccabees: Foundations of Post-Biblical Judaism*, New York, 1962.
   Bright, John, *A History of Israel*, Philadelphia, 1959. A balanced account.
   Chase, Mary E., *Life and Language in the Old Testament*, New York, 1955.
   De Burgh, W. G., *The Legacy of the Ancient World*, 3rd ed., New York, 1960. Includes a good survey of the influence of Hebrew thought.
   Harrison, R. K., *The Dead Sea Scrolls: An Introduction*, New York, 1961. A valuable guide for the beginner.
   Hermann, Siegfried, *A History of Israel in Old Testament Times*, London, 1975. Iconoclastic and challenging.
   Klausner, Joseph, *The Messianic Idea in Israel*, New York, 1955. By one of the greatest Jewish scholars of our age.
   Meek, T. J., *Hebrew Origins*, rev. ed., New York, 1950. Very scholarly and fundamental.
   Noth, Martin, *History of Israel*, 2nd ed., New York, 1960. A basic reappraisal.

[2] See Chapter 11.

Oesterley, W. O. E., and T. H. Robinson, *Hebrew Religion, Its Origin and Development,* New York, 1932.

• Orlinsky, H. M., *Ancient Israel,* 2nd ed., Ithaca, N.Y., 1960. The best brief introduction.

• Roth, Cecil, *The Dead Sea Scrolls,* New York, 1965. Contends that the scrolls were not produced by the Essenes but by the Zealots, a warlike sect deeply involved in the rebellion against Rome in 70 A.D.

Rowley, H. H., *Growth of the Old Testament,* New York, 1963. Helpful account of scholarly opinion on circumstances of origin of all the Old Testament books.

Schürer, E., *The History of the Jewish People in the Time of Jesus,* 5 vols., Edinburgh, 1885–91. An older but irreplaceable work.

• Vaux, Roland de, *Ancient Israel: Its Life and Institutions,* New York, 1962. Especially valuable for archeological data.

SOURCE MATERIALS

Baron, Salo W., and J. L. Blau, eds., *Judaism: Post-Biblical and Talmudic Periods,* New York, 1954.

Gaster, T. H., tr., *The Dead Sea Scriptures in English Translation,* New York, 1964.

The *Old Testament* and the *Apocrypha,* many editions.

Pritchard, J. B., ed., *Ancient Near Eastern Texts Relating to the Old Testament,* rev. ed., Princeton, 1965.

Chapter 5

THE HITTITE, MINOAN, MYCENAEAN, AND LESSER CIVILIZATIONS

But for them among these gods will be bled for annual food:
to the god Karnua one steer and one sheep;
to the goddess Kupapa one steer and one sheep;
to the divinity Sarku one sheep;
and a Kutupalis sheep to the male divinities.

> —Hittite sacrifice formula, translated
> from a hieroglyph by
> H. T. Bossert

A few other ancient civilizations require more than passing attention. Chief among them are the Hittite, the Minoan, the Mycenaean, the Phoenician, and the Lydian. The Hittites are important primarily as intermediaries between East and West. They were one of the main connecting links between the civilizations of Egypt, the Tigris-Euphrates valley, and the region of the Aegean Sea. It appears certain also that they were the original discoverers of iron. The Minoan and the Mycenaean civilizations are the oldest ones of Europe. They are significant above all for their remarkable achievements in the arts and as the starting points of Greek history. As for the Phoenicians, no one could overlook the importance of their distribution of a knowledge of the alphabet and a primitive commercial law to the surrounding civilized world. The Lydians have gone down in history as the originators of the first system of coinage.

Importance of these civilizations

1. THE HITTITES

Until about a century ago little was known of the Hittites except their name. They were commonly assumed to have played no role of any

*The discovery of remains
of the Hittite civilization*

The Hittite Empire

*The mystery of the race
and language of the
Hittites*

*The economic life of the
Hittites*

significance in the drama of history. The slighting references to them in the Bible give the impression that they were little more than a half-barbarian tribe. But in 1870 some curiously inscribed stones were found at Hama in Syria. This was the beginning of an extensive inquiry which has continued with a few interruptions to the present day. It was not long until scores of other monuments and clay tablets were discovered over most of Asia Minor and through the Near East as far as the Tigris-Euphrates valley. In 1907 some evidences of an ancient city were unearthed near the village of Boghaz-Koy in Turkey. Further excavation eventually revealed the ruins of a great fortified capital which was known as Hattusas or Hittite City. Within its walls were discovered more than 20,000 clay tablets, most of them apparently laws and decrees.

On the basis of these finds and other evidences gradually accumulated, it was soon made clear that the Hittites were once the rulers of a mighty empire covering most of Asia Minor and extending to the upper reaches of the Euphrates. Part of the time it included Syria as well and even portions of Phoenicia and Palestine. The Hittites reached the zenith of their power during the years from 1600 to 1200 B.C. In the last century of this period they waged a long and exhausting war with Egypt, which had much to do with the downfall of both empires. Neither was able to regain its strength. After 1200 B.C. Carchemish on the Euphrates River became for a time the leading Hittite city, but as a commercial center rather than as the capital of a great empire. The days of imperial glory were over. Finally, after 717 B.C., all the remaining Hittite territories were conquered and absorbed by the Assyrians, Lydians, and Phrygians.

Where the Hittites came from and what were their relationships to other peoples are problems which still defy a perfect solution. Most modern scholars trace their place of origin to Turkestan and consider them related to the Greeks. Their language was Indo-European. Its secret was unlocked during World War I by the Czech scholar Bedrich Hrozny. Since then thousands of clay tablets making up the laws and official records of the emperors have been deciphered. They reveal a civilization resembling more closely the Old Babylonian than any other.

Hardly enough evidence has yet been collected to make possible an accurate appraisal of Hittite civilization. Some modern historians refer to it as if it were on a level with the Mesopotamian or even with the Egyptian civilization. Such may have been the case from the material standpoint, for the Hittites undoubtedly had an extensive knowledge of agriculture and a highly developed economic life in general. They mined great quantities of silver, copper, and lead, which they sold to surrounding nations. They discovered the mining and use of iron and made that material available for the rest of the civilized world. Trade was also one of their principal economic pursuits. In fact, they seem to have depended almost as much upon commercial penetration as upon war for the expansion of their empire.

The literature of the Hittites consisted chiefly of mythology, including adaptations of creation and flood legends from the Old Babylonians. They had nothing that could be described as philosophy, nor is there any evidence of scientific originality outside of the metallurgical arts. They evidently possessed some talent for the perfection of writing, for in addition to a modified cuneiform adapted from Mesopotamia they also developed a hieroglyphic system which was partly phonetic in character.

One of the most significant achievements of the Hittites was their system of law. Approximately two hundred separate paragraphs or decrees, covering a great variety of subjects, have been translated. They reflect a society comparatively urbane and sophisticated but subject to minute governmental control. The title to all land was vested in the king or in the governments of the cities. Grants were made to individuals only in return for military service and under the strict requirement that the land be cultivated. Prices were fixed in the laws themselves for an enormous number of commodities—not only for articles of luxury and the products of industry, but even for food and clothing. All wages and fees for services were likewise minutely prescribed, with the pay of women fixed at less than half the rate for men.

On the whole, the Hittite law was more humane than that of the Old Babylonians. Death was the punishment for only eight offenses—such as witchcraft, and theft of property from the palace. Even premeditated murder was punishable only by a fine. Mutilation was not specified as a penalty at all except for arson or theft when committed by a slave. The contrast with the cruelties of Assyrian law was more striking. Not a single example is to be found in the Hittite decrees of such fiendish punishments as flaying, castration, and impalement, which the rulers at Nineveh seemed to think necessary for maintaining their authority.

The art of the Hittites was not of outstanding excellence. So far as we know, it included only sculpture and architecture. The former was generally crude, but at the same time it revealed much freshness and vigor. Most of it was in the form of reliefs depicting scenes of war and mythology. Architecture was ponderous and huge. Temples and palaces were squat, unadorned structures with small, two-columned porches and great stone lions guarding the entrance.

Not a great deal is known about the Hittite religion except that it had an elaborate mythology, innumerable deities, and forms of worship of Mesopotamian origin. A sun god was worshiped, along with a host of other deities, some of whom appear to have had no particular function at all. The Hittites seem to have welcomed into the divine company practically all of the gods of the peoples they conquered and even of the nations that bought their wares. The practices of the re-

The intellectual level of Hittite culture

Hittite law

Humane character of Hittite law

The art of the Hittites

Hittite religion

Hittite Sculpture. Perhaps the most highly conventionalized sculpture of the ancient world is found in Hittite reliefs.

ligion included divination, sacrifice, purification ceremonies, and the offering of prayers. Nothing can be found in the records to indicate that the religion was in any sense ethical.

The importance of the Hittites

The chief historical importance of the Hittites probably lies in the role which they played as intermediaries between the Tigris-Euphrates valley and the westernmost portions of the Near East. Doubtless in this way certain culture elements from Mesopotamia were transmitted to the Canaanites and to the peoples of the Aegean islands.

2. THE MINOAN AND MYCENAEAN CIVILIZATIONS

Long-forgotten civilizations

By a strange coincidence the discovery of the existence of the Hittite, Minoan, and Mycenaean civilizations was made at just about the same time. Before 1870 scarcely anyone dreamed that great civilizations had flourished on the Aegean islands and on the shores of Asia Minor for hundreds of years prior to the rise of classical Greek civilization. Students of the *Iliad* knew, of course, of the references to a strange people who were supposed to have dwelt in Troy, to have kidnaped the fair Helen, and to have been punished by the Greeks for this act by the siege and destruction of their city. But it was commonly supposed that these accounts were mere figments of a poetical imagination. Today we are certain that Greek history, and thus European history, began over one thousand years before the Golden Age of Athens.

The discoveries by Schliemann and others

The first discovery of a highly developed Aegean culture center was made not by a professional archeologist but by a retired German businessman, Heinrich Schliemann. Fascinated from early youth by the stories of the Homeric epics, he determined to dedicate his life to archeological research as soon as he had sufficient income to enable

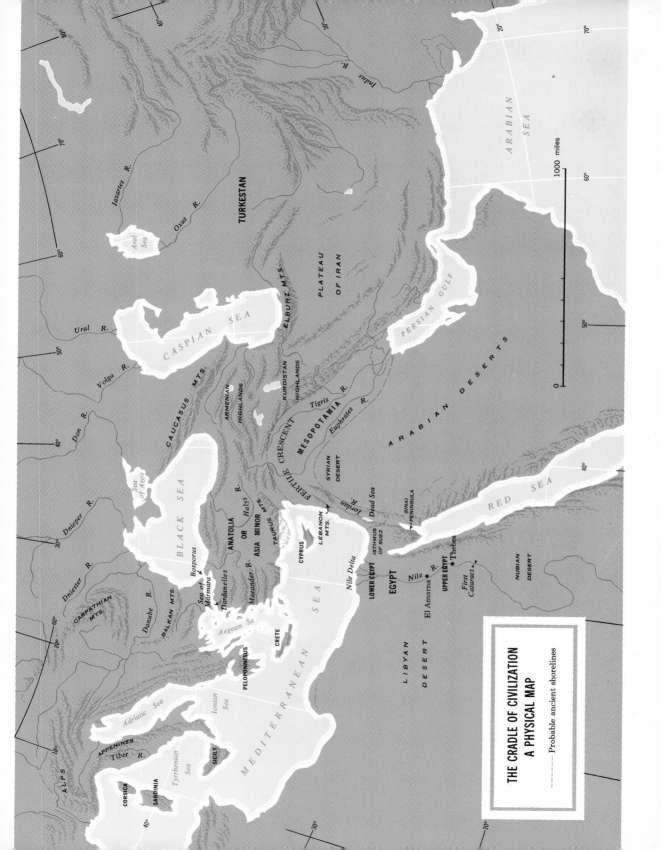

THE CRADLE OF CIVILIZATION
A PHYSICAL MAP

--------- Probable ancient shorelines

1000 miles

ARABIAN SEA

TURKESTAN

Jaxartes R.

Oxus R.

Aral Sea

PLATEAU OF IRAN

ELBURZ MTS.

CASPIAN SEA

Ural R.

Volga R.

Don R.

Sea of Azov

CAUCASUS MTS.

ARMENIAN HIGHLANDS

KURDISTAN HIGHLANDS

Tigris

MESOPOTAMIA

Euphrates R.

FERTILE CRESCENT

SYRIAN DESERT

PERSIAN GULF

ARABIAN DESERTS

BLACK SEA

Halys R.

ANATOLIA OR ASIA MINOR

TAURUS MTS.

CYPRUS

LEBANON MTS.

Jordan R.

Dead Sea

SINAI PENINSULA

ISTHMUS OF SUEZ

RED SEA

Dnieper R.

Bosporus

Dardanelles

Sea of Marmara

Maeander R.

Aegean Se

CRETE

Nile Delta

LOWER EGYPT

EGYPT

Nile   R.

El Amarna

UPPER EGYPT

Thebes

First Cataract

NUBIAN DESERT

Dniester R.

CARPATHIAN MTS.

Danube R.

BALKAN MTS.

PELOPONNESUS

MEDITERRANEAN SEA

LIBYAN DESERT

ALPS

APPENINES

Tiber R.

Adriatic Sea

Ionian Sea

Tyrrhenian Sea

SICILY

CORSICA

SARDINIA

Egyptian Pottery Jar, c. 3600 B.C. It was filled with food or water and placed in the tomb to provide for the afterlife. (MMA)

An Egyptian Official and His Son. Painted limestone, c. 2500 B.C.

Gold and Inlay Pendant of Princess Sit Hat-Hor Yunet. Egyptian, Twelfth Dynasty.

Farm Hand Plowing. Egyptian tomb figures, c. 1900 B.C.

Thutmose III as Amon, 1450 B.C. The Pharaoh wears the crown and the beard of the god, and carries a scimitar and the symbol of "life."

Jeweled Headdress of Gold, Carnelian, and Glass. Egyptian, 1475 B.C.

Part of the Egyptian "Book of the Dead." A collection of magic formulas to enable the deceased to gain admission to the realm of Osiris and to enjoy its eternal benefits.

Silversmiths Working on a Stand and a Jar. Egyptian, c. 1450 B.C.

A scribe writing on a papyrus roll. Egyptian, c. 1415 B.C.

Shawabty ("to answer") Figures, c. 1400 B.C. These were put in the tomb to do any degrading work the rich man might be called upon to do in the next world.

Stele or Grave Marker. It shows the deceased being presented to the Sun god on his throne. She is holding her heart in her hand.

Scarab or Beetle-Shaped Charm of a Pharaoh, c. 1395 B.C. The beetle was sacred in ancient Egypt.

Wall painting of an Egyptian house, c. 1400 B.C.

Painted limestone figures, c. 1300 B.C.

Head of Ramses II, 1324–1258 B.C.

Painted Wood Shrine Box for Shawabty Figures. *Ca.* 1200 B.C.

A hieroglyphic character for the idea "Millions of Years," 500–330 B.C.

A carved sandstone capital, c. 370 B.C., representing a bundle of papyrus reeds.

Silver Figurine of a Kneeling Bull Holding a Vessel. Elamite, c. 3000 B.C.

Gold, Silver, Shell, and Lapis Lazuli Statuette of a Ram in a Thicket. Sumerian, 2500 B.C.

Gold and Lapis Lazuli Lyre with Bull's Head. Sumerian, c. 2500 B.C.

Stone Head of Ur-Ningirsu, Son of Gudea of Lagash. Sumerian, c. 2100 B.C.

Gold Plaque with Animals and Stylized Trees in Relief. Persian, VII cent. B.C.

Bronze Bull, Symbol of Strength. Arabian, VI cent. B.C.

Ivory Screen of Four Winged Figures. Assyrian, VIII cent. B.C.

Geometric Horse, VIII cent. B.C. Greek art of this early period was angular, formal, and conventionalized.

Geometric Jar, VIII cent. B.C. Another example of the stylized decorative patterns of early Greek art.

Sphinx, c. 540–530 B.C. Though doubtless of Oriental derivation, Greek sphinxes had a softer and more human aspect than the Oriental.

Statue of an Amazon, one of the fabled tribe of women warriors, V cent. B.C. (Roman copy)

Departure of a Warrior. Gravestone, c. 530 B.C., a period when naturalism was the dominant note of Greek art.

Athena, c. 460 B.C. The young, graceful patron-goddess of Athens is about to send forth an owl as a sign of victory.

Jar, 500–490 B.C. The figures depicted in a fine black glaze on the natural red clay show athletes in the Panathenaic games.

Chorus of Satyrs, c. 420 B.C. The background is black with the figures in red clay. The satyrs, dressed in fleecy white, with flowing tails, are the chorus of a play.

Toilet Box, 465–460 B.C., showing the Judgment of Paris, an early incident in the Trojan War.

Bronze Mirror Case, V cent. B.C. Greek articles of everyday use were commonly finished with the same delicacy and precision as major works of art.

Diadoumenos, after Polykleitos, V cent. B.C. An idealized statue of a Greek athlete tying the "diadem," or band of victory, around his head.

Bracelet Pendant, IV–III cent. B.C. This tiny figure of the god Pan is a masterpiece of detail and expression.

Woman Arranging Her Hair, 400–300 B.C. Sculptors of antiquity took pride in these statuettes of ordinary people in ordinary activities, which were usually made of terra cotta painted soft blue, pink, or yellow.

Head of an Athlete, c. 440–420 B.C. The sculptor aimed to express manly beauty in perfect harmony with physical and intellectual excellence.

Statuette of Hermarchos, III cent. B.C. An example of the realism of Hellenistic sculpture.

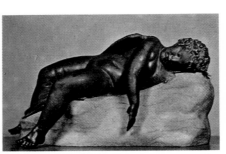

Sleeping Eros, 250–150 B.C. Along with a penchant for realism, Hellenistic sculptors were fond of portraying serenity or repose.

Comic Actor, 200–100 B.C. Hellenistic realism often included portrayal of ugly and even deformed individuals.

Unidentified Man, I cent. B.C. The Romans excelled in portraits of sharp individuality.

Augustus, Reigned 31 B.C.–14 A.D. This portrait suggests the contradictory nature of the genius who gave Rome peace after years of strife.

Constantine, Reigned 306–337 A.D. The head is from a statue sixteen feet in height.

Mummy Portrait, II cent. A.D. A Roman woman buried in Egypt.

Mosaic, I cent. A.D. A floor design composed of small pieces of colored marble fitted together to form a picture.

Wall Painting of a Satyr Mask, I cent. B.C. The belief in satyrs, thought to inhabit forests and pastures, was taken over from the Greeks.

Architectural Wall Painting from a Pompeiian Villa. I cent. B.C., suggesting the Greek origin of Roman forms of architecture.

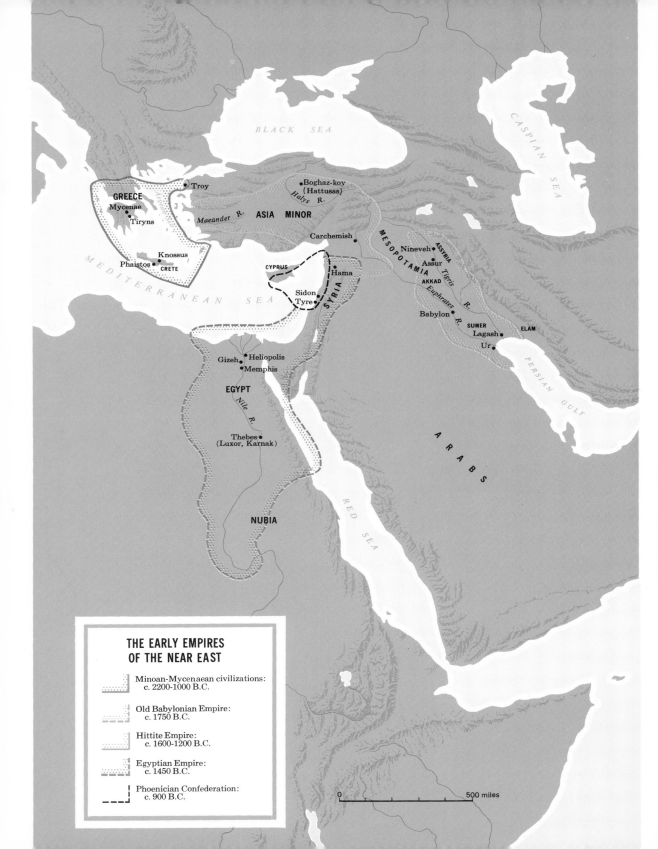

BLACK SEA

CASPIAN SEA

GREECE
•Troy
Mycenae•
Tiryns•
Maeander R.
ASIA MINOR
•Boghaz-koy
(Hattusas)
Halys R.

Carchemish•
MESOPOTAMIA
Nineveh• ASSYRIA
Assur• Tigris R.
AKKAD

CYPRUS
•Hama
SYRIA
Sidon•
Tyre•

Babylon•
Euphrates R.
SUMER
Lagash•
Ur•
ELAM

Knossus•
Phaistos• •
CRETE

MEDITERRANEAN SEA

PERSIAN GULF

Gizeh• •Heliopolis
•Memphis

EGYPT

Nile R.

A R A B S

Thebes •
(Luxor, Karnak)

RED SEA

NUBIA

THE EARLY EMPIRES
OF THE NEAR EAST

Minoan-Mycenaean civilizations:
c. 2200-1000 B.C.

Old Babylonian Empire:
c. 1750 B.C.

Hittite Empire:
c. 1600-1200 B.C.

Egyptian Empire:
c. 1450 B.C.

Phoenician Confederation:
c. 900 B.C.

0   500 miles

PHYSICAL MAP OF EUROPE, WESTERN ASIA, AND NORTHERN AFRICA

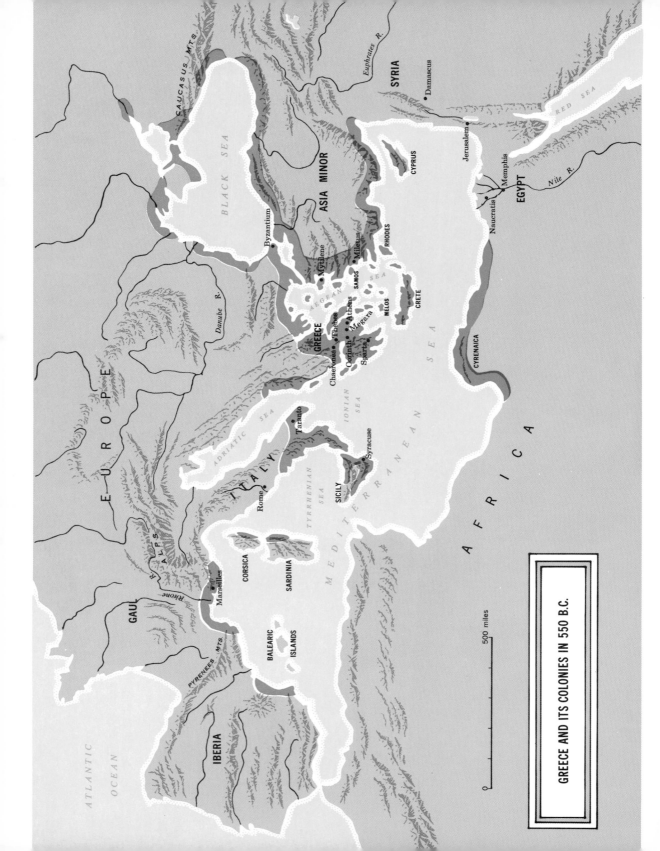

GREECE AND ITS COLONIES IN 550 B.C.

500 miles

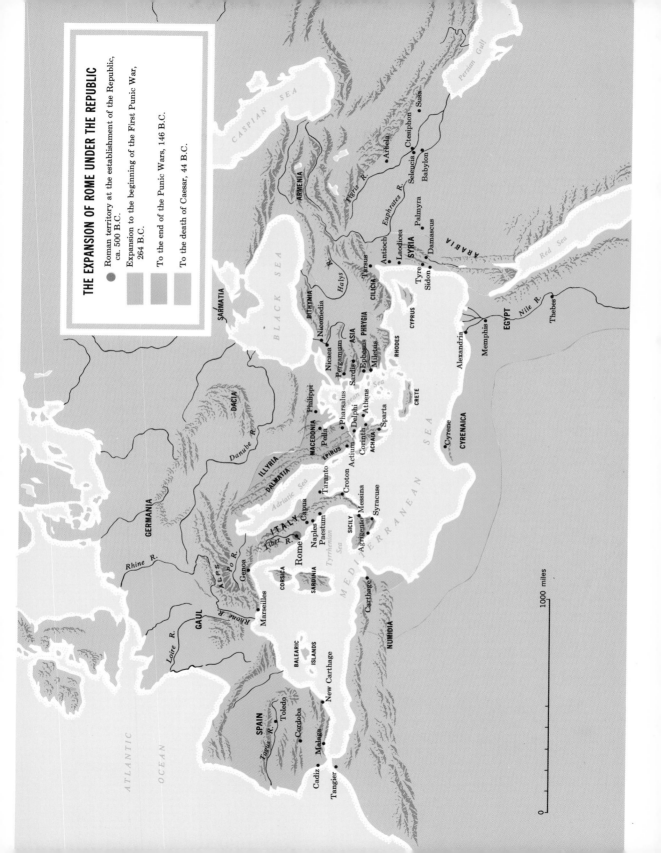

THE EXPANSION OF ROME UNDER THE REPUBLIC

● Roman territory at the establishment of the Republic, ca. 500 B.C.

Expansion to the beginning of the First Punic War, 264 B.C.

To the end of the Punic Wars, 146 B.C.

To the death of Caesar, 44 B.C.

ATLANTIC OCEAN

GERMANIA

GAUL

Rhine R.

Loire R.

Rhône R.

SPAIN

Tagus R.

Toledo
Cordoba
Malaga
Cadiz
Tangier

New Carthage

BALEARIC ISLANDS

Marseilles

ALPS

Genoa

Po R.

CORSICA

SARDINIA

Tiber R.

Rome

ITALY

Naples
Capua
Paestum

Tyrrhenian Sea

Carthage

NUMIDIA

MEDITERRANEAN SEA

SICILY
Agrigento
Messina
Syracuse

Taranto
Croton

Adriatic Sea

ILLYRIA

DALMATIA

MACEDONIA
Pella
Philippi

EPIRUS

Actium
Delphi
Corinth
Athens
ACHAIA
Sparta

Pharsalus

Aegean Sea

CRETE

Cyrene
CYRENAICA

DACIA

Danube R.

SARMATIA

BLACK SEA

BITHYNIA
Nicomedia
Nicaea
Pergamum
ASIA
Sardis
PHRYGIA
Ephesus
Miletus

Halys R.

Tarsus
CILICIA

RHODES

CYPRUS

Alexandria

Memphis

EGYPT

Nile R.

Thebes

CASPIAN SEA

ARMENIA

Tigris R.

Arbela

Ctesiphon
Seleucia
Babylon
Susa

Euphrates R.

Antioch
Laodicea
SYRIA
Palmyra
Damascus

Tyre
Sidon

ARABIA

Red Sea

Persian Gulf

1000 miles

0

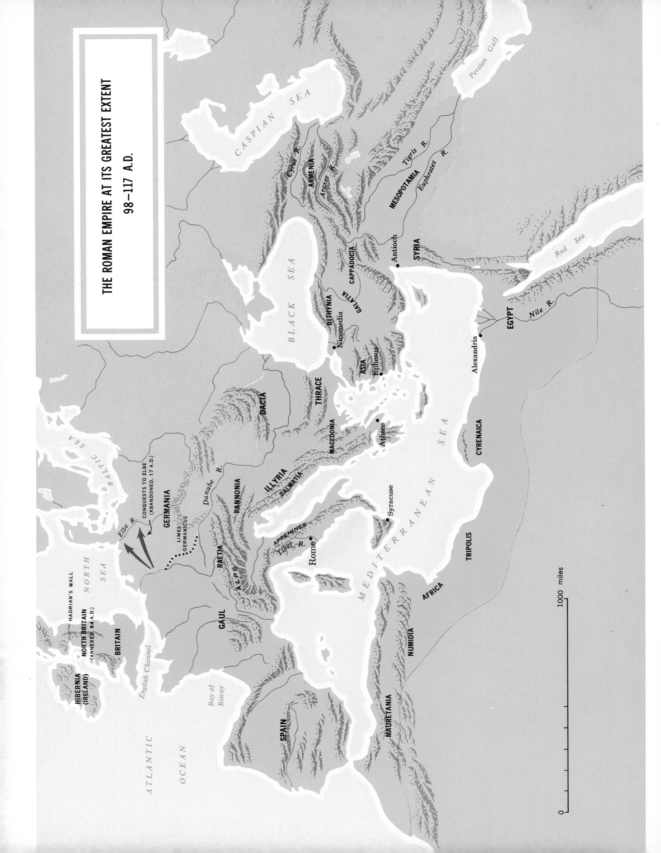

THE ROMAN EMPIRE AT ITS GREATEST EXTENT
98–117 A.D.

CASPIAN SEA

Persian Gulf

Cyrus R.
ARMENIA
Araxes R.
Tigris R.
Euphrates R.
MESOPOTAMIA
CAPPADOCIA
GALATIA
BITHYNIA
Nicomedia
Antioch
SYRIA
Red Sea
EGYPT
Nile R.
Alexandria
ASIA
Ephesus
BLACK SEA
THRACE
MACEDONIA
Athens
CYRENAICA
DACIA
ILLYRIA
DALMATIA
PANNONIA
RAETIA
Danube R.
Syracuse
MEDITERRANEAN SEA
TRIPOLIS
GERMANIA
CONQUESTS TO ELBE
(ABANDONED, 17 A.D.)
Elbe R.
LIMES
GERMANICUS
ALPS
APPENINES
Tiber R.
Rome
AFRICA
NUMIDIA
BALTIC SEA
HADRIAN'S WALL
NORTH BRITAIN
(ANNEXED, 84 A.D.)
BRITAIN
NORTH SEA
HIBERNIA
(IRELAND)
GAUL
English Channel
Bay of Biscay
SPAIN
MAURETANIA
ATLANTIC OCEAN

1000 miles

0

him to do so. Luckily for him and for the world he accumulated a fortune in Russian business ventures and then retired to spend both time
and money in the pursuit of his boyhood dreams. In 1870 he began ex-
cavating at Troy. Within a few years he had uncovered portions of
nine different cities, each built upon the ruins of its predecessor. The
second of these cities he identified as the Troy of the *Iliad,* although it
has been proved since that Troy was the seventh city. After fulfilling
his first great ambition, he started excavations on the mainland of
Greece and eventually uncovered two other Aegean cities, Mycenae
(pronounced My-sée-nee) and Tiryns. The work of Schliemann was
soon followed by that of other investigators, notably the Englishman
Sir Arthur Evans, who discovered Knossos, the resplendent capital of
the Minoan kings of Crete. Up to the present time more than half of
the ancient Aegean sites have been carefully searched, and a wealth of
knowledge has been accumulated about various aspects of the culture.

The Minoan and Mycenaean civilizations originated on the island of
Crete. (See the map on p. 185 below.) In few other cases in history does
the geographic interpretation of culture origins fit so neatly. Crete has
a benign and equable climate. While the soil is fertile, it is not of unlimited area; consequently, as the population increased, people were
impelled to sharpen their wits and to contrive new means of earning a
living. Some emigrated; others took to the sea; but a larger number
remained at home and developed articles for export. The latter included wine and olive oil, pottery, gems and seals, knives and
daggers, and objects of skilled craftsmanship. The chief imports were
foodstuffs and metals. As a result of such trade, prosperity increased
and extensive contacts were made with the surrounding civilized
world. Added to these factors of a favorable environment were the
beauties of nature which abounded almost everywhere, stimulating
the development of a marvelous art.

The Minoan civilization, named after the legendary Cretan ruler

*The favorable natural
environment of Crete*

Central Staircase of the Palace at Knossos

Origins and flowering of
Minoan civilization

Minos, was founded by peoples who emigrated from Asia Minor to Crete around 3000 B.C. In the millennium thereafter they made the transition from the Neolithic stage to the age of metals; by 2000 B.C. they had developed cities and an early form of writing. From then until about 1500 B.C. their civilization developed under the leadership of the cities of Knossos and Phaistos. Recently evidence has been found of the existence of another great city, Kato Zakros, on the east coast of Crete. Here was a huge palace of 250 rooms, with a swimming pool, parquet floors, and thousands of decorated vases. Only severe earthquakes, which periodically shook the island, interrupted the serene existence of the sophisticated Cretans. These quakes caused much devastation, but after each one the inhabitants of the Cretan cities set about the work of rebuilding and usually managed to construct even more splendid palaces than the ones which had been destroyed. So confident were the inhabitants of Knossos that they faced no threat whatsoever of foreign invasion that they left their magnificent city without any protective walls.

Origin of the Mycenaean
civilization

Ultimately such confidence proved to be mistaken. While Cretan civilization was flourishing, a related one was emerging on the mainland of Greece. Around 1900 B.C. Indo-European peoples who spoke the earliest form of Greek invaded the Greek peninsula, and by 1600 B.C. they were beginning to form settled communities. After around 1600 they became greatly influenced in their cultural development by the neighboring civilization of Minoan Crete, with which they had been developing trading relations. The civilization that resulted from the fusion of Greek and Minoan elements is usually called *Mycenaean,* after Mycenae, the leading city of Greece from about 1600 to 1200 B.C. It was this civilization that became dominant in the Aegean world after about 1500 and even gained predominance on the island of Crete itself.

Linear B

One of the greatest scholarly accomplishments of recent times has radically altered our understanding of Cretan and Greek history in the century between 1500 and 1400. It used to be thought that Greece throughout that time was still a semibarbarous economic colony of splendid Crete and that internal changes on Crete between 1500 and 1400 could be attributed to the rise of a "new dynasty." It was known that numerous specimens of the same linear script (called "Linear B") could be found on both Crete and the Greek mainland, but it was simply assumed that the script was Cretan in origin and spread from Crete to Greece. But in 1952 a brilliant young Englishman, Michael Ventris, who was then only thirty years old (and tragically died in an automobile accident four years later), succeeded in deciphering Linear B and demonstrating that it expressed an early form of Greek. Ventris's discovery revolutionized preclassical Greek studies by showing that the mainlanders dominated Crete in the late Minoan period and not vice versa.

A Linear B Tablet from Knossos

The new scholarly consensus is that the Mycenaeans supplanted the Minoans as rulers of the Aegean world sometime shortly after 1500 B.C. Around 1500 a great earthquake on Crete probably brought about sufficient weakness to allow the mainlanders to take control of the island. These Mycenaean Greeks helped to rebuild Knossos and presided over roughly a century of continued prosperity and artistic accomplishment on Crete. Around 1400, however, another wave of Greek invaders crossed over to the island, destroyed Knossos entirely, and put a cataclysmic end to the Minoan civilization. Why this invasion was so destructive cannot be known, but it left mainland Greece unrivaled as the center of civilization in the Aegean world for about another 200 years. Around 1250 B.C. the Mycenaeans waged their successful war with the Trojans of western Asia Minor, but their own demise was now in the offing. In the course of the century between 1200 B.C. and 1100 B.C., the Mycenaeans, whose civilization seems to have been decaying from within, succumbed to the Dorians—barbaric northern Greeks who had iron weapons. (Iron weapons may not at first have been much superior to the bronze ones used by the Mycenaeans, but they were far cheaper, thereby allowing many more fighters to wield them.) Because the Dorians were primitive in all but their weaponry their ascendancy initiated a dark age in Greek history which lasted until about 800 B.C.

The end of the Minoan and Mycenaean civilizations

As can be seen from the foregoing account, the Minoan and Mycenaean civilizations were closely interrelated; even the greatest experts have difficulty in determining exactly where one left off and the other began. The problem is complicated by the fact that two forms of writing which predate Linear B and have been found on Crete alone have not yet been deciphered. (Anyone who wishes to become as famous as Schliemann, Evans, or Ventris may take the decipherment of Cretan writing as his or her goal.) Accordingly, discussions of Minoan civilization before about 1500 B.C. rely exclusively on visual and archeological evidence, leaving much to the realm of speculation. Such evidence, however, does suggest that Cretan civilization was one of the freest and most progressive in all of early history.

The Minoan ruler was no bristling warlord like the Assyrian and Persian kings. He does seem to have commanded a large navy, but

Mycenaean Warrior Vase, c. 1250 B.C. Found in the ruins of Mycenae, this vase displays the warlike aspects of Mycenaean culture: the men might be marching off to the Trojan War.

Difficulty of distinguishing between early Minoan and Mycenaean characteristics

A Minoan Vase, c. 1400 B.C. The potter's wheel, probably invented by the Minoans, allowed a greater variety of shapes for vessels and encouraged Minoan artists to employ new styles and methods of decoration.

Evidences of social equality

The love of sports and games

The matriarchal nature of Minoan religion

this was not for war but for the maintenance of trade. In fact, the king was the chief entrepreneur in the country. The workshops located in the environs of his palace turned out great quantities of fine pottery, textiles, and metal goods. Although private enterprise apparently was not prohibited it seems to have been heavily taxed. Nevertheless there were some privately owned workshops especially in smaller towns, and much agriculture was also in private hands.

The Cretan state is probably best described as a bureaucratic monarchy. The ruler of each leading city and its surrounding territory appears to have been absolute, and towards the end of Minoan history (exactly when is hard to say) the ruler of Knossos appears to have taken over the entire island. The absolute Cretan ruler governed by means of a large administrative class. Scribes, who seem to have had a monopoly of learning, kept close accounts of all aspects of economic life. All agricultural production and manufacturing was closely supervised for purposes of gathering or taxing whatever was owed to the king. Foreign trade too seems to have been closely supervised by the state; most likely the large Cretan ships that put into ports as far away as Syria and Egypt were owned or at least heavily taxed by the ruler and carefully watched over by the bureaucratic administration.

Despite such close supervision, the Cretan people of nearly all classes appear to have led fairly prosperous lives. Although there were great social and economic distinctions between the rulers and the ruled, there were apparently few gradations of wealth or status among the common people. If slavery existed at all, it certainly occupied an unimportant place. The dwellings in the poorest quarters of smaller towns such as Gournia were substantially built and commodious, often with as many as six or eight rooms, but we do not know how many families resided in them. Women seem to have enjoyed equality with men. Regardless of class there was no public activity from which they were debarred, and no occupation which they could not enter. In this, the Minoans were the exception in the ancient world. Crete had female bullfighters and even female pugilists. Women of the upper strata devoted much time to fashion and other leisure activities.

The natives of Crete delighted in games and sports of every description. Dancing, running matches, and boxing rivaled each other in their attraction for the people. The Cretans were the first to build stone theaters where processions and music entertained large audiences.

So far as we know, Minoan religion was a medley of strange characteristics. First of all it was apparently matriarchal. The chief deity was not a god but a goddess, who was the ruler of the entire universe—the sea and the sky as well as the earth. Originally no male deity appears to have been worshiped, but later a god was associated with the goddess as her son and consort. Although, like the divine sons in several other religions, he apparently died and rose from the dead, he was

Scenes from the Bull Ring: Minoan Mural, c. 1500 B.C. Evident are the youth, skill, and agility of the Cretan athletes, the center one a male, the other two female. The body and horns of the bull are exaggerated, as are the slenderness of the athletes and their full-face eyes in profile heads. There is probably also some exaggeration in content: modern experts in bull-fighting insist that it is impossible to somersault over the back of a charging bull.

never regarded by the Cretans as of particular importance. In the second place, the Minoan religion was thoroughly monistic. The mother goddess was the source of evil as well as of good, but not in any morbid or terrifying sense. Though she brought the storm and spread destruction in her path, these served for the replenishment of nature. Death itself was interpreted as the prerequisite for life. Whether the religion had any body of ethical precepts is unknown.

Other features of the religion of the Minoans included the worship of animals and birds (the bull, the snake, and the dove); the worship of sacred trees; the veneration of sacred objects which were probably reproductive symbols (the double-axe, the pillar, and the cross); and, in accordance with the matriarchal nature of the belief system, the employment of priestesses instead of priests to administer sacred rites.

Since we cannot yet decipher the early Cretan scripts it is impossible to tell whether the Minoans had any literature or philosophy, although the existence of either seems extremely unlikely because there is none written in Linear B. The problem of scientific achievements is easier to solve, since we have material remains for our guidance. Archeological discoveries on the island of Crete indicate that the ancient inhabitants were gifted inventors and engineers. They built excellent roads of concrete about eleven feet wide. Nearly all the basic principles of modern sanitary engineering were known to the designers of the palace of Knossos, with the result that the royal family of Crete in the seventeenth century B.C. enjoyed comforts and conveniences, such as indoor running water, that were not available to the wealthiest rulers of Western countries in the seventeenth century A.D.

If there was any one achievement of the Minoans that appears more

Minoan Snake Goddess, Sixteenth Century B.C. A statuette made of ivory and gold.

Minoan art

Architecture

"La Parisienne"

than others to emphasize the vitality and freedom of their culture, it was their art. With the exception of the classical Greek, no other art of the ancient world was quite its equal. Its distinguishing features were delicacy, spontaneity, and naturalism. It served not to glorify the ambitions of an arrogant ruling class or to inculcate the doctrines of a religion, but to express the delight of the individual in the beauty and splendor of the Minoan world. As a result, it was remarkably free from the retarding influence of ancient tradition. It was unique, moreover, in the universality of its application, for it extended not merely to paintings and statues but even to the humblest objects of ordinary use.

Of the major arts, architecture was the least developed. The great palaces were not remarkably beautiful buildings but rambling structures designed primarily for capaciousness and comfort. As more and more functions were absorbed by the state, the palaces were enlarged to accommodate them. New quarters were annexed to those already built or piled on top of them without regard for order or symmetry. The interiors, however, were decorated with beautiful paintings and furnishings. The architecture of Crete may be said to have resembled the modern international style in its subordination of form to utility and in its emphasis upon a pleasing and livable interior as more important than external beauty.

Painting was the supreme Cretan art. Nearly all of it consisted of murals done in fresco, although painted reliefs were occasionally to be found. The murals in the palaces of Crete were by all odds the best that have survived from ancient times. They revealed almost perfectly the remarkable gifts of the Minoan artist—an instinct for the dramatic, a sense of rhythm, a feeling for nature in its most characteristic moods. So sophisticated and elegant was Cretan art that a Frenchman who was unearthing the remains of a fresco at Knossos could not help exclaiming when he saw a painting of a striking woman portrayed with curls, vivid eyes, and sensuous lips: "Mais, c'est la Parisienne!" ("Why, she's just like a woman from Paris!").

Sculpture and the ceramic and gem-carving arts were also developed to a high stage of perfection. The sculpture of the Cretans differed from that of any other people in the ancient Near East. It never relied upon size as a device to convey the idea of power. The Cretans produced no colossi like those of Egypt or reliefs like those of Babylonia depicting a king of gigantic proportions smiting his puny enemies. Instead, they preferred sculpture in miniature. Nearly all of the statues of human beings or of deities that the archeologists have found are smaller than life-size.

Mycenaean civilization appears to have been more warlike and less refined than the Minoan, but the most recent scholarship warns us to beware of exaggerating these differences. As on Crete, so on mainland Greece, the city was the center of civilization—the leading Mycenaean cities being Mycenae itself (according to Homer the home of the leading Greek king Agamemnon), Pylos (according to Homer the home of the wise Nestor), and Tiryns. Each city and its surrounding area was ruled over by a king called a *wanax*, who in many respects ruled like an oriental despot. As on Crete, the Mycenaean state was a bureaucratic monarchy. We know for certain about some of the workings of this monarchy because of the decipherment of numerous Linear B tablets, all of which are records of a highly regulatory bureaucratic apparatus. Linear B tablets from Pylos report the minutest details of the economic lives of the king's subjects: the exact acreage of a given estate; the number of cooking utensils owned by so-and-so; the personal names given to somebody else's two oxen ("Glossy" and "Blackie"). Such detailed inventories show us that the state was highly centralized and that it was as supreme in its control over the economic activities of its citizens as any other in the Near East.

Although the bureaucratic monarchies of Crete and Mycenaean Greece were probably similar, there were still at least a few notable differences between the two related civilizations. One was that the Mycenaeans definitely had a slave system and another was that they did not award equal status to women. Mycenaean society too was geared much more greatly toward warfare. Because Mycenaean cities were frequently at war with one another they were built on hilltops and heavily fortified. In keeping with a somewhat more rugged and barbaric style of life than that which obtained on Crete, Mycenaean kings built themselves ostentatious graves in which they buried their best inlaid bronze daggers and other signs of their power and wealth.

It is also true that Mycenaean art is less elegant than Minoan. Without question the Mycenaeans never equaled the artistic delicacy and grace of their Minoan predecessors. Nevertheless, Mycenaean artwork done in Knossos between 1500 and 1400 B.C., while stiffer and more symmetrical in composition than earlier Minoan work, is by no means wholly different in kind. Moreover, the "Parisian woman" of Minoan Knossos has some very close stylistic relatives in a female procession fresco from about 1300 B.C. found in Mycenaean Tiryns. Nor should it be thought that all the best traits of Mycenaean art can merely be seen as debased borrowings from the Minoans: the superbly executed and exquisite Mycenaean inlaid daggers have no antecedents anywhere on Crete.

The significance of the Minoan and the Mycenaean civilizations should not be estimated primarily in terms of subsequent influences. Minoan culture hardly influenced any peoples other than the Mycenaeans and it was then destroyed more or less without a trace after about 1400 B.C. The Mycenaeans left behind a few more traces, but still not very many. Later Greeks retained some Mycenaean gods and goddesses like Zeus, Hera, Hermes, and Poseidon, but they com-

Similarities between the Minoan and Mycenaean civilizations

Differences between the Minoan and Mycenaean civilizations

Detail from a Procession Fresco at Tiryns, c. 1300 B.C. Note the similarity of this Mycenaean female profile to the Minoan "La Parisienne" shown on p. 102.

Influence of the Minoan and Mycenaean civilizations

pletely altered their role in the religious pantheon. It may also be that
the later Greeks gained from the Mycenaeans their devotion to ath-
letics and their system of weights and measures, but these connections
remain uncertain. Homer definitely remembered the successful Mycenaean siege of Troy, but it is just as important to realize how much
Homer forgot: writing in the eighth century B.C. Homer (actually several different writers who have come down to us under that name) entirely forgot the whole pattern of Mycenaean bureacratic monarchy
which we know from the Linear B tablets. It may well be that the
break between the Mycenaeans and Homer was all for the good. Some
historians maintain that the destruction of despotic Mycenae by the
Dorians was a necessary prelude to the emergence of the freer and
more enlightened later Greek outlook.

*Importance of the Minoan
and Mycenaean
civilizations*

Although the Minoan and Mycenaean civilizations had little subsequent influence, they are still noteworthy for at least four reasons.
First of all, they were the earliest civilizations of Europe. Before the
Cretan accomplishments all civilizations had existed further east, but
afterwards Europe was to witness the development of one highly
impressive civilization after another. Secondly, in some respects the
Minoans and the Mycenaeans seem to have looked forward to certain
later European values and accomplishments even if they did not directly influence them. Minoan and Mycenaean political organization
was similar to that of many Asian states but Minoan art in particular
seems very different and more characteristic of later European patterns. Unlike most ancient Near-Eastern artists, the Minoan gloried
not in portraying the slaughter of armies or the sacking of cities but in
picturing flowery landscapes, joyous festivals, thrilling exhibitions of
athletic prowess, and similar scenes of a free and peaceful existence.
Thirdly, the Minoan civilization, and to a lesser degree also the Mycenaean one, is significant for its worldly and progressive outlook.
This is exemplified in the devotion of the Aegean peoples to comfort
and opulence, in their love of amusement, zest for life, and courage for
experimentation. And finally, the Minoan civilization is particularly
remarkable for having flourished so long in peace. If there has never
again been as peaceful a civilization as the Minoan then that is a fact we
should not celebrate but deplore.

3. THE LYDIANS AND THE PHOENICIANS

The Kingdom of Lydia

After the last remnants of the Hittite Empire fell in the eighth century
B.C., one of the successor states in Asia Minor was the Kingdom of
Lydia. The Lydians established their rule in what is now the western
part of Turkey. They quickly secured control of the Greek cities on

the coast of Asia Minor and of the entire plateau west of the Halys River. But their power was short-lived. In 547 B.C. their king, Croesus, fancied he saw a good opportunity to add to his domain the territory of the Medes east of the Halys. The Median king had just been deposed by Cyrus the Great of Persia. Thinking this meant an easy triumph for his own armies, Croesus set out to capture the territory beyond the river. After an indecisive battle with Cyrus, he returned to his own capital (Sardis) for reinforcements. Here Cyrus caught him unprepared in a surprise attack and captured and burned the city. The Lydians never recovered from the blow, and soon afterward all of their territory, including the Greek cities on the coast, passed under the dominion of Cyrus.

The Lydians were a people of Indo-European speech, who were probably a mixture of native peoples of Asia Minor with migrant stocks from eastern Europe. Benefiting from the advantages of favorable location and abundance of resources, they enjoyed one of the highest standards of living of ancient times. They were famous for the splendor of their armored chariots and the quantities of gold and articles of luxury possessed by the citizens. The wealth of their kings was legendary, as attested by the simile "rich as Croesus." The chief sources of this prosperity were gold from the streams, wool from the thousands of sheep on the hills, and the profits of the extensive commerce which passed overland from the Tigris-Euphrates valley to the Aegean Sea. But with all their wealth and opportunities for leisure, they succeeded in making only one original contribution to civilization. This was the coinage of money from electrum or "white gold," a natural mixture of gold and silver found in the sands of one of their rivers. Hitherto all systems of money had consisted of weighed rings or bars of metal. The new coins, of varying sizes, were stamped with a definite value more or less arbitrarily given by the ruler who issued them.

The Lydian people and their culture

In contrast with the Lydians, who gained their ascendancy as a result of the downfall of the Hittites, were the Phoenicians, who benefited from the break-up of Aegean supremacy. But the Phoenicians were neither conquerors nor the builders of an empire. They exerted their influence through the arts of peace, especially through commerce. During most of their history their political system was a loose confederation of city-states, which frequently bought their security by paying tribute to foreign powers. The territory they occupied was the narrow strip north of Palestine between the Lebanon Mountains and the Mediterranean Sea and the islands off the coast. With good harbors and a central location, it was admirably situated for trade. The great centers of commerce included Tyre and Sidon. Under the leadership of Tyre, Phoenicia reached the zenith of its accomplishments from the tenth to the eighth century B.C. During the sixth century it passed under the domination of the Chaldeans and then of the Persians. In

The Phoenician cities and confederation

332 B.C. Tyre was destroyed by Alexander the Great after a siege of seven months.

Achievements of the Phoenicians

The Phoenicians were a people of Semitic language, closely related to the Canaanites. They displayed very little creative genius, but were remarkable adapters of the achievements of others. They produced no original art worthy of the name, and they made but slight contributions to literature. Their religion, like that of the Canaanites, was characterized by human sacrifice to the god Moloch and by licentious fertility rites. They excelled, however, in specialized manufactures, in geography and navigation. They founded colonies at Carthage and Utica in North Africa, near modern-day Palermo on the island of Sicily, on the Balearic Islands, and at Cadiz and Malaga in Spain. They were renowned throughout the ancient world for their glass and metal industries and for their purple dye obtained from a mollusk in the adjacent seas. They developed the art of navigation to such a stage that they could sail by the stars at night. To less venturesome peoples, the North Star was known for some time as the Phoenicians' star. Phoenician ships and sailors were recruited by all the great powers. The most lasting achievement of the Phoenicians, however, was the completion and diffusion of an alphabet based upon principles discovered by the Egyptians. The Phoenician contribution was the adoption of a system of signs representing the sounds of the human voice, and the elimination of all pictographic and syllabic characters. This alphabet was taken up by the Greeks, who adapted it for their own language.

An Early Lydian Coin, Probably Struck During the Reign of Croesus

4. LESSONS FROM THE HISTORY OF THE NEAR-EASTERN STATES

Defects of the Near-Eastern empires

Like most other periods in world history, the period of the states we have studied thus far was an era of contention and strife. Nearly all of the great empires, and the majority of the smaller states as well, devoted their energies most of the time to policies of expansion and aggression. The only notable exceptions were the Minoan and Egyptian, but even the Egyptians, in the later period of their history, yielded to no one in their addiction to imperialism. The causes were largely geographic. Each nation grew accustomed to the pursuit of its own interests in some fertile river valley or on some easily defended plateau. Isolation bred fear of foreigners and an incapacity to think of one's own people as members of a common humanity. The feelings of insecurity that resulted seemed to justify aggressive foreign policies and the annexation of neighboring states to serve as buffers against a hostile world.

It seems possible to trace nearly all of the woes of the Near-Eastern nations to wars of aggression and imperialist greed. Arnold J. Toynbee has shown this in devastating fashion in the case of the Assyrians. He contends that it was no less true of such later peoples as the Spartans, the Carthaginians, the Macedonians, and the Ottoman Turks. Each made militarism and conquest its gods and wrought such destruction upon itself that when it made its last heroic stand against its enemies, it was a mere "corpse in armor." Not death by foreign conquest but national suicide was the fate which befell it.[1] The way of the warrior brought racism, a love of ease and luxury, crime and racketeering, and crushing burdens of taxation. Expansion of empire promoted a fictitious prosperity, at least for the upper classes, and aroused enough envy among poorer nations to make them willing conspirators against a rich neighbor who could easily be portrayed as an oppressor. The use of hungry and discontented allies against powerful rivals is not new in history.

*Results of Near-Eastern
imperialism*

SELECTED READINGS

• *Items so designated are available in paperback editions.*

Alsop, Joseph, *From the Silent Earth: A Report on the Greek Bronze Age,* New York, 1964. An enthusiastic account by a modern political reporter of some of the most exciting recent discoveries and hypotheses. Favors the Mycenaeans in discussions of their relationships to the Minoans.

Blegen, C. W., *Troy and the Trojans,* New York, 1963. The most reliable archeological appraisal.

Ceram, C. W., *The Secret of the Hittites,* New York, 1956. The best popular account.

• Chadwick, John, *The Decipherment of Linear B,* 2nd ed., New York, 1968. Chadwick was a research colleague of Michael Ventris and here gives the most accessible account of Ventris's brilliant work.

• ———, *The Mycenaean World,* New York, 1976.

• Gordon, Cyrus H., *The Ancient Near East,* New York, 1965.

• ———, *The Common Background of Greek and Hebrew Civilizations,* New York, 1965. Very controversial. Gordon believes that Greek culture was in its origins Semitic.

Gurney, O. R., *The Hittites,* Baltimore, 1961. More scholarly than Ceram.

Harden, Donald, *The Phoenicians,* New York, 1962. Best account of the Phoenicians at home and abroad.

Higgins, Reynold, *Minoan and Mycenaean Art,* New York, 1967.

History of the Hellenic World, Vol. I, *Prehistory and Protohistory,* University Park, Pa., 1974.

Hutchinson, R. W., *Prehistoric Crete,* Baltimore, 1962.

Lloyd, Seton, *Early Anatolia,* Baltimore, 1956.

• MacDonald, William A., *Progress into the Past: The Rediscovery of Mycenaean Civilization,* New York, 1967.

[1] D. C. Somervell (ed.), A. J. Toynbee's *A Study of History,* I, 338–43.

Palmer, L. R., *Mycenaeans and Minoans,* New York, 1962. Includes bold statements on many debatable problems of interpretation.

• Pendlebury, J. D. S., *The Archaeology of Crete,* New York, 1939.

• Vermeule, Emily, *Greece in the Bronze Age,* Chicago, 1964. The best book on the subject.

Chapter 6

ANCIENT INDIAN CIVILIZATION

Hinduism does not distinguish ideas of God as true and false, adopting
one particular idea as the standard for the whole human race. It accepts
the obvious fact that mankind seeks its goal of God at various levels and
in various directions, and feels sympathy with every stage of the search.
— S. Radhakrishnan, *The Hindu View of Life*

The subcontinent of India has an area slightly more than half
that of the United States and is inhabited by more than three
times as many people. Not only is India a vast and densely
populated region but it includes many different levels of culture, different religions, languages, and economic conditions, and its history
is extremely complex. Five or six separate families of languages are
represented among its people. The population contains admixtures of
all of the three great races of mankind—black, yellow, and white—in
various combinations and proportions. One of the most ancient peoples, a Negrito strain related to the Pygmies of Africa, has almost
disappeared from India but is still found in the Andaman Islands to
the east. In striking contrast to this type are the fair-skinned Mediter-
raneans of the north and northwest, descendants of the Indo-Aryans
who invaded the country some 3,500 years ago. The most widespread
group in southern India is that known as Dravidian, but because the
term is applied to all whose language belongs to the Dravidian family,
it no longer denotes a single ethnic stock. Another type, perhaps more
ancient than the Dravidians, is called Australoid, because of its relationship with primitive peoples extending over parts of southeastern
Asia and as far east as Australia. The Mongolian element is confined
chiefly to the border region of the north and northeast. Alpine types
are found along the western coast, sometimes with a slight Nordic
admixture (evidenced by gray or blue eyes). Thus the common practice of referring to the natives of India as "colored" or "brown-
skinned" is misleading. Their skins are indeed of various shades, but

The peoples of India

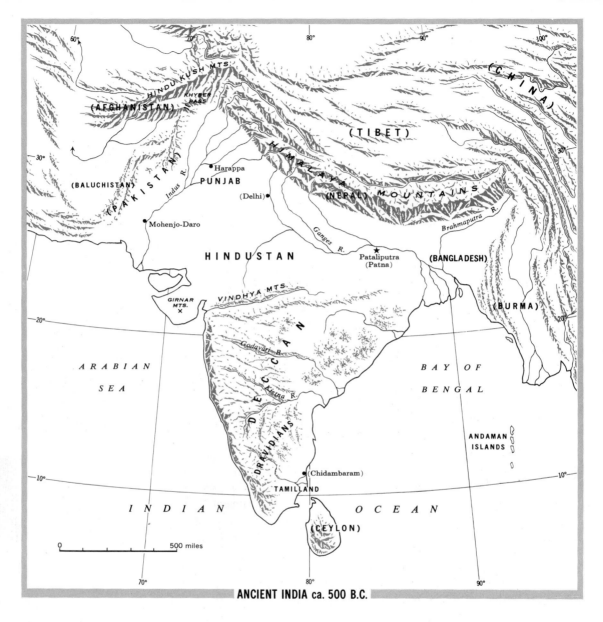

ANCIENT INDIA ca. 500 B.C.

since early times white stocks have been conspicuously present, especially in northern India. Even today some of the most typical examples of the tall variety of the Mediterranean white race can be seen in the Punjab and the northwest frontier. Yet they exist in close proximity to people who reveal Alpine, Australoid, Mongoloid, or Negrito features. Over the course of centuries, and in spite of the inexorable segregation of the caste system in historic times, India has been a human melting pot.

Geographically India falls into two main divisions. The southern triangle or peninsular portion, known as the Deccan, lies entirely within the tropics. The northern or continental half, also triangular in shape, is in the same latitudes as Mexico and the southern United States and has temperatures ranging from tropical heat to the intense cold of the northern mountain peaks. The northern Deccan is semi-mountainous and heavily forested, and shelters some of the primitive hill tribes whose ancestors were crowded into the wilderness by the pressure of expansion from more civilized communities. The greater part of the peninsula, however, is a gently sloping plateau, traversed by rivers, and containing rich agricultural lands. The northern half of India, called Hindustan, is bounded on the north by the lofty Himalayan range and is separated from the Deccan by the low-lying Vindhya Mountains. Most of Hindustan is a level plain comprising an area about as large as France, Germany, and Italy combined, drained by the great river systems of the Indus and the Ganges. The rivers of Hindustan take their rise in the Himalayas or beyond and are fed by snows and glaciers. The Indus and the Brahmaputra each originate in Tibet and flow in opposite directions around the mountain ranges until they turn south into India, bringing with them virgin soil from the highlands which is deposited on the plain. The gently flowing Ganges, less subject to floods than the Indus, is the most beneficent of all. Referred to as "Mother Ganges," it has long been the sacred river of the Hindus. It is no wonder that its central valley, where every inch of soil is productive and no stone even the size of a pebble can be found, is one of the most densely populated spots in the world. The

The geography of India

The Srinagar Valley. Lowlying areas are regularly inundated by the floodwaters of the Jhelum River, a tributary of the Indus River in northwestern India. The floodwaters leave rich soil in their wake.

mouths of the Ganges (in Bengal) are surrounded by forbidding jungle, and a desert separates the lower Indus valley from the Ganges and its tributaries; but the Indo-Gangetic region as a whole is lavishly endowed by nature. Here the most influential centers of Indian civilization have been located.

India a geographic unit

All India enjoys the advantage of the monsoon rains, and the greater part of the country is suitable for cultivation. Moreover, there is no impenetrable barrier between Hindustan and the Deccan and there has always been communication between the two sections. In spite of its size and contrasting terrain, India is a natural geographic unit. That its peoples have been united politically only during relatively brief periods of their history is attributable to many factors, including disturbances from without, but it cannot be ascribed to geographic necessity.

1. THE VEDIC AGE IN INDIA

The earliest civilization of India

Remains of Neolithic and of early metal-age cultures have been discovered both in Hindustan and the Deccan. The first highly advanced civilization began its history as early as 3000 B.C. and reached its peak between 2500 and 2000 B.C. It covered a large area extending 1000 miles through the Indus valley and along the coast of the Arabian Sea both to the east and west of the mouth of the Indus. It was essentially an urban civilization, with a cosmopolitan society and extensive trade with the outside world. Among some 70 metropolitan centers thus far uncovered, the two principal sites are Mohenjo–Daro, about 300 miles from the seacoast, and Harappa, about 400 miles farther up the river.

Excavations at Harappa. These digs have provided the means of reconstructing the urban civilization of the Indus Valley between 3000 B.C. and 2000 B.C. Note the extensive use of brick in the buildings of the period.

Skeletons at Mohenjo-Daro. Although the downfall of this culture is a mystery, barbarian conquest was an important factor.

Both were durably constructed of brick and laid out in accordance with ambitious and intelligent planning. Private houses were solidly built and equipped with bathrooms which drained into sewer pipes running underneath the principal streets and discharging into the river. Evidences of intellectual achievement are scanty, although proofs are available that standards of weight and measurement and a system of writing had been developed. The writing, which has not yet been deciphered, is in the form of pictographic signs on delicately carved stone seals. A group of Scandinavian scholars who are studying it believe that the language of the Indus valley inscriptions can be classified as Proto-Dravidian. Several of the arts reflected a high degree of skill, especially the fabrication of small objects for personal adornment. Some examples of sculpture, also, indicate a talent for grace and naturalness. The religion of this early civilization centered upon the worship of fertility deities, notably a mother goddess. The principal rite was animal sacrifice.

Bull Seal. Impression of stone seal from Mohenjo-Daro, 2500 B.C., probably used as a signature. The animal figure (of a Brahmani bull or zebu) is assumed to have had religious significance.

Archeological evidence supports the conclusion that the Indus valley civilization was one of the earliest in the world and that it was comparable in level of achievement to those of contemporary Egypt and Mesopotamia. Whether it was indigenous to India or was introduced by settlers from the west is still a matter of speculation. It long maintained intercourse with other civilized regions, especially Mesopotamia, where Indus-type stone seals and other objects belonging to the period about 2300–2000 B.C. have been discovered. For reasons not entirely clear, the Indus valley civilization decayed and disappeared from the scene of history about 1600 B.C. Probably a major cause was a series of floods and earthquakes which altered the course of the Indus River and inundated densely inhabited cities. Whatever

Dyers' Troughs or Drains Uncovered at Mohenjo-Daro.

Unicorn Seal. The "unicorn" (perhaps actually the profile of an ox) is the animal most frequently depicted on the Indus civilization seals. The object under the animal's head may represent a brazier or incense holder. The inscription has not been deciphered. This specimen was found in the Deccan, some 600 miles from the Indus Valley.

the causes, the civilization went down to so complete an oblivion that no one was aware of its existence until evidences were unearthed by archeologists about sixty years ago. Shortly before the downfall of the Indus valley cities, India was invaded by seminomadic tribes who were destined to be the founders of a more enduring civilization. These were the so-called Aryans,[1] or Indo-Aryans, who came in by way of Afghanistan through the passes of the Hindu Kush Mountains. For many centuries the Aryan influence was confined to northern India, and here it developed the distinctive Hindu pattern of society, culture, and religion. Though the Aryan (Indo-European) languages never became dominant in the south, they are the most widely spoken group of languages in India today.

For some 1,000 years following the Indo-Aryan invasions the political history of India is largely unknown. There is no reason to assume a wholesale displacement of population. As the invading tribes extended their sway over northern India they intermingled with the inhabitants of the conquered regions. The process of assimilation between conquerors and conquered affected the culture of the invaders to a degree that cannot be clearly determined but which undoubtedly was profound, especially in the development of religion and social structure. The absence of reliable historical records for such a long period of time, among people who achieved a variegated, colorful, and highly intellectual civilization, is extraordinary. The scarcity of historical information is not entirely accidental, although it is partly

---

[1] "Aryan" was the name by which these invaders identified themselves. The theory of a distinctive Aryan race, expounded from time to time by various propagandists, has been exploded. In current usage the term "Aryan" is properly applied only to a family of related languages (the Indo-European group).

accounted for by the fact that the Indo-Aryans had no system of writing until about 1,000 years after their settlement in India. A more potent cause was the character of their civilization itself and especially of their philosophy, which stressed the importance of timeless qualities and the relative insignificance of temporal events and conditions. When they looked back to the past, they were inclined to give free scope to their imagination and to reckon in terms of vast eras and aeons, symmetrical but fantastic, extending to millions or even billions of years. The failure to produce factual chronicles does not mean that no changes or exciting events occurred. On the contrary, the available evidence suggests the normal amount of conflict, turmoil, and upheaval.

The sources of information for early Indo-Aryan civilization are almost exclusively in literary tradition. The oldest literary monument is the collection of religious poems and hymns called the *Vedas*. No one knows when they were composed. The oldest portions may have originated as early as 3000 B.C., and they were passed on orally without any written aids whatsoever until several centuries after the collection was complete. The *Vedas* reflect the culture of the primitive Aryan communities in the upper Indus valley and the "Middle Land" between the two rivers, or roughly the period from 2000 to 800 B.C., which is accordingly called the Vedic age. The latter portion of the *Vedas,* however, shows that profound changes had taken place during these centuries. The second major literary landmark consists of two long epic poems, the *Ramayana* and the *Mahabharata*. Like the *Vedas,* and in spite of their tremendous bulk, the epics were preserved by memory and oral repetition for many generations, but they reflect a different set of conditions, customs, and beliefs from those most typical of the *Vedas*. The epics reveal that by the close of the Vedic age Indo-Aryan culture had been transformed into a complex and stratified social and religious system. It had become Hinduism.

In the early Vedic period the Indo-Aryan tribes had a simple, largely pastoral economy. They cultivated barley and probably other grains, using a wooden plow drawn by bullocks. They ate the flesh of sheep, goats, and oxen, usually at the time of sacrificing these animals to the gods, but their favorite foods were dairy products—milk, cream, and ghee (melted butter). Cattle were the most prized possessions and served as a medium of exchange. Apparently they were not yet worshiped, nor was their slaughter forbidden. Domesticated animals also included the horse, used to pull the war chariot and also for chariot racing. All the common handicrafts, including metal work, were practiced. Music, both vocal and instrumental—with flutes, drums, cymbals, and stringed lutes or harps—was a popular source of entertainment, as was dancing. Gambling with dice was a national pastime and seems to have come close to being a national obsession.

In its typical features this early Indian society was vigorous and uninhibited, its members delighting in song and dance, in feasting,

Scantiness of the early records

Vedas and epics

Dancing Girl. Bronze statuette of a female dancer, from Mohenjo-Daro, a striking example of the art of the ancient Indus civilization. Bracelets and bangles have retained their popularity among the women of India to the present day.

carousing, and feats of strength. Warfare was frequent, and many stories have been preserved of the incredible powers of strong-armed heroes. The social unit was the patriarchal family, in which woman's position was inferior, although considerably freer than in later Indian society. Women were not permitted to participate in religious sacrifice and only sons could inherit property. Polygamy was permissible, but such later Hindu institutions as the immolation of a widow upon her husband's funeral pyre (suttee) and child marriage were completely unknown.

Political institutions

As might be expected, political and legal institutions were rudimentary among the primitive Aryans. Each tribe had its king (raja), whose chief function was to lead his warriors in battle. Associated with the king in ruling was an assembly. Its composition and duties are not at all clear, but its existence suggests a limitation upon the royal authority. Some of the tribes were organized as aristocratic republics rather than hereditary monarchies, with government resting with the heads of the clans or an elected raja. In the early days the raja's powers could hardly have been awe-inspiring in any case. He had no populous cities from which to extract riches, only country villages; and the villages managed their own internal affairs, paying part of their produce to the raja for "protection." The handling of crime and punishment followed patterns similar to those of many other primitive societies. The injured party or his family was expected to take the initiative in prosecuting an offender. Compensation for injuries was usually a payment in money or commodities to the plaintiff or, in the case of murder, to the victim's family. Theft was the most frequent complaint, especially cattle stealing, even though this crime was looked upon as highly reprehensible. An insolvent debtor—usually one who had gambled too recklessly—might be enslaved to his creditor.

The Vedas *as literature*

The most significant achievement of the Vedic age was the composition of the poetry and prose which give the period its name. Ultimately there were four *Vedas,* each containing a large collection of prayers, chants, or hymns, supplemented by prose commentary. The literal meaning of *Veda* is "knowledge" or "wisdom," and the entire collection was believed to have been imparted to ancient seers by the gods rather than invented by men. The *Vedas* constitute the canonical books of the Indo-Aryan—and of the later Hindu—religion; they were considered divinely inspired and uniquely sacred, as were the Hebrew and Christian Scriptures by the members of those faiths. However, because the early Aryans were illiterate, their sacred books were said to have been "heard" rather than "revealed." The *Vedas* cover an amazing variety and range of subjects. Some portions are litanies intended to be chanted by priests during a sacrifice. Others are catalogues of spells and charms, including alleged remedies for fever and snake bite, love formulas, and recipes for exterminating one's enemies. Still others incorporate customs and folklore or display a profound insight into philosophical or religious truth. Although much of the content of the *Vedas* is repetitious and monotonous, in vividness and imagination the best verses deserve to rank with the *Iliad* of Homer.

The religion of the early Aryans as illustrated in the *Vedas* was a comprehensive polytheism, with little ethical significance. Their gods—*deva,* or "shining ones"—were the forces of nature or personifications of these forces. No images or temples were erected, and worship consisted chiefly in performing sacrifices to the gods. Grain and milk were sacrificed, animal flesh was burned upon the altars (the worshipers themselves eating the flesh), but the choicest offering was *soma,* an alcoholic or psychedelic beverage fermented from the juice of a mountain plant. The gods were looked upon in much the same way as the Olympian deities were regarded by the Greeks. They were conceived as splendid and powerful creatures, with human attributes but immortal as long as they drank the *soma* juice, and, on the whole, benevolent. It was assumed that they would reward men out of gratitude for the homage and gifts presented to them. Gradually, however, the insidious notion took root that if the holy rites were conducted with unfailing accuracy they would compel the god to obedience, whether he was willing or not. It is easy to see how such an interpretation would enhance the prestige and authority of the priests who controlled the wonder-working formulas.

Religion of the early Aryans

The roster of gods was a large one and tended to increase. While several deities can be identified with those of other Indo-European peoples, they did not have as clear-cut personalities as the Greek or Norse gods. The Indian mind ran toward specialization and abstraction, tending to invent a new god or a new variant of an old god for every conceivable occasion. Dyaus, lord of the bright sky, was equivalent to the Greek Zeus (though less important). Varuna represented the sky or heaven in its capacity to encompass all things and hold the universe together. He was called Asura, a term which suggests close kinship with the supreme Persian deity, Ahura-Mazda. At least five different divinities were identified with the sun. One of them, Mitra, shared a common origin with the Persian Mithras, but this deity did not assume the prominence in India that Mithras attained in Persia and the West. Surya was the sun's golden disk, Pushan embodied its power to assist vegetation and animal growth, and Vishnu personified the swift-moving orb that traverses the sky in three strides.

The roster of gods

The most popular deity of all in Vedic times was Indra, whose original significance is uncertain. He was alleged to have benefited mankind by slaying a malignant serpent, the demon of drought, thus releasing the pent-up waters to refresh the earth. Also, it was said, he discovered the light, made a path for the sun, and created lightning. He was chiefly honored as a mighty warrior and god of battle, the slayer of demons and the "black-skinned" enemies of the Aryans. Indra was supposed to be particularly fond of *soma,* which fired his blood for combat, and he was reputed to be able to drink three lakes

Indra

of this potent fluid at one draft while devouring the flesh of 300 buffaloes. *Soma,* the sacred liquor, was also deified, as was the sacrificial fire, Agni. Agni was conceived both as a god and as the mouth of the gods or as the servant who carried their savory food offerings up to the heavens for them.

Although religion in the Vedic age was hardly spiritual, it contained traces of such a quality. Some hymns to Varuna are remarkable for their devoutness and ethical content. Varuna is described as the great regulator of the universe, who keeps the rivers in their courses and the sun and planets in their proper orbits. He is also pictured as the upholder of rules and ordinances for both gods and men, capable of binding sinners with fetters. To him were addressed prayers for forgiveness of sin. Offenses likely to incur divine wrath included not only infractions of religious taboos but also violations of the moral code, such as adultery, witchcraft, gambling, and drunkenness. However, despite intimations of a belief in life after death, by far the greater emphasis was placed upon the enjoyment of life here and now.

Associated with each of the *Vedas* is a prose manual called a *Brahmana* because it was for the instruction and assistance of the Brahmans (priests) who officiated at the sacrifices. While the Vedic hymns are generally unaffected and artless, the *Brahmanas* betray a shrewd calculation on the part of the custodians of the sacred traditions and also illustrate the tendency of such traditions to degenerate into empty mechanical formulas. A modern Indian scholar describes the *Brahmanas* as "an arid desert of puerile speculations on ritual ceremonies," and even as "filthy and repulsive," with a morality "no higher than that of primitive medicine-men."[2] The greed and arrogance of the Brahmans is illustrated by such assertions as that judgment should always be awarded to a Brahman in every dispute with a layman and that murder is not actually murder unless the victim is a Brahman.

In view of the decadent tendencies evident in the *Brahmanas* it is all the more notable that the concluding portion of Vedic literature is of an elevated philosophical character, giving proof both of intellectual maturity and of ethical and spiritual insight. Evidently, side by side with the naïve popular cults and with the mechanical rituals of priestcraft had grown up a tradition of skepticism and bold speculation, which attempted to delve beneath the surface of sense experience and formulate answers to eternally recurring questions. This concluding portion, called *Vedanta* ("end of the *Vedas*"), comprises the famous *Upanishads,* of which there are some 200. The *Upanishads* (the word means a "sitting down near" or session with a teacher) are treatises or rambling discourses in prose and poetry, dealing with the nature of being, man, and the universe. Their content varies in subject matter

Spiritual and ethical elements

The Brahmanas

The Upanishads

[2] B. K. Ghosh, in *The History and Culture of the Indian People,* Vol. II, *The Vedic Age,* pp. 225, 418.

and in quality of thought, ranging from the trivial and absurd to the sublime. Scholars and philosophers from the Occident as well as from the Orient have long been attracted by the subtle probing, the sweeping imagination, and the idealistic concepts evident in the *Upanishads,* the best of which rival the products of Greek philosophical genius. However, if the end of ancient Greek inquiry was knowledge for its own sake, that of the *Upanishads* was knowledge as the means to power: true wisdom could give its possessor mastery not only of self, but of the entire cosmos. Although part of the *Vedas,* the *Upanishads* largely ignore the popular mythology of the Vedic hymns and also challenge the presumptuousness of Brahmans and their reliance on ritual and ceremony.

While the *Upanishads* do not fall into a single pattern of thought, their most essential philosophical teachings are fairly consistent. The key concepts, which may be described as idealistic, monistic, and pantheistic, are (1) the supreme reality of the World Soul or Absolute Being; (2) the unreality of the material world; (3) transmigration, or the rebirth of individual souls; and (4) the attainment of serenity through escape from the cycle of recurring births by union with Absolute Being. Evil and suffering are explained on the ground that they are incidental to matter and material creatures. But matter is held to be an illusion (*maya*); the only true reality is the soul or spirit. If the soul could manage to disentangle itself from matter (which actually is only an appearance anyway), it would be free from discord and suffering. Not only does life in the flesh entail sorrow and pain, but, according to this philosophy, death fails to provide relief because the soul will be born again into another body. In developing the theory of an endless chain of births, the philosophers of the *Upanishads* insisted that the process was not purely accidental and uncontrollable. They taught that a person's conduct in life determined the type of body and condition which he would experience in his next incarnation. He might go down in the scale—even to the animal or insect level—or he might go up—to the state of a noble, king, or saint. This is the *karma* doctrine, which holds that actions, thoughts, and motives bear fruit. It resembles the Christian teaching "Whatsoever a man soweth, that shall he also reap"—except that the retribution or reward for actions is held over to another earthly existence. However, if it is assumed that all physical existence is unsatisfactory and illusory, obviously there is not much to be gained from moving a few rungs up the ladder of human wretchedness. Hence the *Upanishads* taught that preferable even to the faithful performance of *dharma* (moral uprightness and the conscientious discharge of one's duties) was a deliberate break with the habits and engagements which lead to the renewal of births. Separation from the chain of births could be achieved only by following a standard of conduct higher than that of righteousness in the ordinary sense of the term. Evil action would

Philosophy of the Upanishads

produce evil fruit or *karma,* and righteous action would produce good *karma;* but still more desirable was conduct which, being "neither black nor white," could lead to the extinction of *karma* altogether. In other words, only when a person acts with complete disinterestedness, detaching himself entirely from the idea of reward for his merit, do the fetters which bind him to the world of sense begin to loosen and ultimately dissolve. When this happens, the liberated soul attains blessedness or *nirvana,*[3] which does not mean either annihilation or entrance into a heaven, but a union with *Brahma,* the undefinable Universal Soul or eternal Absolute Being.

Pessimism and optimism

The philosophy of the *Upanishads* is pessimistic regarding the world and man's present state, because it depreciates everything material and holds that the natural physical life is a burden. However, it is optimistic as to ultimate ends and as to the possibility of human emancipation. It teaches that there is in every man an indestructible fragment of reality. The basic precept is that *atman* (the individual soul) is actually a part of *Brahma* (the Universal Soul or rational principle which pervades the universe); and that although the soul has been separated from its source, it can be reunited with it—not through a miracle, but through the individual's own efforts. Moreover, the state of *nirvana,* while a remote goal for the majority, is declared to be attainable during the mortal existence of a sufficiently dedicated person.

2. THE EPIC AGE: THE EMERGENCE OF HINDUISM

The Indian epics

Long before the *Vedas* were completed, the two Indian epics were in process of development. The epics were not cast into their final form until sometime between 400 B.C. and 200 A.D., but they refer to events of a much earlier date, and the Epic age overlaps with the Vedic. The epics were composed in Sanskrit, a dialect which is derived from but not identical with that of the *Vedas,* and which came to be regarded as the "classical" form of the Indo-Aryan speech, somewhat as Latin is regarded as classical by the Indo-European peoples of Europe. Furthermore, in spite of the lack of precise dividing dates, it is clear that the epics represent a later stage of social and cultural evolution than do the *Vedas.*

Content of the epics

The Indian epics are comparable to the epic poems of the ancient Greeks in that they celebrate the deeds of legendary national heroes, but they are much more encyclopedic and diffuse than the Homeric poems. The *Mahabharata,* the longer of the two Indian epics, is more than seven times the length of the *Iliad* and *Odyssey* combined. While the epics treat of bloody conflicts and amazing exploits, they also

[3] Although not appearing in the genuine *Upanishads, nirvana* became the popular term for the concept of liberation from the cycle of rebirths. Its literal meaning is "extinction."

Ravana, Rama, and Lakshmana. An Indian painting of the eighteenth century depicting an incident from the *Ramayana.* Rama, the epic hero, and his brother Lakshmana are fighting against Ravana, the demon king of Ceylon, who carried off Rama's faithful wife Sita.

incorporate quantities of religious lore, and through the centuries they, rather than the *Vedas,* have served as a Bible for the common people. This is partly because the Brahmans imposed restrictions upon the study of the sacred Vedic texts, whereas anyone could listen to a recitation of the epics.

The *Ramayana* has as its central theme the story of Prince Rama, who, with his beautiful wife Sita, was exiled through the jealous intrigue of a wicked stepmother. It relates how Sita was carried off to Ceylon by the demon king of that country and finally recovered by Rama with the help of a monkey general. The narrative is highly artificial as well as fantastic, and easily lends itself to allegorical interpretation. The poem indicates some familiarity with both southern India and Ceylon and provides evidence that Aryan influence, if not extensive conquests, had penetrated into the Deccan. The story was reworked many times in later Indian literature and embellished with symbolism. Rama and Sita came to be idealized as the perfect types of manly courage and feminine purity and devotion, respectively, and Rama was traditionally regarded as an incarnation of the god Vishnu. It is possible that the poem may be, in part, an allegory of the progress of agriculture, in which Rama represents the plow and Sita the furrow. (In the epic, after returning to her husband's kingdom she is swallowed up by the earth.)

The Ramayana

The *Mahabharata* is just as enigmatic as the *Ramayana,* though livelier in its story and richer in the variety and scope of its subject matter. "If it is not in the *Mahabharata,* it is not in India," has become a proverb. A narrative core, which gives the poem its name, is the account

The Mahabharata

of a great battle between two related but feuding families, the Pandavas and the Kauravas, of Bharata descent. The "Great Bharata War" probably commemorates a historic battle fought near the modern city of Delhi about 1400 B.C., but the epic version is a tissue of myth and fable. Some scholars believe that the Pandavas (who on the whole are the heroes of the story) were not really kinsmen of the Kauravas but a different tribe altogether, perhaps of Mongolian race. The five Pandava brothers are described as having one wife in common, an obvious reference to the institution of polyandry, which was foreign to the Aryan communities but which is still practiced by the Tibetans. As a chronicle of battle the poetic version is gory enough but still full of odd contradictions. Acts of ruthlessness and chicanery are recorded along with examples of exaggerated chivalry and scrupulousness. The god Krishna (supposedly one of the incarnations of Vishnu) takes part in the encounter with rare impartiality—serving as charioteer for one of the Pandava princes but sending his own forces to fight on the other side. The battle is described as raging furiously for eighteen days, by which time practically all the antagonists on both sides have been killed. Finally the five royal Pandava brothers, victorious but the sole survivors of their line, renounce the world and, with their wife and dog, set off for the Himalayas in search of Paradise. Some of the contradictions and inconsistencies in the account can be explained by the fact that the poem was several centuries in the making. Ethical sensibilities and the warriors' code of conduct changed considerably during this period until rough-and-ready practices which were once considered normal came to be looked upon with disapproval.

The Bhagavad-Gita

Interpolated in the story of the great war is a philosophical dialogue which contrasts startlingly with the rapid pace and bloody tone of the main narrative. This passage, which like the rest of the *Mahabharata* is of unknown authorship, is called the *Bhagavad-Gita* or "the Lord's Song." In form, it is a discourse between the warrior Arjuna and his charioteer Krishna (who represents the god Vishnu), precipitated by Arjuna's reluctance to begin the slaughter of his relatives when the lines of battle are drawn up. In substance, it is a dramatic and colorful exposition of some of the most fertile ideas of the *Upanishads,* with greater emotional impact because it speaks not in abstractions but in terms of love for a personal god. At the outset of the dialogue Arjuna expresses his aversion to combat, saying flatly that he will not engage in it: "Better I deem it . . . to face them weaponless, and bare my breast to shaft and spear, than answer blow with blow." Krishna assures him that he must fight, not because there is any virtue in it but because as a member of the warrior caste fighting is his duty (*dharma*). Similarly, Arjuna is reminded that both death and birth are only incidents and that the soul is indestructible: "Life is not slain." Soon, however, the conversation proceeds to a penetrating discussion of the value of different types of action, suggestive of Christian arguments over the respective merits of "faith" and "works." Krishna outlines

Cotton Tapestry. Embroidered with colored silks and silver (eighteenth century), it illustrates scenes from the *Mahabharata.*

four levels of conduct or four paths to virtue. At the lowest level are good works, prescribed by reason. Better than works of diligence is knowledge: "The right act is less than the right-thinking mind." Still higher is worship or pure devotion, meditation which is above the bonds of sense and "troubled no longer by the priestly lore." But on the very highest level is placed the renunciation of self. The ideal worshiper, while not neglecting his duty, will play his part "with unyoked soul," "with spirit unattached." He acts "unmoved by passion and unbound by deeds, setting result aside"—that is, with no thought of reward either material or spiritual. Although in the dialogue the warrior is enjoined to fulfill his warlike function—with complete indifference to victory or defeat—the *Bhagavad-Gita* verses have been interpreted by some Hindus, including Mahatma Gandhi, as a text for pacifism.

Aside from their narrative and philosophical interest, the epics reveal that during the 1000 or 1500 years since the settlement of the Indo-Aryans in India extensive changes had taken place among the people, especially in religion and the organization of society. The carefree, boisterous optimism of the early Vedic period was giving way to attitudes of pessimism, discouragement, and resignation; society, instead of being flexible and largely uninhibited, was tending toward a rigid stratification of functions and privileges. The causes of such marked change are not entirely clear. But whatever the reasons, before the close of the Epic age Indian society had assumed many of the characteristics which have distinguished it down to modern times. Together they make up the culture complex which is Hinduism.

Significance of the epics

Popular religion had changed from a simple polytheism to an intricate network of beliefs and rituals with a tremendous hierarchy of gods. The catalogue and ranking of deities and the forms of worship

Shiva. The dance of Shiva portrayed in this eleventh-century bronze is symbolic of the destructive forces in the world.

Three Faces of Shiva. An eighth-century traditional representation of "the Destroyer," with three faces and four arms.

varied from one locality to another and among different strata of the population. With a few exceptions, the more prominent of the early Aryan deities faded into the background as new gods were added to the pantheon with the absorption of local pre-Aryan cults. Eventually the number of divine and semidivine beings accorded recognition ran into the thousands, or possibly millions. Thus, while philosophy was tending toward monotheism, the popular faiths were moving in the opposite direction. Three gods, however, came to be considered as paramount, although without agreement as to their qualities and import. Vishnu, the old solar deity, believed to have had many incarnations, was worshiped under several names. He was still conceived as a benevolent and cheerful god, "the Preserver," representing the creative or formative principle in the universe. Because he was supposed to disapprove of bloodshed, Vishnu received no animal sacrifice but was offered garlands of flowers. Quite different was Shiva, "the Destroyer" (perhaps identical with one of the Indus valley deities), who, in spite of his frightening aspects, has proved to be a more widely favored object of worship than Vishnu. Typically Shiva was pictured as five-faced and four-armed. He was regarded as beneficent in some aspects because destructive force—symbolized by the dance of Shiva—is a necessary agency in the evolution of the world and living forms, but his power could be prostrating. While some devotees of Shiva were ascetics and mystics, among other groups his worship called for bloody sacrifice, and was also associated with a fertility cult employing orgiastic rites. The third and least influential of the major deities was Brahma, a personification of the Absolute Being or World Soul of the philosophers. Representing an abstract principle, Brahma did not seize upon the popular imagination as did Vishnu and Shiva. He was visualized as a tiny figure who could sit on a lotus leaf. This god, however, has stimulated mystic contemplation. The avowed end of the famous *yoga* discipline is to attain a union of the soul with Brahma.

In many respects Hinduism differs from the pattern of religion familiar to Western peoples. It has no creed, no set of dogmas, no single congregation of the faithful, no established church. It assumes that divine truth wears many faces and that the paths to salvation are myriad. Hinduism is actually a social and religious complex, presenting a wide range of variations from region to region and from one social level to another, but given coherence by the authority accorded to the Brahmans or priests. Throughout India the Brahmans established themselves as ministrants of the rites and recipients of reverence and material compensation. They did not enforce any orthodox creed or crusade against heretics, but they insisted successfully that only they could mediate between gods and men. The chief points of emphasis in Hinduism as a social discipline came to be: (1) respect for and support of the Brahmans; (2) noninjury to animal life, especially cattle (although there are many exceptions to this rule); (3) the inferior status of women; and (4) acceptance of the regulations of caste.

The chief distinguishing characteristic of Hindu religious and social life is the institution of caste, the most rigorous and refined instrument of segregation ever invented. Caste is much more complex than the typical division of a nation into social or economic classes, even when these classes are hereditary. Aside from heredity, membership in a caste is not based upon any single principle nor does it follow a logical pattern. The best definition of caste is a simple one: "A group of families internally united by peculiar rules for the observance of ceremonial purity, especially in the matters of diet and marriage." Typically, a person must marry within his or her caste and should not accept food from a member of a lower caste. Caste is the antithesis of democracy. It is a vast hierarchy, exalting the Brahmans at the top and degrading the "untouchables" or outcastes at the bottom of the social pyramid.

According to orthodox Hindu tradition, caste has always existed; it is part of the order of nature. The word used to denote it (*jat*) literally means "species." Historical evidence, however, shows that caste developed gradually over a long period of time. Caste was unknown to the Indo-Aryan society of the early Vedic age, but by the time of the epics it was already regarded as an ancient institution. Thus the system has probably been operating in India for the past 3000 years, and its origins are lost in obscurity. Its starting point, undoubtedly, was the racial pride of the Aryan conquerors, who were determined to prevent contamination by intermarriage with the supposedly inferior "black-skinned" peoples whom they were fighting and reducing to subjection. In this case the distinction was based on color (*varna*); but as time went on various other criteria entered into the drawing of caste lines, including occupations, religious deviation, migrations from one section of India to another, and later invasions by non-Hindu peoples who could not be expelled but who might be prevented from destroying the Hindu system by assigning them a place within it. While the origins of caste are obscure and its causes multiple, the development and final acceptance of the institution was probably influenced by the exertions of the Brahmans in their struggle for a position of dominance over all other groups, a struggle in which they did not scruple to use religious weapons to discomfit their competitors. The keenest rivalry was between the Brahmans and the warrior nobles (including rajas). The nobles had the advantage of being recognized wielders of authority backed by force; but the Brahmans had the advantage of education, mastery of the sacred *Vedas,* and wonder-working powers in the eyes of the people. Socially the Brahmans and nobles were on a par. There are records of Brahman kings and of kings or nobles who became skilled in the *Vedas.* But eventually the Brahmans won recognition for their claim to the highest rank

The major castes

of all, and the nobles were forced to accept classification as the second caste (*kshatriya*). As the price of their pre-eminence, the Brahmans were expected to devote themselves more unreservedly to their religious and educational functions, adopting a modest and mildly ascetic manner of life and leaving political dominion to the *kshatriyas*. However, as tutors and advisers to kings, the Brahmans managed to retain considerable political influence.

Once the principle of caste was accepted by the leading groups in society, it was not difficult to impose it upon the others. Originating in northern India, the institution was extended among the Dravidians and other peoples of the Deccan as Aryan influence permeated that region. Many occupational groups or guilds became castes, but division does not always follow vocational lines. Brahmans may, without incurring disapproval, engage in a variety of occupations, including comparatively humble ones. At the same time, members of the higher castes avoid tasks which are considered defiling, such as the disposal of corpses, butchering animals, or preparing hides. It is impossible to enumerate precisely the castes of India because the number is enormous and fluctuates from time to time. Theoretically, there are four great castes with subdivisions: *brahmans* (priests), *kshatriyas* (warriors), *vaisyas* (farmers, herdsmen, and artisans), and *sudras* (laborers, servants, and slaves). Actually, except for the first, these categories have little significance. Probably they once represented the general classes of Aryan society before caste had taken hold, but they are much too broad to define caste as it has existed in historic times. The effective

Dravidian Temple of Nataraja at Chidambaram. The gorgeously sculptured spire is a gem of Dravidian art; the temple is believed to be the oldest in South India.

divisions are more minute. There are some 1,800 subdivisions of Brahmans alone, and the total number of castes and subcastes in India has been reckoned at more than 3,000.

Undeniably caste has had a stultifying effect upon Indian society. The rules of caste observance are arbitrary, tedious, and time-consuming, especially in the everyday matters of social intercourse and eating. The fear of pollution becomes an obsession. Not only are there varying degrees of uncleanness in food (depending on the ingredients and the method of cooking as well as who has prepared it), but absolute prohibitions on certain foods restrict the diet unduly, impairing the health of the population. Whether or not a consequence of caste, the position of women in the patriarchal society of India became degraded as the caste system solidified. A man might in some cases marry beneath his caste; for a woman to do so was considered shameful. Caste duty for a woman lay in absolute obedience to her father and then to her husband. The custom of child marriage was introduced, defended with the argument that it saved a girl from the monstrous crime of falling in love with any other man than her future husband. Although child marriages made it inevitable that there would be a large number of widows, a widow was shamed by the belief that some sin of hers had caused her husband's death. She was forbidden to remarry and could best redeem her reputation by committing suicide in flames on her husband's pyre. The most inhumane feature of caste was the treatment accorded the lowest groups in the scale, especially the "Untouchables," who were considered to be outside the border of even the lowest caste, and therefore hardly human beings at all. In southern India the greatest humiliation of the "Untouchables" took place. Their shadow, it was thought, would pollute a well. They were required to live in segregated quarters and to warn people of their approach by uttering cries.

The fact that the caste system has endured in India for tens of centuries and is still operative (though with important changes) is a testimony to the toughness of social institutions, once they have become established. At the same time it should be pointed out that the role of caste in India was not wholly negative. On the positive side it gave the Indian people a sense of identity when confronted with alien cultures or conquerors. It also offered the individual a feeling of security within his group and fostered various forms of mutual assistance. In spite of intercaste rivalries, the separate castes learned to cooperate with one another, notably in the constitution and administration of local village councils. Eventually caste came to be looked upon as a normal and necessary arrangement, especially as it was hedged about by religious sanctions. Particularly effectual were the twin beliefs: *karma* and the transmigration or rebirth of souls. These concepts, which were given an idealistic interpretation by the philosophers of the *Upanishads,* served in the popular imagination to explain and justify caste. If a person was born into a high caste he was thought to be receiving his reward for meritorious behavior in a previous existence. He had produced good *karma,* which carried him upward on the ladder. Similarly, a member of the despised castes was supposed to have incurred his lot because of misdeeds in a previous incarnation. Unfair as the distinctions of caste seemed to be, they were accepted as a just and precise recognition of the individual's deserts. The person who suffered abuse was told to blame only himself and to strive for perfection within the prescribed limits of his present caste in order that his condition would be improved the next time his soul returned to earth. Since it was possible to go either up or down in the succession of births, patience, diligence, and conformity became supreme virtues. Devotion to duty and the certainty of retribution—*dharma* and *karma*—were the cement which held the caste structure together.

3. REFORM MOVEMENTS: THE RISE OF BUDDHISM

The revolt against Brahmanism

In the sixth century B.C. the stratification of society and the hardening of religious ritual provoked a simmering discontent that found an outlet in several protest movements, led by members of the nobility. Because these protests were directed against the extravagant claims of the Brahmans, they assumed at the outset a heretical or even antireligious form. Most of them proved to be only temporary, but two resulted in philosophical and religious schools of enduring influence— Jainism and Buddhism. There were many parallels between these two movements. They originated in the same section of India, north of the Ganges in eastern Hindustan, and the leader of each was a member of the noble or *kshatriya* caste. Each repudiated the authority of priests and *Vedas,* rejecting all the paraphernalia of religion and replacing it by a system of philosophy. At the same time each was ethical and reformist, attempting to provide moral and personal satisfaction to its adherents. Each drew heavily upon the background of Hindu philosophic tradition and formulated goals which, though original in form, were not alien to the spirit of this tradition. And, ironically, each finally turned into a religion, Jainism taking its place within Hinduism, and Buddhism becoming a separate faith. Although Buddhism carried within itself many elements of Hindu thought, it ultimately obtained its widest following in Asian lands outside India and practically disappeared in the country of its birth. However, Buddhism flourished in India for 1000 years after the life of its founder; it helped to liberalize Hinduism and to keep it from becoming an agency of unlimited exploitation in the hands of the Brahmans. Buddhism also contributed heavily to Indian architecture and sculpture, and the Buddhist sacred texts were the first works committed to writing in India.

Jainism is associated with a figure known as Mahavira ("Great Hero"), who, although probably not its founder, gave it a distinctive form. Mahavira expounded a complex metaphysics which embraced the notion that not only living creatures but almost every object possesses a soul. Employing the familiar concepts of transmigration and *karma,* he held that the soul when attached to matter is in bondage and that it will never be content until freed from and entirely independent of the physical body. The purport of his message was to point out the way to the soul's liberation. Insisting that prayers and worship were of no avail, he prescribed a course of mental and moral discipline, the highest stage of which was withdrawal into a state of meditation with complete denial of the claims of the flesh. The exalting of extreme asceticism remained one of the chief characteristics of Jainism, and particular honor was reserved for the zealot who was able to carry self-denial to the point of starving himself to death, as a number of Jain saints are reputed to have done. Another cardinal emphasis among the Jains (derived from their animistic belief in a multiplicity of souls) is the doctrine of *ahimsa,* or the necessity of refraining from injury to any living creature. This doctrine has led to commendable efforts to prevent cruelty to animals, although it has sometimes been carried to extremes in attempting to protect even pests and vermin. Surrounded by the atmosphere of Hinduism, the Jains relinquished their early antireligious tenets, instituting prayers to various deities, including the deified Mahavira. The Jain sect, which numbers slightly more than a million members, is monastic in organization. The monks are bound by five vows, while the laity, who are considered part of the order although not of the same degree of holiness as the monks, may subscribe to "small vows." Through plying the trade of moneylending the Jains became a wealthy order, in spite of their rigorous asceticism.

Much more significant than Jainism was the contemporary movement destined to be known as Buddhism because its founder, Gautama, was accorded the title of Buddha, "the Enlightened One."

Jain Temples on Girnar Mountain. These temples exhibit the lavish sculpture characteristic of Indian architecture.

Gautama (c. 563–483 B.C.) was the son of the head of a small state located on the slopes of the Himalayas in what is now Nepal. This tribal state, like many others of that time, elected its ruler; hence Gautama, although of noble blood, was not a hereditary prince as later tradition claimed. Little is known about the events of his life, but legends have supplied innumerable details, most of them miraculous. There is factual evidence to support the conclusion that he was one of those rare personalities who deliberately relinquished a safe and comfortable existence in order to devote himself to the quest of higher values and the service of his fellow men. Tradition has it that at the age of twenty-nine he left his sumptuous abode in the middle of the night after a fond glance at his young wife and infant son, cut off his hair, and sent back his jewels and fine clothes to his father. Then came years of wandering and disappointment in which he found no answer to the problem that vexed him—the cause and cure of human suffering. After studying philosophy with the Brahmans he concluded that this was a vain pursuit. Next, it is said, he spent six years practicing an extreme asceticism, until his body had almost wasted away. This course he also abandoned as leading only to despair. The climax of his life came when, discouraged and weary, he sat down under a large Bo tree to meditate. Suddenly he had an overwhelming experience, a revelation or a flash of insight in which he seemed to penetrate the mystery of evil and suffering. Henceforth he was free from doubts, but, instead of retiring to enjoy his state of Enlightenment, he determined to teach others how they might also secure it. For the next forty years until his death at the age of eighty, he wandered through the Ganges valley, relying upon charity for his livelihood and instructing the disciples who gathered about him.

Gautama Buddha in the State of Nirvana. A fragment from the Early Khmer period.

The substance of Gautama Buddha's teachings has been better preserved than the facts of his life. Some scholars consider him the most intellectual of all the founders of the world's great religions. He had no intention of establishing a religion, and his ideas, although conditioned by his Hindu religious background, were not sectarian. His doctrines embodied a philosophy or metaphysics, a psychology, and an ethics, of which the last is most important. The basis of his philosophy was materialism. In direct opposition to the absolute idealism of the *Upanishads* and in contrast to Mahavira's teaching, he held that nothing exists except matter and denied the actuality of the soul. Because matter is in a state of flux, constantly changing its form, he said that all things are impermanent. Hence, there is no Absolute Being or fixed universal principle other than the law of change—growth and decay. Buddha's psychological principles followed logically from his materialist metaphysics. If there is no soul, no permanent entity, there can be no distinct individual personality or being. Not only the soul but the *self* is an illusion, he affirmed. What seems to be an individual personality is only a bundle of attributes (such as sense experience and consciousness) held together temporarily as the spokes of a wheel are fastened around the hub.

Gautama's negative and deflating intellectual doctrines were intended to be encouraging rather than discouraging, as shown in the development of his system of ethics. The source of human anguish is, as he saw it, the individual's attempt to attain the unattainable. Desire or craving is the root of all evil. It can never be satisfied because the desired objects and emotional states are transitory; but the abandonment of desire can bring satisfaction and peace (the state of *nirvana*). The most persistent and futile craving, underlying a multitude of vain desires, is the ego impulse—the struggle to enhance and perpetuate the self. Since, according to Gautama, the self is only an illusion, the egoist is doomed to chase a will-o'-the-wisp. Thus it follows that selflessness is more realistic as well as more satisfying than selfishness. Oddly enough, Gautama, while denying the existence of the soul, retained the doctrine of *karma*, insisting that a person's actions would affect the condition of another person yet unborn—just as an expiring lamp can light the flame of another lamp. The ultimate goal which he projected was, like that of the Vedic philosophers, the complete extinction of *karma* through the cultivation of selflessness, so that the cycle of births, travail, and tragedy would be no more.

In his ethical teachings Gautama's emphasis was positive rather than negative. He proclaimed the ideal of universal love, to be exemplified by service and helpfulness. Rather than a saintly hermit, he was apparently a gifted teacher, with a stock of homely illustrations and parables. He gave sensible advice in regard to domestic and marital relations, occupations, business matters, and so on. As a rule of personal conduct he advocated "the Middle Path," by which he meant the avoidance of extremes—renouncing both indulgence and injurious asceticism, rejecting prayers and ritual and also the idea of escape into a heaven of bliss. Gautama repeatedly declared that dogmas are much less important than behavior and inner attitudes. And he was firmly opposed to forcing ideas upon anyone, believing that discussion and the power of example are the only valid means of establishing truth. Although he was an ethical rather than a social reformer and made no direct attack upon the caste system, caste distinctions were dissolved among his own group of disciples. He admonished his followers to develop their faculties to the full and to exert themselves for the benefit of others. His last words are said to have been, "Work out your emancipation with diligence."

*Gautama's ethical
teachings*

The Buddhist movement in Gautama's lifetime had few of the characteristics of a religion. In the course of a century or two, however, it developed its own rites, mystic symbols, and other supernatural elements. The Buddhists in India gradually became an order of monks and nuns. Candidates for admission to the order were required to undergo a long period of training. After completing the training, the

Gautama: monasticism

novitiate shaved his head, put on the yellow robes, and took the monastic vows of poverty and chastity. In contrast to Christian monks, he did not take a vow of obedience, because membership was considered a matter of free choice. The monks customarily remained in a monastery during the three months of the rainy season, which Gautama had devoted to instructing his disciples; for the rest of the year they lived as wandering mendicants, dependent upon the alms which they received in their beggars' bowls as they passed from village to village. Lay men or women who accepted the Buddhist teachings and contributed to the support of the monks were considered adherents of the faith and entitled to its benefits.

Buddhist sects: Hinayana *and* Mahayana

Various sects of Buddhism arose as the movement spread. The two principal schools, representing a cleavage which apparently began soon after Gautama's death, are the *Hinayana* ("Lesser Vehicle") and the *Mahayana* ("Great Vehicle"). The term *Hinayana* was at first applied reproachfully, because the members of this group were bent upon their own self-perfection, claiming that it was possible for the diligent individual to attain *nirvana* in three lifetimes. The *Mahayana* school was characterized by the doctrine of the buddha-elect—a person who had won Enlightenment but chose deliberately to remain in the world of sorrow in order to work for the liberation of all mankind. In spite of its noble beginning, however, the *Mahayana* tradition became more corrupted than the *Hinayana* as time went on. The *Hinayana* school of Buddhism is represented in its purest form in Ceylon, where it was established as early as the third century B.C., and it is also the prevailing religion of Burma and Thailand. In these countries, Gautama is still theoretically regarded as a man, but in actual practice he is worshiped as a deity, and offerings of flowers or incense are made to his image. The intellectual vigor and the moral challenge of Gautama's teachings have been greatly obscured, and elements of primitive religions have retained their hold on the people. However, the Buddha's emphasis upon kindliness, patience, and the avoidance of injury to living creatures is still prominent. *Mahayana* Buddhism was eventually developed in many different forms in Nepal, Tibet, and eastern Asia. It came to include the worship not only of Buddha but of his several supposed reincarnations, and it also transformed the concept of *nirvana* into a conventional paradise of bliss.

Intellectual achievements in ancient India

During the period so far discussed, covering more than 1000 years, the physical and external aspects of Indian civilization were still elementary. Writing was unknown until the eighth, or perhaps the seventh, century B.C., and even then it was used only for business purposes. The people lived in villages or small towns rather than cities, architecture was very simple, and political units were small. There was none of the magnificence which characterized ancient Egypt, Mesopotamia, or the extinct Indus valley civilization. To a remarkable degree the achievements of the ancient Indians were in the fields of the imagination and intellect, expressed in song and poetry, in the epics, and in philosophical and religious speculation. Their intellectual achievements also included considerable scientific progress. Medicine was highly developed as early as the Vedic age. Not only were many specific remedies listed, but dissection was practiced and delicate operations were performed. The knowledge of human anatomy was extensive, and a beginning had been made in the study of embryology. Medical science and the surgeon's vocation were held in high respect, until the caste system introduced a fear of pollution through bodily contact with unclean persons. Many fanciful elements, however, were intermingled with medical lore. An appreciable knowledge of astronomy was acquired in spite of its perversion into astrology. The suggestion that the earth revolves on its axis and that the sun only appears to rise and set was put forward in the *Vedas,* apparently without being taken very seriously. The most brilliant scientific attainments were those in mathematics. The ancient Indians were able to handle extremely large numbers in their calculations and knew how to extract square and cube roots. Besides using the decimal system they invented the all-important principle of the zero, which was eventually adopted by the rest of the world. In geometry their progress was not equal to that of the Greeks, but they surpassed the Greeks in the development of algebra.

During the fourth and third centuries B.C., partly in response to stimulation from without, political developments in India led temporarily in the direction of greater efficiency and unification. As a result of the conquests of the Persian king, Darius I, about 500 B.C., the Indus valley had become a province (satrapy) of the Persian Empire, furnishing mercenary soldiers and an annual tribute in gold. After Alexander the Great, the famous Macedonian conqueror, overthrew the Persian Empire, he conducted his troops eastward through the passes of the Hindu Kush Mountains into the upper Indus valley (327–326 B.C.). He spent less than two years in India but traversed most of the Punjab, fought and negotiated with local rajas, and installed Macedonian officials in the region. Although Alexander's invasion provides the first verifiable date in Indian history, it made so little impression upon the Hindus that their contemporary records do not even mention his name. However, the invasion promoted cultural exchange between the Hindus and the Greek-speaking world, and, more immediately, it paved the way for the erection of a powerful state in India.

*Conquest of the Indus
valley by Alexander the
Great*

In the revolts and confusion that followed the death of Alexander in 323 B.C., an Indian adventurer named Chandragupta Maurya seized the opportunity to found a dynasty. Chandragupta had profited from observing Greek military tactics and led in the movement to expel the Macedonian officials from India. Then he turned his army against the Magadha kingdom, which was the strongest state in Hindustan at this

*The rise of the Maurya
Dynasty*

time. He defeated and killed the Magadhan king and established him-self as ruler with his capital at Pataliputra (now Patna), a magnificent city eight miles long commanding the south bank of the Ganges. When Seleucus (Alexander's successor in Syria and Persia) tried to recover the lost Indian territory, Chandragupta defeated him soundly and forced him to cede Baluchistan and part of Afghanistan. Chandra-gupta extended his power over most of northern India and founded the first empire in Indian history. Although his dynasty, known as the Maurya, lasted less than a century and a half, its record is a distin-guished one.

The reign of Chandragupta

Chandragupta was a much more imposing figure than the rajas of the Vedic age. His government was efficient but very harsh. Social and economic activities were carefully regulated, an elaborate tax sys-tem had been devised, and the death penalty was meted out freely, sometimes through the administering of poison. The king kept a large standing army, with divisions of infantry, cavalry, chariots, and ele-phants. In spite of his far-reaching authority, and his maintenance of secret police or spies, he seems to have lived in dread of assassination and took the precaution to change his sleeping quarters every night. On the credit side was his construction and improvement of public irrigation works and the building of roads. The Royal Road, from the capital to the western frontier, was 1,200 miles long.

King Asoka: Buddhist conqueror

The greatest member of the Maurya Dynasty, and one of the most remarkable rulers in the annals of any civilization, was Chandra-gupta's grandson, King Asoka, the royal patron of Buddhism, whose beneficent reign lasted some forty years (c. 273–232 B.C.). Merely as a conqueror Asoka could lay claim to fame, because he held under Mauryan rule not only Hindustan and the region northwest of the Indus but most of the Deccan as well, thus bringing the greater part of India into one administration. His conquests, however, were the aspect of his reign that he considered least important. In fact, he fought only one major war—by which he was enabled to gain control of the Deccan—and he felt remorseful ever after for the bloodshed which accompanied this campaign. Attracted to the Buddhist teach-ings, he at first became a lay adherent and later took the formal vows and joined the order but without relinquishing his position as king. He attempted, rather, to exemplify the precepts of Buddhism in his personal life and to apply them to the administration of the empire. Thus, without being a theocrat or divine-right ruler, he provides an almost unique example of the injection of religious idealism into state-craft.

The benevolent reign of King Asoka

It is impossible to know how completely Asoka's benign purposes were carried out. He was particularly active in establishing rest houses for travelers, in having trees planted, wells dug, and watering places built along the roads for the refreshment of man and beast, and in improving facilities for the treatment of the sick. He sent commission-

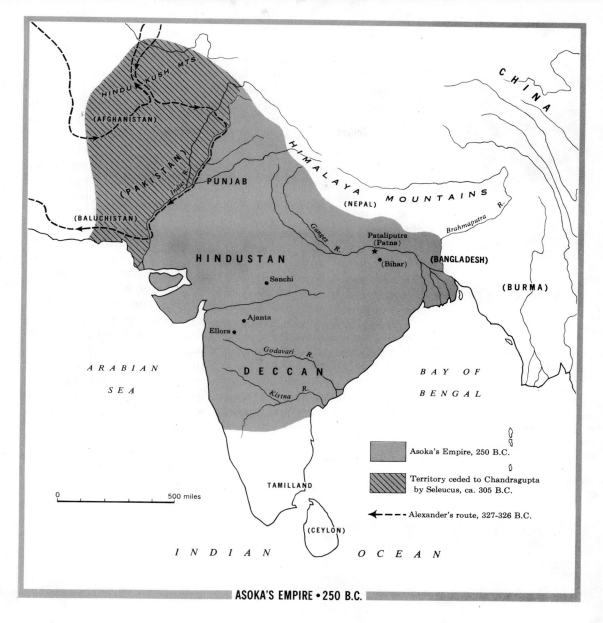

ASOKA'S EMPIRE • 250 B.C.

ers throughout the kingdom to inquire into the needs of the people, teach them religion, and report on their spiritual progress. In deference to the Buddhist injunction against taking life, Asoka gave up hunting (replacing this sport by "pious tours" or pilgrimages) and gradually reduced the meat consumption in the royal household until—according to his announcement—only a vegetable diet was permitted. He reformed the harsh system of punishments which his grandfather had used, but he did not entirely abolish the death penalty. There is no evidence of any trend toward democracy in Asoka's

Asokan Bull Capital. From Rampurva, Bihar (north-eastern India), third century B.C. Emperor Asoka erected huge stone pillars and utilized some already standing as impressive memorials to his own authority and to the law of Buddha. The bell-shaped capital shows the influence of contemporary Persian architecture.

government. He adhered to the tradition of autocratic rule, but exercised it with conscience and benevolence. Although he was earnest in his support of Buddhism, Asoka opposed fanaticism. He made religious toleration a state policy and urged that the Brahmans of all the Hindu sects be treated with respect. He stated that he cared less about what his subjects believed than he did about their actions and attitudes. To commemorate his authority he had erected in various parts of his empire gigantic sandstone pillars, each cut from a single block of stone and standing forty or fifty feet high. The capitals of animal figures and the beautifully polished surface of these columns—some of which are still preserved—testify to the engineering and artistic skill of the royal workmen.

Asoka's patronage during his long reign contributed markedly to the growth of the Buddhist religion. He sent missionaries of the faith to Ceylon, Burma, Kashmir, Nepal, and apparently even west to Macedonia, Syria, and Egypt. The king's own son was the missionary to Ceylon. Buddhist monks held a general council in 250 B.C. at Asoka's capital, Pataliputra, where they agreed upon the basic texts that should be regarded as authentic. This "Council of Patna" established the canonical books of Buddhism, especially for the *Hinayana* school. The Buddhist scriptures are the oldest written literature of India—that is, they were the first to be committed to writing. However, although the texts were settled upon in 250 B.C., they were still memorized and transmitted only by word of mouth. Except for the excerpts in Asoka's rock carvings, the texts were not actually written out in full until about 80 B.C. in Ceylon.

Asoka's extraordinary administrative system did not long survive him. His successors seem to have been mediocrities who lacked both his reforming zeal and his organizing ability. In 184 B.C. the last

Laughing Boy. Terracotta head of a laughing male, from Pataliputra (Patna). An example of the realistic sculpture of the Maurya period.

Maurya ruler was assassinated by the army commander, an ambitious Brahman who seated his own family on the throne. The efficiency of Asoka's government was not duplicated until about 500 years after the end of his dynasty.

SELECTED READINGS

• *Items so designated are available in paperback editions.*
• Basham, A. L., *The Wonder That Was India: A Survey of the Culture of the Indian Sub-Continent before the Coming of the Muslims,* New York, 1955. Illustrated.

———, ed., *A Cultural History of India,* New York, 1975.
• Brown, W. N., *The United States and India, Pakistan, Bangladesh,* Cambridge, Mass. 1972. An excellent general introduction.

Cambridge History of India, Supplementary Volume: Wheeler, Mortimer, *The Indus Civilization,* 3d ed., Cambridge, 1968.

Conze, Edward, *Buddhist Thought in India,* London, 1962.
• Coomaraswamy, A. K., *History of Indian and Indonesian Art,* New York, 1927.

Eliot Charles, *Hinduism and Buddhism: An Historical Sketch,* 3 vols., New York, 1954. A standard work.

Fairservis, W. A., Jr., *The Roots of Ancient India: The Archaeology of Early Indian Civilization,* New York, 1971. An interesting and provocative account.

Garratt, G. T., ed., *The Legacy of India,* Oxford, 1937.

Hutton, J. S., *Caste in India,* 3rd ed., Oxford, 1961.

Kabir, Humayun, *The Indian Heritage,* New York, 1955.

Kramrisch, Stella, *The Art of India: Traditions of Indian Sculpture, Painting, and Architecture,* New York, 1954. Admirable photographs, with brief introduction.

Lee, S. E., *A History of Far Eastern Art,* New York, 1965.

Majumdar, R. C., ed., *The History and Culture of the Indian People,* Vol. I, London, 1951; Vol. II, 2d ed., Bombay, 1953.
• Moore, C. A., ed., *The Indian Mind: Essentials of Indian Philosophy and Culture,* Honolulu, 1967.

Moreland, W. H., and A. C. Chatterjee, *A Short History of India,* 4th ed., New York, 1957.
• Piggott, Stuart, *Prehistoric India,* Baltimore, 1950.
• Prabhavananda, Swami, and F. Manchester, *The Upanishads, Breath of the Eternal,* New York, 1957.

Prebish, C. S., ed., *Buddhism: A Modern Perspective,* University Park, Pa., 1975. A useful account.
• Rawlinson, H. G., *India, a Short Cultural History,* rev. ed., New York, 1952. An excellent interpretive study.

———, *A Concise History of the Indian People,* 2d ed., New York, 1950.

Rowland, Benjamin, *The Art and Architecture of India: Buddhist, Hindu, Jain,* Baltimore, 1953. Informative and discriminating.

Smith, V. A., *Asoka,* Oxford, 1920.

Spear, Percival, ed., *The Oxford History of India,* 2d ed., New York, 1979.
• Wheeler, Mortimer, *Civilizations of the Indus Valley and Beyond,* London, 1966.
———, *Early India and Pakistan to Ashoka,* New York, 1959.
• Wolpert, Stanley, *A New History of India,* New York, 1977. An admirable survey, informative, and well written.

SOURCE MATERIALS

• Arnold, Edwin, tr., *The Song Celestial—The Bhagavad-Gita,* Boston, 1885.
• de Bary, W. T., ed., *Sources of Indian Tradition,* "Brahmanism"; "Jainism and Buddhism"; "Hinduism," New York, 1958.
• Edgerton, Franklin, *The Beginnings of Indian Philosophy,* Cambridge, Mass., 1965. Carefully selected examples with a valuable introduction.
• ———, tr., *The Bhagavad Gita,* Chicago, 1925. Translation and interpretation.
• Hamilton, C. H., ed., *Buddhism, a Religion of Infinite Compassion,* New York, 1952.
Lin Yutang, ed., *The Wisdom of China and India,* New York, 1942. Hymns from the *Rigveda,* Selections from the *Upanishads.*
• Mueller, Max, tr., *The Upanishads,* 2 vols.
• Narayan, R. K., *Gods, Demons and Others,* London, 1964. Fine translation of ancient Indian stories.
The *Ramayana* and the *Mahabharata.*
Sastri, S. R., tr., *The Bhagavadgita,* New York, 1959. An accurate translation with explanatory and critical comment.

Chapter 7

ANCIENT CHINESE CIVILIZATION

There have been many kings, emperors, and great men in history who enjoyed fame and honor while they lived and came to nothing at their death, while Confucius, who was but a common scholar clad in a plain gown, became the acknowledged Master of scholars for over ten generations. All people in China who discuss the six arts, from the emperors, kings, and princes down, regard the Master as the final authority. He may be called the Supreme Sage.

        —*Historical Records* of Ssu-ma Ch'ien (145–c. 85 B.C.)

T
he beginning of a high civilization in China did not occur until about a thousand years after the flowering of the Indus-valley civilization in India. However, when once established the Far Eastern culture continued—not without changes and interruptions but with its essential features intact—into the twentieth century of our own era. The civilization of China, although it took form much later than that of Egypt, Mesopotamia, or the Indus valley, is one of the oldest in existence. Furthermore, its foundations rest upon a population that has retained its identity to a remarkable degree. Throughout successive cultural epochs, in spite of political upheavals and invasions, the Chinese have remained basically the same people since Neolithic times. In contrast to such regions as the Near East, the Mediterranean basin, and Europe, the area of China yielded a civilization that was both independent in origins and unmatched in durability. This does not mean that the Chinese were isolated from the rest of the world or that they did not benefit from foreign contacts. They did their share of conquering, but the lands they annexed were almost exclusively undeveloped territories. They rarely attempted to impose their will upon conquered peoples by force, but considered it their mission to assimilate them and make them the beneficiaries of their superior ethical system.

Reasons for long survival of Chinese civilization

I. THE FORMATIVE STAGE

Early man in China: Peking man

In our study of preliterate cultures we have learned already that China was the home of one of the earliest human species, the so-called Peking man. His skeletal remains were found between 1926 and 1930 in a cave about 25 miles southwest of Peking. Fossilized fragments of over forty separate individuals were discovered, but, unfortunately, after being stored in a warehouse, most were lost during World War II. Anthropologists estimate that Peking man lived at least 500,000 years ago, and that he was probably a contemporary of Java man, one of the oldest human types. His culture was, of course, extremely primitive, but there is evidence that he used stone and bone tools, had a knowledge of fire, and buried his dead. Archeological research—interrupted by World War II but pursued vigorously since 1949 under the People's Republic—has yielded a wealth of information concerning early man in China. Recent excavations at the site where the bones of Peking man were first discovered have unearthed new specimens of the same human type but belonging to a period some 200,000 years later than that assigned to the first appearance of Peking man. Study of these recent finds reveals significant evolutionary changes in the course of 200 millennia. While the creature's teeth and jaws diminished in size, brain capacity increased by as much as 20 percent, indicating a growth in intelligence as well as changes in dietary habits. Contrary to what was formerly believed, it is now known that much of the area of China was continuously occupied by subhuman or human types throughout the Stone Ages. *Homo sapiens* appeared perhaps as early as 50,000 years ago. A later Paleolithic culture—the remains of which have not yet been fully excavated and classified—is identified with people who apparently were Mongoloid in race.

The Neolithic Age in China can be dated from the sixth millennium

The Loess Highlands of Northern China

B.C. At least two Neolithic cultures have been discovered, one centered in the great highland plain that surrounds the Yellow River valley, the other predominant in the southeast coastal area, including the island of Taiwan. Both were developed by communities of farmers, with millet the chief crop in the north and roots and tubers in the southeast, and each produced a distinctive type of pottery.

There is still disagreement as to where and when Neolithic culture advanced to the level of civilization, characterized by metal working, city living, writing, and effective political organization. One contemporary scholar contends that the cradle of Chinese civilization was the semiarid northern plain. He asserts that, in contrast to the inhabitants of the well-watered Nile and Tigris-Euphrates valleys, the Chinese began as dry-land farmers and may have lacked irrigation facilities until the sixth century B.C. The highlands bordering the middle reaches of the Yellow River are covered with a type of soil known as loess, composed of fine particles of loam and dust borne by northwest winds from the central plateaus of Asia and deposited in the valley and along the northeastern coast. This soil, which from its color has given rise to such geographical names as Yellow River and Yellow Sea, is pliable enough to be easily worked with primitive digging sticks, and also has the advantage of being free from a heavy growth of forest or grasses. In choosing farm sites close to the river or its tributaries but on high ground, the early inhabitants avoided the danger of floods. But they had to depend on plants capable of surviving with a minimum of rainfall. The principal crops of northern China in the Neolithic Age were several varieties of millet, hemp, and the mulberry (for raising silkworms). Rice, too, was grown in the marsh areas of the northern plain, probably introduced from the Yangtze region to the south, where it was indigenous.[1] In view of the wide extent of Neolithic communities in China, however, it is quite possible that an advance behind this cultural level took place in more than one area. At any rate, contacts between regions were sufficient to promote the growth and spread of a homogeneous civilization.

Archeological finds in China have thrown light not only on preliterate epochs but on the early historical period as well. They have established that the Bronze Age—universally associated with the oldest civilizations—began in China somewhere around 2000 B.C. Excavations of Bronze Age remains in northern China supply concrete evidence concerning the Shang Dynasty, which according to tradition was the second of China's ruling houses (c. 1766–1027 B.C.). Long regarded by scholars as almost purely legendary, the Shang (or Yin) Dynasty has been verified and impressive examples of its workmanship recovered. Precise dates are not yet determined, but the civiliza-

---

[1] Ping-ti Ho, "The Loess and the Origin of Chinese Agriculture," *American Historical Review,* October 1969, pp. 1–36.

tion was flourishing by 1400 B.C. A study of objects that have been unearthed and especially the all-important deciphering of inscriptions make it possible to construct a fairly complete picture of this formative period of Chinese history.

Shang civilization

Shang culture was based upon that of the Neolithic farming communities. Presumably the dynasty was inaugurated by the conquest of a military chieftain, with no extensive displacement of population. Distinctive aspects of the civilization included the construction of fortified cities, the use of horse-drawn chariots in warfare, a highly developed bronze metallurgy, an elaborate system of writing, and a sharply stratified society composed of an aristocracy, craftsmen, and farmers. The Shang kingdom evidently controlled only a small part of China—the plain surrounding the middle Yellow River valley—but its influence extended over a wide area. The Shang people carried on trade with other regions, including the Yangtze valley to the south, and they had to defend themselves against nomadic tribes from the north and west. The last capital of the dynasty was a city located at the northern tip of Honan Province, about 80 miles north of the Yellow River (the site of modern An-yang).

The economy: agriculture

Though developing in close proximity to the wandering herdsmen of Mongolia, the Chinese were primarily a nation of farmers. Agriculture was the chief source of livelihood of the Shang people, although their tools for cultivating the soil were still quite primitive. Grains were the principal crop; wheat and barley were grown in addition to millet. Hunting and herding contributed to the food supply. Many animals had been domesticated, including not only the dog, pig, goat, sheep, ox, horse, and chicken, but also the water buffalo, monkey, and probably the elephant. Dog flesh as well as pork was a popular item of diet.

Shang housing

The houses the Shang people constructed show an intelligent adaptation to the environment. The Neolithic inhabitants of the region commonly lived in pits hollowed out of the loess. In Shang times rural villagers apparently also occupied pit dwellings, but the city residents built more comfortable houses above ground. For a foundation the firmly packed earth served admirably. Upon the rectangular foundation was erected a gabled-roof structure, with wooden poles holding up the central ridge of the roof and shorter posts supporting each of the two sides at the eaves. Thatching was used for the roof and packed earth for the outside walls of the house. This type of dwelling, which by coincidence is closer in design to the European style of home than to the tents of Mongolia or the mud-brick houses of Egypt and Mesopotamia, has been employed by the Chinese throughout their history.

Material culture

The specimens of Shang craftsmanship that archeologists have recovered reveal a high degree of skill and versatility. In spite of familiarity with metal, Shang artisans still made many objects of

Bronze Ritual Vessel. Shang Dynasty (1523–1027 B.C.).

stone—knives, axes, and even dishes—as well as of bone, shell, and horn. Bone implements inlaid with turquoise and exquisitely carved pieces of ivory were produced in abundance. Cowrie shells were used for jewelry and probably also served as money. The bow and arrow was the most formidable weapon for the hunt or for combat. Bamboo arrows were feathered and tipped with bronze or bone points. The bow was of the composite or reflex type, formed of two separate arcs of wood held together with horn, and said to be almost twice as powerful as the famous English long bow. Two-horse chariots, of elaborate workmanship and with spoked wheels, were probably the exclusive property of the aristocracy. Armor was made of leather, sometimes reinforced with wooden slats. Evidently the people were fond of music. For musical instruments they employed drums, stones emitting a bell-like tone when struck, and a small pipe of hollow bone with five finger-holes.

The artistry of the Shang people is illustrated most strikingly by their sculpture and engraving. The examples of sculpture thus far discovered are generally of small dimensions. Shang metal work was truly remarkable, especially the superb bronze castings of intricate design. Bronze articles included weapons and chariot and harness fittings, but most impressive were the objects intended for religious and ceremonial functions—tripods, libation bowls, drinking cups, and grotesquely figured masks. The technique employed in their making was superlative. A leading American specialist in early Chinese culture asserts that it was more flawless than the technique employed for bronze sculpture at the height of the Italian Renaissance.

Bronze Tripod Cup. Shang Dynasty. This cup was used in sacrificial ceremonies.

Art of the Shang people

Bronze Ritual Vessel with Removable Top. Shang Dynasty.

Oracle Bone. Dating from 1300 B.C., this artifact records the appearance of a new star. Note the pictographic characters.

As has already been mentioned, this early civilization possessed a system of writing. The writing brush and an ink made of soot had been invented. Writing materials included silk cloth and wood, and it is quite possible that books were compiled from narrow strips of bamboo joined together by a thong. Fortunately, a great many specimens of writing have been preserved inscribed on pieces of animal bone, horn, and tortoise shells and pottery. These served in a process of divination by the king and priests; hence they are referred to as "oracle bones." After a question had been directed to the spirits, a flat piece of split cattle bone or a tortoise shell was heated until it cracked; then the shape of the crack was studied to ascertain the answer from the spirit world. The majority of the oracle bones contain no writing; but in about 10 percent of the cases the question was engraved upon the object after the divination rite had been performed. Although the inscriptions are brief, a careful study of them has thrown light upon many aspects of Shang society and activities.

The Shang writing was not primitive but in an advanced pictographic stage. While the Shang symbols are the earliest examples found in the Far East, they presuppose a long period of evolution from more rudimentary forms. Each character represented an entire word, as it does in the classical Chinese. In some cases, only the shape of the sign has changed. For example, the Shang character for *sun* was round—obviously a picture of the sun—while now it is square. Practically all the principles which the Chinese literary language employs in the process of character formation were already in use. The Shang characters were not only pictographs but sometimes ideographs, in which the meaning was conveyed by combining different symbols or concepts (the sun and moon joined together represent *bright* or *brightness;* the sun rising behind a tree stands for *east*). The phonetic principle was also applied. A character having one meaning might be used to indicate a word of different meaning but pronounced the same way. To avoid confusion, the phonetic symbol was combined with a conceptual symbol in the same character. Not surprisingly, fewer characters were employed in Shang times than later, although it is probable that the list compiled from the oracle bones is only partial. About 3,000 characters have been distinguished in the Shang records; the written language eventually came to include more than fifteen times that number.

Little definite information is available as to the political and social institutions of the Shang period. In addition to military activities, the king probably supervised public works and was important as the chief religious functionary. He was assisted by an educated class of priests, who served as astrologers, performed the divination rites, and supervised the calendar. Because the calendar was a lunar one, it frequently had to be adjusted to bring it into harmony with the solar year. There is some evidence from the oracle bones that the Shang priests had made considerable achievements in mathematics and astronomy. As early as the fourteenth century B.C. they recorded eclipses and perhaps had already conceived the decimal system.

The family was the basic social institution. The king, or a great aristocrat, might have several wives, but monogamy seems to have been the more usual practice even in the royal family, as it almost certainly was among the people generally. Slavery existed and there were gradations in the ranks of society, but there is no evidence of a feudal system during this period.

The family

Ample testimony exists for the religious practices of the Shang people. They worshiped many natural objects and forces—the earth, rivers, the winds, even the directions. To these gods they performed sacrifices in temples. Burnt offerings of animal flesh were common, and a kind of wine or beer made from millet was also considered acceptable. Although the Shang were in some ways highly civilized, there is gruesome evidence that they practiced human sacrifice on a large scale. Apparently the victims were usually captives who had been taken in battle, and sometimes raiding expeditions were sent out for the express purpose of securing a batch of foreign tribesmen to be offered in sacrifice. The principal deity seems to have been a god concerned primarily with rainfall, the crops, and war. His name, Shang Ti, has persisted into later times. There is no evidence that Shang religion was essentially spiritual or ethical; it was directed toward the procuring of human prosperity, as among the Sumerians and Babylonians. The king was not a divinity like the Egyptian pharaoh, but he became an object of worship after his death, and sacrifices were performed to the departed spirits of both kings and queens. The royal tombs were sumptuous affairs. A large pit was excavated, provided with stairways, and a wooden tomb chamber was constructed at the bottom. The royal corpse was surrounded with magnificent furnishings, including figured bronzes and pottery, marble statuary, and richly adorned implements and jewels. After the funeral ceremonies the entire excavation was filled with firmly tamped earth.

Religion of the Shang period

It is noteworthy that the typical Chinese institution of ancestor worship was already in existence, at least in the circle of the court. Ancestral spirits were believed to possess the power of helping or hurting their descendants, and yet they depended upon their living representatives for nourishment in the form of food offerings. It was also customary, even among people of humble circumstance, to bury valuable objects with the deceased. Divination by means of the oracle bones—the practice which bequeathed so many valuable inscriptions—was a by-product of the cult of ancestor worship and the belief in the potency of departed spirits.

Ancestor worship

The Shang society represents the earliest genuine civilization of Eastern Asia for which historical records are available. In addition, it laid the foundation and provided materials for the distinctive Chinese culture pattern, as illustrated by methods of agriculture, handicrafts, artistic and architectural forms, emphasis upon the family as the basic social unit, religious concepts, and a system of writing. About 1027 B.C.[2] the city of Shang was captured and the dynasty overthrown, but the new rulers preserved basic institutions, encouraged cultural progress, and gave their name (Chou) to the longest dynasty in China's history.

2. THE CHOU DYNASTY, THE CLASSICAL AGE OF CHINA (c. 1100–256 B.C.)

While the civilization of the Vedic Age in India was still in its early stages, in the Yellow River valley of China the Shang Dynasty was succeeded by the Chou. However, the advent of a new ruling house brought no such profound change in the character of society as did the Indo-Aryan invasion of India. The Chou people, located west of the Shang frontier, were of the same ethnic stock (possibly with a trace of Turkish or Tibetan influence added) and possessed a culture similar to that of the Shang, with whom they had had considerable contact. The demise of the Shang Dynasty was probably the result of an internal power struggle and bore little resemblance to a barbarian conquest.[3] Cultural developments continued uninterruptedly on foundations already laid and eventually completed the pattern of Chinese civilization for centuries to come.

The new dynasty exerted zealous efforts to convince the people that it was a legitimate succession rather than a usurpation. Its spokesmen advanced the claim that the last Shang ruler had been incompetent and debauched, and that the divine powers had used the Chou as an instrument for his removal. The "Mandate of Heaven," they alleged, had been transferred from the Shang house to the Chou. There is no evidence that the Shang king was guilty of the faults ascribed to him, but the charge, even if a fabrication, shows the desire of the conquerors to fit their authority into accepted conventions rather than to break with the past. And the concept of governmental power as a commission from Heaven rather than an absolute and inalienable right—although possibly invented by the Chou for propaganda purposes—was to become a persistent element in Chinese political history.

The Chou form of government was a monarchy, although not identical with that of the Shang. The early Chou rulers maintained their capital near modern Sian (Shensi province) in the Wei valley, where their power had already been established. In addition to the Shang territory they added other conquests, especially southward in the middle Yangtze valley. The king exercised direct rule over the

[2] The exact date is in dispute among scholars. Estimates range from 1122 to 1018 B.C.
[3] K. C. Chang, *The Archaeology of Ancient China*, 3d ed., p. 383.

ANCIENT CHINA DURING THE CHOU DYNASTY · 1100-256 B.C.

region surrounding his capital but administered the outlying areas indirectly, through appoined officials who were given almost complete jurisdiction within their own districts. The Chou administrative system was roughly similar to that which developed in Europe in the age of feudalism some 2,000 years later. The district governors, originally members of the royal family or generals of proved competence, were the king's vassals, but they were also great territorial lords, exercising wide military and judicial powers, and they gradually transformed their position from that of appointive official to hereditary ruler. Chou feudalism—like the later European variety—contained elements of danger for the central government, although for two or three centuries the Chou court was strong enough to remove overly ambitious officials and keep its own authority paramount.

By the eighth century B.C. the vigor of the ruling house had declined to the point where it was no longer able to protect the western frontier effectively against the attacks of barbarians. The fortunes of the dynasty seemed to reach their lowest point in 771 B.C., when a worthless king almost duplicated the villainies that had been unjustifiably attributed to the last of the Shang rulers. King Yu, particularly through his extravagant efforts to amuse his favorite concubine, angered the nobles beyond endurance. When he lit the beacon fires to summon aid in the face of a combined attack by barbarian tribes and one of the outraged nobles, his men refused to answer the summons. King Yu was killed and his palace looted. The dynasty might have been ended then and there, but the nobles of the realm found it expedient to install the king's son as nominal head, keeping in their own hands the actual authority over their respective dominions. This event marks the close of the "Western Chou" period. The royal seat of government was now moved about 100 miles east into safer territory (near the modern city of Honan), and the ensuing period (771–c. 250 B.C.) is known accordingly as the "Eastern Chou."

During the 500 years of the Eastern Chou Dynasty, China suffered from political disunity and internal strife. The king actually ruled over a domain much smaller than that of some of the great hereditary princes. For the kingdom as a whole his powers, while theoretically supreme (he was officially styled "Son of Heaven"), were limited to religious and ceremonial functions and to adjudicating disputes concerning precedence and the rights of succession in the various states. In spite of these conditions, however, it is not quite accurate to describe the Eastern Chou era as an age of feudalism. It is true that hereditary nobles enjoyed social prominence, wealth, and power, and acquired different degrees of rank, roughly equivalent to the European titles of duke, marquis, count, viscount, and baron. They became lords and vassals, held fiefs for which they owed military service, and were supported by the labor of the peasants on their lands. These warrior aristocrats not only raised armies and collected revenues from their dominions but also administered justice. Custom supplied the greater part of law, but severe penalties, including fines, mutilation, and death, were inflicted upon offenders. Nevertheless, a number of factors prevented the complete ascendancy of a feudal regime. In the first place, a large proportion of the nobility failed to acquire estates of their own and remained jealous of the great territorial lords. The lesser aristocracy, generally well educated and frequently unemployed, constituted a sort of middle class that could not fit comfortably into a feudalized society. More important still, towns were growing and trade increasing throughout the Chou period, and the merchants (including part of the aristocracy) attained economic

Ceremonial Bronze Basin. Chou Dynasty (1100–256 B.C.). The inscription on this bronze piece, known as the *San P'an,* records the settlement of a territorial dispute between the feudal states of San and Nieh in Western Shensi Province.

importance. Moreover, rulers of the larger states successfully pushed forward a program of centralization within their own dominions. They introduced regular systems of taxation based upon agriculture. To offset the entrenched position of the nobles they developed their own administrative bureaucracies and staffed them with trained officials, recruited largely from the ranks of the lesser aristocracy. In spite of the disorganized condition of China as a whole, the period provided valuable experience in the art of government which could eventually be drawn upon in the task of reuniting the country.

Expansion of the frontiers

Although China was divided during the Eastern Chou period into many principalities with shifting boundaries and frequent wars, a few of the larger states held the balance of power, especially four which were located on the outer frontiers to the north, west, and south. Usually one state at a time was recognized as paramount and its ruler, designated as "First Noble," took the lead in organizing the defense of the kingdom as a whole and even in collecting the revenues. The boundaries of Chinese civilization were extended by the aggressive initiative of the rulers of the frontier states. The Shantung peninsula, the seacoast as far south as modern Shanghai and Hangchow, and the rich Yangtze valley were all brought under Chinese jurisdiction. Thus the total area was much larger than the old Shang kingdom and included more than half of the eighteen provinces which have constituted the state of China during the greater portion of its history. The southern part of Manchuria was also occupied, and walls of earth— the first stages of the famous Great Wall of China—were constructed both south and north of the Yellow River for protection against the nomads of Mongolia.

Beginning about the middle of the fifth century B.C., internal conditions became extremely chaotic, inaugurating a bloody period

Ancient Chinese Civilization

*The period of the
"Warring States"*

Bronze Ceremonial Vessel. Chou
Dynasty.

known as that of "the Warring States." The relatively restrained competition which the feudal principalities had carried on with one another gave way to a struggle for supremacy in which proprieties and recognized codes were disregarded. The rulers of several of the states even assumed the title of "king" (*wang*), previously reserved for the prince of Chou. In the fourth and third centuries B.C. the state of Ch'in, seated in the Wei valley on the western frontier, gained ascendancy over the others. Not only were the Ch'in rulers aggressive, but within their own dominions they had developed the most effectively centralized government in China. After annexing the fertile plain lying south of the Wei valley (in modern Szechwan province), they constructed a splendid irrigation system which has lasted until the present day. Probably the Ch'in people had also mingled with and absorbed some of the barbarian tribesmen, but they were no less Chinese in culture than their rivals. In spite of alliances formed against them by other feudal princes, the Ch'in forces, employing ruthlessness, massacre, and treachery, annexed one region after another. Finally, in 256 B.C., they seized the tiny remaining portion of the royal domain and ended the Chou Dynasty. Within thirty-five years the Ch'in prince had brought all the Chinese territories under his control and, to indicate the extent of his triumph, assumed the imposing title of "First Emperor" (Shih Huang Ti). Although the Ch'in Dynasty hardly outlasted its founder, it did China the valuable service of abolishing the remnants of feudalism. The highly centralized government which the Ch'in emperor established did not prove to be permanent, but the feudal system never reappeared.

During the 800 or 900 years of the Chou Dynasty, in spite of inter-

Ancient Irrigation Canal. Still in use, this is part of one of the oldest and most elaborate irrigation systems in the world.

Left: *Drum Stand of Lacquered Wood*. Late Chou Dynasty. Right: *Ceremonial Bronze Tripod*. Late Chou Dynasty, fourth century B.C. This piece is thought to have been part of the Li-Yu treasure.

nal conflicts, cultural progress was almost continuous. The period is regarded as the classical age of Chinese civilization, and its contributions were fundamental to the whole subsequent history of the Far East. As has already been indicated, the culture of the Chou was based upon foundations that had been laid by their predecessors. Handicraft techniques improved under the Chou and the smelting of iron was introduced, although iron did not entirely displace bronze. While the great majority of the population lived in rural villages, there were some large towns and the merchant class assumed importance. Trade was by no means exclusively local. With the introduction of the donkey, and especially the camel (probably not before the third century B.C.), it became possible to develop caravan trade routes across Central Asia for the transportation of grain, salt, silk, and other commodities. Coined copper money came into use before the close of the fifth century B.C. The manufacture of silk, already an old industry, was increased, and the fibers of several domestic plants were also employed in making textiles.

Cultural progress under the Chou

From time immemorial the all-important Chinese enterprise has been farming. It was extended under the Chou by reclamation measures—the building of irrigation canals and reservoirs and the draining of swamps—and also by acquisition of the moist and fertile rice-producing lands of the Yangtze valley. The soybean—valuable not only as a food but for restoring fertility to the soil—was added to the

Agriculture under the Chou

list of crops. The methods of cultivation developed during the Shang and Chou periods have remained essentially unchanged ever since.

The persistence of unvarying techniques over 3,000 years is attributable not to the inability of the Chinese to progress but to the fact that these techniques were admirably adapted to the terrain and to the objectives of Chinese society. While they were primitive in some ways, they embodied a great deal of experience and foresight. China has been said to possess a "vegetable civilization," because its people, while not socially or intellectually stagnant, adapted themselves so completely to the potentialities of their environment. The typical Chinese farming village—with fields of various sizes, often tiny but all carefully tended—appears almost as if it were part of the natural landscape instead of being an effort on man's part to manipulate nature for his own benefit. Although China is a large country, the relative scarcity of arable land made it difficult for food production to keep pace with an expanding population. Much of the country is hilly or mountainous, and the north and west portions are subject to drought which cannot be entirely overcome by irrigation. Consequently, attention was lavished upon every suitable plot that could be found. The bulk of labor was done by hand, with simple tools but in such a way as to produce the greatest possible yield. Wastes which had fertilizing value were collected and returned to the soil, as were ashes and even powdered sun-dried bricks when no longer serviceable for building purposes. Crops were rotated to avoid soil exhaustion, and hillsides were terraced to conserve moisture and prevent erosion.

Although draft animals had been known from early times and the ox-drawn plow was introduced about the sixth century B.C., their use was restricted because of the cheapness and—on small plots—greater efficiency of human labor. Besides, hayfields or grazing lands to provide animal fodder represented a curtailment of the area devoted to producing foodstuffs for human beings. The Chinese have subsisted largely on a vegetable diet, not because they had religious scruples against eating flesh as did the Hindus, but for practical reasons of economy. Instead of raising crops to feed cattle and then eating the cattle, they preferred to consume the crops directly themselves. For meats they chose animals that could be reared inexpensively—chickens, ducks, and especially pigs, which were also useful scavengers, and fish, with which even temporary ponds could be profitably stocked. Chinese methods of agriculture thus were intensive rather than extensive. As compared with modern Western countries, particularly the United States and Canada, the yield was low in proportion to the number of men employed and the hours of labor, but high in terms of acreage. While Chinese farming demanded exacting and arduous toil on the part of the cultivators, it made possible the growth of a large population.

Society during the Chou period had a decidedly aristocratic character. There was a tremendous gulf between the great landowners and the peasants, who comprised the vast majority of the people. But while class lines were rigidly drawn, Chinese society was never stratified by a caste system like that of India. There were only two clearly distinguished classes, the commoners or serfs and the nobles; and as civilization became more complex the nobility included contrasting interests and conditions rather than remaining a solidly united order. Because the numbers of the aristocracy tended to increase, many of them consequently possessed little or no landed property. They were forced to seek administrative employment with a powerful noble, to engage in trade, or even to undertake menial occupations, thereby undermining the fiction of the inherent superiority of the hereditary aristocracy. Unfortunately, very little is known about the condition of the lower classes. Evidently before the close of the Chou period a considerable number of peasants had become landowners. Others, however, were actually slaves, and most of the commoners were serfs, attached to the soil without having legal title to it and compelled to give the lord a large share of the produce.

Labor intensive farming

While the family is always a basic social institution, it has been so to an almost unique degree in China. Here the family was a tightly organized unit, bent upon preserving the welfare of its members against any outside agency, official or unofficial, and was probably the only safeguard of any consequence against the unlimited exploitation of the lower classes. Typically the Chinese family was large because it embraced several generations. When a son married he customarily brought his bride home to live under the paternal roof or in a closely neighboring house. Theoretically the family also included the departed ancestral spirits, thus extending vertically into time as well as horizontally among contemporary relatives. Authority was vested in the father (or grandfather), and the utmost emphasis was placed upon respect for elders, so that even grown men were bound by their parents' wishes. Such a custom led to extreme conservatism and sometimes inflicted hardships upon youth, but it had the advantage of developing qualities of patience, loyalty, and consideration for the helpless aged.

The family as a social institution

Women became definitely subordinate to men in the patriarchal family and in Chinese society at large, although their position was not utterly intolerable. Allegedly, in early Chou times the young men and maidens of the peasant class were allowed to choose their mates freely after a Spring Festival characterized by complete license. However that may be, among the aristocracy neither men nor women had freedom of choice in marriage unless they defied convention and parental authority. Marriages were arranged by the parents of the respective parties, usually with the assistance of a matchmaker or go-between. After the bride was brought to her husband's home she was considered as on probation for a three-month period, after which if she had

Subordination of women

*The family as a religious
and political institution*

Large Bronze Bell. This bell, with bosses or nipples, decorative panels, and inscriptions, is typical of the Middle Chou style (ninth century B.C.). It was hung from the ring at the base of the shaft and was sounded by striking with a wooden mallet. The bell has a scooped mouth instead of being even at the bottom. (In the picture it is resting on a cushion.)

proved satisfactory she was allowed to participate in the ancestral sacrifice and became an accepted member of the family. In regard to the laxity of conduct permitted and the right of divorce, the woman was also at a disadvantage. Only the husband could have recourse to divorce, and he could obtain it on any one of a number of grounds, including that his wife talked too much. Actually, however, divorces were rare, especially among people of humble circumstance. Undoubtedly the practices of polygamy and concubinage, permitting a man to have more than one consort, added to the hardships and humiliation of women. But these practices were confined to the wealthy classes and were by no means universal among them. In spite of the inferior position of woman in Chinese society, she had definite rights and privileges and on the whole was much better off than in the caste-ridden society of India. It is strange that, in a predominantly agrarian economy such as China's, labor in the fields was not regarded as woman's normal work, although among poor families she often had to assist. The wife's own family did not renounce all interest in her when she left their home for her husband's and might interfere in case she was abused. Children were taught to love and venerate both parents, and as a woman grew older she shared in the honors accorded to age. The domineering position which a grandmother or mother-in-law sometimes assumed became proverbial.

The Chinese family was not only an economic and sociological unit but a religious and political one as well. Some scholars maintain that during the Chou period the servile peasants were not permitted the dignity of having surnames, and that they had no share in the cult of ancestor worship. However, that condition could not endure in view of the tremendous emphasis placed upon family relationships among the dominant classes, in public administration, and in the literature of the age. Throughout the greater part of Chinese history, religion for the ordinary person consisted largely in caring for his family graves and making prayers and offerings to the spirits of his ancestors. As a political unit the family enforced discipline and considered misconduct on the part of one of its members as a collective disgrace. Very commonly the inflicting of punishment for minor offenses was left to the head of a family rather than to a public official. The strong solidarity and sense of collective responsibility of the family had disadvantages as well as advantages. Because the family was answerable for the behavior of its members, one of them might be punished for the misconduct of another if the true offender was not apprehended by the authorities, or a whole family might be wiped out for a crime committed by one person. On the whole, however, the family gave the individual a greater feeling of security and support than has been typical in most societies.

Religion was fundamentally the same as it had been in Shang times. Many deities were worshiped, ranging from local spirits and nature gods with limited powers to such majestic divinities as Earth and

Heaven. The practice of human sacrifice gradually disappeared and came to be strongly condemned, but animals, agricultural produce, and liquor were offered upon the altars. Evidence of a "chariot sacrifice" was uncovered by archeologists north of the Yellow River when they excavated a deep pit about 30 feet square. In this instance seventy-two horses harnessed to twelve chariots, and eight dogs with bells fastened to their necks, had apparently been placed in the pit and buried alive. While worship did not necessarily include prayer, prayers were sometimes written out and burned with the sacrificial offering. A prominent deity from Chou times on was the one called T'ien, translated as "Heaven." Although of separate origin, this divinity was similar to and became practically identical with the earlier Shang Ti. T'ien was not conceived of primarily as a personal god but as representing the supreme spiritual powers collectively, the universal moral law, or an underlying impersonal cosmic force. It was by the "Mandate of Heaven" (*T'ien-ming*) that the king was supposed to rule, and he was referred to as "Son of Heaven," without, however, implying that he was divine. The worship of the earth as an agricultural deity came to be supplemented by the veneration of a specific locality with which the fortunes of the worshipers were associated. Every village had its sacred mound of earth; the lord of large territories had a mound to represent his domain; and the mound of the king was believed to have significance for the whole land of China. The most important rituals took place either at these mounds or in ancestral temples.

Religion in the Chou period

Among the Chinese at this time, as among the Hindus, there was no clear-cut religious system, no fixed creed, and no church. In contrast to Hindu society, however, the Chinese priests did not become a sacrosanct class in a position to dominate other groups. The priests, like those of the ancient Greeks, were merely assistants in the ritual. The indispensable religious functionaries were the heads of families, including, of course, the king, whose ancestral spirits were particularly formidable, and who propitiated the great deities of the rivers, earth, and sky. For most of the people religion was either a family affair, consisting of social functions invested with sentiment and emphasizing filial piety, or a matter of state, maintained by the proper authorities to ensure the general welfare. Sacrifices to the greatest gods were ordinarily performed only by the highest officials, to lesser deities by lower officials, and so on down to the ordinary folk who sacrificed to their own ancestors in the form of wooden tablets. They believed that the spirits of these ancestors could bring prosperity to the family and that dire consequences would follow any neglect of the rites. Aside from traditional ceremonies, everyday life was complicated by a medley of folklore and superstition hardly classifiable as religion but exerting a potent influence. This included the belief in witchcraft, in good and evil omens, in divination and spirit messages conveyed through mediums, and in the necessity of avoiding offense to numerous malignant beings. "Hungry ghosts," whose sacrifices

Extraordinary characteristics of Chinese religion

had been neglected or cut off through the extinction of a family, were considered especially dangerous. In spite of the strong faith that the soul outlived the body, the notion of rewards and punishments in an afterlife was almost entirely lacking. The worst fate that could happen to a disembodied spirit, it was thought, was for it to be deprived of the nourishment supplied by sacrificial offerings.

By far the most significant contributions of the Chou period were in the fields of literature and philosophy. The Shang system of writing, already highly advanced, was continued with slight modifications. Evidently the Chinese now considered written records as indispensable to the conduct of both public and private affairs. They sometimes recorded important transactions in lengthy inscriptions on bronze vessels, but they more frequently wrote with the brush upon wood or cloth of silk. Books composed of thin strips of bamboo were produced in abundance. Although only a minority of the population was literate, it must have been a large minority and included the feudal nobility as well as the merchants. In contrast to the feudal age of western Europe when writing was confined almost entirely to the clergy, the Chou aristocrats were versed in literature and kept full records of their properties, their dependents, and sometimes of their personal activities. Not only the king but the head of every feudal state maintained archives to preserve the luster of family traditions and to aid in settling disputes with rival princes. The Chinese, even in ancient times, were at the opposite pole from the Hindus in their attitude toward the importance of chronology and the recording of factual events (although this does not mean that Chinese documents were entirely accurate or free from fanciful elements). A young nobleman or prince, in the process of his education, was reminded by his tutors that later generations would study the annals of his administration and that he should, accordingly, choose his actions with care. Princes were regularly given instruction in history "to stimulate them to good conduct and warn them against evil"—apparently with no better results than have attended most modern efforts in this direction.

Of the tremendous output of Chou literature, only a few authentic portions have survived (aside from the imperishable bronze inscriptions). Some of them, however, are from a date earlier than 600 B.C. Probably the most ancient work is the *Book of Changes*. It contains a collection of hexagrams formed of straight and broken lines arranged in different combinations, with accompanying text. The figures, like the earlier Shang oracle bones, were used for divination. Thus the book was originally hardly more than a sorcerer's manual, but it came to be venerated as a work of mystic and occult wisdom.[4] Very differ-

Written records of the Chou period

Literature of the Chou period

---

[4] For a contrary view see H. Wilhelm, *Change: Eight Lectures on the I Ching,* 1960. Wilhelm interprets the classic as an affirmation of man's ability to control his own destiny.

ent is the *Document Classic* (less accurately called *Book of History*), which is a collection of official documents, proclamations, and speeches purporting to be from the early Chou period. The *Book of Etiquette,* dealing with ceremonial behavior, formal occasions, and preparation for adult responsibilities, was intended to assist in the education of the lesser aristocracy. Most interesting of all is the *Book of Poetry,* an anthology of about 300 poems covering a wide range of subjects and moods. Some of the poems are religious, in the nature of prayers or hymns to accompany the rites of sacrifice; others celebrate the exploits of heroes; still others are lyrical in quality, voicing the laments of a discharged official, a soldier's homesickness, delight in the beauties of nature, and the frustration or rapture of young lovers. Neither in quantity nor in profundity do these odes approach the *Vedas* of India, but they are graceful in expression and show vividly the practical down-to-earth temperament of the Chinese and their lively interest in and optimistic attitude toward the business of living—at least among the aristocracy. While the poems on the whole are neither philosophical nor spiritual, a few suggest the reforming fervor of the Hebrew prophets.

In view of the extent and the variety of writing during the Chou period, the literary collections which have survived are rather disappointing. But this deficiency is amply compensated for by achievements in the realm of philosophy, which reached a brilliant climax between the sixth and third centuries B.C. For some unexplained reason—perhaps by mere coincidence—philosophical activity of a high order was carried on at about the same time in three widely separated regions of the ancient world. While the Greeks were inquiring into the nature of the physical universe, and Indian thinkers were pondering the relationship of the soul to Absolute Being, Chinese sages were attempting to discover the basis of human society and the underlying principles of good government. The Chinese thinkers were not much interested in either physical science or metaphysics; the philosophy they propounded was social, political, and ethical. Exhortatory and reformist in tone, it undoubtedly, reflected the influence of the recurrent strife and political disorders of a period when feudal ideas and institutions were becoming increasingly irrelevant but had not yet been clearly repudiated. Against the background of upheaval which marked the late Chou era, philosophers sought to formulate principles for the stabilizing of society and the betterment of the individual. The leaders in this intellectual activity were largely from the lesser aristocracy, a scholarly group, fond of disputation, but also maintaining an interest in the practice of government and sometimes holding administrative posts or coaching pupils who aspired to such posts. It was a time of lively interchange of ideas, and a great variety of opinions was put forward. Out of this intellectual ferment and debate—one of the most productive in the annals of human thought—four main philo-

Philosophy

Confucius in Royal Dress. A traditional representation in bronze.

Confucius as a teacher

sophic schools emerged, the most important being the Confucianist and the Taoist.

Confucius (c. 551–479 B.C.), who has proved to be one of the most influential men in all history, was largely a failure from the standpoint of what he hoped to accomplish. He spent his life advocating reforms that were not adopted; yet he left an indelible stamp upon the thought and political institutions of China and other lands that came under Chinese influence. He was a native of the state of Lu (in modern Shantung province) and was reputed to have been the child of an aged father, a gentleman soldier named K'ung (Confucius is the Latinized form of the name K'ung Fu-tzu, or "Master K'ung"). Probably his family was of the lesser aristocracy, respectable but poor. When he was only about twenty-one he began to teach informally a group of young friends who were attracted by his alert mind and by his precocious knowledge of traditional forms and usages. Although his reputation spread rapidly, little is known concerning the incidents of his career. Possibly as a mature man he held office for a short time under the Duke of Lu. For more than ten years, until old age overtook him, he wandered from state to state, refusing to be employed as a timeserving flatterer but continually hoping that some ruler would give him a chance to apply his ideals and thus set in motion a tide of reform that might sweep the entire country. Although revered by his small band of disciples, some of whom became officeholders, Confucius received no offer of appointment that he could accept in good conscience. Finally he returned to his native country where he died, discouraged, at the age of seventy-two.

Frustrated as a statesman, Confucius made his real contribution as a teacher. The memoranda of his conversations with his disciples (the *Analects*)—which are considered on the whole authentic, even though not written down in the master's lifetime—convey the impression of a lively and untrammeled mind which challenged those with whom it came in contact. Like his contemporary Gautama Buddha, and like his near-contemporary Socrates, Confucius earnestly believed that knowledge was the key to happiness and successful conduct. He also believed that almost anyone was capable of acquiring knowledge, but only through unrelenting effort. He insisted that his student-disciples should think for themselves, saying that if he had demonstrated one corner of a subject it was up to them to work out the other three corners, and constantly pricking their complacency. While no ascetic, he frowned on indulgence and urged his associates to strive continually for improvement. Though he had moments of petulance and harshness, the nobility of his character is unmistakable, and he refused to let his disappointments make him cynical. His regret, he said, was not that he was misunderstood but that he did not understand others sufficiently.

The doctrines of Confucius centered upon the good life and the good community. He respected religious ceremonies as part of established custom, but he refused to speculate on religious or supernatural questions, saying, in substance: "We do not know life; how can we understand death? We do not fully understand our obligations to the living; what can we know of our obligations to the dead?" He was optimistic regarding the material world and regarding human nature, which he thought was essentially good; but he believed that the individual's worth would not be realized unless he was properly guided in the development of his faculties. For this reason he stressed propriety and the observance of ceremonial forms—which he thought were helpful in the acquisition of self-discipline—although he was really more concerned with sincerity and intelligence than with appearances. Impressed as he was by the evils of feudal contention, Confucius advocated the restoration of central authority in the kingdom, combined however, with a logical distribution of power. He visualized the ideal state as a benevolent paternalism, with the ruler not only commanding but also setting an example of conduct for the people to follow. He did not believe in equality and, rather than democracy, advocated an aristocracy of talent and high principles from whom officials would be selected to guide the ruler in his administration. The health of the entire state would depend upon the welfare of each village, and harmony would be achieved by the combined efforts of the common people from below and of the scholar-officials from above.

The doctrines of Confucius

Confucius' teachings therefore embodied a political philosophy, which regarded the state as a natural institution but modifiable by man, and devoted to promoting the general well-being and the fullest growth of individual personalities. The state existed for man, not man for the state. On the ethical side he emphasized fellow feeling or reciprocity, the cultivation of sympathy and cooperation, which must begin in the family and then extend by degrees into the larger areas of association. He stressed the importance of the five cardinal human relationships which were already traditional among the Chinese: (1) ruler and subject, (2) father and son, (3) elder brother and younger brother, (4) husband and wife, and (5) friend and friend. These could be expanded indefinitely and were not bounded even by Chinese lines. The logic of this train of thought was summarized in the famous saying, "All men are brothers." But Confucius argued that a person must be a worthy member of his own community before he could think in terms of world citizenship. Laying no claim to originality, Confucius urged a return to an ideal order which he attributed to the ancients but which actually had never existed. Unknowingly, he was supplying guiding principles which could be utilized in the future.

The political and ethical philosophy of Confucius

Aside from its founder, the ablest exponent of the Confucianist school was Mencius (Meng-tzu), who lived about a century later (c. 373–288 B.C.). Like his master, Mencius affirmed the inherent goodness of human nature and the necessity of exemplary leadership to develop it. He looked upon government primarily as a moral enterprise, and he was more emphatic than Confucius in insisting that the material condition of the people should be improved. He wanted the government to take the initiative in lessening inequalities and in raising the living standards of the common folk. Perhaps because political confusion had increased since Confucius' day, he was outspoken in criticizing contemporary rulers. He taught that only a benevolent government, resting upon the tacit consent of the people, can possess the "Mandate of Heaven," and he defended the people's right to depose a corrupt or despotic sovereign. Hsün-tzu (c. 300–237 B.C.) is usually classified as a Confucianist, although his precepts diverged radically from those of Mencius. While both Confucius and Mencius had started with the assumption that man has a natural propensity for good, Hsün-tzu regarded human nature as basically evil. However, like the earlier Confucianists he believed that man can be improved by proper education and rigorous discipline. He laid great stress upon observance of ritual, formal training in the classics and a strictly hierarchical ordering of society. In spite of his gloomy view of the natural man, he was far from a complete pessimist. He recommended vigorous action by the state to institute reforms and, like Mencius, favored the regulation of economic activities.

The Taoist philosophical school was in many ways the opposite of the Confucianist. Its traditional founder was Lao-tzu ("Old Sage"), a shadowy figure of the sixth century B.C. Little is known about the facts of his life, and some scholars doubt that he was an actual historical person. According to tradition he served as an official at the Chou capital in charge of the archives until, becoming weary of the world, he set out for the western mountains in quest of peace and, at the request of a guard at the mountain pass, set down his words of wisdom in a little book before he disappeared. But the real authorship of the *Tao Teh Ching* (Classic of Nature and Virtue), from which the principles of Taoism are derived, is undetermined, and it may not have been written earlier than the third century B.C. The book is not only brief but enigmatical, paradoxical, and perhaps ironical. With its terse and cryptic style it seems almost like an intentional antidote to the Confucian glorification of scholarship, exhortation, and patient explanation. On the whole the Taoist book exalts nature (sometimes in the sense of impersonal cosmic force, "the Boundless" or Absolute) and deprecates human efforts. Its spirit is romantic, mystical, anti-intellectual. It not only lauds the perfection of nature but idealizes the primitive, suggesting that people would be better off without the arts of civilization, living in blissful ignorance and keeping records by means of knotted cords rather than writing. Wealth creates avarice and laws produce criminals, it asserts. It is useless to try to improve society by preachment, ritual, or elaborate regulations; the more virtue is talked about the less it is practiced. "Those who teach don't know anything; those who know don't teach." A person learns more by staying home than by traveling; the wise man sits and meditates instead of bustling about trying to reform the world.

As a political philosophy, Taoism advocates laissez faire. Unlike Confucius, Lao-tzu believed that governmental interference was the source of iniquity and that, if people were left to follow their intuition, they would live in harmony with nature and with one another. Nevertheless, Lao-tzu's ideal was not pure anarchism. Like Confucius he assumed the necessity of a wise and benevolent (although largely passive) ruler, and agreed that the only legitimate purpose of government was to promote human happiness. Perhaps his thought also reflects a rural protest against both the self-important aristocracy and the artificial society of the rapidly growing towns. In Lao-tzu's teachings there are strains of pacifism and the doctrine of nonretaliation for injury ("The virtuous man is for patching up; the vicious man is for fixing guilt"); of the efficacy of love in human relations ("Heaven arms with love those it would not see destroyed"); and of equalitarianism ("It is the way of Heaven to take away from those that have too much and give to those that have not enough"). The Taoist school produced several able thinkers in late Chou times and played a part in the shaping of Chinese philosophical traditions. However, in contrast to Confucianism, the Taoist doctrines were eventually transformed into a religious system, with a priesthood, temples, ritual, and emotional elements. But the Taoism that became one of the prominent religions of China had little connection with the principles expounded in the *Tao Teh Ching*.

Taoist political and ethical philosophy

A third school of political and ethical philosophy was associated with Mo Ti (or Mo-tzu), whose career is placed in the middle of the fifth century B.C. A man of decided originality, Mo Ti may have been of peasant stock; his sympathies lay with the downtrodden, and he regarded luxury and extravagance with aversion. The distinguishing feature of his thought is that he combined the doctrine of utilitarianism—insisting that everything should be judged by its usefulness—with a sweeping idealism that drew inspiration from religious faith. He condemned elaborate ceremonies dear to Confucianists, including the traditional three-year period of mourning, on the ground that they entailed needless expense. Sports, amusements, and even music met his disapproval because they were unproductive, absorbing energies which might be employed in useful labor. The pressing need, as he saw it, was to increase the supply of food and basic commodities to improve the health, longevity, and numbers of the population; and

Mo Ti

such a program called for hard work on the part of both common people and officials. His strong denunciation of offensive warfare was also rooted in utilitarianism.

Mo Ti's ethics were by far the boldest of any of the Chinese philosophers. In place of the Confucian system of an expanding series of loyalties beginning with the family and radiating outward, he proclaimed the universal and impartial love of all mankind and declared that there can be no satisfactory community until the distinction between "self" and "other" is completely transcended. Applying his utilitarian yardstick, he reasoned that, by cultivating sympathy and mutual helpfulness with everyone, the individual was ensuring his own welfare as well as contributing to the security of others. But while his doctrine of universal and impartial affection linked altruism to self-interest, it called for a rare degree of discipline and high-mindedness, and its similarity to the ethics of Christianity has often been remarked. Mo Ti believed that the state, like other human institutions, was created by divine ordinance and that it was the duty of the ruler to carry out the will of Heaven, which he interpreted to mean promoting the common welfare. Although the Mohist school, as it is called, was prominent for a while and attracted many adherents, it practically disappeared after the downfall of the Chou Dynasty—partly because of the enmity of the Confucianists—and the teachings of the utilitarian philosopher were almost entirely forgotten until modern times.

A fourth philosophical school, known as the "Legalist," stood far removed both from the bold idealism of Mo Ti and the optimistic humanism of Confucius. Formulated during the hectic period which witnessed the final collapse of the Chou Dynasty and the triumph of the Ch'in, it reflects Hsün-tzu's harsh view of human nature and his emphasis upon coercive discipline. At the same time the Legalists were indebted to Taoism in their contempt for scholarship, the intelligentsia, and conventional ethics; and in their preference for a simple agrarian society over a mobile, sophisticated, and economically diversified one. But, unlike the Taoists, they did not exalt nature or any supernatural agency, and they completely rejected laissez faire. Rather than mystics they were hardheaded realists, or even cynics. Asserting that man is by nature hopelessly selfish and incorrigible, they prescribed complete and unquestioning submission to the ruler. People's behavior, they argued, could be controlled only by carefully defined rewards and punishments, by a code of laws which was fundamentally punitive and which derived not from custom or natural instinct but from the will of the sovereign. Of all the schools of Chinese political thought, the Legalist was the most uncompromisingly authoritarian. Although its principles were systematically applied only during the short-lived Ch'in Dynasty, they exerted a continuing influence upon later dynasties also—tempered somewhat by the opposing Confucian tradition—and they find perhaps more than an echo in the present Chinese totalitarian regime.

Although the later centuries of the Chou Dynasty were marked by strife and unrest and encumbered by the remnants of decaying feudal institutions, the material basis for a productive society had been laid and intellectual progress had reached a high point. An abundant and many-sided literature was in existence. Philosophers had come to grips in mature fashion with fundamental problems of individual and group behavior. Scholarship was an honorable profession, and scholars were considered indispensable to the business of government. There was a growing tradition—not yet very effective—that government entailed moral responsibilities as well as privileges, that those who exercised authority did so on sufferance and only so long as they conformed to the "Decree of Heaven." Moreover, the Chinese had come to think of themselves as composing a unique society, not merely a political affiliation but the "Middle Kingdom"—the heart of civilization as contrasted with outlying "barbarian" areas. They had already mingled with and partially absorbed many non-Chinese tribes, and it is significant that the distinction between their civilization and the "barbarian" regions was not based upon race or nationality. The attitude of superiority which they adopted sometimes made them arrogant, but it gave them a toughness in resisting the shock of invasion and other adversities.

Significance of the Chou period

SELECTED READINGS

• *Items so designated are available in paperback editions.*

Chang Kwang-chih, *Early Chinese Civilization: Anthropological Perspectives,* Cambridge, Mass., 1972. Provocative essays on Shang and Chou civilizations.

• ———, *The Archaeology of Ancient China,* 3d ed., New Haven, 1977. The best account to date.

• Creel, H. G., *The Birth of China,* New York, 1937. A fascinating account of archeological exploration of Shang civilization, and an excellent introduction to the basic culture pattern of ancient China.

• ———, *Chinese Thought from Confucius to Mao Tse-tung,* Chicago, 1953.

• ———, *Confucius and the Chinese Way,* New York, 1960.

———, *The Origins of Statecraft in China,* Vol. I: *The Western Chou Empire,* Chicago, 1970. A valuable contribution.

• Eberhard, Wolfram, *A History of China,* 4th ed., Berkeley, 1977.

• Elvin, Mark, *The Pattern of the Chinese Past,* Stanford, 1975.

Fairbank, J. K., E. O. Reischauer, and A. M. Craig, *East Asia: Tradition and Transformation,* rev. ed., Boston, 1978. A shortened edition of a major text.

• Fitzgerald, C. P., *China, a Short Cultural History,* 3d ed., New York, 1961. Frequently unconventional in viewpoint.

- Fung Yu-lan, *A Short History of Chinese Philosophy,* ed. Derk Bodde, New York, 1948.
- Goodrich, L. C., *Short History of the Chinese People,* 3d ed., New York, 1959. Brief but informative; fulfills the promise of its title.

  Harrison, J. A., *The Chinese Empire: A Short History of China from Neolithic Times to the End of the Eighteenth Century,* New York, 1972. A good synthesis.

  Ho Ping-ti, *The Cradle of the East: An Enquiry into the Indigenous Origins of Techniques and Ideas of Neolithic and Early Historic China, 5000–1000 B.C.,* Chicago, 1976.

  Hucker, C. O., *China's Imperial Past: An Introduction to Chinese History and Culture,* Stanford, 1975. Remarkably clear, comprehensive, and readable.
- ———, *China to 1850: A Short History,* Stanford, 1978.

  Keightley, D. N., *Sources of Shang History: The Oracle Bone Inscriptions of Bronze Age China,* Berkeley, 1978. Synthesizes the research of earlier scholars.

  King, F. H., *Farmers of Forty Centuries, or Permanent Agriculture in China, Korea and Japan,* Emmaus, Pa., 1948. A classic description.
- Moore, C. A., ed., *The Chinese Mind: Essentials of Chinese Philosophy and Culture,* Honolulu, 1967.
- Munro, D. J., *The Concept of Man in Early China,* Stanford, 1975.

  Ronan, C. A., ed., *The Shorter Science and Civilization in China,* New York, 1978. Abridgement of the first two volumes of a monumental study by Joseph Needham.

  Treistman, Judith, *The Prehistory of China: An Archaeological Exploration,* Garden City, N.Y., 1972.
- Watson, Burton, *Early Chinese Literature,* New York, 1962.

  Wheatley, Paul, *The Pivot of the Four Quarters: A Preliminary Enquiry into the Origins of the Character of the Ancient Chinese City,* Chicago, 1971.
- Wilhelm, Hellmut, *Change: Eight Lectures on the I Ching,* tr. C. F. Baynes, New York, 1960 (Princeton, 1973).

SOURCE MATERIALS

- de Bary, W. T., ed., *Sources of Chinese Tradition,* "The Classical Period," New York, 1960.

  Chai Ch'u, and Winberg Chai, *A Treasury of Chinese Literature,* New York, 1961.

  Chan Wing-tsit, ed. and tr., *A Source Book in Chinese Philosophy,* Princeton, 1963. Traces the history of Chinese philosophy from Confucianism to Communism.
- Giles, H. A., ed., *Gems of Chinese Literature,* Shanghai, 1922.
- Legge, James, tr., *The I Ching (The Book of Changes),* Oxford, 1891.
- ———, *The Works of Mencius.*

  Lin Yutang, ed., *The Wisdom of China and India,* "Laotse, the Book of Tao," New York, 1942.

  Mei, Y. P., tr., *The Ethical and Political Works of Motse,* London, 1929.

  Soothill, W. E., tr., *The Analects of Confucius,* Yokohama, 1910.

  Waley, Arthur, ed. and tr., *The Book of Songs,* London, 1937.

————, *The Way and Its Power,* London, 1934.

————, *Three Ways of Thought in Ancient China,* London, 1939.

• Watson, Burton, tr., *Mo Tzu: Basic Writings,* New York, 1967.

Wilhelm, Richard, and C. F. Baynes, trs., *The I Ching, or Book of Changes,* Princeton, 1967.

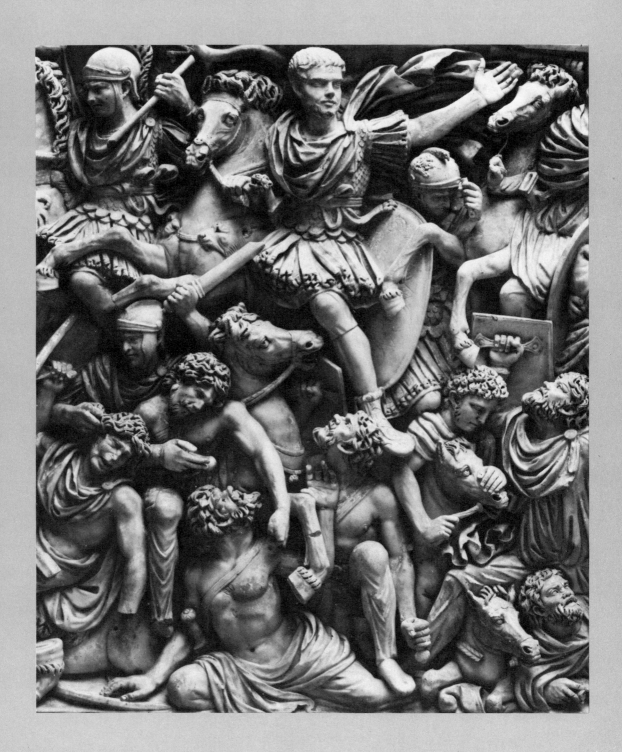

Part Two

THE WORLD IN
THE CLASSICAL ERA

After 600 B.C. the centers of civilization in the Western world were no longer mainly located in the Near East. By that time new cultures were already growing to maturity in Greece and in Italy. Both had started their evolution considerably earlier, but the civilization of Greece did not begin to ripen until about 600 B.C., while the Romans showed little promise of original achievement before 500. About 300 B.C. Greek civilization, properly speaking, came to an end and was superseded by a new culture representing a fusion of elements derived from Greece and the Near East. This was the Hellenistic civilization, which lasted until about the beginning of the Christian era and included not only the Greek peninsula but Egypt and most of Asia west of the Indus River. The outstanding characteristic which serves to distinguish these three civilizations from the ones that had gone before is secularism. No longer does religion absorb the interests of humans to the extent that it did in ancient Egypt or in the nations of Mesopotamia. The state is now above the church, and the power of the priests to determine the direction of cultural evolution has been greatly reduced. Furthermore, ideals of human freedom and an emphasis on the welfare of the individual have largely superseded the despotism and collectivism of the ancient Near East. Only late in Roman history, around the third century A.D., did Near-Eastern despotism begin to reassert itself within the confines of imperial Rome. Around that time too, a new religion, Christianity, began to reshape the life of the West. Somewhat similar developments were taking place in the Far East. In India, Hinduism and the dominance of the Brahman caste were challenged by the ethical and nontheological system of Gautama Buddha. Buddhism also spread to China and Japan and became a major stimulus of cultural vitality in all three countries.

The World in the Classical Era

	POLITICS	PHILOSOPHY AND SCIENCE
800 **B.C.**	Dark Ages of Greek history, 1100–800 Feudalism in China, c. 800–250 Beginning of city-states in Greece, c. 800 Rome founded, c. 750	Thales of Miletus, c. 640–546 Pythagoras, c. 582–c. 507 Confucius, c. 551–479 Lao-tzu, c. 550
	Age of the tyrants in Greece, c. 650–c. 500 Reforms of Solon in Athens, 594 Tyranny of Peisistratus, 560 Reforms of Cleisthenes, 508	
500 **B.C.**	Establishment of Roman Republic, c. 500 Greco-Persian War, 490–479	Protagoras, c. 490–c. 420 Socrates, 469–399
	Delian League, 479–404 Perfection of Athenian democracy, 461–429 Law of the Twelve Tables, Rome, c. 450 Peloponnesian War, 431–404	Hippocrates, 460–c. 377 Democritus, c. 460–c. 362 The Sophists, c. 450–c. 400
400 **B.C.**		Plato, 427–347 Aristotle, 384–322
	Theban supremacy in Greece, 371–362 Macedonian conquest of Greece, 338–337 Conquests of Alexander the Great, 336–323 Division of Alexander's empire, 323	Mencius, c. 373–288 Epicurus, 342–270 Zeno the Stoic, c. 320–c. 250 Euclid, c. 323–285
300 **B.C.**	Reign of Emperor Asoka in India, c. 273–232 Punic Wars between Rome and Carthage, 264–146 Ch'in Dynasty in China, 221–207 Building of Great Wall in China, c. 220	Aristarchus, 310–230 Archimedes, c. 287–212 Eratosthenes, c. 276–c. 195
200 **B.C.**	Han Dynasty in China, 206 B.C. –220 A.D. Reforms of the Gracchi, 133–121 Beginning of Japanese state, c. 100 Dictatorship of Julius Caesar, 46–44 Principate of Augustus Caesar, 27 B.C.–14 A.D.	Herophilus, c. 220–c. 150 Polybius, c. 205–118 The Skeptics, c. 200–c. 100 Introduction of Stoicism into Rome, c. 140 Cicero, 106–43
100 **B.C.**	Dictatorship of Julius Caesar, 46–44 Principate of Augustus Caesar, 27 B.C.–14 A.D.	
		Lucretius, 98–55
		Seneca, 34 B.C.–65 A.D.
100 **A.D.**	"Five Good Emperors," 96–180 Completion of Roman jurisprudence by great	Marcus Aurelius, 121–180
200 **A.D.**	jurists, c. 200 Civil war in Roman Empire, 235–284 Diocletian, 284–305	Galen, 130–c. 200 Plotinus, c. 204–270
300 **A.D.**	Constantine I, 306–337 Theodosius I, 379–395	
400 **A.D.**	Visigoths sack Rome, 410 West African kingdom of Ghana, c. 450	
500 **A.D.**	Deposition of last of Western Roman emperors, 476 Theodoric the Ostrogoth king of Italy, 493–526 Justinian, 527–565 *Corpus* of Roman law, c. 550	Boethius, c. 480–524

ECONOMICS	RELIGION	ARTS AND LETTERS	
Rise of caste system in India, 1000–500		*Vedas* in India, 1200–800	
		Upanishads, 800–600	**800 B.C.**
Economic revolution and colonization in Greece, c. 750–c. 600		*Iliad* and *Odyssey,* c. 750	
Rise of middle class in Greece, c. 750–c. 600		Doric architectural style, c. 650–c. 500	
	Gautama Buddha, c. 563–483	Aeschylus, 525–456	
		Phidias, c. 500–c. 432	
Use of iron in China, c. 500	Orphic and Eleusinian mystery cults, c. 500–c. 100	Ionic architectural style, c. 500–c. 400	**500 B.C.**
		Sophocles, 496–406	
		Herodotus, c. 484–c. 420	
		Euripides, 480–406	
		Thucydides, c. 471–c. 400	
		The Parthenon, c. 460	
		Aristophanes, c. 448–c. 380	
Development of coinage in China, c. 400		Corinthian architectural style, c. 400–c. 300	**400 B.C.**
		Praxiteles, c. 370–c. 310	
Hellenistic international trade and growth of large cities, c. 300 B.C.–c. 100 A.D.			
Use of iron in sub-Saharan Africa, 200			**300 B.C.**
Growth of slavery, rise of middle class, decline of small farmer in Rome, c. 250–100	Oriental mystery cults in Rome, c. 250–50		
			200 B.C.
Manufacture of paper in China, c. 100	Spread of Mithraism in Rome, 27 B.C.–270 A.D.		**100 B.C.**
Decline of slavery in Rome, c. 120–c. 476	The Crucifixion, c. 30 A.D.	Virgil, 70–19	
Growth of serfdom in Rome, c. 200–500	St. Paul's missionary work, c. 35–c. 67	Horace, 65–8	
		Livy, 59 B.C.–17 A.D.	
		Ovid, c. 43 B.C.–17 A.D.	
Sharp economic contraction in Rome, c. 200–c. 300		Tacitus, c. 55 A.D.–c. 117 A.D.	**100 A.D.**
	Development of Buddhism in China, 200–500	The Colosseum, c. 80 A.D.	
Expansion of Bantu people in Africa, 200–900	Beginning of toleration of Christians in the Roman Empire, 311	The Pantheon, c. 120	**200 A.D.**
Use of camel for transport in Africa, 300		Height of Roman portrait statuary, c. 120–c. 250	
	St. Augustine, 354–430	Classical age of Hindu culture, c. 300–800	**300 A.D.**
	Christianity made official Roman religion, 380		**400 A.D.**
		Adoption of Chinese system of writing in Japan, c. 405	
Manufacture of glass and invention of gunpowder and magnetic compass in China, c. 500	Benedictine monastic rule, c. 520	Spread of Buddhism in Japan, c. 552	**500 A.D.**

Chapter 8

THE HELLENIC CIVILIZATION

There Lawfulness dwells and her sisters,
Safe foundation of cities,
Justice and Peace, who was bred with her,
Dispensers of wealth to men
Golden daughters of wise-counseling Right.
                    —Pindar, on the city of Corinth, *Olympian Ode XIII*

Now, what is characteristic of any nature is that which is best for it and
gives most joy. Such to man is the life according to reason, since it is this
that makes him man.

                    —Aristotle, *Nichomachean Ethics*

Among all the peoples of the ancient world, the one whose culture
most clearly exemplified the spirit of Western man was the
Hellenic or Greek. No one of these nations had so strong a
devotion to liberty, at least for itself, or so firm a belief in the nobility
of human achievement. The Greeks glorified man as the most important creature in the universe and refused to submit to the dictation of
priests or despots or even to humble themselves before their gods.
Their attitude was essentially secular and rationalistic; they exalted the
spirit of free inquiry and made knowledge supreme over faith. It was
largely for these reasons that they advanced their culture to the highest
stage which the ancient world was destined to reach.

The character of Hellenic civilization

1. THE GREEK DARK AGES

The fall of the Mycenaean civilization was a major catastrophe for the
Greek world. It ushered in a period usually called by historians the
Dark Ages, which lasted from about 1100 to 800 B.C. Written records
disappeared, except where accidentally preserved, and culture re-
verted to simpler forms than had been known for centuries. Toward

The Dark Ages

Bronze Centaur and Man. These figures date from about 750 B.C. They are no more than about five inches high.

Bronze Statuette. Perhaps representing Apollo, this work dates from about 750 B.C.

the end of the period some decorated pottery and skillfully designed metal objects began to appear on the islands of the Aegean Sea, but essentially the period was a long night. Aside from the development of writing at the very end, intellectual accomplishment was limited to ballads, and short epics sung and embellished by bards as they wandered from one village to another. A large part of this material was finally woven into a great epic cycle by one or more poets in the eighth century B.C. Though not all the poems of this cycle have come down to us, the two most important, the *Iliad* and the *Odyssey,* the so-called Homeric epics, provide us with a rich store of information about many of the customs and institutions of the Dark Ages.

The political institutions of the Dark Ages were exceedingly primitive. Each little community of villages was independent of external control, but political authority was so tenuous that it would not be too much to say that the state scarcely existed at all. The *basileus* or ruler was not much more than a tribal leader. He could not make or enforce laws or administer justice. He received no remuneration of any kind, and had to cultivate his farm for a living the same as any other citizen. Practically his only functions were military and priestly. He commanded the army in time of war and offered sacrifices to keep the gods on the good side of the community. Although each little community had its council of nobles and assembly of warriors, neither of these bodies had any definite membership or status as an organ of government. Almost without exception custom took the place of law, and the administration of justice was private. Even willful murder was punishable only by the family of the victim. While it is true that disputes were sometimes submitted to the ruler for settlement, he acted in such cases merely as an arbitrator, not as a judge. As a matter of fact, the political consciousness of the Greeks of this time was so poorly developed that they had no conception of government as an indispensable agency for the preservation of social order. When Odysseus, ruler of Ithaca, was absent for twenty years, no regent was appointed in his place, and no session of the council or assembly was held. No one seemed to think that the complete suspension of government, even for so long a time, was a matter of critical importance.

The pattern of social and economic life was amazingly simple. Though the general tone of the society portrayed in the epics is aristocratic, there was actually no rigid stratification of classes. Manual labor was not looked upon as degrading, and there were apparently no idle rich. That there were dependent laborers of some kind who worked on the lands of the nobles and served them as faithful warriors seems clear from the Homeric epics, but they appear to have been serfs rather than slaves. The slaves were chiefly women, employed as servants, wool-processors, or concubines. Many were war captives, but they do not appear to have been badly treated. Agriculture and herding were the basic occupations of free men. Except for a few skilled crafts like those of wagonmaker, swordsmith, goldsmith, and potter, there was no specialization of labor. For the most part every household made its own tools, wove its own clothing, and raised its own food. So far were the Greeks of this time from being a trading people that they had no word in their language for "merchant," and barter was the only method of exchange that was practiced.

To the Greeks of the Dark Ages religion meant chiefly a system for: (1) explaining the physical world in such a way as to remove its awesome mysteries and give man a feeling of intimate relationship with it; (2) accounting for the tempestuous passions that seized man's nature and made him lose that self-control which the Greeks considered essential for success as a warrior; and (3) obtaining such tangible benefits as good fortune, long life, skill in craftsmanship, and abundant harvests. The Greeks did not expect that their religion would save them from sin or endow them with spiritual blessings. As they conceived it, piety was neither a matter of conduct nor of faith. Their religion, accordingly, had no commandments, dogmas, or sacraments. Every man was at liberty to believe what he pleased and to conduct his own life as he chose without fear of the wrath of the gods.

Religious conceptions in the Dark Ages

As is commonly known, the deities of the early Greek religion were merely human beings writ large. It was really necessary that this should be so if the Greek was to feel at home in the world over which they ruled. Remote, omnipotent beings like the gods of most oriental religions would have inspired fear rather than a sense of security. What the Greek wanted was not necessarily gods of great power, but deities who could be bargained with on equal terms. Consequently gods were endowed with attributes similar to human ones—with human bodies and human weaknesses and wants. The early Greek imagined the great company of divinities as frequently quarreling with one another, needing food and sleep, mingling freely with mortals, and even occasionally procreating children by mortal women. They differed from humans only in the fact that they subsisted on ambrosia and nectar, which made them immortal. They dwelt not in the sky or in the stars but on the summit of Mount Olympus, a peak in northern Greece with an altitude of about 10,000 feet.

Human qualities of the deities

The religion was thoroughly polytheistic, and no one deity was elevated very high above any of the others. Zeus, the sky god and wielder of the thunderbolt, who was sometimes referred to as the father of the gods and of men, frequently received less attention than did Poseidon, the sea god, Aphrodite, goddess of love, or Athena, variously considered goddess of wisdom and war and patroness of handicrafts. Since the Greeks had no Satan, their religion cannot be described as dualistic. All of the deities were capable of malevolence as well as good.

Poseidon or Zeus. Detail from an Athenian statue of about 470 B.C., larger than life size.

The Greeks of the Dark Ages were almost completely indifferent to what happened to them after death. They did assume, however, that shades or ghosts survived for a time after the death of their bodies. All, with a few exceptions, went to the same abode—to the murky realm of Hades situated beneath the earth. This was neither a paradise nor a hell: no one was rewarded for good deeds, and no one was punished for sins. Each of the shades appeared to continue the same kind of life its human embodiment had lived on earth. The Homeric poems make casual mention of two other realms, the Elysian Plain and the realm of Tartarus, which seem at first glance to contradict the idea of no rewards and punishments in the hereafter. But the few individuals who enjoyed the ease and comfort of the Elysian Plain had done nothing to deserve such blessings: they were simply persons whom the gods had chosen to favor. The realm of Tartarus was not really an abode of the dead but a place of imprisonment for rebellious deities.

Worship in early Greek religion consisted primarily of sacrifice. The offerings were made, however, not as an atonement for sin, but chiefly in order to please the gods and induce them to grant favors. In other words, religious practice was external and mechanical and not far removed from magic. Reverence, humility, and purity of heart were not essentials in it. The worshiper just made the proper sacrifice and then hoped for the best. For a religion such as this no elaborate institutions were required. Even a professional priesthood was unnecessary. Since there were no mysteries and no sacraments, one man could perform the simple rites about as well as another. The Greek temple was not a church or place of religious assemblage, and no ceremonies were performed within it. Instead it was a shrine which the god might visit occasionally and use as a temporary house.

As intimated already, the morality of the Greeks in the Dark Ages had only the vaguest connection with their religion. While it is true that the gods were generally disposed to support the right, they did not consider it their duty to combat evil and make righteousness prevail. In meting out rewards to humans, they appear to have been influenced more by their own whims and by gratitude for sacrifices offered than by any consideration for moral character. The only crime they punished was perjury, and that none too consistently. Nearly all the virtues extolled in the epics were those which would make the individual a better soldier—bravery, self-control, patriotism, wisdom (in the sense of cunning), love of one's friends, and hatred of one's enemies. There was no conception of sin in the Christian sense of wrongful acts to be repented of or atoned for.

At the end of the Dark Ages the Greeks were already well started along the road of social ideals that they were destined to follow in later centuries. They were optimists, convinced that life was worth living for its own sake, and could see no reason for looking forward to death as a glad release. They were egotists, striving for the fulfillment of self. As a consequence, mortification of the flesh and all forms of denial which would imply the frustration of life were rejected. They

Man Carrying a Calf for Sacrifice. A life-size Athenian sculpture from about 570 B.C.

Battle between the Gods and the Giants. This frieze dates from before 525 B.C. and is from the sanctuary of Apollo at Delphi.

could see no merit in humility or in turning the other cheek. They were humanists, who worshiped the finite and the natural rather than the otherworldly or sublime. For this reason they refused to invest their gods with awe-inspiring qualities, or to invent any conception of humans as depraved and sinful creatures. Finally, they were devoted to liberty in an even more extreme form than most of their descendants in the classical period were willing to accept.

The basic Greek ideals

2. THE EVOLUTION OF THE CITY-STATES

About 800 B.C. the village communities which had been founded mainly upon tribal or clan organization, began to give way to larger political units. As trade and the need for defense increased, cities grew up around market-places and defensive fortifications as seats of government for whole communities. Thus emerged the city-state, the most famous unit of political society developed by the Greeks. Examples were to be found in almost every section of the Hellenic world. Athens, Thebes, and Megara on the mainland; Sparta and Corinth on the Peloponnesus; Miletus on the shore of Asia Minor; and Mitylene and Samos on the islands of the Aegean Sea—these were among the best known. They varied enormously in both area and population. Sparta with more than 3,000 square miles and Athens with 1,060 had by far the greatest extent; the others averaged less than 100. At the peak of their power Athens and Sparta, each with a population of about 400,000, had approximately three times the numerical strength of most of their neighboring states.

The origin and nature of the city-states

More important is the fact that the Greek city-states varied widely in cultural evolution. From 800 to 500 B.C., commonly called the Archaic period, the Peloponnesian cities of Corinth and Argos were leaders in the development of literature and the arts. In the seventh century Sparta outshone many of its rivals. Preeminent above all were the Greek-speaking cities on the coast of Asia Minor and the islands of the Aegean Sea. Foremost among them was Miletus, where, as we shall see, a brilliant flowering of philosophy and science occurred as early as the sixth century. Athens lagged behind until at least one hundred years later.

With a few exceptions the Greek city-states went through a similar political evolution. They began their histories as monarchies. During the eighth century they were changed into oligarchies. About a hundred years later, on the average, most of the oligarchies were overthrown by dictators, or "tyrants," as the Greeks called them, meaning usurpers who ruled without legal right whether oppressively or not. Finally, in the sixth and fifth centuries, democracies were set up, or in some cases "timocracies," that is, governments based upon a property qualification for the exercise of political rights, or in which love of honor and glory was the ruling principle.

On the whole, it is not difficult to determine the causes of this political evolution. The first change came about as a result of the concentration of landed wealth. As the owners of great estates gained ever greater economic power, they determined to wrest political authority from the ruler, now commonly called king, and vest it in the council, which they generally controlled. In the end they abolished the kingship entirely. Then followed a period of sweeping economic changes and political turmoil.

These developments affected not only Greece itself but many other parts of the Mediterranean world. For they were accompanied and followed by a vast overseas expansion. The chief causes were an increasing scarcity of agricultural land, internal strife, and a general temper of restlessness and discontent. The Greeks rapidly learned of numerous areas, thinly populated, with climate and soil similar to those of the homelands. The parent states most active in the expansion movement were Corinth, Chalcis, and Miletus. Their citizens founded colonies along the Aegean shores and even in Italy and Sicily. Of the latter the best known were Taras (modern Taranto) and Syracuse. They also established trading centers on the coast of Egypt and as far east as Babylon. The results of this expansionist movement were momentous. Commerce and industry grew to be leading pursuits, the urban population increased, and wealth assumed new forms. The rising middle class now joined with dispossessed farmers in an attack upon the landholding oligarchy. The natural fruit of the bitter class conflicts that ensued was dictatorship. By encouraging extravagant hopes and promising relief from chaos, ambitious demagogues attracted enough popular support to enable them to ride into power in defiance of constitutions and laws. Ultimately, however, dissatisfaction with tyrannical rule and the increasing economic power and political consciousness of the common citizens led to the establishment of democracies or liberal oligarchies.

Unfortunately space does not permit an analysis of the political history of each of the Greek city-states. Except in the more backward sections of Thessaly and the Peloponnesus, it is safe to conclude that the internal development of all of them paralleled the account given above, although minor variations due to local conditions doubtless occurred. The two most important of the Hellenic states, Sparta and Athens, deserve more detailed study.

3. THE ARMED CAMP OF SPARTA

The history of Sparta[1] was the great exception to the political evolution of the city-states. Despite the fact that its citizens sprang from the same origins as most of the other Greeks, Sparta failed to make any progress in the direction of democratic rule. Instead, its government gradually evolved into a form more closely resembling a modern elite dictatorship. Culturally, also, the nation stagnated after the sixth century. The causes were due partly to isolation. Hemmed in by mountains on the northeast and west and lacking good harbors, the Spartan people had little opportunity to profit from the advances made in the outside world. Besides, no middle class arose to aid the masses in the struggle for freedom.

The major explanation is to be found, however, in militarism. The Spartans were originally Dorians who had come into the eastern Peloponnesus as an invading army. At first they attempted to amalgamate with the Mycenaeans they found there. But conflicts arose, and the Spartans resorted to conquest. Though by the end of the ninth century they had gained dominion over all of Laconia, they were not satisfied. West of the Taygetus Mountains lay the fertile plain of Messenia. The Spartans determined to conquer it. The venture was successful, and the Messenian territory was annexed to Laconia. About 640 B.C. the Messenians enlisted the aid of Argos and launched a revolt. The war that followed was desperately fought, Laconia itself was invaded, and apparently it was only the death of the Argive commander and the patriotic pleas of the fire-eating poet Tyrtaeus that saved the day for the Spartans. This time the victors took no chances. They confiscated the lands of the Messenians, murdered or expelled their leaders, and turned the masses into serfs called *helots*. Thereafter Spartan foreign policy was defensive. Following the Messenian wars the Spartans feared that further foreign warfare would provide the opportunities

[1]Sparta was the leading city of a district called Laconia or Lacedaemonia; sometimes the *state* was referred to by one or the other of these names. The people, also, were frequently called Laconians or Lacedaemonians. (The modern adjective "laconic" comes from the reputation of the ancient Spartans for being sparing with words.)

The results of Spartan militarism

The Spartan government

The class system in Sparta

for a helot uprising; consequently Sparta devoted itself to keeping what it had already gained.

There was scarcely a feature of the life of the Spartans that was not the result of their wars with the Messenians. In subduing and despoiling their enemies they unwittingly enslaved themselves, for they lived through the remaining centuries of their history in deadly fear of insurrections. It was this fear which explains their conservatism, their stubborn resistance to change, lest any innovation result in a fatal weakening of the system. Their provincialism can also be attributed to the same cause. Frightened by the prospect that dangerous ideas might be brought into their country, they discouraged travel and prohibited trade with the outside world. The necessity of maintaining the absolute supremacy of the citizen class over an enormous population of serfs required an iron discipline and a strict subordination of the individual; hence the Spartan collectivism, which extended into every branch of the social and economic life. Finally, much of the cultural backwardness of Sparta grew out of the atmosphere of restraint which inevitably resulted from the bitter struggle to conquer the Messenians and hold them under stern repression.

The Spartan constitution provided for a government preserving the forms of the old system of the Dark Ages. Instead of one king, however, there were two, representing separate families of exalted rank. The Spartan kings enjoyed but few powers and those were chiefly of a military and priestly character. A second branch of the government was the council, composed of the two kings and twenty-eight nobles sixty years of age and over. This body supervised the work of administration, prepared measures for submission to the assembly, and served as the highest court for criminal trials. The third organ of government, the assembly, composed of all adult male citizens, approved or rejected the proposals of the council and elected all public officials except the kings. But the highest authority under the Spartan constitution was vested in a board of five men known as the *ephorate*. The ephors virtually were the government. They presided over the council and the assembly, controlled the educational system and the distribution of property, censored the lives of the citizens, and exercised a veto power over all legislation. They had power also to determine the fate of newborn infants, to conduct prosecutions before the council, and even to depose the kings if the religious omens appeared unfavorable. The Spartan government dominated by the ephors was thus in effect an oligarchy.

The population of Sparta was divided into three main classes. The ruling element was made up of the Spartiates, or descendants of the original conquerors. Though never exceeding one-twentieth of the total population, the Spartiates alone had political privileges. Next in order of rank were the *perioeci,* or "dwellers around." The origin of this class is uncertain, but it was probably composed of peoples that had at one time been allies of the Spartans or had submitted voluntarily to Spartan domination. In return for service as a buffer population between the ruling class and the helots, the perioeci were allowed to carry on trade and to engage in manufacturing. At the bottom of the scale were the helots, or serfs, bound to the soil.

Among these classes only the perioeci enjoyed any appreciable measure of comfort and freedom. While it is true that the economic condition of the helots cannot be described in terms of absolute misery, since they were permitted to keep for themselves a good share of what they produced on the estates of their masters, they were personally subjected to such shameful treatment that they were constantly wretched and rebellious. To guard against rebellion young Spartiates were sometimes sent to live among the helots in disguise and act like a secret police with the power to murder whom they pleased. The brutalizing effects on both sides can be easily imagined.

Perioeci and helots

Those who were born into the Spartiate class were doomed to a respectable slavery for the major part of their lives. Forced to submit to the severest discipline and to sacrifice individual interests, they were little more than cogs in a vast machine. Spartan babies were examined for hardiness at birth and those who were thought to be potential weaklings were carried off to the hills to die of neglect. The education of Spartan males was limited almost entirely to military training, which began at the age of seven, supplemented by merciless floggings to harden the boys for the duties of war. Between the ages of twenty and sixty the men gave almost all their time to state service. Although marriage was practically compulsory there was little family life: young men had to live in barracks, and after the age of thirty they still had to eat in military messes. The husbands carried off their wives on their wedding nights by a show of force. Because they saw so little of them afterwards it sometimes happened that men "had children before they ever saw their wives' faces in daylight."[2] The production of vigorous offspring was the wives' main duty, but mothers had to accept the fact that children were virtually the property of the state. It may be doubted that the Spartiates resented these hardships and deprivations. Pride in their status as the ruling class probably compensated in their minds for harsh discipline and denial of privileges.

Discipline for the benefit of the state

The economic organization of Sparta was designed almost solely for the ends of military efficiency and the supremacy of the citizen class. The best land was owned by the state and was originally divided into equal plots which were assigned to the Spartiate class as inalienable estates. Later these holdings as well as the inferior lands were permitted to be sold and exchanged, with the result that some of the citizens became richer than others. The helots, who did all the work of cultivating the soil, also belonged to the state and were assigned to their mas-

Economic regulations

[2] Plutarch, "Lycurgus," *Lives of Illustrious Men*, I, 81.

ters along with the land. Their masters were forbidden to emancipate them or to sell them outside of the country. The labor of the helots provided for the support of the whole citizen class, whose members were not allowed to be associated with any economic enterprise other than agriculture. The minimal trade and industry of the Spartan state were reserved exclusively for the perioeci.

Description of the Spartan system

The Spartan economic system is frequently described by modern historians as communistic. It is true that some of the means of production (the helots and the land) were collectively owned, in theory at least, and that the Spartiate males contributed from their incomes to provide for their common military messes. But with these exceptions the system was as far removed from communism as it was from anarchy. Essentials of the communist ideal include the doctrines that all the instruments of production shall be owned by the community, that no one shall live by exploiting the labor of others, and that all shall work for the benefit of the community and share the wealth in proportion to need. In Sparta commerce and industry were in private hands; the helots were forced to contribute a portion of what they produced to provide for the subsistence of their masters; and political privileges were restricted to a governing class whose members performed no socially useful labor. With its militarism, its secret police, its minority rule, and its closed economy, the Spartan system resembled fascism more nearly than true communism.

4. THE ATHENIAN TRIUMPH AND TRAGEDY

Athens began its history under conditions quite different from those which prevailed in Sparta. The district of Attica in which Athens is situated had not been the scene of an armed invasion or of bitter conflict between opposing peoples. As a result, no military caste imposed its rule upon a vanquished nation. Furthermore, the wealth of Attica consisted of mineral deposits and splendid harbors in addition to agricultural resources. Athens, consequently, never remained a predominantly agrarian state but rapidly developed a prosperous trade and an essentially urban culture.

Advantages enjoyed by the Athenians

From monarchy to oligarchy in Athens

Until the middle of the eighth century B.C. Athens, like the other Greek states, had a monarchical form of government. During the century that followed, the council of nobles, or Council of the Areopagus, as it came to be called, gradually divested the king of his powers. The transition to rule by the few was both the cause and the result of an increasing concentration of wealth. The introduction of vine and olive culture about this time led to the growth of agriculture as a large-scale enterprise. Since vineyards and olive orchards require considerable time to become profitable, only those farmers with abundant resources were able to survive in the business. Their poorer and less thrifty neighbors sank rapidly into debt, especially since grain was now coming to be imported at ruinous prices. The small farmer had no alternative but to mortgage his land, and then his family and himself, in the vain hope that some day a way of escape would be found. Ultimately many of this class became serfs when the mortgages could not be paid; those without land to mortgage were sold into slavery.

Bitter cries of distress now arose and threats of revolution were heard. The urban middle classes espoused the cause of the peasants in demanding liberalization of the government. Finally, in 594 B.C., all parties agreed upon the appointment of the aristocrat Solon as chief magistrate with absolute power to carry out reforms. The measures Solon enacted provided for both political and economic adjustments. The former included: (1) the establishment of a new council, the Council of Four Hundred, and the admission of the middle classes to membership in it; (2) the enfranchisement of the lower classes by making them eligible for service in the assembly; and (3) the organization of a final court of appeals in criminal cases, open to all citizens and elected by universal manhood suffrage. The economic reforms benefited the poor farmers by canceling existing mortgages, prohibiting enslavement for debt in the future, and limiting the amount of land any one individual could own. Nor did Solon neglect the middle classes. He introduced a new system of coinage designed to give Athens an advantage in foreign trade, imposed heavy penalties for idleness, ordered every man to teach his son a trade, and offered full privileges of citizenship to alien craftsmen who would become permanent residents of the country.

*Threats of revolution and
the reforms of Solon*

Significant though these reforms were, they did not allay the discontent. The nobles were disgruntled because some of their privileges had been taken away. The middle and lower classes were dissatisfied because they were still excluded from the offices of magistracy, and because the Council of the Areopagus was left with its powers intact. The chaos and disillusionment that followed paved the way in 560 B.C. for the triumph of Peisistratus, the first of the Athenian tyrants. Although he proved to be a benevolent despot who patronized culture, reduced the power of the aristocracy, and raised the standard of living of the average Athenian, his son Hippias, who succeeded him, was a ruthless and spiteful oppressor.

The rise of dictatorship

In 510 B.C. Hippias's tyranny was overthrown by a group of nobles with aid from Sparta. Factional conflict raged for another two years until Cleisthenes, an intelligent aristocrat, enlisted the support of the masses to eliminate his rivals from the scene. Having promised concessions to the people as a reward for their help, he proceeded to reform the government in so sweeping a fashion that he has since been known as the father of Athenian democracy. Cleisthenes, who dominated Athenian politics from 508 to 502, enlarged the citizen population by granting full rights to all free men who resided in the country

*The reforms of
Cleisthenes*

Greeks at War. A battle scene from the interior of a drinking cup, done in Athens between about 530 and 500 B.C.

The Owl of Athens. An Athenian silver coin of around 470 B.C., showing the owl, thought to be sacred to Athens's protectress, the goddess Athena. The name Athens appears in the Greek letters ΑΘΣ.

at that time. He established a new council and made it the chief organ of government with power to prepare measures for submission to the assembly and with supreme control over executive and administrative functions. Members of this body were to be chosen by lot. Any male citizen over thirty years of age was eligible. Cleisthenes also expanded the authority of the assembly, giving it power to debate and pass or reject the measures submitted by the Council, to declare war, to appropriate money, and to audit the accounts of retiring magistrates. Lastly, not long after the time of Cleisthenes, in 487, the Athenians instituted the device of ostracism, whereby any citizen who might be dangerous to the state could be sent into honorable exile for a ten-year period. The device was meant to eliminate men who were suspected of cherishing dictatorial ambitions, but too often its effect was to eliminate exceptional personalities and to allow mediocrity to flourish.

The Athenian democracy attained its full perfection in the Age of Pericles (461–429 B.C.). It was during this period that the assembly acquired the authority to initiate legislation in addition to its power to ratify or reject proposals of the council. It was during this time also that the Board of Ten Generals rose to a position roughly comparable to that of the British cabinet. The generals were chosen by the assembly for one-year terms and were eligible for reelection indefinitely. Pericles held the position of chief strategus or president of the Board of Generals for more than thirty years. The generals were not simply commanders of the army but the chief legislative and executive officials in the state. Though wielding enormous power, they could not become tyrants, for their policies were subject to review by the assembly, and they could easily be recalled at the end of their one-year terms or indicted for malfeasance at any time. Finally, it was in the Age of Pericles that the Athenian system of courts was developed to completion. No longer was there merely a supreme court to hear appeals from the decisions of magistrates, but an array of popular courts with authority to try all kinds of cases. At the beginning of each year a list of 6,000 citizens was chosen by lot from the various sections of the country. From this list separate juries, varying in size from 201 to 1,001, were made up for particular trials. Each of these juries constituted a court with power to decide by majority vote every question involved in the case. Although one of the magistrates presided, he had none of the prerogatives of a judge; the jury itself was the judge, and from its decision there was no appeal.

The perfection of Athenian democracy

The Athenian democracy differed from the modern form in various ways. First of all, it entirely excluded women. Even taking that into account, it did not extend to the whole population, but only to the citizen class. While it is true that in the time of Cleisthenes the citizens probably included a majority of the inhabitants because of his enfranchisement of resident aliens, in the Age of Pericles the citizens were distinctly a minority. It may be well to observe, however, that within its limits Athenian democracy was more thoroughly applied than is the modern form. The choice by lot of nearly all magistrates except the Ten Generals, the restriction of all terms of public officials to one year, and the uncompromising adherence to the principle of majority rule even in judicial trials were examples of a confidence in the political capacity of the citizen which few modern nations would be willing to accept. The democracy of Athens differed from the contemporary ideal also in the fact that it was direct, not representative. The Athenians were not interested in being governed by a few men of reputation and ability; what vitally concerned them was the assurance to every citizen of an actual voice in the control of all public affairs.

Athenian democracy compared with modern democracy

In the century of its greatest expansion and creativity, Athens fought two major wars. The first, the war with Persia, was an outgrowth of the expansion of that empire into the eastern Mediterranean area. The Athenians resented the oppression of the Greek-speaking cities in Asia Minor and aided them in their struggle for freedom. (These cities shared with Athens a common Greek dialect—Ionian—a fact which made the Athenians feel a particularly close kinship with them.) The Persians retaliated by sending a powerful army and fleet to attack the Greeks. Although all Greece was in danger of conquest, Athens bore the chief burden of repelling the invader. The war, which began in 490 B.C. and lasted with interludes of peace until 479, is commonly regarded as one of the most significant in the history of the world. The heroic victories of the Greeks in such battles as Marathon (490) and Salamis (480) put an end to the menace of Persian conquest and forestalled the submergence of Hellenic ideals of freedom in Near-Eastern despotism. The war also had the effect of strengthening de-

The Persian War and its results

mocracy in Athens and making that state the leading power in Greece.

The other of the great struggles, the Peloponnesian War with Sparta, had results of a quite different character. Instead of being another milestone in the Athenian march to power, it ended in tragedy. The causes of this war are of particular interest to the student of the downfall of civilizations. First and most important was the growth of Athenian imperialism. In the last year of the war with Persia, Athens had joined with a number of other Greek states in the formation of an offensive and defensive alliance known as the Delian League. When peace was concluded the league was not dissolved, for many of the Greeks feared that the Persians might come back. As time went on, Athens gradually transformed the league into a naval empire for the advancement of its own interests. It used some of the funds in the common treasury for its own purposes. It tried to reduce all the other members to a condition of vassalage, and when one of them rebelled, Athens overwhelmed it by force, seized its navy, and imposed tribute upon it as if it were a conquered state. Such high-handed methods aroused the suspicions of the Spartans, who feared that an Athenian hegemony would soon be extended over all of Greece.

A second major cause was to be found in the social and cultural differences between Athens and Sparta. Athens was democratic, progressive, urban, imperialist, and intellectually and artistically advanced. Sparta was aristocratic, conservative, agrarian, provincial, and culturally backward. Where such sharply contrasting systems exist side by side, conflicts are almost bound to occur. The attitude of the Athenians and Spartans had been hostile for some time. The former looked upon the latter as uncouth barbarians. The Spartans accused the Athenians of attempting to gain control over the northern Peloponnesian states and of encouraging the helots to rebel. Economic factors also played a large part in bringing the conflict to a head. Athens was ambitious to dominate the Corinthian Gulf, the principal avenue of trade with Sicily and southern Italy. This made Athens the deadly enemy of Corinth, the chief ally of Sparta.

The war, which broke out in 431 B.C. and lasted until 404, was a record of frightful calamities for Athens. Athenian trade was destroyed, its democracy overthrown, and the population decimated by a terrible pestilence. Quite as bad was the moral degradation which followed in the wake of the military reverses. Treason, corruption, and brutality were among the hastening ills of the last few years of the conflict. On one occasion the Athenians even slaughtered the whole male population of the island of Melos, and enslaved the women and children, for no other crime than refusing to abandon neutrality. Ultimately, deserted by all its allies except Samos and with its food supply cut off, Athens was left with no alternative but to surrender or starve. The terms imposed upon the Athenians were drastic enough: destruction of their fortifications, surrender of all foreign possessions

Athenian imperialism and the Peloponnesian War

Other causes of the Peloponnesian War

The defeat of Athens

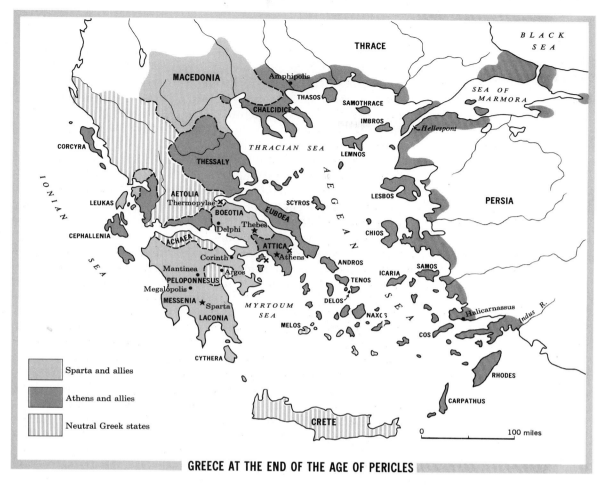

GREECE AT THE END OF THE AGE OF PERICLES

and practically their entire navy, and submission to Sparta as a subject
state. Though Athens recovered its leadership for a time in the fourth
century, its period of glory was approaching its end.

5. POLITICAL DEBACLE—THE LAST DAYS

Not only did the Peloponnesian War put an end to the political supremacy of Athens, it annihilated freedom throughout the Greek
world and sealed the doom of the Hellenic political genius. Following
the war, Sparta asserted its power over all of Greece. Oligarchies supported by Spartan troops replaced democracies wherever they existed.
Confiscation of property and assassination were the methods regularly
employed to combat opposition. Although in Athens the tyrants were
overthrown after a time and free government restored, Sparta was
able to dominate the remainder of Greece for more than thirty years.
In 371 B.C., however, Epaminondas of Thebes defeated the Spartan

*Continuing conflict among
the city-states*

army at Leuctra and thereby inaugurated a period of Theban supremacy. Unfortunately Thebes showed little more wisdom and tolerance in governing than Sparta, and nine years later a combination was formed to free the Greek cities from their new oppressor. Failing to break up the alliance, the Thebans gave battle on the field of Mantinea. Both sides claimed the victory, but Epaminondas was slain, and his empire soon afterward collapsed.

The Macedonian conquest

The long succession of wars had now brought the Greek states to the point of exhaustion. Though the glory of their culture was yet undimmed, politically they were prostrate and helpless. Their fate was soon decided for them by the rise of Philip of Macedon. Except for a thin veneer of Hellenic culture, the Macedonians were barbarians; but Philip, before becoming their king, had learned how to lead an army while a hostage at Thebes. Perceiving the weakness of the states to the south, he determined to conquer them. A series of early successes led to a decisive victory in 338 B.C. and soon afterward to dominion over all of Greece except Sparta. Two years later Philip was murdered as the sequel to a family brawl.

Alexander the Great

Rule over Greece now passed into the hands of his son Alexander, a youth of twenty years. After putting to death all possible aspirants to the throne and quelling some feeble revolts of the Greeks, Alexander, subsequently known as "the Great," conceived the grandiose scheme of conquering Persia. One victory followed another until, in the short space of twelve years, all the eastern territory from the Indus River to the Nile had been annexed to Greece as the personal domain of one man. Alexander did not live to enjoy it long. In 323 B.C. he fell ill of Babylonian swamp fever and died at the age of thirty-two.

The significance of Alexander's career

It is difficult to gauge the significance of Alexander's career. Historians have differed widely in their interpretations. Some have seen him as one of the supreme galvanizing forces in history. Others would limit his genius to military strategy and organization and deny that he made a single major contribution of benefit to humanity. There can be no doubt that he was a master of the art of war (he never lost a battle), and that he was intelligent and endowed with charm and physical courage. Unquestionably, also, he was a man of vibrant energy and overpowering ambitions. Just what these ambitions were is not certain. Evidence eludes us that he aspired to conquer the world or to advance the Hellenic ideals of freedom and justice. It seems doubtful that he had much interest in lofty ideals or in using military force to extend them. His main goal was to enhance his own power and glory. The primary significance of his military accomplishment lay in the fact that he carried the Hellenic drive into Asia farther and faster than would otherwise have occurred. He undoubtedly caused the Greek influence to be more widely felt. At the same time he appears to have placed too great a strain upon Hellenism with the result of encouraging a sweeping tide of Eastern influences into the West. Within a short period

Hellenic and Eastern cultures interpenetrated to such an extent as to produce a new civilization. This was the Hellenistic civilization, to be discussed in the chapter that follows.

6. HELLENIC THOUGHT AND CULTURE

From what has been said in preceding chapters it should be clear that the popular notion that all philosophy originated with the Greeks is fallacious. Centuries earlier the Egyptians had given much thought to the nature of the universe and to the social and ethical problems of humanity. The achievement of the Greeks was rather the development of philosophy in a more inclusive manner than it had ever possessed before. They attempted to find answers to every conceivable question about the nature of the universe, the problem of truth, and the meaning and purpose of life. The magnitude of their accomplishment is attested by the fact that philosophy ever since has been largely a debate over the validity of their conclusions.

The antecedents of Greek philosophy

Greek philosophy had its origins in the sixth century B.C. in the work of the so-called Milesian school, whose members were natives of the commercial city of Miletus on the shore of Asia Minor. Their philosophy was fundamentally scientific and materialistic. The problem which chiefly engaged their attention was to discover the nature of the physical world. They believed that all things could be reduced to some primary substance or original matter which was the source of worlds, stars, animals, plants, and men and women, and to which all would ultimately return. Thales, the founder of the school, perceiving that all things contained moisture, taught that the primary substance is water. Anaximander insisted that it could not be any particular thing such as water or fire but some substance "ungendered and imperishable" which "contains and directs all things." He called this substance the Indefinite or the Boundless. A third member of the school, Anaximenes, declared that the original material of the universe is air. Air when rarefied becomes fire; when condensed it turns successively to wind, vapor, water, earth, and stone.

The philosophy of the Milesian school

Although seemingly naive in its conclusions, the philosophy of the Milesian school was of real significance. It broke through the mythological beliefs of the Greeks about the origin of the world and substituted purely rational explanations. It expanded the Egyptian ideas of the eternity of the universe and the indestructibility of matter. It suggested very clearly, especially in the teachings of Anaximander, the concept of evolution in the sense of rhythmic change, of continuing creation and decay.

Significance of the teachings of the Milesian school

Before the end of the sixth century Greek philosophy developed a metaphysical turn; it ceased to be occupied solely with problems of the physical world and shifted its attention to abstruse questions about the nature of being, the meaning of truth, and the position of the divine in the scheme of things. First to exemplify the new tendency were the Pythagoreans, who interpreted philosophy largely in terms of religion. Little is known about them except that their leader, Pythagoras, migrated from the island of Samos to southern Italy and founded a religious community at Croton in 530 B.C. He and his followers taught that the speculative life is the highest good, but that in order to pursue it, the individual must be purified of the evil desires of the flesh. They held that the essence of things is not a material substance but an abstract principle, number. Their chief significance lies in the sharp distinctions they drew between spirit and matter, harmony and discord, good and evil. Perhaps it is accurate to regard the Pythagoreans as the real founders of dualism in Greek thought.

A consequence of the work of the Pythagoreans was to intensify the debate over the nature of the universe. Some of their contemporaries, notably Parmenides, argued that stability or permanence is the real nature of things; change and diversity are simply illusions of the senses. Directly opposed to this conception was the position taken by Heracleitus, who argued that permanence is an illusion, that change alone is real. The universe, he maintained, is in a condition of constant flux; therefore "it is impossible to step twice into the same stream." Creation and destruction, life and death, are but the obverse and reverse sides of the same picture. In affirming such views Heracleitus was really contending that the things we see and hear and feel are all that there is to reality. Evolution or constant change is the law of the universe. The tree or the stone that is here today is gone tomorrow; no underlying substance exists immutable through all eternity.

The eventual answer to the question of the underlying character of the universe was provided by the atomists. The philosopher chiefly responsible for the development of the atomic theory was Democritus, who lived in Abdera on the Thracian coast in the second half of the fifth century. As their name implies, the atomists held that the ultimate constituents of the universe are atoms, infinite in number, indestructible, and indivisible. Although these differ in size and shape, they are exactly alike in composition. Because of the motion inherent in them, they are eternally uniting, separating, and reuniting in different arrangements. Every individual object or organism in the universe is thus the product of a fortuitous concourse of atoms. The only difference between a man and a tree is the difference in the number and arrangement of their atoms. Here was a philosophy which represented the final fruition of the materialistic tendencies of early Greek thought. Democritus denied the immortality of the soul and the existence of any spiritual world. Strange as it may appear to some people, he was a moral idealist, affirming that "Good means not merely not to do wrong, but rather not to desire to do wrong."

About the middle of the fifth century B.C. an intellectual revolution began in Greece. It accompanied the high point of democracy in Athens. The rise in the power of the citizen, the growth of individualism, and the demand for the solution of practical problems produced a reaction against the old ways of thinking. As a result philosophers abandoned the study of the physical universe and turned to consideration of subjects more intimately related to the individual. The first exponents of the new intellectual trend were the Sophists. Originally the term meant "those who are wise," but later it came to be used in the derogatory sense of men who employ specious reasoning. Since most of our knowledge of the Sophists was derived, until comparatively recently, from Plato, one of their severest critics, they were commonly considered to have been the enemies of all that was best in Hellenic culture. Modern research has exposed the fallacy of so extreme a conclusion. Some members of the group, however, did lack a sense of social responsibility and were quite unscrupulous in "making the worse appear the better case."

The intellectual revolution begun by the Sophists

One of the leading Sophists was Protagoras, a native of Abdera who did most of his teaching in Athens. His famous dictum, "Man is the measure of all things," comprehends the essence of the Sophist philosophy. By this he meant that goodness, truth, justice, and beauty are relative to the needs and interests of man. There are no absolute truths or eternal standards of right and justice. Since sense perception is the exclusive source of knowledge, there can be only particular truths valid for a given time and place. Morality likewise varies from one people to another, for there are no absolute canons of right and wrong eternally decreed in the heavens to fit all cases.

The doctrines of Protagoras

Some of the later Sophists went far beyond the teachings of Protagoras. The individualism which was necessarily implicit in the teachings of Protagoras was twisted by Thrasymachus into the doctrine that all laws and customs are merely expressions of the will of the strongest and shrewdest for their own advantage, and that therefore the wise man is the "perfectly unjust man" who is above the law and concerned with the gratification of his own desires. (It should also be mentioned that man, in the sense of the male, was the primary focus of this and all other Greek philosophy dealing with the individual.)

The extremist doctrines of the later Sophists

Yet there was much that was admirable in the teachings of the Sophists, even of those who were the most extreme. Without exception they condemned slavery and the racial exclusiveness of the Greeks. They were champions of liberty, the rights of the common man, and the practical and progressive point of view. They perceived the folly of war and ridiculed the chauvinism of many Athenian citizens. Perhaps their most important work was the extension of philosophy to include not only physics and metaphysics, but ethics and politics as well. As the Roman Cicero expressed it, they "brought philosophy down from heaven to the dwellings of men."

The valuable contributions of the Sophists

It was inevitable that the relativism, skepticism, and individualism

Socrates. According to Plato, Socrates looked like a goat-man but spoke like a god.

The philosophy of Socrates

Plato

of the Sophists should have aroused strenuous opposition. In the judgment of the more conservative Greeks these doctrines appeared to lead straight to atheism and anarchy. If there is no final truth, and if goodness and justice are merely relative to the whims of the individual, then neither religion, morality, the state, nor society itself can long be maintained. The result of this conviction was the growth of a new philosophic movement grounded upon the theory that truth is real and that absolute standards do exist. The leaders of this movement were perhaps the three most famous individuals in the history of thought—Socrates, Plato, and Aristotle.

Socrates was born in Athens in 469 B.C. of humble parentage; his father was a sculptor, his mother a midwife. How he obtained an education no one knows, but he was certainly familiar with the teachings of earlier Greek thinkers. The impression that he was a mere gabbler in the marketplace is quite unfounded. He became a philosopher on his own account chiefly to combat the doctrines of the Sophists. In 399 B.C. he was condemned to death on a charge of "corrupting the youth and introducing new gods." The real reason for the unjust sentence was the tragic outcome for Athens of the Peloponnesian War. Overwhelmed by resentment, the Athenian citizens turned against Socrates because of his associations with aristocrats, including the traitor Alcibiades, and because of his criticism of popular belief. There is also evidence that he disparaged democracy and contended that no government was worthy of the name except intellectual aristocracy.

Because Socrates wrote nothing himself, historians find it difficult to determine the exact scope of his teachings. He is generally regarded as primarily a teacher of ethics with no interest in abstract philosophy. Certain passages in Plato, however, raise the possibility that Plato's abstract doctrine of Ideas was ultimately of Socratic origin. At any rate we can be reasonably sure that Socrates believed in a stable and universally valid knowledge, which man could possess if he would only pursue the right method. This method would consist in the exchange and analysis of opinions, in the setting up and testing of provisional definitions, until finally an essence of truth recognizable by all could be distilled from them. Socrates argued that in similar fashion man could discover enduring principles of right and justice independent of the selfish desires of human beings. He believed, moreover, that the discovery of such rational principles of conduct would prove an infallible guide to virtuous living, for he denied that anyone who truly knows the good can ever choose the evil.

By far the most distinguished of Socrates's pupils was Plato, who was born in Athens around 429 B.C., the son of noble parents. When he was twenty years old he joined the Socratic circle, remaining a member until the tragic death of his teacher. Unlike his great mentor he was a prolific writer, though some of the works attributed to him are of doubtful authorship. The most noted of his writings are such dialogues as the *Apology,* the *Phaedo,* the *Phaedrus,* the *Symposium,* and the *Republic.* He was engaged in the completion of another great work, the *Laws,* when death overtook him in his eighty-first year.

Plato's objectives in developing his philosophy were similar to those of Socrates although somewhat broader: (1) to combat the theory of reality as a disordered flux and to substitute an interpretation of the universe as essentially spiritual and purposeful; (2) to refute the Sophist doctrines of relativism and skepticism; and (3) to provide a secure foundation for ethics. In order to realize these objectives he developed his doctrine of Ideas. He admitted that relativity and constant change are characteristics of the world of physical things, of the world we perceive with our senses. But he denied that this world is the complete universe. There is a higher, spiritual realm composed of eternal forms or Ideas which only the mind can conceive. These are not, however, mere abstractions invented by the mind, but spiritual things. Each is the pattern of some particular class of objects or relation between objects on earth. Thus there are Ideas of man, tree, shape, size, color, proportion, beauty, and justice. Highest of them all is the Idea of the Good, which is the active cause and guiding purpose of the whole universe. The things we perceive through our senses are merely imperfect copies of the supreme realities, Ideas.

Plato's philosophy of Ideas

Plato's ethical and religious philosophy was closely related to his doctrine of Ideas. Like Socrates he believed that true virtue has its basis in knowledge. But the knowledge derived from the senses is limited and variable; hence true virtue must consist in rational apprehension of the eternal Ideas of goodness and justice. By relegating the physical to an inferior place, he gave to his ethics an ascetic tinge. He regarded the body as a hindrance to the mind and taught that only the rational part of man's nature is noble and good. Yet in contrast with some of his later followers, he did not demand that appetites and emotions should be denied altogether, but urged that they should be strictly subordinated to the reason. Plato never made his conception of God entirely clear, but it is certain that he conceived of the universe as spiritual in nature and governed by intelligent purpose. He rejected both materialism and mechanism. As for the soul, he regarded it not only as immortal but as preexisting through all eternity.

Plato's ethical and religious philosophy

Plato

As a political philosopher Plato was motivated by the ideal of constructing a state which would be free from turbulence and self-seeking on the part of individuals and classes. Neither democracy nor liberty but harmony and efficiency were the ends he desired to achieve. Accordingly, he proposed in his *Republic* a famous plan for society which would have divided the population into three principal classes corresponding to the functions of the soul. The lowest class, representing the appetitive function, would include the farmers, artisans, and merchants. The second class, representing the spirited element or will, would consist of the soldiers. The highest class, representing the func-

Plato as a political philosopher

tion of reason, would be composed of the intellectual aristocracy. Each of these classes would perform those tasks for which it was best fitted. The function of the lowest class would be the production and distribution of goods for the benefit of the whole community; that of the soldiers, defense; the aristocracy, by reason of special aptitude for philosophy, would enjoy a monopoly of political power. The division of the people into these several ranks would not be made on the basis of birth or wealth, but through a sifting process that would take into account the ability of each individual to profit from education. Thus the farmers, artisans, and merchants would be those who had shown the least intellectual capacity, whereas the philosopher-kings would be those who had shown the greatest.

Aristotle

The last of the great champions of the Socratic tradition was Aristotle, a native of Stagira, born in 384 B.C. At the age of seventeen he entered Plato's Academy,[3] continuing as student and teacher there for twenty years. In 343 he was invited by Philip of Macedon to serve as tutor to the young Alexander. History affords few more conspicuous examples of wasted effort, except for the fact that the young prince acquired an enthusiasm for science and for some other elements of Hellenic culture. Seven years later Aristotle returned to Athens, where he conducted a school of his own, known as the Lyceum, until his death in 322 B.C. Aristotle wrote even more voluminously than Plato and on a greater variety of subjects. His principal works include treatises on logic, metaphysics, rhetoric, ethics, natural sciences, and politics.

Aristotle compared with Plato and Socrates

Though Aristotle was as much interested as Plato and Socrates in absolute knowledge and eternal standards, his philosophy differed from theirs in several outstanding respects. To begin with, he had a higher regard for the concrete and the practical. In contrast with Plato, the aesthete, and Socrates, who declared he could learn nothing from trees and stones, Aristotle was an empirical scientist with a compelling interest in biology, medicine, and astronomy. Moreover, he was less inclined than his predecessors to a spiritual outlook. And lastly, he did not share their strong aristocratic sympathies.

Aristotle's conception of the universe

Aristotle agreed with Plato that universals, Ideas (or forms as he called them), are real, and that knowledge derived from the senses is limited and inaccurate. But he refused to go along with his teacher in ascribing an independent existence to universals and in reducing material things to pale reflections of their spiritual patterns. On the contrary, he asserted that form and matter are of equal importance; both are eternal, and neither can exist inseparable from the other. It is the union of the two which gives to the universe its essential character. Forms are the causes of all things; they are the purposive forces that shape the world of matter into the infinitely varied objects and orga-

---

[3] So called from the grove of Academus, where Plato and his disciples met to discuss philosophic problems.

nisms around us. All evolution, both cosmic and organic, results from the interaction of form and matter upon each other. Thus the presence of the form *man* in the human embryo molds and directs the development of the latter until it ultimately evolves as a human being. Aristotle's philosophy may be regarded as halfway between the spiritualism and transcendentalism of Plato, on the one hand, and the mechanistic materialism of the atomists on the other. His conception of the universe was *teleological*—that is, governed by purpose; but he refused to regard the spiritual as completely overshadowing its material embodiment.

That Aristotle should have conceived of God primarily as a First Cause is no more than we should expect from the dominance of the scientific attitude in his philosophy. Aristotle's God was simply the Prime Mover, the original source of the purposive motion contained in the forms. In no sense was he a personal God, for his nature was pure intelligence, devoid of all feelings, will, or desire. Aristotle seems to have left no place in his religious scheme for individual immortality: all the functions of the soul, except the creative reason which is not individual at all, are dependent upon the body and perish with it.

Aristotle's religious doctrines

Aristotle's ethical philosophy was less ascetic than Plato's. He did not regard the body as the prison of the soul, nor did he believe that physical appetites are necessarily evil in themselves. He taught that the highest good consists in self-realization, that is, in the exercise of that part of man's nature which most truly distinguishes him as a human being. Self-realization would therefore be identical with the life of reason. But the life of reason is dependent upon the proper combination of physical and mental conditions. The body must be kept in good health and the emotions under adequate control. The solution is to be found in the *golden mean,* in preserving a balance between excessive indulgence on the one hand and ascetic denial on the other. This was simply a reaffirmation of the characteristic Hellenic ideal of *sophrosyne,* "nothing too much."

Aristotle's ethical philosophy of the golden mean

Although Aristotle included in his *Politics* much descriptive and analytical material on the structure and functions of government, he dealt primarily with the broader aspects of political theory. He considered the state as the supreme institution for the promotion of the good life, and he was therefore vitally interested in its origin and development and in the best forms it could be made to assume. Declaring that man is by nature a political animal, he denied that the state is an artificial product of the ambitions of the few or of the desires of the many. On the contrary, he asserted that it is rooted in the instincts of man himself, and that civilized life outside of its limits is impossible. He considered the best state to be neither a monarchy, an aristocracy, nor a democracy, but a *polity*—which he defined as a commonwealth intermediate between oligarchy and democracy. Essentially it would be a state under the control of the middle class, but Aristotle intended to make sure that the members of that class would be fairly numerous,

The golden mean applied to politics

for he advocated measures to prevent the concentration of wealth. He defended the institution of private property, but he opposed the heaping up of riches beyond what is necessary for intelligent living. He recommended that the government should provide the poor with money to buy small farms or to "make a beginning in trade and husbandry" and thus promote their prosperity and self-respect.

Hellenic science

Contrary to a popular belief, the period of Hellenic civilization, strictly speaking, was not a great age of science. The vast majority of the scientific achievements commonly thought of as Greek were made during the Hellenistic period, when the culture was no longer predominantly Hellenic but a mixture of Hellenic and Near-Eastern. The interests of the Greeks in the Periclean age and in the century that followed were chiefly speculative and artistic; they were not deeply concerned with material comforts or with mastery of the physical universe. Consequently, with the exception of some important developments in mathematics, biology, and medicine, scientific progress was relatively slight.

Mathematics

The founder of Greek mathematics was apparently Thales of Miletus, who is supposed to have originated several theorems which were later included in the geometry of Euclid. Perhaps more significant was the work of the Pythagoreans, who developed an elaborate theory of numbers, classifying them into various categories, such as odd, even, prime, composite, perfect, and so forth. They are also supposed to have discovered the theory of proportion and to have proved for the first time that the sum of the three angles of any triangle is equal to two right angles. But the most famous of their achievements was the discovery of the theorem attributed to Pythagoras himself: the square of the hypotenuse of any right-angled triangle is equal to the sum of the squares on the other two sides.

Biology

The first of the Greeks to manifest an interest in biology was the philosopher Anaximander, who developed a crude theory of organic evolution based upon the principle of survival through progressive adaptations to the environment. The earliest ancestral animals, he asserted, lived in the sea, which originally covered the whole face of the earth. As the waters receded, some organisms were able to adjust themselves to their new environment and became land animals. The final product of this evolutionary process was man himself. The real founder of the science of biology, however, was Aristotle. Devoting many years of his life to painstaking study of the structure, habits, and growth of animals, he revealed many facts which were not destined to be discovered anew until the seventeenth century or later. The metamorphoses of various insects, the reproductive habits of the eel, the embryological development of the dog-fish—these are only samples of the amazing extent of his knowledge. Unfortunately he committed some errors. He denied the sexuality of plants, and although he subscribed to the general theory of evolution, he believed in the spontaneous generation of certain species of worms and insects.

Greek medicine also had its origin with the philosophers. A pioneer was Empedocles, exponent of the theory of the four elements (earth, air, fire, and water). He discovered that blood flows to and from the heart, and that the pores of the skin supplement the work of the respiratory passages in breathing. More important was the work of Hippocrates of Cos in the fifth and fourth centuries. By general consensus he is regarded as the father of medicine. He dinned into the ears of his pupils the doctrine that "Every disease has a natural cause, and without natural causes, nothing ever happens." In addition, by his methods of careful study and comparison of symptoms he laid the foundations for clinical medicine. He discovered the phenomenon of crisis in disease and improved the practice of surgery. Though he had a wide knowledge of drugs, his chief reliances in treatment were diet and rest. The main fact to his discredit was his development of the theory of the four humors—the notion that illness is due to excessive amounts of yellow bile, black bile, blood, and phlegm in the system. The practice of bleeding the patient was the regrettable outgrowth of this theory.

Generally the most common medium of literary expression in the formative age of a people is the epic of heroic deeds. The most famous of the Greek epics, the *Iliad* and the *Odyssey,* were put into written form at the end of the Dark Ages and commonly attributed to Homer. The first, which deals with the Trojan War, has its theme in the wrath of Achilles; the second describes the wanderings and return of Odysseus. Both have supreme literary merit in their carefully woven plots, in the realism of their character portrayals, and in their mastery of the full range of emotional intensity. They exerted an almost incalculable influence upon later writers. Their style and language inspired the fervid emotional poetry of the sixth century, and they were an unfailing source of plots and themes for the great tragedians of the Golden Age of the fifth century.

The three centuries which followed the Dark Ages were distinguished, as we have already seen, by tremendous social changes. The

Medicine

The Homeric epics

Interior of a Greek Cup. Depicted is the friendship of leading characters from the *Iliad:* Patroklus and Achilles. Here Achilles is bandaging Patroklus's wounds.

rural pattern of life gave way to an urban society of steadily increasing complexity. The founding of colonies and the growth of commerce provided new interests and new habits of living. Individuals hitherto submerged rose to a consciousness of their power and importance. It was inevitable that these changes should be reflected in new forms of literature, especially of a more personal type. The first to be developed was the elegy, which was probably intended to be declaimed rather than sung to the accompaniment of music. Elegies varied in theme from individual reactions toward love to the idealism of patriots and reformers. Generally, however, they were devoted to melancholy reflection on the disillusionments of life or to bitter lament over loss of prestige. Outstanding among the authors of elegiac verse was Solon the legislator.

In the sixth century and the early part of the fifth, the elegy was gradually displaced by the lyric, which derives its name from the fact that it was sung to the music of the lyre. The new type of poetry was particularly well adapted to the expression of passionate feelings, the violent loves and hates engendered by the strife of classes. It was employed for other purposes also. Both Alcaeus and Sappho, the latter a woman poet from the island of Lesbos, used it to describe the poignant beauty of love, the delicate grace of spring, and the starlit splendor of a summer night. Meanwhile other poets developed the choral lyric, intended to express the feelings of the community rather than the sentiments of any one individual. Greatest of all the writers of this group was Pindar of Thebes, who wrote during the first half of the fifth century. The lyrics of Pindar took the form of odes celebrating the victories of athletes and the glories of Hellenic civilization.

The supreme literary achievement of the Greeks was the tragic drama. Like so many of their other great works, it had its roots in religion. At the festivals dedicated to the worship of Dionysus, the god of spring and of wine, a chorus of men dressed as satyrs, or goat-men, sang and danced around an altar, enacting the various parts of a dithyramb or choral lyric that related the story of the god's career. In time a leader came to be separated from the chorus to recite the main parts of the story. The true drama was born about the beginning of the fifth century when Aeschylus introduced a second "actor" and relegated the chorus to the background. The name "tragedy," which came to be applied to this drama, was probably derived from the Greek word *tragos* meaning "goat."

Greek tragedy stands out in marked contrast to the tragedies of Shakespeare or modern playwrights. There was, first of all, little action presented on the stage; the main business of the actors was to recite the incidents of a plot which was already familiar to the audience, for the story was drawn from popular legends. Secondly, Greek tragedy devoted little attention to the study of complicated individual personality. There was no development of personal character as

Greek Theater in Epidauros. The construction, to take advantage of the slope of the hill, and the arrangement of the stage are of particular interest. Greek dramas were invariably presented in the open air.

shaped by the vicissitudes of a long career. Those involved in the plot were scarcely individuals at all, but types. On the stage they wore masks to disguise any characteristics which might serve to distinguish them too sharply from the rest of humanity. In addition, Greek tragedies differed from the modern variety in having as their theme the conflict between the individual and the universe, not the clash between personalities, or the internal conflicts of one person. The tragic fate that befell the main characters in these plays was external to individuals. It was brought on by the fact that someone had committed a crime against society, or against the gods, thereby offending the moral scheme of the universe. Punishment must follow in order to balance the scale of justice. Finally, the purpose of Greek tragedies was not merely to depict suffering and to interpret human actions, but to purify the emotions of the audience by representing the triumph of justice.

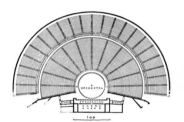

Epidauros Plan

As already indicated, the first of the tragic dramatists was Aeschylus (525–456 B.C.). Though he is known to have written about eighty plays, only seven have survived in complete form, among them *The Persians, Seven against Thebes, Prometheus Bound,* and a trilogy known as *The Oresteia.* Guilt and punishment is the recurrent theme of nearly all of them. The second of the leading tragedians whose works have survived, Sophocles (496–406), is often considered the greatest. His style was more polished and his philosophy more profound than that of his predecessor. He was the author of over a hundred plays. More than any other writer in Greek history, he personified the Hellenic ideal of "nothing too much." His attitude was distinguished by love of harmony and peace, intelligent respect for democracy, and pro-

Aeschylus and Sophocles

found sympathy for human weakness. The most famous of his plays now extant are *Oedipus Rex, Antigone,* and *Electra.*

The work of the last of the great tragedians, Euripides (480–406), reflects a far different spirit. He was a skeptic, an individualist, a humanist, who took delight in ridiculing the ancient myths and the "sacred cows" of his time. An embittered pessimist who suffered from the barbs of his conservative critics, he loved to humble the proud in his plays and to exalt the lowly. He was the first to give the ordinary man, even the beggar and the peasant, a place in the drama. Euripides is also noted for his sympathy for the slave, for his condemnation of war, and for his protests against the exclusion of women from social and intellectual life. Because of his humanism, his tendency to portray men as they actually were (or even a little worse), and his introduction of the love motif into drama, he is often considered a modernist. It must be remembered, however, that in other respects his plays were perfectly consistent with the Hellenic model. They did not exhibit the evolution of individual character or the conflict of egos to any more notable extent than did the works of Sophocles or Aeschylus. Nevertheless, he has been called the most tragic of the Greek dramatists because he dealt with situations having analogues in real life. Among the best-known tragedies of Euripides are *Alcestis, Medea,* and *The Trojan Women.*

Hellenic comedy, in common with tragedy, appears to have grown out of the Dionysiac festivals, but it did not attain full development until late in the fifth century B.C. Its outstanding representative was Aristophanes (448?–380?), a somewhat coarse and belligerent aristocrat who lived in Athens. Most of his plays were written to satirize the political and intellectual ideals of the radical democracy of his time. In *The Knights* he pilloried the incompetent and greedy politicians for their reckless adventures in imperialism. In *The Frogs* he lampooned Euripides for the innovations the latter had made in the drama. *The Clouds* he reserved for ridicule of the Sophists, ignorantly or maliciously classifying Socrates as one of them. While he was undoubtedly a clever poet with a mastery of subtle humor and imaginative skill, his ideas were founded largely upon prejudice. He is deserving of much credit, however, for his sharp criticisms of the policies of the warhawks of Athens during the struggle with Sparta. Though written as a farce, his *Lysistrata* cleverly pointed a way—however infeasible—to the termination of any war: in this play wives refuse to have sexual relations with their husbands until the latter agree to make peace with their foreign enemies.

No account of Greek literature would be complete without some mention of the two great historians of the Golden Age. Herodotus, the "father of history" (c. 484–c. 420), was a native of Halicarnassus in Asia Minor. He traveled extensively through the Persian empire, Egypt, Greece, and Italy, collecting a multitude of interesting data about various peoples. His famous account of the great war between the Greeks and the Persians included so much background that the work seems almost a history of the world. He regarded that war as an epic struggle between East and West, with Zeus giving victory to the Greeks against a mighty host of barbarians.

If Herodotus deserves to be called the father of history, much more does his younger contemporary, Thucydides (c. 460–c. 400), deserve to be considered the founder of scientific history. Influenced by the skepticism and practicality of the Sophists, Thucydides chose to work on the basis of carefully sifted evidence, rejecting opinion, legends, and hearsay. The subject of his *History* was the war between Sparta and Athens, which he described scientifically and dispassionately, emphasizing the complexity of causes which led to the fateful clash. His aim was to present an accurate record which could be studied with profit by statesmen and generals of all time, and it must be said that he was in full measure successful. If there were any defects in his historical method, they consisted in overemphasizing political factors to the neglect of the social and economic and in failing to consider the importance of emotions in history. He also had a prejudice against the democratic factions in Athens after the death of Pericles.

Thucydides

7. THE MEANING OF GREEK ART

Art as well as literature reflected the basic character of Hellenic civilization. The Greek was essentially a materialist who conceived of the world in physical terms. Plato and the followers of the mystic religions were, of course, exceptions, but few other Greeks had much interest in a universe of spiritual realities. It would be natural therefore to find that the material emblems of architecture and sculpture should exemplify best the ideals the Greek held before him.

Greek art as an expression of the Greek spirit

What did Greek art express? Above all, it symbolized humanism—the glorification of man as the most important creature in the universe. Though much of the sculpture depicted gods, and also goddesses, this did not detract in the slightest from its humanistic quality. The Greek deities existed for the benefit of man; in glorifying them he thus glorified himself. Both architecture and sculpture embodied the ideals of balance, harmony, order, and moderation. Anarchy and excess were abhorrent to the mind of the Greek, but so was absolute repression. Consequently, Greek art exhibited qualities of simplicity and dignified restraint—free from decorative extravagance, on the one hand, and from restrictive conventions on the other. Moreover, Greek art was an expression of the national life. Its purpose was not merely aesthetic but political: to symbolize the pride of the people in their city and to enhance their consciousness of unity. The Parthenon at Athens, for example, was the temple of Athena, the protecting goddess who

The ideals embodied in Greek art

See color plates following page 96

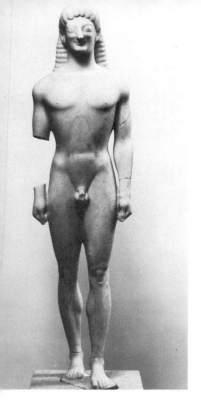

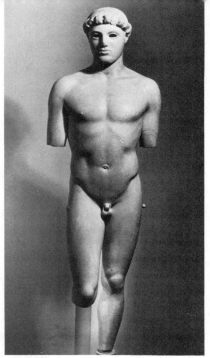

Apollo of Tenea; Apollo of Piombino; "The Critian Boy." These three statues, dating from about 560, 500, and 480 B.C. respectively, display the progressive "unfreezing" of Greek statuary art. The first stiff and symmetrical statue is imitative of Egyptian sculpture (see statue of the Pharoah Mycerinus, p. 38 above). Roughly half a century later it is succeeded by a figure which begins to display motion, as if awakening from a sleep of centuries in a fairy tale. The last figure introduces genuine naturalism in its delicate twists and depiction of the subject's weight resting on one leg.

Greek art compared with that of later peoples

presided over the corporate life of the state. In providing her with a beautiful shrine which she might frequently visit, the Athenians were giving evidence of their love for their city and their hope for its continuing welfare.

The art of the Greeks differed from that of nearly every people since their time in an interesting variety of ways. Like most of the tragedies of Aeschylus and Sophocles, it was universal. It included few portraits of personalities either in sculpture or in painting. (Most of the portrait busts commonly considered Greek really belong to the Hellenistic Age.) The human beings depicted were generally types, not individuals. Again, Greek art differed from that of most later peoples in its ethical purpose. It was not art for the sake of mere decoration or for the expression of the artist's individual philosophy, but a medium for the ennoblement of humanity. This does not mean that it was didactic in the sense that its merit was determined by the moral lesson it taught, but rather that it was supposed to exemplify qualities of living essentially artistic in themselves. The Athenian, at least, drew no sharp distinction between the ethical and aesthetic spheres; the beautiful and the good were really identical. True morality, therefore, consisted in rational living, in the avoidance of grossness, disgusting excesses, and other forms of conduct aesthetically offensive. Finally, Greek art may be contrasted with most later forms in the fact that it was not "naturalistic." Although the utmost attention was given to the depiction of beautiful bodies, this had little to do with fidelity to nature. The Greek was not interested in interpreting nature for its own sake, but in expressing *human* ideals.

The history of Greek art divides itself naturally into three great periods. The first, which can be called the archaic period, covered the seventh and sixth centuries. During the greater part of this age sculpture was dominated by Egyptian influence, as can be seen in the frontality and rigidity of the statues, with their square shoulders and one foot slightly advanced. Toward the end, however, these conventions were thrown aside. The chief architectural styles also had their origin in this period, and several crude temples were built. The second period, which occupied the fifth century, witnessed the full perfection of both architecture and sculpture. The art of this time was completely idealistic. During the fourth century, the last period of Hellenic art, architecture lost some of its balance and simplicity and sculpture assumed new characteristics. It came to reflect more clearly the reactions of the individual artist, to incorporate more realism, and to lose some of its quality as an expression of civic pride.

The three periods of Greek art

For all its artistic excellence, Greek temple architecture was one of the simplest of structural forms. Its essential elements were really only five in number: (1) the cella or nucleus of the building, which was a rectangular chamber to house the statue of the god; (2) the columns, which formed the porch and surrounded the cella; (3) the entablature, which rested upon the columns and supported the roof; (4) the gabled roof itself; and (5) the pediment or triangular section under the gable of the roof. Two different architectural styles were developed, representing modifications of certain of these elements. The more common was the Doric, which made use of a rather heavy, sharply fluted column surmounted by a plain capital. The other, the Ionic, had more slender and more graceful columns with flat flutings, a triple base, and a scroll or volute capital. The so-called Corinthian style, which was chiefly Hellenistic, differed from the Ionic primarily

Greek architecture

Details of the Three Orders of Greek Architecture

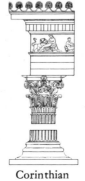

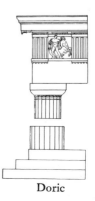

Corinthian   Ionic   Doric

The Parthenon. The largest and most famous of Athenian temples, the Parthenon is considered the classic example of Doric architecture. Its columns were made more graceful by tapering them in a slight curve toward the top. Its friezes and pediments were decorated with lifelike sculptures of prancing horses (see below), fighting giants, and benign and confident deities.

Parthenon Frieze

in being more ornate. The three styles differed also in their treatment of the entablature. In the Ionic style it was left almost plain. In the Doric and Corinthian styles it bore sculptured reliefs. The Parthenon, the best example of Greek architecture, was essentially a Doric building, but it reflected some of the grace and subtlety of Ionic influence.

According to the prevailing opinion among his contemporaries, Greek sculpture attained its acme of development in the work of Phidias (c. 500–c. 432). His masterpieces were the statue of Athena in the Parthenon and the statue of Zeus in the Temple of Olympian Zeus. In addition, he designed and supervised the execution of the Parthenon reliefs. The main qualities of his work are grandeur of conception, patriotism, proportion, dignity, and restraint. Nearly all of his figures are idealized representations of deities and mythological creatures in human form. The second most renowned fifth-century sculptor was Myron, noted for his statue of the discus thrower and for his glorification of other athletic types. The names of three great sculptors in the fourth century have come down to us. The most gifted of them was Praxiteles, renowned for his portrayal of humanized deities with slender, graceful bodies and countenances of philosophic repose. The best known of his works is the statue of Hermes with the infant Dionysus. His older contemporary, Scopas, gained distinction as an emotional sculptor. One of his most successful creations was the statue of a religious ecstatic, a worshiper of Dionysus, in a condition of mystic frenzy. At the end of the century Lysippus introduced even stronger qualities of realism and individualism into sculpture. He was the first great master of the realistic portrait as a study of personal character.

8. ATHENIAN LIFE IN THE GOLDEN AGE

The population of Athens in the fifth and fourth centuries was divided into three distinct groups: the citizens, the metics, and the slaves. The citizens, who numbered at the most about 160,000, included only those males born of citizen parents, except for the few who were occasionally enfranchised by special law. The metics, who probably did not exceed a total of 35,000, were resident aliens, chiefly non-Athenian Greeks. Save for the fact that they had no political privileges and generally were not permitted to own land, male metics had equal opportunities with citizens. They could engage in any occupation they desired and participate in any social or intellectual activities. Contrary to a popular tradition, the slaves in Athens were never a majority of the population. Their maximum number does not seem to have exceeded 110,000. Urban slaves, at least, were very well treated and were sometimes rewarded for faithful service by being set free. The males could work for wages and own property, and some of them

Athenian classes

Left: *The Discobolus or Discus Thrower of Myron.* The statue reflects the glorification of the human body characteristic of Athens in the Golden Age. Now in the Vatican Museum. Right: *Hermes with the Infant Dionysus, by Praxiteles, Fourth Century B.C.* Original in the Olympia Museum, Greece.

held responsible positions as minor public officials and as managers of banks. The treatment of slaves who worked in the mines, however, was often cruel.

Life in Athens stands out in rather sharp contrast to that in most other civilizations. One of its leading features was the amazing degree of social and economic equality that prevailed among all the inhabitants. Although there were many who were poor, there were few who were very rich. Nearly everyone, whether citizen, metic, or slave, ate the same kind of food, wore the same kind of clothing, and participated in the same kind of amusement. This substantial equality was enforced in part by the system of *liturgies,* which were services to the state rendered by wealthy men, chiefly in the form of contributions to support the drama, equip the navy, or provide for the poor.

A second outstanding characteristic of Athenian life was its poverty in comforts and luxuries. Part of this was a result of the low income of the mass of the people. Teachers, sculptors, masons, carpenters, and common laborers all received the same standard wage of one drachma per day. Part of it may have been a consequence also of the mild climate, which made possible a life of simplicity. But whatever the cause, the fact remains that, in comparison with modern standards, the Athenians endured an exceedingly impoverished existence. They knew nothing of such common commodities as watches, soap, newspapers, cotton cloth, sugar, tea, or coffee. Their beds had no springs, their houses had no drains, and their food consisted chiefly of barley cakes, onions, and fish, washed down with diluted wine. From the standpoint of clothing they were no better off. A rectangular piece of cloth wrapped around the body and fastened with pins at the shoulders and with a rope around the waist served as the main garment. A larger piece was draped around the body as an extra garment for outdoor wear. No one wore either stockings or socks, and few had any footgear except sandals.

But lack of comforts and luxuries was a matter of little consequence to the Athenian citizen. He was totally unable to regard these as the most important things in life. His aim was to live as interestingly and contentedly as possible without spending all his days in grinding toil for the sake of a little more comfort for his family. Nor was he interested in piling up riches as a source of power or prestige. What each citizen really wanted was a small farm or business that would provide him with a reasonable income and at the same time allow him an abundance of leisure for politics, for gossip in the marketplace, and for intellectual or artistic activities if he had the talent to enjoy them.

It is frequently supposed that the Athenian was too lazy or too snobbish to work hard for luxury and security. But this was not quite the case. True, there were some occupations in which he would not engage because he considered them degrading or destructive of moral freedom. He would not break his back digging silver or copper out of

Young Men Baiting a Dog and Cat. This Athenian relief from about 510 B.C. depicts an odd form of leisure-time amusement.

a mine; such work was fit only for slaves. On the other hand, there is plenty of evidence to show that the great majority of Athenian citizens did not look with disdain upon manual labor. Most of them worked on their farms or in their shops as independent craftsmen.

In spite of expansion of trade and increase in population, the economic organization of Athenian society remained comparatively simple. Agriculture and commerce were by far the most important enterprises. Even in Pericles's day the majority of the citizens still lived in the country. Industry was not highly developed. Very few examples of large-scale production are on record, and those chiefly in the manufacture of pottery and implements of war. The largest establishment that ever existed was apparently a shield factory owned by a metic and employing 120 slaves. No other was more than half as large. The enterprises which absorbed the most labor were the mines, but they were owned by the state and were leased in sections to petty contractors to be worked by slaves. The bulk of industry was carried on in small shops owned by individual craftsmen who produced their wares directly to the order of the consumer.

The basic economic activities

Religion underwent some notable changes in the Golden Age of the fifth and fourth centuries. The primitive polytheism and anthropomorphism of the Homeric myths were largely supplanted by a belief in one God as the creator and sustainer of the moral law. Such a doctrine was taught by many of the philosophers, by the poet Pindar, and by the dramatists Aeschylus and Sophocles. Other significant consequences flowed from the mystery cults. These new forms of religion first became popular in the sixth century because of the craving for an emotional faith to make up for the disappointments of life. One was the Orphic cult, which revolved around the myth of the death and resurrection of Dionysus. Another, the Eleusinian cult, had as its central

Changes in religion

theme the abduction of Persephone by Hades, god of the nether world, and her ultimate redemption by Demeter, the great Earth Mother. Both of these cults had as their original purpose the promotion of the life-giving powers of nature, but in time they came to be fraught with a much deeper significance. They expressed to their followers the ideas of vicarious atonement, salvation in an afterlife, and ecstatic union with the divine. Although entirely inconsistent with the spirit of the ancient religion, they made a powerful appeal to certain classes and were largely responsible for the spread of the belief in personal immortality. The more thoughtful Greeks, however, seem to have persisted in their adherence to the worldly, optimistic, and mechanical faith of their ancestors and to have shown little concern about a conviction of sin or a desire for salvation in a life to come.

The family in Athens in the Golden Age

It remains to consider briefly the position of the family in Athens in the fifth and fourth centuries. Though marriage was still an important institution for the procreation of children who would become citizens of the state, there is reason to believe that family life had declined. Men of the more prosperous classes, at least, now spent the greater part of their time away from their families. Wives were relegated to an inferior position and required to remain secluded in their homes. Their place as social and intellectual companions for their husbands was taken by alien women, the *hetaerae,* many of whom were highly cultured natives of the Ionian cities of Asia Minor. Marriage itself assumed the character of a political and economic arrangement devoid of romantic elements. Men married wives so as to ensure that at least some of their children would be legitimate and in order to obtain property in the form of a dowry. It was important also, of course, to have someone to care for the household. But husbands did not consider their wives as their equals and did not appear in public with them or encourage their participation in any form of social or intellectual activity.

9. THE GREEK ACHIEVEMENT AND ITS SIGNIFICANCE FOR US

The magnitude of the Greek achievement

No historian would deny that the achievement of the Greeks was one of the most remarkable in the history of the world. With no great expanse of fertile soil or abundance of mineral resources, they succeeded in developing a higher and more varied civilization than any of the most richly favored nations of the Near East. With only a limited cultural inheritance from the past to build upon as a foundation, they produced intellectual and artistic achievements which have served ever since as models of perfection for the culture of the West. It seems reasonable to conclude also that the Greeks achieved a more normal and more rational mode of living than most other peoples who strutted and fretted their hour upon this planet. The infrequency of brutal crimes and the contentment with simple amusements and modest wealth all point to a comparatively happy and satisfied existence.

It is necessary to be on our guard, however, against uncritical judgments that are sometimes expressed in reference to the achievement of the Greeks. We must not assume that all of the natives of Hellas were as cultured, wise, and free as the citizens of Athens and of the Ionian states across the Aegean. The Spartans, the Arcadians, the Thessalians, and probably the majority of the Boeotians remained much less culturally advanced. Further, the Athenian civilization itself was not without its defects. It permitted some exploitation of the weak, especially of the slaves who toiled in the mines. It was based upon a principle of racial exclusiveness which reckoned every man a foreigner whose parents were not both Athenians, and consequently denied political rights to the majority of the inhabitants. It was also characterized by the overt repression of the female members of the society. Its statecraft was not sufficiently enlightened to avoid the pitfalls of imperialism and even of aggressive war. Finally, the attitude of its citizens was not always tolerant and just. Socrates was put to death for his opinions, and two other philosophers, Anaxagoras and Protagoras, were forced to leave the city. It must be conceded, however, that the record of the Athenians for tolerance was better than that of most other nations, both ancient and modern. There was probably more freedom of expression in Athens during the war with Sparta than there was in the United States during World War I.

Undesirable features of Greek life

Nor is it true that the Hellenic influence has really been as great as is commonly supposed. No well-informed student could accept the sentimental verdict of Shelley: "We are all Greeks; our laws, our literature, our religion, our arts have their roots in Greece." Our laws do not really have their roots in Greece but chiefly in Hellenistic and Roman sources. Much of our poetry is undoubtedly Greek in inspiration, but such is not the case with most of our prose literature. Our religion is no more than partly Greek; except as it was influenced by Plato, Aristotle, and the Romans, it reflects primarily the spirit of the Near East. Even our arts derive from other sources almost as much as from Greece. Actually, modern civilization has been the result of the convergence of numerous influences coming from many different places and periods of time.

Hellenic influence sometimes exaggerated

In spite of all this, the Hellenic adventure was of profound significance for the history of the world. For the Greeks were the founders of nearly all those ideals we commonly think of as peculiar to the West. The civilizations of the ancient Near East, with the exception, to a certain extent, of the Hebrew and Egyptian, were dominated by absolutism, supernaturalism, ecclesiasticism, the denial of both body and mind, and the subjection of the individual to the group. It is noteworthy that the Greek word for freedom—*eleutheria*—cannot be

The influence of the Greeks on the West

The Acropolis Today. Occupying the commanding position is the Parthenon. To the left is the Erechtheum with its Porch of the Maidens facing the Parthenon.

translated into any ancient Near-Eastern language, not even Hebrew. The typical political regime of the Near East was that of an absolute monarch supported by a powerful priesthood. Culture in the Near-Eastern empires served mainly as an instrument to magnify the power of the state and to enhance the prestige of rulers and priests.

Contrast of Greek and Near-Eastern ideals

By contrast, the civilization of Greece, notably in its Athenian form, was founded upon ideals of freedom, optimism, secularism, rationalism, the glorification of both body and mind, and a high regard for the dignity and worth of the individual man. Insofar as the individual was subjected at all, his subjection was to the rule of the majority. This, of course, was not always good, especially in times of crisis, when the majority might be swayed by prejudice. Religion was worldly and practical, serving the interests of human beings. Worship of the gods was a means for the ennoblement of man. As opposed to the ecclesiasticism of the Near East, the Greeks had no organized priesthood at all. They kept their priests in the background and refused under any circumstances to allow them to define dogma or to govern the realm of intellect. In addition, they excluded them from control over the sphere of morality. The culture of the Greeks was the first to be based upon the primacy of intellect—upon the supremacy of the spirit of free inquiry. There was no subject they feared to investigate, or any question they regarded as excluded from the province of reason. To an extent never before realized, mind was supreme over faith, logic and science over superstition.

The tragedy of Hellenic history

The supreme tragedy of the Greeks was, of course, their failure to solve the problem of political conflict. To a large degree, this conflict was the product of social and cultural dissimilarities. Because of different geographic and economic conditions the Greek city-states developed at an uneven pace. Some went forward rapidly to high levels of cultural superiority, while others lagged behind and made little or no intellectual progress. The consequences were discord and suspicion, which gave rise eventually to hatred and fear. Though some of the more advanced thinkers made efforts to propagate the notion that the Hellenes were one people who should reserve their contempt for non-Hellenes, or "barbarians," the conception never became part of a national ethos. Athenians hated Spartans, and vice versa, just as vehemently as they hated Lydians or Persians. Not even the danger of Asian conquest was sufficient to dispel the distrust and antagonism of Greeks for one another. The war that finally broke out between Athenians and Spartans sealed the doom of Hellenic civilization just as effectively as could ever have resulted from foreign conquest.

SELECTED READINGS

• *Items so designated are available in paperback editions.*

• Andrewes, A., *The Greeks,* New York, 1967. An excellent, up-to-date account of archaic and classical Greek history from about 750 to 350 B.C.

• ———, *The Greek Tyrants,* New York, 1956.

• Boardman, J., *Greek Art,* New York, 1964.

———, *The Greeks Overseas,* Baltimore, 1964. The standard treatment of Greek colonization.

Bowra, C. M., *Ancient Greek Literature,* New York, 1960. Bowra is the modern master of this field.

Burn, A. R., *The Lyric Age of Greece,* New York, 1961. A lively introduction to the seventh and sixth centuries.

Dodds, E. R., *The Greeks and the Irrational,* Berkeley, Calif., 1963. A novel approach to classical Greek culture.

Dover, K. J., *Greek Homosexuality,* Cambridge, Mass., 1978. A serious analysis of a basic aspect of classical Greek life.

• Ehrenberg, V., *From Solon to Socrates,* New York, 1967. An excellent treatment of early Athenian history by one of the twentieth-century's leading authorities.

• ———, *The Greek State,* New York, 1960.

Farrington, B., *Greek Science,* rev. ed., Baltimore, 1961.

Finley, M. I., *The Ancient Greeks: An Introduction to Their Life and Thought,* New York, 1963. An expert brief introduction to the Greeks.

• ———, *Early Greece: The Bronze and Archaic Ages,* New York, 1970. The best recent survey of the earlier periods.

———, *The World of Odysseus,* rev. ed., New York, 1965. Attempts to use the Homeric poems as a guide to Dark Ages Greece.

• Forrest, W. G., *A History of Sparta, 950–152 B.C.,* London, 1968.

• Guthrie, W. K. C., *The Greeks and Their Gods,* Boston, 1965.

Jones, A. H. M., *Athenian Democracy,* New York, 1957. Concentrates on actual political practice.

• Kitto, H. D. F., *The Greeks,* Baltimore, 1957. A delightfully written, highly personal interpretation.

• Lloyd, G. E. R., *Early Greek Science: Thales to Aristotle,* London, 1970.

Marrou, H. I., *A History of Education in Antiquity*, New York, 1964. A modern classic that covers the entire ancient world.

Meiggs, R., *The Athenian Empire*, Oxford, 1972. The major study of fifth-century Athenian imperialism. A monumental work.

Michell, H., *The Economics of Ancient Greece*, rev. ed., Cambridge, 1956.

• Nilsson, M. P., *A History of Greek Religion*, New York, 1964.

• Pollitt, J. J., *Art and Experience in Classical Greece*, Cambridge, 1972. The best introduction to the social and intellectual forces behind Greek art.

• Pomeroy, Sarah, B., *Goddesses, Whores, Wives, and Slaves: Women in Classical Antiquity*, New York, 1975. The best treatment of the role of women in Greece and Rome. Relies on a variety of source material and covers women of all classes.

Rose, H. J., *A Handbook of Greek Literature*, New York, 1960.

• ———, *A Handbook of Greek Mythology*, sixth ed., New York, 1960.

• Sealey, R., *A History of the Greek City States, ca. 700–338 B.C.*, Berkeley, Calif., 1977. Provocative essays that reconsider older assumptions about Greek political life.

• Sinclair, T. A., *A History of Greek Political Thought*, London, 1951.

Snell, Bruno, *The Discovery of the Mind: The Greek Origins of European Thought*, Cambridge, Mass., 1953. Stimulating essays.

• Starr, C. G., *The Economic and Social Growth of Early Greece: 800–500 B.C.*, New York, 1978. An excellent study of this difficult but important topic.

———, *The Origins of Greek Civilization, 1100–650 B.C.*, New York, 1961. The best detailed treatment of the early periods.

• Zimmern, A. E., *The Greek Commonwealth*, 5th ed., New York, 1931. A classic study, perhaps too uncritical of the Athenians.

SOURCE MATERIALS

Most Greek authors have been translated in the appropriate volumes of the Loeb Classical Library, Harvard University Press.

In addition the following may be helpful:

• Barnstone, Willis, tr., *Greek Lyric Poetry*, New York, 1962.

Kagan, Donald, *Sources in Greek Political Thought*, Glencoe, Ill., 1965.

• Kirk, G. S., and J. E. Raven, *The Presocratic Philosophers*, Cambridge, 1957.

Chapter 9

THE HELLENISTIC
CIVILIZATION

Beauty and virtue and the like are to be honored, if they give pleasure, but
if they do not give pleasure, we must bid them farewell.

—Epicurus, "On the End of Life"

I agree that Alexander was carried away so far as to copy oriental luxury. I
hold that no mighty deeds, not even conquering the whole world, is of
any good unless the man has learned mastery of himself.

—Arrian, *Anabasis of Alexander*

The death of Alexander the Great in 323 B.C. constituted a watershed in the development of world history. Hellenic civilization as it had existed in its prime now came to an end. Of
course, the old institutions and ways of life did not suddenly disappear, but Alexander's career had cut so deeply into the old order that it
was inconceivable that it could be restored intact. The fusion of cultures and intermingling of peoples resulting from Alexander's conquests accomplished the overthrow of many of the ideals the Greeks
had developed in their Golden Age of the fifth and fourth centuries.
Gradually a new pattern of civilization emerged, based upon a mixture
of Greek and Eastern elements. To this new civilization, which lasted
until about the beginning of the Christian era, the name Hellenistic is
most commonly applied.

Though the break between the Hellenic and Hellenistic eras was as
sharp as that between any two other civilizations, it would be a mistake to deny all continuity. The language of the new cultured classes
was predominantly Greek, and even the hordes of people whose heritage was non-Greek considered it desirable to have some Hellenic culture. Hellenic achievements in science provided a foundation for the
great scientific revolution of the Hellenistic Age. Greek emphasis
upon logic was likewise carried over into Hellenistic philosophy,
though the objectives of the latter were in many cases quite different.

A new stage in world history

Comparison of the Hellenistic Age with the Golden Age of Greece

In the spheres of the political, social, and economic the resemblances were few indeed. The classical ideal of democracy was now superseded by despotism perhaps as rigorous as any that Egypt or Persia had ever produced. The Greek city-state survived in some parts of Greece itself, but elsewhere it was replaced by large-scale monarchy, and in the minds of some leaders by notions of a world state. The Hellenic devotion to simplicity and the golden mean gave way to extravagance in the arts and to a love of luxury. In the economic realm there was a growing stress on big business and vigorous competition for profits. In view of these changes it seems valid to conclude that the Hellenistic Age was sufficiently distinct from the Golden Age of Greece to justify its being considered the era of a new civilization.

I. POLITICAL HISTORY AND INSTITUTIONS

The Hellenistic states

When Alexander died in 323 B.C., he left no legitimate heir to succeed him. His nearest male relative was a feeble-minded half-brother. Tradition relates that when his friends requested him on his deathbed to designate a successor, he replied "To the strongest." After his death his highest-ranking generals proceeded to divide the empire among them. Some of the younger commanders contested this arrangement, and a series of wars followed which culminated in the decisive battle of Ipsus in 301 B.C. The result of this battle was a new division among the victors. Seleucus took possession of Persia, Mesopotamia, and Syria; Lysimachus assumed control over Asia Minor and Thrace; Cas-

Alexander in Battle. A scene from a sarcophagus of about 300 B.C. Alexander is shown on horseback at the left.

sander established himself in Macedonia; and Ptolemy added Phoenicia and Palestine to his original domain of Egypt. Twenty years later these four states were reduced to three when Seleucus defeated and killed Lysimachus in battle and appropriated his territory in Asia Minor. In the meantime most of the Greek states had revolted against the attempts of Macedon to extend its power over them. By banding together in defensive leagues several of them succeeded in maintaining their independence for nearly a century. Finally, between 146 and 30 B.C. nearly all of the Hellenistic territory passed under Roman rule.

The dominant form of government in the Hellenistic Age was the despotism of rulers who represented themselves as at least semi-divine. Alexander himself was recognized as a son of God in Egypt and was worshiped as a god in Greece. His most powerful successors, the Seleucid kings in western Asia and the Ptolemies in Egypt, made systematic attempts to deify themselves. A Seleucid monarch, Antiochus IV, adopted the title "Epiphanes" or "God Manifest." The later members of the dynasty of the Ptolemies signed their decrees "Theos" (God) and revived the practice of sister marriage which had been followed by the pharaohs as a means of preserving the divine blood of the royal family from contamination. Only in the kingdom of Macedonia was despotism tempered by a modicum of respect for the liberties of the citizens.

Alexander the Great. Shown here is a silver coin struck in Thrace by King Lysimachus about 300 B.C.

Two other political institutions developed as by-products of Hellenistic civilization: the Achaean and Aetolian Leagues. We have already seen that most of the Greek states rebelled against Macedonian rule following the division of Alexander's empire. The better to preserve their independence, several of these states formed alliances among themselves, which were gradually expanded to become confederate leagues. The organization of these leagues was essentially the same in all cases. Each had a federal council composed of representatives of the member cities with power to enact laws on subjects of general concern. An assembly which all of the citizens in the federated states could attend decided questions of war and peace and elected officials. Executive and military authority was vested in the hands of a general, elected for one year and eligible for reelection only in alternate years. Although these leagues are frequently described as federal states, they were scarcely more than confederacies. The central authority, like the government of the American States under the Articles of Confederation, was dependent upon the local governments for contributions of revenue and troops. Furthermore, the powers delegated to the central government were limited primarily to matters of war and peace, coinage, and weights and measures. The chief significance of these leagues is to be found in the fact that they constituted the nearest approach ever made in Greece to voluntary national union before modern times.

The Achaean and Aetolian Leagues

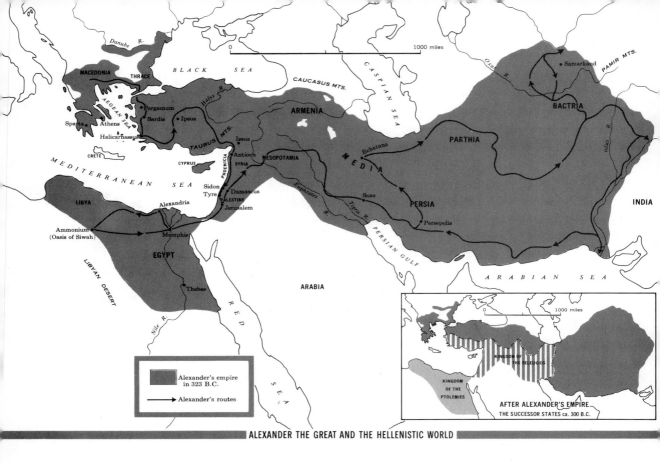

2. SIGNIFICANT ECONOMIC AND SOCIAL DEVELOPMENTS

The economic revolution and its causes

The history of the Hellenistic civilization was marked by economic developments second only in magnitude to the Commercial and Industrial Revolutions of the modern era. Several important causes can be distinguished: (1) the opening up of a vast area of trade from the Indus River to the Nile as a result of the Alexandrian conquests; (2) the rise in prices as a consequence of the release of the enormous Persian hoard of gold and silver into the channels of circulation, resulting in an increase in investment and speculation; and (3) the promotion of trade and industry by governments as a means of augmenting the revenues of the state. The net result was the growth of a system of large-scale production, trade, and finance, with the state as the principal entrepreneur.

The concentration of land ownership

Agriculture was as profoundly affected by the new developments as any other branch of the economic life. The most striking phenomena were the concentration of holdings of land and the degradation of the agricultural population. One of the first things the successors of Alexander did was to confiscate the estates of the chief landowners and add them to the royal domain. The lands thus acquired were either granted to the favorites of the king or leased to tenants under an arrangement calculated to ensure an abundant income for the crown. The tenants were generally forbidden to leave the lands they cultivated until after the harvest and were not allowed to dispose of their grain until after the ruler had had a chance to sell the share he received as rent at the highest price the market would bring. When some of the tenants were on strike or attempted to run away, they were all bound to the soil as hereditary serfs. Many of the small independent farmers also became serfs when they got into debt as a result of inability to compete with large-scale production.

In an effort to make all of the resources of the state contribute to the profit of the government, the rulers of Egypt and the Seleucid Empire promoted and regulated industry and trade. The Ptolemies established factories and shops in nearly every village and town to be owned and operated by the government for its own financial benefit. In addition, they assumed control over all of the enterprises that were privately owned, fixing the prices the owners could charge and manipulating markets to the advantage of the crown. A similar plan of regimentation for industry, although not on quite so ambitious a scale, was enforced by the Seleucid rulers of western Asia. Trade was left by both of these governments very largely in private hands, but it was heavily taxed and regulated in such a way as to make sure that an ample share of the profits went to the ruler. Every facility was provided by the government for the encouragement of new trading ventures. Harbors were improved, warships were sent out to police the seas, and roads and canals were built. Moreover, the Ptolemies employed famous geographers to discover new routes to distant lands and thereby gain access to valuable markets. As a result of such methods Egypt developed a flourishing commerce in the widest variety of products. Into the port of Alexandria came spices from Arabia, copper from Cyprus, gold from Ethiopia and India, tin from Britain, elephants and ivory from Nubia, silver from the northern Aegean and Spain, fine carpets from Asia Minor, and even silk from China. Profits for the government and for some of the merchants were often as high as 20 or 30 percent.

State regimentation of industry and trade

Further evidence of the significant economic development of the Hellenistic Age is to be found in the growth of finance. An international money economy, based upon gold and silver coins, now became general throughout the Near East. Banks, usually owned by the government, developed as the chief institutions of credit for business ventures of every description. Speculation, cornering of markets, intense competition, the growth of large business houses, and the development of insurance and advertising were other significant phenomena of this remarkable age.

The growth of finance

According to the available evidence, the Hellenistic Age, during the first two centuries at least, was a period of prosperity. Although

Hellenistic Coins. Obverse and reverse sides of the silver tetradrachma of Macedon, 336–323 B.C. Objects of common use from this period often show as much beauty of design as formal works of art.

The disparity between rich and poor

serious crises frequently followed the collapse of speculative booms, they appear to have been of short duration. But the prosperity that existed seems to have been limited chiefly to the rulers, the upper classes, and the merchants. It certainly did not extend to the peasants or even to the workers in the towns. The daily wages of both skilled and unskilled workers in Athens in the third century had dropped to less than half of what they had been in the Age of Pericles. The cost of living, on the other hand, had risen considerably. To make matters worse, unemployment in the large cities was so serious a problem that the government had to provide free grain for many of the inhabitants. Slavery declined in the Hellenistic world, partly because of the influence of the Stoic philosophy, but mainly for the reason that wages were now so low that it was cheaper to hire a free laborer than to purchase and maintain a slave.

The growth of large cities

An interesting result of social and economic conditions in the Hellenistic Age was the growth of large cities. Despite the fact that a majority of the people still lived in the country, there was an increasing tendency for men to become dissatisfied with the dullness of rural living and to flock into the cities, where life, if not easier, was at least more exciting. But the chief reasons are to be found in the expansion of industry and commerce, in the enlargement of governmental functions, and in the desire of former independent farmers to escape the hardships of serfdom. Cities multiplied and grew in the Hellenistic empires almost as rapidly as in nineteenth- and twentieth-century America. Antioch in Syria quadrupled its population during a single century. Seleucia on the Tigris grew from nothing to a metropolis of several hundred thousand in less than two centuries. The largest and most famous of all the Hellenistic cities was Alexandria in Egypt, with over 500,000 inhabitants and possibly as many as 1,000,000. No other city in ancient times before imperial Rome, surpassed it in size or in magnificence. Its streets were well paved and laid out in regular order. It had splendid public buildings and parks, a museum, and a library of

700,000 scrolls. It was the most brilliant center of Hellenistic cultural achievement, especially in the field of scientific research. The masses of its people, however, had no share in the brilliant and luxurious life around them, although it was paid for in part out of the fruits of their labor.

3. HELLENISTIC CULTURE: PHILOSOPHY, LITERATURE, AND ART

Hellenistic philosophy exhibited two trends that ran almost parallel throughout the civilization. The major trend, exemplified by Stoicism and Epicureanism, showed a fundamental regard for reason as the key to the solution of human problems. This trend was a manifestation of Greek influence, though philosophy and science, as combined in Aristotle, had now come to a parting of the ways. The minor trend, exemplified by the Skeptics, Cynics, and various Asian cults, tended to reject reason, to deny the possibility of attaining truth, and in some cases to turn toward mysticism and a reliance upon faith. Despite the differences in their teachings, the philosophers of the Hellenistic Age were generally agreed upon one thing: the necessity of finding some way of salvation from the hardships and evils of human existence.

Trends in philosophy

The first of the Hellenistic philosophers were the Cynics, who had their origin about 350 B.C. Their foremost leader was Diogenes, who won fame by his ceaseless quest for an "honest" man. Essentially this meant the adoption of the "natural" life and the repudiation of everything conventional and artificial. The Cynics adopted as their principal goal the cultivation of "self-sufficiency": everyone should cultivate within himself the ability to satisfy his own needs. Obviously the Cynics bore some resemblance to other movements that have cropped up through the ages—the hippie movement of the 1960s, for example. There were notable differences, however. The Cynics spurned music and art as manifestations of artificiality, and they were not representative of a youth generation. But all such movements seem to reflect a sense of frustration and hopeless conflict in society. According to one story, Alexander the Great once asked Diogenes's disciple Crates whether the city of Thebes, recently destroyed in war, should be rebuilt: "Why?" replied the Cynic, "another Alexander will surely tear it down again."

The Cynics

Epicureanism and Stoicism both originated about 300 B.C. The founders were, respectively, Epicurus (c. 342–270) and Zeno (fl. after 300), who were residents of Athens. Epicureanism and Stoicism had several features in common. Both were individualistic, concerned not with the welfare of society but with the good of the individual. Both were materialistic, denying categorically the existence of any spiritual substances; even divine beings and the soul were declared to be formed of matter. In Stoicism and Epicureanism alike there were defi-

Epicureanism and Stoicism

*The Stoics' pursuit of
tranquility of mind through
fatalism*

nite elements of universalism, since both implied that men are the same the world over and recognized no distinctions between Greeks and "barbarians."

But in many ways the two systems were quite different. Zeno and his disciples taught that the cosmos is an ordered whole in which all contradictions are resolved for ultimate good. Evil is, therefore, relative; the particular misfortunes which befall human beings are but necessary incidents to the final perfection of the universe. Everything that happens is rigidly determined in accordance with rational purpose. No individual is master of his fate; human destiny is a link in an unbroken chain. People are free only in the sense that they can accept their fate or rebel against it. But whether they accept or rebel, they cannot overcome it. Their supreme duty is to submit to the order of the universe in the knowledge that that order is good; in other words, to resign themselves as graciously as possible to their fate. Through such an act of resignation the highest happiness will be attained, which consists in tranquility of mind. The individual who is most truly happy is therefore the one who by the assertion of his rational nature has accomplished a perfect adjustment of his life to the cosmic purpose and has purged his soul of all bitterness and whining protest against evil turns of fortune.

The Stoics developed an ethical and social theory that accorded well with their general philosophy. Believing that the highest good consists in serenity of mind, they naturally emphasized duty and self-discipline as cardinal virtues. Recognizing the prevalence of particular evil, they taught tolerance for and forgiveness of one another. Unlike the Cynics, they did not recommend withdrawal from society but urged participation in public affairs as a duty for the citizen of rational mind. They condemned slavery and war, but it was far from their purpose to preach any crusade against these evils. They were disposed to think that the results that would flow from violent measures of social change would be worse than the diseases they were supposed to cure. Besides, what difference did it make if the body were in bondage so long as the mind was free? Despite its negative character, the Stoic philosophy was the noblest product of the Hellenistic Age. Its equalitarianism, pacifism, and humanitarianism were important factors in mitigating the harshness not only of that time but of later centuries as well.

The Epicureans derived their metaphysics chiefly from Democritus. Epicurus taught that the basic ingredients of all things are minute, indivisible atoms, and that change and growth are the results of the combination and separation of these particles. Nevertheless, while accepting the materialism of the atomists, Epicurus rejected their absolute mechanism. He denied that an automatic, mechanical motion of the atoms can be the cause of all things in the universe. Though he taught that the atoms move downward in perpendicular lines because of their weight, he insisted upon endowing them with a spontaneous ability to swerve from the perpendicular and thereby to combine with one another. The chief reason for this peculiar modification of the atomic theory was to make possible a belief in human freedom. If the atoms were capable only of mechanical motion, then a human being, who is made up of atoms, would be reduced to the status of an automaton, and fatalism would be the law of the universe. In this repudiation of the mechanistic interpretation of life, Epicurus was probably closer to the Hellenic spirit than either Democritus or the Stoics.

The ethical philosophy of the Epicureans was based upon the doctrine that the highest good is pleasure. But they did not include all forms of indulgence in the category of genuine pleasure. The so-called pleasures of the flesh should be avoided, since every excess of carnality must be balanced by its portion of pain. On the other hand, a moderate satisfaction of bodily appetites is permissible and may be regarded as a good in itself. Better than this is mental pleasure, sober contemplation of the reasons for the choice of some things and the avoidance of others, and mature reflection upon satisfactions previously enjoyed. The highest of all pleasures, however, consists in serenity of soul, in the complete absence of both mental and physical pain. This end can be best achieved through the elimination of fear, especially fear of the supernatural, since that is the sovereign source of mental pain. The individual must recognize from the study of philosophy that the soul is material and therefore cannot survive the body, that the universe operates of itself, and that the gods do not intervene in human affairs. The gods live remote from the world and are too intent upon their own happiness to bother about what takes place on earth. Since they do not reward or punish mortals either in this life or in a life to come there is no reason why they should be feared. The Epicureans thus came by a different route to the same general conclusion as the Stoics—the supreme good is tranquillity of mind.

The Epicurean pursuit of tranquility of mind through overcoming fear of the supernatural

The ethics of the Epicureans as well as their political theory rested squarely upon a utilitarian basis. In contrast with the Stoics, they did not insist upon virtue as an end in itself but taught that the only reason why one should be good is to increase his own happiness. In like manner, they denied that there is any such thing as absolute justice: laws and institutions are just only insofar as they contribute to the welfare of the individual. Certain rules have been found necessary in every complex society for the maintenance of security and order. These rules are obeyed solely because it is to each individual's advantage to do so. Epicurus held no high regard for either political or social life. He considered the state as a mere convenience and taught that the wise man should take no active part in politics. Unlike the Cynics, he did not propose that civilization should be abandoned; yet his conception of the happiest life was essentially passive and defeatist. Epicurus taught that the thinking person will recognize that evils in the world

The ethical and political theories of the Epicureans

cannot be eradicated by human effort; the individual will therefore withdraw to study philosophy and enjoy the fellowship of a few congenial friends.

A more radically defeatist philosophy was that propounded by the Skeptics. Skepticism reached the zenith of its popularity about 200 B.C. under the influence of Carneades. The chief source of its inspiration was the Sophist teaching that all knowledge is derived from sense perception and therefore must be limited and relative. From this was deduced the conclusion that we cannot prove anything. Since the impressions of our senses deceive us, no truth can be certain. All we can say is that things *appear* to be such and such; we do not know what they really *are*. We have no definite knowledge of the supernatural, of the meaning of life, or even of right and wrong. It follows that the sensible course to pursue is suspension of judgment: this alone can lead to happiness. If we will abandon the fruitless quest for absolute truth and cease worrying about good and evil, we will attain that equanimity of mind which is the highest satisfaction that life affords. The Skeptics were even less concerned than the Epicureans with political and social problems. Their ideal was the typically Hellenistic one of escape for the individual from a world neither understandable nor capable of reform.

The nonrational trend in Hellenistic thought reached its farthest extreme in the philosophies of Philo Judaeus and the Neo-Pythagoreans in the last century B.C. and the first century A.D. The proponents of the two systems were in general agreement as to their basic teachings, especially in their predominantly religious viewpoint. They believed in a transcendent God so far removed from the world as to be utterly unknowable to mortal minds. They conceived the universe as being sharply divided between spirit and matter. They considered everything physical and material as evil; the soul is imprisoned in the body, from which an escape can be effected only through rigorous denial and mortification of the flesh. Their attitude was mystical and nonintellectual: truth comes neither from science nor from reason but from revelation. Philo, a Jew who lived in Alexandria, maintained that the books of the Old Testament were of absolute divine authority and contained all truth; the ultimate aim in life is to accomplish a mystic union with God, to lose one's self in the divine. Both Philo and the Neo-Pythagoreans influenced the development of Christian theology—Philo, in particular, with his dualism of matter and spirit and his doctrine of the Logos, the word, or highest intermediary between God and the universe.

Hellenistic literature is significant mainly for the light it throws upon the character of the civilization. Most of the writings showed little originality or depth of thought. But they poured forth from the hands of the copyists in a profusion that is almost incredible when we consider that the art of printing by movable type was unknown. We know the names of at least 1,100 authors. Much of what they wrote was trash, comparable to some of the cheap novels of our own day. Nevertheless, there were several works of more than mediocre quality and a few which met the highest standards ever set by the Greeks.

Among the leading types of Hellenistic literature were the drama and the pastoral. Drama was almost exclusively comedy, represented mainly by the plays of Menander. His plays were very different from the comedy of Aristophanes. They were distinguished by naturalism rather than by satire, by preoccupation with the seamy side of life rather than with political or intellectual issues. Their dominant theme was romantic love, with its pains and pleasures, its intrigues and seductions, and its culmination in happy marriage. The greatest author of pastorals was Theocritus of Syracuse, who wrote in the first half of the third century B.C. His pastorals, as the name implies, celebrate the charm of life in the country and idealize the simple pleasures of rustic folk. Theocritus later found greater imitators in the Roman poet Vergil and the Elizabethan poet Edmund Spenser.

The field of prose literature was dominated by the historians, the biographers, and the authors of utopias. By far the ablest of the writers of history was Polybius of Megalopolis, who lived during the second century B.C. From the standpoint of his scientific approach and his zeal for truth, he probably deserves to be ranked second only to Thucydides among all the historians in ancient times; but he excelled Thucydides in his grasp of the importance of social and economic forces. Although most of the biographies were of a light and gossipy character, their tremendous popularity bears eloquent testimony to the literary tastes of the time. Even more significant was the popularity of the

Hellenistic poetry

Historians, biographers, and authors of utopias

The Dying Gaul. A good example of Hellenistic realism in sculpture, which often reflected a preoccupation with the morbid and sensational. Every detail of the warrior's agony is dramatically portrayed. Now in the Capitoline Museum, Rome.

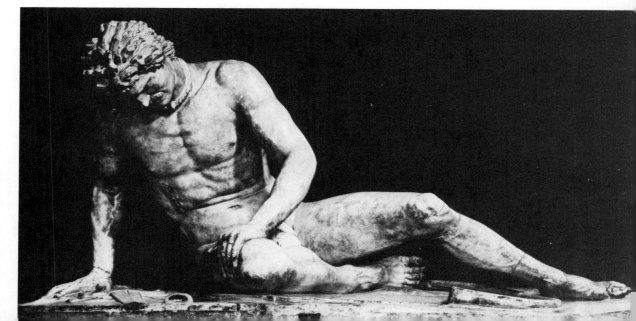

Left: *The Winged Victory of Samothrace*. In this figure, done around 200 B.C., a Hellenistic sculptor preserved some of the calmness and devotion to grace and proportion characteristic of Hellenic art in the Golden Age. Right: *Laocoön*. In sharp contrast to the serenity of the Winged Victory is this famous sculpture group from the late second century B.C., depicting the death of Laocoön. According to legend, Laocoön warned the Trojans not to touch the wooden horse sent by the Greeks and was punished by Poseidon, who sent two serpents to kill him and his sons. The intense emotionalism of this work later had a great influence on western European art from Michelangelo onwards.

utopias, or descriptive accounts of ideal states. Virtually all of them depicted a life of social and economic equality, free from greed, oppression, and strife, on an imaginary island or in some distant, unfamiliar region. Generally in these paradises money was considered to be unknown, trade was prohibited, all property was held in common, and all were required to work with their hands in producing the necessities of life. We are probably justified in assuming that the profusion of this utopian literature was a direct result of the evils and injustices of Hellenistic society and a consciousness of the need for reform.

Hellenistic art

Hellenistic art did not preserve all of the characteristic qualities of the art of the Greeks. In place of the humanism, balance, and restraint which had distinguished the architecture and sculpture of the Golden Age, qualities of exaggerated realism, sensationalism, and voluptuousness now became dominant. The simple and dignified Doric and Ionic temples gave way to luxurious palaces, costly mansions, and elaborate public buildings and monuments symbolic of power and wealth. A typical example was the great lighthouse of Alexandria, which rose to a height of nearly four hundred feet, with three diminishing stories and eight columns to support the light at the top. Sculpture likewise exhibited extravagant and sentimental tendencies. Many of the statues and figures in relief were huge and some of them almost grotesque. Violent emotionalism and exaggerated realism were features common to the majority. But by no means all of Hellenistic sculpture was overwrought and grotesque. Some of it was distinguished by a calmness and poise and compassion for human suffering reminiscent of the best work of the great fourth-century artists. Statues which exemplify these superior qualities include the *Aphrodite of Melos* (*Venus de Milo*) and the *Winged Victory of Samothrace*.

See color plates following page 96

4. THE FIRST GREAT AGE OF SCIENCE

The most brilliant age in the history of science prior to the seventeenth century A.D. was the period of the Hellenistic civilization. Indeed, many of the achievements of the modern age would scarcely have been possible without the discoveries of the scientists of Alexandria, Syracuse, Pergamum, and other great cities of the Hellenistic world. The reasons for the impressive development of science in the centuries after the downfall of Alexander's empire are not difficult to discover. Alexander himself had given some financial encouragement to the progress of research. More important was the stimulus provided for intellectual inquiry by the fusion of Chaldean and Egyptian science with the learning of the Greeks. Possibly a third factor was the new interest in luxury and comfort and the demand for practical knowledge which would enable the scientific thinker to solve the problems of a disordered and unsatisfying existence.

Factors responsible for the remarkable progress of science

The sciences which received major attention in the Hellenistic Age were astronomy, mathematics, geography, medicine, and physics. Chemistry, aside from metallurgy, was practically unknown. Except for the work of Theophrastus, who was the first to recognize the sexuality of plants, biology was also largely neglected. Neither chemistry nor biology bore any definite relationship to trade or to the forms of industry then in existence, and apparently they were not regarded as having much practical value.

The most popular sciences

The most renowned of the earlier astronomers of this time was Aristarchus of Samos (310–230 B.C.), who is sometimes called the "Hellenistic Copernicus." His chief title to fame comes from his deduction that the earth and the other planets revolve around the sun. Unfortunately this deduction was not accepted by his successors. It conflicted with the teachings of Aristotle and with the conviction of the Greeks that man, and therefore the earth, must be at the center of the universe. Besides, it was not in harmony with the beliefs of the Jews and other Eastern peoples who made up so large a percentage of

Astronomy

the Hellenistic population. Another important Hellenistic astronomer was Hipparchus, who did his most valuable work in Alexandria in the latter half of the second century B.C. His chief contributions were the invention of the astrolabe and the approximately correct calculation of the diameter of the moon and its distance from the earth. His fame was eventually overshadowed, however, by the reputation of Ptolemy of Alexandria (second century A.D.). Although Ptolemy made few original discoveries, he systematized the work of others. His principal writing, the *Almagest,* based upon the geocentric theory (the view that all heavenly bodies revolve around the earth), was handed down to medieval Europe as the classic summary of ancient astronomy. Ptolemy's geography too had a considerable influence on medieval and Renaissance thought.

Mathematics and geography

Closely allied with astronomy were two other sciences, mathematics and geography. The Hellenistic mathematician of greatest renown was, of course, Euclid (c. 323–c. 285 B.C.), the master of geometry. Until the middle of the nineteenth century his *Elements of Geometry* remained the accepted basis for the study of that branch of mathematics. Much of the material in this work was not original but was a synthesis of the discoveries of others. The most original of the Hellenistic mathematicians was probably Hipparchus, who laid the foundations of both plane and spherical trigonometry. Hellenistic geography owed most of its development to Eratosthenes (c. 276–c. 196 B.C.), astronomer, poet, philologist, and librarian of Alexandria. By means of sundials placed some hundreds of miles apart, he calculated the circumference of the earth with an error of less than 200 miles. He produced the most accurate map that had yet been devised, with the surface of the earth divided into degrees of latitude and longitude. He propounded the theory that all of the oceans are really one, and he was the first to suggest the possibility of reaching India by sailing west. One of his successors divided the earth into the five climatic zones which are still recognized, and explained the ebb and flow of the tides as due to the influence of the moon.

Medicine: the development of anatomy

Perhaps none of the Hellenistic advances in science surpassed in importance the progress in medicine. Especially significant was the work of Herophilus of Chalcedon, who conducted his researches in Alexandria about the beginning of the second century. Without question he was the greatest anatomist of antiquity and probably the first to practice human dissection. Among his most important achievements were a detailed description of the brain, with an attempt to distinguish between the functions of its various parts; the discovery of the significance of the pulse and its use in diagnosing illness; and the discovery that the arteries contain blood alone, not a mixture of blood and air as Aristotle had taught, and that their function is to carry blood from the heart to all parts of the body. The value of this last discovery in laying the basis for a knowledge of the circulation of the blood can hardly be overestimated.

The ablest of the colleagues of Herophilus was Erasistratus, who flourished in Alexandria about the middle of the third century. He is considered the founder of physiology as a separate science. Not only did he practice dissection, but he is believed to have gained a great deal of his knowledge of bodily functions from vivisection. He discovered the valves of the heart, distinguished between motor and sensory nerves, and taught that the ultimate branches of the arteries and veins are connected. He was the first to reject absolutely the humoral theory of disease and to condemn excessive blood-letting as a method of cure. Unfortunately this theory was revived by Galen, the great encyclopedist of medicine who lived in the Roman Empire in the second century A.D.

Physiology

Prior to the third century B.C. physics had been a branch of philosophy. It was made a separate experimental science by Archimedes of Syracuse (c. 287–212 B.C.). Archimedes discovered the law of floating bodies, or specific gravity, and formulated with scientific exactness the principles of the lever, the pulley, and the screw. Among his memorable inventions were the compound pulley, the tubular screw for pumping water, the screw propeller for ships, and the burning lens. Although he has been called the "technical Yankee of antiquity," there is evidence that he set no high value upon his ingenious mechanical contraptions and preferred to devote his time to pure scientific research.

Physics

Certain other individuals in the Hellenistic Age were quite willing to give all their attention to applied science. Preeminent among them was Hero of Alexandria, who lived in the last century B.C. The record of inventions credited to him almost passes belief. The list includes a fire engine, a siphon, a jet engine, a hydraulic organ, a slot machine, and a catapult operated by compressed air. How many of these inventions were really his own is impossible to say, but there appears to be no question that such contrivances were actually in existence in his time or soon thereafter. Nevertheless, the total progress in applied science was comparatively slight, probably for the reason that human labor continued to be so abundant and cheap that it was not worthwhile to substitute the work of machines.

Applied science

5. RELIGION IN THE HELLENISTIC AGE

If there was one aspect of the Hellenistic civilization which served more than others to accent the contrast with Hellenic culture, it was the new trend in religion. The civic religion of the Greeks as it was in the age of the city-states had now almost entirely disappeared. For the majority of the intellectuals its place was taken by the philosophies of Stoicism, Epicureanism, and Skepticism. Some who were less philosophically inclined turned to the worship of Fortune.

The new trend in religion

Among the common people a tendency to embrace emotional religions was even more clearly manifest. The Orphic and Eleusinian mystery cults attracted more votaries than ever before. The worship of the Egyptian mother-goddess, Isis, threatened for a time to become dominant throughout the Near East. The astral religion of the Chaldeans likewise spread rapidly, with the result that its chief product, astrology, was received with fanatical enthusiasm throughout the Hellenistic world. But the most powerful influence of all came from the offshoots of Zoroastrianism, especially from Mithraism and Gnosticism. While all of the cults of Oriental origin resembled each other in their promises of salvation in a life to come, Mithraism and Gnosticism had a more ethically significant mythology, a deeper contempt for this world, and a more clearly defined doctrine of redemption through a personal savior. These were the ideas which satisfied the emotional cravings of the common people, convinced as they were of the worthlessness of this life and ready to be lured by extravagant promises of better things in a world to come. If we can judge by conditions in our own time, some of the doctrines of these cults must have exerted their influence upon members of the upper classes also. Even the most casual observer of modern society knows that pessimism, mysticism, and otherworldliness are not confined to the downtrodden. In some cases the keenest disgust with this life and the deepest mystical yearnings are to be found among those whose pockets bulge the most.

A factor by no means unimportant in the religious developments of the Hellenistic Age was the dispersion of the Jews. As a result of Alexander's conquest of Palestine in 332 B.C. and the Roman conquest about three centuries later, thousands of Jews migrated to various sections of the Mediterranean world. It has been estimated that 1,000,000 of them lived in Egypt in the first century A.D. and 200,000 in Asia Minor. They mingled freely with other peoples, adopting the Greek language and no small amount of the Hellenic culture which still survived from earlier days. At the same time they played a major part in the diffusion of Eastern beliefs. Some of the Hellenistic Jews eventually became converts to Christianity and were largely instrumental in the spread of that religion outside of Palestine. A notable example, of course, was Saul of Tarsus, known in Christian history as St. Paul.

6. A FORETASTE OF MODERNITY?

With the possible exception of the Roman, no great culture of ancient times appears to suggest the spirit of the modern age quite so emphatically as does the Hellenistic civilization. Here, as in the world of the twentieth century, were to be found a considerable variety of forms of government, the growth of militarism, and a trend in the direction of authoritarian rule. Many of the characteristic economic and social de-

Statue of an Old Market Woman. In the Hellenistic Age the idealism and restraint of Hellenic art were succeeded by a tendency to portray the humble aspects of life and to express compassion for human suffering. Original in the Metropolitan Museum of Art, New York.

velopments of the Hellenistic Age are equally suggestive of contemporary experience: the growth of big business, the expansion of trade, the zeal for exploration and discovery, the interest in technology, the devotion to comfort and the craze for material prosperity, the growth of cities with congested slums, and the widening gulf between rich and poor. In the realms of intellect and art the Hellenistic civilization also bore a distinctly modern flavor. This was exemplified by the emphasis upon science, the narrow specialization of learning, the penchant for realism and naturalism, the vast production of mediocre literature, and the popularity of mysticism side by side with extreme skepticism and dogmatic unbelief.

Because of these resemblances there has been a tendency among certain writers to regard our own civilization as decadent. But this is based partly upon the false assumption that the Hellenistic culture was merely a degenerate phase of Greek civilization. Instead, it was a new social and cultural organism born of a fusion of Greek and Near-Eastern elements. Moreover, the differences between the Hellenistic civilization and that of the contemporary world are perhaps just as important as the resemblances. The Hellenistic political outlook was es-

Basic differences

sentially cosmopolitan; nothing comparable to the national patriotism of modern times really prevailed. Despite the remarkable expansion of trade in the Hellenistic Age, no industrial revolution ever took place, for reasons which have already been noted. Finally, Hellenistic science was more limited than that of the present day. Modern pure science is to a very large extent a species of philosophy—an adventure of the mind in the realm of the unknown. Notwithstanding frequent assertions to the contrary, much of it is gloriously impractical and will probably remain so.

SELECTED READINGS

- *Items so designated are available in paperback editions.*
  Burn, A. R., *Alexander the Great and the Hellenistic World*, New York, 1962. A good brief biography.
- Bury, J. B., et al., *The Hellenistic Age*, New York, 1923.
  Cary, Max, *The Legacy of Alexander: A History of the Greek World from 323 to 146 B.C.*, New York, 1932. Best on the complicated political history of the period.
  Clagett, M., *Greek Science in Antiquity*, New York, 1963.
  Festugière, A. J., *Epicurus and His Gods*, Cambridge, Mass., 1956.
- Finley, M. I., *The Ancient Economy*, Berkeley, Calif., 1973. A fundamental topical treatment.
  Grant, F. C., *Hellenistic Religions*, New York, 1963.
- Hadas, M., *Hellenistic Culture*, New York, 1964.
  Larsen, J. A. O., *Greek Federal States*, Oxford, 1968.
  Rostovtzeff, M., *The Social and Economic History of the Hellenistic World*, 3 vols., Oxford, 1941. An authoritative mine of information.
- Tarn, W. W., *Alexander the Great*, Cambridge, 1948. Tarn was the leading English expert on Alexander and the Hellenistic period.
- ———, *Hellenistic Civilization*, 3rd ed., London, 1952. Still indispensible.
- Wilcken, U., *Alexander the Great*, New York, 1932. A fundamental older interpretation, translated from the German.

SOURCE MATERIALS

Greek source materials for the Hellenistic period are available in the appropriate volumes of the Loeb Classical Library, Harvard University Press.

Chapter 10

ROMAN CIVILIZATION

My city and country, so far as I am Antoninus, is Rome, but so far as I am
a man, it is the world.

—Marcus Aurelius Antoninus, *Meditations*

For the categories into which you divide the world are not Hellenes and
Barbarians. . . . The division which you substituted is one into Romans
and non-Romans. To such a degree have you expanded the name of your
city.

—Aelius Aristides, *Oration to Rome*

Well before the glory that was Greece had begun to fade,
another civilization, ultimately much influenced by Greek
culture, had started its growth in the West on the banks of
the Tiber. Around the time of Alexander's conquests the new civilization of Rome was already a dominant force on the Italian peninsula.
For five centuries thereafter Rome's power increased. By the end of
the first century B.C. it had imposed its rule over the entire Hellenistic
world as well as over most of modern-day western Europe. By conquering the old Hellenistic states and destroying the North African
civilization of Carthage, Rome was able to make the Mediterranean a
"Roman lake." In so doing it brought Greek institutions and ideas to
the western half of the Mediterranean world. And by pushing northwards to the Rhine and Danube rivers it brought Mediterranean urban
culture to lands still sunk in the Iron Age. Rome, then, was the builder
of a great historical bridge between East and West.

The rise of Rome

Of course Rome would not have been able to play this role had it
not followed its own peculiar course of development. This was
marked by the tension between two different cultural outlooks. On
the one hand Romans throughout most of their history tended to be
conservative: they revered their old agricultural traditions, household
gods, and ruggedly warlike ways. But they also wanted to be
builders and could not resist the attractions of Greek culture and lux-

The Roman synthesis

ury. For a few centuries their greatness was based on a synthesis of these different traits: respect for tradition, order, and military prowess, together with Greek urbanization and cultivation of the mind. The synthesis could not last forever, but as long as it did the glory that was Greece was replaced by the grandeur that was Rome.

1. EARLY ITALY AND THE ROMAN MONARCHY

The impact of geography on Roman history

The geographical character of the Italian peninsula contributed significantly to the course of Roman history. Except for some excellent marble and small quantities of tin, copper, iron, and gold, Italy has no mineral resources. The extensive coastline is broken by few good harbors. On the other hand, the amount of fertile land is much larger than that of Greece. As a result, the Romans were destined to remain a predominantly agrarian people through the greater part of their history. They seldom enjoyed the intellectual stimulus which comes from extensive trading with other areas. In addition, the Italian peninsula was more open to invasion than was Greece. The Alps posed no effective barrier to the influx of peoples from central Europe, and the low-lying coast in many places invited conquest by sea. Domination of the country by force was therefore more common than peaceful intermingling of immigrants with original settlers. The Romans became absorbed in military pursuits almost from the moment of their settlement on Italian soil, for they were forced to defend their own conquests against other invaders.

The earliest inhabitants of Italy

Archeological evidence indicates that Italy was inhabited at least as far back as the later Paleolithic Age. At this time the territory was occupied by a people closely related to the Cro-Magnons of southern France. In the Neolithic period people of Mediterranean stock entered the land, some coming in from northern Africa and others from Spain and Gaul. The beginning of the Bronze Age witnessed several new incursions. From north of the Alps came the first of the immigrants of

An Etruscan Sarcophagus. The Etruscans often depicted social events, sports, funeral banquets, and processions, either in painting or relief, on their tombs. Seen here are preparations for a funeral.

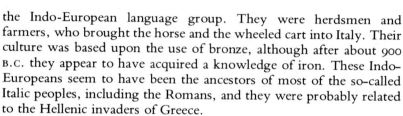

Etruscan Sarcophagus. This work of the fourth century B.C. depicts a husband and wife: note the sympathetic portrayal of the woman and the sense of equality between the two figures.

the Indo-European language group. They were herdsmen and farmers, who brought the horse and the wheeled cart into Italy. Their culture was based upon the use of bronze, although after about 900 B.C. they appear to have acquired a knowledge of iron. These Indo-Europeans seem to have been the ancestors of most of the so-called Italic peoples, including the Romans, and they were probably related to the Hellenic invaders of Greece.

Probably during the eighth century B.C. two other nations of immigrants occupied different portions of the Italian peninsula: the Etruscans and the Greeks. Where the Etruscans came from is a question which has never been satisfactorily answered, although it is certain that they were not Indo-Europeans. Most authorities believe that they were natives of Asia Minor. Whatever their origins, we know that by the sixth century B.C. they had established a great federation of cities that stretched over most of northern and central Italy. Although their writing has never been completely deciphered, enough materials survive to indicate the nature of their culture. They had an alphabet based upon the Greek, a high degree of skill in metalwork, great artistic talents, a flourishing trade with the East, and a religion based upon the worship of gods in human form. They bequeathed to the Romans a knowledge of the arch and the vault, the cruel amusement of gladiatorial combats, and the practice of foretelling the future by supernatural means such as studying the entrails of animals or the flight of birds. One of their most distinctive traits was the comparatively great respect they showed for women. Etruscan wives, unlike those in other contemporary societies, ate with their husbands, and some Etruscan families listed descent through the maternal line.

The Greeks settled mainly along the southern and southwestern shores of Italy and the island of Sicily, as well as along the southern coast of Gaul. Their most important settlements were Taranto, Na-

The Etruscans and the Greeks

The Greeks in Italy

ples, and Syracuse, each of which was an independent city-state. Greek civilization in Italy and Sicily was as advanced as it was in Greece itself. Such famous Greeks as Pythagoras, Archimedes, and even Plato for a time, actually lived in the Italian West. From the Greeks the Romans derived their alphabet, a number of their religious concepts, and much of their art and mythology.

The founding of Rome

The founders of Rome itself were Italic peoples who lived in the area south of the Tiber River. Though the exact year of the founding of the city is unknown, recent archeological research places the event quite near the traditional date of 753 B.C. By reason of its strategic location, Rome came to exercise an effective suzerainty over several of the most important neighboring cities. One conquest followed another until, by the sixth century B.C., Rome came to dominate most of the surrounding area. But just then Etruscans took over power in Rome.

The government of Rome under the monarchy; the powers of the king

The political evolution of Rome in this early period resembled in some ways the governmental development of the Greek communities, although it was far from being exactly the same. The Romans appear from the first to have had a much stronger interest in authority and stability than in liberty or democracy. Their state was essentially an application of the idea of the patriarchal family to the whole community, with the king exercising a jurisdiction over his subjects comparable to that of the head of the family over the members of his household. But just as the authority of the father was limited by custom and by the requirement that he respect the wishes of his adult sons, the authority of the king was limited by the ancient constitution, which he was powerless to change without the consent of the chief men of the realm. His prerogatives were not primarily legislative but executive, priestly, military, and judicial. He judged all civil and criminal cases, but he had no authority to pardon without the consent of the assembly. Although his accession to office had to be confirmed by the people, he could not be deposed, and there was no one who could really challenge the exercise of his powers.

The Senate and the assembly

In addition to the kingship, the Roman government of this time included an assembly and a Senate. The former was composed of all the male citizens of military age. As one of the chief sources of sovereign power, according to the theory, this body could veto any proposal for a change in the law which the king might make. Besides, it determined whether pardons should be granted and whether aggressive war should be declared. But it was essentially a ratifying body with no right to initiate legislation or recommend changes of policy. The Senate, or council of elders, comprised in its membership the heads of the various clans which formed the community. Even more than the common citizens, the rulers of the clans embodied the sovereign power of the state. The king was only one of their number to whom they had delegated the active exercise of their authority. When the royal office became vacant, the powers of the king immediately re-verted to the Senate until the succession of a new monarch had been confirmed by the people. In ordinary times the chief function of the Senate was to examine proposals of the king which had been ratified by the assembly and to veto them if they violated rights established by ancient custom. It was thus almost impossible for fundamental changes to be made in the law even when the majority of the citizens were ready to sanction them. This extremely conservative attitude of the ruling classes persisted until the end of Roman history.

Toward the end of the sixth century (the date traditionally given is 509 B.C.) the monarchy was overthrown and replaced by a republic. Legend has it that this revolution was provoked by the crimes of the Tarquins, an Etruscan family that had taken over the kingship in Rome around the middle of the century. After suffering numerous indignities, the last and worst of which was the rape and subsequent suicide of a virtuous Roman matron, Lucretia, by a lustful Tarquin prince, the native Romans could stand no more and rose up to expel their alien oppressors. In fact the story of the rape of Lucretia is fictional but the change in government was probably in part a native uprising against foreigners, as well as a successful movement of the Roman senatorial aristocracy to gain full power for itself. The result was the beginning of Etruscan decline in Italy, as well as a lasting conviction among Romans that kingship was evil.

End of the monarchy

2. THE EARLY REPUBLIC

The history of the Roman Republic for more than two centuries after its establishment was one of almost constant warfare. Many of the most familiar Roman legends, such as that of the brave Horatio, who with only two friends held off an entire army in front of a bridge, date from this period. At first the Romans were on the defensive. The overthrow of the Tarquins resulted in acts of reprisal by their allies in neighboring regions, and other peoples on the borders took advantage of the confusion accompanying the change of regime to slice off portions of Roman territory. After Rome managed to ward off these attacks it began to expand in order to gain more land and satisfy a rapidly growing population. As time went on Rome steadily conquered all the Etruscan territories and then took over all the Greek cities in the southernmost portion of the Italian mainland. Not only did the latter add to the Roman domain, they also brought the Romans into fruitful contact with Greek culture. The Romans were then frequently confronted with revolts of peoples previously conquered. The suppression of these revolts awakened the suspicions of surrounding states and sharpened the appetite of the victors for further triumphs. New wars followed each other in what seemed an unending succession, until by 265 B.C. Rome had conquered the entire Italian peninsula.

This long series of military conflicts had profound social, economic,

Early Roman expansion

See color map following page 96

Roman Battle Sarcophagus. This relief displays the glories of war and expresses the Roman military ideal.

Effects of the early military conflicts

and cultural effects upon the subsequent history of Rome. It affected adversely the interests of the poorer citizens and furthered the concentration of land in the possession of wealthy proprietors. Long service in the army forced the ordinary farmers to neglect the cultivation of the soil, with the result that they fell into debt and frequently lost their farms. Many took refuge in the city, until they were settled later as tenants on great estates in the conquered territories. The wars had the effect also of confirming the agrarian character of the Roman nation. The repeated acquisition of new lands made it possible to absorb the entire population into agricultural pursuits. As a consequence Romans saw no need for the development of industry and commerce. Lastly, the continual warfare of this formative period served to develop among the Romans a strong military ideal: along with Horatio, another of Rome's great early legendary heroes was Cincinnatus, who supposedly left his farm at a moment's notice for the battlefield.

Political changes following the overthrow of the monarchy

During this same period of the early Republic, Rome underwent some significant political changes. These were not products so much of the revolution of the sixth century as of the developments of later years. The revolution which overthrew the monarchy was about as conservative as it is possible for a revolution to be. Its chief effect was to substitute two elected officials called consuls for the king and to exalt the position of the Senate by granting it control over the public funds and a veto on all actions of the assembly. The consuls themselves were usually senators and acted as the agents of their class. They did not rule jointly, but each was supposed to possess the full executive and judicial authority which had previously been wielded by the king. If a conflict arose between them, the Senate might be called upon to decide; or, in time of grave emergency, a dictator might be appointed for a term not greater than six months. In other respects the government remained the same as in the days of the monarchy.

Not long after the establishment of the Republic a struggle for power began among factions of the common citizens. Before the end of the monarchy the Roman population had come to be divided into two great classes—the patricians and the plebeians. The former were the aristocracy, wealthy landowners who monopolized the seats in the Senate and the offices of magistracy. Among the plebeians were some wealthy families who were barred from the patriciate because they were of recent foreign origin, but most plebeians were common people—small farmers, craftsmen, and tradesmen. Many were clients or dependents of the patricians, obliged to fight for them, to render them political support, and to cultivate their estates in return for protection. The grievances of the plebeians were numerous. Compelled to pay heavy taxes and forced to serve in the army in time of war, they were nevertheless excluded from all part in the government except membership in the assembly. Moreover, they felt themselves the victims of discriminatory decisions in judicial trials. They did not even know what legal rights they were supposed to enjoy, for the laws were unwritten, and no one but the consuls had the power to interpret them. In suits for debt the creditor was frequently allowed to sell the debtor into slavery.

The struggle between patricians and plebeians

In order to obtain a redress of these grievances the plebeians rebelled soon after the beginning of the fifth century B.C. They gained their first victory about 494 B.C., when they forced the patricians to agree to the election of a number of officers known as tribunes with power to protect the citizens by means of a veto over unlawful acts of the magistrates. This victory was followed by a successful demand for codification of the laws about 450 B.C. The result was the publication of the famous Law of the Twelve Tables, so called because it was written on tablets of wood. Although the Twelve Tables came to be revered by the Romans of later times as a kind of charter of the people's liberties, they were really nothing of the sort. For the most part they merely perpetuated ancient custom without even abolishing enslavement for debt. They did, however, enable the people to know where they stood in relation to the law, and they permitted an appeal to the assembly against a magistrate's sentence of capital punishment. About a generation later the plebeians won eligibility to positions as lesser magistrates, and about 367 B.C. the first plebeian consul was elected. Since ancient custom provided that, upon completing their term of office, consuls should automatically enter the Senate, the patrician monopoly of seats in that body was broken. The final plebeian victory came in 287 B.C. with the passage of a law which provided that measures enacted by the assembly should become binding upon the state whether the Senate approved them or not.

The victories of the plebeians

The significance of these changes must not be misinterpreted. They did not constitute a revolution to gain more liberty for the individual but merely to curb the power of the magistrates and to win for the plebeians a larger share in government. The state as a whole remained

Significance of the plebeian victories

as despotic as ever, for its authority over the citizens was not even challenged. Indeed, the Romans of the early Republic "never really abandoned the principle that the people were not to govern but to be governed."[1] Because of this attitude the grant of full legislative powers to the assembly seems to have meant little more than a formality; the Senate continued to rule as before. Nor did the admission of plebeians to membership in the Senate have any effect in liberalizing that body. So high was its prestige and so deep was the veneration of the Roman for authority, that the new members were soon swallowed up in the conservatism of the old. Moreover, the fact that the magistrates received no salaries prevented most of the poorer citizens from seeking public office.

Roman society and culture still rather primitive

Intellectually and culturally the Romans developed very slowly. Life in Rome was still harsh and crude. Though writing had been adopted as early as the sixth century, little use was made of it except for the copying of laws, treaties, and funerary inscriptions. Inasmuch as education was limited to instruction imparted by the father in manly sports, practical arts, and soldierly virtues, the great majority of the people were still illiterate. War and agriculture continued as the chief occupations for the bulk of the citizens. A few craftsmen were to be found in the cities, and a minor development of trade had occurred. But the comparative insignificance of Roman commerce at this time is pretty clearly revealed by the fact that the country had no standard system of coinage until 269 B.C.

The religion of the Romans compared with that of the Greeks

During the period of the early Republic Roman religion assumed the character it was destined to retain through the greater part of Roman history. In several ways this religion resembled that of the Greeks, partly for the reason that the Etruscan religion was deeply indebted to the Greek, and the Romans, in turn, were influenced by the Etruscans. Both the Greek and Roman religions emphasized the performances of rites in order to gain benefits from the gods or keep them from anger. The deities in both religions performed similar functions: Jupiter corresponded roughly to Zeus as god of the sky, Minerva to Athena as goddess of wisdom and patroness of crafts, Venus to Aphrodite as goddess of love, Neptune to Poseidon as god of the sea, and so on. The Roman religion, like the Greek, had no dogmas or sacraments or belief in rewards and punishments in an afterlife.

Contrasts with Greek religion

But there were significant differences also. The Roman religion was distinctly more political and less humanist in purpose. It served not to glorify humanity or establish a comfortable relationship between human beings and their world but to protect the state from its enemies and to augment its power and prosperity. The gods were less human; indeed, it was only as a result of Greek and Etruscan influences that they were made personal deities at all, having previously been worshiped as animistic spirits. The Romans never conceived of their dei-

---

[1] Theodor Mommsen, *The History of Rome*, I, 313.

Intervention of Jupiter. This scene from the first century A.D. depicts Jupiter, god of the sky, supporting the Romans in a battle against Germanic barbarians.

ties as quarreling among themselves or mingling with human beings after the fashion of the Homeric divinities. Finally, the Roman religion contained a much stronger element of priestliness than the Greek. The priests, or pontiffs as they were called, formed an organized class, a branch of the government itself. They not only supervised the offering of sacrifices, they were also guardians of an elaborate body of sacred traditions and laws which they alone could interpret. It must be understood, however, that these pontiffs were not priests in the sense of intermediaries between the individual Roman and the gods; they heard no confessions, forgave no sins, and administered no sacraments.

The morality of the Romans in this as in later periods had almost no connection with religion. The Romans did not ask their gods to make them good, but to bestow upon the community and upon their families material blessings. Morality was a matter of patriotism and of respect for authority and tradition. The chief virtues were bravery, honor, self-discipline, reverence for the gods and for one's ancestors, and duty to country and family. Loyalty to Rome took precedence over everything else. For the good of the state the citizen had to be ready to sacrifice not only his own life but, if necessary, the lives of his family and friends. The courage of certain consuls who dutifully put their sons to death for breaches of military discipline was a subject of profound admiration. Few peoples in European history with the exception of the Spartans and modern totalitarians have ever taken the problems of national interest so seriously or subordinated the individual so completely to the welfare of the state.

Morality in the early Republic

3. THE FATEFUL WARS WITH CARTHAGE

The beginning of imperialism on a major scale

By 265 B.C., as we have already learned, Rome had conquered and annexed the whole mainland of Italy south of the Po. Proud and confident of its strength, it was almost certain to strike out into new fields of empire. The prosperous island of Sicily was not yet within its grasp, nor could it regard with indifference the situation in other parts of the Mediterranean world. Rome was now prone to interpret almost any change in the status quo as a threat to its own power and security. It was for such reasons that Rome after 264 B.C. became involved in a series of wars with other great nations which decidedly altered the course of Roman history.

Carthage

The first and most important of these wars was the struggle with Carthage, a great maritime empire that stretched along the northern coast of Africa from modern-day Tunisia to the Strait of Gibraltar. Carthage had originally been founded about 800 B.C. as a Phoenician colony. In the sixth century it severed its ties with the homeland and gradually developed into a rich and powerful state. The prosperity of its upper classes was founded upon commerce and upon exploitation of the silver and tin resources of Spain and the tropical products of north central Africa. Carthaginian government was oligarchic. The real rulers were thirty merchant princes who constituted an inner council of the Senate. These men controlled elections and dominated every other branch of the government. The remaining 270 members of the Senate appear to have been summoned to meet only on special occasions. In spite of these political deficiencies and a cruel religion that demanded blood sacrifices, Carthage had a civilization superior in luxury and scientific attainment to that of Rome when the struggle between the two states began.

Causes of the First Punic War

The initial clash with Carthage started in 264 B.C.[2] The primary cause was Roman jealousy over Carthaginian expansion in Sicily. Carthage already controlled the western portion of the island and was threatening the Greek cities of Syracuse and Messina on the eastern coast. If these cities should be captured, all chances of Roman occupation of Sicily would be lost. Faced with this danger, Rome declared war upon Carthage with the hope of forcing it back into its African domain. Twenty-three years of fighting finally brought victory to the Roman generals. Carthage was compelled to surrender its possessions in Sicily and to pay an indemnity of 3,200 talents, or about 13 million dollars at present silver prices.

The Second Punic War

But the Romans were unable to stand the strain of this triumph. They had had to put forth such heroic efforts to win that when victory was finally secured it made them more arrogant and acquisitive than

[2] The wars with Carthage are known as the Punic Wars. The Romans called the Carthaginians *Poeni,* i.e., Phoenicians, whence is derived the adjective "Punic."

ever. As a result, the struggle with Carthage was renewed on two different occasions thereafter. In 218 B.C., the Romans interpreted the Carthaginian attempt to rebuild an empire in Spain as a threat to their interests and responded with a declaration of war. This struggle raged through a period of sixteen years. Italy was ravaged by the armies of Hannibal, the famous Carthaginian commander, who crossed the Alps with sixty elephants, and whose tactics have been copied by military experts to the present day. Rome escaped defeat by the narrowest of margins. Only the durability of its system of alliances in Italy saved the day. As long as these alliances held, Hannibal dared not besiege the city of Rome itself for fear of being attacked from the rear. In the end Carthage was more completely humbled than before. Carthage was compelled to abandon all its possessions except the capital city and its surrounding territory in Africa, and to pay an indemnity of 10,000 talents, or, very roughly, 39 million dollars.

Roman vindictiveness reached its peak about the middle of the second century B.C. By this time Carthage had recovered a modicum of its former prosperity—enough to excite the displeasure of its conquerors. Nothing would now satisfy the senatorial magnates but the complete destruction of Carthage and the expropriation of its land. In 149 B.C. the Senate dispatched an ultimatum demanding that the Carthaginians abandon their city and settle at least ten miles from the coast. Since this demand was tantamount to a death sentence for a nation dependent upon commerce, it was refused—as the Romans probably hoped it would be. The result was the Third Punic War, a brutal conflict which was fought between 149 and 146 B.C. The final Roman assault upon the city was carried into the houses of the inhabitants and a frightful butchery took place. When the victorious Roman general saw Carthage going up in flames he said: "It is a glorious moment, but I have a strange feeling that some day the same fate will befall my own homeland." After the resistance of the Carthaginians was finally broken, the few citizens who were left to surrender were sold into slavery, their once magnificent city was razed, and the ground was plowed over with salt. Carthaginian territory was then organized into a Roman province, with the best areas parceled out as senatorial estates.

The wars with Carthage had momentous effects on Rome. First, victory in the Second Punic War led to Roman occupation of Spain. This not only brought great new wealth—above all from Spanish silver—but was the beginning of a policy of westward expansion that was to be one of the great formative influences on the history of Europe. Then too the wars brought Rome into conflict with eastern Mediterranean powers and thereby paved the way for still greater dominion. During the Second Punic War, Philip V of Macedon had entered into an alliance with Carthage and had plotted with the king of Syria to divide Egypt between them. In order to forestall the execution of Philip's plans, Rome sent an army into the East. The result was

Hannibal. A coin from Carthage representing Hannibal as a victorious general, with an elephant on the reverse.

The Third Punic War and the destruction of Carthage

Results of the wars with Carthage: (1) conquest of Spain and the Hellenistic East

the conquest of Greece and Asia Minor and the establishment of a protectorate over Egypt. Thus before the end of the second century B.C. virtually the entire Mediterranean area had been brought under Roman control. The conquest of the Hellenistic East led to the introduction of Greek ideas and customs into Rome. Despite formidable resistance, these novelties exerted considerable influence in changing some aspects of social and cultural life.

(2) a social and economic revolution

Still another effect of the Punic Wars was a great social and economic revolution that swept over Rome in the third and second centuries B.C. The changes wrought by this revolution may be enumerated as follows: (1) a marked increase in slavery due to the capture and sale of prisoners of war; (2) the decline of the small farmer as a result of the establishment of the plantation system in conquered areas and the influx of cheap grain from the provinces; (3) the growth of a helpless urban element composed of impoverished farmers and workers displaced by slave labor; (4) the appearance of a middle class comprising merchants, moneylenders, and men who held government contracts to operate mines, build roads, or collect taxes; and (5) an increase in luxury and vulgar display, particularly among the newly rich who fattened themselves on the profits of war.

Cato's attempt to prevent the transformation of Roman society

As a consequence of this social and economic revolution, Rome was changed from a republic of yeoman farmers into a complex society with new habits of luxury and indulgence. Though property had never been evenly distributed, the gulf which separated rich and poor now yawned more widely than before. The old-fashioned ideals of discipline and devotion to the service of the state were weakened, and people began to live more for pleasure. A few members of the senatorial aristocracy exerted efforts to check these tendencies and to restore the simple virtues of the past. The leader of this movement was the dour Cato the Elder, who inveighed against the new rich for their soft living and strove to set an example to his countrymen by performing hard labor on his farm and dwelling in a house with a dirt floor and no plaster on the walls. In addition he was a prude who showed contempt for women and boasted that his wife never came into his arms except when there was great thunder. Cato also strove, often cantankerously, to prevent the influx of Greek intellectual influences. But his efforts on all fronts had no lasting effect because the clock could not be turned back.

4. THE SOCIAL STRUGGLES OF THE LATE REPUBLIC

The new period of turbulence

The period from the end of the Punic Wars in 146 B.C. to about 30 B.C. was one of the most turbulent in the history of Rome. It was between these years that the nation reaped the full harvest of the seeds of violence sown during the wars of conquest. Bitter class conflicts, assassinations, desperate struggles between rival dictators, wars, and insurrections were the all too common occurrences of this time. Even the slaves contributed their part to the general disorder: first, in 104 B.C. when they ravaged Sicily; and again in 73 B.C. when 70,000 of them under the leadership of a slave named Spartacus held the consuls at bay for more than a year. Spartacus was finally slain in battle and 6,000 of his followers were captured and left crucified along the length of a long road to provide a warning for others.

The first stage in the conflict between classes of citizens began with the revolt of the Gracchi brothers. The Gracchi were leaders of the liberal, pro-Greek elements in Rome and had the support of the middle classes and a number of influential senators as well. Though of aristocratic lineage themselves, they strove for a program of reforms to alleviate the country's ills. They considered these to be a result of the decline of the free peasantry, and proposed the simple remedy of dividing state lands among the landless. The first of the brothers to take up the cause of reform was Tiberius. Elected tribune in 133 B.C., he proposed a law that restricted the current renters or holders of state lands to a maximum of 640 acres. The excess was to be confiscated by the government and given to the poor in small plots. Conservative aristocrats bitterly opposed this proposal and brought about its veto by Tiberius's colleague in the tribunate, Octavius. Tiberius removed Octavius from office, and when his own term expired attempted to stand for reelection. Both of these moves were unconstitutional and gave the conservative senators an excuse for violence. Armed with clubs, they went on a rampage during the elections and murdered Tiberius and 300 of his followers.

The revolt of the Gracchi: the land program of Tiberius

Nine years later Gaius Gracchus, the younger brother of Tiberius, renewed the struggle for reform. Though Tiberius's land law had finally been enacted by the Senate, Gaius believed that the campaign had to go further. Elected tribune in 123 B.C., and reelected in 122, he procured the enactment of various laws for the benefit of the less privileged. The first provided for stabilizing the price of grain in Rome. For this purpose great public granaries were built along the Tiber. A second law proposed to extend the franchise to Roman allies, giving them the rights of Latin citizens. Still a third gave the middle class the right to make up the juries that tried governors accused of exploiting the provinces. These and similar measures provoked so much anger and contention among the classes that civil war broke out. Gaius was proclaimed an enemy of the state, and the Senate authorized the consuls to take all necessary steps for the defense of the Republic. In the ensuing conflict Gaius committed suicide and about 3,000 of his followers were killed.

Gaius Gracchus and the renewed fight for reform

The Gracchan revolt had a broad significance. It demonstrated, first of all, that the Roman Republic had outgrown its constitution. Over the years the assembly had gained powers almost equal to those of the Senate. Instead of working out a peaceful accommodation to these changes, both sides resorted to violence. By so doing they set a prece-

Significance of the Gracchan revolt

Pompey

Julius Caesar

Pompey and Julius Caesar

dent for the unbridled use of force by any politician ambitious for supreme power and thereby paved the way for the destruction of the Republic. The Romans had shown a remarkable capacity for organizing an empire and for adapting the Greek idea of a city-state to a large territory, but the narrow conservatism of their upper classes was a fatal hindrance to the health of the state. They appeared to regard all reform as evil. They failed to understand the reasons for internal discord and seemed to think that repression was its only remedy.

After the downfall of the Gracchi, two military leaders who had won fame in foreign wars successively made themselves rulers of the state. The first was Marius, who was elevated to the consulship by the masses in 107 B.C. and reelected six times thereafter. Unfortunately, Marius was no statesman and accomplished nothing for his followers beyond demonstrating the ease with which a general with an army at his back could override opposition. Following his death in 86 B.C. the aristocrats took a turn at government by force. Their champion was Sulla, another victorious commander. Appointed dictator in 82 B.C. for an unlimited term, Sulla ruthlessly proceeded to exterminate his opponents and to restore to the Senate its original powers. Even the senatorial veto over acts of the assembly was revived, and the authority of the tribunes was sharply curtailed. After three years of rule Sulla decided to exchange the pomp of power for the pleasures of the senses and retired to a life of luxury and ease on his country estate.

It was not to be expected that the "reforms" of Sulla would stand unchallenged after he had relinquished his office, for the effect of his decrees was to give control to a selfish aristocracy. Several new leaders now emerged to espouse the cause of the people. The most famous of them were Pompey (106–48 B.C.) and Julius Caesar (100–44 B.C.). For a time they pooled their energies and resources in a plot to gain control of the government, but later they became rivals and sought to outdo each other in bids for popular support. Pompey won fame as the conqueror of Syria and Palestine, while Caesar devoted his talents to a series of brilliant forays against the Gauls, adding to the Roman state the territory of modern Belgium, Germany west of the Rhine, and France. In 52 B.C., after a series of mob disorders in Rome, the Senate turned to Pompey and caused his election as sole consul. Caesar, stationed in Gaul, was eventually branded an enemy of the state, and Pompey conspired with the senatorial faction to deprive him of political power. The result was a deadly war between the two men. In 49 B.C. Caesar crossed the Rubicon River into Italy (ever since then an image for a fateful decision) and marched on Rome. Pompey fled to the East in the hope of gathering a large enough army to regain control of Italy. In 48 B.C. the forces of the two rivals met at Pharsalus in Greece. Pompey was defeated and soon afterward was murdered by agents of the ruler of Egypt.

Caesar then intervened in Egyptian politics at the court of Cleopatra (whom he left pregnant). Then he conducted another military campaign in Asia Minor in which victory was so swift that he could report "I came, I saw, I conquered" (*veni, vidi, vici*). After that Caesar returned to Rome. There was now no one who dared to challenge his power. With the aid of his veterans he cowed the Senate into granting his every desire. In 46 B.C. he became dictator for ten years, and two years later for life. In addition, he assumed nearly every other title that would augment his power. He obtained from the Senate full authority to make war and peace and to control the revenues of the state. For all practical purposes he was above the law, and the other agents of the government were merely his servants. It seems unquestionable that he had little respect for the constitution, and there were rumors that he intended to make himself king. At any rate, it was on such a charge that he was assassinated on the Ides of March in 44 B.C. by a group of conspirators, under the leadership of Brutus and Cassius, who hoped to rid Rome of the dictatorship.

Caesar's achievements

Although Caesar used to be revered by historians as a superhuman hero, it is now customary to dismiss him as insignificant. But both extremes of interpretation should be avoided. Certainly he did not "save Rome" and was not the greatest statesman of all time, for he treated the Republic with contempt and made the problem of governing more difficult for those who came after him. Yet some of the measures he took as dictator did have lasting effects. With the aid of a Greek astronomer he revised the calendar so as to make a year last for 365 days (with an extra day added every fourth year). This "Julian" calendar—subject to adjustments made by Pope Gregory XIII in 1582—is still with us. It is thus only proper that the seventh month is named after Julius as "July." By conferring citizenship upon thousands of Spaniards and Gauls, Caesar took an important step toward eliminating the distinction between Italians and provincials. He also helped relieve economic inequities by settling many of his veterans and some of the urban poor on unused lands. Vastly more important than these reforms, however, was Caesar's far-sighted resolve, made before he seized power, to invest his efforts in the West. While Pompey, and before him Alexander, went to the East to gain fame and fortune, Caesar was the first great leader to recognize the potential significance of northwestern Europe. By incorporating Gaul into the Roman world he brought Rome great agricultural wealth and helped bring urban life and culture to what was then the wild West. Western European civilization, later to be anchored in just those regions that Caesar conquered, might not have been the same without him.

Ides of March Coin. This coin was struck by Brutus to commemorate the assassination of Julius Caesar. Brutus is depicted on the obverse; on the reverse is a liberty cap between two daggers and the Latin abbreviation for the Ides of March.

5. ROME BECOMES SOPHISTICATED

The culture that Rome brought to Gaul was itself taken from the Greek East. During the last two centuries of republican history Rome came under the influence of Hellenistic civilization. The result was a flowering of intellectual activity and a further impetus to social change beyond what the Punic Wars had produced. The fact must be noted, however, that several of the components of the Hellenistic pattern of culture were never adopted by the Romans. The science of the Hellenistic Age, for example, was largely ignored, and the same was true of some of its art.

One of the most notable effects of Hellenistic influence was the adoption of Epicureanism and, above all, Stoicism by numerous Romans of the upper classes. The most renowned of the Roman exponents of Epicureanism was Lucretius (98–55 B.C.), author of a book-length philosophical poem entitled *On the Nature of Things*. In writing this work Lucretius was moved to explain the universe in such a way as to remove all fear of the supernatural, which he regarded as the chief obstacle to peace of mind. Worlds and all things in them, he taught, are the results of fortuitous combinations of atoms. Though he admitted the existence of the gods, he conceived of them as living in eternal peace, neither creating nor governing the universe. Everything is a product of mechanical evolution, including human beings, and their habits, institutions, and beliefs. Since mind is indissolubly linked with matter, death means utter extinction; consequently, no part of the human personality can survive to be rewarded or punished in an afterlife. Lucretius's conception of the good life was simple: what one needs, he asserted, is not enjoyment but "peace and a pure heart." Whether one agrees with Lucretius's philosophy or not, there is no doubt that he was an extraordinarily fine poet. In fact his musical cadences, sustained majesty of expression, and infectious enthusiasm earn him a rank among the greatest poets who ever lived.

Stoicism was introduced into Rome about 140 B.C. and soon came to include among its converts numerous influential leaders of public life. The greatest of these was Cicero (106–43 B.C.), the "father of Roman eloquence." Although Cicero adopted doctrines from a number of philosophers, including both Plato and Aristotle, he derived more of his ideas from the Stoics than from any other source. Cicero's ethical philosophy was based on the Stoic premises that virtue is sufficient for happiness and that tranquility of mind is the highest good. He conceived of the ideal human being as one who has been guided by reason to an indifference toward sorrow and pain. Where Cicero diverged from the Greek Stoics was in his greater approval of the active, political life. To this degree he still spoke for the older Roman tradition of service to the state. Cicero never claimed to be an original philosopher but rather conceived his goal to be that of bringing the best of Greek philosophy to the West. In this he was remarkably successful, for he wrote in a rich and elegant Latin prose style that has never been surpassed. Cicero's prose immediately became a standard for composition and has remained so until the present century. Thus even though not a truly great thinker Cicero was the most influential Latin transmitter of ancient thought to the medieval and modern western European worlds.

Lucretius and Cicero were the two leading exponents of Greek thought but not the only two fine writers of the later Roman Republic. It now became the fashion among the upper classes to learn Greek and to strive to reproduce in Latin some of the more popular forms of Greek literature. Some results of enduring literary merit were the ribald comedies of Plautus (257?–184 B.C.), the passionate love poems of Catullus (84?–54? B.C.), and the crisp military memoirs of Julius Caesar, the opening of which all beginning students of Latin used to know as well as the pledge of allegiance.

Roman literary achievements

The conquest of the Hellenistic world accelerated the process of social change which the Punic Wars had begun. The effects were most clearly evident in the growth of luxury, in a widened cleavage between classes, and in a further increase in slavery. The Italian people, numbering about eight million at the end of the Republic, had come to be divided into four main castes: the aristocracy, the equestrians, the common citizens, and the slaves. The aristocracy included the senatorial class with a total membership of 300 citizens and their families. The majority of them inherited their status, although occasionally a plebeian would gain admission to the Senate through serving a term as consul. Most of the aristocrats gained their living as office-holders and as owners of great landed estates. The equestrian order was made up of government contractors, bankers, and the wealthier merchants. Originally this class had been composed of those citizens with incomes sufficient to enable them to serve in the cavalry at their own ex-

Social conditions in the late Republic

Left: *Atrium of an Upper-class House in Pompeii, Seen from the Interior.* Around the atrium or central court were grouped suites of living rooms. The marble columns and decorated walls still give an idea of the luxury and refinement enjoyed by the privileged minority. Right: *A Street in Ostia.* This town was the seaport of ancient Rome. The round arches and masonry columns form the balcony of a rich man's house.

pense, but the term equestrian had now come to be applied to all outside of the senatorial class who possessed property in substantial amount. The equestrians were the chief offenders in the indulgence of vulgar tastes and in the exploitation of the poor and the provincials. As bankers they regularly charged exorbitant interest rates whenever they could get them. By far the largest number of the citizens were mere commoners or plebeians. Some of these were independent farmers, a few were industrial workers, but the majority were members of the city mob. When Julius Caesar became dictator, 320,000 citizens were receiving free grain from the state.

The status of the slaves

The Roman slaves were scarcely considered people at all but instruments of production like cattle or horses to be worked for the profit of their masters. Notwithstanding the fact that some of them were cultivated foreigners taken as prisoners of war, they had none of the privileges granted to slaves in Athens. The policy of many of their owners was to get as much work out of them as possible during their prime and then to turn them loose to be fed by the state when they became old and useless. Of course, there were exceptions, especially as a result of the civilizing effects of Stoicism. Cicero, for example, reported himself very fond of his slaves. It is, nevertheless, a sad commentary on Roman civilization that nearly all of the productive labor in the country was done by slaves. They produced practically all of the nation's food supply, for the amount contributed by the few surviving independent farmers was quite insignificant. At least 80 percent of the workers employed in shops were slaves or former slaves. But many of the members of the servile population were engaged in nonproductive activities. A lucrative form of investment for the business classes was ownership of slaves trained as gladiators, who could be rented to the government or to aspiring politicians for the amusement of the people. The growth of luxury also required the employment of thousands of slaves in domestic service. The man of great wealth must have his doorkeepers, his litter-bearers, his couriers (for the government of the Republic had no postal service), his valets, and his tutors for his children. In some great households there were special servants with no other duties than to rub the master down after his bath or to care for his sandals.

Changes in religion

The religious beliefs of the Romans were altered in various ways in the last two centuries of the Republic—again mainly because of the extension of Roman power over most of the Hellenistic states. There was, first of all, a tendency of the upper classes to abandon the traditional religion for the philosophies of Stoicism and, to a lesser degree, Epicureanism. But many of the common people also found worship of the ancient gods no longer satisfying. It was too formal and mechanical and demanded too much in the way of duty and self-sacrifice to meet the needs of the masses, whose lives were now empty and meaningless. Furthermore, Italy had attracted a stream of immigrants from the East, most of whom had a religious background totally different from that of the Romans. The result was the spread of Eastern mystery cults, which satisfied the craving for a more emotional religion and offered the reward of immortality to the wretched and downtrodden of the earth. From Egypt came the cult of Osiris (or Serapis, as the god was now more commonly called), while from Phrygia in Asia Minor was introduced the worship of the Great Mother, with her eunuch priests and wild, symbolic orgies. So strong was the appeal of these cults that the decrees of the Senate against them proved almost impossible to enforce. In the last century B.C. the Persian cult of Mithraism, which came to surpass all the others in popularity, gained a foothold in Italy.

6. THE PRINCIPATE OR EARLY EMPIRE (27 B.C.–180 A.D.)

Shortly before his death in 44 B.C., Julius Caesar had adopted as his sole heir his grandnephew Octavian (63 B.C.–14 A.D.), then a young man of eighteen quietly pursuing his studies in Illyria across the Adriatic Sea. Upon learning of his uncle's death, Octavian hastened to Rome to take control of the government. He soon found that he had to share his ambition with two of Caesar's powerful friends, Mark Antony and Lepidus. The following year the three men formed an alliance for the purpose of crushing the power of the aristocratic group responsible for Caesar's murder. The methods employed were not to the new leaders' credit. Prominent members of the aristocracy were hunted down and slain and their property confiscated. The most noted of the victims was Cicero, brutally slain by Mark Antony's thugs though he had taken no part in the conspiracy against Caesar's life. The real murderers, Brutus and Cassius, escaped and organized an army, but were finally defeated by Octavian and his colleagues near Philippi in 42 B.C.

An alliance to avenge Caesar's death

Thereafter a quarrel developed between the members of the alliance, inspired primarily by Antony's jealousy of Octavian. The subsequent struggle became a contest between East and West. Antony went to the East and made an alliance with Cleopatra that was dedicated to introducing principles of Oriental despotism into Roman rule. Octavian consolidated the forces of the West and came forward as the champion of Greek cultural traditions. As in the earlier contest between Caesar and Pompey the victory again was for the West. In the naval battle of Actium (31 B.C.) Octavian's forces defeated those of Antony and Cleopatra, both of whom soon afterwards committed suicide. It was now clear that Rome would not be swallowed up by the East. Actium guaranteed that there would be several more centuries for the consolidation of Greek ideals and urban life, a development important above all for the future of western Europe.

The struggle between Antony and Octavian

The victory of Octavian ushered in a new period in Roman history, the most glorious and the most prosperous that the nation experi-

*The revival of
constitutional government*

The reforms of Augustus

enced. Although problems of peace and order were still far from being completely solved, the deadly civil strife was ended, and the people now had their first decent opportunity to show what their talents could achieve. Octavian was determined to preserve the forms if not the substance of constitutional government. He accepted the titles of Augustus and emperor (which then only meant "victorious general") conferred upon him by the Senate and the army. He held the authority of proconsul and tribune permanently; but he refused to make himself dictator or even consul for life, despite the pleas of the populace that he do so. In his view the Senate and the people were the supreme sovereigns, as they had been under the early Republic. The title by which he preferred to have his authority designated was princeps, or first citizen of the state. For this reason the period of his rule and that of his successors is properly called the Principate, or early Empire, to distinguish it from the periods of the Republic (sixth century B.C. to 27 B.C.), the time of upheavals (180 A.D. to 284 A.D.), and the period of the late Empire (284 A.D. to 610 A.D.).

Octavian, or Augustus as he was now more commonly called, ruled over Italy and the provinces for forty-four years (31 B.C.–14 A.D.). At the beginning of the period he governed by military power and by common consent, but in 27 B.C. the Senate bestowed upon him the series of offices and titles described above. His work as a statesman at least equaled in importance that of Julius Caesar. Among the reforms of Augustus were the establishment of a new coinage system, the creation of a centralized system of courts under his own supervision, and the bestowal of a large measure of local self-government upon cities and provinces. He insisted upon experience and intelligence as qualifi-

The Emperor Augustus Receiving the Submission of German Barbarians. A drinking cup of the first century A.D.

Trajan Addressing His Troops. This relief on the column of Trajan dates from the first century A.D.

cations for appointment to administrative office. By virtue of his proconsular authority he assumed direct control over the provincial governors and punished them severely for graft and extortion. He abolished the old system of farming out the collection of taxes in the provinces, which had led to great abuses, and appointed his own personal representatives as collectors at regular salaries. But he did not stop with political reforms. He enacted laws designed to check the more glaring social and moral evils of the time. By his own example of temperate living he sought to discourage luxurious habits and to set the precedent for a return to the ancient virtues.

After the death of Augustus in 14 A.D. until almost the end of the century Rome had no really capable rulers, with the single exception of Claudius (41–54). Several of Augustus's successors, most infamously Caligula (37–41) and Nero (54–68), were brutal tyrants who squandered the resources of the state and kept the city of Rome in an uproar by their deeds of bloody violence. But starting in 96 A.D., a period of strong and stable government returned with the advent of "five good emperors": Nerva (96–98), Trajan (98–117), Hadrian (117–138), Antoninus Pius (138–161), and Marcus Aurelius (161–180). These five ruled in harmony with the Senate, displayed great gifts as administrators, and, each in their turn, were able to bequeath a well-ordered and united realm to their designated successors.

From the time of Augustus until that of Trajan, the Roman Empire continued to expand. Augustus gained more land for Rome than did any other Roman ruler. His generals advanced into central Europe, conquering the territories known today as Switzerland, Austria, and

Augustus

Bulgaria. Only in modern-day central Germany did Roman troops meet defeat, a setback which convinced Augustus to hold the Roman borders at the Rhine and Danube. Subsequently, in 43 A.D., the Emperor Claudius began the conquest of Britain, and at the beginning of the next century Trajan pushed beyond the Danube to add Dacia (now Rumania) to the Roman realms. Trajan also conquered territories in Mesopotamia but thereby incurred the enmity of the Persians, causing his successor Hadrian to embark on a defensive policy. The Roman Empire had now reached its ultimate territorial limits; in the third century these limits would begin to recede.

Territorial expansion under the empire

Rome's peaceful sway over a vast empire for about two centuries from the time of Augustus to that of Marcus Aurelius was certainly one of its most impressive accomplishments. As the historian Gibbon said, "the Empire of Rome comprehended the fairest part of the earth and the most civilized portion of mankind." The celebrated *Pax Romana,* or Roman peace, was unprecedented. The Mediterranean was now under the control of one power (as it has never been before or since) and experienced the passage of centuries without a single naval battle. On land one rule held without contention from the borders of Scotland to those of Persia. A contemporary orator justly boasted that "the whole civilized world lays down the arms which were its ancient load, as if on holiday . . . all places are full of gymnasia, fountains, monumental approaches, temples, workshops, schools; one can say that the civilized world, which had been sick from the beginning . . . , has been brought by the right knowledge to a state of health." But much of this health, as we will see, proved illusory.

The Pax Romana

See color map following page 96

7. CULTURE AND LIFE IN THE PERIOD OF THE PRINCIPATE

From the standpoint of variety of intellectual and artistic interests the period of the Principate outshone all other ages in the history of Rome. From 27 B.C. to about 200 A.D. Roman philosophy attained its most characteristic form. The same period also witnessed the production of outstanding literary works, the growth of a distinctive architecture and art, and the greatest triumphs of Roman engineering.

Cultural progress under the Principate

The form of philosophy that appealed most strongly to the Romans was Stoicism. The reasons for Stoicism's popularity are easy to discover. With its emphasis upon duty, self-discipline, and subjection to the natural order of things, it accorded well with the ancient virtues of the Romans and with their habits of conservatism. Moreover, its insistence upon civic obligations and its doctrine of cosmopolitanism appealed to the Roman political-mindedness and pride in world empire. It is necessary to observe, however, that the Stoicism developed in the days of the Principate was somewhat different from that of

Roman Stoicism

Marcus Aurelius. The mounted figure of the emperor-philosopher, now standing on the Piazza del Campidoglio in Rome, is the only full-sized equestrian statue surviving from the ancient world. The Christians destroyed other such statues because they seemed to stand for ruler worship, but they saved this one on the mistaken assumption that it represented Constantine, the first Christian Roman emperor.

Zeno and his school. The old physical theories borrowed from Heracleitus were now discarded, and in their place was substituted a broader interest in politics and ethics. There was a tendency also for Roman Stoicism to assume a more distinctly religious flavor than that which had characterized the original philosophy.

Three eminent apostles of Stoicism lived and taught in Rome in the two centuries that followed the rule of Augustus: Seneca (4 B.C.–65 A.D.), millionaire adviser for a time to Nero; Epictetus, the slave (60?–120 A.D.); and the Emperor Marcus Aurelius (121–180 A.D.). All of them agreed that inner serenity is the ultimate goal to be sought, that true happiness can be found only in surrender to the benevolent order of the universe. They preached the ideal of virtue for virtue's sake, deplored the sinfulness of human nature, and urged obedience to conscience as the voice of duty. Seneca and Epictetus adulterated their philosophy with such deep mystical yearnings as to make it almost a religion. They worshiped the cosmos as divine, governed by an all-powerful Providence who ordains all that happens for ultimate good. The last of the Roman Stoics, Marcus Aurelius, was more fatalistic and less hopeful. Although he did not reject the conception of an ordered and rational universe, he shared neither the faith nor the dogmatism of the earlier Stoics. He was confident of no blessed immortality to balance the sufferings of one's earthly career and was inclined to think of humans as creatures buffeted by evil fortune for which no distant perfection of the whole could fully atone. He urged, nevertheless, that people should continue to live nobly, that they should neither abandon themselves to gross indulgence nor break down in angry protest, but that they should derive what contentment they could from dignified resignation to suffering and tranquil submission to death.

The literary achievements of the Romans bore a definite relation to

Seneca, Epictetus, and Marcus Aurelius

their philosophy. This was especially true of the works of the most distinguished writers of the Augustan Age. Horace (65–8 B.C.), for example, in his famous *Odes* drew copiously from the teachings of both Epicureans and Stoics. He confined his attention, however, to their doctrines of a way of life, for like most of the Romans he had little curiosity about the nature of the world. He developed a philosophy which combined the Epicurean justification of pleasure with the Stoic bravery in the face of trouble. While he never reduced pleasure to the mere absence of pain, he was sophisticated enough to know that the highest enjoyment is possible only through the exercise of rational control.

Virgil (70–19 B.C.) likewise reflects a measure of the philosophical temper of his age. Though his *Eclogues* convey something of the Epicurean ideal of quiet pleasure, Virgil was much more of a Stoic. His utopian vision of an age of peace and abundance, his brooding sense of the tragedy of human fate, and his idealization of a life in harmony with nature indicate an intellectual heritage similar to that of Seneca and Epictetus. Virgil's most noted work, the *Aeneid,* like several of the *Odes* of Horace, was a purposeful glorification of Roman imperialism. The *Aeneid* in fact was an epic of empire recounting the toils and triumphs of the founding of the state, its glorious traditions, and its magnificent destiny. Other major writers of the Augustan Age were Ovid (43 B.C.?–17 A.D.) and Livy (59 B.C.–17 A.D.). The former was the chief representative of the cynical and individualist tendencies of his day. His brilliant and witty writings often reflected the dissolute tastes of the time. The chief claim of Livy to fame rests upon his skill as a prose stylist. As a historian he was woefully deficient. His main work, a history of Rome, is replete with dramatic and picturesque narrative, designed to appeal to the patriotic emotions rather than to present an accurate record of events.

The literature of the period which followed the death of Augustus also exemplified conflicting social and intellectual tendencies. The novels of Petronius and Apuleius and the epigrams of Martial describe the more exotic and sometimes sordid aspects of Roman life. The attitude of the authors is not to instruct or uplift but chiefly to tell an entertaining story or turn a witty phrase. An entirely different viewpoint is presented in the works of the other most important writers of this age: Juvenal, the satirist (60?–140 A.D.), and Tacitus, the historian (55?–117? A.D.). Juvenal wrote under the influence of the Stoics but with narrow vision. Convinced that the troubles of the nation were due to moral degeneracy, he lashed the vices of his countrymen with the fury of an evangelist. A somewhat similar attitude characterized the writing of his younger contemporary, Tacitus. The best-known of Roman historians, Tacitus described the events of his age not with a view to dispassionate analysis but largely for the purpose of moral indictment. His description of the customs of the ancient Germans in his

Germania served to heighten the contrast between the manly virtues of an unspoiled race and the effeminate vices of the decadent Romans. Whatever his failings as a historian, he was a master of ironic wit and brilliant aphorism. Referring to the boasted *Pax Romana,* he makes a barbarian chieftain say: "They create a wilderness and call it peace."

Roman art first assumed its distinctive character during the period of the Principate. Before this time what passed for an art of Rome was really an importation from the Hellenistic East. Conquering armies brought back to Italy wagonloads of statues, reliefs, and marble columns as part of the plunder from Greece and Asia Minor. These became the property of wealthy businessmen and were used to embellish their sumptuous mansions. As the demand increased, hundreds of copies were made, with the result that Rome came to have by the end of the Republic a profusion of objects of art which had no more cultural significance than the Picassos in the home of some modern stockbroker. The aura of national glory which surrounded the early Principate stimulated the growth of an art that was more indigenous. Augustus himself boasted that he found Rome a city of brick and left it a city of marble. Nevertheless, much of the old Hellenistic influence remained until the talent of the Romans themselves was exhausted.

The arts most truly expressive of the Roman character were architecture and sculpture. Architecture was monumental, designed to symbolize power and grandeur. It contained as its leading elements the round arch, the vault, and the dome, although at times the Corinthian column was employed, especially in the construction of temples. The materials most commonly used were brick, squared stone blocks, and concrete, the last a Roman invention. As a further adornment of public buildings, sculptured entablatures and facades, built up of tiers of colonnades or arcades, were frequently added. Roman architecture was devoted primarily to utilitarian purposes. The foremost examples were government buildings, amphitheaters, baths, race courses, and private houses. Nearly all were of massive proportions and solid construction. Among the largest and most noted were the Pantheon, with its dome having a diameter of 142 feet, and the Colosseum, which

Achievements in art

See color plates following page 96

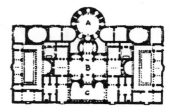

Floor Plan of the Baths of Caracalla

The Baths of Caracalla, Rome. The gigantic scale is typical of late empire buildings. Elaborate and luxurious public baths like these were often presented to the public by the emperor or rich citizens. The floor plan above indicates the separate chambers for hot tub baths.

The Pantheon in Rome. Built by the Emperor Hadrian it boasted the largest dome without interior supports of the ancient world. The dome forms a perfect sphere, exactly as high as it is wide.

could accommodate 65,000 spectators at the gladiatorial combats. Roman sculpture included as its main forms triumphal arches and columns, narrative reliefs, altars, and portrait busts and statues. Its distinguishing characteristics were individuality and naturalism. Sometimes Roman statues and busts served only to express the vanity of the aristocracy, but the best Roman sculptured portraiture succeeded in conveying qualities of simple human dignity similar to those espoused in the philosophy of the Stoics.

Roman engineering

Closely related to their achievements in architecture were Roman triumphs in engineering and public services. The imperial Romans built marvelous roads and bridges, many of which still survive. In the time of Trajan eleven aqueducts brought water into Rome from the nearby hills and provided the city with 300 million gallons daily for drinking and bathing as well as for flushing a well-designed sewage system. Water was cleverly funneled into the homes of the rich for their private gardens, fountains, and pools. Romans also established the first hospitals in the Western world and the first system of state medicine for the benefit of the poor.

As impressive as the Romans were in engineering, they accomplished little in science. They excelled, as has been jokingly but not inaccurately said, in drains, not brains. Scarcely an original discovery of fundamental importance was made by anyone of Latin nationality. This fact seems strange when we consider that the Romans had the advantage of Hellenistic science as a foundation upon which to build. But they neglected their opportunity almost completely because they had no vigorous curiosity about the natural world in which they lived. Roman writers on scientific subjects were hopelessly devoid of critical intelligence. The most renowned and typical of them was Pliny the Elder (23–79 A.D.), who completed about 77 A.D. a voluminous encyclopedia of "science" which he called *Natural History*. The subjects discussed varied from cosmology to economics. Despite the wealth of material it contains, Pliny's work is of limited value. He was totally unable to distinguish between fact and fable. In his estimation, the weirdest tales of wonders and portents were to be accepted as of equal value with the most solidly established facts.

Pliny

The only real scientific advance made during the period of the Principate was the work of Hellenistic scientists who lived in Italy or in the provinces. One of these was the astronomer Ptolemy, who flourished in Alexandria around the middle of the second century (see above, p. 162). Another was the physician Galen, active in Rome at various times during the latter half of the second century. While Galen's fame rests primarily on his medical encyclopedia, systematizing the learn-

Galen

Roman Aqueduct at Segovia, Spain. Aqueducts conveyed water from mountains to the larger cities.

ing of others, he is deserving of more credit for his own experiments which brought him close to a discovery of the circulation of the blood. He not only taught but proved that the arteries carry blood, and that severance of even a small one is sufficient to drain away all of the blood of the body in little more than half an hour.

Roman women

Roman society exhibited the same general tendencies under the Principate as in the last days of the Republic. One of the least attractive of its traits was the low status it accorded to women. The historian M. I. Finley has remarked that the two most famous women in Roman history were Cleopatra, who was not even a Roman, and the fictional Lucretia, who earned her fame by being raped and killing herself. Seldom have women been so confined to domesticity and obscurity. Roman women did not even really have their own names but were given family names with feminine endings—for example, Julia from Julius, Claudia from Claudius, and Livia from Livius. When there were two daughters in a family they would be distinguished only as "Julia the elder" and "Julia the younger," and when several as "Julia the first," "second," and "third." Women were expected to be subservient to their fathers and husbands, were valued to the degree they produced progeny, and were expected to stay at home. A typical tomb epitaph might say: "She loved her husband . . . she bore two sons . . . she was pleasant to talk with . . . she kept the house and worked in wool. That is all." During the Principate Roman women from imperial families not surprisingly tried to escape these limitations by taking a backstage and often literally murderous role in politics. Less highly placed women sought outlets in the excitement of gladiatorial shows—making gladiators the equivalent of modern rock-and-roll stars—or in the ceremonies of religious cults.

Gladiatorial combat

Along with the confinement of women, the most serious indictment which can be brought against the age was the further growth of the passion for cruelty. Whereas the Greeks entertained themselves with theatre, the Romans more and more preferred "circuses," which were really exhibitions of human slaughter. In the period of the Principate the great games and spectacles became bloodier than ever. The Romans could no longer obtain a sufficient thrill from mere exhibitions of athletic prowess: pugilists were now required to have their hands wrapped with thongs of leather loaded with iron or lead. The most popular amusement of all was watching the gladiatorial combats in the Colosseum or in other amphitheaters capable of accommodating thousands of spectators. Fights between gladiators were nothing new, but they were now presented on a much more elaborate scale. Not only the common people attended them, but wealthy aristocrats also, and frequently the head of the government himself. The gladiators fought to the accompaniment of savage cries and curses from the audience. When one went down with a disabling wound, it was the privilege of the crowd to decide whether his life should be spared or whether the weapon of his opponent should be plunged into

The Colosseum. Built by the Roman emperors between 75 and 80 A.D. as a place of entertainment, it was the scene of gladiatorial combats. The most common form of Greek secular architecture was the theater (see p. 197), but the most common Roman form was the amphitheater.

his heart. One contest after another, often featuring the sacrifice of men to wild animals, was staged in the course of a single exhibition. Should the arena become too sodden with blood, it was covered over with a fresh layer of sand, and the revolting performance went on. Most of the gladiators were condemned criminals or slaves, but some were volunteers even from the respectable classes. Commodus, the worthless son of Marcus Aurelius, entered the arena several times for the sake of the plaudits of the mob: this was his idea of a Roman holiday.

Notwithstanding its low moral tone, the age of the Principate was characterized by an even deeper interest in salvationist religions than that which had prevailed under the Republic. Mithraism now gained adherents by the thousands, absorbing many of the followers of the cults of the Great Mother and of Serapis. About 40 A.D. the first Christians appeared in Rome. The new sect grew steadily and eventually succeeded in displacing Mithraism as the most popular of the salvationist faiths. We will read more about its nature and success in the next chapter.

The spread of Mithraism and Christianity

The establishment of stable government by Augustus ushered in a

The Maison Carrée at Nîmes, France. The most perfect example of a Roman temple extant. Reflecting possible Etruscan influence, it was built on a high base or podium with great steps leading to the entrance. It dates from the beginning of the Christian era.

period of prosperity for Italy which lasted for more than two centuries. Trade was now extended to all parts of the known world, even to Arabia, India, and China. Manufacturing increased somewhat, especially in the production of pottery, textiles, and articles of metal and glass. In spite of all this, the economic order was far from healthy. Prosperity was not evenly distributed but was confined primarily to the upper classes. Since the stigma attached to manual labor persisted as strongly as ever, production was bound to decline as the supply of slaves diminished. Perhaps worse was the fact that Italy had a decidedly unfavorable balance of trade. The meager industrial development was by no means sufficient to provide enough articles of export to meet the demand for luxuries imported from the provinces and from the outside world. As a consequence, Italy was gradually drained of its supply of precious metals. By the third century the Western Roman economy began to collapse.

Portrait Bust of a Roman Lady. The ostentatiousness of upper-class culture during the period of the Principate is well displayed by this sculpture, done around 90 A.D.

8. ROMAN LAW

There is general agreement that one of the most important legacies which the Romans left to succeeding cultures was their system of law. This was the result of a gradual evolution which may be considered to have begun with the publication of the Twelve Tables about 450 B.C. In the later centuries of the Republic the law of the Twelve Tables was modified and practically superseded by the growth of new precedents and principles. These emanated from different sources: from changes in custom, from the teachings of the Stoics, from the decisions of judges, but especially from the edicts of the *praetors*. The Roman praetors were magistrates who had authority to define and interpret the law in a particular suit and issue instructions to the jury for the decision of the case. The jury merely decided questions of fact; all issues of law were settled by the praetor, and generally his interpretations became precedents for the decision of similar cases in the future. Thus a system of judicial practice was built up in somewhat the same fashion as the English common law.

The early development of Roman law

It was under the Principate, however, that the Roman law attained its highest stage of development. This later progress was the result in part of the extension of the law over a wider field of jurisdiction, over the lives and properties of aliens in strange environments as well as over the citizens of Italy. But the major reason was the fact that Augustus and his successors gave to certain eminent jurists the right to deliver opinions on the legal issues of cases under trial in the courts. The most prominent of the men thus designated from time to time were Gaius, Ulpian, Papinian, and Paulus. Although most of them held high judicial office, they had gained their reputations primarily as lawyers and writers on legal subjects. The responses of these jurists came to embody a science and philosophy of law and were accepted as the basis of Roman jurisprudence. It was typical of the Roman respect for authority that the ideas of these men should have been adopted so readily even when they upset, as they occasionally did, time-honored beliefs.

Roman law under the Principate; the great jurists

The Roman law as it was developed under the influence of the jurists comprised three great branches or divisions: the civil law, the law of peoples, and the natural law. The civil law was the law of Rome and its citizens. As such it existed in both written and unwritten forms. It included the statutes of the Senate, the decrees of the princeps, the edicts of the praetors, and also certain ancient customs operating with the force of law. The law of peoples, was the law that was held to be common to all people regardless of nationality. It was the law which authorized the institutions of slavery and private ownership of property and defined the principles of purchase and sale, partnership, and contract. It was not superior to the civil law but supplemented it as especially applicable to the alien inhabitants of the empire.

The three divisions of Roman law

The most interesting and in many ways the most important branch of the Roman law was the natural law. This was not a product of judicial practice, but of philosophy. The Stoics had developed the idea of a rational order of nature which is the embodiment of justice and right. They had affirmed that all men are by nature equal, and that

The natural law

they are entitled to certain basic rights which governments have no authority to transgress. The father of the law of nature as a legal principle, however, was not one of the Hellenistic Stoics, but Cicero. "True law," he declared, "is right reason consonant with nature, diffused among all men, constant, eternal. To make enactments infringing this law, religion forbids, neither may it be repealed even in part, nor have we power through Senate or people to free ourselves from it." This law is prior to the state itself, and any ruler who defies it automatically becomes a tyrant. Most of the great jurists subscribed to conceptions of the law of nature very similar to those of the philosophers. Although the jurists did not regard this law as an automatic limitation upon the civil law, they thought of it nevertheless as a great ideal to which the statutes and decrees of men ought to conform. This development of the concept of abstract justice as a legal principle was one of the noblest achievements of the Roman civilization.

9. THE CRISIS OF THE THIRD CENTURY (180–284 A.D.)

The problems of imperial succession

With the death of Marcus Aurelius in 180 A.D. the period of beneficent imperial rule came to an end. One reason for the success of the "five good emperors" was that the first four designated particularly promising young men, rather than sons or close relatives, for the succession. But Marcus Aurelius broke this pattern with results that were to prove fateful. Although he was one of the most philosophic and thoughtful rulers who ever reigned, he was not wise enough to recognize that his son Commodus was a vicious incompetent. Made emperor by his father's wishes, Commodus indulged his taste for perversities, showed open contempt for the Senate, and ruled so brutally that a palace clique finally had him murdered by strangling in 192. Matters thereafter became worse. With the lack of an obvious successor to Commodus, the armies of the provinces raised their own candidates and civil war ensued. Although a provincial general, Septimius Severus (193–211), emerged victorious, it now became clear that provincial armies could interfere in imperial politics at will. Severus and some of his successors aggravated the problem by eliminating even the theoretical rights of the Senate and ruling frankly as military dictators. Once the role of brute force was openly revealed any aspiring general could try his luck at seizing power. Hence civil war became endemic. From 235 to 284 there were no less than twenty-six "barracks emperors," of whom only one managed to escape a violent death.

Commodus. The self-deluded ruler encouraged artists to portray him as the equal of Hercules.

The half-century between 235 and 284 was certainly the worst for Rome since its rise to world power. In addition to political chaos, a number of other factors combined to bring the empire to the brink of ruin. One was that civil war had disastrous economic effects. Not only did constant warfare interfere with agriculture and trade, but the

Arch of Septimius Severus. This monument to the feats of Septimius Severus was constructed about 200 A.D.

rivalry of aspirants to rule led them to drain the wealth of their territories in order to gain favor with their armies. Following the maxim of "enriching the soldiers and scorning the rest," they could only raise funds by debasing the coinage and by nearly confiscatory taxation of civilians. Landlords, small tenants, and manufacturers thus had little motive to produce at a time when production was most necessary. In human terms the poorest, as is usual in times of economic contraction, were hurt the worst. Often they were driven to the most wretched extremes of destitution. In the wake of war and hunger, disease then became rampant. Already in the reign of Marcus Aurelius a terrible plague had swept through the empire, decimating the army and the population at large. In the middle of the third century pestilence returned and struck at the population with its fearful scythe for fifteen years.

Consequences of civil war

The resulting strain on human resources came at a time when Rome could least afford it, for still another threat to the empire in the middle of the third century was the advance of Rome's external enemies. With Roman ranks thinned by disease and Roman armies fighting each other, Germans in the West and Persians in the East were able to break through the old Roman defense lines. In 251 the Goths defeated and slew the Emperor Decius, crossed the Danube, and marauded at will in the Balkans. A more humiliating disaster came in 260 when the Emperor Valerian was captured in battle by the Persians and made to kneel as a footstool for their ruler. When he died his body was stuffed

The Emperor Decius. The extreme naturalism and furrowed brow is typical of the portraits of this period.

The Emperor Philip the Arab. An artistic legacy of the Roman "age of anxiety."

Plotinus

Turning point in 284

and hung on exhibition. Clearly the days of Caesar and Augustus were very far off.

Understandably enough the culture of the third century was marked by pervasive anxiety. One can even see expressions of worry in the surviving statuary, as in the bust of the Emperor Philip (244–249) who appears almost to realize that he would soon be killed in battle. Suiting the spirit of the age, the Neoplatonic philosophy of otherworldlyism came to the fore. Neoplatonism (meaning "New Platonism") drew the spiritualist tendency of Plato's thought to extremes. The first of its basic teachings was emanationism: everything that exists proceeds from God in a continuing stream of emanations. The initial stage in the process is the emanation of the world-soul. From this come the divine Ideas or spiritual patterns, and then the souls of particular things. The final emanation is matter. But matter has no form or quality of its own; it is simply the privation of spirit, the residue which is left after the spiritual rays from God have burned themselves out. It follows that matter is to be despised as the symbol of evil and darkness. The second major doctrine was mysticism. The human soul was originally a part of God, but it has become separated from its divine source through its union with matter. The highest goal of life should be mystic reunion with the divine, which can be accomplished through contemplation and through emancipation of the soul from bondage to matter. Human beings should be ashamed of the fact that they possess a physical body and should seek to subjugate it in every way possible. Asceticism was therefore the third main teaching of this philosophy.

The real founder of Neoplatonism was Plotinus, who was born in Egypt about 204 A.D. In the later years of his life he taught in Rome and won many followers among the upper classes before he died in 270. His principal successors diluted the philosophy with more and more bizarre superstitions. In spite of its antirational viewpoint and its utter indifference to the state, Neoplatonism became so popular in Rome in the third and fourth centuries A.D. that it almost completely supplanted Stoicism. No fact could have expressed more eloquently the turn of Rome away from the realities of the here and now.

10. CAUSES FOR ROME'S DECLINE

As Rome was not built in a day, so it was not lost in one. As we will see in the next chapter, strong rule returned in 284. Thereafter the Roman Empire endured in the West for two hundred years more and in the East for a millennium. But the restored Roman state was extremely different from the old one—so much so that it is proper to end the story of characteristically Roman civilization here and review the reasons for Rome's decline.

More has been written on the fall of Rome than on the death of any other civilization. The theories offered to account for the decline have been many and varied. A popular recent one is that Rome fell from the effects of lead poisoning, but this cannot be accepted for many reasons, one of which is that most Roman pipes were not made of lead but of *terra cotta*. Moralists have found the explanation for Rome's fall in the descriptions of lechery and gluttony presented in the writings of such authors as Juvenal and Petronius. Such an approach, however, overlooks the facts that much of this evidence is patently overdrawn, and that nearly all of it comes from the period of the early Principate: in the later centuries, when the empire was more obviously collapsing, morality became more austere through the influence of ascetic religions. One of the simplest explanations is that Rome fell only because of the severity of German attacks. But barbarians had always stood ready to attack Rome throughout its long history: German pressures indeed mounted at certain times but German invasions would never have succeeded had they not come at moments when Rome was already weakened internally.

It is best then, to concentrate on Rome's most serious internal problems. Some of these were political. The most obvious political failing of the Roman constitution under the Principate was the lack of a clear law of succession. Especially when a ruler died suddenly there was no certainty about who was to follow him. In modern America the deaths of a Lincoln or Kennedy might shock the nation, but people at least knew what would happen next; in imperial Rome no one knew and civil war was generally the result. From 235 to 284 such warfare fed upon itself. Civil war was also nurtured by the lack of constitutional means for reform. If regimes became unpopular, as most did after 180, the only means to alter them was to overthrow them. But the resort to violence always bred more violence. In addition to those problems, imperial Rome's greatest political weakness may ultimately have been that it did not involve enough people in the work of government. The vast majority of the empire's inhabitants were subjects who did not participate in the government in any way. Hence they looked on the empire at best with indifference and often with hostility, especially when tax-collectors appeared. Loyalty to Rome was needed to keep the empire going, but when the tests came such loyalty was lacking.

Even without political problems the Roman Empire would probably have been fated to extinction for economic reasons. Rome's worst economic problems derived from its slave system and from manpower shortages. Roman civilization was based on cities, and Roman cities existed largely by virtue of an agricultural surplus produced by slaves. Slaves were worked so hard that they did not normally reproduce to fill their own ranks. Until the time of Trajan Roman victories in war and fresh conquests provided fresh supplies of

Theories of decline

Internal causes of decline

Economic causes

slaves to keep the system going, but thereafter the economy began to run out of human fuel. Landlords could no longer be so profligate of human life, barracks slavery came to an end, and the countryside produced less of a surplus to feed the towns. The fact that no technological advance took up the slack may also be attributed to slavery. Later in Western history agricultural surpluses were produced by technological revolutions but Roman landlords were indifferent to technology because interest in it was thought to be demeaning. As long as there were slaves to do the work there was no interest in labor-saving devices, and attention to any sort of machinery was deemed a sign of slavishness. Landlords proved their nobility by their interest in "higher things," but while they were contemplating these heights their agricultural surpluses gradually became depleted.

Inadequate manpower

Manpower shortages greatly aggravated Rome's economic problems. With the end of foreign conquests and the decline of slavery there was a pressing need for people to stay on the farm, but because of constant barbarian pressures there was also a steady need for men to serve in the army. The plagues of the second and third centuries sharply reduced the population just at the worst time. It has been estimated that between the reign of Marcus Aurelius and the restoration of strong rule in 284 the population of the Roman Empire was reduced by one third. (Demoralization seems also to have lowered the birthrate.) The result was that there were neither sufficient forces to work the land nor men to fight Rome's enemies. No wonder Rome began to lose battles as it had seldom lost them before.

Lack of civic ideals

Enormous dedication and exertion on the part of large numbers might just possibly have saved Rome, but few were willing to work hard for the public good. For this cultural explanations may be posited. Most simply stated the Roman Empire of the third century could not draw upon commonly shared civic ideals. By then the old republican and senatorial traditions had been rendered manifestly obsolete. Worse, provincials could hardly be expected to fight or work hard for Roman ideals of any sort, especially when the Roman state no longer stood for beneficent peace but only brought recurrent war and oppressive taxation. Regional differences, the lack of public education, and social stratification were further barriers to the development of any unifying public spirit. As the empire foundered new ideals indeed emerged, but they were religious, otherworldly ones. Ultimately, then, the decline of Rome was accompanied by disinterest, and the Roman world slowly came to an end not so much with a bang as with a whimper.

11. THE ROMAN HERITAGE

It is tempting to believe that we today have many similarities to the Romans: first of all, because Rome is nearer to us in time than any of the other civilizations of antiquity; and secondly, because Rome seems to bear such a close kinship to the modern temper. The resemblances between Roman history and the history of Great Britain or the United States in the nineteenth and twentieth centuries have often been noted. The Roman economic evolution progressed all the way from a simple agrarianism to a complex urban system with problems of unemployment, gross disparities of wealth, and financial crises. The Roman Empire, in common with the British, was founded upon conquest. It must not be forgotten, however, that the heritage of Rome was an ancient heritage and that consequently, the similarities between the Roman and modern civilizations are not so important as they seem. As we have noted already, the Romans disdained industrial activities, and they were not interested in science. Neither did they have any idea of the modern national state; the provinces were really colonies, not integral parts of a body politic. The Romans also never developed an adequate system of representative government. Finally, the Roman conception of religion was vastly different from our own. Their system of worship, like that of the Greeks, was external and mechanical, not inward or spiritual. What Christians consider the highest ideal of piety—an emotional attitude of love for the divine—the Romans regarded as gross superstition.

Comparison of Rome with the modern world

The Forum, the Civic Center of Ancient Rome. In addition to public squares, the Forum included triumphal arches, magnificent temples, and government buildings. In the foreground is the Temple of Saturn. Behind it is the Temple of Antoninus and Faustina. The three columns at the extreme right are what is left of the Temple of Castor and Pollux, and in the farthest background is the arch of Titus.

Nevertheless, the civilization of Rome exerted a great influence upon later cultures. The form, if not the spirit, of Roman architecture was preserved in the ecclesiastical architecture of the Middle Ages and survives to this day in the design of many of our government buildings. The sculpture of the Augustan Age also lives on in the equestrian statues, the memorial arches and columns, and in the portraits in stone of statesmen and generals that adorn our streets and parks. Although subjected to new interpretations, the law of the great jurists became an important part of the Code of Justinian and was thus handed down to the Middle Ages and modern times. American judges frequently cite maxims originally invented by Gaius or Ulpian. Further, the legal systems of nearly all continental European countries today incorporate much of the Roman law. This law was one of the grandest of the Romans' achievements and reflected their genius for governing a vast and diverse empire. It should not be forgotten either that Roman literary achievements furnished much of the inspiration for the revival of learning that spread over Europe in the twelfth century and reached its zenith in the Renaissance. Perhaps not so well known is the fact that the organization of the Catholic Church, to say nothing of part of its ritual, was adapted from the structure of the Roman state and the complex of the Roman religion. For example, the pope still bears the title of supreme pontiff (*pontifex maximus*), which was used to designate the authority of the emperor as head of the civic religion.

Most important of all Rome's contributions to the future was the transmission of Greek civilization to the European West. The development in Italy of a culture that was highly suffused by Greek ideals from the second century B.C. onwards was in itself an important counterweight to the earlier predominance of Greek-oriented civilization in the East. Then, following the path of Julius Caesar, this culture advanced still further West. Before the coming of Rome the culture of northwestern Europe (modern France, the Benelux countries, western and southern Germany, and England) was tribal. Rome brought cities and Greek ideas, above all conceptions of human freedom and individual autonomy that went along with the development of highly differentiated urban life. It is true that ideals of freedom were often ignored in practice—they did not temper Roman dependence on slavery and subjugation of women, or prevent Roman rule in conquered territories from being exploitative and sometimes oppressive. Nonetheless, Roman history is the real beginning of Western history as we now know it. Greek civilization brought to the East by Alexander was not enduring, but the same civilization brought West by the work of such men as Caesar, Cicero, and Augustus was the starting point for many of the subsequent accomplishments of western Europe. As we will see, the development was not continuous and there were many other ingredients to later European success, but the influence of Rome was no less profound.

SELECTED READINGS

• *Items so designated are available in paperback editions.*

POLITICAL HISTORY

• Adcock, F. E., *Roman Political Ideas and Practice,* Ann Arbor, Mich., 1964.

Bloch, Raymond, *The Origins of Rome,* New York, 1960.

Cary, M., and H. H. Scullard, *A History of Rome,* 3rd ed., New York, 1975. A basic college-level textbook.

Chambers, M., ed., *The Fall of Rome,* New York, 1970. A collection of readings on this perennially fascinating subject.

Cowell, F. R., *Cicero and the Roman Republic,* New York, 1948.

Gruen, E. S., *The Last Generation of the Roman Republic,* Berkeley, Calif., 1964.

Haywood, R. M., *The Myth of Rome's Fall,* New York, 1962.

Mommsen, Theodor, *The History of Rome,* Chicago, 1957. An abridged reissue of one of the greatest historical works of the nineteenth century. Emphasizes personalities, especially that of Julius Caesar.

Ogilvie, R. M., *Early Rome and the Etruscans,* Atlantic Highlands, N.J., 1976. Now the best specialized review of the earliest period.

• Scullard, H. H., *From the Gracchi to Nero,* New York, 1959. Good survey of events in this central period.

Sinnigen, W., and A. E. R. Boak, *A History of Rome to A.D. 565,* 6th ed., New York, 1977. A good alternative to Cary and Scullard as a basic textbook.

• Starr, C. G., *The Emergence of Rome,* Ithaca, N.Y., 1953. A brief elementary introduction.

• Syme, Ronald, *The Roman Revolution,* New York, 1939. A pathfinding work on the late Republic and early empire that stresses power politics and the role of factions rather than the clash of institutional principles. Also extremely well written.

• Taylor, Lily Ross, *Party Politics in the Age of Caesar,* Berkeley, Calif., 1949. Still the best introduction to society and politics in the late republican period.

Warmington, B. H., *Carthage,* Baltimore, 1965.

CULTURAL AND SOCIAL HISTORY

Africa, T., *Rome of the Caesars,* New York, 1965. An entertaining approach to the history of imperial Rome by means of short biographies.

Arnold, E. V., *Roman Stoicism,* New York, 1911.

• Badian, Ernst, *Roman Imperialism in the Late Republic,* Oxford, 1967. Very sophisticated analysis.

Bailey, Cyril, ed., *The Legacy of Rome,* New York, 1924. An older collection of readings on different aspects of the Roman legacy to later times.

Balston, J. P. V. D., *Life and Leisure in Ancient Rome,* New York, 1969.

• Brunt, P. A., *Social Conflicts in the Roman Republic,* London, 1971.

• Carcopino, Jerome, *Daily Life in Ancient Rome,* New Haven, Conn., 1960.

Dill, Samuel, *Roman Society from Nero to Marcus Aurelius,* New York, 1905.

Duff, J. W., *A Literary History of Rome in the Golden Age,* New York, 1964.
———, *A Literary History of Rome in the Silver Age,* New York, 1960.
Earl, Donald, *The Moral and Political Tradition of Rome,* Ithaca, N.Y., 1967.
Frank, Tenney, *Economic History of Rome,* Baltimore, 1927. Still valuable.
Grant, M., *Roman Literature,* New York, 1954.
Laistner, M. L. W., *The Greater Roman Historians,* Berkeley, Calif., 1947.
McMullen, R., *Enemies of the Roman Order,* Cambridge, Mass., 1966.
———, *Roman Social Relations, 50 B.C. to A.D. 284,* New Haven, Conn., 1974.
Rostovtzeff, M. I., *Social and Economic History of the Roman Empire,* 2nd ed., 2 vols., New York, 1957. By one of the greatest historians of the early twentieth century. Important both for its interpretations and the wealth of information it contains.
• Sandbach, F. H., *The Stoics,* London, 1975.
Scullard, H. H., *The Etruscan Cities and Rome,* Ithaca, N.Y., 1967.
• Starr, C. G., *Civilization and the Caesars,* Ithaca, N.Y., 1954. Surveys Roman intellectual developments in the four centuries after Cicero.
Toynbee, A. J., *Hannibal's Legacy,* 2 vols., London, 1965.
Westermann, W. L., *The Slave Systems of Greek and Roman Antiquity,* Philadelphia, 1955. The best overview of this basic subject.
• Wheeler, Mortimer, *The Art of Rome,* New York, 1964.
Yavetz, Z., *Plebs and Princeps,* London, 1969.

SOURCE MATERIALS

Translations of Roman authors are available in the appropriate volumes of the Loeb Classical Library, Harvard University Press.

See also:

• Lewis, Naphtali, and M. Reinhold, *Roman Civilization,* 2 vols., New York, 1955.
MacKendrick, P., *The Roman Mind at Work,* Princeton, N.J., 1958.

Chapter 11

CHRISTIANITY AND THE TRANSFORMATION OF THE ROMAN WORLD

Who will hereafter credit the fact . . . that Rome has to fight within her own borders not for glory but for bare life? . . . The poet Lucan describing the power of the city in a glowing passage says: "If Rome be weak, where shall we look for strength?" We may vary his words and say: "If Rome be lost, where shall we look for help?"

For mortals this life is a race: we run it on earth that we may receive our crown elsewhere. No man can walk secure amid serpents and scorpions.

—St. Jerome, *Letters*

The Roman Empire declined after 180 A.D. but it did not collapse. In 284 the vigorous soldier-emperor Diocletian began a reorganization of the empire which gave it a new lease on life. Thereafter, throughout the fourth century the Roman state continued to surround the Mediterranean. In the fifth century the western half of the empire did fall to invading Germans, but even then Roman institutions were not entirely destroyed, and in the sixth century the eastern half of the empire managed to reconquer a good part of the western Mediterranean shoreline. Only in the seventh century did it become fully clear that the Roman Empire could only hope to survive by turning away from the West and consolidating its strength in the East. When that happened ancient history clearly came to an end.

The protracted decline of the Roman Empire

Historians used to underestimate the longevity of Roman institutions and begin their discussions of medieval history in the third, fourth, or fifth century. Since historical periodization is always approximate and depends largely on what aspects of development a historian wishes to emphasize, this approach cannot be dismissed. Certainly the transition from ancient to medieval history was gradual and

The age of late antiquity (284–610)

*Christianity and the
Transformation of the Roman
World*

*Rise of Christianity and
decline of urban life*

many "medieval" ways were slowly emerging in the West as early as the third century. But it is now more customary to conceive of ancient history continuing after 284 and lasting until the Roman Empire lost control over the Mediterranean in the seventh century. The period from 284 to about 610, although transitional (as, of course, all ages are), has certain common themes of its own and is perhaps best described as neither Roman nor medieval but as the age of late antiquity.

The major cultural trend of late antique history was the spread and triumph of Christianity throughout the Roman world. At first Christianity was just one of several manifestations of the turn toward other-worldlyism, but in the fourth century it was adopted as the Roman state religion and thereafter became one of the greatest shaping forces in the development of the West. While Christianity was spreading, the Roman Empire was indubitably declining. Central to this decline was a contraction of the urban life on which the empire had been based. Once the empire began to experience severe pressures it was inevitable that contraction would be most pronounced in the European northwest because city civilization there was least deeply rooted and because the area was far away from the empire's major trade and communications lifelines on the Mediterranean. Contraction was also felt in parts of the West that were closer to the Mediterranean because western cities depended far more on declining agricultural production than eastern ones. The East relied more on trade in luxury goods and industry. Consequently the entire period saw a steady shift in the weight of civilization and imperial government from West to East. The most visible manifestations of this shift were the German successes of the fifth century. These surely helped open a new chapter in Western political history, but their immediate impact should not be exaggerated. Even with the influx of Germans, Roman institutions continued to decline gradually. Particularly in areas that were on or close to the Mediterranean, Roman city life persisted, albeit with steadily declining vigor, until the Mediterranean was no longer a Roman lake.

1. THE REORGANIZED EMPIRE

The reforms of Diocletian

Before we examine the emergence and triumph of Christianity, it is best to survey the nature of the government and society in which the new religion became a dominant force. The fifty years of chaos that threatened to destroy Rome in the third century were ended by the energetic work of a remarkable soldier named Diocletian, who ruled as emperor from 284 to 305. Conscious of some of the more obvious problems that had undone his predecessors, Diocletian embarked on a number of fundamental political and economic reforms. Recognizing that the dominance of the army in the life of the state had hitherto been too great, he introduced measures to separate military from civilian administrative chains of command. Aware that new pressures, both external and internal, had made it nearly impossible for one man to govern the entire Roman Empire, he divided his realm in half, granting the western part to a trusted colleague, Maximian, who recognized Diocletian as the senior ruler. The two then chose lieutenants, called *caesars,* to govern large subsections of their territories. This system was also meant to provide for an orderly succession, for the caesars were supposed to inherit the major rule of either East or West and then appoint new caesars in their stead. In the economic sphere Diocletian stabilized the badly debased currency, introduced a new system of taxation, and issued legislation designed to keep agricultural workers and town-dwellers at their jobs so that the basic work necessary to support the empire would continue to be done.

Diocletian. His short hair is in the Roman military style.

Although Diocletian's program of reorganization was remarkably successful insofar as it restored an empire that had been on the verge of expiring, it also helped to transform the empire. Essentially Diocletian changed the empire by "orientalizing" it in three primary and lasting ways. Most literally, he began a geographical orientalization of the empire by shifting its administrative weight toward the East. Since he was a "Roman" emperor we would assume that he must have ruled from Rome, but in fact between 284 and 303 he was never there, ruling instead from Nicomedia, a city in modern-day Turkey. This he did in tacit recognition of the fact that the wealthier and more vital part of the empire was clearly in the East. Second, as befitting one who turned his back on Rome, Diocletian adopted the titles and ceremonies of an Oriental potentate. Probably he did this less because he had Eastern tastes than because he wished to avoid the fate of his predecessors who were insufficiently respected. Most likely he thought that if he were feared and worshiped he would stand a greater chance of dying in bed. Accordingly, Diocletian completely abandoned Augustus's policy of appearing to be a constitutional ruler and came forward as an undisguised autocrat. He took the title not of princeps, or first citizen, but of *dominus,* or lord, and he introduced Oriental ceremony into his court. He wore a diadem and a purple gown of silk interwoven with gold. Those who gained an audience had to prostrate themselves before him; a privileged few were allowed to kiss his robe.

Diocletian's easternizing policy

The third aspect of orientalization in Diocletian's policy was his growing reliance on an imperial bureaucracy. By separating civilian from military commands and legislating on a wide variety of economic and social matters, Diocletian created the need for many new officials. Not surprisingly, by the end of his reign subjects were complaining that "there were more tax-collectors than taxpayers." The officials did keep the empire going but the new bureaucracy was prone—as all are—to graft and corruption; worse, the growth of of-

The growth of imperial bureaucracy

The Emperor Honorius. An example of the impassive portrait sculpture brought in by the age of Diocletian. Compare the lack of individuality of this bust to the portraits of Decius and Philip the Arab, above, pp. 261–62.

The reign of Constantine

ficialdom called for reservoirs of manpower and wealth at a time when the Roman Empire no longer had large supplies of either. Taken together, the various aspects of Diocletian's easternizing made him seem more like a pharaoh than a Roman ruler: it was almost as if the defeat of Antony and Cleopatra at Actium was now being avenged.

The new coercive regime of Diocletian left no room for the cultivation of individual spontaneity or freedom. The results can be seen most clearly in the building and art of the age. Diocletian himself preferred a colossal bombastic style of building that was meant to emphasize his own power. The baths he had constructed in Rome, when he finally arrived there in 303, were the largest yet known, encompassing about thirty acres. When he retired in 305 Diocletian built a palace for himself in what is now Split (Yugoslavia) that was laid out along a rectilinear grid like an army camp. A plan of this palace shows clearly how Diocletian favored regimentation in everything.

Also in the age of Diocletian, Roman portrait statuary, which had hitherto featured striking naturalism and individuality, became impersonal. Human faces became impassive and symmetrical rather than reflecting a free play of emotions. Porphyry, a particularly hard and dark stone that had to be imported from Egypt—itself a sign of easternization—often replaced marble for imperial busts. Porphyry groups of Diocletian, Maximian, and their two caesars show the new hardness and symmetry at their fullest, for the figures were made to look so similar that they are indistinguishable from each other.

In 305 Diocletian decided to abdicate to raise cabbages—an unprecedented achievement for a late-Roman ruler. At the same time he obliged his colleague Maximian to retire as well, and their two caesars moved peacefully up the ladders of succession. Such concord, however, could not last. Soon civil war broke out among Diocletian's successors and continued until Constantine, the son of one of the original caesars, emerged victorious. From 312 until 324 Constantine ruled only in the West, but from the latter year until his death in 337 he did

Diocletian's Palace in Split. An artistic reconstruction.

Left: *Porphyry Sculptures of Diocletian and His Colleagues in Rule.* Every effort is made to make the two senior rulers and their two junior colleagues look identical by means of stylization. Note also the emphasis on military strength. Right: *Colossal Head of Constantine.* In the head of Constantine the eyes are enlarged as if to emphasize the ruler's spiritual vision. The head is approximately ten times larger than life.

away with the sharing of powers and ruled over a reunited empire. Except for the fact that he favored Christianity, an epoch-making decision to be treated in the next section, Constantine otherwise continued to govern along the lines laid down by Diocletian. Bureaucracy proliferated and the state became so vigilant in keeping town-dwellers and agricultural laborers at their posts that society began to harden into a caste system. Although Constantine was a Christian, he never thought for a moment of acting with any Christlike humility: on the contrary, he made court ceremonials more elaborate and generally behaved as if he were a god. In keeping with this he built a new capital in 330 and named it Constantinople, after himself. Although he declared that he moved his government from Rome to Constantinople in order to demonstrate his abandonment of paganism, self-esteem was no doubt a major factor, and the shift was the most visible manifestation of the continued move of Roman civilization to the East. Situated on the border of Europe and Asia, Constantinople had commanding advantages as a center for eastern-oriented communications, trade, and defense. Surrounded on three sides by water and protected on land by walls, it was to prove nearly impregnable and would remain the center of "Roman" government for as long as the Roman Empire was to endure.

Constantine also made the succession hereditary. By so doing he

274

*Christianity and the
Transformation of the Roman
World*

*Dynastic disputes of the
fourth century*

Theodosius. Detail from a silver plate. The emperor is shown with an orb in his hand, symbolizing his worldly power, and a halo, symbolizing his supernatural strength.

brought Rome back to the principle of dynastic monarchy that it had thrown off about eight hundred years earlier. But Constantine, who treated the empire as if it were his private property, did not pass on united rule to one son. Instead he divided his realm among three of them. Not surprisingly his three sons started fighting each other upon their father's death, a conflict exacerbated by religious differences. The warfare and succeeding dynastic squabbles that continued on and off for most of the fourth century need not detain us here. Suffice it to say that they were not as serious as the civil wars of the third century, and that from time to time one or another contestant was able to reunite the empire for a period of years. The last to do so was Theodosius I (379–395), who butchered thousands of innocent citizens of Thessalonica in retribution for the death of one of his officers, but whose energies in preserving the empire by holding off Germanic barbarians still gave him some claim to his surname "the Great."

The period between Constantine and Theodosius saw the steady development of earlier tendencies. With Constantinople now the leading city of the empire, the center of commerce and administration was located clearly in the East. Regionalism too was becoming more pronounced: the Latin-speaking West was losing a sense of rapport and contact with the Greek-speaking East, and in both West and East local differences were becoming accentuated. In economic life the hallmark of the age was the growing gap between rich and poor. In the West large landowners were able to consolidate their holdings, and in the East some individuals became prosperous by rising through the bureaucracy and enriching themselves with graft, or by trading in luxury goods. But the taxation system initiated by Diocletian and maintained throughout the fourth century weighed down heavily on the poor, forcing them to carry the burden of supporting the bureaucracy, the army, and the lavish imperial court or courts. The poor, moreover, had no chance to escape their poverty, for legislation demanded that they and their heirs stay at their unrewarding and heavily taxed jobs. Since most people in the fourth century were poor, most people lived in desperate and unrelenting poverty against a backdrop of ostentatious wealth. The Roman Empire may have been restored in the years from 284 to 395, but it was nonetheless a fertile breeding-ground for a new religion of otherworldly salvation.

2. THE EMERGENCE AND TRIUMPH OF CHRISTIANITY

The origins and spread of Christianity

Christian beginnings of course go back several centuries before Constantine to the time of Jesus. Christianity was formed primarily by Jesus and St. Paul and gained converts steadily thereafter. But the new religion only became really widespread during the chaos of the third century and only triumphed in the Roman Empire during the demoralization of the fourth. At the time of its humble beginnings nobody could have known that Christianity would be decreed the sole religion of the Roman Empire by the year 380.

Jesus of Nazareth was born in Bethlehem, a small town of Judea, sometime near the beginning of the Christian era (but not exactly in the "year one"—we owe this mistake in our dating system to a sixth-century monk). While Jesus was growing up Judea was under Roman rule. The atmosphere of the country was charged with religious emotionalism and political discontent. Some of the people, notably the Pharisees, concentrated on preserving the Jewish law and looked forward to the coming of a political messiah who would rescue the country from Rome. Most extreme of those who sought hope in politics were the "Zealots," who wished to overthrow the Romans by means of armed force. Some groups, on the other hand, were not interested in politics at all. Typical of these were the Essenes, who hoped for spiritual deliverance through asceticism, repentance, and mystical union with God. The ministry of Jesus was clearly more allied to this pacific orientation.

Jesus of Nazareth; his milieu

When Jesus was about thirty years old, he was acclaimed by an ascetic evangelist, John the Baptist, as one "mightier than I, whose shoes I am not worthy to bear." Thenceforth for about three years his career, according to the New Testament accounts, was a continuous course of preaching and teaching and of healing the sick, "casting out devils," restoring sight to the blind, and raising the dead. He not only denounced shame, greed, and licentious living but set the example himself by a life of humility and self-denial. Though the conception he held of himself is somewhat obscure, he apparently believed that he had a mission to save humanity from error and sin. His preaching and other activities eventually aroused the antagonism of some of the chief priests and conservative rabbis. They disliked his caustic references to the legalism of the Pharisees, his contempt for form and ceremony, and his scorn for pomp and luxury. They feared also that his active leadership would cause trouble with the Romans. Accordingly, they brought him into the highest court in Jerusalem, where he was solemnly condemned for blasphemy and for setting himself up as "king of the Jews" and turned over to Pontius Pilate, the Roman governor, for execution of the sentence. After hours of agony he died on the cross between two thieves on the hill of Golgotha outside Jerusalem.

Jesus's career

The crucifixion of Jesus marked a great climax in Christian history. At first his death was viewed by his followers as the end of their hopes. Their despair soon vanished, however, for rumors began to spread that the Master was alive, and that he had been seen by certain of his faithful disciples. The remainder of his followers were quickly convinced that he had risen from the dead, and that he was truly a divine being. With their courage restored, they organized their little

Jesus Christ. An artist's conception from a sixth-century mosaic in Ravenna.

A Carved Tablet, c. 400 A.D., Depicting Christ's Tomb and Ascension into Heaven

St. Paul. From a Ravenna mosaic.

band and began preaching and testifying in the name of their martyred leader. Thus one of the world's great religions was launched on a career that would ultimately convert an empire no less mighty than Rome.

There has never been perfect agreement among Christians as to the precise teachings of Jesus of Nazareth. The only dependable records are the four Gospels, but the earliest of these was not written until at least a generation after Jesus's death. According to the beliefs of his orthodox followers, the founder of Christianity revealed himself as the Christ, the divine Son of God, who was sent on this earth to suffer and die for the sins of humanity. They were convinced that after three days in the tomb, he had risen from the dead and ascended into heaven, whence he would come again to judge the world. The Gospels at least make it clear that he included the following among his basic teachings: (1) the fatherhood of God and the brotherhood of humanity; (2) the Golden Rule; (3) forgiveness and love of one's enemies; (4) repayment of evil with good; (5) self-denial; (6) condemnation of hypocrisy and greed; (7) opposition to ceremonialism as the essence of religion; (8) the imminent approach of the end of the world; and (9) the resurrection of the dead and the establishment of the kingdom of heaven. Recent research has tended to emphasize the last two of these points as being at the center of Jesus's mission.

Christianity was broadened and invested with a more elaborate theology by some of the successors of Jesus, above all the Apostle Paul, originally known as Saul of Tarsus (10?–67?A.D.). Although of Jewish nationality, Paul was not a native of Palestine but a Jew born in the city of Tarsus in southeastern Asia Minor. Originally a persecutor of Christians, he was later converted to Christianity, and devoted his limitless energy to propagating that faith throughout the Near East. It would be almost impossible to overestimate the significance of his work. Denying that Jesus was sent merely as the redeemer of the Jews, Paul proclaimed Christianity to be a universal religion. But this was not all. He gave major emphasis to the idea of Jesus as the Christ, as the anointed God-man whose death on the cross was an atonement for the sins of humanity. Not only did he reject the works of the Law (i.e., Jewish ritualism) as of primary importance in religion, but he declared them to be utterly worthless in procuring salvation. Human beings are sinners by nature, and can therefore be saved only by faith and by the grace of God "through the redemption that is in Christ Jesus." It follows, according to Paul, that human fate in the life to come is almost entirely dependent upon the will of God; for "Hath not the potter power over the clay, of the same lump to make one vessel unto honor, and another unto dishonor?" (Romans 9:21). God has mercy "on whom he will have mercy, and whom he will he hardeneth" (Romans 9:18).

Although it may be something of a simplification, it seems basically true to say that Jesus proclaimed the imminent coming of the kingdom of God, whereas Paul laid the basis for a religion of personal salvation through Christ and the ministry of the Church. Therefore, after the time of Paul the development of Christianity was marked by the development of ceremonies, or sacraments, to bring the believer closer to Christ, as well as the development of an organization of priests to administer those sacraments. In teaching that priests who administered sacraments were endowed with supernatural powers, Christianity gradually developed a distinction between clergy and laity that was much sharper than that which had existed in most earlier religions. This would become the basis of subsequent Western controversies and divisions between "Church" and "State." In the meantime, Christianity's emphasis on otherworldly salvation ministered by a worldly priestly organization helped it greatly to grow and ultimately to flourish.

The beginnings of Church organization

Christianity grew steadily in the first two centuries after Christ but only really began to flourish in the third. To understand this we must recall that the third century in Roman history was an "age of anxiety." At a time of extreme political turbulence and economic hardship people understandably began to treat life on earth as an illusion and place their hopes in the beyond. The human body and the material world were more and more regarded as either evil or basically unreal. As the Neoplatonic philosopher and leading thinker of that age, Plotinus, wrote, "when I come to myself, I wonder how it is that I have a body . . . by what deterioration did this happen?" Plotinus devised a whole philosophical system to answer this question, but this system was far too abstruse to have much meaning for large numbers of people. Instead, as we have seen, several religions that emphasized the dominance in this world of spiritual forces and the absolute preeminence of otherworldly salvation gained hold as never before.

The growth of Christianity in the "age of anxiety"

At first Christianity was just another of these religions; Mithraism, Gnosticism, and the cults of Isis and Serapis were others. It is natural to ask, therefore, why Christianity gained converts in the third century at the expense of its rivals. A number of answers may be posited. One of the simplest, but not therefore the least important, is that even though Christianity borrowed elements from older religions—above all Judaism and Gnosticism—it was new and therefore possessed of a sense of dynamism that was lacking among the other salvationist religions which had existed for centuries. (It is noteworthy in this regard that one of Christianity's most serious rivals in the period from 276 to about 400 was Manicheanism, which was even newer than itself.) Christianity's dynamism was also enhanced by its rigorous exclusiveness. Hitherto people took on religions as today we might take on insurance policies, piling one on another in order to feel more secure. The fact that Christianity strictly prohibited this, demanding that the Christian God be worshiped alone, made the new religion most ap-

Other reasons for the success of Christianity

A Medieval Christian Conception of the Torments of the Damned in Hell

An Early-Christian Woman. A wall-painting from the cata-comb of Priscilla, Rome, third century A.D.

pealing at a time when people were searching desperately for absolutes. Similarly, Christianity alone among its rivals (with the later exception of Manicheanism) had an all-embracing theory to explain evil on earth, namely as the work of demons governed by the devil. When Christian missionaries sought converts they successfully emphasized the new faith's ability to combat these demons by reputed miracles.

Although Christianity's novelty, exclusiveness, and theory of evil help greatly to explain its success, probably the greatest attractions of the religion had to do with three other traits: its view of salvation, its social dimensions, and its organizational structure. Exorcism of demons might help to make life more tolerable on earth but ultimately people in the later Roman Empire were most concerned with other-worldly salvation. Rival religions also promised an afterlife, but Christianity's doctrine on this subject was the most far-reaching. Christian preachers who warned that nonbelievers would "liquefy in fierce fires" for eternity and that believers would enjoy eternal blessedness understandably made many converts in an age of fears. They made converts too among all classes because Christianity had from its origins been a religion of the humble—carpenters, fishermen, and tent-makers—which promised the exaltation of the lowly. As the religion grew it gained a few wealthy patrons but it continued to find its greatest strength among the lower and middle classes who comprised the greatest numbers in the Roman Empire. Moreover, while Christianity forbade women to become priests or discuss the faith, and, as we will see, took on many attitudes hostile to women, it at least accorded women some rights of participation in worship and equal hope with men for salvation. This fact gave it an advantage over Mithraism, which excluded women from its cult entirely. In addition to all these considerations, a final reason for Christianity's success lay in its organization. Unlike the rival mystery religions, it had by the third century developed an organized hierarchy of priests to direct the life of the faith. More than that, Christian congregations were tightly knit communities that provided services to their members—such as nursing, support of the unprotected, and burial—that went beyond strictly religious concerns. Those who became Christians found human contacts and a sense of mission while the rest of the world seemed to be collapsing about them.

Christianity was never as brutally persecuted by the Roman state as used to be thought. In fact the attitude of Rome was usually one of indifference: Christians were customarily tolerated unless certain magistrates decided to prosecute them for refusing to worship the official state gods. From time to time there were more concerted persecutions, but these were highly intermittent and never lasted long enough to do irreparable damage: on the contrary they served to give Christianity some helpful publicity. To this degree the blood of martyrs really was the seed of the Church, but only because the blood did not flow too freely. One last great persecution took place toward the end of the reign of Diocletian and was continued by one of his immediate successors, a particularly bitter enemy of Christianity named Galerius. But by then the religion was far too strong to be wiped out by persecution, a fact that Galerius finally recognized by issuing an edict of toleration right before his death in 311. Thereafter Christianity was to be supported by the Roman state rather than persecuted by it.

Roman persecution of Christians relatively moderate

The adoption of Christianity by the Roman Empire was initiated by Constantine and completed by Theodosius. Constantine did not yet make Christianity the official religion of the empire, but he clearly favored it. Probably he did so both because he associated his own conversion to the faith (around the year 312) with a rise of his political for-

The triumph of Christianity

Jonah under the Gourd. A Christian marble statue done around the time of Constantine's conversion. Jonah resting after leaving the whale's belly was a symbol for the risen Christ.

Christ and the Apostles in the Heavenly Jerusalem. Noteworthy is how this fourth-century mosaic (heavily restored) portrays Roman dress and Roman buildings, showing how quickly after Constantine's conversion the Romans were able to conceive Jesus as one of their own.

tunes, and because he hoped that Christianity might bring a spiritual unity to an empire that had been badly demoralized and religiously divided. Some of his successors, who were brought up in the Christian religion, went much further to achieve this end by ordering the persecution of pagans more ruthlessly than some pagan emperors had formerly persecuted Christians. Christianity probably would have triumphed anyway merely with official support because aspiring functionaries were usually quick to accept the religion of their rulers. The masses too were easily converts to the faith once it was supported by the state because, even though the fourth century was politically more stable than the third, the reorganization of the empire weighed most heavily on the lower classes and made them as much concerned about otherworldly salvation as they had been in the century before. Substantial numbers, too, simply followed the lead of authority. Christians probably comprised no more than a fifth of the population of the Roman Empire at the time of the conversion of Constantine at the beginning of the fourth century; with state support they quickly became an overwhelming majority. When Theodosius the Great forbade the worship of all religions other than Christianity by an edict of 380, paganism, already disappearing, was soon wiped out in all but the most rural backlands of the Roman realms.

3. THE NEW CONTOURS OF CHRISTIANITY

Changes in the Christian religion

Once the new faith became dominant within the Roman Empire it underwent some major changes in forms of thought, organization, and conduct. These changes all bore relationships to earlier tendencies, but the triumph of the faith greatly accelerated certain trends and altered the course of others. The result was that in many basic respects the

Christianity of the late fourth century was a very different religion from the one persecuted by Diocletian and Galerius.

One consequence of Christianity's triumph was the flaring up of bitter doctrinal disputes. These brought great turmoil to the Church but resulted in the hammering out of dogma and discipline. Before the conversion of Constantine there had of course been disagreements among Christians about doctrinal matters, but as long as Christianity was a minority religion it managed to control its internal divisions in order to present a united front against hostile outsiders. Hardly had the new faith emerged victorious, however, than sharp splits developed within its own ranks. These were due partly to the fact that there had always been a tension between the intellectual and emotional tendencies within the religion which could now come more fully into the open, and partly to the fact that different regions of the empire tried to preserve a sense of their separate identities by preferring different theological formulas.

Controversy over doctrinal matters

The first of the bitter disputes was between the Arians and Athanasians over the nature of the Trinity. The Arians—not to be confused with Aryans (a racial term)—were followers of a priest named Arius and were the more intellectual group. Under the influence of Greek philosophy they rejected the idea that Christ could be equal with God. Instead they maintained that the Son was created by the Father and therefore was not co-eternal with Him or formed of the same substance. The followers of St. Athanasius, indifferent to human logic, held that even though Christ was the Son he was fully God: that Father, Son, and Holy Ghost were all absolutely equal and composed of an identical substance. After protracted struggles Athanasius's side won out and the Athanasian doctrine became the dogma of the Church, as it remains today.

Division between the Arians and Athanasians

The struggle between the Arians and Athanasians was followed by numerous other doctrinal quarrels which succeeded each other for the next few centuries. The issues at stake were generally too abstruse to warrant explaining here, but the results were momentous. One was that the the dogmas of the Catholic faith steadily began to become fixed. It should be emphasized that this was a slow development and that many basic tenets of Catholicism were only defined much later (for example, the theory of the Mass was not formally promulgated until 1215; the doctrine of the Immaculate Conception of the Virgin Mary until 1854; and that of the Bodily Assumption of the Virgin until 1950). Nonetheless the faith was beginning to take on a sharply defined form that was unprecedented in the history of earlier religions. Above all, this meant that any who differed from a certain formulation would be excluded from the community and often persecuted as a heretic. In the subsequent history of Christianity this concern for doctrinal uniformity was to result in both strengths and weaknesses for the Church.

Consequences of persisting doctrinal disputes

282

*Christianity and the
Transformation of the Roman
World*

Two other results of the doctrinal quarrels were that they aggravated regional hostilities and provoked secular interference into the government of the Church. In the fourth century differences among Christians increased alienation between West and East and also aggravated hostilities between one region and another within the East. Although the Roman Empire was evolving toward regionalism for many different reasons, including economic and administrative ones, and although regionalism was partly a cause of religious differences, the sharper and more frequent religious quarrels became, the more they serve to intensify regional hostilities.

At the same time the Roman state was inevitably drawn into these religious conflicts. The same Constantine who favored Christianity as a unifying force was horrified by the prompt emergence of the Arian conflict and intervened in it by calling the Council of Nicea (325), which condemned Arius. It is noteworthy that this council—the first general council of the Church—was not only convened by a Roman emperor, but that Constantine served during its meetings as a presiding officer. Thereafter secular interference in Church matters continued, above all in the East. There were two major reasons for this: First, religious disputes were more prevalent in the East than the West and quarreling parties often appealed to the emperor for support. Second, the weight of imperial government was generally heavier in the East, and after 476 there were no Roman emperors in the West at all. When Eastern emperors were not appealed to by quarreling parties they interfered in religious disputes themselves, as Constantine had done before them, in order to preserve unity. The result was that in the East the emperor assumed great religious authority and control, but in the West the future of relations between State and Church was more open.

Even while emperors were interfering in religious matters, however, the Church's own internal organization was becoming more complex and articulated. We have seen that a clear distinction between clergy and laity was already a hallmark of the early Christian religion after the time of St. Paul. The next step was the development of a hierarchical organization within the ranks of the clergy. The superiority of bishops over priests was recognized before Christianity's triumph. Christian organization was centered in cities and one bishop in each important city became the authority to which all the clergy in the surrounding vicinity answered. This organization was sufficient for a minority religion but as the number of congregations multiplied, and as the influence of the Church increased due to the adoption of Christianity as the official religion of Rome, distinctions of rank among the bishops themselves began to appear. Those who had their headquarters in the larger cities came to be called metropolitans (today known in the West as archbishops), with authority over the clergy of an entire province. In the fourth century the still higher rank of patriarch was established to designate those bishops who ruled over the oldest and largest of Christian communities—such cities as Rome, Jerusalem, Constantinople, Antioch, and Alexandria, and their surrounding districts. Thus the Christian clergy by 400 A.D. had come to embrace a definite hierarchy of patriarchs, metropolitans, bishops, and priests.

The climax of all this development—still largely in the future—was the growth of the primacy of the bishop of Rome, or in other words the rise of the papacy. For several reasons the bishop of Rome enjoyed a preeminence over the other patriarchs of the Church. The city in which he ruled was venerated by the faithful as a scene of the missionary activities of the Apostles Peter and Paul. The tradition was widely accepted that Peter had founded the bishopric of Rome, and that therefore all of his successors were heirs of his authority and prestige. This tradition was supplemented by the theory that Peter had been commissioned by Christ as his vicar on earth and had been given the keys of the kingdom of heaven with power to punish people for their sins and even to absolve them from guilt (Matthew 16:18–19). This theory, known as the doctrine of the Petrine Succession, has been used by popes ever since as a basis for their claims to authority over the Church. The bishops of Rome had an advantage also in the fact that after the transfer of the imperial capital to Constantinople there was seldom any emperor with effective sovereignty in the West. Finally, in 445 the Emperor Valentinian III issued a decree commanding all western bishops to submit to the jurisdiction of the pope. It must not be supposed, however, that the Church was by any means yet under a monarchical form of government. The patriarchs in the East regarded the extreme assertions of papal claims as brazen effrontery, and even many bishops in the West continued to ignore them for some time. The clearest example of the papacy's early weakness is the fact that the popes did not even attend the first eight general councils of the Church (from 325 to 869) although later they were to convene and preside over all the others.

The rise of the papacy

The growth of ecclesiastical organization helped the Church to conquer the Roman world in the fourth century and to minister to the needs of the faithful thereafter. The existence of an episcopal administrative structure was particularly influential in the West as the Roman Empire decayed and finally collapsed in the fifth century. Since there was always a bishop in every city who was trained to some degree in the arts of administration, the Church in the West took over many of the functions of government and helped to preserve order amid the deepening chaos. But the new emphasis on administration also had its inevitably deleterious effects: with the Church developing its own rationalized administrative structure it inevitably became more worldly and distant in spirit from the simple faith of Jesus and the Apostles.

Effects of the rationalization of ecclesiastical administration

The clearest reaction to this trend was expressed in the spread of

*Christianity and the
Transformation of the Roman
World*

The rise of monasticism

*The extremes of
monastic asceticism*

*The communal
monasticism of St. Basil*

monasticism. Today we are accustomed to thinking of monks as groups of priests who live communally in order to dedicate themselves primarily to lives of contemplation and prayer. In their origins, however, monks were not priests but laymen, who almost always lived alone and who sought extremes of self-torture rather than ordered lives of spirituality. Monasticism began to emerge in the third century as a response to the anxieties of that age, but it only became a dominant movement within Christianity in the fourth century. Two obvious reasons for this fact stand out. First of all, the choice of extreme hermitlike asceticism was a substitute for martyrdom. With the conversion of Constantine and the abandonment of persecution, most chances of winning a crown of glory in heaven by undergoing death for the faith were eliminated. But the desire to prove one's religious ardor by self-abasement and suffering was still present. Second, as the fourth century progressed the priesthood became more and more enmired in worldly concerns. Those who wished to avoid secular temptations fled to the deserts and woods to practice an asceticism that priests and bishops were forgetting. (Monks customarily became priests only later during the Middle Ages.) In this way even while Christianity was accommodating itself to practical needs, monasticism satisfied the inclinations of ascetic extremists who otherwise might have become Gnostics or Manicheans and who looked forward to lives of torture and deprivation that far outstripped those of Christ and the Apostles.

Monasticism first emerged in the East, where for about one hundred years after Constantine's conversion it spread like a mania. Hermit monks of Egypt and Syria vied with each other in their pursuit of the most inhuman and humiliating excesses. Some grazed in the fields after the manner of cows, others penned themselves into small cages, and others hung heavy weights around their necks. A monk named Cyriacus stood for hours on one leg like a crane until he could bear it no more. The most extravagant of these monastic ascetics was St. Simeon Stylites, who performed self-punishing exercises—such as touching his feet with his head 1,244 times in succession—on top of a high pillar for thirty-seven years, while crowds gathered below to worship "the worms that dropped from his body."

In time such ascetic hysteria subsided and it became recognized that monasticism would be more enduring if monks lived in a community and did not concentrate on self-torture. The most successful architect of communal monasticism in the East was St. Basil (330?–379), who started his monastic career as a hermit and ascetic extremist but came to prefer communal and more moderate forms of life. Basil expressed this preference in writings for monks that laid down the basic guidelines for eastern monasticism from then until the present time. Rather than encouraging extremes of self-torture, Basil encouraged monks to discipline themselves by useful labor. Although his teachings were

A Monastery of the Basilian Order on Mt. Athos. The asceticism of the Basilian monks caused them to build their monasteries in almost inaccessible places on lofty crags or on the steep sides of rugged mountains.

still extremely severe by modern standards, he prohibited monks from engaging in prolonged fasts or lacerating their flesh. In place of that he urged them to submit to obligations of poverty and humility, and to spend many hours of the day in silent religious meditation. With the triumph of St. Basil's ideas, eastern monasticism became more organized and subdued, but even so Basilian monks preferred to live as far away from the "world" as they could and never had the same civilizing influence on external society as did their brothers in western Europe.

Monasticism did not at first spread so quickly in the West as it did in the East because the West was not as attracted by severe asceticism. Most often whatever monasticism was introduced in the West was too ascetic to have any widespread appeal. This situation was only remedied in the sixth century when St. Benedict (480?–547?) drafted his famous Latin rule which ultimately became the guide for nearly all the monks in the West. Recent research has shown that Benedict copied much of his rule from an earlier Latin text, but he still produced a document that is notable for its brevity, flexibility, and moderation. The Benedictine rule imposed obligations similar to those laid down by St. Basil: poverty, obedience, labor, and religious devotion. Yet Benedict prescribed less austerity than Basil did: the monks were granted a sufficiency of simple food, clothing, and enough sleep; they were even allowed to drink a small amount of wine, although meat was only granted to the sick. The abbot's authority was absolute and the abbot was allowed to flog monks for disobedience, yet Benedict urged him

The rule of St. Benedict

286

*Christianity and the
Transformation of the Roman
World*

to try "to be loved rather than feared," and ordained that the abbot take counsel before making decisions "because the Lord often reveals to a younger member what is best." For such reasons the Benedictine monastery became a center of deep religious enrichment rather than a school for punishment.

*The significance of
Benedictine monasticism:
(1) missionary activities
and attitude towards
manual labor*

We will have occasion for continuing the story of Benedictine monasticism later on, but here we may point in advance to some of its greatest contributions to the development of Western civilization. One was that Benedictine monks were committed from an early date to missionary work: they were primarily responsible for the conversion of England and later most of Germany. Such activities not only helped to spread the faith but also served to create a sense of cultural unity for western Europe. Another positive contribution lay in the attitude of the Benedictines towards work. Whereas the highest goal for ancient philosophers and aristocrats was to have enough leisure time for unimpeded contemplation, St. Benedict wanted his monks always to keep busy, for he believed that "idleness is an enemy of the soul." Therefore he prescribed that they should be occupied at certain times in manual labor, a prescription that would have horrified most thinkers of earlier times. Accordingly, early Benedictines worked hard themselves and spread the idea of the dignity of labor to others. With Benedictine support acceptance of this idea would become one of the most distinctive traits of Western culture. We read of Benedictines who gladly milked cows, threshed, plowed, and hammered: in so doing they increased the prosperity of their own monasteries and provided good examples for others. Benedictine monasteries became particularly successful in farming and later in estate-managing. Thus they often helped to advance the level of the western European economy and sometimes even to provide wealth that could be drawn upon by emerging western European states.

The fact that Benedictine monasteries were often islands of culture when literacy and learning were all but forgotten in the secular world is better known. St. Benedict himself was no admirer of classical culture. Quite the contrary, he wanted his monks only to serve Christ—not literature or philosophy. But he did assume that monks would have to read well enough to say their prayers. That meant that there would have to be some teaching in the monasteries because it was seldom available outside, and because boys were often given over from birth to the monastic profession. Once there was teaching there would obviously be at least a few writing implements and books. This explains why Benedictines always maintained some literacy but not why some of them became devoted to perpetuating classical culture. The

A Monk Working in the Fields.
From an eleventh-century manuscript.

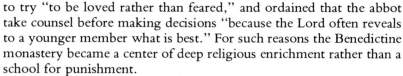

impetus behind the latter development was the work of a monastic thinker named Cassiodorus (477?–570?). Inspired by St. Augustine, whom we will treat in more detail later, Cassiodorus believed that some basic classical learning was necessary for the proper understanding of the Bible; this justified the study of the classics by monks. Furthermore, Cassiodorus recognized that copying manuscripts was in itself "manual labor" (literally work with the hands) and might be even more appropriate for monks than hard work in the fields. As Benedictines began to subscribe to these ideas, Benedictine monasteries became centers for learning and transcribing that were without rival for centuries. No work of classical Latin literature, including such "licentious" writings as the poems of Catullus and Ovid, would survive today had they not been copied and preserved during the early Middle Ages by Benedictine monks.

(2) the preservation of classical culture; Cassiodorus

Love of women was of course, however, not a Benedictine preference. Returning to our original subject—the changes that took place in Christian institutions and attitudes during the fourth century—we may count a final fateful trend to have been the development of a negative attitude toward the role of women in human life. Compared to most other religions, Christianity was favorable to women. Female souls were regarded as being equal to male ones in the eyes of God, and human nature was deemed to be complete only in both sexes. St. Paul even went so far as to say that after baptism "there is neither male nor female" (Galatians 3:28), a spiritual equalitarianism which meant that women could be saved as fully as men. But Christians from earliest times shared the view of their contemporaries that in everyday life and in marriage women were to be strictly subject to men. Not only did early Christians believe, with all male supremacists of the ancient world, that women should be excluded from positions of leadership or decision-making, meaning that they should be "silent in Church" (I Corinthians 14:34–35), but they added to this the view that women were more "fleshly" than men and therefore should be subjected to men as the flesh is subjected to the spirit (Ephesians 5:21–33).

Christian attitudes toward women

With the growth of the ascetic movement in the third and fourth centuries, the denigration of women as dangerously "fleshly" creatures became more and more pronounced. Since sexual abstinence lay at the heart of asceticism, the most perfect men were expected to shun women. Monks, of course, shunned women the most. This was a primary reason why they fled to deserts and forests. One eastern ascetic was struck by the need for virginity in the midst of his marriage ceremony, ran off to a hermit's cell and blocked the entrance; another monk who was forced to carry his aged mother across a stream swaddled her up as thoroughly as he could so that he would not catch any "fire" and no thoughts of other women attack him. With monks taking such an uncompromising attitude, the call for continence was extended to the priesthood. Originally priests could be married; it seems

The emergence of the doctrine of celibacy

288

*Christianity and the
Transformation of the Roman
World*

that even some of the Apostles were (I Corinthians 9:5). But in the course of the fourth century the doctrine spread that priests could not be married after ordination, and that if they had been married before then they were expected to live continently with their wives afterwards.

Once virginity was accepted as the highest standard, marriage was taken to be only second-best. St. Jerome expressed this view most earthily when he said that virginity was wheat, marriage barley, and fornication cow-dung: since people should not eat cow-dung he would permit them barley. The major purposes of marriage were to keep men from "burning" and to propagate the species. (St. Jerome went so far as to praise marriage above all because it brought more virgins into the world!) Thus Christianity reinforced the ancient view that woman's major earthly purpose was to serve as mother. Men and women were warned not to take pleasure even in marital intercourse but to indulge in it only for the purpose of procreation. Women were to be "saved in childbearing" (I Timothy 2:15). Since they could not become priests and only a very few could become nuns (female monasticism was regarded as being a very expensive luxury in the premodern world), almost all women were expected to become submissive wives and mothers. As wives they were not expected to have their own careers and were not meant to be educated or even literate. Hence, even though they had full hopes for salvation, they were treated as inferiors in the everyday affairs of the world, a treatment that would endure until modern times.

4. THE GERMANIC INVASIONS AND THE FALL OF THE ROMAN EMPIRE IN THE WEST

While Christianity was conquering the Roman Empire from within, another force, that of the Germanic barbarians, was threatening it from without. The Germans, who had already almost brought Rome to its knees in the third century, were held off from the time of Diocletian until shortly before the reign of Theodosius the Great. But thereafter they demolished Western Roman resistance and, by the end of the fifth century, succeeded in conquering all of the Roman West. Germanic kingdoms then became the new form of government in territories once ruled over by Caesar and Augustus.

It is customary to think, perhaps with the encouragement of grade-B movies, that the Germans who destroyed the Western Roman Empire were fierce and thoroughly uncouth savages. But that is a misunderstanding. The Germans were barbarians in the sense that they did not live in cities and were customarily illiterate, but they were not therefore savages. On the contrary, they often practiced settled agriculture—although they preferred hunting and grazing—and were adept at making iron tools and weapons as well as at other metal and clay crafts. Physically they looked enough like Romans so that they could intermarry without causing much comment, and their language belonged to the Indo-European group, and therefore was related to Latin and Greek. Prolonged interaction with the Romans had a decisive civilizing influence on the Germans before they started their final conquests. Germans and Romans who shared common borders along the Rhine and Danube had steady trading relations with each other. Even during times of war Romans were often allied with some German tribes while they fought others. By the fourth century German tribes often served as auxiliaries of depleted Roman armies and were sometimes allowed to settle on borderlands of the empire where Roman farmers had given up trying to cultivate the land. Many German tribes too had been converted to Christianity in the fourth century, although the Christianity they accepted was of the heretical Arian version. All these interactions made the Germans very familiar with Roman civilization and substantially favorable to it.

The Germans began their final push not to destroy Rome but to find more and better land. The first breakthrough occurred in 378 when one tribe, the Visigoths, who had recently settled on some Roman lands in the Danube region, revolted against mistreatment by Roman officials and then decisively defeated a punitive Roman army in the Battle of Adrianople. The Visigoths did not immediately follow up this victory because they were cleverly bought off and made allies of the empire by Theodosius the Great. But when Theodosius died in 395 he divided his realm between his two sons, neither of whom was as competent as he was, and both halves of the empire were weakened by political intrigues. The Visigoths under their leader Alaric took advantage of this situation to wander through Roman realms almost at will, looking for the best land and provisions. In 410 they sacked Rome itself—a great shock to some contemporaries—and in the following years marched into southern Gaul. Meanwhile, in December of 406, a group of allied German tribes led by the Vandals crossed the frozen Rhine and capitalized on Roman preoccupation with the Visigoths by streaming through Gaul into Spain. Later they were able to cross the straits into northwest Africa, then one of the richest agricultural regions of the empire. From Africa they took control of the central Mediterranean, even sacking Rome from the sea in 455. By 476 the entirely ineffectual Western Roman emperor, a mere boy derisively nicknamed Augustulus ("little Augustus"), was easily deposed by a leader of a mixed band of Germans who then assumed the title of king of Rome. Accordingly, 476 is conventionally given as the date for the end of the Western Roman Empire. But it must be remembered that a Roman emperor, who maintained some claims to authority in the West, continued to rule in Constantinople.

Two questions that historians of the German invasions customarily

The Visigoths and the Vandals

Reasons for the German success

Why the Eastern Roman Empire survived and the Western collapsed

Consequences of the Germanic invasions

ask are: How did the Germans manage to triumph so easily? Why was it that they were particularly successful in the West rather than the East? The ease of the German victories appears particularly striking when it is recognized that the German armies were remarkably small: the Goths who won at Adrianople numbered no more than 10,000 men, and the total number of the Vandal "hordes" (including women and children) was about 80,000—a population about the same as that of an average-sized American suburb. But the Roman armies themselves were depleted because of declining population and the need for manpower in other occupations, above all in the new bureaucracies. More than that, German armies often won by default (Adrianople was one of the few pitched battles in the history of their advance) because the Romans were no longer zealous about defending themselves. Germans were seldom regarded with horror—many German soldiers had even risen to positions of leadership within Roman ranks—and the coercive regime begun by Diocletian was not deemed to be worth fighting for.

The reasons why the Germans fared best in the West are complex—some having to do with personalities and mistakes of the moment, and others with geographical considerations. But the primary explanation why the Eastern Roman Empire survived while the Western did not is that the East was simply richer. By the fifth century most Western Roman cities had shrunk both in terms of population and space to a small fraction of their earlier size and were often little more than empty administrative shells or fortifications. The economy of the West was becoming more and more strictly agricultural, and agricultural produce served only to feed farm laborers and keep rich landlords in luxuries. In the East, on the other hand, cities like Constantinople, Antioch, and Alexandria were still teeming metropolises because of their trade and industry. Because the eastern state had greater reserves of wealth to tax, it was more vigorous. It could also afford to buy off the barbarians with tribute money, which it did with increasing regularity. So Constantinople was able to stay afloat while Rome floundered and then sank.

The effects of the Germanic conquests in the West were not cataclysmic. The greatest difference between the Germans and the Romans had been that the former did not live in cities, but since the Western Roman cities were already in a state of decline, the invasions only served at most to accelerate the progress of urban decay. On the land Germans replaced Roman landlords without interrupting basic Roman agricultural patterns. Moreover, since the Germans never comprised very large numbers, they usually never took over more than a part of Roman lands. Germans also tried to avail themselves of Roman administrative apparatuses, but these tended to diminish gradually because of the diminishing of wealth and literacy. Thus the only major German innovation was to create separate tribal kingdoms in the West in place of a united empire.

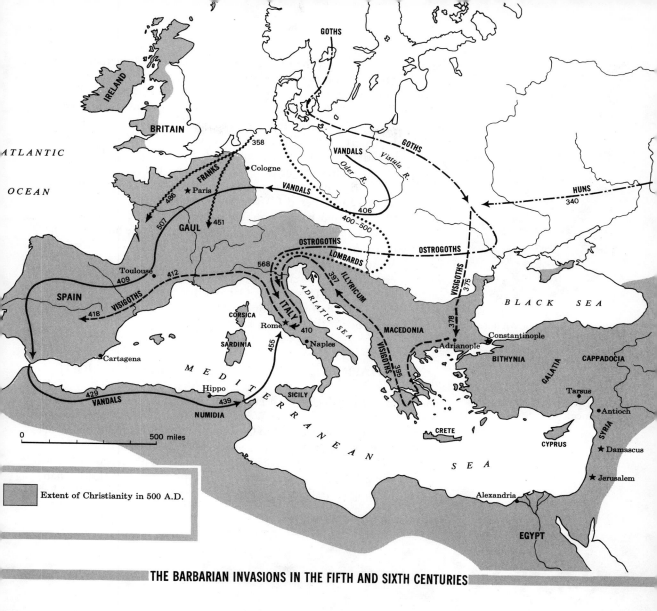

GOTHS

IRELAND

BRITAIN

ATLANTIC

OCEAN

VANDALS

GOTHS

Vistula R.

Oder R.

FRANKS

358

• Cologne

486

★ Paris

507

451

GAUL

VANDALS

406

400–500

HUNS

340

OSTROGOTHS

Toulouse

409

412

SPAIN

VISIGOTHS

418

CORSICA

SARDINIA

Cartagena

429

VANDALS

439

NUMIDIA

OSTROGOTHS

LOMBARDS

568

397

ILLYRICUM

ITALY

ADRIATIC SEA

Rome ★

410

• Naples

455

VISIGOTHS

375

VISIGOTHS

378

395

MACEDONIA

Adrianople

Constantinople

BITHYNIA

BLACK SEA

GALATIA

CAPPADOCIA

Tarsus

• Antioch

SYRIA

★ Damascus

★ Jerusalem

Hippo •

SICILY

M E D I T E R R A N E A N

CRETE

CYPRUS

0   500 miles

S E A

Alexandria •

EGYPT

Extent of Christianity in 500 A.D.

THE BARBARIAN INVASIONS IN THE FIFTH AND SIXTH CENTURIES

The map of western Europe around the year 500 reveals the following major political divisions. Germanic tribes of Anglo-Saxons, who had crossed the English Channel in the middle of the fifth century, were extending their rule on the island of Britain. In the northern part of Gaul, around Paris and east to the Rhine, the growing kingdom of the Franks was ruled over by a crafty warrior named Clovis. South of the Franks were the Visigoths, who ruled the southern half of Gaul and most of Spain. South of them were the Vandals, who ruled throughout previously Roman northwest Africa. In all of Italy the Ostrogoths, eastern relatives of the Visigoths, held sway under their impressive King Theodoric. Of these kingdoms the Frankish would

Germanic kingdoms in the year 500

292

*Christianity and the
Transformation of the Roman
World*

Theodoric the Ostrogoth. The barbarian ruler is shown here in Roman dress, with an ornate Roman hairstyle and a Roman symbol of victory in his hand. The inscription reads REX THEODERICVS PIVS PRINCIS, Latin for King Theodoric, pious prince.

be most promising for the future (for that reason it will be taken up in the next chapter) and the seemingly strongest for the present was that of the Ostrogoths.

Theodoric the Ostrogoth, who ruled in Italy from 493 to 526, was a great admirer of Roman civilization; this he tried to preserve as best he could. He fostered agriculture and commerce, repaired public buildings and roads, patronized learning, and maintained a policy of religious toleration. In short he gave Italy a more enlightened rule than it had known under most of its earlier emperors. But since Theodoric and his sparsely numbered Ostrogoths were Arian Christians while the local bishops and native population were Catholics, his rule, no matter how tolerant and benign, was viewed with some hostility. The "Roman" rulers in Constantinople were also hostile to Theodoric because he was an Arian and because they had not given up hopes of reconquering Italy themselves. All these circumstances led, as we will see, to the demise of Theodoric's Ostrogothic kingdom not long after his death. In fact, all of the continental barbarian kingdoms would not last long except for that of the Franks.

5. THE SHAPING OF WESTERN CHRISTIAN THOUGHT

The period of the decline and fall of the Roman Empire in the West was also the time when a few Western Christian thinkers formulated an approach to the world and to God that was to guide the thought of the West for roughly the next 800 years. This concurrence of political decline and theological advance is not surprising. With the empire falling and being replaced by barbarian kingdoms, it seemed clearer than ever to thinking Christians both that the classical inheritance had to be

Mosaic of Theodoric's Palace at Ravenna. At the right is a stylized conception of the ruler's palace, with the Latin inscription PALA TIVM; to the left of it is a row of saints, who would be indistinguishable were it not for the initials on their clothing: for early Christian artists, supernatural merits rather than individual personality traits were of the essence.

reexamined and that God had not intended the world to be anything more than a transistory testing place. The consequences of these assumptions accordingly became questions of most pressing concern. Between about 380 and 525 answers were worked out by Western Christian thinkers whose thought and accomplishments were intimately interrelated. The towering figure among them was St. Augustine, but some others had great influence as well.

Three contemporaries who all knew and influenced each other—St. Jerome (340?–420), St. Ambrose (340?–397), and St. Augustine (354–430)—count as three of the four greatest "fathers" of the Western, Latin Church. (The fourth, St. Gregory the Great, came later and will be discussed in the next chapter.) St. Jerome's greatest single contribution to the future was his translation of the Bible from Hebrew and Greek into Latin. His version, known as the "Vulgate" (or "common" version), became the standard Latin Bible used throughout the Middle Ages; with minor variations it continued to be used long afterwards by the Roman Catholic Church. Fortunately Jerome was one of the best writers of his day, and endowed his translation with vigorous, often colloquial prose and, occasionally, fine poetry. Since the Vulgate was the most widely read work in Latin for centuries, Jerome's writing had as much influence on Latin style and thought as the King James Bible has had on English literature. Jerome, who was the least original thinker of the great Latin fathers, also influenced the Western Christian future by his contentious but eloquent formulations of contemporary views. Among the most important of these were the beliefs that much of the Bible was to be understood allegorically rather than literally, that classical learning could only be valid for Christians if it was thoroughly subordinated to Christian aims, and that the most perfect Christians were those who were rigorously ascetic. In keeping with the last position Jerome was an avid supporter of monasticism. He also taught that women should not take baths so that they would not see their own bodies naked.

Unlike Jerome, who was primarily a scholar, St. Ambrose was most active in the concerns of the world as archbishop of Milan. In this office he was the most influential Church official in the West— more so even than the pope. Guided by his practical concerns, Ambrose wrote an ethical work, *On the Duties of Ministers,* which followed closely upon Cicero's *On Duties* in title and form, and also drew heavily on Cicero's Stoic ethics. But Ambrose differed from Cicero and most of traditional classical thought on two major points. One was that the beginning and end of human conduct should be the reverence and search for God rather than any self-concern or interest in social adjustment. The other—Ambrose's most original contribution—was that God helps some Christians but not others in this pursuit by the gift of grace, a point that was to be greatly refined and enlarged upon by St. Augustine. Ambrose put his concern for proper conduct into action by his most famous act, his confrontation with the Emperor Theodosius the Great for massacring innocent civilians.

St. Jerome

St. Ambrose

294

*Christianity and the
Transformation of the Roman
World*

St. Augustine

Augustine's theology

Ambrose argued that by violating divine commandments Theodosius had made himself subject to Church discipline. Remarkably the archbishop succeeded in forcing the sovereign emperor to do penance. This was the first time that a churchman had subordinated the Roman secular power in matters of morality. Consequently it symbolized the Church's claim to preeminence in this sphere, and particularly the *Western* Church's developing sense of autonomy and moral superiority that would subsequently make it so much more independent and influential on the secular world than the Eastern Church.

St. Ambrose's disciple, St. Augustine, was the greatest of all the Latin fathers; indeed he was one of the most powerful Christian intellects of all time. Augustine's influence on subsequent medieval thought was incalculable. Even after the Middle Ages his theology had a profound influence on the development of Protestantism; in the twentieth century many leading Christian thinkers have called themselves Neo-Augustinians. It may be that one reason why Augustine's Christianity was so searching was because he began his career by searching for it. Nominally a Christian from birth, he hesitated until he was thirty-three to be baptized but passed from one system of thought to another without being able to find intellectual or spiritual satisfaction in any. Only increasing doubts about all other alternatives, the appeals of St. Ambrose's teachings, and a mystical experience movingly described in his *Confessions* led Augustine to embrace the faith without reserve in 387. Thereafter he advanced rapidly in ecclesiastical positions, becoming bishop of the North African city of Hippo in 395. Although he led a most active life in this office, he still found time to write a large number of profound, complex, and powerful treatises in which he set forth his convictions concerning the most fundamental problems of Christian thought and action.

St. Augustine's theology revolved around the principles of divine omnipotence and the profound sinfulness of humanity. Ever since humankind turned away from God in the Garden of Eden humans have remained basically sinful. One of Augustine's most vivid examples of this comes from a passage in the *Confessions,* where he tells how he and some other boys once were driven to steal pears from a neighbor's garden, not because they were hungry or because the pears were beautiful, but for the sake of the evil itself. God would be purely just if He condemned all human beings to hell, but since He is also merciful He has elected to save a few. Ultimately human will has nothing to do with this choice: although one has the power to choose between good and evil, one does not have the power to decide whether he will be saved. God alone, from eternity, predestined a portion of the human race to be saved, and left the remainder to be damned. In other words, God fixed for all time the number of human inhabitants of heaven. If any mere mortals were to respond that this seems unfair, the answer is first that strict "fairness" would confine all to perdition, and second that the basis for God's choice is a mystery wrapped up in His omnipotence—far beyond the realm of human comprehension.

Even though it might seem to us that the practical consequences of this rigorous doctrine of predestination would be lethargy and fatalism, Augustine and subsequent medieval Christians did not see it that way at all. Humans themselves must do good, and if they are "chosen" they will do good; since no one knows who is chosen and who is not, all should try to do good in the hope that they are among the chosen. For Augustine the central guide to doing good was the doctrine of "charity," which meant leading a life devoted to loving God and loving one's neighbor for the sake of God. Seen from the opposite, humans should avoid "cupidity," or loving earthly things for their own sake. Put in other terms, Augustine taught that humans should behave on earth as if they were travelers or "pilgrims," keeping their eyes at all times on their heavenly home, and avoiding all materialistic concerns.

Augustine built an interpretation of history on this view in one of his major works, *On the City of God*. In this, he argued that the entire human race from the Creation until the Last Judgment was and will be composed of two warring societies, those who "live according to man" and love themselves, and those who "live according to God." The former belong to the "City of Earth," and will be damned, while the blessed few who compose the "City of God" will on Judgment Day put on the garment of immortality. This reading of history subsequently went unquestioned throughout the Middle Ages.

Although Augustine worked out for the first time major new aspects of Christian theology, he believed that he was only putting together truths that he found in the Bible. Indeed, he was convinced that the Bible alone contained all the wisdom worth knowing. But he also believed that much of the Bible was expressed very difficultly, and that it was therefore necessary to have a certain amount of education in order to understand it thoroughly. This conviction led him to a modified acceptance of classical learning. The ancient world had already worked out an educational system based on the "liberal arts," or those subjects necessary for the worldly success and intellectual growth of free men. Augustine argued that privileged Christians could learn the fundamentals of these subjects, but only in a limited way and for a completely different end—study of the Bible. Since nonreligious schools existed in his day which taught these subjects, he permitted a Christian elite to attend them; later, when such schools died out, their place was taken by schools in monasteries and cathedrals. Thus Augustine's teaching laid the groundwork for some continuity of educational practice as well as for the theory behind the preservation of some classical treatises. But we must qualify this by remarking that Augustine intended liberal education only for an elite;

296

*Christianity and the
Transformation of the Roman
World*

Boethius

all others were simply to be catechized, or drilled, in the faith. He also thought it far worse that anyone should become engaged in classical thought for its own sake than that someone might not know any classical thought at all. The true wisdom of mortals, he insisted, was piety.

Augustine had many followers, of whom the most interesting and influential was Boethius, a Roman aristocrat who lived from about 480 to 524. To say that Boethius was a follower of St. Augustine might until recently have been regarded as controversial because some of his works make no explicit mention of Christianity. Indeed, since Boethius was indisputably interested in ancient philosophy, wrote in a polished, almost Ciceronian style, and came from a noble Roman family, it has been customary to view him as the "last of the Romans." But in fact he meant the classics to serve Christian purposes, just as Augustine had prescribed, and his own teachings were basically Augustinian.

*Boethius's intellectual
contributions*

Because Boethius lived a century after Augustine he could see far more clearly that the ancient world was coming to an end. Therefore he made it his first goal to preserve as much of the best ancient learning as he could by a series of handbooks, translations, and commentaries. Accepting a contemporary division of the liberal arts into seven subjects—grammar, rhetoric, logic, arithmetic, geometry, astronomy, and music—he wrote handbooks on two: arithmetic and music. These summaries were meant to convey all the basic aspects of the subject matter that a Christian might need to know. Had Boethius lived longer he probably would have written similar treatments of the other liberal arts, but as it was he concentrated his efforts on the subject that was his favorite: logic. In order to preserve the best of classical logic, he translated from Greek into Latin some of Aristotle's logical treatises as well as an introductory work on logic by Porphyry (another ancient philosopher). He also wrote his own explanatory commentaries on these works in order to help beginners. Since Latin writers had never been interested in logic, even in the most flourishing periods of Roman culture, Boethius's translations and commentaries became a crucial link between the Greeks and the Middle Ages. Boethius helped endow the Latin language with a logical vocabulary, and when interest in logic was revived in the twelfth-century West it rested first on a Boethian basis.

Boethius. A twelfth-century artist's conception of Boethius as a musician, a reputation he earned because of his treatise on music.

Although Boethius was an exponent of Aristotle's logic, his worldview was not Aristotelian but Augustinian. This can be seen both in his several orthodox treatises on Christian theology and above all in his masterpiece, *The Consolation of Philosophy*. Boethius wrote the *Consolation* at the end of his life, after he had been condemned to death for treason by Theodoric the Ostrogoth, whom he had served as an official. (Historians are unsure about the justice of the charges.) In it Boethius asks the age-old question of what is human happiness, and concludes that it is not found in earthly rewards such as riches or fame but only in the "highest good," which is God. Human life, then, should be spent in pursuit of God. Since Boethius speaks in the *Consolation* as a philosopher rather than a theologian, he does not refer to Christian revelation or to the role of divine grace in salvation. But his basically Augustinian message is unmistakable. *The Consolation of Philosophy* became one of the most popular books of the Middle Ages because it was extremely well written, because it showed how classical expression and some classical ideas could be appropriated and subordinated into a clearly Christian framework, and most of all, because it seemed to offer a real meaning to life. In times when all earthly things really did seem crude or fleeting it was a genuine consolation to be told eloquently and "philosophically" that life has purpose if it is led for the sake of God.

The Consolation of Philosophy

At a climactic moment in the *Consolation* Boethius retold in verse the myth of Orpheus in a way that might stand for the common position of the four writers we have just discussed; i.e., how Christian thinkers were willing to accept and maintain some continuity with the classical tradition. But Boethius also made new sense of the story. According to Boethius Orpheus's wife, Eurydice, symbolized hell; since Orpheus could not refrain from looking at her he was forced to die and was condemned to hell himself. In other words, Orpheus was too worldly and material; he should not have loved a woman but instead have sought God. True Christians, on the other hand, know that "happy is he who can look into the shining spring of good [i.e., the divine vision]; happy is he who can break the heavy chains of earth."

The myth of Orpheus as a symbol for Christian truths

6. EASTERN ROME AND THE WEST

Boethius's execution by Theodoric the Ostrogoth in 524 was in many ways an important historical turning point. For one, Boethius was both the last noteworthy philosopher and last writer of cultivated Latin prose the West was to have for many hundreds of years. Then too Boethius was a layman, and for hundreds of years afterwards almost all western European writers would be priests or monks. In the political sphere Boethius's execution was symptomatic as well because it was the harbinger of the collapse of the Ostrogothic kingdom in Italy. Whether or not he was justly condemned, Boethius's execution showed that the Arian Ostrogoths could not live in perfect harmony with Catholic Christians such as himself. Soon afterwards, therefore, the Ostrogoths were overthrown by the Eastern Roman Empire. That event in turn was to be a major factor in the ultimate divorce between East and West and the consequent final disintegration of the old Roman World.

Boethius's execution a turning point

The conquest of the Ostrogoths was part of a larger plan for Roman revival conceived and directed by the Eastern Roman Emperor Justinian (527–565). Eastern Rome, with its capital at Constantinople, had faced many external pressures from barbarians and internal re-

The Emperor Justinian

Justinian and Theodora. Sixth-century mosaics from the church of San Vitale, Ravenna. The emperor and empress are conceived here to have supernatural, almost priestly powers: they are advancing toward the altar, bringing the communion dish and chalice respectively. Both rulers are set off from their

ligious dissensions since the time of Theodosius. But throughout the fifth century it had managed to weather these, and by the time of Justinian's accession had regained much of its strength. Although the Eastern Roman Empire—which then encompassed the modern-day territories of Greece, Turkey, most of the Middle East, and Egypt—was largely Greek- and Syriac-speaking, Justinian himself came from a westernmost province (modern-day Yugoslavia) and spoke Latin. Not surprisingly, therefore, he concentrated his interests on the West. He saw himself as the heir of imperial Rome, whose ancient power and western territory he was resolved to restore. Aided by his astute and determined wife, Theodora, who, unlike earlier imperial Roman consorts, played an influential role in his reign, Justinian took great strides toward this goal. But ultimately his policy of recovering the West proved unrealistic.

See color map facing page 384

Codification and revision of Roman law; the Corpus Juris Civilis

One of Justinian's most impressive and lasting accomplishments was his codification of Roman law. This project was part of his attempt to emphasize continuities with earlier imperial Rome and the Latin legal tradition. It was also meant to enhance his own prestige and absolute power. Codification of the law was necessary because between the third and sixth centuries the volume of statutes had continued to grow, with the result that the vast body of enactments contained many contradictory or obsolete elements. Moreover, conditions had changed so radically that many of the old legal principles could no longer be applied, due to the establishment of an Oriental despotism and the adoption of Christianity as the offical religion.

retinues by their haloes. The observant viewer is also meant to note the representation of the "three wise kings from the East" at the hem of Theodora's gown: just as the "three magi" once had supernatural knowledge of Christ, so now do their counterparts, Justinian and Theodora.

When Justinian came to the throne in 527, he immediately decided upon a revision and codification of the existing law to bring it into harmony with the new conditions and to establish it as an authoritative basis of his rule. To carry out the actual work he appointed a commission of lawyers under the supervision of his minister, Tribonian. Within two years the commission published the first result of its labors. This was the Code, a systematic revision of all of the statutory laws which had been issued from the reign of Hadrian to the reign of Justinian. The Code was later supplemented by the Novels, which contained the legislation of Justinian and his immediate successors. By 532 the commission had completed the Digest, representing a summary of all of the writings of the great jurists. The final product of the work of revision was the Institutes, a textbook of the legal principles which were reflected in both the Digest and the Code. The combination of all four of these results of the program of revision constitutes the *Corpus Juris Civilis,* or the body of the civil law.

Justinian's *Corpus* was a brilliant achievement in its own terms: the Digest alone has been justly called "the most remarkable and important lawbook that the world has ever seen." In addition, the *Corpus* had an extraordinarily great, often almost monopolistic influence, on subsequent legal and governmental history. Revived and restudied in western Europe from the eleventh century on, Justinian's *Corpus* became the basis of all the law and jurisprudence of European states, exclusive of England (which followed its own "common law"). The nineteenth-century Napoleonic Code, which provided the basis for

General significance of Justinian's Corpus

Christianity and the
Transformation of the Roman
World

Other influences

the laws of modern European countries and also of Latin America, is fundamentally the Institutes of Justinian in modern dress.

Only a few of the more specific influences of Justinian's legal work can be alluded to here. One is that in its basic governmental theory it was a bastion of absolutism. Starting from the maxim that "what pleases the prince has the force of law," it granted untrammeled powers to the imperial sovereign and therefore was adopted with alacrity by later European monarchs and autocrats. But the *Corpus* also provided some theoretical support for constitutionalism because it maintained that the sovereign originally obtained his powers from the people rather than from God. Since government came from the people it could in theory be given back to them. Perhaps most important and influential was the *Corpus*'s view of the state as an abstract public and secular entity. In the Middle Ages rival views of the state as the private property of the ruler or as a supernatural creation meant to control sin often predominated. The modern conception of the state as a public entity concerned not with the future life but with secular, everyday affairs gained strength towards the end of the Middle Ages largely because of the revival of assumptions found in Justinian's legal compilations.

Justinian's policy of reconquest in the West

Justinian aimed to be a full Roman emperor in geographical practice as well as in legal theory. To this end he sent out armies to reconquer the West. At first they were quickly successful. In 533 Justinian's brilliant general Belisarius conquered the Vandal kingdom in northwest Africa, and in 536 Belisarius seemed to have won all Italy, where he was welcomed by the Catholic subjects of the Ostrogoths. But the first victories of the Italian campaign were illusory. After their initial defeats the Ostrogoths put up stubborn resistance and the war dragged on for decades until the exhausted Eastern Romans finally reduced the last Gothic outposts in 563. Shortly before he died Justinian became master of all Italy as well as northwest Africa and coastal parts of Spain that his troops had also managed to recapture. The Mediterranean was once more briefly a "Roman" lake. But the cost of the endeavor was soon going to call the very existence of the Eastern Roman Empire into question.

The Western campaigns unwise

There were two major reasons why Justinian's western campaigns were ill-advised. One was that his realm really could not afford them. Belisarius seldom had enough troops to do his job properly: he began his Italian campaign with only 8,000 men. Later, when Justinian did grant his generals enough troops, it was only at the cost of oppressive taxation. But additional troops would probably have been insufficient to hold the new lines in the West because the empire had greater interests, as well as enemies, to the East. While the Eastern Roman Empire was exhausting itself in Italy the Persians were gathering strength. Justinian's successors had to pull away from the West in order to meet the threat of a revived Persia, but even so, by the beginning of the seventh century, it seemed as if the Persians would be able to march all the way to the waters that faced Constantinople. Only a heroic reorganization of the empire after 610 saved the day, but it was one that helped withdraw Eastern Rome from the West and helped the West begin to lead a life of its own.

In the meantime Justinian's wars had left most of Italy in a shambles. In the course of the protracted fighting much devastation had been wrought. Around Rome aqueducts were cut and the countryside returned to marshes that would not be drained until the time of Mussolini. In 568, only three years after Justinian's death, another Germanic tribe, the Lombards, invaded the country and took much of it away from the Eastern Romans. They met little resistance because the latter were now properly paying more attention to the East, but the Lombards were still too weak to conquer the whole Italian peninsula. Instead, Italy became divided between Lombard, Eastern Roman, and papal territories. At the same time Slavs took advantage of Eastern Roman weakness to sweep into the Balkans. Further west the Franks in Gaul were fighting among themselves, and it would be only a matter of time before northwest Africa and most of Spain would fall to Arabs. So the Roman unity had finally come to an end. The future in this decentralized world may have looked bleak, but new forces in the separate areas would soon be gathering strength.

The end of Roman unity

SELECTED READINGS

• *Items so designated are available in paperback editions.*
• Anderson, Hugh, *Jesus,* Englewood Cliffs, N.J., 1967. An excellent collection of readings displaying many different scholarly points of view.

   Bonner, Gerald, *St. Augustine of Hippo,* London, 1963. The best biography for beginners.
• Brown, Peter, *Augustine of Hippo,* Berkeley, Calif., 1967. An extremely subtle study.
• ———, *The World of Late Antiquity,* New York, 1971. A survey that approaches the period in its own terms rather than as a prelude to the Middle Ages.
• Bultmann, Rudolf, *Primitive Christianity in Its Contemporary Setting,* New York, 1956. Summarizes the ideas of one of our century's most important biblical scholars.
• Bury, J. B., *The Invasion of Europe by the Barbarians,* London, 1928. A straightforward narrative.
• Chadwick, Henry, *The Early Church,* Baltimore, 1967.
• Cochrane, C. N., *Christianity and Classical Culture,* Oxford, 1940. Difficult but fundamental.

   Daniélou, J., and H. I. Marrou, *The Christian Centuries; I: The First Six Hundred Years,* London, 1964. A survey from the Roman Catholic perspective.

   Dill, Samuel, *Roman Society in the Last Century of the Western Empire,* London, 1921.
• Dodds, E. R., *Pagan and Christian in an Age of Anxiety,* Cambridge, 1965. A

short but brilliant study of what pagans and Christians had in common as well as what made Christianity ultimately successful.

• Enslin, M. S., *The Prophet from Nazareth*, New York, 1961.

  Gibbon, Edward, *The Decline and Fall of the Roman Empire*. (Many editions, including several abridged ones.)

• Jones, A. H. M., *The Decline of the Ancient World*, New York, 1966. A survey that emphasizes economic and social factors.

• Katz, Solomon, *The Decline of Rome*, Ithaca, N.Y., 1955. The best brief introduction.

• Knowles, David, *Christian Monasticism*, New York, 1969.

• Latourette, K. S., *A History of Christianity*, New York, 1953.

• L'Orange, H. P., *Art Forms and Civic Life in the Late Roman Empire*, Princeton, N.J., 1965. An imaginative and stimulating essay displaying how developments in art reflected developments in political and social life.

• Lot, Ferdinand, *The End of the Ancient World*, New York, 1931. The best detailed treatment of the political history of the period.

• Lyon, Bryce, *The Origins of the Middle Ages*, New York, 1971.

  MacMullen, Ramsay, *Constantine*, New York, 1969. A good popular biography.

  Markus, R. A., *Christianity in the Roman World*, New York, 1974.

• Mattingly, Harold, *Christianity in the Roman Empire*, New York, 1967.

  Momigliano, A., *The Conflict between Paganism and Christianity*, New York, 1963.

  Pelikan, J., *The Christian Tradition; I: The Emergence of the Catholic Tradition*, Chicago, 1971. An advanced survey of doctrine.

• Rand, E. K., *Founders of the Middle Ages*, Cambridge, Mass., 1928. A thoroughly engaging account of the early Christian reactions to the classics.

• Riché, Pierre, *Education and Culture in the Barbarian West*, Columbia, S.C., 1976. A magisterial survey of learning in the Christian West from the fall of Rome to about 800.

• White, Lynn T., Jr., *The Transformation of the Roman World*, Berkeley, Calif., 1966. Stimulating essays.

  Workman, H. B., *The Evolution of the Monastic Ideal*, London, 1913. Highly interpretative but still one of the best works on the subject.

SOURCE MATERIALS

• St. Augustine, *City of God*, tr. H. Bettenson, Baltimore, 1972.
• ———, *Confessions*, tr. R. S. Pine-Coffin, Baltimore, 1961.
• ———, *The Enchiridion on Faith, Hope and Love*, ed. H. Paolucci, Chicago, 1961.
• ———, *On Christian Doctrine*, tr. D. W. Robertson, Jr., New York, 1958.
• Boethius, *The Consolation of Philosophy*, tr. R. Green, Indianapolis, 1962.
• Cassiodorus, *An Introduction to Divine and Human Readings*, tr. L. W. Jones, New York, 1946.
• *Early Christian Writings: The Apostolic Fathers*, tr. M. Staniforth, Baltimore, 1968.
• Eusebius, *The History of the Church*, tr. G. A. Williamson, Baltimore, 1965.
  Procopius, *The Secret History*, tr. G. A. Williamson, Baltimore, 1966.

Chapter 12

THE FAR EAST AND AFRICA IN TRANSITION (c. 200 B.C.- 900 A.D.)

If brave and ambitious men have sincere understanding and awareness; if they fear and heed the warnings of disaster and use transcendent vision and profound judgment; if they . . . rid themselves of the blind notion that the mandate of Heaven can be pursued like a deer in chase and realize that the sacred vessel of rule must be given from on high; . . . then will fortune and blessing flow to their sons and grandsons, and the rewards of Heaven will be with them to the end of their days.

—Pan Piao, *History of the Former Han Dynasty*

During the period when the Greco-Roman classical civilization was being extended throughout the Mediterranean world under the auspices of the Roman Empire, a high stage of cultural development had been reached in both India and China. The disturbances that characterized the downfall of the Roman Empire in the West had their parallels in Asia too. However, the invasions and political upheavals in the Far East did not produce the same drastic changes as those in the West. The structure of society continued without serious modification in India and China, and the cultures of these two countries attained a brilliant peak while Europe was experiencing its Dark Ages. In India a combination of commercial prosperity—which encouraged the growth of large cities—and the religious enthusiasm accompanying the spread of Buddhism stimulated an outpouring of artistic talent. During this period Indian influence extended far beyond the borders of the country. Buddhism was planted in Central Asia and from there carried to China, Korea, and Japan. Indian colonization led to the introduction of both Buddhism and Hinduism, together with their art and literature, in Southeast Asia and the Malay Archipelago (which is still called Indonesia). China, while importing a major religion from India, showed much greater success in achieving political unification and an effective administrative system. So great was the prestige of imperial China that its culture was studied and eagerly assimilated by the Japanese in the sixth and succeeding centuries A.D. At the same time the West received some impact from the

Contrasts of East and West

civilization of Asia by way of the Hellenistic and imperial Roman commercial centers and, later, through the initiative of the Arabs. In sub-Saharan Africa civilization developed slowly. Geographic isolation limited cultural and commercial exchange to a far greater degree than it did in the case of Japan. Contact with the Romans was negligible and Arab incursions south of the Sahara were intermittent.

1. THE FLOWERING OF HINDU CIVILIZATION

Conflict in post-Maurya India

The Maurya Dynasty, under the energetic and devout King Asoka, had projected a common rule over the greater part of India. Upon the overthrow of this dynasty early in the second century B.C., the empire quickly fell apart, leaving India in a condition of political discord. For the next several hundred years the most powerful kingdoms were centered not in the Indo-Gangetic plain but in the Deccan, where a succession of dynasties contended with one another, and some of them emerged as major states with extensive territories and resources. It is clear that by this time the arts of civilization were well advanced in southern India, even though the most distinctive historic influences—Vedic literature and philosophy, the traditional religious and social concepts of Hinduism, and the creative force of Buddhism—had originated in the north. Moreover, the invasions which began to trouble northern India did not penetrate into the Deccan. The states of the Deccan carried on commercial intercourse with neighboring and even distant areas but were not seriously threatened with hostile assaults from foreign powers. On the contrary, their merchants and missionaries were ensuring the cultural ascendancy of India over Southeast Asia.

The Gupta Dynasty

After a period of domination by nomadic tribes from Turkestan, the political initiative in India was recovered by a native house which established a highly effective rule and was even more remarkable for its advancement of culture. The Gupta Dynasty, as it was called, governed most of northern India during the fourth and fifth centuries A.D. The dynasty's founder, Chandragupta I, was probably not descended from the Chandragupta who had instituted the Maurya Dynasty after the death of Alexander the Great, but the Guptas ruled from the same capital—Pataliputra (Patna) on the Ganges—and also revived some of the principles of the renowned King Asoka. The climax of the Gupta period came in the reign of Vikramaditya ("Sun of Power"), 375–413 A.D., which inaugurated a golden age not unworthy of comparison with Athens' Golden Age in the days of Pericles. Valuable information on conditions in northern India at this time has been preserved in the brief account written by a Chinese pilgrim, Fa Hsien, who spent six years in the realm of Vikramaditya. Buddhism had already spread into China, and the monk Fa Hsien undertook his hazardous journey to acquire sacred texts and firsthand knowledge of the religion in the land of its birth. His comments, however, were not restricted to religious matters, and because he was an intelligent and civilized foreigner, his observations may be taken as objective and generally reliable. The travels of Fa Hsien in themselves represent no mean undertaking. He made his way on foot across Sinkiang and the mountain passes, taking six years to reach India (399–405 A.D.). Here he taught himself the Sanskrit language, procured texts, drawings, and relics at the Gupta capital, and then returned to his native land by sea, spending two years in Ceylon en route and also visiting Java on the voyage. Altogether, during the fiteen years of his pilgrimage he traversed a distance of some 8,000 miles.

According to Fa Hsien's testimony, Buddhism was flourishing in India, especially in the Gupta empire, but all the Hindu cults were tolerated and the rivalry among the different religions was not embittered by persecution. Evidently the impact of Buddhism and the traditions of Asoka had stimulated the growth of humane sentiments, given practical expression in public hospitals, rest houses, and other charitable institutions receiving state support. Fa Hsien asserted that the Indians scrupulously refrained from the use of liquor and were vegetarians to such an extent that they slaughtered no living creatures—undoubtedly a pious exaggeration. Apparently, also, the caste system had not become utterly rigid, probably because Buddhism was still vigorous and also because segregation was impracticable in the cosmopolitan society of the thriving commercial centers. Fa Hsien, who had no reason to bestow unmerited praise (he does not even mention the name of the great king Vikramaditya), described the government as just and beneficent. The roads, he indicated, were well maintained, brigandage was rare, taxes were relatively light, and capital punishment was unknown. He testified to a generally high level of prosperity, social contentment, and intellectual vitality at a time when the nations of western Europe were sinking into a state of semibarbarism.

Another invasion of India destroyed the Gupta power and brought a period of confusion lasting for more than a century. Almost simultaneously with the formal demise of the Roman Empire in the West, a group of nomads called "White Huns" defeated the Gupta forces and made themselves masters of northern India (480 A.D.). By the early sixth century the White Huns had staked out an empire extending from Bengal in the east into Afghanistan and Central Asia. However, it was much more barbaric than its predecessors, and disrupted the splendid administrative system of the Guptas. The Huns in India were gradually absorbed by the native population, but on the northwestern borders a promising artistic movement was blighted before the Hunnish power disintegrated in accordance with the usual cycle of hastily constructed nomadic states. After the Hunnish menace receded, an able government was re-established by one of the most famous rulers in Indian history, King Harsha (606–648 A.D.).

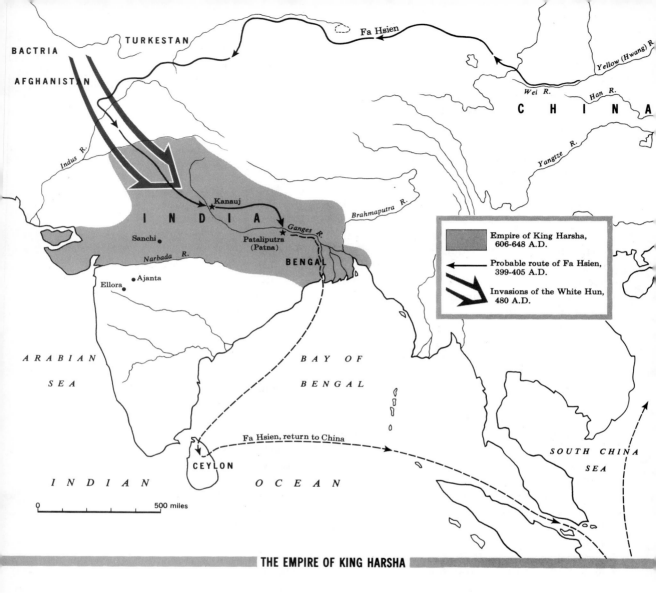

The reign of King Harsha (606–648 A.D.)

Although Harsha's state was not literally a continuation of the Gupta, it was so similar in important features that the term "Gupta" is often used to designate the civilization of northern India from the fourth to the seventh century, a period of cultural maturity despite the devastating interlude of the Hunnish invasion. King Harsha was a mighty conqueror who, with a huge army efficiently organized in divisions of infantry, cavalry, and elephants, reunited most of northern India. He was also a capable administrator, an intelligent and prudent statesman, and a generous patron of art, literature, and religion. His capital, Kanauj, extending four miles along the river in the central Ganges valley, was a splendid city, adorned with hundreds of temples and imposing public buildings, and enlivened with festive pageantry. As in the reign of Vikramaditya, the account of a Chinese Buddhist pilgrim throws revealing light upon Harsha's administration.

According to the narrative of this pilgrim (Hsün-tsang or Yuan Chwang) and other contemporary records, Harsha's administration was in the Gupta tradition but slightly less gentle. The state revenue was derived chiefly from taxes on the royal domains, which amounted to one-sixth of the produce of the villages and could hardly be regarded as oppressive. Harsha allotted only one-fourth of his income to administrative expenses, devoting the remainder to the rewarding of public servants, to charity, and to the promotion of education, religion, and the arts. In contrast to the mild punishments employed by the earlier Gupta regime, King Harsha inflicted such severe penalties as mutilation and death through starvation. Nevertheless, crimes of violence seem to have become more numerous. Religious toleration was still the official policy. Although Harsha is supposed to have been converted to the *Mahayana* school of Buddhism, he continued to worship the Sun and Shiva, and no attempt was made to enforce a religious orthodoxy. Despite this policy, the Brahmans were beginning to recover their ascendancy, and it was only a question of time before Buddhism, with its universalist and caste-dissolving tendencies, would be crowded out or absorbed by the cults so deeply rooted in Indian local tradition, literature, and social institutions. During the upheaval which followed the death of Harsha, this trend became more pronounced.

Harsha's administrative policies

During the first seven or eight centuries of the Christian era, in spite of invasions and disunity, political vigor and artistic and intellectual creativity in India reached their height. This period, in which Hindu civilization attained its full maturity, ranks as a major era in the history of the world's cultures. What the Periclean Age and the Augustan Age were for the classical civilizations of the West the reigns of Vikramaditya and Harsha were for India and, to a considerable extent, for other portions of Southern Asia. Undoubtedly the development of industry and commerce helps explain the generally prosperous state of Indian society and the cultural advances. At this time, and later also, India was the center of an intercontinental market, and her merchants took the initiative in navigation on the high seas. During the first two centuries A.D. there was extensive intercourse between India and the Near East, especially with the city of Alexandria. Many products were also being exported from India to the Roman West, including jewels, ivory, tortoise shells, pepper, cinnamon and other spices, fine muslin cloth, and silks of both Indian and Chinese manufacture. In exchange the Indians imported linens, glass, copper, wines, and other items, but the trade balance was so decidedly in India's favor that the Roman emperors became alarmed at the drainage of gold to the East and tried to curtail the use of silk for wearing apparel. Some of this trade was

The climax of Hindu culture

overland, but Indian merchants had from early days sailed across the Arabian Sea and up the Red Sea to Egypt. Not until the first century A.D. did Western traders discover the monsoon winds which enabled them to sail east to the Indian coast during the summer and then return when the wind direction changed in October. Traffic between the Near Eastern ports and southern India was probably even greater than with northern India. Pearls and beryls from the Deccan were especially prized, and Roman coins, testifying to a once flourishing trade, have been discovered along both the southwestern and southeastern coasts of the Indian peninsula. Apparently no obstacles were placed by the Indian rulers in the way of foreign intercourse or even against settlement by foreign traders, some of whom took up permanent residence in India. Southern India acquired small colonies of Romans, Jews, Nestorian Christians from Syria and Persia (a Syriac-speaking Christian church still exists in south-western India), and Arabs.

Influence upon the West

Through commercial contacts India probably exerted more influence upon the West than has been generally recognized, although much of it came somewhat later and with the Arabs as intermediaries. The Indian numerals ("Arabic"), which were not adopted by Europeans until the late Middle Ages, were perhaps known in Alexandria as early as the second century A.D. In the eighth and ninth centuries important scientific and medical treatises were translated from Sanskrit into Arabic. In addition, it is quite possible that familiarity with Indian philosophy and religion contributed a stimulus to the growth of Christian monasticism. The earliest Christian hermit-ascetics appeared in Eygpt, where there was considerable knowledge of Hinduism and Buddhism, both of which religions stressed the concepts of renunciation and mystic exaltation.

Buddhist patronage of education

The manifold intellectual activity of this period of Indian history reflected the interests of a cosmopolitan society, the patronage of wealthy rulers, and—most strongly of all—the incentives of religious faith. High levels of scholarship were maintained both by the Brahmans and by Buddhist monks, and large libraries came into being. Particularly noteworthy were the educational foundations, for which the chief credit should be given to the Buddhists. The role of the Buddhist monks in education was comparable to that of the Christian monks of the West during the early Middle Ages, but the scope of their studies was broader because the general level of knowledge was far higher in India than in the West at this time. Some Buddhist monasteries were internationally famous centers of learning, unmatched in Europe until the rise of such universities as Paris, Montpellier, and Oxford in the late Middle Ages. One of the greatest Buddhist universities, at Nalanda in the Ganges valley (in modern Bihar), was functioning as early as the fourth or fifth century A.D. Endowed by the Gupta rulers with a substantial income, it maintained residence halls for students—with free tuition, board, lodging, and medical care

Ruins at Nalanda. The remains of the ancient university town, early seat of Buddhist learning.

for poor boys who were able to pass the entrance examinations—and had a library that occupied three buildings. Pilgrims visiting the university in the seventh century reported that 5,000 students were in attendance, including some from Tibet, China, and Korea. Although Nalanda was a Buddhist foundation and provided instruction in eighteen different schools of Buddhism, its faculty also offered courses in Hindu philosophy, grammar, medicine, mathematics, and in both Vedic and contemporary literature.

While the literary output was prolific and uninhibited, it betrayed a veneration for the past in that Sanskrit—the ancient language of the Epic Age—became the universally accepted literary vehicle, in the Deccan as well as in Hindustan. Even the Buddhists felt constrained to translate their sacred texts from *Pali* (the dialect of King Asoka's day) into Sanskrit, and it was the Sanskrit versions which were carried by missionaries into Central Asia, China, Korea, and ultimately Japan. Literature of the Gupta Age, in both prose and poetry, ranged from scientific treatises and biographies to tales for popular entertainment. The latter included long romantic narratives suggestive of—and perhaps the prototype of—the *Arabian Nights;* and also "Beast Fables" comparable to those attributed to Aesop. The most impressive literary medium was the drama, which, as in Europe somewhat later, evolved out of a popular type of religious instruction and entertainment. The Sanskrit drama, in its perfected form, combined song, dance, and gesture with narrative and dialogue, and thus resembled the Western opera or cantata more than the typical stage play. The plots, often diffuse, were usually concerned with romantic love, drew heavily upon legendary themes from the epics, and resorted to miracles when-

Literature: romantic narratives, fables, and drama

ever necessary to resolve a difficulty in the story. Although they employed pathos, the dramas were never tragedies, always ending happily. They also utilized the peculiarly artificial device of having the principal characters speak in classical Sanskrit while women and lesser figures used the less elegant dialect of ordinary conversation. Although the Sanskrit drama never provided the suspense or realism characteristic of the modern Western theater, it did attain undeniable beauty, both in descriptions of nature and in lyrical passages expressing human emotions of tenderness and anguish.

The most superb expression of the Indian creative faculties during these centuries was in art, especially architecture and sculpture, although some excellent paintings were also produced. By the Gupta era, architecture was nearing a point of perfection, as evidenced by imposing stone structures in all sections of India. As in so many other fields, the Buddhists pioneered in the development of artistic forms. The evolution of the Buddhist monasteries and temples set the pattern for practically the whole of Hindu architecture (and sculpture also). During the early centuries when *Hinayana* Buddhism was dominant, neither temples nor images of Gautama were made. Hence the first typical Buddhist monument was the *stupa,* a simple burial mound in the shape of a dome or hemisphere crowned with an umbrella—the Indian symbol of sovereignty. Inside the brick- or rock-faced mound was buried a sacred relic, usually some object associated with Gautama or with a revered Buddhist saint. The most famous *stupa* is the large one at Sanchi in the very center of India, still in an excellent state of preservation, although it was begun in Asoka's reign and substantially completed during the first century B.C. More impressive than the stone-faced mound (which has a diameter at the base of 120 feet) are the four carved gateways surrounding the *stupa.* These massive fences of stone are supported by pillars 35 feet high and, in spite of their huge proportions, are adorned with intricate carvings, both pictorial and symbolic, with a profusion of delicately formed human and animal figures. After the *stupa,* the next step in the evolution of religious architecture was the assembly hall, where monks and lay disciples gathered to honor the memory of Gautama, the "Master of the Law." These halls were commonly tunneled out of solid rock in a mountain or the side of a cliff. Their general plan was similar to that of the Roman basilica and early Christian church in that it emphasized a central passageway or nave separated from aisles on either side by round columns. Paralleling the evolution of the temple was the development of the Buddhist monastery. Like the assembly hall or temple, the monastery was often carved out of a single mass of rock, with successive stories of cells or cubicles so arranged that the structure as a whole appeared to be a terraced pyramid. Devotees of the Hindu cults soon began to construct temples in imitation of the Buddhist and eventually even more elaborate.

Buddhist Missionary. A sixth-century carving supposed to represent the first Indian Buddhist missionary to China. Buddhism had probably been introduced into China as early as the first century A.D.

Great Stupa at Sanchi. Begun by Asoka and completed under the Andhra Dynasty (72–25 B.C.), it was originally a burial mound containing relics of the Buddha. The fully developed stupa, designed with mathematical precision, became an architectural symbol of the cosmos. The tiered mast on top of the structure represents the earth's axis penetrating the dome of heaven.

Although some free-standing temples were erected as early as the first century A.D., for several centuries the Indians seemed to prefer the more arduous method of hewing their edifices out of the solid rock of caves and cliffs. More than 1,200 rock-cut temples and monasteries were executed in various sections of India, the larger proportion being along the western coast. The two most remarkable groups of cliff excavations are located at Ajanta and Ellora, about 70 miles apart, in the northern part of what later became Hyderabad. The Ajanta caves were Buddhist sanctuaries, some of them dating from the second century B.C. and some from as late as the fifth century A.D. They include both assembly halls and monasteries, complete with stone beds, tables, water cisterns, and niches for oil reading lamps. The even more splendid caves at Ellora represent about 900 years of architectural and sculptural enterprise, extending from the fourth to the thirteenth century. The Buddhists were the first to utilize the site, but some of the caves were the work of Jains and the largest number were constructed as Hindu temples, of tremendous size and lavish design.

Temples composed of separate stone blocks, in contrast to the cave type, began to be more common in Gupta times and were typical of the most active period of Hindu temple building, between the sixth and the thirteenth centuries. The essential architectural features of these free-standing Hindu temples are (1) a base consisting of a square

Ajanta. A section of the gorge from which more than thirty cave chambers of worship, assembly, and residence were cut and decorated over a period of 700 years, beginning in the second century B. C.

Sculpture and Indian ideals

or rectangular chamber to house the image of the god, and (2) a lofty tower which rises from the roof of the chamber and dominates the entire edifice. The shape of the tower distinguishes the two main styles of Hindu temples. The "Dravidian" style, found only in the tropics, is identified by a terraced steeple divided into stories like a step pyramid and decidedly reminiscent of the early Buddhist rock-cut monasteries. The "Indo-Aryan" style, prevalent in northern India, has a curvilinear tower with vertical ribs which may possibly be derived from the Buddhist *stupa*.

Sculpture usually develops in close conjunction with architecture, and this was especially true in India, where so many sacred halls and chambers were literally carved out of stone. Decorative engravings, including figures in relief, were typically an integral part of the building itself. Chiseled decorations were very successfully applied to the gateways and pillars surrounding some of the early Buddhist *stupas*. The figures on the gates of the great *stupa* at Sanchi (first century B.C.) are particularly fine examples. Although they were intended to commemorate events of sacred tradition and embody pious symbolism, they are invested with vigor, freshness, and spontaneity, suggesting an uninhibited delight in the natural world rather than a brooding melancholy. Meanwhile a significant school of sculpture was arising in northwestern India and beyond the borders in Afghanistan and Bactria. The initial stimulus undoubtedly was Greek or Hellenistic, but Persian and other influences played a part, and the school developed its own original characteristics with Buddhist concepts predominant. It was in this region that the figure of Gautama was delineated for the first time, and relief sculptures depicted the legendary incidents of his life from infancy to Enlightenment. The large statues of the Buddha clearly revealed Greek influence at the beginning: the head resembled an Apollo or Zeus and the garment was draped like a toga rather than a monk's robe. However, there was a gradual approach toward the conventional form—in cross-legged posture and an attitude of benign repose—which eventually came to represent the Buddha all over the Far East. This Greco-Buddhist school of sculpture continued to flourish in the border regions of Central Asia, acquiring a more and more hearty realism, until it was snuffed out by the Hun invasions in the early sixth century.

During the Gutpa Age, Indian sculpture largely emancipated itself from foreign influences and assumed characteristics peculiarly expressive of Indian ideals. The treatment of the human form was handled with a subtle delicacy, conveying a sense both of rhythmic movement and tranquility. Garments on the figures were shown as almost transparent or suggested only in faint outline so that the effect is that of nudity, although chaste rather than voluptuous. The harmonious proportions and graceful curves of the limbs were derived from a study of plant forms as well as from human anatomy. Thus Gupta art, particularly as exemplified in the statues of Buddha, was idealistic and spiritual rather than realistic.

The richest creations of the Hindu artistic genius are to be found in the relief sculpture and fresco paintings executed in the rock-cut temples upon which so much energy was expended during the period

Eastern Gateway of the Great Stupa at Sanchi. The relief carvings, depicting incidents from the life of the Buddha, are remarkable for their fine detail, vitality, and naturalism.

Entrance to the Ajanta Caves. The Gupta period (fourth to seventh centuries A.D.) constitutes the Golden Age of Indian art—in sculpture, architecture, and painting—as well as the climax of classical Sanskrit literature.

Left: *Yakshi or "Tree Spirit."* A female figure derived from an early fertility cult but here symbolizing the transition from the sensuous world of illusion to the world of the spirit. Right: *Cast Bronze Buddha from Sultanganj in Bengal.* This 7-foot 6-inch representation of Buddha, dating from the fifth century, is typical of Gupta art and metallurgy at its peak.

Relief sculpture and painting

corresponding to the Classical and Medieval ages of the West. The Buddhist caves at Ajanta contain the most important surviving collection of wall paintings. Religious in inspiration, they are at the same time spontaneous and unrestrained, proclaiming an unabashed delight in physical beauty. Although long neglected and damaged by the ravages of bats, insects, smoke, and water seepage, they are still magnificent. (The Indian government is taking steps to clean and conserve this priceless heritage.) In the Hindu temples, which increased in number from the seventh century on as Buddhism began to decline, decoration was usually in sculpture rather than painting. Relief sculptures in the Ellora cave temples and in Hindu and Jain temples erected during the tenth and eleventh centuries at Khajuraho in east central India rank among masterpieces of the world's art. In these carvings not only the gods but a galaxy of figures and dramatic episodes out of India's historic and legendary past seem to come alive. Many scenes are boldly realistic, but the Hindu tendency toward abstraction is also evident in the practice of depicting gods with several pairs of arms or several faces to signify their separate attributes. The themes portrayed range from voluptuous ecstasy and heroic struggle to attitudes of piety and mystic contemplation.

The spread of Indian culture

While the Indian communities were bringing their civilization to a point of refinement, they were also implanting it among various other peoples of Southeast Asia. Indian navigators and merchants were active in the eastern waters of the Indian Ocean as well as in the Arabian Sea to the west and apparently led the world in maritime enterprise during this period. Some of the Indian states maintained navies and had a Board of Shipping as a governmental department. They not only promoted commerce but chartered companies of merchants, giving them trade monopolies in certain areas and authority to establish colonies. During the early centuries A.D. Indian colonies were planted in the Malay Peninsula, Annam (eastern Indochina), Java, Sumatra, and many other islands of the Malay Archipelago. Between the fifth and tenth centuries an empire ruled by a Buddhist dynasty and possessing formidable naval strength was based on the island of Sumatra. It also controlled western Java, extended into the Malay Peninsula, sent colonists to Borneo and from thence to the Philippine Islands. It dominated the Strait of Malacca and effectively policed the waters of this area against piracy. Although weakened by a long struggle with one of the Hindu mainland states, the empire (known as the Srivijaya) remained intact until the fourteenth century. Indian influence was extensive in the peninsula of Indochina—in the Cham state on the southeastern coast (later absorbed into the Annamese empire), in the Cambodian kingdoms of the lower Mekong valley, and among the Thais (Siamese) to the northwest.

The political vicissitudes of these various Eastern states were too complex to be enumerated here, but the entire region long remained an outpost of Indian culture. Sanskrit literature was introduced, along with Buddhism and the leading cults of Hinduism. Art and architecture, originating in Indian prototypes, were assiduously cultivated and attained considerable individuality. During the eighth and ninth centuries the Srivijaya empire in Sumatra and Java was perhaps the foremost center of Buddhist art. The colossal temple of Borobudur in central Java, one of the world's architectural marvels, is actually a

Art in the Srivijaya and Khmer Empires

Relief Sculpture in the Hindu Cave at Ellora, Hyderabad (eighth century A.D.) The central figures are the god Shiva and his consort Parvati.

stone-encased hill rising 150 feet high, with nine terraces, staircases, covered gateways, and four galleries containing 1,500 sculptured panels. This "great picture bible of the Mahayana creed" is currently being restored under the sponsorship of UNESCO. In the ninth century, building on an ambitious scale was in progress in the Cambodian empire established by the Khmers, a native people who wielded dominion over a large part of Indochina between the ninth and the fourteenth centuries, and who responded energetically to the stimulus of Indian cultural contacts. Their capital city, Angkor (recovered from the jungle by French archeologists in the twentieth century), was of almost incredible magnificence in its heyday. Among several huge temples the most imposing was that of Angkor Wat, about a mile south of the capital, built during the twelfth century and said to be the largest work of its kind in the world, surpassing in mass even Luxor and Karnak of ancient Egypt. Angkor Wat was dedicated to the Hindu god Vishnu and was also designed as a tomb for the emperor, who was deified after his death and identified in some way with Vishnu. Eastern Asia for which historical records are available. In addition, it warned sinners of the numerous hells awaiting the wicked, celebrated the king's earthly conquests, and depicted scenes from the classic Sanskrit epics of India. While Hindu influence was ascendant in Cambodia, Buddhism was also a potent force there. Khmer statues of Buddha are distinguished by the "smile of Angkor"—a countenance expressing the height of benevolence and the supreme peace associated with the attainment of an inner state of enlightenment or *nirvana*.

Flourishing culture of "Greater India"

During the Middle Ages the whole region surrounding the Bay of Bengal, while comprising separate political units, was dominated by Indian culture, imparted through commercial contacts and manifest in the fields of religion, literature, and art. The creative activity in this

Angkor Wat. Built in the twelfth century by Suryavarman II as a sepulcher and monument to the divinity of the monarch, this temple is one of the largest religious structures in the world. The architecture of Angkor Wat is derived from the Indian stupa form.

Wall Carvings at Angkor Wat. The walls of this twelfth-century monument to the god Vishnu are covered with bas reliefs of celestial dancers, parading kings, and marching armies.

"Greater India" was not inferior to that of the motherland. In some ways it was even bolder, more vigorous and experimental, and it continued to flourish after the onslaught of fanatical Muslim conquerors from Afghanistan had brought a decay in India. However, a decline finally overtook the Buddhist and Hindu civilizations of Southeast Asia as the result of exhausting struggles among the competing states, pressure from China to the north, and—more decisive—the impact of Arab and other Muslim adventurers who traded, proselytized, and conquered successfully in this area during the fourteenth, fifteenth, and sixteenth centuries.

2. THE TERRITORIAL, POLITICAL, AND CULTURAL GROWTH OF CHINA

The Ch'in Dynasty, inaugurated after the overthrow of the Chou, lasted only fourteen years (221–207 B.C.), but it was one of the most important in Chinese history because it carried out a drastic reorganization of the government with permanent effects upon the character of the state. The founder of the dynasty, who assumed the title of "First Emperor" (Shih Huang Ti), was a man of iron will and administrative genius. He did away with the rival kingdoms, divided the country into provinces, and instituted an elaborate bureaucracy directly responsible to himself. The centralized administration and effective military organization that had been carefully cultivated in the state of Ch'in was now applied to all of China, thus effecting a momentous break with the past. The feudal institutions of 500 years'

The Ch'in Dynasty (221–207 B.C.)

standing were almost completely extinguished, and the government was brought into direct contact with the people. Determined to eliminate any competition for authority, the emperor's chief minister forbade the philosophic schools to continue their discussions and commanded their writings to be destroyed. His order for the burning of the books was a sweeping one, carrying the death penalty for disobedience, although copies of the forbidden works were locked up in the imperial library. Some Taoist writings were exempted from the proscription because the emperor was attracted by their reputed magic-working formulas. He was particularly anxious to root out the Confucianist and Mohist teachings because they emphasized moral restraints upon the ruler and his dependence upon the advice of learned counselors.

Shih Huang Ti, "First Emperor"

Every aspect of Shih Huang Ti's reign reveals tremendous force of personality and a ruthless determination. He carried out conquests in all directions. In the south he not only annexed regions but built canals, one of which linked the Yangtze to the West River (of which Canton is the principal port). While raising large armies by conscription he disarmed the bulk of the Chinese people as a precautionary measure. With forced labor he executed an ambitious building program that included a network of military roads radiating from his capital. His most impressive engineering project was to complete and join together the series of fortifications in the north, by which he created the Great Wall of China, reaching from the seacoast some 1,400 miles inland. At his capital (near Sian, the site of the old Western Chou capital) he had constructed a sumptuous palace measuring 2,500 by 500 feet and capable of accommodating 10,000 people. In addition to such undertakings he and his ministers found time to standardize weights, measures, and even the axle length of carts, and—still more important—to unify the style of writing in China, with the result that communication among the various sections was made easy in spite of the diversity of spoken dialects. In his administrative policies the First Emperor probably borrowed some features from the Persian monarchs and from the Indian ruler Chandragupta Maurya. That he made a great impression not only upon the Chinese but upon foreign powers is illustrated by the fact that his country came to be known in other lands as "China"—after the name of his dynasty. This indomitable monarch's chief weakness was his addiction to superstitious fancies. He undertook several journeys in search of the elixir of immortality and died on one of these expeditions. Three years later his dynasty ended in a round of court conspiracies and assassinations, and his great palace was burned to the ground.

The Ch'in emperor had aimed at a social as well as political reconstruction, and although this was a more difficult undertaking it succeeded in part. On the whole his policy was to encourage and promote agriculture above commerce, assisting the farmers and holding the merchant class in check. Officially he abolished serfdom, decreeing that the peasants should be owners of the lands they worked. It is doubtful, however, that their lot was actually much better than before. Not only were there great differences between the small and the large proprietors, but the poor peasants became burdened with debts contracted with the merchants and moneylenders, the very group the government had intended to restrain. The Ch'in ruler exacted heavy taxes of various sorts, including a poll tax, and conscripted men for military and labor service with a callous disregard for human suffering. Thus, while the state was concerning itself more directly and actively than ever before with the welfare of the whole community, it reduced the dignity and freedom of the individual to a minimum. Large numbers of the population were forcibly moved from one region to another and many were made slaves of the state. People's actions and, as far as possible, their thoughts also were controlled by the government. The Ch'in rule carried into practice the Legalist doctrines of coercion, punishment, and fear, and bore a striking resemblance to the European totalitarian regimes of the twentieth century.

The overthrow of the Ch'in Dynasty was followed soon afterward by the establishment of the Han, founded by a military adventurer who had risen from the ranks. In the course of Chinese history many dynasties came and went—some very brief and some with only a local jurisdiction—but most of them tended to follow a similar course and met with a similar fate. From time to time a new ruling house was inaugurated by force or usurpation, sometimes by an alien or by a leader of lowly birth (the founder of the Han Dynasty was said to have come from a poor peasant family). If he could vindicate his authority and maintain order, he was looked upon as a legitimate ruler entitled to all the imperial dignities, regardless of the previous status

Social reforms and totalitarian methods of Shih Huang Ti

The Han Dynasty (206 B.C.–220 A.D.)

The Great Wall of China at Nankow Pass. The wall was erected about 221–207 B.C. for defense against northern invaders.

of his family. To be accepted, however, the dynasty had to promote general prosperity as well as defend the country and suppress internal strife. The typical dynastic cycle of China illustrates not only the rise and fall of successive ruling families but also the close relationship between the condition of society and the durability of a political regime. Usually during the early years of a dynasty vigorous and efficient rule was accompanied by internal peace, prosperity, and an increase in population. When the imperial court and its officers became venal and corrupt, neglected administrative problems, and demanded exorbitant taxes, domestic upheaval ensued, frequently joined to the threat of attack from without. If the dynasty failed to resolve the crisis, it went down in bloodshed, and a new firm hand seized control, cleared away the debris, and began the process all over again under a new dynastic name. The rise and fall of the Han Dynasty (206 B.C.–220 A.D.) illustrates the general pattern which was typical of China's successive political episodes. At the same time the Han Dynasty marks one of the most splendid periods in Chinese history, characterized by cultural progress and by the development of a form of government so satisfactory that its essential features remained unchanged—except for temporary interruptions—until the present century.

Centralized government

The Han government was a centralized bureaucracy but conducted with some regard for local differences and with deference to ancient traditions. Certain aspects of feudalism were reintroduced as the first Han emperor granted estates in the form of fiefs to his relatives and other prominent figures. However, the danger of feudal principalities becoming powerful and independent, as had happened in Chou times, was circumvented by a decree requiring the estates of nobles to be divided among the heirs instead of passing intact to the eldest son. Chinese society was still far from being equalitarian, but its aristocratic structure had been severely jolted. The imperial administration cut across class lines, and there was little danger that it would ever again be constituted on feudal principles. The power of the old Chou states was broken beyond recovery. Obviously, the Han rulers were profiting from and continuing the work begun by the hated house of Ch'in, although they softened the harshest features of the Ch'in regime. Whereas the Ch'in emperor had antagonized the class of scholars, the Han ruler sought their favor and support and instructed his officials to recommend to the public service young men of ability irrespective of birth. The Confucianists profited most from the government's policy of toleration toward the philosophical schools. Some of their books had escaped the flames, and the scholars had long memories. Under the patronage of the emperor, Confucianist teachings were reinterpreted, with more emphasis upon the supremacy of the central authority than Confucius had probably intended. Thus, instead of serving as a stumbling block, they assisted in the creation of an efficient imperial government.

The Han rule, while energetic, efficient, and relatively enlightened, was sufficiently severe. As under the Ch'in, ambitious public works of reclamation and canal- and road-building entailed enormous labor, much of which was performed by slaves. Taxes were high, the salt and iron industries were made state monopolies, and the currency was debased to yield a profit to the government at the expense of the people. At the same time, the emperor attempted to regulate prices, not merely for the protection of the poorer consumers but to divert the middleman's profit into the imperial coffers. The government also participated in the rapidly expanding foreign commerce of the empire.

As under most strong dynasties, efforts were directed to expanding the territorial frontiers. The Huns after many campaigns were forced to acknowledge Han suzerainty and compelled to furnish tribute and military support. Chinese control was established over much of Central Asia, including not only the Tarim basin of Sinkiang but parts of Turkestan beyond the mountains. Southern Manchuria and northern Korea were annexed, and Chinese settlers and culture penetrated this area. The provinces south of the Yangtze were secured and also northeastern Indochina (Tonkin). Both in territorial extent and in power, China under the Han was almost equal to the contemporary Roman Empire. Nor was China isolated from other civilized areas. Her trade connections were far-reaching, especially by the caravan routes which traversed Sinkiang and Turkestan. The Chinese had also begun to venture on the high seas, although ocean traffic was conducted chiefly by Indian navigators who sailed to the South China Sea and the Gulf of Tonkin. Chinese merchants exchanged products not only with India and Ceylon, but also with Japan, Persia, Arabia, Syria, and—indirectly—with Rome. The trade balance was generally favorable to China because of the high price commanded by her leading export, silk, frequently paid for in gold or precious stones.

The Han Dynasty reached its climax in the latter half of the second century B.C., under the able leadership of an emperor who ruled for more than fifty years (Han Wu Ti, 140–87 B.C.). At the opening of the first century A.D. a court minister named Wang Mang, without military backing but with wide popular support, seized the imperial throne and proclaimed a new dynasty, which lasted only until the usurper's death fourteen years later (23 A.D.). During his brief and disastrous reign Wang Mang launched a radical reform program, sometimes described as an abortive attempt to establish a socialist society but which was actually inspired by Confucianist precepts as interpreted by Wang. He tried to re-establish early Chou institutions, including a semifeudal nobility, while at the same time alleviating the condition of slaves. Invoking the ancient doctrine that all land belongs to the ruler, he confiscated the property of great landowners to provide a farm plot for every family. However benevolent in intent, Wang's reforms were vitiated by his own inflexibility, inefficiency, and corruption through the exercise of power. He alienated almost all sections of the population, including those he was trying to help, and must go down as one of the supreme failures in the history of public administration. After he was murdered by rebels who broke into the palace, his program was scrapped. In 25 A.D. the Han family recovered the throne and retained it for two more centuries—a period known as the Later or Eastern Han because the capital was moved eastward to the site of Honan. The Later Han period exhibited the typical symptoms of decay at court and within the ruling house, although the administrative system remained intact and China's reputation in foreign parts was upheld by skillful diplomacy and force of arms. The dynasty crumbled as rebellions broke out and power passed into the hands of warlords, one of whom deposed the Han emperor in 220 A.D.

*A period of turbulence and
disunity*

For almost four centuries after the collapse of the Han Dynasty, China was in a state of turbulence and upheaval. The country was divided, warfare was frequent, and it seemed that all the gains of the previous era were in jeopardy. Although the dates are not identical, this period of political disunity in China is comparable to the time of confusion which Europe experienced after the fall of the Roman Empire in the West. As in Europe during the early Middle Ages, the central government was weak or nonexistent; barbarian invasions affected a wide area; and, just as Christianity became rooted among the Latin and Germanic peoples of the West, a new otherworldly religion—Buddhism—made tremendous headway in China. Aside from these parallels, however, China's period of disunion was very different from the early Middle Ages in Europe. In China there was no appreciable decline in commerce or in city life, nor was there a serious modification of culture and institutions. The absence of a strong central authority was the only real disadvantage from which the country suffered, and this defect could be remedied by reviving the administrative machinery which had been temporarily disrupted. The Han state had been a practical and effective expression of Chinese experience, utilizing existing social and economic institutions and emphasizing ancient traditions. Consequently, even a long period of semianarchy could not destroy China's civilization. This period, dismal as it was, gave evidence of the toughness of Chinese society and culture, embodied in the patriarchal family, the village organization, and the sturdy enterprise of farmers who literally worshiped the soil on which they labored and were determined to make it support them regardless of the political controversies that raged on all sides.

*Nomadic invaders from the
north*

As might be expected, the nomadic peoples on China's northern borders took advantage of her internal weakness to overrun the country. For about 250 years, from the fourth to the late sixth century A.D., practically all northern China including the Wei and Yellow River valleys was ruled by nomad dynasties of Hunnish, Turkish, and related stocks. It was not, however, successfully incorporated into any of the extensive but short-lived empires which arose in Central Asia and often impinged upon India as well as China. The dominance of non-Chinese rulers over the Yellow River valley—the historic center of Chinese culture—did not by any means destroy this culture. On the contrary, the rulers seemed eager to be accepted as custodians and defenders of civilization, and in the Far East civilization was synonymous with Chinese institutions. The nomads who settled south of the Great Wall assimilated the speech and customs of the older inhabitants. One of the few permanent changes in the habits of the Chinese people that can be attributed to their contact with the steppe nomads was in costume. During the fourth and fifth centuries they adopted trousers and boots similar to those worn by the northern horsemen, and this style of dress gradually supplanted the flowing tunic even in south China.

The contrast between China and western Europe during the medieval era is accentuated by the fact that four centuries of disunity in China were followed by another vigorous and highly successful dynasty, the T'ang (618–907), which re-established the imperial administration, again pushed back the territorial frontiers, and promoted brilliant cultural achievements. Thus, at the very time when feudalism was taking root in Europe and a new type of civilization was in process of formation there, China was resuming the course that had been marked out in Han times. Although it followed so closely upon the period of invasion and division, the T'ang Dynasty in many respects marked the culmination of China's cultural evolution.[1]

The T'ang Dynasty was at its height during the first half of the eighth century, covered almost entirely by one distinguished reign, when the area under Chinese control was slightly greater than the Han dominions and greater than it has ever been since under a native Chinese monarch. Wars in Mongolia broke the power of the Turks, who had been dominant there for about 150 years, and some of them became allies of the T'ang emperor. Parts of Manchuria were annexed, all Korea was tributary for a brief span, and control was again asserted over northern Indochina. The most redoubtable advances were in Central Asia. Chinese jurisdiction was recognized as far west as the Caspian Sea and the borders of Afghanistan and India, and some of the Indus valley princes accepted Chinese suzerainty. In carrying out their military exploits the T'ang rulers relied heavily upon the assistance of the non-Chinese peoples with whom their subjects were by this time familiar, either as friends or as foes. Now that the Chinese dragon was in the ascendancy, Mongols, Turks, and Huns were glad to be accepted as allies.

[1] Actually the brief Sui Dynasty (589–618) had already reunited China and inaugurated the new era of progess.

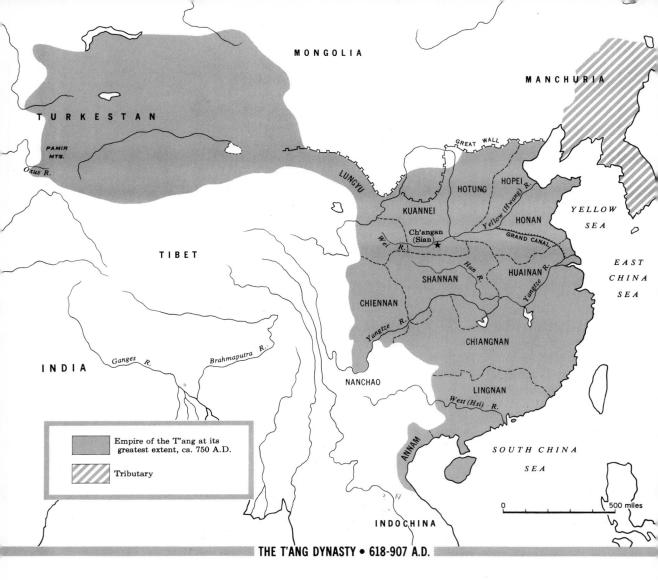

MONGOLIA

MANCHURIA

TURKESTAN

PAMIR
MTS.

Oxus R.

GREAT WALL

LUNGYU

HOTUNG

HOPEI

Yellow (Hwang) R.

KUANNEI

HONAN

YELLOW
SEA

TIBET

Wei R.

Ch'angan
(Sian)

GRAND CANAL

EAST
CHINA
SEA

Han R.

HUAINAN

SHANNAN

Yangtze R.

CHIENNAN

Yangtze R.

CHIANGNAN

INDIA

Ganges R.

Brahmaputra R.

NANCHAO

LINGNAN

West (Hsi) R.

ANNAM

SOUTH CHINA
SEA

	Empire of the T'ang at its greatest extent, ca. 750 A.D.
	Tributary

0   500 miles

INDOCHINA

THE T'ANG DYNASTY • 618-907 A.D.

Decline of the T'ang empire

Imposing as was the T'ang hegemony over Central Asia, it could not be maintained indefinitely. When the rapid expansion of Islam began under Arab leadership in the seventh century, it seemed for a while that China, in spite of her remoteness from the West, was the only power to offer effective resistance. The last Sassanid king of Persia, fleeing from the Arabs, sought refuge at the T'ang court, and T'ang forces with the assistance of local princes checked the Muslim advance in Turkestan. The check was only temporary, however. When the T'ang administration passed its zenith (about 750), the Arabs gained control of Turkestan—bequeathing the religion of Islam as a permanent heritage—and for a time their influence extended as far east as the border of China's Kansu province. The T'ang rulers also encountered trouble with Tibet, which previously had remained in isolation from the turbulent politics of Central Asia. Early in the seventh century a kingdom was founded in the highland country by a leader who attained sufficient prestige to be given both a Chinese and an Indian princess in marriage. The Tibetans invaded Chinese territory several times, allied themselves alternately with the Turks and with the Arabs, and interrupted trade between China and Persia by blocking the passes through the Pamir Mountains. In 798 the T'ang court succeeded in obtaining a treaty of alliance with the famous Harun-al-Raschid, caliph of Baghdad, and the Tibetan power subsided in the ninth century. Meanwhile, a division of Turks had reoccupied Mongolia, and in spite of a long struggle the Chinese were unable to hold their northern and western frontiers inviolate. By the end of the ninth century internal rebellions, together with governmental corruption and decadence in the ruling house, had led again to a state of general disorder.

The T'ang administrative machinery, similar to the Han, was centralized under the emperor and staffed by a large bureaucracy. China proper was divided into fifteen provinces, which were subdivided into prefectures, and these again into smaller units or sub-prefectures, and each of the units was headed by an official appointed from the capital. The Han practice of recruiting talent for the imperial service had now developed into a rudimentary civil-service system in which written examinations were offered periodically throughout the provinces, and officeholders were chosen from among the successful candidates. Appointments were not confined solely to those who had taken the examinations, nor were all successful candidates rewarded with positions; but the system did provide opportunities for public service to young men of ability from every class of the population, in keeping with the policy advocated by Confucius a thousand years earlier.

Development of the civil service

Since the abolition of feudalism and the establishment of peasant proprietorship by the Ch'in emperor, the character of Chinese society had not greatly changed. Many peasants were tenants rather than independent owners, and slavery had not entirely disappeared, although the percentage of slaves in the population was small. Inequalities in wealth and distinctions of rank were conspicuous. The T'ang emperors supported a titled nobility of several grades, but its prestige was based upon governmental favor rather than upon the possession of landed estates. Instead of hereditary titles carrying administrative power as in a feudal regime, the titles were bestowed upon eminent officials as a reward for their services. Ordinarily the emperor did not rule as a military despot but maintained a clear separation between the civil and military authority. It was only during periods of weakness and disorder that warlords usurped political functions. By T'ang times the Chinese had acquired a conviction that military regimes were incompatible with a normal, civilized state of

Chinese society under the T'ang

affairs. By tradition society was believed to be properly composed of five classes ranked in the order of their value to the commonwealth. These were, first, scholars; second, farmers; third, artisans; fourth, merchants; and last, soldiers, lumped together with beggars, thieves, and bandits.[2] The notable aspects of this classification are the high recognition granted to intellectual ability, the deprecation of violence and of nonproductive occupations, and the fact that the categories are based upon individual talents and capacities rather than upon birth. The five-class system was never fully realized or perfectly respected, but it was an ideal which tended to lessen the rigidity of Chinese institutions. On the more practical side, the prominence of scholars in the administration and the system of competitive examinations helped to prevent the dominance of aristocratic families. In addition, the circumstance that the imperial throne did not remain in any one family for more than a few centuries provided an object lesson not to be forgotten.

Agriculture

Continuing the policy of encouraging agriculture, every vigorous dynasty gave attention to irrigation works, usually maintained public granaries to provide food distribution in famine years, and sometimes attempted to relieve the farmers from their heavy burden of debt and taxes. Nevertheless, while China was already one of the world's leading agricultural countries, the poorer peasants undoubtedly suffered from a miserably low standard of living as has been the case throughout history. Furthermore, the farmer bore the chief burden of supporting the state. Theoretically the emperor reserved the right to redistribute holdings, but in practice he was usually content to break the power of overly ambitious wealthy houses that might challenge his own authority. Too often the interest of officials in the peasants centered upon the fact that they constituted the most lucrative and dependable source of taxation, collectible either in produce or labor, the latter including conscription for military service.

Commerce and urban growth

Curiously enough, in spite of the honored position of the farmer and the pro-agrarian policies of the government, the merchant class attained a prominence far superior to that of European merchants during this period, and the steady increase of trade induced the growth of thriving cities. During the eighth century the T'ang capital in the Wei valley (on the site of Sian, but known during this period as Ch'ang-an), the eastern terminus of the trans-Asiatic caravan routes, apparently had a population of close to 2 million, while the population of China as a whole was between 40 and 50 million—about 5 percent of the present number. Foreign commerce was greater under the T'ang than ever before, and an increasing proportion of it was oceanic, the leading ports of exchange being Canton and other cities along the

---

[2] A famous ancient Chinese proverb is "Good iron is not used to make a nail; a good man is not used to make a soldier."

southeast coast, where merchants of various nationalities from the Near and Middle East were to be found. In addition to silk and spices, porcelain ware was becoming a notable item in China's export trade.

Significant developments in religion took place during the period under consideration. The most important was the introduction of Buddhism, which brought the Chinese for the first time into contact with a complex religion with an elaborate theology, ecclesiastical organization, and emphasis upon personal salvation. For several centuries following the life of Gautama, the Buddhist faith gained such momentum in the regions surrounding India that it was bound to reach China. It was brought in over the northern trade routes as early as the first century A.D. and made rapid headway during the period of disunion that followed the collapse of the Han Dynasty. Buddhism met with a mixed reception in China, arousing both enthusiastic interest and repugnance. Mysticism, asceticism, contempt for the physical world, and the concept of transmigration of souls were quite alien to Chinese tradition; and the monastic life seemed to involve a repudiation of sacred family loyalties. On the other hand, Buddhism offered consolations not found in the native Chinese cults or philosophical disciplines. It was nonaristocratic, open to all classes, and—in contrast to the Confucian emphasis upon the inflexible will of Heaven—its *karma* doctrine affirmed that anyone could improve his chances in a future existence by diligent application. Converts were attracted by the rich symbolism of the new religion, and the voluminous scriptures which the Buddhist missionaries brought with them impressed the Chinese, who venerated scholarship. Buddhism's otherworldly orientation appealed particularly to the downtrodden and oppressed. In spite of violent opposition from some Chinese rulers, Buddhism continued to recruit adherents; congregations of women as well as of men were organized; pilgrims went to India to study and returned with copies of the Buddhist canons. By about 500 A.D. China had practically become a Buddhist country.

It might be supposed that after the restoration of a strong monarchy the interest in this imported salvationist faith would have subsided, but such was not the case. Although a few of the T'ang emperors tried to root out Buddhism (one emperor is reputed to have destroyed 40,000 temples), several of them encouraged it, and it was under the T'ang Dynasty that Chinese Buddhism reached its height as a creative influence. Many varieties of the religion had been brought into China—chiefly of the *Mahayana* school—and others were developed on Chinese soil, appealing to different temperaments and degrees of education. One of the most popular sects, called the "Pure Land" or "Lotus" school, promised an easy salvation in a western paradise to all who invoked the name of Amida (or Amitabha). Amida, theoretically an incarnation of Buddha, was actually visualized as a god, alleged to have been born of a lotus in the heavenly western realm of

The introduction of Buddhism

Head of Buddha. T'ang Dynasty (618–907). This stone head was found in the caves of Lung Men.

Varieties of Chinese Buddhism

bliss. Several of the sects, however, encouraged a zeal for scholarship and also stimulated interest in the problems of government and society. The most vigorous philosophical speculation under the T'ang was found in Buddhist circles. But in spite of the great success of Buddhism its triumph was not comparable to the ascendancy of Christianity in western Europe during this same period. The Chinese Buddhists were not united in a common discipline, had no coercive power, and their organization did not replace or challenge the authority of the state as did the Christian hierarchy in the West. And the fact that Buddhism was practiced in almost all parts of the country did not mean that other religions had ceased to exist. The idea of an inclusive universal church was foreign to Chinese conceptions.

Taoism as a religion

Paralleling the spread of Buddhism, Taoism, which had originated as a philosophical school, acquired the characteristic features of an otherworldly religion with wide popular appeal. Taoism developed not only a priesthood but an ecclesiastical hierarchy headed by a "Prince Celestial Master," who established pontifical headquarters in south central China. This Taoist hierarchy was given official recognition in the eighth century and was not formally abolished until 1927. The religion, incorporating many primitive beliefs, expounded the Way (*Tao*), which was interpreted to mean the road to individual happiness defined usually in material terms, although it offered elements to attract intellectuals and encouraged acts of charity. Taoism was greatly affected by Buddhism and borrowed ideas from the foreign faith, including the concepts of *karma* and transmigration and the belief in thirty-three heavens and eighteen hells. Its priesthood was modeled after the Buddhist monastic order, except that the Taoists did not practice celibacy; and the later Taoist scriptures show a strong resemblance to Buddhist texts. Inevitably rivalry sprang up between the two competing religions, but neither was able to eliminate the other and both received imperial as well as popular support. Some Taoist apologists claimed that their master, Lao-tzu, had actually been the Buddha or else had instructed him; while Buddhists countered with the assertion that Lao-tzu had rendered homage to Gautama.

Confucianism as a state cult

In spite of the popularity of Taoism and the temporary ascendancy of Buddhism, Confucianism began to be revived in the later T'ang period and retained its hold upon the allegiance of the Chinese. Although usually described as one of the three great religions of China, Confucianism was not and never became a religion in the strict sense of the term. It was a body of ethical principles, of etiquette and formal ceremony, and also—as a result of the policies of Han and T'ang emperors—a code of government, strengthened by the practice of recruiting officials from scholars versed in the Confucian classics. Veneration for the great teacher finally became part of the state cult and was invested with formal religious observances. The later Han emperors had prescribed sacrifices to Confucius in every large city,

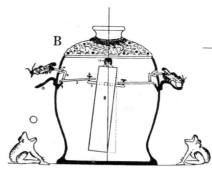

The Ancestor of All Seismographs. Invented by a Chinese mathematician and geographer in 132 A.D., it was described in a contemporary document as an "earthquake weathercock." These conjectural reconstructions show the interior of the bronze, bell-shaped instrument. (A) The pendulum carries jointed arms radiating in eight directions, each arm ending in a crank connected with a dragon head. (B) When an earth tremor causes the pendulum to swing, one of the dragon heads is raised and releases a ball, which drops into the mouth of a toad below. After the swing of the pendulum, a catch mechanism immobilizes the instrument. Thus, by observing which ball has fallen, it is possible to determine the direction of the initial shock wave.

and a T'ang ruler of the seventh century ordered temples to be built in his honor in each prefecture and subprefecture. Thus the sage, together with other famous men of antiquity, revered rulers, outstanding generals, etc., was ensured perpetual homage and respect, but he was not worshiped as were the Buddhist and Taoist deities. The Chinese idea of religion, it should be remembered, was different from that of most other peoples. The typical Chinese would be a Confucianist as a matter of course; but he might also be a Taoist, a Buddhist, or a combination of both.

Many economic and cultural changes took place during the thousand years between the Ch'in Dynasty and the end of the T'ang. Some items were borrowed from Western lands—grapes and alfalfa among the agricultural products, astrological concepts and the seven-day week from the Manicheans. The Chinese began to use coal for fuel and for smelting iron in the fourth century A.D., far in advance of Europeans. Their astrologers had observed sunspots as early as 28 B.C.; a crude seismograph was constructed in 132 A.D. The magnetic compass, apparently developed by the Taoists around 500 A.D., was used chiefly to determine favorable locations for grave sites. The properties of gunpowder had also been discovered. At this time, however, gunpowder was employed not to blow people to bits but in the manufacture of firecrackers to frighten away evil spirits. The highly important invention of paper (made of bark, hemp, and rags) was achieved by the beginning of the second century A.D., and printing from blocks was introduced about 500 years later. By the tenth century the printing of books was common not only in China but in Korea and Japan.

Porcelain Ewer or Pitcher, in the Form of a Court Lady. T'ang Dynasty.

Economic and cultural changes

Two Carved Wood Bodhisattvas. T'ang Dynasty. The bodhisattva, or Buddha-to-be, represented a person eligible for enlightenment but who remained in the world to help others on the upward path. In Mahayana Buddhism a number of bodhisattvas came to be worshiped as deities.

A great deal of the intellectual and artistic progress of this era must be credited to the Buddhists, whose contributions were not confined to religion exclusively. Buddhism enriched Chinese music by the introduction of a liturgy of vocal chants and also with several new musical instruments, including the psaltery, guitar or mandolin and other stringed instruments, the reed organ, clarinet, and a type of flute. It was in the visual arts, however, that the impetus of Buddhism was most notable. The Buddhists of northern India, who had absorbed artistic motifs from the Greeks and Persians, spread them into Central Asia and thence into China. During the period of disunion and the early T'ang Dynasty, Chinese sculpture reached its climax, successfully blending together Indian, Iranian, and Hellenic characteristics into a distinctive Chinese style. Superbly beautiful examples of this sculpture have survived, the best of which were produced in the late sixth and early seventh centuries. The most impressive works of architecture were Buddhist temples or sacred grottoes in northwestern China, carved out of rock caves after the Indian manner. Painting, too, reached a peak of realism and sensitivity which has rarely been surpassed. Skill in this medium was stimulated by the Chinese habit of writing with brush and ink, and pictorial figures or scenes were often combined with masterly specimens of calligraphy executed on scrolls of silk. Some paintings in fresco have been preserved from T'ang times and, like the sculpture, they show Buddhist influence. Outstanding among the minor arts was the production of pottery figurines representing human beings and animals with grace and naturalness, used chiefly as funeral presents to the departed. The manufacture of white porcelain—the beginning of the world-famous "china" ware—apparently began in the sixth or seventh century.

As early as Chou times, the Chinese civilization was highly literary, and by the T'ang period China had probably the most abundant collection of writings of any nation in the world. Philosophical activity did not equal the creative age of Confucius, Mo Ti, and Mencius, but a great variety of literary forms had come into existence, showing maturity of thought, sophistication, and aesthetic sensitivity. Writers of the T'ang period produced histories, essays, dictionaries, short stories and romances for popular entertainers, an embryonic form of the drama, and—outshining all the rest—poetry. Poetry had been developed prolifically during the centuries of disunion and civil strife. The influence of Buddhism and Taoism imparted emotional intensity and a quality of mysticism conducive to lyrical richness. The final result was a flowering in the eighth and ninth centuries which made the T'ang the supreme age of Chinese poetry. The verse forms were usually short, with words carefully chosen to evoke beauty of tone as well as to convey pithy thought and vivid imagery. While sometimes expressing philosophical ideas, they were frequently poignant in mood and romantic in theme, treating especially of nature, love, and friendship. A few of the best examples were tinged with a deep melancholy, expressing compassion for the miserable lot of the poor, distress over abuses in government, revulsion against the senseless brutality of war, and bewilderment at the apparent triumph of evil over good.

3. EARLY CIVILIZATION IN JAPAN

Of the great civilizations of the Far East, Japan's was the latest to develop. In origin it was derived from and was largely an adaptation of cultures from the mainland, especially from China. However, the fact that the Japanese lagged many centuries behind China and India and made their most rapid progress under the stimulus of borrowings from China does not prove that the island dwellers were lacking in ability or originality. Not only did the Japanese display remarkable ingenuity in assimilating foreign elements and in modifying them to meet their particular needs, but during some periods of history they seemed to possess more initiative than any of the other Far Eastern nations. The backwardness of Japan in early times is explained, at least in part, by the geographical circumstance of its isolation from the continent of Asia. Before oceanic commerce was well advanced, the Japanese islands could not be readily affected by political and cultural changes taking place on the mainland. These islands stand in the same relationship to Asia as do the British Isles to Europe. Just as European civilization was slowly extended from the Near Eastern centers westward to Italy and then to the northern countries, reaching Britain last of all, so Far Eastern civilization gradually radiated from the Yellow River valley to the south, west, and northeast, and necessarily reached Japan belatedly. Actually Japan is much more remote from the neighboring continent than is Britain from Continental Europe. At the narrowest point the Strait of Dover is only about 20 miles wide, while more than 100 miles separate the islands of Japan from the closest point on the Korean peninsula.

The retarded development of civilization in Japan

Japan's geographic setting is in some ways very favorable. Of the approximately 3,000 islands composing the group, only about 600 are inhabited, and the bulk of the population is concentrated on the four principal islands. The entire archipelago lies within the temperate zone, and the largest island, Honshu, holding about half of the Japanese people, lies between almost exactly the same latitudes as the state of California. The Black Current, drifting northward from tropical seas, moderates the severity of winter; and cyclonic storms, while sometimes destructive, bring fluctuations in temperature that are conducive to physical and mental vigor. Their proximity to the ocean encouraged the Japanese to develop navigation and to become hardy fishermen. With its expanse of seacoast, mountains, volcanoes and

Geographic advantages and disadvantages

snow-capped peaks, the region is scenically one of the most beautiful in the world, a factor which has undoubtedly contributed to the keen aesthetic sensibilities of the Japanese people. At the same time Japan is by no means perfectly endowed by nature and suffers from several disadvantages. Except for having fair deposits of coal, the islands are poor in mineral resources. Even more serious has been the scarcity of good agricultural land, owing to the rocky or mountainous character of much of the country. Although throughout most of their history the Japanese have been a nation of farmers, only about 16 percent of their soil is cultivable. This sufficed when the population was small and generally stationary; it has posed a tremendous problem in modern times.

Racial stocks in Japan

Small as is the land area of Japan (slightly less than that of California) and in spite of its relative isolation, it was inhabited even in early times by people of various stocks as the result of successive migrations from the continent. The earliest inhabitants, so far as is known, were a primitive people who possessed a Neolithic culture, crude in many respects but distinguished by pottery of striking design and skillfully fashioned weapons. They are represented today by the Ainu, a light-colored, flat-faced, and hairy people, who have largely disappeared except from Hokkaido and the Kuril Islands to the north. For the most part the Japanese nation is descended from Mongoloid invaders who crossed over to the islands at various times during the Neolithic Age and even later, chiefly by way of Korea. From the time of the Ch'in Dynasty on, the settlers in Japan possessed some knowledge of Chinese culture, which had already penetrated into Korea. Bronze mirrors, carved jewels, and swords of Chinese or Mongolian type appear in graves dating from the second and first centuries B.C. By the close of the first century B.C. the Japanese had begun to use iron as well as bronze.

The beginnings of Japanese society

Quite understandably, the leading centers of cultural evolution were in the south and west of Japan—the areas closest to Korea, from which the chief migrations came—and developments in this region gradually spread to the north and east. The real nucleus of the Japanese state was the peninsula of Yamato, on the southeastern side of the great island of Honshu, to which a group of families had migrated from Kyushu (opposite Korea) perhaps as early as the first century A.D. The Japanese communities at this time were very primitive. People wore clothing made from hemp or bark, although silk was not entirely unknown. They carried on trade by barter only and had no system of writing. The chief unit of society was the clan, a group of families claiming to be related by blood. Each clan venerated some particular deity, who was supposed to be the ancestor of the group; but the worship of human ancestors had not yet become an institution. The headship of the clan was vested hereditarily in a specific family, and the clan leader served both as a warrior chieftain and as

EARLY JAPAN

priest. In primitive Japanese society women seem to have held a position of prominence, perhaps even of superiority. The clan head was sometimes a woman, and evidence points to the conclusion that originally the family was matriarchal, with descent traced through the mother—a remarkable circumstance in view of the rigid subordination of women in later times. The transition to a patriarchal system, however, was effected at an early date. According to Chinese accounts from the third century A.D., polygamy was a common practice, especially among men of the higher classes. Various crafts and skills were organized as occupational groups in the form of guilds with hereditary membership. Each guild was attached to a clan and tended to merge with it eventually, although a few guilds whose members performed distinctive services, such as administering religious rites, retained an independent existence and honorable status. Members of the agricultural and artisans' guilds, on the other hand, were practically serfs. Society was decidedly aristocratic, rank was generally hereditary, and slavery existed, although the number of slaves was relatively small.

The foundations of Shintoism

Japanese religion, while comparable to that of other primitive peoples, was in some ways unique. It was basically animistic, a type of unreflecting and almost universal nature worship, with no well-defined conception of the nature of divine being. In a general way it was polytheistic, except that the term probably suggests too definite a catalogue of gods or too precise a theology. The Japanese later gave their religion the name of *Shinto* ("the way of the Gods"), simply because they needed to distinguish it from Buddhism when this articulate and mature faith began to compete with the native cult. Although the Japanese recognized some great deities, associated with the sun, moon, earth, crops, and storms, these were not endowed with distinct personalities and were not represented by images. Objects of worship were designated as *kami,* a term meaning "superior" but which was applied to almost anything having mysterious or interesting properties, ranging from heavenly phenomena to irregularly shaped stones and such lowly objects as sand, mud, and vermin. No sharp line was drawn between the natural and the supernatural or between magic and worship. The notion of life after death was extremely shadowy, and religion was largely devoid of ethical content. It involved taboos and scrupulous concern for ceremonial cleanness, with purification rites to remove contamination, but the requirements were not based on considerations of morality or even always of health. Uncleanness, for example, was associated with childbirth, with contact with the dead, and with wounds whether inflicted honorably or not. To placate the gods, respectful gestures, prayers, and sacrifices were employed. Offerings of food and drink gradually tended to be superseded by symbolic objects—of pottery, wood, and eventually paper.

Attractive elements in native Japanese religion

In spite of its diffuse and elementary character, the native Japanese religion was not lacking in attractive elements. It reflected an attitude of cheerfulness and a rare sympathy for and appreciation of nature. The gods were not thought of as cruel and terrifying creatures; even the god of the storm was generally conceived as benign. On the whole, the religion of the Japanese was one "of love and gratitude rather than of fear, and the purpose of their religious rites was to praise and thank as much as to placate and mollify their divinities."[3] It was

---

[3] G. B. Sansom, *Japan, a Short Cultural History,* p. 47.

enlivened also with picturesque legends and poetic phrases that suggest a spontaneous delight in the natural world.

The clan which was dominant on the plain of Yamato, and gradually acquired an ascendancy over adjacent regions, probably came from Kyushu and claimed descent from the Sun Goddess. There was nothing remarkable in such a claim because all important families traced their ancestry to gods or goddesses. However, myths associated with the Sun Goddess assumed greater significance as the Yamato clan extended its political power and attempted to secure fuller recognition of its paramountcy over the other clans, for which purpose it was helpful to foster the legend that the Yamato chief had been divinely appointed to rule over Japan (even though most of it was still unconquered from the aborigines). According to this legend the Sun Goddess had sent down to earth her own grandson, Ninigino-Mikoto. Ninigi, "thrusting apart the many-piled clouds of Heaven, clove his way with an awful way-cleaving" to land on the western island of Kyushu, carrying with him the three symbols of Japanese royalty—a jewel, a sword, and a mirror. The grandson of this Ninigi, it was related, advanced along the coast of the larger island to Yamato, where he began to rule as Jimmu, the "first emperor." National tradition dates the empire from February 11, 660 B.C. Actually, it was at least 600 or 700 years later that the Yamato state was established, and then it was anything but imperial. The saga of the Sun Goddess and her descendants did not become a distinctive element in the national cult of Japan until the sixth century A.D., and not until the modern era was it deliberately exploited on a national scale for the purpose of instilling a fanatical and unquestioning patriotism among the people.

For many centuries the Japanese maintained contact with and continued to receive cultural impetus from Korea, which means that they were being influenced indirectly by the older and richer civilization of China of the Han and later dynasties. The Japanese even controlled a small section at the southern tip of Korea from about 100 to 560 A.D. and intervened in Korean politics to maintain a balance of power, siding with one and then another of the three kingdoms into which Korea was divided during this time. Of fundamental importance for the later history of Japan was the introduction, by way of Korea, of the Chinese system of writing (about 405 A.D.) and of Buddhism (about 552 A.D.).

While the technique of writing was essential to the advance of civilization, it was unfortunate for the Japanese that they acquired it from China. If they had been able to devise or borrow a phonetic or alphabetic system, the problem of writing their language would have been comparatively simple. The Chinese characters—fundamentally pictographic or ideographic, with very little apparent relationship to pronunciation of the words for which they stand—had been developed to a state of complexity and utilized in producing masterpieces of Chinese literature; but they were ill suited to represent Japanese. The

Founding of the Japanese state

Japanese Tomb Culture. Clay grave statues of ordinary people, such as this soldier, surrounded the tombs of more important people. This reflects the influence of Korean culture. Such statuary began to appear in the third and fourth centuries A.D.

Japanese writing

Japanese language is phonetically quite different from the Chinese, and the attempt to write it with Chinese characters was a feat as difficult as it would be to try to write English in Chinese characters. Nevertheless, the Japanese struggled heroically with the task and eventually developed a script of their own, or, rather, two varieties of script. Although the original Chinese characters were abbreviated considerably and, during the ninth and tenth centuries, given phonetic value by identification with individual Japanese syllables, the resulting product was still cumbersome. Hence, the process of learning to write Japanese—in which 48 phonetic symbols plus 1,850 Chinese characters must be mastered—was and still is a laborious undertaking. The fact that the system of writing is alien to the structure, inflection, and idiosyncrasies of the spoken language hampered clarity of expression. To compensate for these disadvantages, however, along with the Chinese-derived script a great many Chinese words were adopted bodily by the Japanese, enriching their language in vocabulary and concepts. In view of the circumstances in which writing was introduced in Japan, a person who wished to become educated was almost bound to learn the Chinese language, especially since it was the vehicle of all literature considered worthy of the name. For several centuries Japanese scholars, officials, and men of letters wrote in classical Chinese, in somewhat the same manner that educated Europeans used Latin during the Middle Ages and later—except that while Latin was

Japanese and Chinese Writing. The text on the right is a passage from Mencius in Chinese with kaeriten added on the left hand side of each column to indicate the sequence in which the characters should be read to transcribe the passage into Japanese. This adaptation of Chinese writing is called Kambun. The text on the left is the same passage in Japanese. The hiragana written between the characters indicate the appropriate verbal inflections and postpositions. The small hiragana beside each character indicate the correct Japanese pronunciation. Note the use of Chinese characters in the Japanese text.

Great Buddha, Todaiji Temple, Nara. This statue, cast in the middle of the eighth century A.D., is one of the two largest bronze statues in the world. The seated Buddha is 53 feet high.

both written and spoken by educated Europeans, few Japanese scholars or literati learned to *speak* Chinese.[4]

In the middle of the sixth century Buddhism began to obtain a foothold in Japan. The first Buddhist missionary is said to have come from Korea; other evangelists of the new faith arrived not only from Korea but from China and even from India. As in the case of China, the *Mahayana* school of Buddhism, with its elaborate theology and emphasis upon the soul's redemption, was most in evidence. And, just as had happened in China, a number of different sects arose in Japan from time to time. The appearance of Buddhism in Japan produced perhaps even greater agitation than had accompanied its introduction into China a few centuries earlier. The Chinese were at least familiar with mystical concepts through Taoism, but the Japanese had had no previous experience either with this type of otherworldly religion or with any analogous philosophy. Part of the appeal of Buddhism to the Japanese lay in its novelty. The Buddhist scriptures raised questions that had apparently never occurred to the Japanese before—as to the soul, the nature of the immaterial world, rewards and punishments after death—and then proceeded to answer them with impressive eloquence. For a while, sharp controversy raged over the acceptability of the foreign faith (the first statue of the Buddha sent from Korea was thrown into a canal when an epidemic of disease broke out). However, one prominent aristocratic family in Yamato, the Soga, adopted and championed the cause of Buddhism and prevailed upon the imperial clan to favor it, so that before the close of the sixth century the success of the religion was assured. To some extent its success was attributable to political maneuvers and expediency. In

The establishment of Buddhism in Japan

---

[4]For an illuminating discussion of the Japanese language, see E. O. Reischauer, *The Japanese,* chapter 37.

patronizing the scholarly faith the Soga family sought to enhance its own prestige and, through the benefit of whatever supernatural power the religion contained, to secure an advantage in the struggle against rival families. Buddhism rapidly acquired a wide following both among the common people and the aristocracy and became so firmly entrenched that it would survive any shift in equilibrium among the contending clans. Probably its popularity is largely explained by its being interpreted as a miraculous protector against disasters both in this world and the next rather than by its philosophical heritage. Nevertheless, the increasing familiarity with Buddhist doctrines stimulated intellectual activity and was conducive to the cultivation of attitudes of sympathy and humaneness.

Buddhism a medium for disseminating Chinese culture

One of the most significant aspects of the spread of Buddhism in Japan was that it proved to be a highly effective medium for disseminating Chinese culture, especially art, architecture, and literature. Temples and shrines were erected, paintings and images of the Buddha were produced, and libraries of the sacred texts were accumulated. Converts from the aristocratic class frequently went to China to study, returning with a broadened viewpoint and refined tastes. The native Japanese cult, now beginning to be called *Shinto,* was by no means extinguished, but it was influenced considerably by contact with Buddhism. There was very little antagonism between the two religions. Buddhism in Japan became tinged with national traditions, and frequently the same shrine was regarded as sacred to both faiths. The Japanese priests, whether Buddhist or Shinto, did not constitute a hierarchy with coercive powers over the people any more than did the priests in China, although the Buddhist monasteries gained in economic importance as they were endowed with lands.

During the most vigorous period of the T'ang Dynasty, the impact

Horyuji Temple, Nara. The Horyuji Temple, founded in 607 A.D. by Prince Shotoku, Regent of the Empress-Regnant Suiko, is a complex of about forty buildings and includes some of the oldest wooden structures in the world.

of Chinese civilization upon Japan reached such a climax that it marks a turning point in the evolution of Japanese institutions. It is not at all strange that the Japanese turned avidly to China for tutelage at this time. China under the early T'ang rulers was one of the most highly civilized states in the world, as well as the most powerful, and in the Far East had no close rivals for such a distinction. Throughout the seventh and eighth centuries the government in Yamato sent a succession of official embassies to the T'ang court, largely for the purpose of recruiting personnel trained in the sciences, arts, and letters. The result was a wholesale copying of Chinese techniques and ideas, affecting almost every aspect of Japanese life and society. Chinese medical practices, military tactics, and methods of road building were introduced; also styles of architecture, of household furniture, and even of dress. A system of weights and measures was adopted, and copper coins came into limited circulation, although a genuine money economy did not replace barter until centuries later. Many works of art had previously been imported and copied, but now Japanese painters and sculptors began to display both technical proficiency and originality. The Chinese classics, especially the Confucian writings, were studied intently, since every well-bred person was expected to be familiar with them. Along with these concrete and visible innovations came an attempt to fit the social structure into the Chinese pattern. A new emphasis was placed upon family solidarity and filial devotion, including the duty of sacrificing to ancestral spirits.[5] Japanese leaders and intellectuals seemed determined to remake their country in the image of China.

The most comprehensive project involved nothing less than reconstituting the government according to the T'ang model. It was announced by a decree known as the Taika Reform Edict, issued in 645 A.D. by the Yamato ruler at the instigation of a clique of scholar-reformers. This declaration, rather than the mythical events of 660 B.C., represents the founding of the Japanese imperial system. By the Taika Edict the ruler assumed the role not of a mere clan leader but of an emperor, with absolute power, although professedly honoring Confucian principles. All Japan was to be divided into provinces, prefectures, and subprefectures, which would be administered by a centrally appointed bureaucracy recruited from the populace. Faithful to the example of China, the reformers instituted a civil service, offering examinations to candidates for government posts, whose selection would be based not on familiarity with the problems of Japan but on proficiency in Chinese philosophy and classical literature. To give the new administration an economic foundation and to bring it to bear directly upon the people, the Reform Edict proclaimed that all the

Japanese Religious Sculpture. This wooden figure of Bishamon, revered as one of the Four Guardian Kings of the Budhist kingdom, dates from the twelfth century or earlier.

Chinese influence on Japanese government

---

[5] Some Japanese scholars deny that the custom of ancestor worship was an importation; but in any case it was intensified by contacts with the Chinese. An unfortunate consequence was the increasing subordination of women to male authority in the patriarchal family and in society at large.

land belonged to the emperor, and that it would be divided equitably among the farmers and redistributed every six years. In return, every landholder would be required to pay taxes (in commodities, money, or labor) directly to the state.

*Consolidation of the
Japanese government*

Altogether, the reform program of the seventh century was one of the most ambitious that any government has ever attempted. It sought to graft upon a still fairly primitive society an administrative system that was the product of almost a thousand years of evolution among a people with cultural maturity and deeply entrenched traditions. Similarly, it involved an effort on the part of one corner of Japan to impose its regime on the entire area, much of which had hardly advanced beyond the Neolithic stage. In adopting the scheme of a centralized paternalism, one aspect of the Chinese prototype was studiously avoided: namely, the concept that imperial authority is conditional upon the promotion of public welfare and that it may be terminated—by rebellion as a last resort—if it fails in this objective. The Yamato group tried to attach a bureaucracy of scholar-officials to a government that called for perpetual rule by one family, whose head occupied a position of inviolable sanctity. To strengthen the prestige of the emperor, greater emphasis than ever before was placed upon his reputed descent from the Sun Goddess. He was represented as the embodiment of a "lineal succession unbroken for ages eternal" and as divine in his own person—a significantly different concept from that of the "Mandate of Heaven," the conditional and temporary divinity that hedged the Chinese emperor. In addition to this fundamental contrast between the official Chinese and Japanese theories as to the ultimate basis and limits of political authority, there was a notable divergence in practice also. China knew many different dynasties, most of them begun through rebellion or usurpation; but when a vigorous emperor sat on the throne, he usually ruled effectively and sometimes autocratically, as is attested by the records of the first few rulers of every major dynasty. In Japan, on the other hand, while the imperial family was never dethroned in spite of violent or revolutionary changes within society and in foreign relations, and while the fiction of imperial sanctity was carefully preserved, the actual power for the most part was exercised by some other family, agency, or clique, using the sacred imperial office as a front. Indirect government, sometimes removed by several stages from the nominal sovereign, has been the rule rather than the exception in Japan ever since its attempt to incorporate the Chinese political machinery.

*Partial failure of the
reform program*

In view of the inherent difficulties, it is not surprising that the reform program of the seventh century was not entirely successful. The new administrative system existed on paper but not as an operating reality. The imperial clan, which had previously enjoyed only a limited and largely ceremonial authority over the others, could not compel absolute obedience from remote areas, and aristocratic traditions were too strong to be broken immediately. The emperor made it a practice to appoint clan heads as officials in their own territories instead of replacing them by loyal servants sent out from the capital. Thus the local magnates acquired new titles and kept much of their former power. Examinations were provided for candidates desiring posts in the government service, but important positions were almost always reserved for members of the aristocracy, while capable men of the lower class found themselves employed as underlings and clerks. The announced policy of land equalization, which was intended to serve as the basis for a uniform tax system, was the most dismal failure of all. It had been inspired by the Chinese ideal of community interest in the land, a sentiment which condemned the appropriation of land for the exclusive benefit of any individual and taught that it should be distributed equally among the cultivators. This was only a theory in China, and in Japan it was thoroughly unrealistic. Later large proprietors managed to evade taxation and so increased the burden upon the poorer farmers that some of them ran away from their homes in sheer desperation. In this manner the amount of taxable land diminished, and the emperors themselves contributed to the process by giving away estates to courtiers or to endow Buddhist monasteries. Furthermore, the decree regarding periodic redistribution of land applied only to the fields that had already been brought under rice cultivation, a relatively small area. As the frontier clans added to their domains either by conquest from the aborigines or by reclaiming waste lands for cultivation, these new territories were regarded as personal holdings not directly subject to imperial assessment. Consequently, economic progress lessened rather than increased the proportion of the land under effective control by the central government. Instead of securing large funds from taxation, the court became more and more dependent for revenue upon estates that were owned outright by the imperial family.

Although the central government failed in its political objectives, it succeeded in promoting cultural progress to an appreciable degree. Before the seventh century there had been no fixed Japanese capital even in Yamato, or in fact no cities at all. Impressed with the splendor of the T'ang capital, the great city of Ch'ang-an, the Japanese determined to build one like it to serve as the imperial headquarters. Their city, begun in 710 and located near the modern town of Nara, followed the Chinese model faithfully in its broad streets and carefully aligned squares of equal size, although it was unwalled and much smaller than Ch'ang-an. Even so, its plan was too large for the population that occupied it. In 794 a more imposing capital was built at Kyoto, which has been an important city ever since. The construction of these cities under imperial patronage, with palaces, temples, and other public buildings, provided a stimulus to all the arts. Scholarship, bent on the production of histories, treatises, and literary criticism,

Governmental stimulation of culture

Benten Playing on a Biwa. A Japanese painting on silk by an artist of the Heian (Fujiwara) period, 893–1185.

also flourished at the imperial court. If the bureaucracy had little real public responsibility, its members could find satisfaction and enhanced social prestige in polishing their classical Chinese, translating Buddhist sutras, painting, or composing poetry of a rather strained and artificial type. The refinement of ceremony and etiquette also received much attention. Life in court circles tended to become effete and frivolous, but it harbored some artistic and intellectual talent of high caliber. Odd as it may seem, the best Japanese literature of this period was produced by women of the nobility and of the imperial household. Their contributions, outstanding in the tenth and eleventh centuries, were chiefly prose, typically in the form of diaries but including one justly famous romantic novel (*Tale of Genji*). In this instance it was fortunate that women, even of the court, were not held to the same educational standards as men. "While the men of the period were pompously writing bad Chinese, their ladies consoled themselves for their lack of education by writing good Japanese, and created, incidentally, Japan's first great prose literature."[6]

4. THE FOUNDATION OF CIVILIZATIONS IN AFRICA SOUTH OF THE SAHARA

The advance of civilization in sub-Saharan Africa was relatively slow. Africa's lack of early development, like Japan's, may be explained in

[6] E. O. Reischauer, *Japan, the Story of a Nation*, pp. 34–35.

part by its geographical isolation. The continent possessed few natural harbors, leaching of the soil's nutrients contributed to a general scarcity of good agricultural land, and the vast Sahara inhibited meaningful cultural and profitable commercial exchange. Desert transportation was dangerous and unreliable with horses or oxen.

Before 200 B.C. nearly all Africans south of the Sahara functioned on a nomadic hunting and gathering level. Religion, deeply rooted in superstition, remained basically animistic. Leadership was exercised by priests or family elders. Population density was exceedingly low everywhere, obviating the need to form large, centralized governing units. With an abundance of unoccupied land. Africans found permanent settlements unnecessary, and in the absence of external threats, there was no compulsion to organize military cadres for defense. Government was therefore rudimentary. Many clans engaged in ancestor worship for the purpose of establishing a sense of continuity and exerting a measure of moral control. Intermediaries were chosen from among elders in the group to interpret the will of the ancestors and gods and to lead rituals in their honor.

*Early mechanisms for
social control*

From very early times, some Africans developed exceptionally advanced skills in metallurgy. At least 1,500 years ago Africans on the western shore of Lake Victoria in East Africa produced medium carbon steel in forced-draft furnaces. Their sophisticated technique would not be matched by Europeans for centuries. Inexplicably, the African practice did not seem to have radiated beyond the ancestors of the present Haya people of modern Tanzania. Of greater consequence to Africa was the smelting of iron.

Metallurgy

The Iron Age wrought revolutionary changes in African life styles after about 200 B.C. At that time, small bands of Bantu-speaking Negroes living along the modern Nigerian-Cameroon border in West Africa learned how to forge iron ore into spears and hoes. We do not yet know whether they developed the ability to smelt iron independently or whether the technique was introduced by immigrants from North Africa or from the lands of Kush. In any case, it endowed the Bantu with an immediate technological advantage over others. With their superior iron implements they expanded southward into the equatorial woodlands of West Central Africa. Then in approximately 1 A.D., in the watershed of the Congo-Zambezi river systems, they encountered high-yield food crops, including the nutritious banana, coco-yam and plantain. These plants had probably spread up the Zambezi River valley from Madagascar island. They were brought to Madagascar by seaborne southeast Asian immigrants of Javanese origin. The Bantu, possessing sturdy iron hoes, were in an excellent position to cultivate these new food crops.

*Iron and the Bantu
dispersion*

Iron metallurgy, together with superior southeast Asian crops, greatly accelerated the transition from a food-gathering to a food-producing economy. By 200 A.D. agricultural surpluses had triggered a population explosion among the Bantu, propelling them in easterly

The Iron Age in Africa. An iron smelter in Tanzania such as those that enabled th Bantu to create iron tools and weapons.

and westerly directions across the breadth of equatorial Africa from coast to coast. Small, segmented Neolithic populations were either absorbed or eliminated by the Bantu, who enjoyed greater social cohesion and practiced efficient methods of farming and pastoralism. With plentiful food and meat, they could support many wives and large, extended families. Consequently, their numbers quickly multiplied.

Southeast Asian food crops trigger population explosions

Food-producing economies led to the emergence of village life. Trade became a necessary handmaiden to agriculture as metallurgists bartered their finished tools for iron ore, copper, salt, and other essential commodities. By the close of the tenth century, most Africans were using iron implements; and from the Cameroons to the South African veld they spoke Bantu-related languages. Bantu peoples had thus initiated an agricultural revolution and accelerated the development of new mechanisms for social organization and control in East, Central, and Southern Africa. In effect, they laid the necessary foundations for the civilizations which emerged in the millennium after 900 A.D.

The emergence of village life and trading activity

The impact of iron in West Africa

Iron technology brought forth similar changes in West Africa, even though the Bantu diaspora did not extend there. For centuries Nubians from the Upper Nile and Saharan Berbers, bearing iron tools and weapons, had infiltrated Negro cultures of the West African grasslands. Marrying local women, they quickly lost their ethnic identity. An excellent environment for fishing and cereal cultivation in the Niger River area and Chad basin had already stimulated a dramatic growth of the indigenous population.

Before the introduction of the camel, Carthaginians and later Romans had conducted a minuscule Saharan trade by horse-drawn chariot. But few if any of them ever established direct commercial connections with West Africans. Their small purchases of gold, ivory, slaves, and pepper were made through the middlemen of Garamante in the Fezzan oases of central Sahara. The clever Garamantes received glass beads, fine cloth, and dates which they passed on to the West African producers. By 300 A.D. camels had come into wide use in the Sahara as transport vehicles. Camels possessed an exceptional capacity for carrying heavy loads over long distances and maneuvering effectively under sandy conditions. They became, in effect, ships of the desert and greatly facilitated the movement of peoples and goods between North and West Africa. An ensuing revival and expansion of trans-Saharan trade led to the eventual flowering of market centers and coherent civilizations in the grassland expanse between southern Mauretania and Lake Chad.

Roman departure from North Africa in the fourth century A.D. seems to have coincided with the organization by desert Berbers of the first West African kingdom, called Ghana, or Awkar. This Negro-Berber state, located in the southeastern corner of modern Mauretania, thrived on its middleman position between the gold miners of the southern forests and the Berber traders of North Africa. By the eighth century the "Ghana," or king, of Awkar was a Negro, and his people were known in North Africa and the Middle East as the world's major gold exporters.

Trans-Saharan traffic remained small and informally organized until the mid-seventh century when Muslim Arabs overran the strategic Fezzan oases. By 740 A.D. desert Berbers had begun to embrace Islam and to withdraw more deeply into the Sahara where they set up new

Introduction of the camel in the trans-Saharan trade

Foundation of Ghana, West Africa's first kingdom

The Arab invasion of North Africa

Agriculture. A Ndebele granary in southern Zimbabwe. The ability to sustain sedentary village life depended on the community's ability to stockpile foodstuffs.

trade centers. At Sijilmasa they exchanged Ghanaian gold with the Arabs for Saharan salt. The salt was resold in the south to perspiring miners while the Arabs carried their gold into North Africa and Europe.

The Berbers in West Africa

The Arab presence in North Africa encouraged Berbers to probe more deeply into West Africa in search of gold or to seek refuge from Islamic persecution. Zaghawa Berbers established communities of highly cultured farmers and fishermen around Lake Chad. In 846 A.D. they founded a ruling dynasty, based on concepts of divine kingship. Like the Berbers in Ghana, they readily married into local families and were ethnically absorbed within a few generations.

The West African Sudan: Land of the Blacks

Small chieftaincies were gradually coalescing into larger governing units from the upper Senegal eastward to the shores of Lake Chad. By about 800 A.D. trade routes had reached the upper Niger River, where caravan paths from Morocco, Algeria, Tunis, Tripoli, and Egypt converged at the emporium of Gao. West Africa's rolling grasslands had become famous in Arab commercial circles as the Bilad-as-Sudan or "Land of the Blacks."

Indo-Shirazi penetration along the East African coast

Similar commercial and political trends were discernible along the coast of East Africa. The rise of Persian sea power in the late seventh century resulted in the eclipse of Ethiopian trade in the Red Sea and western Indian Ocean. Arabs from the Persian Shiraz swarmed along the Banadir coast of modern Somalia, where they established permanent trading settlements. Within a few generations they turned their sailing boats, or dhows, southward along the coast of modern Kenya and Tanzania. There they encountered Bantu-speaking people who, centuries before, had reached the coast from the equatorial savanna. By 900 A.D. the Bantu were beginning to marry into Arab Shirazi and Indian families, who had only recently converted to Islam. Together

Gateway to a Medieval City in the Sultanate of Morocco. Morocco was a major trading partner of the Western Sudanic cities and had a significant architectural impact on the area.

they founded dynasties and organized a formal seaborne trade propelled by monsoon winds. As of old, turtle shells, ivory, rhinoceros
horns, and small numbers of slaves were exported to Arabian ports
and northwestern India. But by 900 A.D. increasing quantities of Central African copper had begun to arrive on the Mozambique coast.
Growing Asian demands for copper led to trading operations through
the Zambezi valley to reach the mines of Katanga. Indian Ocean trade,
like that of the Sahara, acted as a powerful catalyst for the centralization of authority among groups engaged in mining and marketing
activities.

*The catalytic effect of
Indian Ocean Trade*

Meanwhile, in the sixth century along the upper reaches of the Nile,
a number of Christian Nubian kingdoms appeared. The Nubians,
though influenced by Byzantine Greece, developed their own language, laid out beautiful cities, constructed impressive brick monasteries and cathedrals, and adorned them with paintings. They also
enjoyed a highly sophisticated tradition of ceramic art, with pottery
of outstanding design. Their civilization reached its zenith during the
ninth and tenth centuries. Powerful Nubian armies were strong
enough to resist Muslim intrusions for nearly four centuries afterward.

*The flowering of Nubian
civilization*

SELECTED READINGS

• *Items so designated are available in paperback editions.*
• Binyon, Laurence, *Painting in the Far East,* 3d ed., New York, 1923.
• ———, *The Spirit of Man in Asian Art,* New York, 1935.
• Nakamura Hajime, *Ways of Thinking of Eastern Peoples: India, China, Tibet,
    Japan,* ed. P. P. Wiener, Honolulu, 1964.

INDIA—*See also Readings for Chapter 6*

Devahuti, D., *Harsha: A Political Study,* Oxford, 1970.
Panikkar, K. M., *India and the Indian Ocean,* New York, 1945.
Sen, Gertrude E., *The Pageant of India's History,* Vol. I, New York, 1948.
van Leur, J. C., *Indonesian Trade and Society,* New York, 1955.

CHINA—*See also Readings for Chapter 7*

Bagchi, P. C., *India and China, a Thousand Years of Cultural Relations,* rev.
    ed., New York, 1951.
Balazs, Etienne, *Chinese Civilization and Bureaucracy,* New Haven, 1964. An
    important interpretation of Chinese society.
Carter, T. F., and L. C. Goodrich, *The Invention of Printing in China and Its
    Spread Westward,* 2d ed., New York, 1955.
• Ch'en, Kenneth, *Buddhism in China, A Historical Survey,* Princeton, 1974. A
    solid and lucid study.
Ching, Julia, *Confucianism and Christianity: A Comparative Study,* New York,
    1977.

- Lattimore, Owen, *The Inner Asian Frontiers of China*, 2d ed., New York, 1951.
- Levenson, J. R., and F. Schurmann, *China, an Interpretive History: From the Beginnings to the Fall of Han*, Berkeley, 1969.

Schafer, E. H., *The Golden Peaches of Samarkand: A Study of T'ang Exotics*, Berkeley, 1963.

Shryock, J. K., *The Origin and Development of the State Cult of Confucius*, New York, 1932.

Sickman, L., and A. Soper, *The Art and Architecture of China*, Baltimore, 1956. Reliable; richly illustrated.
- Sullivan, Michael, *The Arts of China*, rev. ed., Berkeley, 1978. Incorporates recent archeological discoveries.

Sun, E. Z., and John De Francis, *Chinese Social History*, Washington, 1956. Translations of articles by modern Chinese scholars.
- Wittfogel, K. A., *Oriental Despotism: A Comparative Study of Total Power*, New Haven, 1957. Attempts to explain the despotic character of the Chinese imperial government by the necessities of a "hydraulic society," in which flood control and efficient irrigation systems were imperative.

Wright, Arthur F., *Buddhism in Chinese History*, Stanford, 1959. Brief but good.

Zurcher, E., *The Buddhist Conquest of China: The Spread and Adaptation of Buddhism in Early Medieval China*, 2 vols., Leiden, 1959. An illuminating study of the interaction between Chinese culture and Buddhism to the early fifth century A.D.

JAPAN

Anesaki, Masaharu, *Art, Life and Nature in Japan*, Boston, 1933.

———, *History of Japanese Religion*, London, 1930.

Brower, R. H., and E. Miner, *Japanese Court Poetry*, Stanford, 1961. Covers the period from the sixth to the fourteenth centuries.

Cole, Wendell, *Kyoto in the Momoyama Period*, Norman, Okla., 1967.

Eliot, Charles, *Japanese Buddhism*, New York, 1959. A standard text.
- Fenollosa, E. F., *Epochs of Chinese and Japanese Art*, New York, 1927.
- Hall, J. W., *Japan: From Prehistory to Modern Times*, New York, 1971.

Langer, P. F., *Japan, Yesterday and Today*, New York, 1966. An excellent summary.
- Moore, C. A., ed., *The Japanese Mind: Essentials of Japanese Philosophy and Culture*, Honolulu, 1967.
- Morris, Ivan, *The World of the Shining Prince*, Baltimore, 1969.
- Munsterberg, Hugo, *The Arts of Japan: An Illustrated History*, Rutland, Vt., 1957.
- Reischauer, E. O., *Japan: The Story of a Nation*, New York, 1979. Lucid and well organized.

Sansom, George B., *A History of Japan to 1934*, Stanford, 1958. An outstanding work by an eminent British scholar.

———, *Japan: A Short Cultural History*, rev. ed., New York, 1962.

Swann, Peter C., *An Introduction to the Arts of Japan*, New York, 1958.
- Warner, Langdon, *The Enduring Art of Japan*, Cambridge, Mass., 1952.

Wheatley, Paul, and Thomas See, *From Court to Capital: A Tentative Interpretation of the Origins of the Japanese Urban Tradition*, Chicago, 1978.

Whitney, J. H., and R. K. Beardsley, *Twelve Doors to Japan,* New York, 1965.

AFRICA

Adams, William Y., *Nubia—Corridor to Africa,* London, 1977.
- Bovill, E. W., *The Golden Trade of the Moors.* New York, 1958.
- Oliver, Roland, ed., *The Dawn of African History,* New York, 1968.
  Oliver, Roland, and Brian Fagan, eds., *Africa in the Iron Age c. 500 B.C. to A.D. 1400,* Cambridge, 1975.
- Posnansky, Merrick, ed., *Prelude to East African History,* London, 1966.
  Shaw, Thurstan C., *Nigeria: Its Archaeology and Early History,* London, 1977.

SOURCE MATERIALS

Aston, W. G., tr., *Nihongi: Chronicles of Japan from the Earliest Times to* A.D. *697,* 2 vols., London, 1896.

Ayscough, Florence, ed., *Tu Fu, the Autobiography of a Chinese Poet,* London, 1934.

Beal, Samuel, tr., *Buddhist Records of the Western World,* 2 vols., London, 1884.

Bynner, Witter, and Kiang Kanghu, trs., *The Jade Mountain, a Chinese Anthology,* New York, 1929.

- de Bary, W. T., ed., *Sources of Chinese Tradition,* "The Imperial Age: Ch'in and Han"; "Neo-Taoism and Buddhism," New York, 1960.
- ————, ed., *Sources of Indian Tradition,* "Hinduism," New York, 1958.
- ————, ed., *Sources of Japanese Tradition,* "Ancient Japan"; "The Heian Period," New York, 1964.
- Fage, J. D., and R. A. Oliver, eds., *Papers in African Prehistory,* New York, 1979.
- Keene, Donald, ed., *Anthology of Japanese Literature, from the Earliest Era to the Mid-Nineteenth Century,* New York, 1956.

Lu, David, ed., *Sources of Japanese History,* Vol. I, New York, 1973.

Morris, Ivan., tr., *As I Crossed the Bridge of Dreams: Recollections of a Woman in Eleventh-Century Japan.*

Sanskrit Dramas: *Sakuntala, The Little Clay Cart.*

- Thompson, L., and J. Ferguson, eds., *Africa in Classical Antiquity,* New York, 1969.
- van Buitenen, J. A. B., *Tales of Ancient India,* Chicago, 1959.

Waley, Arthur, tr., *Ballads and Stories from Tun-Huang, an Anthology* (T'ang era); *The Tale of Genji; Translations from the Chinese,* New York, 1960.

Watson, Burton, tr., *Records of the Grand Historian of China, Translated from the Shih Chi of Ssu-ma Ch'ien,* 2 vols., New York, 1961.

- Whitehouse, W., and E. Yanagisawa, trs., *The Tale of Lady Ochikubo,* Kobe, 1934.

Part Three

THE WORLD IN
THE MIDDLE AGES

The "Middle Ages" was a term coined by Europeans in the seventeenth century to express their view that a long and dismal period of interruption extended between the glorious accomplishments of classical Greece and Rome and their own "modern age." Because the term became so widespread, it is now an ineradicable part of our historical vocabulary; but no serious scholar uses it with the sense of contempt it once had. Between about 600 and 1500—the rough opening and closing dates of the Middle Ages—too many different things happened to be characterized in any single way. In the eastern parts of the old Roman Empire two new civilizations emerged, the Byzantine and the Islamic, which must rank among the most impressive civilizations of all time. Although the Byzantine civilization came to an end in 1453, the Islamic one has continued to exist without major interruption right up to the present. Seen from an Islamic perspective, therefore, the "Middle Ages" was not a middle period at all but a marvelous time of birth and vigorous early youth. The history of western Europe in the Middle Ages is conventionally divided into three parts: the early Middle Ages; the High Middle Ages; and the later Middle Ages. Throughout the early, High, and later Middle Ages the Christian religion played an extraordinarily important role in human life, but otherwise there are few common denominators. The early Middle Ages, from about 600 to about 1050, came closest to appearing like an interval of darkness, for the level of material and intellectual accomplishment was, in fact, very low. Nonetheless, even during the early Middle Ages important foundations were being laid for the future: above all, western Europe was beginning to develop its own distinct sense of cultural identity. The High Middle Ages, from about 1050 to 1300, was one of the most creative epochs in the history of human endeavor. Europeans greatly improved their standard of living, established enduring national states, developed new institutions of learning and modes of thought, and created magnificent works of literature and art. During the later Middle Ages, from about 1300 to 1500, the survival of many high-medieval accomplishments was called into question by the onslaught of numerous disasters, particularly profound economic depression and lethal plague. But people in the later Middle Ages rose above adversity, tenaciously held on to what was most valuable in their prior inheritance, and, where necessary, created new institutions and thought-patterns to fit their altered circumstances. The Middle Ages thus were really many hundred years of enormous diversity. They may be studied profitably both for their own intrinsic interest and for the fundamental contributions they made to the development of modern times. During these same "medieval" centuries, the great nations of southern and eastern Asia continued their cultural evolution along lines already established. Both India and China were invaded, however, by Mongols from the West and North who introduced alien elements originally derived from Muslim sources. Japan adopted political feudalism and more and more aspects of Chinese culture. The spread of the religion of Islam in Africa promoted political and cultural progress in several regions of that vast continent.

POLITICS	PHILOSOPHY AND SCIENCE	
Byzantine Emperor Heraclius, 610–641		**600**
Muhammad enters Mecca in triumph, 630		
Muslims conquer Syria, Persia, and Egypt, 636–651		
Muslims conquer Spain, 711		
Muslim attack on Constantinople repulsed, 717		**700**
Charles Martel defeats Muslims at Poitiers, 732		
Abbasid dynasty in Islam, 750–1258		
Pepin the Short anointed king of the Franks, 751		
Charlemagne, 768–814		
Charlemagne crowned emperor, 800		**800**
Carolingian Empire disintegrates, c. 850–911		
Alfred the Great of England, 871–899		
High point of Viking raids in Europe, c. 880–911	Al-Farabi, d. 950	
Otto the Great of Germany, 936–973	Avicenna, d. 1037	**900**
	Peter Abelard, 1079–1142	**1000**
Norman Conquest of England, 1066		
Seljuk Turks defeat Byzantines at Manzikert, 1071		
Penance of Henry IV at Canossa, 1077		
Henry I of England, 1100–1135	Origins of universities in the West, c. 1100–c. 1300	**1100**
Louis VI of France, 1108–1137	Translation of Aristotle's works into Latin, c. 1140–c. 1260	
Frederick I (Barbarossa) of Germany, 1152–1190	Peter Lombard's *Sentences,* c. 1155	
Henry II of England, 1154–1189	Robert Grosseteste, c. 1168–1253	
Philip Augustus of France, 1180–1223	Windmill invented, c. 1180	
	Averroës, d. 1198	
Crusaders take Constantinople (Fourth Crusade), 1204	Maimonides, d. 1204	**1200**
Spanish victory over Muslims at Las Navas de Tolosa, 1212		
Frederick II of Germany and Sicily, 1212–1250	Roger Bacon, c. 1214–1294	
	St. Thomas Aquinas, 1225–1274	
Magna Carta, 1215	Height of Scholasticism, c. 1250–c. 1277	
Louis IX (St. Louis) of France, 1226–1270	William of Ockham, c. 1285–1349	
	Mechanical clock invented, c. 1290	
Edward I of England, 1272–1307		
Philip IV (the Fair) of France, 1285–1314	Master Eckhart, active c. 1300–c. 1327	**1300**
Hundred Years' War, 1337–1453	Height of nominalism, c. 1320–c. 1500	
Political chaos in Germany, c. 1350–c. 1450		
Appearance of Joan of Arc, 1429–1431		**1400**
Reassertion of royal power in France, c. 1143–c. 1513	Printing with movable type, c. 1450	
Rise of princes in Germany, c. 1450–c. 1500	Heavy artillery helps Turks capture Constantinople and French end Hundred Years' War, 1453	
Capture of Constantinople by Ottoman Turks, 1453		
Wars of the Roses in England, 1455–1485		
Peace among northern Italian states, 1454–1485		
Marriage of Ferdinand and Isabella, 1469		
Strong Tudor dynasty in England, 1485–1603		

The European Middle Ages (continued)

	ECONOMICS	RELIGION	ARTS AND LETTERS
600	Decline of towns and trade in the West, c. 500–c. 700	Muhammad, c. 570–632 Pope Gregory I, 590–604 Muhammad's *Hijrah,* 622 Split in Islam between Shiites and Sunnites, c. 656	Byzantine church of Santa Sophia, 532–537
700	Height of Islamic commerce and industry, c. 700–c. 1300 Predominantly agrarian economy in the West, c. 700–c. 1050	Missionary work of St. Boniface in Germany, c. 715–754 Iconoclasm in Byzantine Empire, 726–843	
800	Height of Byzantine commerce and industry, c. 800–c. 1000	Foundation of Cluny, 910	The Venerable Bede, d. 735 *Beowulf,* c. 750 Irish "Book of Kells," c. 750 Carolingian Renaissance, c. 800–c. 850
900		Byzantine conversion of Russia, c. 988	
1000	Destruction of Byzantine free peasantry, c. 1025–c. 1100 Agricultural advance, revival of towns and trade in the West, c. 1050– c. 1300	Beginning of Reform Papacy, 1046 Schism between Roman and Eastern Orthodox Churches, 1054 Pope Gregory VII, 1073–1085 St. Bernard of Clairvaux, 1090–1153 First Crusade, 1095–1099	Romanesque style in architecture and art, c. 1000–c. 1200
1100		Height of Cistercian monasticism, c. 1115–c. 1153 Concordat of Worms ends investiture struggle, 1122 Crusaders lose Jerusalem to Saladin, 1187 Pope Innocent III, 1198–1216 Albigensian Crusade, 1208–1213 Founding of Franciscan Order, 1210 Fourth Lateran Council, 1215 Founding of Dominican Order, 1216	*Song of Roland,* c. 1095 Troubadour poetry, c. 1100–c. 1220 *Rubaiyat* of Umar Khayyam, c. 1120 Anna Comnena's biography of Alexius, 1148 Gothic style in architecture and art, c. 1150–c. 1500 Poetry of Chretien de Troyes, c. 1165–c. 1190 Development of polyphony in Paris, c. 1170 Wolfram von Eschenbach, c. 1200
1200		Fall of last Christian outposts in Holy Land, 1291 Pope Boniface VIII, 1294–1303	Gottfried von Strassburg, c. 1210 Persian poetry of Sadi, c. 1250 *Romance of the Rose,* c. 1270
1300	European economic depression, c. 1300–c. 1450 Floods through western Europe, 1315 Black Death, 1347–1350 Height of Hanseatic League, c. 1350–c. 1450 English Peasants' Revolt, 1381 Medici Bank, 1397–1494	Babylonian Captivity of papacy, 1305–1378 John Wyclif, c. 1330–1384 Great Schism of papacy, 1378–1417 John Hus preaches in Bohemia, c. 1408–1415 Council of Constance, 1414–1417 Hussite Revolt, 1420–1434 *Imitation of Christ,* c. 1427 Council of Basel, defeat of conciliarism, 1431–1449	Paintings of Giotto, c. 1305–1337 Dante's *Divine Comedy,* c. 1310 Boccaccio's *Decameron,* c. 1350 Persian poetry of Hafiz, c. 1370 Chaucer's *Canterbury Tales,* c. 1390 Paintings of Jan van Eyck, c. 1400–c. 1441
1400			

The Nonwestern World, 600–1600

AFRICA	INDIA	THE FAR EAST	
Expansion of Bantu people, 200–900	Great stone temple architecture, c. 550–1250 Sanskrit drama, c. 600–1000 King Harsha, 606–648	T'ang Dynasty in China, 618–907 Taika Reform Edict, creating imperial government in Japan, 645	**600** **700**
			800
		Wood-block printing of books in China, Japan, and Korea, c. 900	**900**
Expansion of Islam, 1000–1500 Consolidation of states, 1000–1500	Muslim invasions, 1000–1500	Sung Dynasty in China, 960–1279	**1000**
Bantu, Arab, and Indian cultures blend in Swahili civilization along eastern coast, c. 1100–1500		Neo-Confucianism, 1130–1200 Highest development of landscape painting in China, 1141–1279 Explosive powder used in weapons in China, c. 1150 Genghis Khan, 1162?–1227 Establishment of Shogunate in Japan, 1192 Zen Buddhism in Japan, c. 1200	**1100**
	Turkish Sultanate at Delhi, 1206–1526	Inoculation for smallpox in China, c. 1200 Development of Chinese drama, c. 1235 Marco Polo in China, 1275–1292	**1200**
Decline of Kingdom of Ghana, c. 1224 Mali empire in middle Niger region, c. 1300–1500 University of Timbuktu, c. 1330		Mongol (Yüan) Dynasty in China, 1279–1368 Rise of daimyo in Japan, 1300–1500	**1300**
		Ming Dynasty in China, 1368–1644	
	Sack of Delhi by Timur, 1398		**1400**
Expansion of Songhay, c. 1493–1582			

The Nonwestern World, 600–1600 (continued)

AFRICA	INDIA	THE FAR EAST

1500

Founding of Sikh religious
sect, c. 1500

Introduction of Christianity
into Japan, 1549–1551

Decline of Songhay after
defeat by Moroccans, 1591

Chapter 13

ROME'S THREE HEIRS: THE BYZANTINE, ISLAMIC, AND EARLY-MEDIEVAL WESTERN WORLDS

Constantinople is a bustling city, and merchants come to it from all over, by sea or land, and there is none like it in the world except Baghdad, the great city of Islam. In Constantinople is the church of Santa Sophia, and the seat of the Pope of the Greeks, since the Greeks do not obey the Pope of Rome. There are also as many churches as there are days of the year. A quantity of wealth is brought to them from the islands, and the like of this wealth is not to be found in any other church in the world.

—Benjamin of Tudela, *Travels*

You have become the best community ever raised up for mankind, enjoining the right and forbidding the wrong, and having faith in God.

—The Koran, III, 110

He who ordains the fate of kingdoms and the march of events, the almighty Disposer, having destroyed one extraordinary image, that of the Romans, which had feet of iron, or even feet of clay, then raised up among the Franks the golden head of a second image, just as remarkable, in the person of the glorious Charlemagne.

—A monk of St. Gall

A new period in the history of Western civilizations began in the seventh century when it became clear that there would no longer be a single empire ruling over all the territories bordering on the Mediterranean. By about 700 A.D., in place of a united Rome, there were three successor civilizations that stood as rivals on different Mediterranean shores: the Byzantine, the Islamic, and the Western Christian. Each of these had its own language and distinctive forms of life. The Byzantine civilization, which descended directly from the Eastern Roman Empire, was Greek-speaking and dedicated to combining Roman governmental traditions with intense pursuit of

The successors of Rome

the Christian faith. The Islamic civilization was based on Arabic and inspired in government as well as culture by the idealism of a dynamic new religion. Western Christian civilization in comparison to the others was a laggard. It was the least economically advanced and faced organizational weaknesses in both government and religion. But it did have some base of unity in Christianity and the Latin language, and it would soon begin to find greater political and religious cohesiveness.

The reappraisal of the Byzantine and Islamic civilizations

Because the Western Christian civilization ultimately outstripped its rivals, Western writers until recently have tended to denigrate the Byzantine and Islamic civilizations as backward and even irrational. Of the three, however, the Western Christian was certainly the most backward from about the seventh to the eleventh centuries. For some four or five hundred years the West lived in the shadow of Constantinople and Mecca. Scholars are only now beginning to recognize the full measure of Byzantine and Islamic accomplishments. These greatly merit our attention both for their own sakes and because they influenced western European development in many direct and indirect ways.

1. THE BYZANTINE EMPIRE AND ITS CULTURE

The Byzantine achievement impressive despite weaknesses

Once dismissed by the historian Gibbon as "a tedious and uniform tale of weakness and misery," the story of Byzantine history is today recognized to be a most interesting and impressive one. It is true that the Byzantine Empire was in many respects not very innovative; it was also continually beset by grave external threats and internal weaknesses. Nonetheless it managed to survive for a millennium. In fact the empire did not just survive, it frequently prospered and greatly influenced the world around it. Among many other achievements, it helped preserve ancient Greek thought, created magnificent works of art, and brought Christian culture to pagan peoples, above all the Slavs. Simply stated it was one of the most enduring and influential empires the world has ever known.

Problems of periodization in Byzantine history

It is impossible to date the beginning of Byzantine history with any precision because the Byzantine Empire was the uninterrupted successor of the Roman state. For this reason different historians prefer different beginnings. Some argue that "Byzantine" characteristics already emerged in Roman history as a result of the easternizing policy of Diocletian, and others that Byzantine history began when Constantine moved his capital from Rome to Constantinople, the city which subsequently became the center of the Byzantine world. (The old name for the site on which Constantinople was built was Byzantium, from which we get the adjective Byzantine; it would be more accurate but cumbersome to say Constantinopolitine.) Diocletian and Constantine, however, continued to rule a united Roman Empire. As we have seen, as late as the sixth century, after the western part of the empire had fallen to the Germans, the Eastern Roman Emperor Justinian thought of himself as an heir to Augustus and fought hard to win back the West. Justinian's reign was clearly an important turning point in the direction of Byzantine civilization because it saw the crystallization of new forms of thought and art that can be considered more "Byzantine" than "Roman." But this still remains a matter of subjective emphasis: some scholars emphasize these newer forms, while others respond that Justinian continued to speak Latin and dreamed of restoring old Rome. Only after 610 did a new dynasty emerge that came from the East, spoke Greek, and maintained a fully Eastern or properly "Byzantine" policy. Hence although good arguments can be made for beginning Byzantine history with Diocletian, Constantine, or Justinian, we will begin here with the accession in 610 of the Emperor Heraclius.

It is also convenient to begin in 610 because from then until 1071 the main lines of Byzantine military and political history were determined by successful resistance against successive waves of invasions from the East. When Heraclius came to the throne the very existence of the Byzantine Empire was being challenged by the Persians, who had conquered almost all of the empire's Asian territories. As a symbol of their triumph the Persians in 614 even carried off the holy relic believed to be part of the original cross from Jerusalem. By enormous effort Heraclius rallied Byzantine strength and quickly turned the tide, fully routing the Persians and retrieving the cross in 627. Persia was then reduced to a subordinate state and Heraclius reigned in glory until 641. But in his last years new armies began to invade eastern Byzantine territory, swarming out of hitherto placid Arabia. Inspired by the new religion of Islam and profiting from Byzantine exhaustion after the struggle with Persia, the Arabs made astonishingly rapid gains. By 650 they had taken most of the Byzantine territories the Persians had occupied briefly in the early seventh century, had conquered all of Persia itself, and were making their way westward across North Africa. Having become a Mediterranean power, the Arabs also took to the sea. In 677 they tried to conquer Constantinople with a fleet. Failing that, they attempted to take the city again in 717 by means of a concerted land and sea operation.

The Arab threat to Constantinople in 717 was a new low in Byzantine fortunes, but the threat was countered by the Emperor Leo the Isaurian (717–741) with as much resolution as Heraclius had met the Persian threat a century before. With the help of a secret incendiary device known as "Greek fire"[1] and great military ability, Leo was able

The reign of Heraclius; the rise of Islam

Byzantine revival prior to the Battle of Manzikert

---

[1] This is believed to have been a mixture of sulphur, naptha, and quicklime. Bronze tubes placed on the prows of ships, and also on the walls of Constantinople, released this liquid fire at the enemy.

πύρρηχῶρ. Ἡραῶδὲ καὶ τῶῦσκⲇⲁⲅτῶⲡⲣ ⲱⲡⲟⲗⲟⲱⲡⲡⲩⲣⲓ

τⲟⲗⲟⲉⲣ ⲱ ⲙⲟⲩ ⲡⲩⲣⲡⲟⲗ ⲱ ⲧⲟ Ν ⲧⲱ Ν Ε Ν Η Ⲁ Ν ⲡ ⲅ̄ ⲗⲟ Ν ·

Greek Fire

The end of the Byzantine Empire

to defeat the Arab forces on sea and land. Leo's relief of Constantinople in 717 was one of the most significant battles in European history, not just because it allowed the Byzantine Empire to endure for centuries more, but also because it helped to save the West: had the Islamic armies taken Constantinople there would have been little to stop them from sweeping through the rest of Europe. Over the next few decades the Byzantines were able to reconquer most of Asia Minor. This territory, together with Greece, became the heartland of their empire for the next three hundred years. Thereafter the Byzantines achieved a stalemate with Islam until they were able to take the offensive against a decaying Islamic power in the second half of the tenth century. In that period—the greatest in Byzantine history—Byzantine troops reconquered most of Syria. But in the eleventh century a different Islamic people, the Seljuk Turks, cancelled out all the prior Byzantine gains. In 1071 the Seljuks annihilated a Byzantine army at Manzikert in Asia Minor, a stunning victory which allowed them to overrun the remaining Byzantine eastern provinces. Constantinople was now thrown back upon itself more or less as it had been in the days of Heraclius and Leo.

After Manzikert the Byzantine Empire managed to survive, but never regained its earlier vigor. One major reason for this was the fact that, from 1071 until the final destruction of the empire in 1453, Byzantine fortunes were greatly complicated by the rise of western Europe. Hitherto the West had been far too weak to present any major challenge to Byzantium, but that situation changed entirely in the course of the eleventh century. In 1071, the same year that saw the victory of the Seljuks over the Byzantines in Asia Minor, westerners known as Normans expelled the Byzantines from their last holdings in southern Italy. Despite this clear sign of Western enmity, in 1095 a Byzantine emperor named Alexius Comnenus issued a call for Western help against the Turks. He could hardly have made a worse mistake: his call helped inspire the Crusades, and the Crusades became a major cause for the fall of the Byzantine state. Westerners on the First Crusade did help the Byzantines win back Asia Minor but they also carved out territories for themselves in Syria, which the Byzantines considered to be their own. As time went on frictions mounted and the westerners, now militarily superior, looked more and more upon Constantinople as a fruit ripe for the picking. In 1204 they finally picked it: Crusaders who should have been intent on conquering Jerusalem conquered Constantinople instead and sacked the city with ruthless ferocity. A greatly reduced Byzantine government was able to survive nearby and return to Constantinople in 1261, but thereafter the Byzantine state was an "empire" in name and recollection of past glories only. After 1261 it eked out a reduced existence in parts of Greece until 1453, when powerful Turkish successors to the Seljuks, the Ottomans, completed the Crusaders' work of destruction by conquering the last vestiges of the empire and taking Constantinople. Turks rule in Constantinople—now Istanbul—even today.

That Constantinople was finally taken was no surprise. What *is* a cause for wonder is that the Byzantine state survived for so many centuries in the face of so many different hostile forces. This wonder becomes all the greater when it is recognized that the internal political history of the empire was exceedingly tumultuous. Because Byzantine rulers followed their late-Roman predecessors in claiming the powers of divinely appointed absolute monarchs, there was no way of opposing them other than by intrigue and violence. Hence Byzantine history was marked by repeated palace revolts; mutilations, murders, and blindings were almost commonplace. Byzantine politics became so famous for their behind-the-scenes complexity that we still use the word "Byzantine" to refer to highly complex and devious backstage machinations. Fortunately for the empire some very able rulers did emerge from time to time to wield their untrammeled powers with efficiency, and, even more fortunately, a bureaucratic machinery always kept running during times of palace upheaval.

Factors of the stability of the Byzantine Empire: (1) occasional able rulers

Efficient bureaucratic government indeed was one of the major elements of Byzantine success and longevity. The Byzantines could count on having an adequate supply of manpower for their bureaucracy because Byzantine civilization preserved and encouraged the practice of education for the laity. This was one of the major differences between the Byzantine East and the early Latin West: from about 600 to about 1200 there was practically no literate laity in Western Christendom, while lay literacy in the Byzantine East was the basis of governmental accomplishment. Byzantine officialdom regulated many aspects of life, far more than we would think proper

(2) efficient bureaucratic administration

today. Bureaucrats helped supervise education and religion and presided over all forms of economic endeavor. Urban officials in Constantinople, for example, regulated prices and wages, maintained systems of licensing, controlled exports, and enforced the observance of the Sabbath. What is more, they usually did this with comparative efficiency and did not stifle business initiative. Bureaucratic methods too helped regulate the army and navy, the courts, and the diplomatic service, endowing them with organizational strengths incomparable for their age.

(3) firm economic base

Another explanation for Byzantine endurance was the comparatively sound economic base of the state until the eleventh century. As the historian Sir Steven Runciman has said, "if Byzantium owed her strength and security to the efficiency of her Services, it was her trade that enabled her to pay for them." While long-distance trade and urban life all but disappeared in the West for hundreds of years, commerce and cities continued to flourish in the Byzantine East. Above all, in the ninth and tenth centuries Constantinople was a vital trade emporium for Far Eastern luxury goods and Western raw materials. The empire also nurtured and protected its own industries, most notably that of silk-making, and it was renowned until the eleventh century for its stable gold and silver coinage. Among its great urban centers was not only Constantinople, which at times may have had a population of close to a million, but also in certain periods Antioch, and up until the end of Byzantine history the bustling cities of Thessalonica and Trebizond.

The significance of Byzantine agricultural history

Historians emphasize Byzantine trade and industry because these were so advanced for the time and provided most of the surplus wealth which supported the state. But agriculture was really at the heart of the Byzantine economy as it was of all premodern ones. The story of Byzantine agricultural history is mainly one of a struggle of small peasants to stay free of the encroachments of large estates owned by wealthy aristocrats and monasteries. Until the eleventh century the free peasantry just managed to maintain its existence with the help of state legislation, but after 1025 the aristocracy gained power in the government and began to transform the peasants into impoverished tenants. This had many unfortunate results, not the least of which was that the peasants became less interested in resisting the enemy. The defeat at Manzikert was the inevitable result. The destruction of the free peasantry was accompanied and followed in the last centuries of Byzantine history by foreign domination of Byzantine trade. Primarily the Italian cities of Venice and Genoa established trading outposts and privileges within Byzantine realms after 1204, which channeled off much of the wealth on which the state had previously relied. In this way the empire was defeated by the Venetians from within before it was destroyed by the Turks from without.

So far we have spoken about military campaigns, government, and economics as if they were at the center of Byzantine survival. Seen from hindsight they were, but what the Byzantines themselves cared about most was usually religion. Remarkable as it might seem, Byzantines fought over abstruse religious questions as vehemently as we today might argue about politics and sports—indeed more vehemently because the Byzantines were often willing to fight and even die over some words in a religious creed. The intense preoccupation with questions of doctrine is well illustrated by the report of an early Byzantine writer who said that when he asked a baker for the price of bread, the answer came back, "the Father is greater than the Son," and when he asked whether his bath was ready, was told that "the Son proceeds from nothing." Understandably such zealousness could harm the state greatly during times of religious dissension but endow it with a powerful sense of confidence and mission during times of religious concord.

Preoccupation with religion

Byzantine religious dissensions were greatly complicated by the fact that the emperors took an active role in them. Because the emperors carried great power in the life of the Church—emperors were sometimes deemed by churchmen to be "similar to God"—they exerted great influence in religious debates. Nonetheless, especially in the face of provincial separatism, rulers could never force all their subjects to believe what they did. Only after the loss of many eastern provinces and the refinement of doctrinal formulae did religious peace seem near in the eighth century. But then it was shattered for still another century by what is known as the Iconoclastic Controversy.

Imperial participation in religious controversies

The Iconoclasts were those who wished to prohibit the worship of icons—that is, images of Christ and the saints. Since the Iconoclastic movement was initiated by the Emperor Leo the Isaurian, and subsequently directed with even greater energy by his son Constantine V (740–775), historians have discerned in it different motives. One was certainly theological. The worship of images seemed to the Iconoclasts to smack of paganism. They believed that nothing made by human beings should be worshiped by them, that Christ was so divine that he could not be conceived of in terms of human art, and that the prohibition of worshiping "graven images" in the Ten Commandments (Exodus: 20,4) placed the matter beyond dispute.

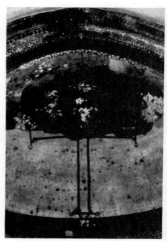

Iconoclasts' Cross. The Iconoclasts covered over beautiful apse mosaics with unadorned crosses. This example survives in St. Irene's church, Greece.

In addition to these theological points, there were probably other considerations. Since Leo the Isaurian was the emperor who saved Constantinople from the onslaught of Islam, and since Muslims zealously shunned images on the grounds that they were "the work of Satan" (Koran: V.92), it has been argued that Leo's Iconoclastic policy was an attempt to answer one of Islam's greatest criticisms of Christianity and thereby deprive Islam of some of its appeal. There may also have been certain internal political and financial motives. By proclaiming a radical new religious movement the emperors may have wished to reassert their control over the Church and combat the

Political and financial motives

Christ as Ruler of the Universe. A twelfth-century Byzantine mosaic from the cathedral of Cefalù in Sicily. Although the Byzantines did not rule in Sicily in the twelfth century, the Norman rulers employed Byzantine workmen. Note the use of Greek—the Byzantine language—on the left-handed Bible page and Latin—the Norman language—on the right.

growing strength of monasteries. In the event, the monasteries did rally behind the cause of images and as a result were bitterly persecuted by Constantine V, who took the opportunity to appropriate much monastic wealth.

Significance of the Iconoclastic Controversy

The Iconoclastic Controversy was resolved in the ninth century by a return to the status quo, namely the worship of images, but the century of turmoil over the issue had some profound results. One was the destruction by imperial order of a large amount of religious art. Pre–eighth-century Byzantine religious art that survives today comes mostly from places like Italy or Palestine, which were beyond the easy reach of the Iconoclastic emperors. When we see how great this art is we can only lament the destruction of the rest. A second consequence of the controversy was the opening of a serious religious breach between East and West. The pope, who until the eighth century had usually been a close ally of the Byzantines, could not accept Iconoclasm for many reasons. The most important of these was that extreme Iconoclasm tended to question the cult of saints, and the claims of papal primacy were based on an assumed descent from St. Peter. Accordingly, the eighth-century popes combated Byzantine Iconoclasm and turned to the Frankish kings for support. This "about-face of the papacy" was both a major step in the worsening of East-West relations and a landmark in the history of western Europe.

Other results: (1) reaffirmation of tradition

Those were some consequences of Iconoclasm's temporary victory; a major consequence of its defeat was the reassertion of some major traits of Byzantine religiosity, which from the ninth century until the end of Byzantine history remained predominant. One of these was the reemphasis of a faith in traditionalism. Even when Byzantines were experimenting in religious matters they consistently stated that they were only restating or developing the implications of tradition. Now, after centuries of turmoil, they abandoned experiment almost entirely and reaffirmed tradition more than ever. As one opponent of Iconoclasm said: "If an angel or an emperor announces to you a gospel other than the one you have received, close your ears." This view gave strength to Byzantine religion internally by ending controversy and heresy, and helped it gain new adherents in the ninth and tenth centuries. But it also inhibited free speculation not just in religion but also in related intellectual matters.

Allied to this development was the triumph of Byzantine contemplative piety. Supporters defended the use of icons not on the grounds that they were meant to be worshiped for themselves but because they helped lead the mind from the material to the immaterial. The emphasis on contemplation as a road to religious enlightenment thereafter became the hallmark of Byzantine spirituality. While westerners did not by any means reject such a path, the typical Western saint was an activist who saw sin as a vice and sought salvation through good works. Byzantine theologians on the other hand saw sin more as ignorance and believed that salvation was to be found in illumination. This led to a certain religious passivity and mysticism in Eastern Christianity which makes it seem different from Western varieties up to the present time.

(2) the triumph of Byzantine contemplative piety

Since religion was so dominant in Byzantine life, certain secular aspects of Byzantine civilization often go unnoticed, but there are good reasons why some of these should not be forgotten. One is Byzantine cultivation of the classics. Commitment to Christianity by no means inhibited the Byzantines from revering their ancient Greek inheritance. Byzantine schools based their instruction on classical Greek literature to the degree that educated people could quote Homer more extensively than we today can quote Shakespeare. Byzantine scholars studied and commented on the philosophy of Plato and Aristotle, and Byzantine writers imitated the prose of Thucydides. Such dedicated classicism both enriched Byzantine intellectual and literary life, which is too often dismissed entirely by moderns because it generally lacked originality, and helped preserve the Greek classics for later ages. The bulk of classical Greek literature that we have today survives only because it was copied by Byzantine scribes.

Byzantine classicism

Byzantine classicism was a product of an educational system for the laity which extended even to the education of women. Given attitudes and practices in the contemporary Christian West and Islam, Byzantine commitment to female education was truly unusual. Girls from aristocratic or prosperous families did not go to schools but were relatively well educated at home by private tutors. We are told, for example, that one Byzantine woman could discourse like a Plato or a Pythagoras. The most famous Byzantine female intellectual was the Princess Anna Comnena, who described the deeds of her father Alexius in an urbane biography in which she freely cited Homer and the ancient tragedians. In addition to such literary figures there were

The education of women

women doctors in the Byzantine Empire, a fact which may serve to remind us that there have hardly been any in America almost to the present day.

Byzantine achievements in the realms of architecture and art are more familiar. The finest example of Byzantine architecture was the Church of Santa Sophia (Holy Wisdom), built at enormous cost in the sixth century. Even though it was built before the date we have taken here to be the beginning of Byzantine history, it was typically Byzantine in both its style and subsequent influence. Although designed by architects of Hellenic descent, it was vastly different from any Greek temple. Its purpose was not to express human pride in the power of the individual, but to symbolize the inward and spiritual character of the Christian religion. It was for this reason that the architects gave little attention to the external appearance of the building. Nothing but plain brick covered with plaster was used for the exterior walls; there were no marble facings, graceful columns, or sculptured entablatures. The interior, however, was decorated with richly colored mosaics, gold leaf, colored marble columns, and bits of tinted glass set on edge to refract the rays of sunlight after the fashion of sparkling gems. To emphasize a sense of the miraculous, the building was constructed in such a way that no light appeared to come from the outside at all but to be manufactured within.

The structural design of Santa Sophia was something altogether new in the history of architecture. Its central feature was the application of the principle of the dome to a building of square shape. The church was designed, first of all, in the form of a cross, and then over the central square was to be erected a magnificent dome, which would dominate the entire structure. The main problem was how to fit the round circumference of the dome to the square area it was supposed to cover. The solution consisted in having four great arches spring from pillars at the four corners of the central square. The rim of the dome

Santa Sophia. The greatest monument of Byzantine architecture. The four minarets were added after the fall of the Byzantine Empire, when the Turks turned the church into a mosque. As the diagram shows, the central dome rests on four massive arches.

was then made to rest on the keystones of the arches, with the curved triangular spaces between the arches filled in with masonry. The result was an architectural framework of marvelous strength, which at the same time made possible a style of imposing grandeur and even some delicacy of treatment. The great dome of Santa Sophia has a diameter of 107 feet and rises to a height of nearly 180 feet from the floor. So many windows are placed around its rim that the dome appears to have no support at all but to be suspended in mid-air.

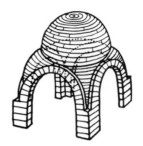

Diagram of Santa Sophia Dome

As in architecture, so in art the Byzantines profoundly altered the earlier Greek classical style. Byzantines excelled in ivory-carving, manuscript illumination, jewelry-making, and, above all, the creation of mosaics—that is, designs of pictures produced by fitting together small pieces of colored glass or stone. Human figures in these mosaics were usually distorted and elongated in a very unclassical fashion to create the impression of intense piety or extreme majesty. Most Byzantine art is marked by highly abstract, formal, and jewel-like qualities. For this reason many consider Byzantine artistic culture to be a model of timeless perfection. The modern poet W. B. Yeats expressed this point of view most eloquently when he wrote in his "Sailing to Byzantium" of artificial birds made by Byzantine goldsmiths ". . . to sing / To lords and ladies of Byzantium / Of what is past, or passing, or to come."

See color plates following page 384

Probably the single greatest testimony to the vitality of Byzantine civilization at its height was the conversion of many Slavic peoples, especially those of Russia. According to the legend, which has a basic kernel of fact, a Russian ruler named Vladimir decided around 988 to abandon the paganism of his ancestors. Accordingly, he sent emissaries to report on the religious practices of Islam, Roman Catholicism, and Byzantine Christianity. When they returned to tell him that only among the Byzantines did God seem to "dwell among men," he promptly agreed to be baptized by a Byzantine missionary. The event was momentous because Russia thereupon became a cultural province of Byzantium. From then until the twentieth century Russia remained a bastion of the Eastern Orthodox religion.

After Constantinople fell in 1453 Russians began to feel that they were chosen to carry on both the faith and the imperial mission of the fallen Byzantine Empire. Thus their ruler took the title of tsar—which simply means caesar—and Russians asserted that Moscow was "the third Rome": "Two Romes have fallen," said a Russian spokesman, "the third is still standing, and a fourth there shall not be." Such ideology helps explain in part the later growth of Russian imperialism. Byzantine traditions also may help explain the dominance of the ruler in the Russian state. Without question Byzantine stylistic principles influenced Russian religious art, and Byzantine ideas influenced the thought of modern Russia's greatest writers, Dostoevsky and Tolstoy.

Byzantine Metalwork. This dish, from about 620, represents literally David and Goliath, and figuratively the New Dispensation (David was the ancestor of Christ) overcoming the Old. The New, Christian, Dispensation is also symbolized by the sun, and the Old by a crescent moon.

Russian Icon. This early–seventeenth-century Russian painting depicts an angel in a distinctly Byzantine style.

Unfortunately, just at the time when relations between Constantinople and Russia were solidifying, relations with the West were deteriorating to a point of no return. After the skirmishes of the Iconoclastic period relations between Eastern and Western Christians remained tense, partly because Constantinople resented Western claims (initiated by Charlemagne in 800) of creating a rival empire, but most of all because cultural and religious differences between the two were growing. From the Byzantine point of view westerners were uncouth and ignorant, while to western European eyes Byzantines were effeminate and prone to heresy. Once the West started to revive, it began to take the offensive against a weakened East in theory and practice. In 1054 extreme papal claims of primacy over the Eastern Church provoked a religious schism which since then has never been healed. Thereafter the Crusades drove home the dividing wedge.

After the sack of Constantinople in 1204 Byzantine hatred of westerners became understandably intense. "Between us and them," one Byzantine wrote, "there is now a deep chasm: we do not have a single thought in common." Westerners called easterners "the dregs of the dregs . . . unworthy of the sun's light," while easterners called westerners the children of darkness, alluding to the fact that the sun sets in the West. The beneficiaries of this hatred were the Turks, who not only conquered Constantinople in 1453, but soon after conquered most of southeastern Europe up to Vienna.

St. Mark's Church, Venice. The most splendid example of Byzantine architecture in Italy.

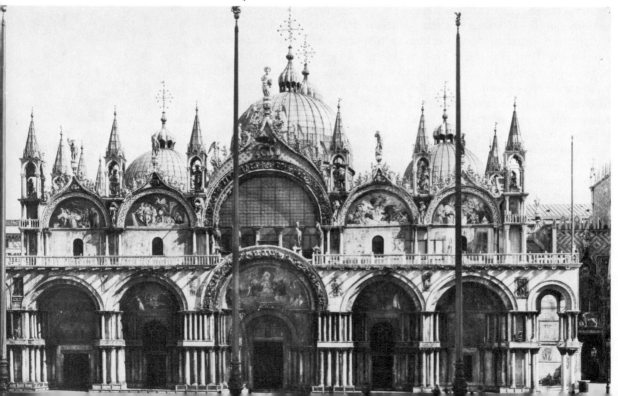

The Interior of St. Mark's, Venice

In view of this sad history of hostility it is best to end our treatment of Byzantine civilization by recalling how much we owe to it. In simple physical terms the Byzantine Empire acted as a bulwark against Islam from the seventh to the eleventh centuries, thus helping to preserve an independent West. If the Byzantines had not prospered and defended Europe, Western Christian civilization might well have been snuffed out. Then too we owe an enormous amount in cultural terms to Byzantine scholars who helped preserve classical Greek learning. The most famous moment of communication between Byzantine and western European scholars came during the Italian Renaissance, when Byzantines helped introduce Italian humanists to the works of Plato. But westerners were already learning from Byzantines before then, and they continued to gain riches from Byzantine manuscripts until the sixteenth century. Similarly, Byzantine art exerted a great influence on the art of western Europe over a long period of time. To take only some of the most famous examples, St. Mark's basilica in Venice was built in close imitation of the Byzantine style, and the art of such great Western painters as Giotto and El Greco owes much in different ways to Byzantine influences. Nor should we stop at listing influences because the great surviving monuments of Byzantine culture retain their imposing appeal in and of themselves. Travelers who view Byzantine mosaics in such cities as Ravenna and Palermo are continually awe-struck; others who make their way to Istanbul still find Santa Sophia to be a marvel. In such jeweled beauty, then, the light from the Byzantine East, which once glowed so brightly, continues to shimmer.

The Byzantine contribution to Western civilization

2. THE FLOWERING OF ISLAM

In contrast to Byzantine history, which has no clearly datable beginning but a definite end in 1453, the history of Islamic civilization has a clear point of origin, beginning with the career of Muhammad in the

The phenomenon of Islam

seventh century, but no end since Islam, Muhammad's religion, is still a major force in the modern world. Believers in Islam, known as Muslims, currently comprise about one-seventh of the global population: in their greatest concentrations they extend from Africa through the Middle East and the Soviet Union to India, Bangladesh, and Indonesia. All these Muslims subscribe both to a common religion and a common way of life, for Islam has always demanded from its followers not just adherence to certain forms of worship but also adherence to set social and cultural norms. Indeed, more than Judaism or Christianity, Islam has been a great experiment in trying to build a worldwide society based on a full identity between religious requirements and a thoroughgoing code for everyday existence. In practice, of course, that experiment has differed in its success and quality according to time and place, but it is still being tested and it accounts for the fact that there remains an extraordinary sense of community between all Muslims regardless of race, language, and geographical distribution. In this section we will trace the early history of the Islamic experiment with primary emphasis on its orientation toward the West. But it must always be remembered that Islam expanded in many directions and that it ultimately had as much influence on the history of Africa and India as it did on that of Europe or western Asia.

Conditions in Arabia before the rise of Islam

Although Islam spread to many lands it was born in Arabia, so the story of its history must begin there. Arabia, a peninsula of deserts, had been so backward before the founding of Islam that the two dominant neighboring empires, the Roman and the Persian, had not deemed it worthwhile to extend their rule over Arabian territories. Most Arabs were Bedouins, wandering camel herdsmen who lived off the milk of their animals and the produce, such as dates, that was grown in desert oases. In the second half of the sixth century there was a quickening of economic life owing to a shift in long-distance trade routes. The protracted wars between the Byzantine and Persian Empires made Arabia a safer transit route for caravans than other areas, and some towns grew to direct and take advantage of this growth of trade. Most prominent of these was Mecca, which owed its position not just to the fact that it lay on the junction of important trade routes, but also because it had long been a center for local religion. In Mecca was located the Kabah, a pilgrimage shrine which served as a central place of worship for many different Arabian clans and tribes. (Within the Kabah was the Black Stone, a meteorite worshiped as a miraculous relic by adherents of many different divinities.) The men who controlled this shrine and also directed the economic life of the Meccan area belonged to the tribe of Quraish, an aristocracy of traders and entrepreneurs who provided the area with whatever little government it knew.

Muhammad, the founder of Islam, was born in Mecca to a family of

The Kabah. It contains the black stone which was supposed to have been miraculously sent down from heaven, and rests in the courtyard of the great mosque in Mecca.

the Quraish about 570. Orphaned early in life he entered the service of a rich widow whom he later married, thereby attaining financial security. Until middle age he lived as a prosperous trader, behaving little differently from his fellow townsmen, but around 610 he underwent a religious experience which changed the course of his life and ultimately that of a good part of the world. Although most Arabs until then had been polytheists who recognized at most the vague superiority of a more powerful god they called Allah, Muhammad in 610 believed he heard a voice from heaven tell him that there was no god but Allah alone. In other words, as the result of a conversion experience he became an uncompromising monotheist. Thereafter he received further messages which served as the basis for a new religion and which commanded him to accept the calling of "Prophet" to proclaim the monotheistic faith to the Quraish. At first he was not very successful in gaining converts beyond a limited circle, perhaps because the leading Quraish tribesmen believed that establishment of a new religion would deprive the Kabah, and therewith Mecca, of its central place in local worship. The town of Yathrib to the north, however, had no such concerns, and its representatives invited Muhammad to emigrate there so that he could serve as a neutral arbiter of local rivalries. In 622 Muhammad and his followers accepted the invitation. Because their migration—called in Arabic the *Hijrah* (or Hegira)—saw the beginning of a change upward in Muhammad's fortunes, it is considered by Muslims to mark the beginning of their era: as Christians begin their era with the birth of Christ so Muslims begin their dating system with the *Hijrah* of 622.

Muhammad changed the name of Yathrib to Medina (the "city of the Prophet") and quickly succeeded in establishing himself as ruler of

Muhammad

*The consolidation of
Muhammad's religion*

the town. In the course of doing this he consciously began to organize his converts into a political as well as religious community. But he still needed to find some means of support for his original Meccan followers, and he also desired to wreak vengeance on the Quraish for not heeding his calls for conversion. Accordingly, he started leading his followers in raids on Quraish caravans traveling beyond Mecca. The Quraish endeavored to defend themselves, but after a few years Muhammad's band, fired by religious enthusiasm, succeeded in defeating them. In 630, after several desert battles, Muhammad entered Mecca in triumph. The Quraish thereupon submitted to the new faith and the Kabah was not only preserved but made the main shrine of Islam, as it remains today. With the taking of Mecca other tribes throughout Arabia in turn accepted the new faith. Thus, although Muhammad died in 632, he lived long enough to see the religion he had founded become a success.

The doctrines of Islam

The doctrines of Islam are very simple. The word *islam* itself means submission, and the faith of Islam called for absolute submission to God. Although the Arabic name for the one God is Allah, it is mistaken to believe that Muslims worship a god like Zeus or Jupiter who is merely one of a pantheon: Allah for Muslims means the Creator God Almighty—the same omnipotent deity worshiped by Christians and Jews. Instead of saying, then, that Muslims believe "there is no god but Allah," it is more correct to say they believe that "there is no divinity but God." In keeping with this, Muslims believe that Muhammad himself was God's last and greatest prophet, but not that he was God himself. In addition to strict monotheism Muhammad taught above all that men and women must surrender themselves entirely to God because divine judgment was imminent. Mortals must make a fundamental choice about whether to begin a new life of divine service: if they decide in favor of this, God will guide them to blessedness, but if they do not, God will turn away from them and they will become irredeemably wicked. On judgment day the pious will be granted eternal life in a fleshly paradise of delights but the damned will be sent to a realm of eternal fire and torture. The practical steps the believer can take are found in the Koran, the purported compilation of the revelations sent by God to Muhammad, and accordingly the definitive Islamic scripture. These steps include thorough dedication to moral rectitude and compassion, and fidelity to set religious observances: i.e., a regimen of prayers and fasts, pilgrimage to Mecca, and frequent recitation of parts of the Koran.

*Judeo-Christian influence
on Islam*

The fact that much in the religion of Islam bears similarity to Judaism and Christianity is not just coincidental; Muhammad was definitely influenced by the two earlier religions. (There were many Jews in Mecca and Medina; Christian thought was also known to Muhammad, although more indirectly.) Islam most resembles the two earlier religions in its strict monotheism, its stress on personal morality and

The Archangel Gabriel Brings Revelation to Muhammad. A much later Persian conception.

compassion, and its reliance on written, revealed scripture. Muhammad proclaimed the Koran as the ultimate source of religious authority but accepted both the Old and New Testaments as divinely inspired books. From Christianity Muhammad seems to have derived his doctrines of the last judgment, the resurrection of the body with subsequent rewards and punishments, and his belief in angels (he thought that God's first message to him had been sent by the angel Gabriel). But although Muhammad accepted Jesus Christ as one of the greatest of a long line of prophets, he did not believe in Christ's divinity and himself laid claim to no miracles other than the writing of the Koran. He also ignored the Christian doctrine of sacrificial love, and, most importantly, preached a religion without sacraments or priests. For Muslims every believer has direct responsibility for living the life of the faith without intermediaries; instead of priests there are only religious scholars who may comment on problems of Islamic faith and law. Muslims are expected to pray together in mosques, but there is nothing like a Muslim mass. The absence of clergy makes Islam more similar to Judaism, a similarity which is enhanced by Islamic stress on the inextricable connection between the religious and sociopolitical life of the divinely inspired community. But, unlike Judaism, Islam laid claim to universalism and a unique role in uniting the world as it started to spread far beyond the confines of Arabia.

The start of this move toward becoming a world force took place immediately upon Muhammad's death. Since he had made no provision for the future, and since the Arabs had no clear concept of political succession, it was unclear whether Muhammad's community would survive at all. But his closest followers, led by his father-in-law Abu-Bakr and a zealous early convert named Umar, forestalled this possibility by quickly taking the initiative and naming Abu-Bakr *ca-*

The unification of Arabia after Muhammad: the caliphs

Two Views of the Dome of the Rock, Jerusalem. According to Muslim tradition, Muhammad made a miraculous journey to Jerusalem before his death and left a footprint in a rock. The mosque which was erected over the site in the seventh century is, after the Kabah, Islam's second holiest shrine.

liph, meaning "deputy of the Prophet." Thereafter, for about three hundred years, the caliph was to serve as the supreme religious and political leader of all Muslims. Immediately after becoming caliph Abu-Bakr began a military campaign to subdue various Arabian tribes which had followed Muhammad but were not willing to accept his successor's authority. In the course of this military action, which was marked by thorough success, Abu-Bakr's forces began to spill northwards over the borders of Arabia. Probably to their surprise they found that they met minimal resistance from Byzantine and Persian forces.

Abu-Bakr died two years after his accession but was succeeded as caliph by Umar, who continued to direct the Arabian invasions of the neighboring empires. In the following years triumph was virtually uninterrupted. In 636 the Arabs routed a Byzantine army in Syria and then quickly swept over the entire area, occupying the leading cities of Antioch, Damascus, and Jerusalem; in 637 they destroyed the main army of the Persians and marched into the Persian capital of Ctesiphon. Once the Persian administrative center was taken, the Persian Empire offered scarcely any more resistance: by 651 the Arabian conquest of the entire Persian realm was complete. Since Byzantium was centered around distant Constantinople, the Arabs were not similarly able to stop its imperial heart from beating. But they did quickly

Arab expansion and conquests

manage to deprive the Byzantine Empire of Egypt by 646 and then swept west across North Africa. In 711 they crossed from there into Spain and quickly took almost all of that area too. Thus within less than a century all of ancient Persia and much of the old Roman world was conquered by Islam.

How can we explain this prodigious expansion? The best approach is to see first what impelled the conquerors and then to see what circumstances helped to ease their way. Contrary to widespread belief the early spread of Islam was not achieved through a religious crusade. At first the Arabs were not at all interested in converting other peoples: to the contrary, they hoped that conquered populations would not convert so that they could maintain their own identity as a community of rulers and tax-gatherers. But although their motives for expansion were not religious, religious enthusiasm played a crucial role in making the hitherto unruly Arabs take orders from the caliph and in instilling a sense that they were carrying out the will of God. What really moved the Arabs out of the desert was the search for richer territory and booty, and what kept them moving ever farther was the ease of acquiring new wealth as they progressed. Fortunately for the Arabs their inspiration by Islam came just at the right time in terms of the weakness of their enemies. The Byzantines and Persians had become so exhausted by their long wars that they could hardly rally for a new effort. Moreover, Persian and Byzantine local populations were hostile to the financial demands made by their bureaucratic empires; also, in the Byzantine lands of Syria and Egypt "heretical" Christians were at odds with the persecuting orthodoxy of Constantinople. Because the Arabs did not demand conversion and exacted fewer taxes than the Byzantines and Persians, they were often welcomed as preferable to the old rulers. One Christian writer in Syria went so far as to say "the God of vengeance delivered us out of the hands of the Romans [i.e., the Byzantine Empire] by means of the Arabs." For all these reasons Islam quickly spread over the vast extent of territory between Egypt and Iran, and has been rooted there ever since.

Reasons for the spread of Islam

While the Arabs were extending their conquests they ran into their first serious political divisions. In 644 the Caliph Umar died; he was replaced by one Uthman, a weak ruler who had the added drawback for many of belonging to the Umayyad family, a wealthy clan from Mecca which had not at first accepted Muhammad's call. Those dissatisfied with Uthman rallied around the Prophet's cousin and son-in-law Ali, whose blood, background, and warrior spirit made him seem a more appropriate leader of the cause. When Uthman was murdered in 656 by mutineers, Ali's partisans raised him up as caliph. But Uthman's powerful family and supporters were unwilling to accept Ali. In subsequent disturbances Ali was murdered and Uthman's party emerged triumphant. In 661 a member of the Umayyad family took over as caliph and that house ruled Islam until 750. Even then, however, Ali's followers did not accept defeat. As time went on they har-

Division between Shiites and Sunnites

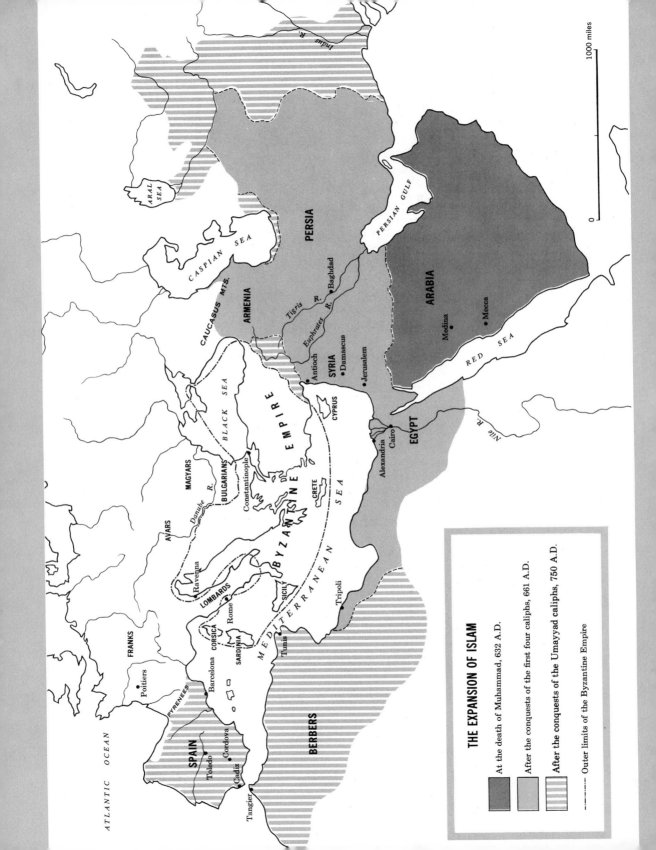

ATLANTIC OCEAN

SPAIN
Toledo
Cordova
Cadiz
Tangier

FRANKS
Poitiers
PYRENEES
Barcelona

AVARS
MAGYARS
BULGARIANS
Danube R.

BLACK SEA

Constantinople

B Y Z A N T I N E   E M P I R E

Ravenna
LOMBARDS
Rome
CORSICA
SARDINIA
SICILY
Tunis

M E D I T E R R A N E A N   S E A

CRETE

CYPRUS

BERBERS

Tripoli

Antioch
SYRIA •Damascus
•Jerusalem

Alexandria
Cairo
EGYPT
Nile R.

RED SEA

CASPIAN SEA

CAUCASUS MTS.
ARMENIA

PERSIA

Tigris R.
•Baghdad
Euphrates R.

PERSIAN GULF

ARABIA
Medina
• Mecca

ARAL SEA

Indus R.

1000 miles

0

THE EXPANSION OF ISLAM

At the death of Muhammad, 632 A.D.

After the conquests of the first four caliphs, 661 A.D.

After the conquests of the Umayyad caliphs, 750 A.D.

Outer limits of the Byzantine Empire

dened into a minority religious party known as Shiites; this group insisted that only descendants of Ali could be caliphs or have any authority over the Muslim community. Those who stood instead for the actual historical development of the caliphate and became committed to its customs were called Sunnites. The cleft between the two parties has been a lasting one in Islamic history. Often persecuted, Shiites developed great militancy and a deep sense of being the only true preservers of the faith. From time to time they were able to seize power in one or another area, but they never succeeded in converting the majority of Muslims. Today they rule in Iran and are very numerous in Iraq but comprise only about one-tenth of the worldwide population of Islam.

The triumph of the Umayyads in 661 began a more settled period in the history of the caliphate, lasting until 945. During that time there were two major governing orientations: that represented by the rule of the Umayyads, and that represented by their successors, the Abbasids. The Umayyads centered their strength in the old Byzantine territories in Syria and continued to use local officials who were not Muslims for their administration. For these reasons the Umayyad caliphate appears to some extent like a Byzantine successor state. With their more Western orientation the Umayyads concentrated their energies on dominating the Mediterranean and conquering Constantinople. When their most massive attack on the Byzantine capital failed in 717, Umayyad strength was seriously weakened; it was only a matter of time before a new orientation would develop.

The Umayyads

This was represented by the takeover of a new family, the Abbasids, in 750. Their rule may be said to have stressed Persian more than Byzantine elements. Characteristic of this change was a shift in capitals, for the second Abbasid caliph built his new capital of Baghdad in Iraq near the ruins of the old Persian capital and even appropriated stones from the ruins. The Abbasids developed their own Muslim administration and imitated Persian absolutism. Abbasid caliphs ruthlessly cut down their enemies, surrounded themselves with elaborate court ceremonies, and lavishly patronized sophisticated literature. This is the world described in the *Arabian Nights,* a collection of stories of dazzling Oriental splendor written in Baghdad under the Abbasids. The dominating presence in those stories, Harun al-Rashid, actually reigned as caliph from 786 to 809 and behaved as extravagantly as he was described, tossing coins in the streets, passing out sumptuous gifts to his favorites and severe punishments to his enemies. From a Western point of view the Abbasid caliphate was of significance not just in creating legends and literature but also because its Eastern orientation took much pressure off the Mediterranean. The Byzantine state, accordingly, was able to revive and the Franks in the far West began to develop some strength of their own. (The greatest Frankish ruler, Charlemagne, maintained diplomatic relations with the cali-

The Abbasids

*Islamic political history
after the fall of the
Abbasid Empire*

phate of Harun al-Rashid, who patronizingly sent the much poorer westerner a gift of an elephant.)

When Abbasid power began to decline in the tenth century there followed an extended period of decentralization. The major cause for growing Abbasid weakness was the gradual impoverishment of their primary economic base, the agricultural wealth of the Tigris-Euphrates basin. Their decline was further accelerated by the later Abbasids' practice of surrounding themselves with Turkish soldiers, who soon realized that they could take over actual power in the state. In 945 the Abbasid Empire fell apart when a Shiite tribe seized Baghdad. Thereafter the Abbasids became powerless figureheads until their caliphate was completely destroyed with the destruction of Baghdad by the Mongols in 1258. From 945 until the sixteenth century Islamic political life was marked by localism, with different petty rulers, most often Turkish, taking command in different areas. It used to be thought that this decentralization also meant decay, but in fact Islamic civilization greatly prospered in the "middle period," above all from about 900 to about 1250, a time also when Islamic rule expanded into modern-day Turkey and India. Later, new Islamic empires developed, the leading one in the West being that of the Ottoman Turks, who controlled much of eastern Europe and the Near East from the fifteenth century until 1918. It is therefore entirely false to believe that Islamic history descended upon an ever downward course sometime shortly after the reign of Harun al-Rashid.

For those who approach Islamic civilization with modern preconceptions, the greatest surprise is to realize that from the time of Muhammad until at least about 1500 Islamic culture and society was extraordinarily cosmopolitan and dynamic. Muhammad himself was not a desert Arab but a town-dweller and trader imbued with advanced ideals. Subsequently, Muslim culture became highly cosmopolitan for several reasons: it inherited the sophistication of Byzantium and Persia; it remained centered at the crossroads of long-distance trade between the Far East and West; and the prosperous town life in most Muslim territories counterbalanced agriculture. Because of the importance of trade there was much geographical mobility. Muhammad's teachings furthermore encouraged social mobility because the Koran stressed the equality of all Muslims. The result was that at the court of Baghdad, and later at those of the decentralized Muslim states, careers were open to those with talent. Since literacy was remarkably widespread—a rough estimate for around the year 1000 is 20 percent of all Muslim males—many could rise through education. Offices were seldom regarded as being hereditary and "new men" could arrive at the top by enterprise and skill. Muslims were also remarkably tolerant of other religions. As stated above, they rarely sought forced conversions, and they generally allowed a place within their own states for Jews and Christians, whom they accepted as "people of the book" because the Bible was seen as a precursor of the Koran. In keeping with this attitude of toleration an early caliph employed a Christian as his chief secretary, the Umayyads patronized a Christian who wrote poetry in Arabic, and Muslim Spain saw the greatest flowering of Jewish culture between ancient and modern times. The greatest fruit of this Jewish flowering was the work of Moses Maimonides (1135–1204), a profound religious thinker, sometimes called "the second Moses," who wrote both in Hebrew and Arabic.

There was one major exception to this rule of Muslim equalitarianism and tolerance: the treatment of women. Perhaps because social status was so fluid, successful men were extremely anxious to preserve and enhance their positions and their "honor." They could accomplish this by maintaining and/or expanding their worldly possessions, which category included women. For a man's females to be most "valuable" to his status, their inviolability had to be assured. The Koran allowed a man to marry four wives, so women were at a premium, and married ones were segregated from other male society. A prominent man would also have a number of female servants and concubines, and he kept all these women in a part of his residence called the harem, where they were guarded by eunuchs, i.e., castrated men. Within these enclaves women vied with each other for preeminence and engaged in intrigues to advance the fortunes of their children. Although large harems could be kept only by the wealthy, the system was imitated so far as possible by all classes. Based on the principle that women were chattel, these practices did much to debase women and to emphasize attitudes of domination in sexual life. Male homosexual relations were tolerated in upper-class society, yet they too were based on patterns of domination, usually that of a powerful adult over an adolescent.

The treatment of women

There were two major Islamic avenues for devotion to the particularly religious life. One was that of the *ulama,* learned men who came closest to being like priests. Their job was to study and offer advice on all aspects of religion and religious law. Not surprisingly they usually stood for tradition and rigorous maintenance of the faith; most often they exerted great influence on the conduct of public life. But complementary to them were the *sufis,* religious mystics who might be equated with Christian monks, were it not for the fact that they were not committed to celibacy and seldom withdrew from the life of the community. Sufis stressed contemplation and ecstasy as the ulama stressed religious law: they had no common program and in practice behaved very differently. Some sufis were "whirling dervishes," known in the West as such because of their dances; others were *faqirs,* associated in the West with snake-charming in marketplaces; and others were quiet meditative men who practiced no exotic rites. Sufis were usually organized into "brotherhoods," which did much to con-

Islamic religious life: the ulama and the sufis

vert outlying areas such as Africa and India. Within all of Islamdom sufism provided a channel for the most intense religious impulses. The ability of the ulama and sufis to coexist is in itself a remarkable index of Islamic cultural pluralism.

More remarkable still is the fact that these two groups often coexisted with representatives of yet another worldview, students and practitioners of philosophy and science. Islamic philosophers were actually called *faylasufs* in Arabic because they were dedicated to the cultivation of what the Greeks had called *philosophia*. Islamic philosophy was based on the study of earlier Greek thought, above all the Aristotelian and Neoplatonic strains. Around the time when the philosophical schools were closed in Athens by order of the Emperor Justinian, Greek philosophers migrated east, and the works of Aristotle and others were translated into Syriac, a Semitic dialect. From that point of transmission Greek philosophy gradually entered the life of Islam and became cultivated by the class of faylasufs, who believed that the universe is rational and that a philosophical approach to life was the highest god-given calling. The faylasufs' profound knowledge of Aristotle can be seen, for example, in the fact that Avicenna (d. 1037), one of the greatest of them, read practically all of Aristotle's works in the Far-Eastern town of Bukhara before he reached the age of eighteen.

The most serious problem faced by the faylasufs was that of reconciling Greek philosophy with Islamic religion because they followed their Greek sources in believing—in opposition to Islamic doctrine—that the world is eternal and that there is no immortality for the individual soul. Different faylasufs reacted to this problem in different ways. Of the three greatest, Al-Farabi (d. 950), who lived mainly in Baghdad, was least concerned by it; he taught that an enlightened elite could philosophize without being distracted by the binding common beliefs of the masses. Even so, he never attacked these beliefs, considering them necessary to hold society together.

Unlike Al-Farabi, Avicenna, who was active further east, taught a less rationalistic philosophy that came close in many points to sufi mysticism. (A later story held that Avicenna said of a sufi "all I know, he sees," while the sufi replied "all I see, he knows.") Finally, Averroës (1126–98) of Cordova, in Spain, was a thoroughgoing Aristotelian who led two lives, one in private as an extreme rationalist and the other in public as a believer in the official faith, indeed even as an official censor. Averroës was the last really important Islamic philosopher: after him rationalism either blended into sufism, the direction pointed to by Avicenna, or became too constrained by religious orthodoxy to lead an independent existence. But in its heyday between about 850 and 1200 Islamic philosophy was far more advanced and sophisticated than anything found in either the Byzantine or Western Christian realms.

Before their decline Islamic faylasufs were as distinguished in study-ing natural science as they were in philosophical speculation. Usually the same men were both philosophers and scientists because they could by no means make a living by commenting on Aristotle (there were no universities in which to teach) but could rise to positions of wealth and power by practicing astrology and medicine. Astrology sounds to us today less like science than superstition, but among the Muslims it was an "applied science" intimately related to accurate as-tronomical observation: after an Islamic astrologer carefully studied and foretold the courses of the heavenly bodies, he would endeavor to apply his knowledge to the course of human events, particularly the fortunes of wealthy patrons. In order to account most simply for heavenly motions, some Muslims considered the possibilities that the earth rotates on its axis and revolves around the sun, but these theories were not accepted because they did not fit in with ancient preconcep-tions such as the assumption of circular planetary orbits. It was there-fore not in these suggestions that Muslim astrologers later influenced the West, but rather in their extremely advanced observations and predictive tables that often went beyond the most careful work of the Greeks.

Islamic science; the practice of astrology

Islamic accomplishments in medicine were equally remarkable. Faylasufs serving as physicians appropriated the knowledge contained in the medical writings of the Hellenistic Age but were rarely content with that. Avicenna discovered the contagious nature of tuberculosis, described pleurisy and several varieties of nervous ailments, and pointed out that disease can be spread through contamination of water and soil. His chief medical writing, the *Canon,* was accepted in Europe as authoritative until late in the seventeenth century. Avicenna's older contemporary, Rhazes (865–925), was the greatest clinical physician of the medieval world. His major achievement was the discovery of the difference between measles and smallpox. Other Islamic physicians discovered the value of cauterization and of styptic agents, diagnosed cancer of the stomach, prescribed antidotes for cases of poisoning, and made notable progress in treating diseases of the eyes. In addition, they recognized the infectious character of bubonic plague, pointing out that it could be transmitted by clothes. Finally, the Mus-lims excelled all other medieval peoples in the organization of hospi-tals and in the control of medical practice. There were at least thirty-four great hospitals located in the principal cities of Persia, Syria, and Egypt, which appear to have been organized in a strikingly modern fashion. Each had wards for particular cases, a dispensary, and a li-brary. The chief physicians and surgeons lectured to the students and graduates, examined them, and issued licenses to practice. Even the owners of leeches, who in most cases were also barbers, had to submit them for inspection at regular intervals.

Islamic contributions to medicine

Other great Islamic scientific achievements were in optics, chemis-

*Optics, chemistry, and
mathematics*

try, and mathematics. Islamic physicists founded the science of optics and drew a number of significant conclusions regarding the theory of magnifying lenses and the velocity, transmission, and refraction of light. Islamic chemistry was an outgrowth of alchemy, an invention of the Hellenistic Greeks, the system of belief that was based upon the principle that all metals were the same in essence, and that baser metals could therefore be transmuted into gold if only the right instrument, the philosopher's stone, could be found. But the efforts of scientists in this field were by no means confined to this fruitless quest; some even denied the whole theory of transmutation of metals. As a result of innumerable experiments by Muslim scientists, various new substances and compounds were discovered; among them carbonate of soda, alum, borax, bichloride of mercury, nitrate of silver, saltpeter, and nitric and sulphuric acids. In addition, Islamic scientists were the first to describe the chemical processes of distillation, filtration, and sublimation. In mathematics Islam's greatest accomplishment was to unite the geometry of the Greeks with the number science of the Hindus. Borrowing what westerners know as "Arabic numerals," including the zero, from the Hindus, Islamic mathematicians were able to develop an arithmetic based on the decimal system and also make advances in algebra (itself an Arabic word). Building upon Greek geometry with reference to heavenly motions, they made great progress in spherical trigonometry. Thus they brought together and advanced all the areas of mathematical knowledge which would later be further developed in the Christian West.

In addition to its philosophers and scientists Islam had its poets too. The primitive Arabs themselves had excelled in writing poetry, and literary accomplishment became recognized as a way to distinguish oneself at court. Probably the greatest of Islamic poets were the Persians (who wrote in their own language), the best known of whom in the West is Umar Khayyam (d. 1123) because his *Rubaiyat* was turned into a popular English poem by the Victorian Edward Fitzgerald. Although Fitzgerald's translation distorts much, Umar's hedonism ("a jug of wine, a loaf of bread—and thou") shows us that all Muslims were by no means dour puritans. Actually Umar's poetry was excelled by the works of Sadi (1193–1292) and Hafiz (d. 1389). And far from Persia lush poetry was cultivated as well in the courts of Muslim Spain. This poetry too was by no means inhibited, as can be seen from lines like "such was my kissing, such my sucking of his mouth / that he was almost made toothless."

In their artistic endeavors Muslims were highly eclectic. Their main source of inspiration came from the art of Byzantium and Persia. The former contributed many of the structural features of Islamic architecture, especially the dome, the column, and the arch. Persian influence was probably responsible for the intricate, nonnaturalistic designs which were used as decorative motifs in practically all of the arts.

The Great Mosque, Qayrawan, Tunisia. This ninth century minaret, from which the criers call the faithful to prayer, is a leading monument of the North African Islamic architectural style.

The Court of the Lions in the Alhambra, Granada, Spain. The palace-fortress of the Alhambra is one of the finest monuments of the Islamic architectural style. Notable are the graceful columns, the horseshoe arches, and the delicate tracery in stone that surmounts the arches.

From both Persia and Byzantium came the tendency to subordinate form to rich and sensuous color. Architecture was the most important of the Islamic arts; the development of both painting and sculpture was inhibited by religious prejudice against representation of the human form. By no means all of the examples of this architecture were mosques; many were palaces, schools, libraries, private dwellings, and hospitals. Indeed, Islamic architecture had a much more decidedly secular character than any in medieval Europe. Among its principal elements were bulbous domes, minarets, horseshoe arches, and twisted columns, together with the use of tracery in stone, alternating stripes of black and white, mosaics, and Arabic script as decorative devices. As in the Byzantine style, comparatively little attention was given to exterior ornamentation. The so-called minor arts of the Muslims included the weaving of gorgeous pile carpets and rugs, magnificent leather tooling, and the making of brocaded silks and tapestries, inlaid metalwork, enameled glassware, and painted pottery. Most of the products of these arts were embellished with complicated patterns of interlacing geometric designs, plants and fruits and flowers, Arabic script, and fantastic animal figures. In general, art laid particular emphasis on pure visual design. Separated from any role in religious teaching, it became highly abstract and nonrepresentational. For these reasons Islamic art often seems more secular and "modern" than any other art of premodern times.

The economic life of the Islamic world varied greatly according to time and place, but underdevelopment was certainly not one of its primary characteristics. On the contrary, in the central areas of Islamic

The eclectic art of the Muslims

The economic development of the Islamic Empire: (1) commerce

civilization from the first Arab conquests until about the fourteenth century mercantile life was extraordinarily advanced. The principal reason for this was that the Arabs inherited in Syria and Persia an area that was already marked by an enterprising urban culture and that was at the crossroads of the world, lying athwart the major trade routes between Africa, Europe, India, and China. Islamic traders and entrepreneurs built venturesomely on these earlier foundations. Muslim merchants penetrated into southern Russia and even into the equatorial regions of Africa, while caravans of thousands of camels traveled to the gates of India and China. (The Muslims used camels as pack animals instead of building roads and drawing wheeled carts.) Ships from Islam established new routes across the Indian Ocean, the Persian Gulf, and the Caspian Sea. For periods of time Islamic ships also dominated parts of the Mediterranean. Indeed, one reason for subsequent Islamic decline was that the Western Christians took hold of the Mediterranean in the eleventh and twelfth centuries and wrested control of the Indian Ocean in the sixteenth century.

(2) industry

The great Islamic expansion of commerce would scarcely have been possible without a corresponding development of industry. It was the ability of the people of one region to turn their natural resources into finished products for sale to other regions which provided a basis for a large part of the trade. Nearly every one of the great cities specialized in some particular variety of manufactures. Mosul, in Syria, was a center of the manufacture of cotton cloth; Baghdad specialized in glassware, jewelry, pottery, and silks; Damascus was famous for its fine steel and for its "damask" or woven figured silk; Morocco was noted for the manufacture of leather; and Toledo, in Spain, for its excellent swords. The products of these cities did not exhaust the list of manufactures. Drugs, perfumes, carpets, tapestries, brocades,

Interior of the Great Mosque at Cordova, Spain. This splendid specimen of Moorish architecture gives an excellent view of the cusped arches and alternating stripes of black and white so commonly used by Islamic architects.

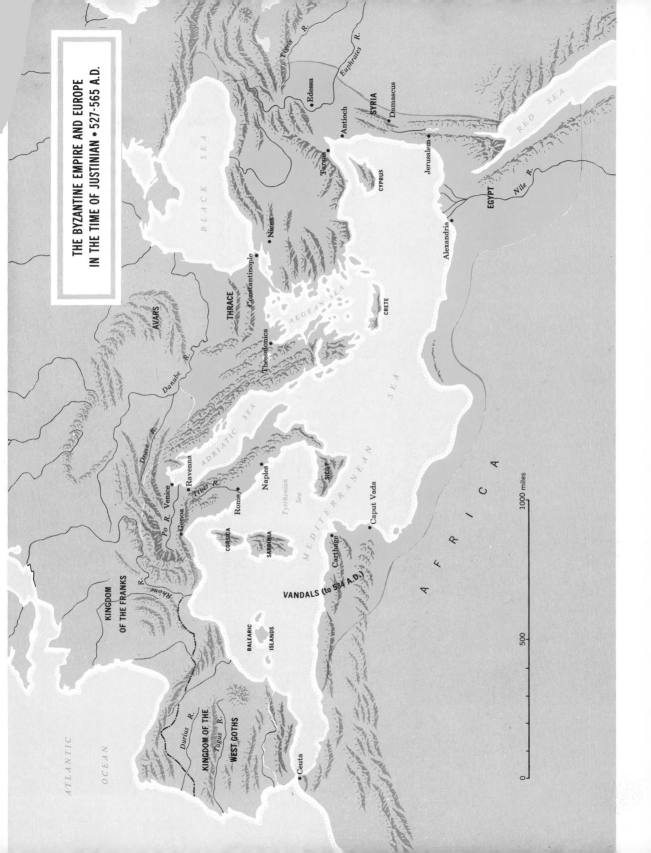

THE BYZANTINE EMPIRE AND EUROPE
IN THE TIME OF JUSTINIAN • 527-565 A.D.

BLACK SEA

ATLANTIC OCEAN

KINGDOM OF THE FRANKS

KINGDOM OF THE WEST GOTHS

Durius R.

Tagus R.

Ceuta

Rhone R.

Po R.

Genoa

Venice

Ravenna

Tiber R.

Rome

Naples

CORSICA

SARDINIA

BALEARIC ISLANDS

Tyrrhenian Sea

SICILY

Carthage

Caput Vada

VANDALS (to 534 A.D.)

MEDITERRANEAN SEA

AFRICA

AVARS

Danube R.

Drave R.

Drave R.

THRACE

Thessalonica

Constantinople

Nicaea

AEGEAN SEA

CRETE

CYPRUS

Tarsus

Antioch

Edessa

Tigris R.

Euphrates R.

SYRIA

Damascus

Jerusalem

Alexandria

Nile R.

EGYPT

RED SEA

1000 miles

500

0

Saint John Writing His Gospel. From an Anglo-Frankish
illuminated manuscript, c. 850, produced in a Carolingian
monastery. The unknown artist knew nothing of perspective, but excelled in coloring and conveying a sense of
vitality and energy. (Morgan Library)

Gold Cup, Byzantine, VI–IX cent.
The figure is a personification of
Constantinople, a queen or goddess
holding the scepter and orb of imperial rule. (MMA)

Merovingian Fibula or Brooch, VII cent.
A fabulous gold-plated animal set with
garnets and colored paste reveals the
lively imagination of the early Middle
Ages. (MMA)

Enthroned Madonna
and Child, Byzantine
School, XIII cent.
The painters of Siena
followed the opulent
and brilliant style of
Byzantine art. Their
madonnas were not
earthly mothers, but
celestial queens reign-
ing in dignified splen-
dor. (National Gal-
lery)

The Young King, Louis IX, XIII cent. Though Louis was widely revered as a saint, the artist has endowed him with distinctively human features. (Morgan Library)

Aquamanile, German, XII–XIII cent. Aquamaniles were water jugs used for handwashing during church ritual, or at meal times. (MMA)

Ivory Plaque, German, X cent. The plaque shows Otto the Great presenting a church to Christ while St. Peter watches, a reference to Otto's building an empire by cooperating with the Church. (MMA)

Kings in Battle, French, c. 1250. A scene depicting, with the trappings of knighthood, Joshua's fight against the five kings of Canaan. In the center Joshua raises his hand, commanding the sun and moon to stand still to enable him to complete his victory. (Morgan Library)

Chalice, German, XIII cent. A beautifully embellished wine cup used in the sacrament of the Eucharist. (MMA)

Building Operations. From a French picture Bible, c. 1250. Note the treadmill, with wheel, ropes, and pulley, by means of which a basket of stones is brought to the construction level. (Morgan Library)

Above: Siege of a City. From the *Universal Chronicle* by Jean de Courcy, Flemish, c. 1470. The cannon meant the end of feudal knights and medieval towered fortresses. (Morgan Library)

A Scholar at Work. From the Flemish manuscript *The Golden Legend*, 1445–1460. (Morgan Library)

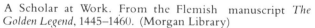

Stained Glass, German, c. 1300. Some stained-glass windows were purely decorative; others told a story. (MMA)

Vespers of the Holy Ghost, with a View of Paris, Jean Fouquet. From the *Book of Hours* of Etienne Chevalier, 1461. Demons in the sky are sent flying by the divine light from Heaven. The cathedral is Notre Dame. (Robert Lehman)

A Sixteenth-Century Map of the World by Paolo dal Toscanelli, Adviser to Columbus. The European continent is in the upper left. (Scala)

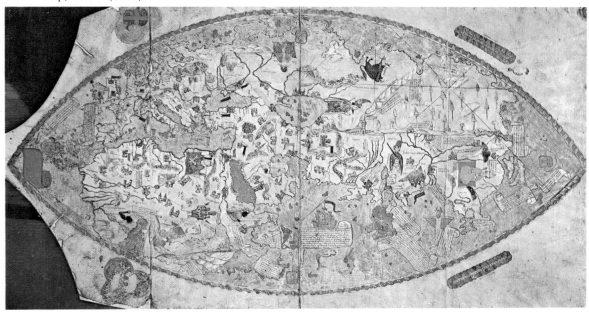

St. Lawrence Enthroned, Fra Lippo Lippi (1406–1469). One of the first of the psychological painters, Fra Lippo Lippi exhibited in this work his gift for portraying pensive melancholy. (MMA)

The Flight into Egypt, Giotto (1276–1337). Giotto is regarded as the founder of the modern tradition in painting. A fresco in the Arena Chapel, Padua. (MMA)

The Birth of Venus, Sandro Botticelli (1444–1510). Botticelli was a mystic as well as a lover of beauty whose works suggest a longing for the glories of the classical world. (Scala)

The Virgin of the Rocks, Leonardo da Vinci. This painting reveals not only Leonardo's interest in human character, but also his absorption in the phenomena of nature. (Louvre)

Mona Lisa, Leonardo da Vinci (1452–1519). Unlike most other Renaissance painters who sought to convey an understandable message, Leonardo created questions to which he gave no answer. Nowhere is this more evident than in the enigmatic countenance of Mona Lisa. (Louvre)

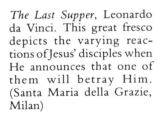

The Last Supper, Leonardo da Vinci. This great fresco depicts the varying reactions of Jesus' disciples when He announces that one of them will betray Him. (Santa Maria della Grazie, Milan)

0   500 miles

NORWAY

SWEDEN

Upsala △

NORTH SEA

SCOTLAND

△ Aberdeen

△ St. Andrews

△ Glasgow

DENMARK

△ Copenhagen

BALTIC SEA

ENGLAND

Cambridge ■

△ Oxford

Rostock △

△ Greifswald

Elbe R.

Vistula R.

Frankfurt △

POLAND

Wittenburg △

Oder R.

Louvain △

Cologne △

Erfurt △

Leipzig △

Cracow △

Rhine R.

Trier △

HOLY ROMAN

△ Würzburg

Prague △

ATLANTIC OCEAN

Caen ●

Seine R.

Paris △

Mainz ●

Heidelberg ●

EMPIRE

Freiburg ●

Ingolstadt ●

Vienna ●

△ Pressburg

Angers △

Orléans △

Tübingen ●

AUSTRIA

Buda ●

HUNGARY

Nantes △

Bourges ●

Loire R.

Besançon ●

Basel ●

SWITZ.

Dôle ●

Danube R.

Poitiers △

FRANCE

Treviso ●

Fünfkirchen ●

Lyons ●

Vercelli ■

Vicenza ●

VENETIAN REPUBLIC

Bordeaux ●

Cahors ●

Grenoble ●

Turin ●

Pavia ■

Padua ■

Valence ●

Piacenza ■

Reggio ●

Ferrara ■

ADRIATIC SEA

Toulouse △

Montpellier △

Orange ●

Avignon ●

Bologna ■

Rhône R.

Aix ●

Florence ●

Arezzo ●

Palencia ■

Ebro R.

Perpignan ●

Siena ■

Perugia ●

PAPAL STATES

● Valladolid

Huesca △

Lérida ●

CORSICA

Rome ●

Coimbra ●

Salamanca ■

Saragossa △

Siguenza △

Barcelona ●

△ Avila

PORTUGAL

Tagus R.

Toledo ●

SPAIN

Naples ■

Lisbon ■

Valencia ●

BALEARIC

SARDINIA

Salerno △

Palma ● △ MAJORCA

ISLANDS

THE TWO

Seville ●

MEDITERRANEAN

Palermo ●

SICILIES

Catania △

SEA

THE RISE OF THE MEDIEVAL UNIVERSITY

△ Founded in the 12th century

■ Founded in the 13th century

● Founded in the 14th century

△ Founded in the 15th century

Boundaries ca. 1500 A.D.

woolens, satins, metal products, and a host of others were turned out by the craftsmen of many cities. From the Chinese the Muslims learned the art of papermaking, and the products of that industry were in great demand, not only within the empire itself but in Europe as well.

In all the areas we have reviewed Islamic civilization so overshadowed that of the Christian West until about the twelfth century that there can be no comparison. When the West did move forward it was partly able to do so because of what it learned from Islam. In the economic sphere westerners profited from absorbing many accomplishments of Islamic technology, such as irrigation techniques, the raising of new crops, papermaking, and the distillation of alcohol. The extent of our debt to Islamic economic influence is well mirrored in the large number of common English words which were originally of Arabic or Persian origin. Among these are traffic, tariff, magazine, alcohol, muslin, orange, lemon, alfalfa, saffron, sugar, syrup, and musk. (Our word admiral also comes from the Arabic—in this case deriving from the title of emir.)

Islamic economic influence on the West

The West was as much indebted to Islam in intellectual and scientific as in economic life. In those areas, too, borrowed words tell some of the story: algebra, cipher, zero, nadir, amalgam, alembic, alchemy, alkali, soda, almanac, and names of many stars such as Aldebaran and Betelgeuse. Islamic civilization both preserved and expanded Greek philosophical and scientific knowledge when such knowledge was almost entirely forgotten in the West. All the important Greek scientific works surviving from ancient times were translated into Arabic and most of these in turn were translated in the medieval West from Arabic into Latin. Above all, the preservation and interpretation of the works of Aristotle was one of Islam's most enduring accomplishments. Not only was Aristotle first reacquired in the West by means of the Arabic translations, but Aristotle was interpreted with Islamic help, above all that of Averroës, whose prestige was so great that he was simply called "the Commentator" by medieval Western writers. Of course Arabic numerals, too, rank as a tremendously important intellectual legacy, as anyone will discover by trying to balance a checkbook with Roman ones.

Intellectual and scientific contributions

Aside from all these specific contributions, the civilization of Islam probably had its greatest influence on the West merely by standing as a powerful rival and spur to the imagination. Byzantine civilization was too closely related to the Christian West and ultimately not strong enough to serve this function. Westerners usually, for right or wrong, looked down on the Byzantine Greeks, but they more often respected and feared the Muslims. And right they were as well, for Islamic civilization at its zenith (to use another Arabic word) was surely one of the world's greatest. Though loosely organized, it united peoples as diverse as Arabs, Persians, Turks, various African tribes, and Hindus by means of a great religion and common institutions. Unity within mul-

General significance of Islamic civilization

tiplicity was an Islamic hallmark, which created both a splendid diverse society and a splendid legacy of original discoveries and achievements.

3. WESTERN CHRISTIAN CIVILIZATION IN THE EARLY MIDDLE AGES

The shaping of a cultural unity in the early-medieval West

Western Europeans in the early Middle Ages (the period between about 600 and 1050) were so backward in comparison to their Byzantine and Islamic neighbors that a tenth-century Arabic geographer could write of them that "they have large bodies, gross natures, harsh manners, and dull intellects . . . those who live farthest north are particularly stupid, gross, and brutish." Material conditions throughout this period were so primitive that we can almost speak of five centuries of camping-out. Yet new and promising patterns were definitely taking shape. Above all, a new center of civilization was emerging in the north Atlantic regions. Around 800 the Frankish monarchy, based in agriculturally rich northwestern Europe, managed to create a western European empire in alliance with the Western Christian Church. Although this empire did not last long, it still managed to hew out a new Western cultural unity that was to be an important building block for the future.

The kingdom of the Franks: the Merovingian period

Once the Eastern Romans under Justinian had destroyed the Ostrogothic and Vandal kingdoms in Italy and Africa, and the Arabs had eliminated the Visigothic kingdom in Spain, the Frankish rulers in Gaul remained as the major surviving barbarian power in western Europe. But it took about two centuries before they began to exercise their full hegemony. The founder of the Frankish state was the brutal and wily chieftain Clovis, who conquered most of modern-day France and Belgium around 500 and cleverly converted to Catholic Christianity, the religion of the local bishops and indigenous population. Clovis founded the Merovingian dynasty (so called from Merovech, the founder of the family to which he belonged). He did not, however, pass on a united realm but followed the typical barbarian custom of dividing up his kingdom among his sons. More or less without interruption for the next two hundred years sons fought sons for a larger share of the Merovingian inheritance. Toward the end of that period the line also began to degenerate and numerous so-called do-nothing kings left their government and fighting to their chief ministers, known as "mayors of the palace." Throughout this era, one of the darkest in the recorded history of Europe, trade contracted, towns declined, literacy was almost forgotten, and violence was endemic. Minimal agricultural self-sufficiency coexisted with the rule of the battle-axe.

Largely unnoticed, however, some hope for the future was coalescing around the institutions of the Roman papacy and Benedictine monasticism. The architect of a new western European religious policy that was based on an alliance between these two institutions was Pope Gregory I (reigned 590–604), known as St. Gregory the Great. Until his time the Roman popes were generally subordinate to the emperors in Constantinople and to the greater religious prestige of the Christian East, but Gregory sought to counteract this situation by creating a more autonomous western-oriented Latin Church. This he tried to do in many ways. As a theologian—the fourth great "Latin father" of the Church—he built upon the work of his three predecessors, Jerome, Ambrose, and especially Augustine, in articulating a theology that had its own distinct characteristics. Among these were emphasis on the idea of penance and the concept of purgatory as a place for purification before admission into heaven. (Western belief in purgatory was thereafter to become one of the major differences in the dogmas of the Eastern and Western Churches.) In addition to his theological work, Gregory pioneered in the writing of a simplified unadorned Latin prose that corresponded to the actual spoken language of his contemporaries, and presided over the creation of a powerful Latin liturgy. If Gregory did not actually invent the "Gregorian chant," it was under his impetus that this new plainsong—forever after a central part of the Roman Catholic ritual—developed. All of these innovations helped to make the Christian West religiously and culturally more independent of the Greek-speaking East than it had ever been before.

Pope Gregory the Great. In this tenth-century German ivory panel the pope is receiving inspiration from the Holy Spirit in the form of a dove.

Gregory the Great was as much a statesman as he was a theologian and shaper of Latin. Within Italy he assured the physical survival of the papacy in the face of the barbarian Lombard threat of his day (the Lombards were natural enemies of the papacy because they were Arian heretics) by clever diplomacy and expert management of papal landed estates. He also began to reemphasize earlier claims of papal primacy, especially over Western bishops, that were in danger of being forgotten. Above all, he patronized the order of Benedictine monks and used them to help evangelize new Western territories. Gregory himself had been a Benedictine—perhaps the first Benedictine monk to become pope—and he wrote the standard life of St. Benedict. Because the Benedictine order was still very young and the times were turbulent, Gregory's patronage helped the order to survive and later to become for centuries the only monastic order in the West. In return the pope could profit from using the Benedictines to carry out special projects. The most significant of these was the conversion of Anglo-Saxon England to Christianity. This was a long-term project which took about a century to complete, but its great result was that it left a Christian outpost to the far northwest that was thoroughly loyal to the papacy and that would soon help to bring together the papacy and the Frankish state. Gregory the Great himself did not live to see that union but it was his policy of invigorating the Western Church that most helped to bring it about.

Gregory's religious policies

Around 700, when the Benedictines were completing their conversion of England, the outlook for Frankish Gaul was becoming somewhat brighter. The most profound reason for this was that the long, troubled period of transition between the ancient and medieval worlds was finally coming to an end. The ancient Roman civilization of cities and Mediterranean trade was in its last gasps in Gaul in the time after Clovis. Then, when the Arabs conquered the southern Mediterranean shore and took to the sea in the seventh century, Gaul and western Europe was finally thrown back upon itself and forced to look away from the Mediterranean. In fact the lands of the north—modern-day northern France, the Low Countries, Germany, and England—were extremely fertile: with adequate farming implements they could yield great natural wealth. Given the proper circumstances, a new power could emerge in the north to make the most of a new pattern of life based predominantly on agrarianism instead of urban commerce and Mediterranean trade. Around 700 that is exactly what happened in Merovingian Gaul.

*The alliance between
Frankish rulers and the
Church; Charles Martel
and St. Boniface*

The proper circumstances were the triumph of a succession of able rulers and their alliance with the Church. In 687 an energetic Merovingian mayor of the palace, Pepin of Heristal, managed to unite all the Frankish lands under his rule and build a new power base for his own family in the region of Belgium and the Rhine. He was succeeded by his aggressive son, Charles Martel ("the Hammer"), who is sometimes considered a second founder of the Frankish state. Charles's claim to this title is twofold. First, in 732 he turned back a Muslim force from Spain at the Battle of Poitiers, some 150 miles from Paris. Although the Muslim contingent was not a real army but merely a marauding band, the incursion was the high-water mark of their progress toward the northwest and Charles's victory won him great prestige. Equally important, around the end of his reign Charles began to develop an alliance with the Church, particularly with the Benedictines of England. Having finished most of their conversion work on their island, the Benedictines, under their idealistic leader St. Boniface, were moving across the English Channel in an attempt to convert central Germany. Charles Martel realized that he and they had common interests, for after he had guarded his southern flank against the Muslims he was seeking to direct Frankish expansion eastward in the direction of Germany. Missionary work and Frankish expansion could go hand in hand, so Charles offered St. Boniface and his Benedictines material aid in return for their support of his territorial aims.

*Solidification of the
alliance in the time of
Pepin the Short*

Once allied with the Franks, St. Boniface provided further service in the next reign in helping to contribute to one of the most momentous events in Western history. Charles Martel had never assumed the royal title, but his son, Pepin the Short, wished to take it. Even though Pepin and not the reigning "do-nothing king" was the real power, Pepin needed the prestige of the Church for supporting a change in dynasties. Fortunately for him the times were highly propitious for obtaining Church support. St. Boniface supported Pepin because the young ruler continued his father's policy of collaborating with the Benedictines in Germany. And Boniface had great influence in Rome because the Anglo-Saxon Benedictines had remained in the closest touch with the papacy since the time of Gregory the Great.

The papacy was now fully prepared to cast its own lots with a strong Frankish ruler because it was in the midst of a bitter fight with the Byzantine emperors over Iconoclasm. The Byzantines until then had offered papal territories in Italy some protection against the Lombards, but the increasingly powerful Franks were now fully able to take over that role. The papacy accordingly made an epochal about-face, turning fully and lastingly to the West. In 750 the pope encouraged Pepin to depose the Merovingian figurehead, and in 751 St. Boniface, acting as papal emissary, anointed Pepin as a divinely sanctioned king. Thus the Frankish monarchy attained a spiritual mandate and was fully integrated into the papal-Benedictine orbit. Shortly afterwards Pepin paid his debt to the pope by conquering the Lombards in Italy. The West was now achieving its own unity based on the Frankish state and the Latin church, not coincidentally just at the time when the Abbasid caliphate was being founded in the East and the Byzantines were going their own fully Greek way.

The "about-face" of the papacy

The ultimate consolidation of the new pattern took place in the reign of Pepin's son, Carolus Magnus or Charlemagne (768–814), from whom the new dynasty takes its name of "Carolingian." Without question Charlemagne ranks as one of the most important rulers of the whole medieval period. Had it been possible to ask him what his greatest accomplishment was, he almost certainly would have replied that it lay in greatly increasing the Frankish realm. Except for the English, there was scarcely a people of western Europe against whom he did not fight. Most of his campaigns were successful; he annexed the greater part of central Europe and northern and central Italy to the Frankish domain. To rule this vast area he bestowed all the powers of local government upon his own appointees, called counts, and tried to remain in control of them by sending representatives of the court to observe them. Among the counts' many duties were the administration of justice and the raising of armies. Although Charlemagne's system in practice was far from perfect, it led to the best government that Europe had seen since the Romans. Because of the military triumphs and internal peace of his reign, Charlemagne was long remembered and revered as a western European folk hero.

Charlemagne. A silver penny struck between 804 and 814 showing Charlemagne in a highly stylized fashion as emperor with Roman toga and laurel. The inscription reads KAROLVS IMP AVG (Charles, Emperor, Augustus).

Primarily to aid his territorial expansion and help administer his realm Charlemagne presided over a revival of learning known as the "Carolingian Renaissance." Charlemagne extended his rule into Germany in the name of Christianity, but in order to proselytize he needed educated monks and priests. More than that, in order to ad-

The Carolingian Renaissance

minister his far-flung territories he needed at least a few people who could read and write. Amazing as it may seem to us, there were hardly any at first in his entire realm who were literate, so thoroughly had the rudiments of learning been forgotten since the decay of Roman city life. Only in Anglo-Saxon England had literacy been cultivated by the Benedictine monks. The reason for this was that the Anglo-Saxons spoke a form of German but the monks needed to learn Latin in order to say their offices and study the Bible. Since they knew no Latin to begin with they had to go about learning it by a very self-conscious program of studies. The greatest Anglo-Saxon Benedictine scholar before Charlemagne's time was the Venerable Bede (d. 735), whose *History of the English Church and People,* written in Latin, was one of the best historical writings of the early-medieval period and can still be read with pleasure. When Charlemagne came to the throne he invited the Anglo-Saxon Benedictine Alcuin—a student of one of Bede's students—to direct a revival of studies on the continent. With Charlemagne's active support Alcuin helped establish new schools to teach reading, directed the copying and correcting of important Latin works, including many Roman classics, and inspired the formulation of a new clear handwriting that is the ancestor of our modern "Roman" print. These were the greatest achievements of the Carolingian Renaissance, which stressed practicality rather than original literary or intellectual endeavors. Thoroughly unpretentious as they were, they established a bridgehead for literacy on the Continent which thereafter would never be completely lost. They also helped to preserve Latin literature, and they made the Latin language the language of state and diplomacy for all of western Europe, as it remained until comparatively modern times.

The climax of Charlemagne's career came in the year 800 when he was crowned emperor on Christmas Day in Rome by the pope. His-

Carolingian Handwriting. Even the untrained reader has no difficulty in reading this excerpt from a Carolingian manuscript.

torians continue to debate whether this was Charlemagne's or the pope's idea, but there is no doubt that the pope did not gain any immediate power from it. Once the Franks ruled Italy they came to dominate the papacy, and indeed the whole Church, to such a degree that by 800 the pope was very close to being Charlemagne's puppet. Charlemagne did not gain any actual new power by taking the imperial title either, but the significance of the event is nonetheless great. Up until 800 the only emperor ruled in Constantinople and could lay claim to being the direct heir of Augustus. Although the Byzantines had lost most of their interest in the West, they still continued to regard it vaguely as an outlying province and were actively opposed to any westerner calling himself emperor. Charlemagne's assumption of the title was virtually a declaration of Western self-confidence and independence. Since Charlemagne's vast realm was fully as large as that of the Byzantines, had great reserves of agricultural wealth, and was defining its own culture based on Western Christianity and the Latin linguistic tradition, the claim to empire was largely justified. More than that, it was never forgotten. Both for its symbolism and its contribution toward giving westerners a sense of unity and purpose it was a major landmark on the road to the making of a great western Europe.

Charlemagne's coronation as emperor

Although the claim to empire was bold and memorable, Charlemagne's actual empire disintegrated quickly after his death for many reasons. The simplest was that hardly any of his successors were as competent and decisive as he was. In order to rule an empire in those still extremely primitive times, one had to have enormous reserves of strength and energy—one had to travel on horseback over enormous distances, fight and win battles at the head of unruly armies, and know how to delegate power to others with vigilance against its abuse. Unfortunately for western Europe few of Charlemagne's heirs had such combinations of energy and talent. To make matters worse, Charlemagne's sole surviving son, Louis the Pious, who inherited the Frankish realm intact, divided his inheritance among his own three sons, thereby bringing civil war back to Frankish Europe. And to make matters worst of all, new waves of invasions began just as Charlemagne's grandsons and great-grandsons started fighting each other: from the north came the Scandinavian Vikings; from the east came the Asiatic Magyars (or Hungarians); and from the south came new attacks by marauding Muslims, attacking now from the sea. Under these pressures the Carolingian Empire completely fell apart and a new political map of Europe was drawn in the tenth century.

The disintegration of Charlemagne's empire

As the Carolingian period was crucial for marking the beginnings of a common north Atlantic western European civilization, so the tenth century was crucial for marking the beginnings of the major modern European political entities. England, which never had been part of Charlemagne's empire, and which hitherto had been divided among

England in the time of Alfred the Great

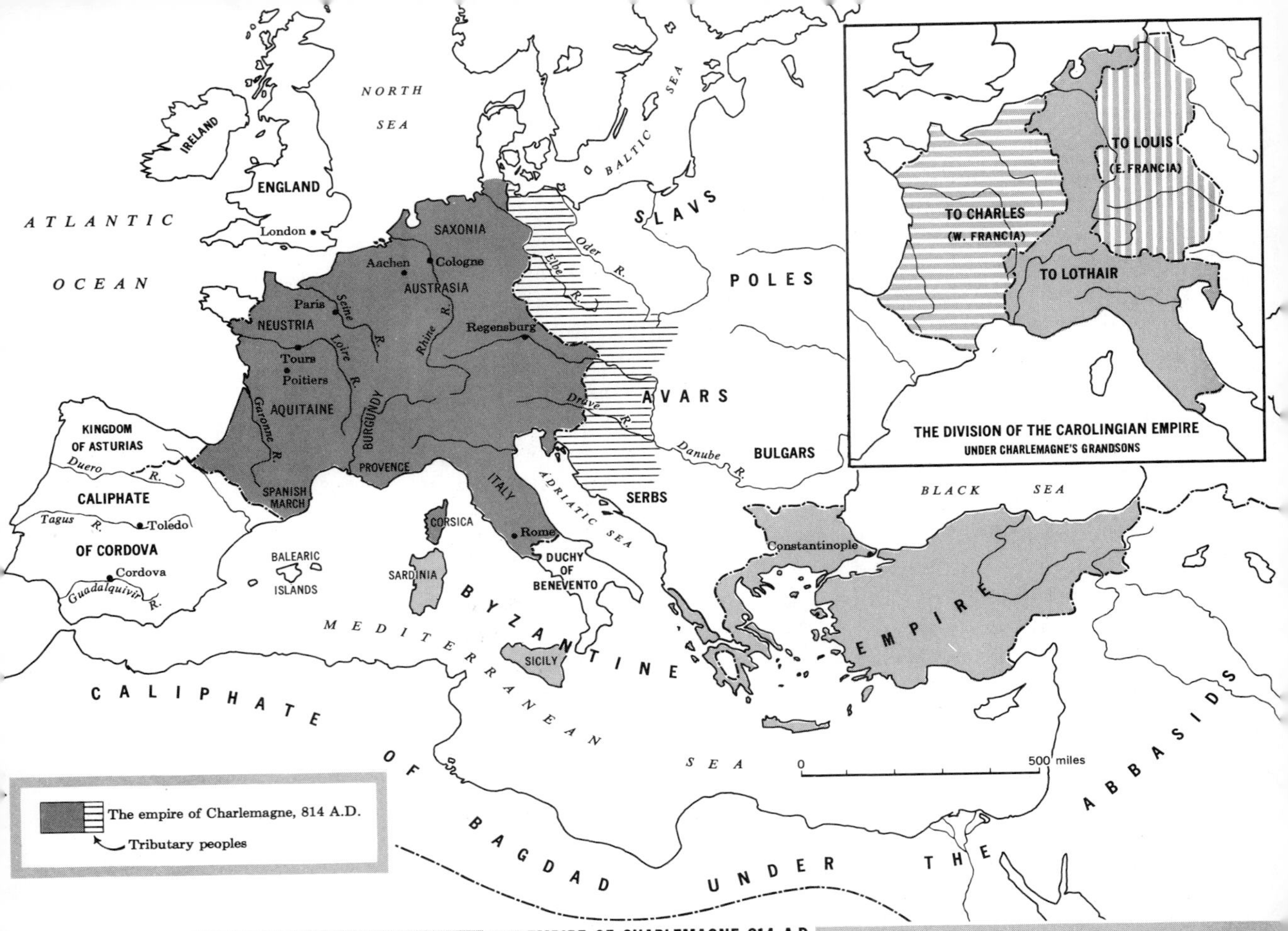
NORTH SEA
IRELAND
ENGLAND
London
ATLANTIC OCEAN
BALTIC SEA
SLAVS
SAXONIA
Aachen
Cologne
AUSTRASIA
Paris
NEUSTRIA
Seine R.
Oder R.
Elbe R.
Rhine R.
Regensburg
POLES
Tours
Poitiers
Loire R.
AQUITAINE
Garonne R.
BURGUNDY
Drave R.
AVARS
KINGDOM OF ASTURIAS
Duero R.
CALIPHATE OF CORDOVA
Tagus R.
Toledo
Cordova
Guadalquivir R.
SPANISH MARCH
PROVENCE
Danube R.
BULGARS
ITALY
CORSICA
ADRIATIC SEA
SERBS
Rome
DUCHY OF BENEVENTO
SARDINIA
BALEARIC ISLANDS
Constantinople
BLACK SEA
BYZANTINE EMPIRE
SICILY
MEDITERRANEAN SEA
CALIPHATE OF BAGDAD UNDER THE ABBASIDS
0
500 miles
The empire of Charlemagne, 814 A.D.
Tributary peoples
TO CHARLES (W. FRANCIA)
TO LOUIS (E. FRANCIA)
TO LOTHAIR
THE DIVISION OF THE CAROLINGIAN EMPIRE UNDER CHARLEMAGNE'S GRANDSONS

THE EMPIRE OF CHARLEMAGNE 814 A.D.

smaller warring Anglo-Saxon states, became unified in the late ninth and the tenth century owing to the work of King Alfred the Great (871–899) and his direct successors. Alfred and his heirs reorganized the army, infused new vigor into local government, and codified the English laws. In addition, Alfred founded schools and fostered an interest in Anglo-Saxon writing and other elements of a national culture.

Political conditions in France and Germany

Across the Channel, France (now the name for the main part of Roman Gaul because it was the original seat of the Frankish monarchy) was most devastated by the invasions of Vikings, who had sailed up the French rivers. For that reason France broke up into small principalities rather than developing a strong national monarchy on the pattern of England. Nonetheless there was a king in France, who, however weak, was recognized as the ruler of the western part of Charlemagne's former territories. Directly to the east, the kings of Germany were the strongest continental monarchs of the tenth century, ruling over an essentially united realm. In addition to Germany, their lands encompassed most of the Low Countries and a good part of modern eastern France.

The most important German ruler of the period was Otto the Great. He became king in 936, resoundingly defeated the Hungarians in 955—thereby relieving Germany of its greatest foreign threat—and took the title of emperor in Rome in 962. By this last act Otto strengthened his claim to being the greatest continental monarch since Charlemagne. Otto and his successors, who continued to call themselves emperors, tried to rule over Italy but barely succeeded in doing so. Instead, Italy in the tenth century saw the greatest western European development of urban life, a pattern on which the Italians would subsequently build.

Otto the Great of Germany

Although Italy did develop some city life in the tenth century, this was by no means typical of the early-medieval period in western Europe as a whole. Quite to the contrary, from the eighth to the eleventh century the European economy was based almost entirely on agriculture and very limited local trade. Roads deteriorated and barter widely replaced the use of money. Whatever cities survived from Roman days were usually empty shells that served at most as administrative centers for bishops and fortified places in case of common danger. The main economic unit throughout the period was the self-supporting large landed estate, usually owned by kings, warrior aristocrats, or large-scale monasteries. Although the northern European soil was rich, farming tools in most places were still too primitive to bring in a fully adequate return on the enormous investment of effort expended by the laboring masses. Agricultural yields in all but the most fertile Carolingian heartlands (and often even in them) were pitifully low, and Europeans, except the rulers and the higher clergy, lived on the edge of subsistence. It is true that some increase in agricultural income had underpinned the Carolingian successes and some progress in farming might have continued had the peace of Charlemagne's reign endured. But the subsequent invasions of the ninth and tenth centuries set agricultural life back and new beginnings would have to be made in the years thereafter.

The economy of western Europe in the early Middle Ages

Given the low level of early-medieval economic life, it is not surprising that the age was not a prosperous time for learning or the arts: if there is scarcely enough wealth to keep most people alive, there is not going to be much to support schools or major artistic projects. Throughout the period, even in the best of years, learning was a privilege for the few: the masses received no formal education, and even most members of the secular aristocracy were illiterate. Learning also consisted mostly of memorization, without regard for criticism or refutation. We have seen that there was some revival of learning under Charlemagne that may be called a "renaissance" but that it did not issue into any real intellectual creativity. Its major accomplishment was the founding of enough schools to educate the clergy in the rudi-

The low level of intellectual life

ments of reading and the training of enough monastic scribes to re-copy and preserve some major works of Roman literature. Even this accomplishment was jeopardized in the period of invasions that accompanied the fall of the Carolingian Empire. Fortunately just enough schools and manuscripts survived to become the basis for another—far greater—revival of learning that began in the eleventh and twelfth centuries.

Literature

In the realm of literature the early Middle Ages had an extremely meager production. This was because few Christians could write and those who could were usually monks and priests, who were not supposed to engage in purely literary endeavors. There was some impressive writing of history in Latin, most notably that of Bede and Charlemagne's eloquent biographer, Einhard, but otherwise Latin composition was little cultivated. Toward the close of the period, however, the vernacular languages, which were either Germanic or based on different regional dialects of Latin (the "Romance" languages, so-called because they were based on "Roman" speech) began to be employed for crude poetic expression, usually first by oral transmission.

Beowulf

The best-known example of this literature in the vernacular is the Anglo-Saxon epic poem *Beowulf.* First put into written form about the eighth century, this poem incorporates ancient legends of the Germanic peoples of northwestern Europe. It is a story of fighting and seafaring and of heroic adventure against deadly dragons and the forces of nature. The background of the epic is pre-Christian, but the author of the work introduced into it some qualities of Christian idealism. *Beowulf* is important not only as one of the earliest specimens of Anglo-Saxon or Old English poetry, but also for the picture it gives of the society of the English and their ancestors in the early Middle Ages.

The artistic history of the early Middle Ages was a story of isolated and interrupted accomplishments because artistic life relied most of all on brief moments of local peace or royal patronage. The earliest enduring monuments of early-medieval art were those created by monks in Ireland—which had its own unique culture—between the sixth and the eighth centuries. Above all in manuscript illumination (i.e., painted illustrations) the Irish monks developed a thoroughly anticlassical and almost surrealistic style, whose origins are most difficult to account for. The greatest surviving product from this school is the stunning "Book of Kells," an illuminated Gospel book that has been called "the most sophisticated work of decorative art in the history of painting." The Irish school declined without subsequent influence and was followed by artistic products of the Carolingian Renaissance.

Irish Art. The opening of a gospel page that shows the Irish style at its most surrealistic.

The art of Charlemagne's period returned for much of its inspiration to classical models, yet it also retained some of the spontaneous vitality of barbarian decoration. When Charlemagne's empire declined and disintegrated there was a corresponding decline and then interruption in the history of Western art. In the tenth century, however, new

Carolingian Art. The fountain of life: an illuminated manuscript page from Gottschalk's Evangeliary (book with four gospels), dating from 781.

regional schools emerged. The greatest of these were the English, which emphasized restless fluency in manuscript illumination; the German, which was more grave but still managed to communicate extreme religious ecstasy; and the northern Spanish, which, though Christian, created a rather strange and independent style mostly influenced by the decorative style of Islamic art. By the very end of the early-medieval period a new European international style was emerging that would be called "Romanesque," but that is a subject for later consideration.

Regional variations in early-medieval art

Just as the Romanesque style bridged the early and subsequent medieval periods, there is no single, obvious terminal date for early-medieval history as a whole. The date 1000 is sometimes given, most of all because it is a convenient round number, but even as late as 1050 Europe had not changed on the surface very much from the way it had been since the end of the Carolingian period. Indeed, looking at Europe as late as 1050 it would at first seem that not much progress had been made over the entire course of the early-medieval centuries. Except for Germany there was hardly any centralized government, because by 1050 the Anglo-Saxon English state created by King Alfred and his successors was falling apart. Throughout Europe, all but the most privileged individuals continued to live on the brink of starvation and cultural attainments were minimal and sparse. But actually much had been accomplished. By shifting its main weight to the Atlantic northwest, European civilization became centered in lands that would soon harvest great agricultural wealth. By preserving some of the traditions developed by Gregory the Great, St. Boniface,

A distinct western European civilization evident in 1050

Left: *Utrecht Psalter.* This Carolingian manuscript of the Psalms from about 820 later provided the basis for the "nervous expressiveness" of the tenth-century English regional school. Right: *Bamberg Apocalypse.* In this manuscript illumination from about 1000 A.D. the fall of Babylon in the Book of Revelation (18: 1–20) is displayed by depicting the city upside down. An example of the grave regional German style.

Pepin, and Charlemagne, European civilization had also developed an enduring sense of cultural unity based on Western Christianity and the Latin inheritance. And in the tenth century the beginnings of the future European kingdoms and city-states started to coalesce. Western European civilization was thus for the first time becoming autonomous and distinctive. From then until now it would become a leading force in the history of the world.

SELECTED READINGS

• *Items so designated are available in paperback editions.*

BYZANTINE CIVILIZATION

    Beckwith, John, *The Art of Constantinople,* 2nd ed., London, 1968. A standard account.

• Diehl, Charles, *Byzantium: Greatness and Decline,* New Brunswick, N.J., 1957. Evaluates strengths and weaknesses of Byzantine civilization.

    Geanakoplos, D. J., *Byzantine East and Latin West,* New York, 1966.

    Hussey, J. M., *The Byzantine World,* London, 1957. Half-narrative, half-topical; a useful short introduction.

• Krautheimer, R., *Early Christian and Byzantine Architecture,* Baltimore, 1970.

Magoulias, H. J., *Byzantine Christianity: Emperor, Church and the West*, Chicago, 1970. Limited to three themes mentioned in title.

Miller, D. A., *The Byzantine Tradition*, New York, 1966. The briefest introduction.

Ostrogorsky, George, *History of the Byzantine State*, New Brunswick, N.J., 1957. The most authoritative longer account of political developments; very scholarly.

• Pelikan, J., *The Christian Tradition; II: The Spirit of Eastern Christendom*, Chicago, 1974. An advanced treatment of religious doctrines.

• Runciman, S., *Byzantine Civilization*, New York, 1933. A topical approach; well written but in parts outdated.

• ———, *Byzantine Style and Civilization*, Baltimore, 1975. A fine study of Byzantine art.

• Vasiliev, A. A., *History of the Byzantine Empire*, 2 vols., Madison, Wisc., 1928. Supplements Ostrogorsky; valuable for its detail on social and intellectual as well as political history.

Vryonis, S., *Byzantium and Europe*, New York, 1967. Noteworthy for its illustrations.

ISLAMIC CIVILIZATION

Arnold, Thomas, and A. Guillaume, *The Legacy of Islam*, New York, 1931.

Gabrieli, F., *Muhammad and the Conquests of Islam*, New York, 1968.

• Gibb, H. A. R., *Arabic Literature: An Introduction*, 2nd ed., Oxford, 1963. An excellent survey.

———, *Mohammedanism: An Historical Survey*, 2nd ed., Oxford, 1953. The best brief interpretation of Islamic religion.

• Goitein, S. D., *Jews and Arabs, Their Contacts through the Ages*, New York, 1955.

Grube, E. J., *The World of Islam*, New York, 1966.

• Hodgson, M., *The Venture of Islam*, 3 vols., Chicago, 1974. A masterwork. One of the greatest works of history written by a modern American. Advanced and sometimes difficult, but always rewarding.

• Lewis, Bernard, *The Arabs in History*, rev. ed., New York, 1966. The best short survey of the conquests and political fortunes of the Arabs.

• Lombard, Maurice, *The Golden Age of Islam*, New York, 1975.

Peters, F. E., *Aristotle and the Arabs*, New York, 1968. A well-written and engaging account.

Watt, W. Montgomery, *Islamic Philosophy and Theology*, Edinburgh, 1962.

• ———, *Muhammad: Prophet and Statesman*, Oxford, 1961. A good short biography.

Watt, W. M., and P. Cachia, *A History of Islamic Spain*, Edinburgh, 1965. Briefly covers an undeservedly neglected subject.

EARLY-MEDIEVAL WESTERN CHRISTIAN CIVILIZATION

• Barraclough, G., *The Crucible of Europe: The Ninth and Tenth Centuries in European History*, Berkeley, Calif., 1976. A controversial and sometimes wrongheaded but clear and stimulating interpretation of political developments.

• Dawson, Christopher, *The Making of Europe,* London, 1932. A brilliant interpretation that emphasizes cultural and religious developments by one of this century's most eminent Catholic historians.

• Duby, G., *The Early Growth of the European Economy,* Ithaca, N.Y., 1974. Emphasizes role of lords and peasants; very sophisticated economic history.

Fichtenau, H., *The Carolingian Empire,* Oxford, 1957. A highly interpretative account that aims to whittle its subject down to size.

• Ganshof, F. L., *Frankish Institutions under Charlemagne,* Providence, 1958. A straightforward technical exposition.

Halphen, L., *Charlemagne and the Carolingian Empire,* New York, 1977. An older French survey recently translated into English.

• Kitzinger, Ernst, *Early Medieval Art,* London, 1940. A very short but masterful introduction.

• Laistner, M. L. W., *Thought and Letters in Western Europe, A.D. 500–900,* rev. ed., Ithaca, N.Y., 1957. An old-fashioned but standard account; should be supplemented by Wolff.

• Pirenne, Henri, *Mohammed and Charlemagne,* New York, 1939. A bold interpretation, now no longer widely accepted but still thought provoking.

Stenton, Frank, *Anglo-Saxon England,* 3rd ed., Oxford, 1971. A standard work.

• Sullivan, Richard E., *Heirs of the Roman Empire,* Ithaca, N.Y., 1960. An elementary introduction.

• Wallace-Hadrill, J. M., *The Barbarian West, A. D. 400–1000,* 2nd ed., London, 1962. A sophisticated short account that emphasizes analysis of the historical sources and questions earlier scholarly assumptions.

Wolff, Philippe, *The Awakening of Europe,* Baltimore, 1968. The "new intellectual history": emphasizes interrelations between the development of thought and material foundations. Masterfully written and organized.

SOURCE MATERIALS

• Arberry, A. J., *The Koran Interpreted,* 2 vols., London, 1955.

• Bede, *A History of the English Church and People,* tr. L. Sherley-Price, Baltimore, 1955.

• Brand, Charles M., ed., *Icon and Minaret: Sources of Byzantine and Islamic Civilization,* Englewood Cliffs, N.J., 1969.

• Brentano, Robert, ed., *The Early Middle Ages: 500–1000,* New York, 1964. The best shorter anthology of the Western Christian sources, enlivened by the editor's subjective commentary.

Davis, Charles T., ed., *The Eagle, the Crescent, and the Cross,* New York, 1967.

• Einhard and Notker the Stammerer, *Two Lives of Charlemagne,* tr. L. Thorpe, Baltimore, 1969.

• Gregory Bishop of Tours, *History of the Franks,* tr. E. Brehaut, New York, 1965.

Chapter 14

THE HIGH MIDDLE AGES (1050–1300): ECONOMIC, SOCIAL, AND POLITICAL INSTITUTIONS

I judge those who write at this time to be in a certain measure happy. For, after the turbulence of the past, an unprecedented brightness of peace has dawned again.

—The historian Otto of
Freising, writing around 1158

The period between about 1050 and 1300, termed by historians the High Middle Ages, was the time when western Europe first clearly emerged from backwardness to become one of the greatest powers on the globe. Around 1050 the West was still less developed in most respects than the Byzantine Empire or the Islamic world, but by 1300 it had forged ahead of these two rivals. From a global perspective, only China was its equal in economic, political, and cultural prosperity. Given the sorry state of western Europe around 1050, this startling leap forward was certainly one of the most impressive achievements of human history. Those who think that the entire Middle Ages were times of stagnation could not be more wrong.

Western Europe emerges from backwardness

The reasons for Europe's enormous progress in the High Middle Ages are predictably complex, yet medieval historians agree upon certain broad lines of interpretation. One is that Europe between 900 and 1050 was already poised for growth and could finally begin to live up to its potential once the devastating invasions of Vikings, Hungarians, and Muslims had ceased. Most of these invasions had tapered off by around 1000, but in the eleventh century England was still troubled by the Danes: the year 1066, more famous as the year of the Norman Conquest, was also the year of the last Viking invasion of England.

Reasons for the "great leap forward"

Once foreign invasions were no longer imminent, western Europeans could concentrate on developing their economic life with much less fear of interruption than before. Because of the relative continuity allowed by this change, extraordinarily important technological breakthroughs were made, above all those that contributed to the first great western European "agricultural revolution." The revolution in agriculture made food more bountiful and provided a solid basis for economic development and diversification in other spheres. Population grew rapidly and towns and cities grew to such a degree that we can speak also of an "urban revolution." At the same time political life in the West became more stable. In the course of the High Middle Ages strong new secular governments began to provide more and more internal peace for their subjects and became the foundations of our modern nation-states. In addition to all these advances, there were also striking new religious and intellectual developments, to be treated in the next chapter, which helped give the West a new sense of mission and self-confidence. Although in this chapter we will treat only the economic, social, and political accomplishments of the High Middle Ages, it is well to bear in mind that religion played a pervasive role in all of medieval life, and that all aspects of the high-medieval "great leap forward" were inextricably interrelated.

1. THE FIRST AGRICULTURAL REVOLUTION

*The state of agriculture
before 1050*

The agricultural worker, the "Man with the Hoe," supported European civilization materially by his labors more than anyone else until the industrialization of modern times. Yet, amazing as it seems, until about 1050 he had hardly so much as a hoe. Inventories of farm implements from the Carolingian period reveal that metal tools on the wealthiest rural estates were extremely rare and even wooden implements were so few in number that many laborers must have had to grapple with nature quite literally with only their bare hands. Between about 1050 and 1250 all that changed. In roughly those two centuries an agricultural revolution took place which entirely altered the nature and vastly increased the output of western European farming.

*Prerequisities for the
medieval agricultural
revolution: (1) shift in
area of cultivation*

Many of the prerequisites for the medieval agricultural revolution had been present before the middle of the eleventh century. The most important was the shift in the weight of European civilization from the Mediterranean to the north Atlantic regions. Most of northern Europe from southern England to the Urals is a vast, wet, and highly fertile alluvial plain. The Romans had hardly begun to cultivate this area because they only ruled part of it, because it lay too far away from the center of their civilization, and because they did not have the proper tools and systems to work the soil. Starting around the time of the Carolingians much more attention was paid to colonizing and cultivating the great alluvial plain. The Carolingians opened up all of western and central Germany to agricultural settlement and started experimenting with new tools and methods that would be most appropriate for cultivating the newly settled lands. The results helped support other Carolingian achievements, but the Carolingian peace, as we have seen, was too brief to allow for any cumulative development. After the invasions of the tenth century, it was necessary to start again in a systematic attempt to exploit the potential wealth of the north. As long as Western civilization was centered in England, northern France, the Low Countries, and Germany, however, the rich lands were right there to be cultivated.

Another prerequisite for agricultural development was improved climate. We know far less about European climatic patterns in past centuries than we would like to, but historians of climate are reasonably certain that there was an "optimum," or period of improved climate for western Europe, lasting from about 700 to 1200. This meant not only that during those centuries the temperature on the average was somewhat warmer than it had been before (at most only a rise of about 1° Centigrade), but also that the weather was somewhat drier. Dryness was of primary advantage to northern Europe, where lands were, if anything, usually too wet for good farming, whereas it was disadvantageous to the Mediterranean south, which was already dry enough. Among other things, the occurrence of this optimum helps explain why there was more agricultural cultivation in northern climes such as Iceland than there has been since then. (Also, with fewer icebergs in the northern seas, Norsemen were able to reach Greenland and Newfoundland, and Greenland then was probably indeed more green than white.) Although the optimum began around 700 and continued through the ninth and tenth centuries, it could not by itself counteract the deleterious effects of the tenth-century invasions. Fortunately the weather stayed propitious when Europeans again were able to take advantage of it.

Similar remarks apply to the fact that the Carolingians knew about many of the technological devices to be discussed presently that later most helped western Europeans accomplish their first agricultural revolution. Although the most basic new devices were known before 1050, all came into widespread use and were brought to greatest perfection between then and about 1200 because only then was there a conjunction of the most favorable circumstances. Not only did the invasions end and good climate continue, but better government gradually provided the more lasting peace necessary for agricultural expansion. Landlords too became more interested in profit-making than mere consumption. Above all, from about 1050 to 1200 there was a greater consolidation of wealth for further investment as one advance helped support another; quite simply, technological devices could now be afforded.

(2) improved climate

(3) technology in conjunction with favorable circumstances

Light Plow and Heavy Plow. Note that the peasant using the light plow has to press his foot on it to give it added weight. The major innovation of the heavy

Technological innovations: (1) the heavy plow

One of the first and most important breakthroughs in agriculture was the use of the heavy plow. The plow itself, of course, is an ancient tool, but the Romans knew only a light "scratch plow" that broke up the surface of the ground without fully turning it over. This implement was sufficient for the light soil of the Mediterranean regions but was virtually useless with the much heavier, wetter soil of the European north. During the course of the early Middle Ages a much heavier and more efficient plow was developed that could cultivate the northern lands. Not only could this heavier plow deal with heavier soils, but it was fitted with new parts that enabled it to turn over furrows and fully aerate the ground. The benefits were immeasurable. In addition to the fact that the plow allowed for the cultivation of hitherto unworkable lands, the furrows it made provided excellent drainage systems for water-logged territories. It also saved labor: whereas the Roman scratch plow had to be dragged over the fields twice in two different directions, the heavy plow did more thorough work in one operation. In short, the opening up of northern Europe for intensive agriculture and everything that followed would have been inconceivable without the heavy plow.

(2) the three-field system

Closely allied to the use of the heavy plow was the introduction of the three-field system of crop rotation. Before modern times, farmers always let a large part of their arable land lie fallow for a year to avoid exhaustion of the soil because there was not enough fertilizer to support more intensive agriculture, and nitrogen-fixing crops such as clover and alfalfa were almost unknown. But the Romans represented an unproductive extreme in their inability to cultivate any more than half of their arable land in any year. The medieval innovation was to reduce the fallow to one-third by introducing a three-field system. In a given year one third of the land would lie fallow, one third would be given to cereal that was sown in the fall and harvested in early sum-

plow was the long moldboard, which turned over the ground after the plowshare cut into it.

mer, and one third to a new crop—oats, barley, or legumes—that would be planted in the late spring and harvested in August or September. The fields were then rotated over a three-year cycle. The major innovation was the planting of the new crop which grew over the summer. The Romans could not have supported this system because their lands were poorer and especially because the Mediterranean area is too dry to support much summer growth at all. In this respect the wetter north obviously had a great advantage. The benefits of the new crop were that it did not deplete the soil as much as cereal like wheat and rye (in fact, it restored nitrogen taken from the soil by these crops); that it provided some insurance against loss from natural disasters by diversifying the growth of the fields; and that it produced new types of food. If the third field was planted with oats, the crop could be consumed by both humans and horses; if planted with legumes, it helped to balance the human diet by providing a source of protein to balance the major intake of cereal carbohydrates. Since the new system also helped to diversify labor over the course of the year and raised production from one-half to two-thirds, it was nothing short of an agricultural miracle.

A third major innovation was the use of mills. The Romans had known about water mills but hardly used them, partly because they had enough slaves to be indifferent to labor-saving devices and partly because most Roman territories were not richly endowed with swiftly flowing streams. Starting around 1050, however, there was a veritable craze in northern Europe for building increasingly efficient water mills. One French area we know of saw a growth from 14 water mills in the eleventh century to 60 in the twelfth; in another part of France about 40 mills were built between 850 and 1080, 40 more between 1080 and 1125, and 245 between 1125 and 1175. Once Europeans had mastered the complex technology of building water mills, they turned

(3) use of mills

their attention to harnessing the power of wind: around 1170 they constructed the first European windmills. Thereafter, in flat lands like Holland that had no swiftly flowing streams, windmills proliferated as rapidly as water-powered ones had spread elsewhere. Although the major use of mills was to grind grain, they were soon adapted for a variety of other important functions: for example, they were employed to drive saws, process cloth, press oil, brew beer, provide power for iron forges, and crush pulp for manufacturing paper. Paper had been made in China and the Islamic world before this but never with the aid of paper mills, which is evidence of the technological sophistication the West was achieving in comparison to other advanced civilizations.

*(4) other technological
developments*

There were other important technological breakthroughs that gathered force around 1050 which should be mentioned. Several related to providing the means for using horses as farm animals. Around 800 a padded collar was first introduced into Europe; this allowed the horse to put his full weight into pulling without choking himself. Roughly a century later iron horseshoes were first used to protect hooves, and perhaps around 1050 tandem harnessing was developed to allow horses to pull behind each other. With these advances and the greater abundance of oats due to the three-field system, horses replaced oxen as farm animals in some parts of Europe and brought with them the advantages of working more quickly and working longer hours. Further inventions were the wheelbarrow and the harrow, a tool drawn over the field after the plow to level the earth and mix in the seed. Important for most of these inventions was the greater use of iron in the High Middle Ages to reinforce all sorts of agricultural implements, most crucially the parts of the heavy plow that came into contact with the soil.

So far we have been speaking of technological developments as if they alone account for the high-medieval agricultural revolution. But that is by no means the case. Along with improved technology came a

Peasants Bringing Grain to Windmills. Shown here are two different kinds of mills: those set to operate by prevailing winds and those that are pivoted to face into chance winds. Note how windmills dot the landscape.

great extension in the amount of land made arable and more intensive cultivation of the land already cleared. Although the Carolingians had begun to open the rich plain of northwestern Europe to tillage, they had only chosen to clear the most easily workable patches: a map of Carolingian agricultural settlements would show numerous tiny islands of cultivated lands surrounded by vast stretches of forests, swamps, and wastes. Starting around 1050, and greatly accelerating in the twelfth century, movements of land-clearing entirely changed the topography of northern Europe. First, greater peace and stability allowed farm workers in northern France and western Germany to begin pushing beyond the islands of settlement, clearing little bits of land at a time. At first they did this surreptitiously because they were poaching on territories that were actually owned by aristocratic lords. But then the aristocratic landowners gave their support to the clearing activities because they demanded their own profits from them. When that happened the work of clearing forests and draining swamps was carried on more swiftly. Thus, as the twelfth century progressed the isolated arable islands of Carolingian times expanded to meet each other. While this was going on, and continuing somewhat later, entirely new areas were colonized and opened to cultivation, for example, in northern England, Holland, and above all the eastern parts of Germany. Finally, in the twelfth and thirteenth centuries, peasants began working all the lands they had cleared more efficiently and intensively in order to gain more income for themselves. They harrowed after plowing, hoed frequently to keep down weeds, and added extra plowings to their yearly cycle, thereby greatly helping to renew the fertility of the soil.

Extension and intense cultivation of arable land

The result of all these changes was an enormous increase in agricultural production. With more land opened for cultivation obviously more crops were raised, but the increase was magnified by the introduction of more efficient farming methods. Thus, average yields from grains of seed sown increased from at best twofold in Carolingian times to three- or fourfold by around 1300. And all the additional grain could be ground far more rapidly than before because a mill could grind grain in the same time that it would have taken forty men to do the same job. Europeans, therefore, could for the first time begin to rely on a regular and stable food supply.

Enormous increase in agricultural productivity

That fact in turn had the profoundest consequences for the further development of European history. To begin with, it meant that more land could be given over to uses other than raising grain. Accordingly, as the High Middle Ages progressed, there was greater agricultural diversification and specialization. Large areas were turned over to sheep-raising, others to viniculture, and others to raising cotton and dyestuffs. Many of the products of these new enterprises were consumed locally, but many were also traded over long distances or used to provide the raw materials for new industries—above all those of cloth-making. The growth of this trade and manufacturing helped ini-

Consequences of the agricultural revolution

tiate and support, as we will see, the growth of towns. The agricultural boom also helped sustain the growth of towns in another way: by supporting a great spurt in population. With more food and a better diet (above all the increase in proteins) life expectancy increased from perhaps as low as an average of thirty years for the poor of Carolingian Europe to between forty and fifty years in the High Middle Ages. Healthier people also increased their birthrate. For these reasons the population of the West grew about threefold between about 1050 and 1300. More people and more labor-saving devices meant that not everybody had to stay on the farm: some could migrate to new towns and cities where they found a new way of life.

Other results

Still other results of the agricultural revolution were that it raised the incomes of lords, thereby underpinning a great increase in the sophistication of aristocratic life, and raised the incomes of monarchs, underpinning the growth of states. European-wide prosperity also helped support the growth of the Church and paid the way for the burgeoning of schools and intellectual enterprises. One final, more intangible, result was that Europeans apparently became more optimistic, more energetic, and more willing to experiment and take risks than any of their rivals on the world scene.

2. LORD AND SERF: SOCIAL CONDITIONS AND QUALITY OF LIFE IN THE MANORIAL REGIME

The meaning of the term
manorialism

While the agricultural revolution was going on, social and economic conditions began to change for both landowners and agricultural laborers. Since for much of the High Middle Ages, however, rural life revolved around the institution of the manor owned by lords and worked by serfs, it is best to describe this manorial regime in its most typical form before describing basic changes. In reading the following it should be understood that the term manorialism is not synonymous with feudalism: manorialism was an economic system in which large agricultural estates were worked by serfs, whereas feudalism, in the sense the word is used by most medieval historians, was a political system in which government was greatly decentralized (see the fourth section of this chapter). It should also be borne in mind that when scholars talk about manorialism based on a "typical manor" they are resorting to a historical approximation: no two manors were ever exactly alike, and many differed enormously in size and basic characteristics. Moreover, in those parts of Europe furthest away from the original centers of Carolingian settlement between the Seine and the Rhine, there were few, if any, manors at all. In Italy there was still much agriculture based on slavery, and in central and eastern Germany there were many smaller farms worked by free peasants.

The manor first clearly emerged in Carolingian times and continued

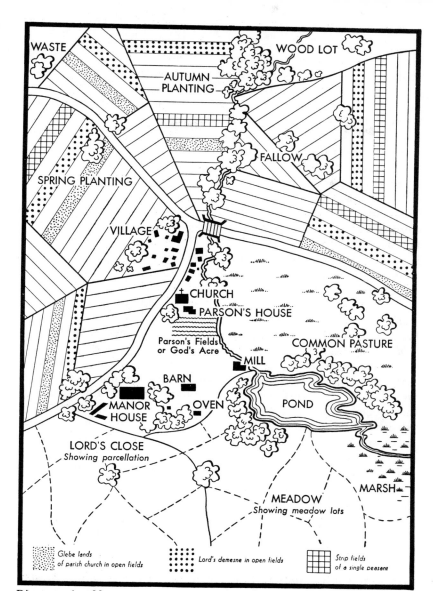

Diagram of a Manor

to be the dominant form of agrarian social and economic organization in most of northwestern Europe until about the thirteenth century. It descended from the large Roman landed estate, but, unlike the Roman estate, the manor was worked by serfs (sometimes called villeins) and not slaves. Serfs were definitely not free in the modern sense: above all, they could not leave their lands, were forced to work for their lords regularly without pay, were subject to numerous humiliating dues, and were most often subject to the jurisdiction of the lord's court. But they were much better off than slaves insofar as they were allocated

The manor; serfs

*The manorial system of
agriculture*

Living conditions of serfs

land which they cultivated to support themselves and which normally could not be taken away from them. Thus, when there were agricultural improvements the serfs themselves could hope to profit at least a little from them. More than that, although the lord theoretically had the right to levy dues at will, in practice obligations tended to remain fixed. Although the lot of the serf was surely terribly hard, he was seldom entirely at his lord's whim.

The lands of the manor, which might run from several hundred to several thousand acres, were divided into those that belonged to the lord and those that were allocated to the serfs. The former, called the lord's *demesne* (pronounced demean), usually comprised between a third and a half of the arable land. It was worked by the serfs on certain days, perhaps three days a week. The demesne did not consist of big parcels but was made up of narrow strips alternating with strips belonging to different peasants (and sometimes also strips set aside for the Church). All these strips were long and narrow because a heavy plow drawn by a yoke of horses or oxen could not be turned around easily. Because all the strips were generally separated only by a narrow band of unplowed turf, the whole regime is sometimes called the *open-field system.* Even when the serfs were working their own lands they almost always worked together because they usually owned farm animals and implements in common. For the same reason, grazing lands were called "commons" because the commonly owned herds grazed there together. In addition to cultivated fields and pastures, the serfs usually had their own small gardens. Most manors also had forests set aside primarily for the lord's hunting but which were also useful for the foraging of pigs and the gathering of firewood. Insofar as serfs were allowed to take advantage of such opportunities they did that too in common: indeed, the entire manorial system emphasized communal enterprise and solidarity.

Communalism must have helped make a barely endurable life seem slightly more bearable. Even though the lot of the medieval serf was surely far superior to that of the Roman slave, and even though it improved from around 1050 to 1300, it was still primitive and pitiful beyond modern comprehension. Dwellings were usually miserable hovels constructed of wattle—braided twigs—smeared over with mud. As late as the thirteenth century an English peasant was convicted of destroying his neighbor's house simply by sawing apart one central beam. The floors of most huts were usually no more than the bare earth, often cold or damp. For beds there was seldom more than bracken, and beyond that there was hardly any furniture. Not entirely jokingly it may be said that a good meal often consisted of two courses: one a porridge very much like gruel and the other a gruel very much like porridge. Fruit was almost unheard of and meager vegetables were limited to such fare as onions, leeks, turnips, and cabbages—all boiled to make a thin soup. Meat came at most a few times a year, either on holidays or deep in winter, when all the fodder for a scrawny ox or pig had run out. Cooking utensils were never cleaned, so as to make sure that there was never any waste. In addition, there was always the possibility of crop failures, which affected the serfs far more than their lords, since the lords demanded the same income as always. At such times the serfs were forced to surrender whatever grain they had and watched their children die slowly of starvation. It is particularly heart-rending to realize that children might be dying while there was still a bit of grain in the granaries: but that grain could not be touched because it was set aside as next year's seed, and without that there would be no future at all.

To counterbalance this grim picture we may now turn to patterns of change and improvement. One, as we have already seen, was dietary. In the High Middle Ages famines were actually far rarer than before and people grew stronger because some protein, mostly in the form of legumes, was added to their fare. There was also a widespread enfranchisement (i.e., freeing) of serfs for many reasons. Once landlords started opening up new lands, they could only attract laborers by guaranteeing their freedom. New centers of free labor usually attracted runaway serfs and became models of a new system whereby landlords asked for fixed rents rather than demanding services. Then, even on the old manors, lords began to realize that they might be able to raise profits by demanding rents instead of duties. Alternatively, serfs might become sufficiently rich by selling their excess produce at free markets to buy their freedom.

Improvements in the condition of serfs

In these different ways serfdom gradually came to an end throughout most of Europe in the course of the thirteenth century. The process, however, moved more or less swiftly in different areas—it was somewhat delayed in England and was seldom so complete that former serfs did not owe some remnant of labor service and dues to powerful local lords. In France some of these continued to exist as nagging indignities right up to the French Revolution in 1789. Serfs who became enfranchised often continued to work communally, but they were now free peasants who produced more for the open market than for their own subsistence.

The lords profited even more than their serfs from the agricultural revolution for several reasons. One was that whenever lords enfranchised serfs they obtained large sums of cash, usually about all the wealth that the serfs had hitherto amassed. Afterwards the lords lived mainly on their rents. Since some of these were levied on lands that the lords had once owned but had never been cultivated, noble income rose greatly. Even more than that, once the lords began to prefer rents to services, they found that rents were easier to increase. In their capacity as rent-collectors the lords did not personally supervise their lands as much as before but traveled more freely, sometimes going off crusading and sometimes living at royal courts. Consequently, added

Benefits of the agricultural revolution for lords

*The medieval nobility;
the rise of chivalry*

wealth allowed them to live better, and greater mobility gave them new ideas for improving their style of life.

Increased sophistication of the nobility was much enhanced by the fact that in the High Middle Ages there was less tumultuous local warfare than before. Until around 1100 the typical European noble was a crude and brutal warrior who spent most of his time engaging in combat with his neighbors and pillaging the defenseless. Much of this violence slackened off in the twelfth century as a result of ecclesiastical constraints, because emerging states were more effectively enforcing local peace, and because the nobles themselves were beginning to enjoy a more settled existence. Nobles continued to go on crusades and to fight in national wars, but they engaged in petty quarrels with each other less frequently. Apparently as an unconscious surrogate for the old fighting spirit the code of *chivalry* was developed. This channeled martial conduct into relatively benign activities. Chivalry literally means "horsemanship," and the chivalrous noble was expected to be thoroughly adept at the equestrian arts. Chivalry also imposed the obligation of fighting in defense of honorable causes; if none were to be found there were opportunities for combat in tournaments, mock battles that at first were quite savage but later became elaborate ceremonial affairs. Above all, the chivalric lord—typically a "knight" who owned less land than the upper aristocracy—was expected to be not only brave and loyal but generous, truthful, reverent, kind to the poor, and disdainful of unfair advantage or sordid gain.

By-products of the increase in noble wealth and the rise of chivalry

Jousting in a Tournament

Aristocratic Table Manners. There are knives but no forks or napkins on the table. The large stars mark these nobles as members of a chivalric order.

were improvements in the quality of living conditions and the treatment of women. Until around 1100 most noble dwellings were made of wood, and burned down frequently because of primitive heating and cooking methods. With increasing wealth and more advanced technology, castles after 1100 were usually built of stone and were thus far less flammable. Moreover, they were now equipped with chimneys and mantled fireplaces, both medieval inventions, which meant that instead of having one large fire in a central great hall, individual rooms could be heated and individuals gained some privacy. Nobles customarily ate fewer vegetables than peasants, but their diet was laden with meat; increased luxury trade also brought costly exotic spices like pepper and saffron to their tables. Although table manners were still atrocious—all used only knives and spoons but no forks and blew their noses on their sleeves—nobles tried to show their superiority to others by dressing elegantly, indeed ostentatiously. During this period snug-fitting clothing also became available because both knitting and the button and buttonhole had just been invented.

Improvements in the quality of noble life

The history of noble attitudes toward women in the High Middle Ages is somewhat controversial for two reasons. One is that most of our evidence comes from literature, and historians differ as to what degree literature actually reflects life. The other is that according to some scholars women were at best put on a pedestal, whereas modern women rightly prefer to move "up from the pedestal." Nonetheless, there can be no question that as the material quality of noble life improved it did so for women as well as men. More than that, there definitely was a revolution in some verbalized attitudes toward the female sex. Until the twelfth century, aside from a few female saints, women were virtually ignored in literature: the typical French epic told of bloody warlike deeds that either made no mention of women or portrayed them only in passing as being totally subservient. But within a few decades after 1100 noblewomen were suddenly turned into objects of veneration by lyric poets and writers of romances (see the following chapter). A typical troubadour poet could write of his lady

Changes in noble attitudes toward women

that "all I do that is fitting I infer from her beautiful body," and that "she is the tree and the branch where joy's fruit ripens."

Although the new "courtly" literature was extremely idealistic and somewhat artificial, it surely expressed the values of a gentler culture wherein upper-class women were in practice more respected than before. Moreover, there is no question that certain royal women in the twelfth and thirteenth centuries actually did rule their states on various occasions when their husbands or sons were dead or unable to do so. The indomitable Eleanor of Aquitaine, wife of Henry II, for example, helped rule England even though she was over seventy years old when her son Richard I went on a crusade from 1190 to 1194, and the strong-willed Blanche of Castile ruled France extremely well twice in the thirteenth century, once during the minority of her son Louis IX and again when he was off crusading. No doubt from a modern perspective high-medieval women were still very constrained, but from the point of view of the past the High Middle Ages was a time of progress for the women of the upper classes. The most striking symbol comes from the history of the game of chess: before the twelfth century chess was played in Eastern countries, but there the equivalent of the queen was a male figure, the king's chief minister, who could only move diagonally one square at a time; in twelfth-century western Europe, however, this piece was turned into a queen, and sometime before the end of the Middle Ages she began to move all over the board.

3. THE REVIVAL OF TRADE AND THE URBAN REVOLUTION

Inseparable from the agricultural revolution, the enfranchisement of serfs, and the growing sophistication of noble life was the revival of trade and the burgeoning of towns. Reviving trade was of many different sorts. Most fundamental was the mundane trade at local markets, where serfs or free peasants sold their excess grain or perhaps a few dozen eggs. But with growing specialization, produce like wine or cotton might be shipped over longer distances. River and sea routes were used wherever possible, but land transport was also necessary and this was aided by improvements in road-building, the introduction of packhorses and mules, and the building of bridges. Whereas the Romans were really only interested in land *communications,* medieval people, starting in the eleventh century, concentrated on land *transport* to the degree that they were much better able to maintain a vigorous land-based trade. And that is not to say that they ignored Mediterranean communications either. On the contrary, starting again in the eleventh century they began to make the former Roman "lake" the intermediary for an extensive seaborne trade that stretched over shorter and longer distances. Between 1050 and 1300 the Italian

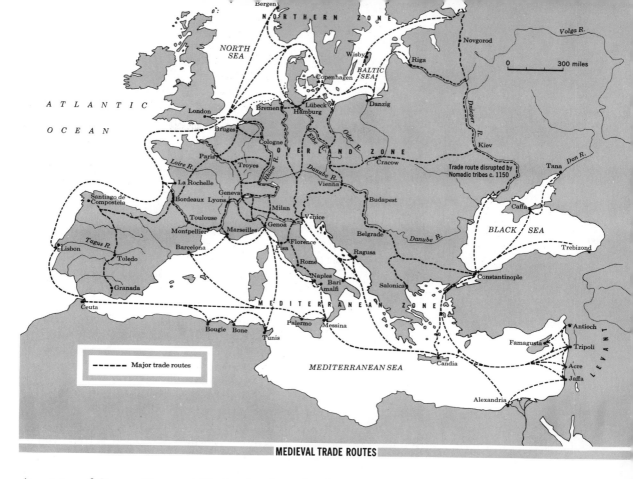

MEDIEVAL TRADE ROUTES

city-states of Genoa, Pisa, and Venice freed much of the Mediterranean from Muslim control, started monopolizing trade on formerly Byzantine waters, and began to establish in eastern Mediterranean outposts a flourishing commerce with the Orient. As a result, luxury goods such as spices, gems, perfumes, and fine cloths began to appear in Western markets and stimulated economic life by inspiring nobles to accelerate the agricultural revolution in order to pay for them.

This revival of trade called for new patterns of payment and the development of new commercial techniques. Most significantly, western Europe returned to a money economy after about four centuries when coined money was hardly used as a medium of exchange. The traditional manor had been almost self-sufficient and the few external items needed could be bartered for. But with the growth of markets coins became indispensable. At first these were coins of only the smallest denominations, but as luxury trade grew in the West the denominations increased apace; by the thirteenth century gold coins were minted by Italian states such as Florence and Venice.

In a similar pattern of development, long-distance traders were first itinerant merchants, often not unlike peddlers, but gradually they

The revival of a money economy

found it best to exhibit and sell their wares at international trade fairs. The most prosperous of these fairs were held in the French province of Champagne, where, for example, cloths from Flanders and spices brought by Italians from the East were exhibited and sold. Later, by around 1300, trade fairs declined because prosperous merchants were now sending out whole fleets from Italy to the north Atlantic and staying at home themselves. To facilitate this more sedentary pattern of business life, merchants perfected modern techniques of business partnerships, letters of credit, and accounting. Because such entrepreneurs invested in trade intentionally for profit and devised and used sophisticated credit mechanisms, most modern historians agree in calling them the first Western commercial capitalists.

In addition to the expansion of money and credit, trade was vastly facilitated by the rapid growth of towns. If we could imagine an aerial view of twelfth-century Europe, the mushrooming of towns would be the most strikingly visible phenomenon after the clearing of forests and wastes. Some historians misleadingly include under the heading of towns the numerous new agricultural village communities of peasants that were established in clearings. These, however, were not really urban in any sense. Putting them aside, many urban agglomerations were built from the ground up in the High Middle Ages, and existing towns that had barely survived from the Roman period grew enormously in size. To take some examples, in central and eastern Germany, which had not been part of the old Roman area of settlement, new towns such as Freiburg, Lübeck, Munich, and Berlin were founded in the twelfth century. Further west, where old Roman towns had become little more than episcopal residences or stockades, formerly insignificant towns like Paris, London, and Cologne roughly doubled in size between 1100 and 1200 and doubled again in the next century. Urban life was above all concentrated in Italy, which encompassed most of Europe's largest cities: Venice, Genoa, Milan, Bologna, Palermo, Florence, and Naples. In the thirteenth century the population of the largest of these—Venice, Genoa, and Milan—was in the range of 100,000. We lack accurate growth figures for other Italian cities, but it seems likely that many at least trebled in population between about 1150 and 1300 because we do know that the smaller Italian town of Imola, near Bologna, grew from some 4,200 in 1210 to 11,500 in 1312. Considering that town life had come very close to disappearing in most of Europe between 750 and 1050, it is warranted to speak of a high-medieval urban revolution. Moreover, from the High Middle Ages until now a vigorous urban life has been a major characteristic of western European and subsequently modern world civilization.

It used to be thought that the primary cause of the medieval urban revolution was the revival of long-distance trade. Theoretically, itinerant peddlers, who had no secure place in the dominantly agrarian so-

View of Paris. The city looked this way at the end of the Middle Ages, around 1480. Note the prominence of the cathedral of Notre Dame in the center and the large number of other church spires; note, too, how closely all the buildings are packed behind the walls.

ciety of Europe, gradually settled together in towns in order to offer each other much-needed protection and establish markets to sell their wares. In fact, the picture is far more complicated than that. While some towns did receive great stimulus from long-distance trade, and the growth of a major city such as Venice would have been unthinkable without it, most towns relied for their origin and early economic vitality far more on the wealth of their surrounding areas. These brought them surplus agricultural goods, raw materials for manufacture, and an influx of population. In other words, the quickening of economic life in general was the major cause of urban growth: towns existed in a symbiotic relationship with the countryside by providing markets and also wares made by artisans, while they lived off the rural food surplus and grew with the migration of surplus serfs or peasants who were seeking a better life. (Escaped serfs were guaranteed their freedom if they stayed in a town a year and a day.) Once towns started to flourish, many of them began to specialize in certain enterprises. Paris and Bologna gained considerable wealth by becoming the homes of leading universities; Venice, Genoa, Cologne, and London became centers of long-distance trade; and Milan, Ghent, and Bruges specialized in manufactures. The most important urban industries were those devoted to cloth-making. Cloth manufacturers sometimes developed techniques of large-scale production and investment that are ancestors of the modern factory system and industrial capitalism. But it must be emphasized that large industrial enterprises were atypical of medieval economic life as a whole.

Medieval cities and towns were not smaller-scale facsimiles of modern ones, and to our own eyes would have still seemed half-rural and uncivilized. Streets were often unpaved, houses had gardens for rais-

Causes of the urban revolution

Old Houses in Strassburg. In the Middle Ages food was stored in attics, with special openings for ventilation, as insurance against famine. Of course there was still much spoilage.

The Great Crane at Bruges. A pulley device operated by human energy. Animals wander through the narrow street in the background.

A Medieval Shoemaker

ing vegetables, and cows and pigs were kept in stables and pigsties. Passing along the streets of a major metropolis one might be stopped by a flock of bleating sheep or a crowd of honking geese. Sanitary conditions were often very poor and the air must often have reeked of excrement—both animal and human. Town-dwellers were cursed by the frequency of fires that swept quickly through closely settled wooden or straw quarters and went unstopped by the lack of fire stations. People were also highly susceptible to contagious diseases bred by unsanitary conditions and crowding. Still another problem was that economic tensions and family rivalries could lead to bloody riots. Yet for all this, urban folk took great pride in their new cities and ways of life. A famous paean to London, for example, written by a twelfth-century denizen of that city, boasted of its prosperity, piety, and perfect climate (!), and claimed that except for frequent fires, London's only nuisance was "the immoderate drinking of fools."

The most distinctive form of economic and social organization in the medieval towns was the guild. This was, roughly speaking, a professional association organized to protect and promote special interests. The main types were merchant guilds and craft guilds. The primary functions of the merchant guild were to maintain a monopoly of the local market for its members and to preserve a stable economic system. To accomplish these ends the merchant guild severely restricted trading by foreigners in the city, guaranteed to its members the right to participate in sales offered by other members, enforced uniform pricing, and did everything possible to ensure that no individual would corner the market for goods produced by its members.

Craft guilds similarly regulated the affairs of artisans. Usually their only full-fledged voting members were so-called master craftsmen, who were experts at their trades and ran their own shops. Hence if these guilds were anything like modern trade unions, they were unions of bosses. Second-class members of craft guilds were journeymen, who had learned their trades but still worked for the masters (*journeyman* is from the French *journée,* meaning "day," or by extension "day's work"), and apprentices. Terms of apprenticeship were carefully regulated: if an apprentice wished to become a master he often had to produce a "masterpiece" for judging by the masters of the guild. Craft guilds, like merchant guilds, sought to preserve monopolies and to limit competition. Thus they established uniformity of prices and wages, prohibited working after hours, and formulated detailed regulations governing methods of production and quality of materials. In addition to all their economic functions, both kinds of guilds served important social ones. Often they acted in the capacity of religious associations, benevolent societies, and social clubs. Wherever possible guilds tried to minister to the human needs of their members. Thus in some cities they came close to becoming miniature governments.

Town merchants and artisans were particularly concerned to protect themselves because they had no accepted role in the older medieval scheme of things. Usually merchants were disdained by the landed aristocracy because they could claim no ancient lineages and were not versed in the ways of chivalry. Worst of all, they were too obviously concerned with pecuniary gain. Although nobles too were gradually becoming interested in making profits, they displayed this less openly: they paid little attention in their daily lives to accounts and made much of their free-spending largesse. Still another reason why medieval

A Medieval Weaver

Medieval attitudes toward merchants

Medieval Walled City of Carcassonne, France. These walls date from 1240 to 1285.

A Medieval Tailor

*Significance of the urban
revolution: (1)
development of the
economy and government*

*(2) towns as a
foundation for intellectual
life*

merchants were on the defensive was that the Church, opposed to il-
licit gain, taught a doctrine of the "just price" that was often at
variance with what the merchants thought they deserved. Clergymen
too condemned usury—i.e., the lending of money for interest—even
though it was often essential for doing business. A decree of the Second Lateran Council of 1139, to take one example, excoriated the "de-
testable, shameful, and insatiable rapacity of moneylenders." As time
went on, however, attitudes slowly changed. In Italy it often became
hard to tell merchants from aristocrats because the latter customarily
lived in towns and often engaged in trade themselves. In the rest of
Europe, the most prosperous town-dwellers, called patricians, developed their own sense of pride verging on that of the nobility. The medieval Church never abandoned its prohibition of usury, but it did
come to approve making profits on commercial risks, which was
often close to the same thing. Moreover, starting around the thirteenth century leading churchmen came to speak more favorably of
merchants. St. Bonaventure, a leading thirteenth-century churchman,
argued that God showed special favors to shepherds like David in the
time of the Old Testament, to fishers like Peter in the time of the
New, and to merchants like St. Francis in the thirteenth century.

All in all, the importance of the high-medieval urban revolution can
scarcely be overestimated. The fact that the new towns were the vital
pumps of the high-medieval economy has already been sufficiently
emphasized: in providing markets and producing wares they kept the
entire economic system thriving. In addition, cities and towns made
important contributions to the development of government because in
many areas they gained their own independence and ruled themselves
as city-states. Primarily in Italy, where urban life was by far the most
advanced, city governments experimented with new systems of tax-
collecting, record-keeping, and public participation in decision-making. Italian city-states were particularly advanced in their administrative techniques and thereby helped influence a general European-wide
growth in governmental sophistication.

Finally, the rise of towns contributed greatly to the quickening of
intellectual life in the West. New schools were invariably located in
towns because towns afforded domiciles and legal protection for
scholars. At first, students and teachers were always clerics, but by the
thirteenth century the needs of merchants to be trained in reading and
accounting led to the foundation of numerous lay primary schools.
Equally momentous for the future was the fact that the stimulating
urban environment helped make advanced schools more open to intellectual experimentation than any in the West since those of the Greeks.
Not coincidentally, Greek intellectual life too was based on thriving
cities. Thus it seems that without commerce in goods there can be
little exciting commerce in ideas.

4. FEUDALISM AND THE RISE OF THE NATIONAL MONARCHIES

If any western European city of around 1200 epitomized Europe's greatest new accomplishments it was Paris: that city was not only a bustling commercial center and an important center of learning, it was also the capital of what was becoming Europe's most powerful government. France, like England and the new Christian kingdoms of the Iberian peninsula, was taking shape in the twelfth and thirteenth centuries as a *national monarchy,* a new form of government which was to dominate Europe's political future. Because the developing national monarchies were the most successful and promising European governments we must concentrate on them, but before we do it is well to see what was happening from the political point of view in Germany and Italy.

*The national monarchy as
a political innovation*

Around 1050 Germany was unquestionably the most centralized and best-ruled territory in Europe, but by 1300 it had fallen into a congeries of warring petty states. Since most other areas of Europe were gaining stronger rule in the very same period, the political decline of Germany becomes an intriguing historical problem. It is also a problem of fundamental importance because from a political point of view Germany only caught up with the rest of Europe in the nineteenth century: in trying to gain its full place in the European political system as late as then it created difficulties that have just come to be resolved in our own age.

*The political decline of
medieval Germany an
intriguing historical
problem*

The major sources of Germany's strength from the reign of Otto the Great in the middle of the tenth century until the latter part of the eleventh century were its succession of strong rulers, its resistance to political fragmentation, and the close alliance of its crown with the Church. By resoundingly defeating the Hungarians and taking the title of emperor, Otto kept the country from falling prey to further invasions and won great prestige for the monarchy. For over a century afterwards there was a nearly uninterrupted succession of rulers as able and vigorous as Otto. Their nearest political rivals were the dukes, military leaders of five large German territories (Lorraine, Saxony, Franconia, Swabia, and Bavaria), but throughout most of this period the dukes were overawed by the emperors' greater power. The latter, in order to rule their wide territories—which included Switzerland, eastern France, and most of the Low Countries, as well as claims to northern Italy—relied heavily on cooperation with the Church. The leading royal administrators were archbishops and bishops whom the emperors appointed without interference from the pope and who often came from their own families. The German emperors were so strong that, when they chose to do so, they could come down to Italy

*The German monarchy in
the tenth and eleventh
centuries*

*The struggle between
Henry IV and Gregory
VII*

and name their own popes. The archbishops and bishops ran the German government fairly well for the times without any elaborate administrative machinery, and they counterbalanced the strength of the dukes. In the course of the eleventh century the emperors were starting tentatively to develop their own secular administration. Had they been allowed to continue this policy, it might have provided a really solid governmental foundation for the future. But just then the whole system shaped by Otto the Great and his successors was dramatically challenged by a revolution within the Church.

The challenge to the German government came in the reign of Henry IV (1056–1106) and was directed by Pope Gregory VII (1073–1085). For reasons that will be discussed in the next chapter, Gregory wished to free the Church from secular control and launched a struggle to achieve this aim against Henry IV. Gregory immediately placed Henry on the defensive by forging an alliance with the dukes and other German princes, who only needed a sufficient pretext to rise up against their ruler. When the princes threatened to depose Henry because of his disobedience to the pope, the hitherto mighty ruler was forced to seek absolution from Gregory VII in one of the most melodramatic scenes of the Middle Ages. In the depths of winter in 1077 Henry hurried over the Alps to abase himself before the pope in the north Italian castle of Canossa. As Gregory described the scene in a letter to the princes: "There on three successive days, standing before the castle gate, laying aside all royal insignia, barefooted and in coarse attire, Henry ceased not with many tears to beseech the apostolic help and comfort." No German ruler had ever been so humiliated. Although the events at Canossa forestalled Henry's deposition, they robbed him of his great prestige. By the time his struggle with the papacy, continued by his son, was over, the princes had won far more practical independence from the crown than they had ever had. More than that, in 1125 they made good their claims to be able to elect a new ruler regardless of hereditary succession—a principle that would thereafter often lead them to choose the weakest successors or to embroil the country in civil war. Meanwhile, the crown had lost much of its control of the Church and thus in effect had its administrative rug pulled out from under it. While France and England were gradually consolidating their centralized governmental apparatuses, Germany was losing its own.

Frederick Barbarossa

A major attempt to stem the tide running against the German monarchy was made in the twelfth century by Frederick I (1152–1190), who came from the family of Hohenstaufen. Frederick, called "Barbarossa" (meaning "red beard"), tried to reassert his imperial dignity by calling his realm the "Holy Roman Empire," on the theory that it was a universal empire descending from Rome and blessed by God. Laying claim to Roman descent, he promulgated old Roman imperial laws—preserved in the Code of Justinian—that gave him much theoretical power. But he could not hope to enforce such laws unless he had his own material base of support. Therefore the major policy of his reign was to balance the power of the princes by carving out his own geographical domain from which he might draw wealth and strength.

Unfortunately for Frederick, his ancestral lands were located in Swabia, a poorer part of Germany that even today still consists of relatively unproductive hill country and the Black Forest. So Frederick decided to make northern Italy his power base in addition to Swabia. In this he could hardly have made a worse decision. Northern Italy was certainly wealthy, but it was also fiercely independent. Its rich towns and cities, led by Milan, offered stiff resistance. They were further lent helpful moral support by the papacy, which had no wish to see a strong German emperor ruling powerfully in Italy. Frederick came very close to overpowering the urban-papal alliance but ultimately the Alps proved to be too great a barrier to allow him to enforce his will in Italy and hope to rule in Germany as well. Whenever he subdued the towns he would shortly afterwards have to leave for home, and the towns, with papal encouragement, would then rise up again. Finally, in 1176, insufficient German imperial forces were resoundingly defeated by the troops of a north Italian urban coalition at Legnano, and Barbarossa was forced to concede the area's de facto independence. In the meantime, the princes in Germany were continuing to gather strength, especially by colonizing the rich agricultural lands east of the Elbe where Frederick really should have busied himself, and the emperor's struggle with the popes further alienated elements within the German church. Because Barbarossa was a dashing figure he was well remembered by Germans, but his reign virtually made it certain that the German empire would not rise again during the medieval period.

The reign of Barbarossa's equally famous grandson, Frederick II (1212–1250), was merely a playing out of Germany's fate. In terms of his personality Frederick was probably the most fascinating of all medieval rulers. Because his father, Henry VI, had inherited through marriage the kingdom of southern Italy and Sicily (later called the Kingdom of the Two Sicilies), Frederick grew up in Palermo, where he absorbed elements of Islamic culture. (Arabs had ruled in Sicily for two and a half centuries, from 831 to 1071.) Frederick II spoke five or six languages, was a patron of learning, and wrote his own book on falconry, which takes an honored place in the early history of Western observational science. He also performed bizarre and brutal "experiments," such as disemboweling men to observe the comparative effects of rest and exercise upon digestion. Such practices corresponded to Frederick's overall policy of trying to rule like an Oriental despot. In his autonomous kingdom of southern Italy he introduced Eastern forms of absolutist and bureaucratic government. He established a

Frederick's Italian policy

Frederick Barbarossa. A stylized contemporary representation.

Frederick II; his personality and policies

The Emperor Frederick II. He is shown holding a *fleur de lis,* as a symbol of rule, with a falcon, his favorite bird, at his side.

The political situation in high-medieval Italy

professional army, levied direct taxation, and promulgated uniform Roman law. Typically, Frederick tried to create a ruler cult and decreed it an act of sacrilege even to discuss his statutes or judgments. For a while these policies seemed successful in ruling southern Italy, but Frederick's power base in Italy led to renewed conflicts with the papacy and the north Italian cities. These dragged on indecisively until his death, but thereafter the papacy was resolved to see no further Hohenstaufens ruling in Italy and proceeded to eliminate the remaining contenders from the line by calling crusades against them. Overtaxed by Frederick's ruthlessness and subsequent wars, southern Italy gradually sank into the backwardness from which it is only barely emerging today. And Frederick's reign was as damaging to Germany as well. Bent on pursuing his Italian policies without hindrance, Frederick formally wrote Germany off to the princes by granting them large areas of sovereignty. Although titular "emperors" afterwards continued to be elected, the princes were the real rulers of the country. Yet they fought with each other so much that peace was rare, and they subdivided their lands among their heirs to such an extent that the map of Germany began to look like a jig-saw puzzle. As the French philosopher Voltaire later said, the German "Holy Roman Empire" had become neither holy, nor Roman, nor an empire.

The story of high-medieval Italian politics may be told more quickly. Southern Italy and Sicily had been welded together into a strong monarchical state in the twelfth century by Norman-French descendants of the Vikings. But then, as we have seen, the area went to the Hohenstaufens and was subsequently brought to ruin. Central Italy was largely ruled by the papacy in the High Middle Ages, but the popes were seldom strong enough to create a really well-governed state, partly because they were at constant loggerheads with the German emperors. Farthest north were the rich commercial and manufacturing cities which had successfully fought off Barbarossa. These were usually organized politically in the form of republics or "communes." They offered much participation in governmental life to their more prosperous inhabitants. But because of diverse economic interests and family antagonisms, the Italian cities were usually riven with internal strife. Moreover, although they could unite in leagues against foreign threats such as those represented by Barbarossa or Frederick II, the cities often fought each other when foreign threats were absent. The result was that although economic and cultural life was very far advanced in the Italian cities, and although the cities made important experiments in administrative techniques, political stability was widely lacking in northern Italy throughout most of the high-medieval period.

If one looks for the centers of growing political stability in Europe, then one has to seek them in high-medieval France and England. Ironically, some of the most basic foundations for future political achievement in France were established without any planning just

GERMAN EMPIRE c. 1200 A.D.

when that area was most politically unstable. These foundations were aspects of a level of political decentralization often referred to by historians as the system of "feudalism." The use of this word is controversial because ever since Marx some historians prefer to use it as a term to describe an agrarian economic and social system wherein large estates are worked by a dependent peasantry. The difficulty with this usage is that it is too imprecise, for such large estates existed in many times and places beyond the European Middle Ages and the medieval agrarian system can best be called manorialism. Some historians on

Feudalism: a controversial term

the other extreme argue that even if the word feudalism is used to describe a medieval political system, medieval realities were so diverse that no one definition of feudalism can accurately or even usefully be extended to cover more than a single case. Nonetheless, for convenience we can retain the use of the word here and apply it to a specific point in medieval political development so long as we bear in mind that, like manorialism, it is only meant to serve as any approximation and that other historians may use it as a term for economic or sociological analysis.

Political feudalism

Political feudalism was essentially a system of extreme political decentralization wherein what we today would call public power was widely vested in private hands. From a historical perspective it was most fully experienced in France during the tenth century when the Carolingian empire had disintegrated and the area was being buffeted by devastating Viking invasions. The Carolingians had maintained a modicum of public authority, but they proved to be no help whatsoever in warding off the invasions. So local landlords had to fend for themselves. In the end, the landlords turned out to offer the best defense against the Vikings and accordingly were able to acquire practically all the old governmental powers. They raised their own small armies, dispensed their own crude justice, and occasionally issued their own primitive coins. Despite such decentralization, however, it was never forgotten that there once had been higher and larger units of government. Above all, no matter how weak the king was (and he was indeed usually very weak), there always remained a king in France who descended directly or indirectly from the western branch of the Carolingians. There also were scattered remaining dukes or counts, who in theory were supposed to have more power and authority than petty landlords or knights. So, by a complicated and hard-to-trace process of rationalization, a vague theory was worked out in the course of the tenth and eleventh centuries that tried to establish some order within feudalism. According to this, minor feudal lords did not hold their powers outright but only held them as so-called *fiefs* (rhymes with reefs), which could be revoked upon noncompliance with certain obligations. In theory—and much of this theory was ignored in practice for long periods of time—the king or higher lords granted fiefs, that is, governmental rights over various lands, to lesser lords in return for a stipulated amount of military service. In turn, the lesser lords could grant some of those fiefs to still lesser lords for military services until the chain stopped at the lowest level of knights. The holder of a fief was called a *vassal* of the granter, but this term had none of the demeaning connotations that it has gained today. Vassalage—much unlike serfdom—was a purely honorable status and all fief-holders were "noble."

Since feudalism was originally a form of decentralization, it once was considered by historians to have been a corrosive or divisive historical force; in common speech today many use the word feudal as a synonym for backward. But scholars more recently have come to the conclusion that feudalism was a force for progress and a fundamental point of departure for the growth of the modern state. They note that in areas such as Germany and Italy, where there was hardly any feudalism, political stabilization and unification came only in later times, whereas in the areas of France and England, which saw full feudalization, stabilization and governmental centralization came rapidly afterwards. Scholars now posit several reasons for this. Because feudalism was originally spontaneous and makeshift, it was highly flexible. Local lords, instead of being bound by anachronistic, procrustean principles, could rule as seemed best at the moment, or could bend to the dictates of particular local customs. Thus their governments, however crude, worked the best for their times and could be used for building an even stronger government as time went on. A second reason for the effectiveness of feudalism was that it drew more people into direct contact with the actual workings of political life than had the old Roman or Carolingian systems. Government on the most local level could most easily be seen or experienced; as it became tangible people began to appreciate and identify with it far more than they had appreciated empires. The result was that feudalism inculcated growing governmental loyalty, and once that loyalty was developed it could be drawn upon by still larger units. Thirdly, feudalism helped lead to certain more modern institutions by its emphasis on courts. As the feudal system became more regularized, it became customary for vassals to appear at the court of their overlords at least once a year. There they were expected to "pay court," i.e., show certain ceremonial signs of loyalty, and also to serve on "courts" in the sense of participating in trials and offering counsel. Thus they became more and more accustomed to performing governmental business and began to behave more like courtiers or politicians. As the monarchical states of France and England themselves developed, kings saw how useful the feudal court was and made it the administrative kernel of their expanding governmental systems. A final reason why feudalism led to political progress is not really intrinsic to the system itself. Because the theory of larger units was never forgotten, it could be drawn upon by greater lords and kings when the right time came to reacquire their rights.

The greatest possibilities for the use of feudalism were first demonstrated in England after the Norman Conquest of 1066. We have seen that England became unified and enjoyed strong kingship under the Saxon Alfred and his successors in the late ninth and tenth centuries. But then the Saxon kingship began to weaken, primarily as the result of renewed Viking invasions and poor leadership. In 1066 William, the duke of Normandy (in western France), laid claim to the English crown and crossed the Channel to conquer what he had claimed. For-

*Feudalism as a cause of
political progress*

The Norman Conquest

Battle of Hastings. A scene from the Bayeux tapestry, embroidered shortly after William the Conqueror's victory. The inscription reads in translation: "Here the English and French have fallen together in battle."

tunately for him the newly installed English king, Harold, had just warded off a Viking attack in the north and thus could not offer resistance at full strength. At the Battle of Hastings Harold and his Saxon troops fought bravely, but ultimately could not withstand the onslaught of the fresher Norman troops. As the day waned Harold fell, mortally wounded by a random arrow, his forces dispersed, and the Normans took the field and with it, England. Duke William now became King William, the Conqueror, and proceeded to rule his new prize as he wished.

The feudal system in Norman England

With hindsight we can say that the Norman Conquest came at just the right time to preserve and enhance political stability. Before 1066 England was threatened with disintegration under warrior aristocrats called earls, but William destroyed their power entirely. In its place he substituted the feudal system, whereby all the land in England was newly granted in the form of fiefs held directly or indirectly from the king. Fief-holders had most of the governmental rights they had obtained less formally on the Continent, but William retained the prerogatives of coining money, collecting a land tax, and supervising justice in major criminal cases. He also retained the Anglo-Saxon officer of local government, known as the sheriff, to help him administer and enforce these rights. In order to make sure that none of his barons (the English term for major fief-holders) became too powerful, William was careful to scatter the fiefs granted to them throughout various parts of the country. In these ways William used feudal practices to help govern England when there were not yet enough trained administrators to allow any real governmental professionalization. But he also retained much royal power and kept the country thoroughly unified under the crown.

The history of English government in the two centuries after William is primarily a story of kings tightening up the feudal system to their advantage until they superseded it and created a strong national monarchy. The first to take steps in this direction was the Conqueror's energetic son Henry I (1100–1135). One of his most important accomplishments was to start a process of specialization at the royal court whereby certain officials began to take full professional responsibility for supervising financial accounts; these officials became known as clerks of the *Exchequer*. Another accomplishment was to institute a system of traveling circuit-judges to administer justice as direct royal representatives in various parts of the realm.

After an intervening period of civil war Henry I was succeeded by his grandson Henry II (1154–1189), who was very much in his grandfather's activist mold. Henry II's reign was certainly one of the most momentous in all of English history. One reason for this was that it saw a great struggle between the king and the flamboyant archbishop of Canterbury, Thomas Becket, over the status of Church courts and Church law. In Henry's time priests and other clerics were tried for any crimes in Church courts under the rules of canon law. Punishment in these courts was notoriously lax. Even murderers were seldom sentenced to more than penance and loss of their clerical status. Also, decisions handed down in English Church courts could be appealed to the papal *curia* in Rome. Henry, who wished to have royal law prevail as far as possible and maintain judicial standards for all subjects in his realm, tried to limit these practices by the Constitutions of Clarendon of 1164. On the matter of clerics accused of crime he was willing to compromise by allowing them to be judged in Church courts but then

The growth of national monarchy in England; the reign of Henry I

The struggle between Henry II and Thomas Becket

Martyrdom of Thomas Becket. From a thirteenth-century English Psalter. One of the knights has struck Becket so mightily that he has broken his sword.

have them sentenced in royal ones. Becket, however, resisted all attempts at change with great determination. The quarrel between king and archbishop was made more bitter by the fact that the two had earlier been close friends. It reached a tragic climax when Becket was murdered in Canterbury Cathedral by four of Henry's knights, after the king, in an outburst of anger, had rebuked them for doing nothing to rid him of his antagonist. The crime so shocked the English public that Becket was quickly revered as a martyr and became the most famous English saint. More important for the history of government, Henry had to abandon most of his program of bringing the Church courts under royal control, and his aims were only fulfilled in the sixteenth century with the coming of the English Reformation.

*The judicial reforms of
Henry II*

Despite this major setback, Henry II made enormous governmental gains in other areas, so much so that some historians maintain that Henry was the greatest king that England has ever known. His most important contributions were judicial. He greatly expanded the use of the itinerant judges instituted by Henry I and began the practice of commanding sheriffs to bring before these judges groups of men who were familiar with local conditions. These were then required to report under oath every case of murder, arson, robbery, or other major crimes known to them to have occurred since the judges' last visit. This was the origin of the grand jury. Henry also for the first time allowed parties in civil disputes to obtain royal justice. In the most prevalent type of case, someone who claimed to have been recently dispossessed of his land could obtain a writ from the crown, which would order the sheriff to bring twelve men who were assumed to know the facts before a judge. The twelve were then asked under oath if the plaintiff's claim was true, and the judge rendered his decision in accordance with their answers. Out of such practices grew the institution of the trial jury.

*The benefits of Henry's
legal work*

Henry II's legal innovations benefited both the crown and the country in several ways. Most obviously, they made justice more uniform and equitable throughout the realm. They also thereby made royal justice sought after and popular. Particularly in disputes over land—the most important and frequent disputes of the day—the weaker party was no longer at the mercy of a strong-arming neighbor. Usually the weaker parties were knights, with whom the crown before then had not been in close touch. In helping defend their rights Henry gained valuable allies in his policy of keeping the stronger barons in tow. Finally, the widespread use of juries in Henry's reign brought more and more people into actual participation in royal government. In so doing it got them more interested in government and more loyal to government. Since these people served without pay, Henry brilliantly managed to expand the competence and popularity of his government at very little cost.

The most concrete proof of Henry II's success is that after his death his government worked so well that it more or less ran on its own.

Henry's son, the swashbuckling Richard I, the "Lionhearted," ruled for ten years, from 1189 to 1199, but in that time he only stayed in England for six months because he was otherwise engaged in crusading or defending his possessions on the Continent. Throughout the time of Richard's absence governmental administration actually became more efficient, owing to the work of capable ministers. The country also raised two huge sums for Richard by taxation: one to pay for his crusade to the Holy Land and the other to buy his ransom when he was captured by an enemy on his return. But later when a new king needed still more money, most Englishmen were disinclined to pay it.

King John. An effigy in Worcester cathedral.

The new king was Richard's brother, John (1199–1216), who has the reputation of being a villain but was more a victim of circumstances. Ever since the time of William the Conqueror, English kings had continued to rule in large portions of modern-day France, but by John's reign the kings of France were becoming strong enough to take back much of these territories. John had the great misfortune of facing the able French King Philip Augustus, who won back Normandy and neighboring lands by force of arms in 1204 and reinsured this victory by military successes in 1214. John needed money both to govern England and to fight in France, but his defeats made his subjects disinclined to give it to him. The barons particularly resented John's financial exigencies and in 1215 they made him renounce these in the subsequently famous Magna Carta (Great Charter), a document which was also designed to redress all the other abuses the barons could think of. Most common conceptions of Magna Carta are erroneous. It was not intended to be a bill of rights or a charter of liberties for the common man. On the contrary, it was basically a feudal document in which the king as overlord pledged to respect the traditional rights of his vassals. Nonetheless, it did enunciate in writing the important principles that large sums of money could not be raised by the crown without consent given by the barons in a common council, and that no free man could be punished by the crown without judgment by his equals and by the law of the land. Above all, Magna Carta was important as an expression of the principle of limited government and of the idea that the king is bound by the law.

As the contemporary American medievalist J. R. Strayer has said, "Magna Carta made arbitrary government difficult, but it did not make centralized government impossible." In the century following its issuance, the progress of centralized government continued apace. In the reign of John's son, Henry III (1216–1277), the barons vied with the weak king for control of the government but did so on the assumption that centralized government itself was a good thing. Throughout that period administrators continued to perfect more efficient legal and administrative institutions. Whereas in the reign of Henry I financial administration began to become a specialized bureau of the royal court, in the reign of Henry III this became true of legal administration (the creation of permanent High Courts) and adminis-

*The progress of
centralized government in
the reign of Henry III*

*Origins of the English
Parliament*

tration of foreign correspondence (the so-called Chancery). English central government was now fully developing a trained officialdom.

The last and most famous branch of the medieval English governmental system was Parliament. This gradually emerged as a separate branch of government in the decades before and after 1300, above all owing to the wishes of Henry III's son, Edward I (1272–1307). Although Parliament later became a check against royal absolutism, nothing could be further from the truth than to think that its first meetings were "demanded by the people." In its origins Parliament actually had little to do with popular representation, but was rather the king's feudal court in its largest gathering. Edward I was a strong king who called Parliaments frequently to raise money as quickly and efficiently as possible in order to help finance his foreign wars. Those present at Parliaments were not only expected to give their consent to taxation—in fact, it was virtually inconceivable for them to refuse—but while they were there they were told why taxes were necessary so that they would pay them less grudgingly. They could also agree upon details of collection and payment. At the same meetings Edward could take advice about pressing concerns, have justice done for exceptional cases, review local administration, and promulgate new laws. Probably the most unusual trait of Edward's Parliaments in comparison to similar assemblies on the Continent was that they began to include representatives from the counties and towns in addition to the higher nobility. These representatives, however, scarcely spoke for "the people" because most of the people of England were unfranchised serfs and peasants—not to mention women, who were never consulted in any way. Most likely, Edward had predominantly financial motives for calling representatives from the "commons." He probably also realized the propaganda value of overawing local representatives with royal grandeur at impressive parliamentary meetings so that they would then spread a favorable impression of the monarchy back home. As time went on, commoners were called to Parliament so often that they became a recognized part of its organization: by the middle of the fourteenth century they sat regularly in their own "house." But they still represented only the prosperous people of countryside and towns and were usually manipulated by the crown or the nobles.

Edward I's reign also saw the culmination of the development of a strong national monarchy in other aspects. By force of arms Edward nearly unified the entire island of Britain, conquering Wales and almost subduing Scotland (which, however, was to rise up again soon after his death). Edward began the practice of regularly issuing statute law, that is, original public legislation designed to apply indefinitely to the entire realm. Because of his role as a law-giver, Edward is sometimes referred to as the "English Justinian." Most important, Edward also curtailed the feudal powers of his barons by limiting their rights

*The English monarchy
under Edward I*

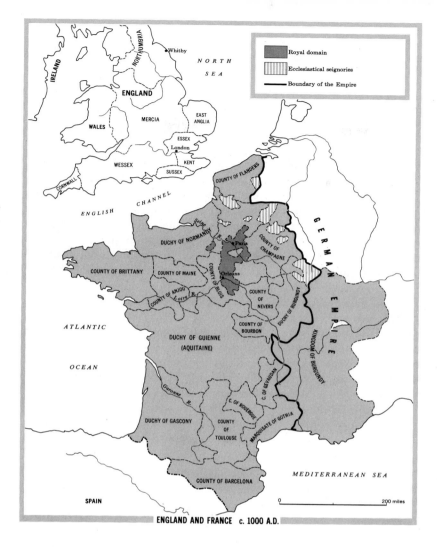

ENGLAND AND FRANCE c. 1000 A.D.

to hold private courts and to grant their own lands as fiefs. Thus, by the end of his reign much of the independent power once consciously vested with the barons by William the Conqueror was being taken away from them. The explanation for this is that in the intervening high-medieval centuries the king was developing his own royal institutions of government to the degree that old-fashioned feudalism was now no longer of any real service. Because Edward pressed his strong government and financial demands somewhat excessively for the spirit of the age, there was an antimonarchical reaction after his death. But it is striking that after Edward's time whenever there were baronial rebellions they were always made on the assumption that England would remain a unified country, governed by the basic high-medieval monarchical institutions. England was unified around the crown in

*The process of political
centralization in France*

the High Middle Ages and would remain a basically well-governed and unified country right up to modern times.

While the process of governmental centralization was making impressive strides in England, it developed more slowly in France. But by around 1300 it had come close to reaching the same point of completion. French governmental unification proceeded more slowly because France in the eleventh century was more decentralized than England and faced greater problems. The last of the weak Carolingian monarchs was replaced in 987 by Hugh Capet, the count of Paris, but the new Capetian dynasty—which was to rule without interruption until 1328—was at first no stronger than the old Carolingian one. Even through most of the twelfth century the kings of France ruled directly only in a small area around Paris known as the Ile-de-France, roughly the size of Vermont. Beyond that territory the kings had shadowy claims to being the feudal overlords of numerous counts and dukes throughout much of the area of modern France, but for practical purposes those counts and dukes were almost entirely independent. It was said that when the king of France demanded homage from the first duke of Normandy, the duke had one of his warriors pretend to kiss the king's foot but then seize the royal leg and pull the king over backwards, to the mockery of all those present. While the French kingship was so weak, the various parts of France were developing their own distinct local traditions and dialects. Thus, whereas William the Conqueror inherited in England a country that had already been unified and was just on the verge of falling apart, the French kings of the High Middle Ages had to unify their country from scratch, with only a vague reminiscence of Carolingian unity to build upon.

*Factors facilitating the
growth of the French
monarchy*

In many respects, however, luck was on their side. First of all, they were fortunate for hundreds of years in having direct male heirs to succeed them. Consequently, there were no deadly quarrels over the right of succession. In the second place, most of the French kings lived to an advanced age, the average period of rule being about thirty years. That meant that sons were already mature men when they came to the throne and there were few regencies to squander the royal power during the minority of a prince. More than that, the kings of France were always highly visible, if sometimes not very imposing, when there were power struggles elsewhere, so people in neighboring areas became accustomed to thinking of the kingship as a force for stability in an unstable world. A third favorable circumstance for the French kings was the growth of agricultural prosperity and trade in their home region; this provided them with important sources of revenue. A fourth fortuitous development was that the kings were able to gain the support of the popes because the latter usually needed allies in their incessant struggles with the German emperors. The popes lent the French kings prestige, as they earlier had done for the Carolingians, and they also allowed them much direct power over the local

Church, thereby bringing the kings further income and influence from patronage. A fifth factor in the French king's favor was the growth in the twelfth and thirteenth centuries of the University of Paris as the leading European center of studies. As foreigners came flocking to the university, they learned of the French king's growing authority and spread their impressions when they returned home. Finally, and by no means least of all, great credit must be given to the shrewdness and vigor of several of the French kings themselves.

The first noteworthy Capetian king was Louis VI, "the Fat" (1108–1137). While accomplishing nothing startling, Louis at least managed to pacify his home base, the Ile-de-France, by driving out or subduing its turbulent "robber barons." Once this was accomplished, agriculture and trade could prosper and the intellectual life of Paris could start to flourish. Thereafter, the French kings had a geographical source of power of exactly the kind that the German ruler Barbarossa sought but never found. The really startling additions to the realm were made by Louis's grandson, Philip Augustus (1180–1223). Philip was wily enough to know how to take advantage of certain feudal rights in order to win large amounts of western French territory from the English King John. He was also decisive enough to know how to defend his gains in battle. Most impressive of all, Philip worked out an excellent formula for governing his new acquisitions. Since these increased his original lands close to fourfold, and since each new area had its own highly distinct local customs, it would have been hopeless to try to enforce strict governmental standardization by means of what was then a very rudimentary administrative system. Instead, Philip allowed his new provinces to maintain most of their indigenous governmental practices but superimposed on them new royal officials known as *baillis*. These officials were entirely loyal to Philip because they never came from the regions in which they served and were paid impressive salaries for the day. They had full judicial, administrative, and military authority in their bailiwicks: on royal orders they tolerated regional diversities but guided them to the king's advantage. Thus there were no revolts in the conquered territories and royal power was enhanced. This pattern of local diversity balanced against bureaucratic centralization was to remain the basic pattern of French government. Thus Philip Augustus can be seen as an important founder of the modern French state.

Foundations of the French monarchy; Louis VI and Philip Augustus

A Seal Depicting Philip Augustus

In the brief reign of Philip's son, Louis VIII (1223–1226), almost all of southern France was added to the crown in the name of intervention against religious heresy. Once incorporated, this territory was governed largely on the same principles laid down by Philip. The next king, Louis IX (1226–1270), was so pious that he was later canonized by the Church and is commonly referred to as St. Louis. He ruled strongly and justly (except for great intolerance of Jews and heretics), decreed a standardized coinage for the country, perfected the judicial

St. Louis

King Philip the Fair of France

*Comparison of England
and France*

system, and brought France a long, golden period of internal peace. Because he was so well-loved, the monarchy lived off his prestige for many years afterwards.

That prestige, however, came close to being squandered by St. Louis's more ruthless grandson, Philip IV, "the Fair" (1285–1314). Philip fought many battles at once, seeking to round out French territories in the northeast and southwest and to gain full control over the French Church instead of sharing it with the pope in Rome. All these activities forced him to accelerate the process of governmental centralization, especially with the aim of trying to raise money. Thus his reign saw the quick formulation of many administrative institutions that came close to completing the development of medieval French government, as the contemporary reign of Edward I did in England. Philip's reign also saw the calling of assemblies that were roughly equivalent to the English Parliaments, but these—later called "Estates General"—never played a central role in the French governmental system. Philip the Fair was successful in most of his ventures; above all, as we will later see, in reducing the pope to the level of a virtual French figurehead. After his death there would be an antimonarchical reaction, as there was at the same time in England, but by his reign France was unquestionably the strongest power in Europe. With only a sixteenth-century interruption, it would remain so until the nineteenth century.

While England and France followed certain similar processes of monarchical centralization and nation-building, they were also marked by basic differences that are worth describing because they were to typify differences in development for centuries after. England, a far smaller country than France, was much better unified. Aside from Wales and Scotland, there were no regions in Britain that had such different languages or traditions that they thought of themselves as separate territories. Correspondingly, there were no aristocrats who could move toward separatism by drawing on regional resentments. This meant that England never really had to face the threat of internal division and could develop strong institutions of united national government such as Parliament. It also meant that the English kings, starting primarily with Henry II, could rely on numerous local dignitaries, above all, the knights, to do much work of local government without pay. The obvious advantage was that local government was cheap, but the hidden implication of the system was that government also had to be popular, or else much of the voluntary work would grind to a halt. This doubtless was the main reason why English kings went out of their way to seek formal consent for their actions. When they did not they could barely rule, so wise kings learned the lesson and as time went on England became most clearly a limited monarchy. The French kings, much to the contrary, ruled a richer and larger country, which gave them—at least in times of peace—sufficient wealth to pay for a more bureaucratic, salaried administration at both the central and local levels. French kings therefore could rule more absolutely. But they were continually faced with serious threats of regional separatism. Different regions continued to cherish their own traditions and often supported centrifugalism in league with the upper aristocracy. So French kings often had to struggle with attempts at regional breakaways and take various measures to subdue their aristocrats. Up to around 1700 the monarchy had to fight a steady battle against regionalism, but it had the resources to win consistently and thereby managed to grow from strength to strength.

The only continental state that would rival France until the rise of Germany in the nineteenth century was Spain. The foundations of Spain's greatness were also laid in the High Middle Ages on the principle of national monarchy, but in the Middle Ages there was not yet one monarchy that ruled through most of the Iberian peninsula. After the Christians started pushing back the forces of Islam around 1100 there were four Spanish Christian kingdoms: the tiny northern mountain state of Navarre, which would always remain comparatively insignificant; Portugal in the west; Aragon in the northeast; and Castile in the center. The main Spanish occupation in the High Middle Ages was the *Reconquista,* i.e., the reconquest of the peninsula for Christianity. This reached its culmination in the year 1212 in a major victory of a combined Aragonese-Castilian army over the Muslims at Las Navas de Tolosa. The rest was mostly mopping up. By the end of the thirteenth century all that remained of earlier Muslim domination was the small state of Granada in the extreme south, and Granada existed largely because it was willing to pay tribute to the Christians. Because Castile had the largest open frontier, it became by far the largest Spanish kingdom, but it was balanced in wealth by the more urban and trade-oriented Aragon. Both kingdoms developed institutions in the thirteenth century that roughly paralleled those of France. But until the union of Aragon and Castile under King Ferdinand and Queen Isabella in the fifteenth century, the Iberian states individually could not hope to be as strong as the much richer and more populous France.

Medieval Spain

Before concluding this chapter it is best to assess the general significance of the rise of the national monarchies in high-medieval western Europe. Until their emergence there had been two basic patterns of government in Europe: city-states and empires. City-states had the advantage of drawing heavily upon citizen participation and loyalty and thus were able to make highly efficient use of their human potential. But they were often divided by economic rivalries and they were not sufficiently large or militarily strong to defend themselves against imperial forces. The empires, on the other hand, could win battles and often had the resources to support an efficient bureaucratic administrative apparatus, but they drew on little voluntary participation and were too far-flung or rapacious to inspire any deep loyal-

Historical role of the national monarchies

ties. The new national monarchies were to prove the "golden mean" between these extremes. They were large enough to have adequate military strength and they developed administrative techniques that would rival and eventually surpass those of the Roman or Byzantine Empires. More than that, building at first upon the bases of feudalism, they drew upon sufficient citizen participation and loyalty to help support them in times of stress when empires would have foundered. By about 1300 the monarchies of England, France, and the Iberian peninsula had gained the primary loyalties of their subjects, superseding loyalties to communities, regions, or to the government of the Church. For all these reasons they brought much internal peace and stability to large parts of Europe where there had been little stability before. Thus they contributed greatly to making life fruitful. The medieval national monarchies were also the ancestors of the modern nation-states—the most effective and equitable governments of our day (the current Soviet Union being something more like an empire). In short, they were one of the Middle Ages' most beneficial bequests to modern times.

SELECTED READINGS

• *Items so designated are available in paperback editions.*

GENERAL STUDIES

• Bloch, Marc, *Feudal Society,* Chicago, 1961. A modern classic, first published in France in 1940. Full of valuable insights but outdated in some respects.
• Heer, Friedrich, *The Medieval World,* London, 1961. A controversial interpretation that opposes an "open" twelfth century to a "closed" thirteenth century. Very detailed.
• Southern, R. W., *The Making of the Middle Ages,* New Haven, Conn., 1953. A subtle and brilliant reading of eleventh- and twelfth-century developments. Difficult but most rewarding.
• Strayer, J. R., *Western Europe in the Middle Ages,* 2nd ed., Pacific Palisades, Calif., 1974. In a class by itself as the best short introduction to medieval political and cultural history.
  Wood, Charles T., *The Age of Chivalry* (also published as *The Quest for Eternity*), London, 1970. A lively work for the beginner that supplements Strayer in its emphasis on economic and social history.

ECONOMIC AND SOCIAL CONDITIONS

• Bautier, R. H., *The Economic Development of Medieval Europe,* London, 1971.
• Duby, G., *Rural Economy and Country Life in the Medieval West,* London, 1968. The best work on agrarian history. Highly recommended as an example of recent French historiography at its highest level.

- Gies, J. and F., *Life in a Medieval City*, New York, 1973. An engaging popular account concentrating on life in thirteenth-century Troyes.

  Labarge, M. W., *A Baronial Household of the Thirteenth Century*, New York, 1965. Particularly valuable for its emphasis on the career of a woman.
- Lopez, Robert S., *The Commercial Revolution of the Middle Ages*, Englewood Cliffs, N.J., 1971.
- Painter, Sidney, *French Chivalry*, Baltimore, 1940.
- Pirenne, H., *Economic and Social History of Medieval Europe*, London, 1936. Many of Pirenne's ideas are no longer accepted but this is still an extremely useful brief account.

  Postan, M. M., *The Medieval Economy and Society: An Economic History of Britain, 1100–1500*, Berkeley, Calif., 1972.
- Power, Eileen, *Medieval Women*, Cambridge, 1975. Very brief but informative.
- White, Lynn, Jr., *Medieval Technology and Social Change*, Oxford, 1962. Controversial but excellently written and thought-provoking.

POLITICAL DEVELOPMENTS

- Barraclough, G., *The Origins of Modern Germany*, 2nd ed., Oxford, 1947. Highly interpretative, should be read in conjunction with Hampe.

  Douglas, David, *The Norman Achievement, 1050–1100*, Berkeley, Calif., 1969.

  ———, *The Norman Fate, 1100–1154*, Berkeley, Calif., 1976.
- Fawtier, R., *The Capetian Kings of France*, London, 1962. The best single volume on medieval French politics.

  Hampe, K., *Germany under the Salian and Hohenstaufen Emperors*, Totowa, N.J., 1973. An older, reliable German work recently translated.

  Hyde, J. K., *Society and Politics in Medieval Italy*, New York, 1973. An excellent survey that integrates political and social history.

  Loyn, H. R., *The Norman Conquest*, London, 1965.

  O'Callaghan, Joseph F., *A History of Medieval Spain*, Ithaca, N.Y., 1975.

  Petit-Dutaillis, Charles, *The Feudal Monarchy in France and England*, London, 1936. An excellent essay in comparative history.
- Poole, Austin L., *From Domesday Book to Magna Carta, 1087–1216*, 2nd ed., Oxford, 1955. Very detailed yet clear.
- Sayles, G. O., *The King's Parliament of England*, New York, 1974. Emphasizes the role of the crown and downplays the importance of the commons.

  ———, *The Medieval Foundations of England*, London, 1952. An excellent interpretation of medieval English political developments.
- Stephenson, Carl, *Mediaeval Feudalism*, Ithaca, N.Y., 1942. Very elementary.
- Strayer, J. R., *On the Medieval Origins of the Modern State*, Princeton, N.J., 1970. A distillation of the ideas of one of America's greatest medievalists.

SOURCE MATERIALS

Herlihy, David, ed., *The History of Feudalism*, New York, 1970.
- Lopez, Robert S., and I. W. Raymond, eds., *Medieval Trade in the Mediterranean World*, New York, 1955.

• Lyon, Bryce, ed., *The High Middle Ages,* New York, 1964.
• Otto of Freising, *The Deeds of Frederick Barbarossa,* tr. C. C. Mierow, New York, 1953. A contemporary chronicle that is interesting enough to read from start to finish.

Strayer, J. R., ed., *Feudalism,* Princeton, N.J., 1965.

Chapter 15

THE HIGH MIDDLE AGES (1050–1300): RELIGIOUS AND INTELLECTUAL DEVELOPMENTS

You would see men and women dragging carts through marshes . . . everywhere miracles daily occurring, jubilant songs rendered to God. . . . You would say that the prophecy was fulfilled, "The Spirit of Life was in the wheels."

—Abbot Robert of Torigni,
on the building of the cathedral
of Chartres, 1145

The religious and intellectual changes that transpired in the West between 1050 and 1300 were as important as the economic, social, and political ones. In the sphere of religion, the most fundamental organizational development was the triumph of the *papal monarchy*. Before the middle of the eleventh century certain popes had laid claim to primacy within the Church, but very few were able to come close to making good on such claims. Indeed, most popes before about 1050 were hardly able to rule effectively as bishops of Rome. But then, most dramatically, the popes emerged as the supreme religious leaders of Western Christendom. They centralized the government of the Church, challenged the sway of emperors and kings, and called forth the crusading movement. By 1300 the temporal success of the papacy had proven to be its own nemesis, but the popes still ruled the Church internally, as they continue to rule the Roman Catholic Church today.

Religious changes

While the papacy was assuming power, a new vitality infused the Christian religion itself, enabling Christianity to capture the human imagination as never before. At the same time too there was a remarkable revival of intellectual and cultural life. In education, thought, and

Intellectual changes

the arts, as in economics and politics, the West before 1050 had been a backwater. Thereafter it emerged swiftly from backwardness to become an intellectual and artistic leader of the globe. Westerners boasted that learning and the arts had moved northwest to them from Egypt, Greece, and Rome—a boast that was largely true. In the High Middle Ages Europeans first started building on ancient intellectual foundations and also contributed major intellectual and artistic innovations of their own.

1. THE CONSOLIDATION OF THE PAPAL MONARCHY

The sorry state of religious life in the tenth and early eleventh centuries

To understand the origins and appreciate the significance of the western European religious revival of the High Middle Ages it is necessary to have some idea of the level to which religion had sunk in the tenth and early eleventh centuries. Around 800 the Emperor Charlemagne had made some valiant attempts to enhance the religious authority of bishops, introduce the parish system into rural regions where there had hardly been any priests before, and provide for the literacy of the clergy. But with the collapse of the Carolingian Empire, religious decentralization and ensuing corruption prevailed throughout most of Europe. Most churches and monasteries became the private property of strong local lords. The latter disposed of Church offices under their control as they wished, often by selling them or by granting them to close relatives. Obviously this was not the best way to find the most worthy candidates, and many priests were quite unqualified for their jobs. They were almost always illiterate, and often they lived openly with concubines. When archbishops or bishops were able to control appointments the results were not much better because such officials were usually close relatives of secular lords and followed their practices of financial or family aggrandizement. As for the popes, they were usually incompetent or corrupt, the sons or tools of powerful families who lived in or around the city of Rome. Some were astonishingly debauched. John XII may have been the worst of them. He was made pope at the age of eighteen in 955 because of the strength of his family. It is certain that he ruled for nine years as a thorough profligate, but there is some uncertainty about the cause of his death: either he was caught *in flagrante delicto* by a jealous husband and murdered on the spot, or else he died in the midst of a carnal act from sheer amorous exertion.

Religious revival: (1) Cluny and monastic reform

Once Europe began to catch its breath from the wave of external invasions that peaked in the tenth century, the wide extent of religious corruption or indifference was bound to call forth some reaction. The first successful measures of reform were taken in the monasteries because the work of a bishop was limited to what he could do in his lifetime, and even more because most archbishops and bishops were unable to disentangle themselves from the political affairs of their day. Monasteries could be somewhat more independent and could count more on the support of their reforms by lay lords, insofar as lords feared for the health of their souls if monks did not serve their proper function in saying offices (i.e., prayers). The movement for monastic reform began with the foundation of the monastery of Cluny in Burgundy in 910 by a pious nobleman. Cluny was a Benedictine house but it introduced two constitutional innovations. One was that, in order to remain free from domination by either local secular or ecclesiastical powers, it was made directly subject to the pope. The other was that it undertook the reform or foundation of numerous "daughter monasteries": whereas formerly all Benedictine houses had been independent and equal, Cluny founded a monastic "family," whose members were suboᵣdinate to it. Owing to the succession of a few extremely pious, active, and long-lived abbots, the congregation of Cluniac houses grew so rapidly that there were sixty-seven by 1049. In all of them dedicated priors were chosen who followed the dictates of the abbot of Cluny rather than being responsible to local potentates. Cluniac monks accordingly became famous for their industry in the saying of offices. And Cluny was only the most famous of the new congregations. Other similar ones spread just as rapidly in the years around 1000 and succeeded in making the reformed monasteries vital centers of religious life and prayer.

Around the middle of the eleventh century, after so many monasteries had been taken out of the control of secular authorities, the leaders of the monastic reform movement started to lobby for the reform of the secular clergy as well. They centered their attacks upon *simony*—i.e., the buying and selling of positions in the Church—and they also demanded celibacy for all levels of clergy. Their entire program was directed toward depriving secular powers of their ability to dictate appointments of bishops, abbots, and priests, and toward making the clerical estate as "pure" and as distinct from the secular one as possible. Once this reform program was appropriated by the papacy, it would begin to change the face of the entire Church.

(2) reform of the secular clergy

Considering that the reformers were greatly opposed to lay interference, it is ironic that their party was first installed in the papacy by a German emperor, namely Henry III. In 1046 this ruler came to Italy, deposed three rival Italian claimants to the papal title, and named as pope a German reformer from his own retinue. Henry III's act brought in a series of reforming popes, who started to promulgate decrees against simony, clerical marriage, and immorality of all sorts throughout the Church. These popes also insisted upon their own role as primates and universal spiritual leaders in order to give strength to their actions. One of the most important steps they took was the issuance in 1059 of a decree on papal elections. This vested the right of naming a new pope solely with the cardinals, thereby depriving the

Emperor Henry III and reform of the papacy

Roman aristocracy or the German emperor of the chance to interfere in the matter. The decree preserved the independence of papal elections thereafter. In granting the right of election to cardinals the decree also became a milestone in the evolution of a special body within the Church. Ever since the tenth century a number of bishops and clerics, known as cardinals, from sees in and near Rome had taken on an important role as advisors and administrative assistants of the popes, but the election decree of 1059 first gave them their clearest powers. Thereafter the "college of cardinals" took on more and more administrative duties and helped create continuity in papal policy, especially when there was a quick succession of pontiffs. The cardinals still elect the pope today.

The ideals of Pope Gregory VII

A new and most momentous phase in the history of the reform movement was initiated during the pontificate of Gregory VII (1073–1085). Scholars disagree about how much Gregory was indebted to the ideas and policies of his predecessors in the reform movement and how much he departed from them. The answer seems to be that Gregory supported reform as much as others, indeed he explicitly renewed his predecessors' decrees against simony and clerical marriage. Yet he was not only more zealous in trying to enforce these decrees—a contemporary even called him a "Holy Satan"—but he brought with him a basically new conception of the role of the Church in human life. Whereas the older Christian ideal had been that of withdrawal, and the perfect "athlete of Christ" had been a passive contemplative, or ascetic monk, Gregory VII conceived of Christianity as being much more activist and believed that the Church was responsible for creating "right order in the world." To this end he demanded absolute obedience and strenuous chastity from his clergy: some of his clerical opponents complained that he wanted clerics to live like angels. Equally important, he thought of kings and emperors as his inferiors, who would carry out his commands obediently and help him reform and evangelize the world. Gregory allowed that secular princes would continue to rule directly and make their own decisions in purely secular matters, but he expected them to accept ultimate papal overlordship. Put in other terms, in contrast to his predecessors who had sought merely a duality of ecclesiastical and secular authority, Gregory VII wanted to create a papal monarchy over both. When told that his ideas were novel, he and his immediate followers replied: "The Lord did not say 'I am custom'; the Lord said 'I am truth.' " Since no pope had spoken like this before, it is proper to accept the judgment of a modern historian who called Gregory "the great innovator, who stood quite alone."

The investiture struggle

Gregory's actual conduct as pope was nothing short of revolutionary. From the start he was determined to enforce a decree against "lay investiture," the practice whereby secular rulers ceremonially granted clerics the symbols of their office. The German Emperor

Henry IV was bound to resist this because the ceremony was a manifestation of his long-accepted rights to appoint and control churchmen: without these his own authority would be greatly weakened. The ensuing fight is often called "the investiture struggle" because the problem of investitures was a central one, but the struggle was really about the relative obedience and strength of pope and emperor. The larger issue was immediately joined when Henry IV flouted Gregory's injunctions against appointing prelates. Whereas earlier popes might have tried to deal with such insubordination diplomatically, Gregory rapidly took the entirely unprecedented step of excommunicating the emperor and suspending him from all his powers as an earthly ruler. This bold act amazed all who learned of it. Between 955 and 1057 German emperors had deposed five and named twelve out of twenty-five popes; now a pope dared to dismiss an emperor! We have seen in the previous chapter that in 1077 Henry IV abased himself before the pope in order to forestall a formal deposition: that act amazed contemporaries even more. Thereafter Henry was able to rally some support and sympathy for himself and a terrible war of words ensued, while on the actual battlefield the emperor was able to place troops supporting the pope on the defensive. In 1085 Gregory died, seemingly defeated. But Gregory's successors continued the struggle with Henry IV and later with his son, Henry V.

The long and bitter contest on investiture only came to an end with the Concordat of Worms (a city in Germany) of 1122. Under this compromise the German emperor was forbidden to invest prelates with the religious symbols of their office but was allowed to invest them with the symbols of their rights as temporal rulers because the emperor was recognized as their temporal overlord. That settlement was ultimately less significant than the fact that the struggle had lastingly impaired the prestige of the emperors and raised that of the popes. In addition, the dramatic struggle helped rally the Western clergy behind the pope and galvanized the attentions of all onlookers. As one chronicler reported, nothing else was talked about "even in the women's spinning-rooms and the artisans' workshops." This meant that people who had earlier been largely indifferent to or excluded from religious issues became much more absorbed by them.

Gregory VII's successors and most of the popes of the twelfth century were fully committed to the goal of papal monarchy. But they were far less impetuous than Gregory had been and were more interested in the everyday administration of the Church. They apparently recognized that there was no point in claiming to rule as papal monarchs unless they could avail themselves of a governmental apparatus to support their claims. To this end they presided over an impressive growth of law and administration. Under papal guidance the twelfth century saw the basic formulation of the canon law of the Church. Canon law claimed ecclesiastical jurisdiction for all sorts of cases pertaining not only to the clergy but also to problems of marriage, inheritance, and rights of widows and orphans. Most of these cases were supposed to originate in the courts of bishops, but the popes insisted that they alone could issue dispensations from the strict letter of the law and that the papal *consistory*—comprised of the pope and cardinals—should serve as a final court of appeals. As the power of the papacy and the prestige of the Church mounted, cases in canon law courts and appeals to Rome rapidly increased; after the middle of the twelfth century legal expertise became so important for exercising the papal office that most popes were trained canon lawyers, whereas previously they had usually been monks. Concurrent with this growth of legalism was the growth of an administrative apparatus to keep records and collect income. As the century wore on, the papacy developed a bureaucratic government that was far in advance of most of the secular governments of the day. This allowed it to become richer, more efficient, and ever stronger. Finally, the popes asserted their powers within the Church by gaining greater control over the election of bishops and by calling general councils in Rome to promulgate laws and demonstrate their leadership.

By common consent the most capable and successful of all high-medieval popes was Innocent III (1198–1216). Innocent, who was elected at the age of thirty-seven, was extremely young and vigorous for a high-medieval pope; more than that, he was expertly trained in both theology and canon law. His major goal was to unify all Christendom under papal hegemony and to bring in the "right order in the world" so fervently desired by Gregory VII. He never questioned the right of kings and princes to rule directly in the secular sphere but believed that he could step in and discipline kings whenever they "sinned," a wide opening for interference. Beyond that, he saw himself as the ultimate overlord of all. In his own words he said that "as every knee is bowed to Jesus . . . so all men should obey His Vicar [i.e., the pope]."

Innocent sought to implement his goals in many different ways. In order to give the papacy a solid territorial base of support, like the one drawn upon by the French kings, he tried to initiate strong rule in the papal territories around Rome by consolidating them where possible and providing for efficient and vigilant administration. For this reason Innocent is often considered to be the real founder of the Papal States. But because some urban communities tenaciously sought to maintain their independence, he never came close to dominating the papal lands in Italy so completely as the French kings controlled the Ile-de-France. In other projects he was more completely successful. He intervened in German politics assertively enough to engineer the triumph of his own candidate for the imperial office, the Hohenstaufen Frederick II. He disciplined the French King Philip Augustus for his marital misconduct and forced John of England to accept an unwanted candidate as archbishop of Canterbury. To demonstrate his superiority and also

Pope Innocent III

Pope Innocent III. A mosaic dating from the thirteenth century.

gain income, Innocent forced John to grant England to the papacy as a fief, and he similarly gained the feudal overlordship of Aragon, Sicily, and Hungary. When southern France was threatened by the spread of the Albigensian heresy (to be discussed later) the pope effectively called a crusade that would extinguish it by force. He also levied the first income tax on the clergy to support a crusade to the Holy Land. The crown of Innocent's religious achievement was the calling of the Fourth Lateran Council in Rome in 1215. This defined central dogmas of the faith and made the leadership of the papacy within Christendom more apparent than ever. The pope was now clearly both disciplining kings and ruling over the Church without hindrance.

Innocent's reign was certainly the zenith of the papal monarchy, but it also sowed some of the seeds of future ruin. Innocent himself could administer the Papal States and seek new sources of income without seeming to compromise the spiritual dignity of his office. But future popes who followed his policies had less of his stature and thus began to appear more like ordinary acquisitive rulers. Moreover, because the Papal States bordered on the Kingdom of Sicily, Innocent's successors quickly came into conflict with the neighboring ruler, who was none other than Innocent's protegé Frederick II. Although Innocent had raised up Frederick, he never dreamed that Frederick would later become an inveterate opponent of paper power in Italy.

Problems for Innocent's successors

At first these and other problems were not fully apparent. The popes of the thirteenth century continued to enhance their powers and centralize the government of the Church. They gradually asserted the right to name candidates for ecclesiastical benefices, both high and low, and they asserted control over the curriculum and doctrine taught at the University of Paris. But they also became involved in a protracted political struggle which led to their own demise as temporal powers. This struggle began with the attempt of the popes to destroy Frederick II. To some degree they were acting in self-defense because Frederick threatened their own rule in central Italy. But in combating him they overemployed their spiritual weapons. Instead of merely excommunicating and deposing Frederick, they also called a crusade against him—the first time a crusade was called on a large scale for blatantly political purposes.

The papacy's struggle with Frederick II and his heirs; political crusades

After Frederick's death in 1250 a succession of popes made a still worse mistake by renewing and maintaining their crusade against all of the emperor's heirs, whom they called the "viper brood." In order to implement this crusade they became preoccupied with raising funds, and they sought and won as their military champion a younger son from the French royal house, Charles of Anjou. But the latter only helped the popes for the purely political motive of winning the Kingdom of Sicily for himself. Charles in fact won Sicily in 1268 by defeating the last of Frederick II's male heirs. But he then taxed the realm so excessively that the Sicilians revolted in the "Sicilian Vespers" of 1282 and offered their crown to the king of Aragon, who had married Fred-

The effects of the political crusades

*Pope Boniface VIII. From a por-
trait by Giotto.*

*Two crucial disputes: (1)
the issue of clerical
taxation*

*(2) quarrel with the king
of France*

erick II's granddaughter. The king of Aragon accordingly entered the
Italian arena and came close to winning Frederick's former kingdom
for himself. To prevent this Charles of Anjou and the reigning pope
prevailed upon the king of France—then Philip III (1270–1285)—to
embark on a crusade against Aragon. This crusade was a terrible failure and Philip III died on it. In the wake of these events Philip's son,
Philip IV, resolved to alter the traditional French pro-papal policy. By
that time France had become so strong that such a decision was fateful.
More than that, by misusing the institution of the crusade and trying
to raise increasingly large sums of money to support it, the popes had
lost much of their prestige. The denouement would be played out at
the very beginning of the next century.

The temporal might of the papacy was toppled almost melodra-
matically in the reign of Boniface VIII (1294–1303). Many of Boniface's troubles were not of his own making. His greatest obstacle was
that the national monarchies had gained more of their subjects' loyalties than the papacy could draw upon because of the steady growth of
royal power and erosion of papal prestige. Boniface also had the misfortune to succeed a particularly pious, although inept, pope who
resigned his office within a year. Since Boniface was entirely lacking
in conventional piety or humility, the contrast turned many Christian
observers against him. Some even maintained—incorrectly—that
Boniface had convinced his predecessor to resign and had murdered
him shortly afterwards. Boniface ruled assertively and presided over
the first papal "jubilee" in Rome in 1300. This was an apparent, but,
as events would show, hollow demonstration of papal might.

Two disputes with the kings of England and France proved to be
Boniface's undoing. The first concerned the clerical taxation that had
been initiated by Innocent III. Although Innocent had levied this tax to
support a crusade and had collected it himself, in the course of the thirteenth century the kings of England and France had begun to levy and
collect clerical taxes on the pretext that they would use them to help
the popes on future crusades to the Holy Land or aid in papal crusades
against the Hohenstaufens. Then, at the end of the century, the kings
started to levy their own war taxes on the clergy without any pretexts
at all. Boniface understandably tried to prohibit this step, but quickly
found that he had lost the support of the English and French clergy.
Thus when the kings offered resistance he had to back down.

Boniface's second dispute was with the king of France alone. Specifically it concerned Philip IV's determination to try a French bishop for
treason. As in the earlier struggle between Gregory VII and Henry IV
of Germany, the real issue was the comparative strength of papal and
secular power, but this time the papacy was decisively defeated. As
before, there was a bitter propaganda war, but now hardly anyone lis-
tened to the pope. The king instead pressed absurd charges of heresy
against Boniface and sent his minions to arrest the pope to stand trial.
At the papal residence of Anagni in 1303 Boniface, who was in his

eighties, was captured and mistreated before he was released by the local citizens. These events exhausted the old man's strength and he died a month later. Immediately thereupon it was said that he had entered the papacy like a fox, reigned like a lion, but died like a dog.

After Boniface VIII's death the papacy became virtually a pawn of French temporal authority for most of the fourteenth century. But the emergence and success of the papal monarchy in the High Middle Ages had several beneficial effects during the course of that period. One was that the international rule of the papacy over the Church enhanced international communications and uniformity of religious practices. Another was that the papal cultivation of canon law aided a growing respect for law of all sorts and often helped protect the causes of otherwise defenseless subjects, like widows and orphans. The popes also managed to advance very far in their campaigns to eliminate the sale of Church offices and to raise the morals of the clergy. By centralizing appointments they made it easier for worthy candidates who had no locally influential relatives to gain advancement. There was of course corruption in the papal government too, but in an age of entrenched localism the triumph of an international force was mainly beneficial. Finally, as we will see later, the growth of the papal monarchy helped bring vitality to popular religion and helped support the revival of learning.

Beneficial effects of the papal monarchy

2. THE CRUSADES

The rise and fall of the crusading movement was closely related to the fortunes of the high-medieval papal monarchy. The First Crusade was initiated by the papacy, and its success a great early victory for the papal monarchy. But the later decline of the crusading movement helped undermine the pope's temporal authority. Thus the Crusades can be seen as part of a chapter in papal and religious history. In addition, the Crusades opened the first chapter in the history of Western imperialism.

Two themes of the crusading movement

The immediate cause of the First Crusade was an appeal for aid in 1095 by the Byzantine Emperor Alexius Comnenus. Alexius hoped to reconquer Byzantine territory in Asia Minor which had recently been lost to the Turks. Since he had already become accustomed to using Western mercenaries as auxiliary troops, he asked the pope to help rally some Western military support. But the emperor soon found, no doubt to his great surprise, that he was receiving not just simple aid but a *crusade*. In other words, instead of a band of mercenaries to fight in Asia Minor, the West sent forth an enormous army of volunteers whose goal was to wrest Jerusalem away from Islam. Since the decision to turn Alexius's call for aid into a crusade was made by the pope, it is well to examine the latter's motives.

The direct cause of the First Crusade

The Roman pope in 1095 was Urban II, an extremely competent

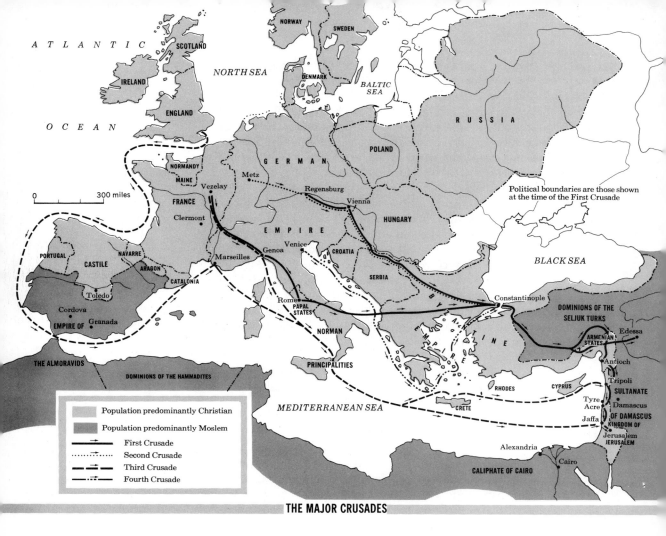

THE MAJOR CRUSADES

Political boundaries are those shown at the time of the First Crusade

Population predominantly Christian
Population predominantly Moslem
First Crusade
Second Crusade
Third Crusade
Fourth Crusade

The Gregorian theory of Christian Warfare

disciple of Gregory VII. Without question, Urban called the First Crusade to help further the policies of the Gregorian papacy. Urban's very patronage of Christian warfare was Gregorian. Early Christianity had been pacifistic: St. Martin, for example, a revered Christian saint of the fourth century, gave up his career as a soldier when he converted with the statement "I am Christ's soldier; I cannot fight." The Latin fathers St. Augustine and St. Gregory worked out theories to justify Christian warfare but only in the eleventh century, with the triumph of the Gregorian movement, were these put into practice. Gregory VII engineered papal support for the Norman Conquest even before he became pope, and he, or popes under his influence, blessed Christian campaigns against Muslims in Spain, Greeks in Italy, and Slavs in the German east. All these campaigns were considered by Gregory VII and his followers to be steps toward gaining "right order in the world."

Following in Gregory VII's footsteps, Urban II probably conceived of a great crusade to the Holy Land as a means for achieving at least four ends. One was to bring the Greek Orthodox Church back into the fold. By sending a mighty volunteer army to the East, Urban might overawe the Byzantines with Western strength and convince them to reaccept Roman primacy. If he was successful in that, he would gain a great victory for the Gregorian program of papal monarchy. A second motive was to embarrass the pope's greatest enemy, the German emperor. In 1095 Henry IV had become so militarily strong that Urban had been forced to flee Italy for France. By calling a mighty crusade of all westerners but Germans, Urban might hope to show up the emperor as a narrow-minded, un-Christian persecutor, and demonstrate his own ability to be the spiritual leader of the West. Thirdly, by sending off a large contingent of fighters Urban might help to achieve peace at home. Earlier, the local French Church had supported a "peace movement" which prohibited attacks on noncombatants (the "Peace of God") and then prohibited fighting on certain holy days (the "Truce of God"). Right before he called the First Crusade Urban promulgated the first full papal approval and extension of this peace movement. Clearly the crusade was linked to the call for peace: in effect, Urban told unruly warriors that if they really wished to fight they could do so justly for a Christian cause overseas. Finally, the goal of Jerusalem itself must have genuinely inspired Urban. Jerusalem was thought to be the center of the earth and was the most sacred shrine of the Christian religion. It must have seemed only proper that pilgrimages to Jerusalem should not be impeded and that Christians should rule the city directly. "Right order in the world" could scarcely mean less.

Urban II's motives

When Urban called his crusade at a Church council in the French town of Clermont in 1095, the response was more enthusiastic than he could possibly have expected. Many in the crowd interrupted the pope's speech with spontaneous cries of "God wills it," and many impetuously rushed off to the East shortly thereafter. All told, there were

Economic and political causes of the First Crusade

French Knights about to Depart on a Crusade. The chief weapons are the long bow and the spear.

Religion the dominant motive: crusades as armed pilgrimages

The brutal conduct of the Crusaders

probably about a hundred thousand men in the main crusading army, an enormous number for the day. Accordingly, the question arises as to why Urban's appeal was so remarkably successful. Certainly there were economic and political reasons. Many of the poorer people who went crusading came from areas that by 1095 were already becoming overpopulated: these crusaders may have hoped to do better for themselves in the East than they could on their crowded lands. Similarly, some lords were feeling the pressures of growing political stability and a growing acceptance of *primogeniture* (inheritance limited to the eldest male heir). Hitherto younger sons might have hoped to make their own fortune in endemic warfare, or at least inherit a small piece of territory for themselves, but now there were more and longer-lived siblings, warfare was becoming limited, and only the eldest son inherited his father's lands. Clearly, leaving for the East was an attractive alternative to chafing at home.

But the dominant motive for going on the First Crusade was definitely religious. Nobody could have gone crusading out of purely calculating motives because nobody could have predicted for certain that new lands would be won. Indeed, any rational caculation would have predicted at best an unremunerative return trip, or, more likely, death at the hands of the Muslims. But the journey offered great solace for the Christian soul. For centuries pilgrimages had been the most popular type of Christian penance, and the pilgrimage to Jerusalem was considered to be the most sacred and efficacious one of all. Obviously the greatest of all spiritual rewards would come from going on an armed pilgrimage to Jerusalem in order to win back the holiest of sacred places for Christianity. To make this point explicit, Urban II at Clermont promised that Crusaders would be freed from all other penances imposed by the Church. Immediately afterwards some Crusade preachers went even further by promising, without Urban's authorization, what became known as a *plenary indulgence*. This was the promise that all Crusaders would be entirely freed from otherworldly punishments in pugatory and that their souls would go straight to heaven if they died on the Crusade. The plenary indulgence was a truly extraordinary offer and crowds streamed in to take advantage of it. As they flocked together they were further whipped up by preachers into a religious frenzy that approached mass hysteria. They were convinced that they had been chosen to cleanse the world of unbelievers. One terrible consequence was that even before they had fully set out for the East they started slaughtering European Jews in the first really virulent outbreak of Western anti-Semitism.

Against great odds the First Crusade was a thorough success. In 1098 the Crusaders captured Antioch and with it most of Syria; in 1099 they took Jerusalem. Their success came mainly from the facts that their Muslim opponents just at that time were internally divided and that the appearance of the strange, uncouth, and terribly savage

Burning of Jews. From a late-medieval German manuscript. After the persecutions of the First Crusade, treatment of Jews in western Europe became worse and worse. These Jews were set upon by the populace because they were suspected of poisoning wells.

westerners took the Muslims by surprise. From the start the Crusaders in the Holy Land acted like imperialists. As soon as they conquered new territories they claimed them as property for themselves, carving out their acquisitions into four different principalities. They also exulted in their own ferocity. When they captured Antioch, instead of taking prisoners they killed all the Turks they laid their hands on. Similarly, when they conquered Jerusalem they ignored Christ's own pacifistic precepts, mercilessly slaughtering all the Muslim inhabitants of the city. Some Crusaders actually boasted in a joint letter home that "in Solomon's Porch and in his temple our men rode in the blood of the Saracens up to the knees of their horses." Those Crusaders who stayed on in the Holy Land gradually became more civilized and tolerant, but new waves of armed pilgrims from the West continued to act brutally. Moreover, even the settled Crusaders never became fully integrated with the local population but remained a separate, exploiting foreign element in the heart of the Islamic world.

Given the fact that the Christian states comprised only an underpopulated, narrow strip of colonies along the coastline of Syria and Palestine, it was only a matter of time before they would be won back for Islam. By 1144 the northernmost principality fell. When Christian warriors led by the king of France and emperor of Germany came East in the Second Crusade to recoup the losses, they were too internally divided to win any victories. Not long afterwards the Islamic lands of the region were united from Egypt by the Sultan Saladin, who recaptured Jerusalem in 1187. Again a force from the West tried to repair the damages: this was the Third Crusade, led by the German Em-

Failure of subsequent crusades; the triumph of Frederick II's diplomacy

Krak des Chevaliers, Northern Syria. This Castle of the Knights is considered the most magnificent of all the Crusader fortresses and one of the best preserved relics of the Middle Ages.

peror Frederick Barbarossa, the French King Philip Augustus, and the English King Richard the Lionhearted. Even this glorious host, however, could not triumph, above all because rival leaders again quarreled among themselves. When Innocent III became pope his main ambition was to win back Jerusalem. He called the Fourth Crusade to that end, but that Crusade was an unprecedented disaster from the point of view of a united Christendom. The pope could not control its direction and the Crusaders in 1204 wound up seizing Orthodox Christian Constantinople instead of marching on the Holy Land. As we have seen, the ultimate result of this act was to help destroy the Byzantine Empire and open up eastern Europe to the Ottoman Turks. Innocent convened the Fourth Lateran Council in 1215 partially to prepare for yet another crusade that would be more directly under papal guidance. That crusade, the fifth, was launched from the sea against Egypt in order to penetrate Muslim power at its base, but after a promising start it too was a failure. Only the Sixth Crusade, led from 1228 to 1229 by the Emperor Frederick II, was a success; this, however, was not for any military reasons. Frederick, who knew Arabic and could communicate easily with the Egyptian sultan, did not fight but skillfully negotiated a treaty whereby Jerusalem and a narrow access route were restored to the Christians. Thus diplomacy triumphed where warfare had failed. But the Christians could not hold on to their gains and Jerusalem fell again in 1244, never to be recaptured by the West until 1917. The Christian "states" were now only a small enclave around the Palestinian city of Acre.

While Frederick II was negotiating for Jerusalem, he was under excommunication by the pope; therefore, when he entered the city, he had to crown himself king of Jerusalem in the Church of the Holy Sepulcher with his own hands. This was indicative of the fact that by then the papacy was becoming more intent on advancing European

The papacy's sacrifice of the crusading ideal to political interests

political aims than on reconquering the Holy Land. The victory of the First Crusade had greatly enhanced the prestige and strength of the papal monarchy, but the subsequent failures were increasingly calling into question the papal ability to unite the West for a great enterprise. The Albigensian Crusade, called by Innocent III in 1208, established the crucial precedent that a believer could receive the same spiritual rewards by crusading within Europe as by going on a much longer and more risky crusade to the East. The Albigensian Crusade did not damage the papacy's religious image, however, because the Albigensian heretics (whose beliefs will be discussed later) were a clear religious threat to the Church. Once the papacy launched its crusade against Frederick II and his heirs, however, it fully sacrificed the crusading ideal to political interests.

It was then that the decline of the crusading movement and the decline of the papacy became most closely interrelated. In the crusades against Frederick and his successors, and later against the king of Aragon, the popes offered the same plenary indulgence that was by then officially offered to all Crusaders against Islam. Worse, they granted the same indulgence to anyone who simply contributed enough money to arm a Crusader for the enterprise. This created a great inflation in indulgences. By 1291 the last Christian outposts in the Holy Land had fallen without any Western help while the papacy was still trying to salvage its losing crusade against Aragon. Boniface VIII's papal jubilee of 1300, which offered a plenary indulgence to all those who made a pilgrimage to Rome, was a tacit recognition that the Eternal City and not the Holy Land would henceforth have to be the central goal of Christian pilgrimage. Boniface fell from power three years later for many reasons, but one was certainly that the prestige of the papacy had become irreparably damaged by the misuses and failures of crusading.

The decline of the crusading movement and the decline of the papacy interrelated

So, while the crusading idea helped build up the papal monarchy, it also helped destroy it. Other than that, what practical significance did the Crusades have? On the credit side, the almost incredible success of the First Crusade greatly helped raise the self-confidence of the medieval West. For centuries western Europe had been on the defensive against Islam; now a Western army could march into a center of Islamic power and take a coveted prize seemingly at will. This dramatic victory contributed to making the twelfth century an age of extraordinary buoyancy and optimism. To Western Christians it must have seemed as if God was on their side and that they could accomplish almost anything they wished. The Crusades also helped broaden Western horizons. Few westerners in the Holy Land ever bothered to learn Arabic or profit from specific Islamic institutions or ideas—the most profitable cultural communications between Christians and Muslims took place in Spain and Sicily—but Crusaders who traveled long distances through foreign lands were bound to become somewhat more sophisticated. The Crusades certainly stimulated interest in hitherto

Positive effects of the Crusades

unknown luxury goods and presented a wealth of subjects for literature and fable.

From an economic point of view, the success of the First Crusade helped open up the eastern Mediterranean to Western commerce. The Italian cities of Venice and Genoa particularly began to dominate trade in that area, thereby helping to enhance Western prosperity as a whole. The need to transfer money over long distances also stimulated early experiments in banking techniques. Politically, the precedent of taxing the clergy for financing crusades was not only quickly turned to the advantage of the Western monarchies, it also stimulated the development of various forms of national taxation. More than that, the very act of organizing a country to help support a royal crusade by raising funds and provisions was an important stimulus to the development of efficient administrative institutions in the emerging nation-states.

But there was a debit as well as a credit side to the crusading balance sheet. There is no excusing the Crusaders' savage butchery—of Jews at home and of Muslims abroad. As we have seen too in Chapter 10, the Crusades greatly accelerated the deterioration of Western relations with the Byzantine Empire and contributed fundamentally to the destruction of that realm, with all the disastrous consequences that followed. And Western imperialism in the Holy Land was only the beginning of a long history of imperialism that has continued until modern times.

3. THE OUTBURST OF RELIGIOUS VITALITY

The First Crusade would never have succeeded if westerners had not become enthusiastic about religion. The growth of that enthusiasm itself was a most remarkable development. Had the First Crusade been called about fifty years earlier it is doubtful that many people would have joined it. But the eleventh-century reform movement and the pontificate of Gregory VII awakened interest in religion in all quarters. Thereafter the entire high-medieval period was to be marked by extraordinary religious vitality.

*The impact of the
Gregorian reform
movement on religious
revival*

The reformers and Gregory VII stimulated a European religious revival for two reasons. One was that the campaign to cleanse the Church actually achieved a large measure of success: the laity could now respect the clergy more and increasingly large numbers of people were inspired to join the clergy themselves. According to a reliable estimate, the number of people who joined monastic orders in England increased tenfold between 1066 and 1200, a statistic that does not include the increase in priests. The other reason why the work of Gregory VII in particular helped inspire a revival was that Gregory explicitly called upon the laity to help discipline their priests. In letters of great propagandistic power he denounced the sins of "fornicating priests" (by which he really meant just married ones) and urged the laity to drive them from their pulpits or boycott their services. Not surprisingly, this touched off something close to a vigilante movement in many parts of Europe. This excitement, taken together with the fact that the papal struggle with Henry IV was really the first European event of universal interest, increased religious commitment immensely. Until about 1050 most western Europeans were Christians in name, but religiosity seems to have been lukewarm and attendance at church services quite rare; after the Gregorian period Christianity was becoming an ideal and practice which really began to direct human lives.

One of the most visible manifestations of the new religiosity was the spread of the Cistercian movement in the twelfth century. By around 1100 the Cluniac monks had begun to sink into the same morass of worldliness and corruption that had engulfed their older Benedictine brothers whom they had set about to reform. The result was the founding of new orders to provide for the fullest expression of monastic idealism. One was the Carthusian order, whose monks were required to live in separate cells, abstain from meat, and fast three days each week on bread, water, and salt. The Carthusians never sought to attract great numbers and therefore remained a small group. But the same was by no means true of the Cistercians. The latter were monks who were first organized around 1100 and who sought to follow the Benedictine Rule in the purest and most austere way possible. In order

The new religiosity: the Carthusian and Cistercian orders; St. Bernard of Clairvaux

St. Bernard of Clairvaux. Here the saint, in the white habit of the Cistercians, has a miraculous vision of Christ during Mass. From a manuscript of about 1290.

to avoid the worldly temptations to which the Cluniacs had succumbed, they founded new monasteries in forests and wastelands as
far away from civilization as possible. They shunned all unnecessary
church decoration and ostentatious utensils, abandoned the Cluniac
stress on an elaborate liturgy in favor of more contemplation and
private prayer, and seriously committed themselves to hard manual
labor. Under the charismatic leadership of St. Bernard of Clairvaux
(1090–1153), a spellbinding preacher, brilliant writer, and the most influential European religious personality of his age, the Cistercian order
grew exponentially. There were only 5 houses in 1115 but no less than
343 on St. Bernard's death in 1153. This growth not only meant that
many more men were becoming monks—the older houses did not
disappear—but that many pious laymen were donating funds and
lands to support the new monasteries.

*New forms of religious
belief and practice*

As more people were entering or patronizing new monasteries, the
very nature of religious belief and devotion was changing. One of
many examples was a shift away from the cult of saints to emphasis on
the worship of Jesus and veneration of the Virgin Mary. Older Benedictine monasteries encouraged the veneration of the relics of local
saints that they housed in order to attract pilgrims and donations. But
the Cluniac and Cistercian orders were both centralized congregations
that allowed only one saintly patron for all their houses: respectively,
St. Peter (to honor the founder of the papacy) and the Virgin. Since
these monasteries contained few relics (the Virgin was thought to have
been taken bodily into heaven, so there were no corporeal relics for
her at all) they deemphasized their cult. The veneration of relics was
replaced by a concentration on the Eucharist, or the sacrament of the
Lord's Supper. Of course celebration of the Eucharist had always been
an important part of the Christian faith, but only in the twelfth century was it made really central, for only then did theologians fully
work out the doctrine of *transubstantiation*. According to this the priest
during mass cooperates with God in the performance of a miracle
whereby the bread and wine on the altar are changed or "transubstantiated" into the body and blood of Christ. Popular reverence for the
Eucharist became so great in the twelfth century that for the first time
the practice of elevating the consecrated host was initiated so that the
whole congregation could see it. The new theology of the Eucharist
greatly enhanced the dignity of the priest and also encouraged the
faithful to meditate on the Passion of Christ. As a result many developed an intense sense of identification with Christ and tried to imitate
his life in different ways.

*The cult of the Virgin
Mary*

Coming a very close second to the renewed worship of Christ in
the twelfth century was veneration of the Virgin Mary. This development was more unprecedented because until then the Virgin had
been only negligibly honored in the Western Church. Exactly why
veneration of the Virgin became so pronounced in the twelfth century

Christ Blessing the Coronation of His Mother, the Virgin Mary. A relief from the cathedral of Notre Dame, Paris.

is not fully clear, but, whatever the explanation, there is no doubt that in the twelfth century the cult of Mary blossomed throughout all of western Europe. Not only did the Cistercians make her their patron saint, but St. Bernard constantly taught about her life and virtues, and practically all the magnificent new cathedrals of the age were dedicated to her: there was Notre Dame ("Our Lady") of Paris, and also a "Notre Dame" of Chartres, Rheims, Amiens, Rouen, Laon, and many other places. Theologically, Mary's role was that of intercessor with her son for the salvation of human souls. It was held that Mary was the mother of all, an infinite repository of mercy who urged the salvation even of sinners so long as they were loving and ultimately contrite. Numerous stories circulated about seeming reprobates who were saved because they venerated Mary and because she then spoke for them at the hour of death.

The significance of the new cult was manifold. It was the first time that a woman was given such a central and honored place in the Christian religion. The fathers of the church still taught that sin had entered the world through the woman Eve; they now counterbalanced this by explaining how the triumph over sin came about with the help of Mary. Then too, this emphasis gave women a religious figure with whom they could identify, thereby enhancing their own religiosity. A third result was that artists and writers who portrayed Mary were able to concentrate on femininity and scenes of human tenderness and family life. This contributed greatly to a general softening of artistic and literary style. But perhaps most important of all, the rise of the cult of Mary was closely associated with a general rise of hopefulness and optimism in the twelfth-century West.

Significance of the cult

The Virgin in Majesty. A representation from a stained-glass window in the cathedral of Chartres.

Sometimes the great religious enthusiasm of the twelfth century went beyond the bounds approved by the Church. After Gregory VII had called upon the laity to help discipline their clergy it was difficult to control lay enthusiasm. As the twelfth century progressed and the papal monarchy concentrated on strengthening its legal and financial administration, some lay people began to wonder whether the Church, which had once been so inspiring, had not begun to lose sight of its idealistic goals. Another difficulty was that the growing emphasis on the miraculous powers of priests tended to inhibit the religious role of the laity and place it in a distinct position of spiritual inferiority. The result was that in the second half of the twelfth century large-scale movements of popular heresy swept over western Europe for the first time in its history. The two major twelfth-century heresies were Albigensianism and Waldensianism. The former, which had its greatest strength in Italy and southern France was a recrudescence of Eastern dualism. Like the Zoroastrians, Gnostics, and Manicheans before them, the Albigensians believed that all matter was created by an evil principle and that therefore the flesh should be thoroughly mortified. This teaching was completely at variance with Christianity, but it seems that most Albigensians believed themselves to be Christians and subscribed to the heresy mainly because it challenged the authority of insufficiently zealous Catholic priests and provided an outlet for intense lay spirituality. More typical of twelfth-century mainstream religious protest was Waldensianism, a heresy that originated in southern France and spread throughout most of Europe. Waldensians wished to imitate the life of Christ and the Apostles to the fullest possible extent. Therefore, they translated and studied the Gospels, and dedicated themselves to lives of poverty and preaching. Since the Waldensians did not attack any actual doctrines or practices of the Church, the ecclesiastical hierarchy did not at first interfere with them. But it was soon recognized that they were becoming too independent and that their simple piety could prove an embarrassing contrast to the life of worldly prelates. So the papacy forbade them to preach without authorization; when they refused to accept this they were condemned for heresy. This only made them more radical and they began to teach that men could be saved by living the simple apostolic life without any need for the sacraments administered by priests.

Innocent III's response to heresy

When Innocent III became pope in 1198 he was faced with a very serious challenge from growing heresies. His response was characteristically decisive and fateful for the future of the Church. Simply stated it was two-pronged. On the one hand, Innocent resolved to crush all disobedience to papal authority, but on the other, he decided to patronize whatever idealistic religious groups he could find that were willing to acknowledge obedience. Papal monarchy would hence no longer be threatened, but there would still be some dynamic spirituality within the Church. Innocent not only launched a full-scale crusade against the Albigensians, he also encouraged the use of judicial procedures against heresy that included ruthless techniques of religious "inquisition." In 1252 the papacy first approved the use of torture in inquisitorial trials, and burning at the stake became the prevalent punishment for religious disobedience. Neither the crusade nor the inquisitorial procedures were fully successful in uprooting the Albigensian heresy in Innocent's own lifetime, but the extension of such measures did result in destroying the heresy by fire and sword after about the middle of the thirteenth century. Waldensians, like Albigensians, were hunted down by inquisitors and their numbers reduced, but scattered Waldensian groups did manage to survive until modern times.

Another aspect of Innocent's program was to pronounce formally the new religious doctrines that enhanced the special status of priests and the ecclesiastical hierarchy. Thus at the Fourth Lateran Council of 1215 he reaffirmed the doctrine that the sacraments administered by the Church were the indispensable means of procuring God's grace, and that no one could be saved without them. The decrees of the Lateran Council emphasized two sacraments: the Eucharist and Penance. The doctrine of transubstantiation was formally defined and it was made a requirement—as it remains today—that all Catholics confess their sins to a priest at least once a year. The council also promulgated other doctrinal definitions and disciplinary measures which served both to oppose heresy and assert the unique dignity of the clergy.

Innocent III's emphasis on the sacraments

As stated above, the other side of Innocent's policy was to support obedient idealistic movements within the Church. The most important of these were the new orders of *friars*—the Dominicans and the Franciscans. Friars were like monks in vowing to follow a rule but they differed greatly from monks in their actual conduct. Above all, they did not retreat from society into monasteries. Assuming that the way of life originally followed by Christ and the Apostles was the most holy, they wandered through the countryside and especially the towns ministering to the sick and poor, preaching, and teaching. In imitation of Christ they also resolved to wed themselves to poverty. In many respects they resembled the Waldensian heretics but they professed absolute obedience to the pope and sought to fight heresy themselves.

The new orders of friars

The Dominican order, founded by St. Dominic in 1216 with Innocent III's approval, was particularly dedicated to the fight against heresy and also to the conversion of Jews and Muslims. At first the Dominicans hoped to achieve this end by preaching and public debate. Hence they became intellectually oriented. Many members of the order gained teaching positions in the infant European universities and contributed much to the development of philosophy and theology. The most influential thinker of the thirteenth century, St. Thomas

The Dominican order

St. Francis of Assisi. By the great Italian painter of the late thirteenth century, Cimabue.

The working relationship between the papal monarchy and the friars

The age of faith

Aquinas, was a Dominican who addressed one of his major theological works to converting the "gentiles" (i.e., all non-Christians). The Dominicans always retained their reputation for learning, but they also came to believe that stubborn heretics were best controlled by legal procedures. Accordingly, they became the leading medieval administrators of inquisitorial trials.

The Franciscan order was in many respects quite different and more radical. Its founder, St. Francis of Assisi (1182–1226), behaved at first remarkably like a social rebel and heretic. The son of a rich Italian merchant, he became dissatisfied with the values of his father and determined to become a servant of the poor. Giving away all of his property, he threw off all of his clothes in public, donned the simple garb of a beggar, and began to preach salvation and minister to outcasts in the darkest corners of Italian cities. He rigorously imitated the life of Christ and displayed indifference to doctrine, form, and ceremony. But he did wish to gain the support of the pope. One day in 1210 he appeared in Rome with a small ragged band to request that Innocent III approve a primitive "rule" that was little more than a collection of Gospel precepts. Some other pope might have rejected the layman Francis as a hopelessly unworldly, perhaps even demented, religious anarchist. But Francis was thoroughly willing to profess obedience, and Innocent had the genius to approve Francis's rule and give him permission to preach. With papal support the Franciscan movement spread rapidly. Thus Innocent managed to harness a vital new force that would help maintain a sense of religious enthusiasm within the Church.

Until the end of the thirteenth century both the Franciscans and Dominicans worked closely together with the papal monarchy in a mutually supportive relationship. The popes helped the friars establish themselves throughout Europe and often allowed them to infringe on the duties of parish priests. On their side the friars combated heresy, helped preach papal crusades, were active in missionary work, and otherwise undertook special missions for the popes. Above all, by the power of their examples and by their vigorous preaching the friars helped maintain religious intensity throughout the thirteenth century.

The entire period from 1050 to 1300 was hence unquestionably a great "age of faith." The products of this faith were both tangible and intangible. We will examine the tangible products—works of theology, literature, art, and architecture—presently. Great as these were, the intangible products were equally important. Until the Christian religion became deeply felt in the High Middle Ages there were hardly any common ideals to inspire average men and women. Life in the Middle Ages was extraordinarily hard, and until about 1050 there was not much to give it meaning. Then, when people began to take Christianity more seriously, an impetus was provided for performing hard work of all sorts. As we have seen in the last chapter, Europeans after

1050 literally had better food than before, and now we have seen that they were better fed figuratively as well. With more spiritual as well as material nourishment they accomplished great feats in all forms of human endeavor.

4. THE MEDIEVAL INTELLECTUAL REVIVAL

The major intellectual accomplishments of the High Middle Ages were of four related but different sorts: the spread of primary education and literacy; the origin and spread of universities; the acquisition of classical and Islamic knowledge, and the actual progress in thought made by westerners. Any one of these accomplishments would have earned the High Middle Ages a signal place in the history of Western learning; taken together they began the era of Western intellectual predominance which became a hallmark of modern times.

Four major intellectual accomplishments

Around 800 Charlemagne ordered that primary schools be established in every bishopic and monastery in his realm. Although it is doubtful that this command was carried out to the letter, many schools were certainly founded during the Carolingian period. But their continued existence was later endangered by the Viking invasions. Primary education in some monasteries and cathedral towns managed to survive, but until around 1050 the extent and quality of basic education in the European West was meager. Thereafter, however, there was a blossoming that paralleled the efflorescence we have seen in other human activities. Even contemporaries were struck by the rapidity with which schools sprang up all over Europe. One French monk writing in 1115 stated that when he was growing up around 1075 there was "such a scarcity of teachers that there were almost none in the villages and hardly any in the cities," but that by his maturity there was "a great number of schools," and the study of grammar was "flourishing far and wide." Similarly, a Flemish chronicle reported that around 1120 there was an extraordinary new passion for the study and practice of rhetoric. Clearly, the economic revival, the growth of towns, and the emergence of strong government allowed Europeans to dedicate themselves to basic education as never before.

The spread of primary education

The high-medieval educational boom was more than just merely a growth of schools, for the nature of the schools changed, and as time went on so did the curriculum and the clientele. The first basic mutation was that monasteries in the twelfth century abandoned their practice of educating outsiders. Earlier, monasteries had taught only a privileged few who were not monks how to read, solely because there were no other schools where those outsiders could go. But by the twelfth century there were sufficient alternatives. The main centers of European education became the cathedral schools located in the growing

Changes in medieval education: (1) the development of cathedral schools

A Woman Representing Grammar Leading a Young Boy into the Palace of the Liberal Arts

towns. The papal monarchy energetically supported this development by ordering in 1179 that all cathedrals should set aside income for one schoolteacher, who could then instruct all who wished, rich or poor, without fee. The papacy believed correctly that this measure would enlarge the number of well-trained clerics and potential administrators.

(2) the broadening of the curriculum

At first the cathedral schools existed almost exclusively for the basic training of priests, and the curriculum was designed to teach only the literacy necessary for reading the Church offices. But soon after 1100 the curriculum was broadened. With the growth of both ecclesiastical and secular governments there was a growing demand for trained officials who had to know more than how to read a few prayers. The revived reliance on law especially made it imperative to improve the quality of primary education in order to train future lawyers. Above all, a thorough knowledge of Latin grammar and composition began to be inculcated, often by studying some of the Roman classics such as the works of Cicero and Vergil. The revived interest in these texts, and attempts to imitate them, has led scholars to refer to a "Renaissance of the Twelfth Century."

(3) the growth of lay education

Until about 1200 the students in the urban schools remained predominantly clerical. Even those who hoped to become lawyers or administrators rather than mere priests usually found it advantageous to take Church orders. But afterwards more pupils entered schools who were not in the clergy and never intended to be. Some were children of the upper classes who began to regard literacy as a badge of status.

Others were future notaries (i.e., men who drew up official documents) or merchants who needed some literacy and/or computational skills to advance their own careers. Customarily, the latter groups would not go to cathedral schools but to alternate ones which were more practically oriented. Such schools grew rapidly in the course of the thirteenth century and became completely independent of ecclesiastical control. Not only were their students recruited from the laity, their teachers were usually laymen as well. At time went on instruction ceased being in Latin, as had hitherto been the case, and was offered in the European vernacular languages instead.

The rise of lay education was an enormously important development in western European history for two related reasons. The first was that the Church lost its monopoly over education for the first time in almost a millennium. Learning and resultant attitudes could now become more secular, and they did just that increasingly over the course of time. Laymen could not only evaluate and criticize the ideas of priests, they could also pursue entirely secular lines of inquiry. Western culture therefore ultimately became more independent of religion, and much of the traditionalism associated with religion, than any other culture in the world. Secondly, the growth of lay schools, taken together with the growth of church schools which trained the laity, led to an enormous growth of lay literacy: by 1340 roughly 40 percent of the Florentine population could read; by the later fifteenth century about 40 percent of the total population of England was literate as well. (These figures include women, who were usually taught to read by tutors at home rather than in schools.) When one considers that literacy around 1050 was almost entirely limited to the clergy, and that the literate comprised less than 1 percent of the population of western Europe, it can be appreciated that an astonishing revolution had taken place. Without it, many of Europe's other accomplishments would have been inconceivable.

*Significance of the rise of
lay education*

The emergence of universities was part of the same high-medieval educational boom. Originally, universities were institutions that gave specialized instruction in advanced studies which could not be pursued in average cathedral schools. In Italy the earliest universities took shape in the eleventh and twelfth centuries. They were those of Salerno, which specialized in medicine, and Bologna, which specialized in law—both Roman law and the canon law of the Church. North of the Alps the earliest and for a long time the most prominent university was that of Paris. The University of Paris started out as a cathedral school like many others, but in the twelfth century it began to become a recognized center of northern intellectual life. One reason for this was that scholars there found necessary conditions of peace and stability provided by the increasingly strong French kingship; another was that food was plentiful because the area was rich in agricultural produce; and another was that the cathedral school of Paris in the first half of the twelfth century boasted the most charismatic and controversial

The origins of universities

See color map following
page 384

teacher of the day, Peter Abelard (1079–1142). Abelard, whose intellectual accomplishments we will discuss later, attracted students from all over Europe in droves. According to an apocryphal story that was told at the time, he was such an exciting teacher that when he was forbidden to teach in French lands, because of his controversial views, he climbed a tree and students flocked under it to hear him lecture; when he was then forbidden to teach from the air he started lecturing from a boat and students massed to hear him from the banks. As a result of his reputation many other teachers settled in Paris and began to offer much more varied and advanced instruction than anything offered in other French cathedral schools. By 1200 Paris was evolving into a university that specialized in liberal arts and theology. Around then Innocent III, who had studied in Paris himself, called the school "the oven that bakes the bread for the entire world."

Nature of the medieval university

It should be emphasized that the institution of the university was really a medieval invention. Of course advanced schools existed in the ancient world, but they did not have fixed curricula or organized faculties, and they did not award degrees. At first, medieval universities themselves were not so much places as groups of scholars. The term university originally meant a corporation or guild. In fact, all of the medieval universities were corporations, either of teachers or students, organized like other guilds to protect their interests and rights. But gradually the word university came to mean an educational institution with a school of liberal arts and one or more faculties in the professional subjects of law, medicine, and theology. Salerno never became more than a medical school, but Bologna and Paris after about 1200 were regarded as the prototypic universities. During the thirteenth century such famous institutions as Oxford, Cambridge, Montpellier, Salamanca, and Naples were founded or granted formal recognition. In Germany there were no universities until the fourteenth century—a reflection of the disorganized condition of that area—but in 1385 Heidelberg, the first university on German soil, was founded and many others quickly followed.

Organization of universities

Every university in medieval Europe was patterned after one or the other of two different models. Throughout Italy, Spain, and southern France the standard was generally the University of Bologna, in which the students themselves constituted the corporation. They hired the teachers, paid their salaries, and fined or discharged them for neglect of duty or inefficient instruction. The universities of northern Europe were modeled after Paris, which was not a guild of students but of teachers. It included four faculties—arts, theology, law, and medicine—each headed by a dean. In the great majority of the northern universities arts and theology were the leading branches of study. Before the end of the thirteenth century separate colleges came to be established within the University of Paris. The original college was nothing more than an endowed home for poor students, but eventually the colleges become centers of instruction as well as residences. While most of these colleges have disappeared from the Continent, the universities of Oxford and Cambridge still retain the pattern of federal organization copied from Paris. The colleges of which they are composed are semi-independent educational units.

Most of our modern degrees as well as our modern university organization derive from the medieval system, but actual courses of study have been greatly altered. No curriculum in the Middle Ages included history or anything like the modern social sciences. The medieval student was assumed to know Latin grammar thoroughly before entrance into a university—this he learned in the primary, or "grammar," schools. Upon admission, limited to males, he was required to spend about four years studying the basic liberal arts, which meant doing advanced work in Latin grammar and rhetoric, and mastering the rules of logic. If he passed his examinations he received the preliminary degree of bachelor of arts (the prototype of our B.A.), which conferred no unusual distinction. To assure himself a place in professional life he then usually had to devote additional years to the pursuit of an advanced degree, such as master of arts (M.A.), or doctor of laws, medicine, or theology. For the M.A. degree three or four years had to be given to the study of mathematics, natural science, and philosophy. This was accomplished by reading and commenting on standard ancient works, such as those of Euclid and especially Aristotle. Abstract analysis was emphasized and there was no such thing as laboratory science. The requirements for the doctors' degrees included more specialized training. Those for the doctorate in theology were particularly arduous: by the end of the Middle Ages the course for the doctorate in theology at the University of Paris had been extended to twelve or thirteen years after the roughly eight years taken for the M.A.! Continuous residence was not required and it was accordingly

The courses of study

A Lecture Class in a Medieval University. Some interesting similarities and contrasts may be observed between this scene and a modern classroom.

rare to become a doctor of theology before the age of forty; statutes in fact forbade awarding the degree to anyone under thirty-five. Strictly speaking, doctor's degrees, including even the one in medicine, only conferred the right to teach. But in practice university degrees of all grades were recognized as standards of attainment and became pathways to nonacademic careers.

Student life

Student life in medieval universities was often very rowdy. Many students were very immature because it was customary to begin university studies between the ages of twelve and fifteen. Moreover, all university students believed that they comprised an independent and privileged community, set aside from that of the local townspeople. Since the latter tried to reap financial profits from the students, and the students were naturally boisterous, there were frequent riots and sometimes pitched battles between "town" and "gown." But actual study was very intense. Because the greatest emphasis was placed on the value of authority and also because books were prohibitively expensive (they were handwritten and made from rare parchment), there was an enormous amount of rote memorization. As students advanced in their disciplines they were also expected to develop their own skills in formal, public disputations. Advanced disputations could become extremely complex and abstract; sometimes they might also last for days. The most important fact pertaining to medieval university students was that, after about 1250, there were so many of them. The University of Paris in the thirteenth century numbered about seven thousand students and Oxford somewhere around two thousand in any given year. This means that a relatively appreciable proportion of male Europeans who were more than peasants or artisans were gaining at least some education at the higher levels.

*Acquisition of Greek and
Arabic knowledge*

As the numbers of those educated at all levels vastly increased during the High Middle Ages, so did the quality of learning. This was owing first and foremost to the reacquisition of Greek knowledge and to the absorption of intellectual advances made by the Muslims. Since practically no western Europeans knew Greek or Arabic, works in those languages had to be transmitted by means of Latin translations. But there were very few of these before about 1140: of all the many works of Aristotle only a few logical treatises were available in Latin translations before the middle of the twelfth century. But then, suddenly, an enormous burst of translating activity made almost all of ancient Greek and Arabic scientific knowledge accessible to western Europeans. This activity transpired in Spain and Sicily because Christians there lived in close proximity with Arabic speakers, or Jews who knew Latin and Arabic, either of whom could aid them in their tasks. Greek works were first translated into Latin from earlier Arabic translations; then many were retranslated directly from the Greek by a few westerners who had managed to learn that language, usually by traveling in Greek-speaking territories. The result was that by about 1260 almost the entire Aristotelian corpus that is known today was made available in Latin. So also were basic works of such important Greek scientific thinkers as Euclid, Galen, and Ptolemy. Only the milestones of Greek literature and the works of Plato were not yet translated because they had not been made available to the Arabs; they existed only in inaccessible Byzantine manuscripts. But in addition to the thought of the Greeks, Western scholars became familiar with the accomplishments of all the major Islamic philosophers and scientists such as Avicenna and Averroës.

Having acquired the best of Greek and Arabic scientific and speculative thought, the West was able to build on it and make its own advances. This progress transpired in different ways. When it came to natural science, westerners were able to start building on the acquired learning without much difficulty because it seldom conflicted with the principles of Christianity. But when it came to philosophy, the basic question arose as to how thoroughly Greek and Arabic thought was compatible with the Christian faith. The most advanced thirteenth-century scientist was the Englishman Robert Grosseteste (c. 1168–1253), who was not only a great thinker but was also very active in public life as bishop of Lincoln. Grosseteste became so proficient at Greek that he translated all of Aristotle's *Ethics*. More important, he made very significant theoretical advances in mathematics, astronomy, and optics. He formulated a sophisticated scientific explanation of the rainbow and he posited the use of lenses for magnification. Grosseteste's leading disciple was Roger Bacon (c. 1214–1294), who is today more famous than his teacher because he seems to have predicted automobiles and flying machines. Bacon in fact had no real interest in machinery, but he did follow up on Grosseteste's work in optics, discussing, for example, further properties of lenses, the rapid speed of light, and the nature of human vision. Grosseteste, Bacon, and some of their followers at the University of Oxford argued that natural knowledge was more certain when it was based on sensory evidence than when it rested on abstract reason. To this degree they can be seen as early forerunners of modern science. But the important qualification remains that they did not yet perform any real laboratory experiments.

The growth of western scientific and speculative thought; Robert Grosseteste and Roger Bacon

The story of the high-medieval encounter between Greek and Arabic philosophy and Christian faith is basically the story of the emergence of Scholasticism. This word can be, and has been, defined in many ways. In its root meaning Scholasticism was simply the method of teaching and learning followed in the medieval schools. That meant that it was highly systematic and also that it was highly respectful of authority. Yet Scholasticism was not only a method of study: it was a worldview. As such, it taught that there was a fundamental compatability between the knowledge humans can obtain naturally, i.e., by experience or reason, and the teachings imparted by

The meaning of Scholasticism

Divine Revelation. Since medieval scholars believed that the Greeks were the masters of natural knowledge and that all revelation was in the Bible, Scholasticism consequently was the theory and practice of reconciling classical philosophy with Christian faith.

Peter Abelard

One of the most important thinkers who paved the way for Scholasticism without yet being fully a Scholastic himself was the stormy petrel Peter Abelard. As a student Abelard was so adept in logic and theology that he publicly humiliated his teachers in and around Paris in debate. Such arrogant conduct made him many enemies. These engineered his first conviction for heresy in 1121. To complicate matters, Abelard entered upon an affair with a young woman, Heloise, herself a scholar, without marrying her. Abelard had been hired to be Heloise's tutor by her uncle, Fulbert, canon of Notre Dame of Paris. A child was the result of the affair, and Heloise's uncle took revenge upon Abelard by having him castrated. Heloise became a nun and Abelard a monk, but Abelard was too restless and cantankerous a personality to find real peace in a monastery. After quarreling and breaking with the monks of two different communities, he set himself up as a teacher in Paris from about 1132 until 1141. This was the peak of his career. In 1141, however, he was again charged with heresy, this time by the highly influential St. Bernard, and condemned by a Church council. Not long afterwards the persecuted thinker abjured, and in 1142 he died in retirement. Abelard recounted many of these trials in a letter called *The Story of My Calamities,* one of the first autobiographical accounts written in the West since St. Augustine's *Confessions.*

The life of the mind as a profession

On first reading, this work appears "modern" because Abelard seems to revel in himself and boast a great deal. But actually he did not write about his calamities in order to boast. Rather, his main intention was to moralize about how he had been appropriately punished for his intellectual pride by his first condemnation, and for his "lechery" by the loss of those parts which had "offended." Abelard certainly represents a reawakening interest in personal introspection, but in this he did not differ much from St. Augustine. More important is the fact that he was the first westerner who sought to make a full profession out of the life of the mind.

Sic et Non and the Scholastic method

Abelard's greatest contributions to the subsequent development of Scholasticism were made in his *Sic et Non* (Yes and No) and in a number of original theological works. In the *Sic et Non* Abelard prepared the way for the Scholastic method by gathering a collection of statements from the Bible and the church fathers that spoke for both sides of 150 theological questions. It used to be thought that the brash Abelard did this in order to embarrass authority, but the contrary is true. What Abelard really hoped to do was begin a process of careful study, whereby it could be shown that the highest authority of the Bible was infallible, and that the best authorities, despite any appearances to the contrary, really agreed with each other. Later Scholastics would follow his method of studying theology by raising fundamental questions and arraying the answers that had been put forth in authoritative texts. Abelard did not propose any solutions of his own in the *Sic et Non*, but he did start to do this in his original theological writings. In these he proposed to treat theology like a science, by studying it as comprehensively as possible and by applying to it the tools of logic, of which he was a master. He did not even shrink from applying logic to the mystery of the Trinity, one of the excesses for which he was condemned. Thus he was one of the first to try to harmonize religion with rationalism and was in this capacity a herald of the Scholastic outlook.

Immediately after Abelard's death two important steps were taken to further prepare for mature Scholasticism. One was the writing of the *Book of Sentences* between 1155 and 1157 by Abelard's student Peter Lombard. This raised all the most fundamental theological questions in rigorously consequential order, adduced answers from the Bible and Christian authorities on both sides of each question, and then proposed a judgment on every case. Within a short time Peter Lombard's work became a standard text. Once formal schools of theology were established in the universities, all aspirants to the doctorate were required to study and comment upon it; not surprisingly theologians also followed its organizational procedures in their own writings. Thus the full Scholastic method was born.

Peter Lombard's Book of Sentences

The other basic step in the development of Scholasticism, as mentioned above, was the reacquisition of classical philosophy that occurred after about 1140. Abelard would probably have been glad to have drawn upon the thought of the Greeks, but he could not because few Greek works were yet available in translation. Later theologians, however, could avail themselves fully of the new knowledge, above all, the works of Aristotle and his Arabic commentators. By around 1250 Aristotle's authority in purely philosophical matters became so great that he was referred to as "the Philosopher" pure and simple. Scholastics of the mid–thirteenth century accordingly adhered to Peter Lombard's organizational method, but added the consideration of Greek and Arabic philosophical authorities to that of purely Christian theological ones. In doing this they tried to construct systems of understanding the entire universe that most fully harmonized the earlier separate realms of faith and natural knowledge.

Influence of Aristotle

By far the greatest accomplishments in this endeavor were made by St. Thomas Aquinas (1225–1274), the leading Scholastic theologian of the University of Paris. As a member of the Dominican order, St. Thomas was committed to the principle that faith could be defended by reason. More important, he believed that natural knowledge and the study of the created universe were legitimate ways of approaching theological wisdom because "nature" complements "grace." By this

St. Thomas Aquinas

St. Thomas Aquinas. A fifteenth-century painting by Justus of Ghent, after an earlier copy.

The achievements of the thirteenth century

he meant to say that because God created the natural world He can be approached through its terms even though ultimate certainty about the highest truths can only be obtained through the supernatural revelation of the Bible. Imbued with a deep confidence in the value of human reason and human experience, as well as in his own ability to harmonize Greek philosophy with Christian theology, Thomas was the most serene of saints. In a long career of teaching at the University of Paris and elsewhere he indulged in few controversies and worked quietly on his two great *Summaries* of theology: the *Summa contra Gentiles* and the much larger *Summa Theologica*. In these he hoped to set down all that could be said about the faith on the firmest of foundations.

Most experts think that St. Thomas came extremely close to fulfilling this extraordinarily ambitious goal. His vast *Summaries* are awesome for their rigorous orderliness and intellectual penetration. He admits in them that there are certain "mysteries of the faith," such as the doctrines of the Trinity and the Incarnation, that cannot be approached by the unaided human intellect; otherwise, he subjects all theological questions to philosophical inquiry. In this, St. Thomas relied heavily on the work of Aristotle, but he is by no means merely "Aristotle baptized." Instead, he fully subordinated Aristotelianism to basic Christian principles and thereby created his own original philosophical and theological system. Scholars disagree about how far this system diverges from the earlier Christian thought of St. Augustine, but there seems little doubt that Aquinas placed a higher value on human reason, on human life in this world, and on the abilities of humans to participate in their own salvation. Not long after his death St. Thomas was canonized, for his intellectual accomplishments seemed like miracles. His influence lives on today insofar as he helped to revive confidence in rationalism and human experience. More directly, philosophy in the modern Roman Catholic Church is supposed to be taught according to the Thomistic method, doctrine, and principles.

With the achievements of St. Thomas Aquinas in the middle of the thirteenth century, Western medieval thought reached its pinnacle. Not coincidentally, other aspects of medieval civilization were reaching their pinnacles at the same time. France was enjoying its ripest period of peace and prosperity under the rule of St. Louis, the University of Paris was defining its basic organizational forms, and the greatest French Gothic cathedrals were being built. Some ardent admirers of medieval culture have fixed on these accomplishments to call the thirteenth the "greatest of centuries." Such a judgment, of course, is a matter of taste, but many of us might respond that life was still too harsh and requirements for religious orthodoxy too great to justify this extreme celebration of the lost past. Whatever our individual judgments, it seems wise to end this section by correcting some false impressions about medieval intellectual life.

It is often thought that medieval thinkers were excessively conservative, but in fact the greatest thinkers of the High Middle Ages were astonishingly receptive to new ideas. As committed Christians they could not allow doubts to be cast upon the principles of their faith, but otherwise they were glad to accept whatever they could from the Greeks and Arabs. Considering that Aristotelian thought was radically different than anything accepted before in its emphasis on rationalism and the fundamental goodness and purposefulness of nature, its rapid acceptance by the Scholastics was a philosophical revolution. Another false impression is that Scholastic thinkers were greatly constrained by authority. Certainly they revered authority more than we do today, but Scholastics like St. Thomas did not regard the mere citation of texts—except biblical revelation concerning the mysteries of the faith—as being sufficient to clinch an argument. Rather, the authorities were brought forth to outline the possibilities, but reason and experience then demonstrated the truth. Finally, it is often believed that Scholastic thinkers were "antihumanistic," but modern scholars are coming to the opposite conclusion. Scholastics unquestionably gave primacy to the soul over the body and to otherworldly salvation over life in the here and now. But they also exalted the dignity of human nature because they viewed it as a glorious divine creation, and they believed in the possibility of a working alliance between themselves and God. Moreover, they had extraordinary faith in the powers of human reason—probably more than we do today.

*False impressions
concerning Scholastic
thinkers*

5. THE BLOSSOMING OF LITERATURE, ART, AND MUSIC

The literature of the High Middle Ages was as varied, lively, and impressive as that produced in any other period in Western history. The revival of grammatical studies in the cathedral schools and universities led to the production of some excellent Latin poetry. The best examples were secular lyrics, especially those written in the twelfth century by a group of poets known as the Goliards. How these poets got their name is uncertain, but it possibly meant followers of the devil. That would have been appropriate because the Goliards were riotous poets who wrote parodies of the liturgy and burlesques of the Gospels. Their lyrics celebrated the beauties of the changing seasons, the carefree life of the open road, the pleasures of drinking and sporting, and especially the joys of love. The authors of these rollicking and satirical songs were mainly wandering students, although some were men in more advanced years. The names of most are unknown. Their poetry is particularly significant both for its robust vitality and for being the first clear counterstatement to the ascetic ideal of Christianity.

In addition to the use of Latin, the vernacular languages of French,

*Medieval Latin literature;
the poetry of the Goliards*

Charlemagne Weeping for His Knights. A scene from the *Song of Roland*.

The growth of vernacular literature; the epic

German, Spanish, and Italian became increasingly popular as media of literary expression. At first, most of the literature in the vernacular languages was written in the form of the heroic epic. Among the leading examples were the French *Song of Roland,* the Norse eddas and sagas, the German *Song of the Nibelungs,* and the Spanish *Poem of the Cid.* Practically all of these works were originally composed between 1050 and 1150, although some were first set down in writing afterwards. These epics portrayed a virile but unpolished warrior society. Blood flowed freely, skulls were cleaved by battleaxes, and heroic warfare, honor, and loyalty were the major themes. If women were mentioned at all, they were subordinate to men. Brides were expected to die for their betrotheds, but husbands were free to beat their wives. In one French epic a queen who tried to influence her husband met with a blow to the nose; even though blood flowed she replied: "Many thanks, when it pleases you, you may do it again." Despite the repugnance we find in such passages, the best of the vernacular epics have much unpretentious literary power. Above all, the *Song of Roland,* though crude, is like an uncut gem.

The love songs of the troubadours

In comparison to the epics, an enormous change in both subject matter and style was introduced in twelfth-century France by the troubadour poets and the writers of courtly romances. The dramatic nature of this change represents further proof that high-medieval culture was not at all conservative. The troubadours were courtier poets who came from southern France and wrote in the dialect of French known as Provençal. The origin of their inspiration is debated, but there can be no doubt that they initiated a movement of profound importance for all subsequent Western literature. Their style was far more finely wrought and sophisticated than that of the epic poets, and the most eloquent of their lyrics, which were meant to be sung to music, originated the theme of romantic love. The troubadours idealized women as marvelous beings who could grant intense spiritual and sensual gratification. Whatever greatness the poets found in themselves they usually attributed to the inspiration they found in love. But they also assumed that their love would lose its magic if it were too easily or frequently gratified. Therefore, they wrote more often of longing than of romantic fulfillment.

In addition to their love lyrics, the troubadours wrote several other kinds of short poems. Some were simply bawdy. In these, love is not mentioned at all but the poet revels in thoughts of carnality, comparing, for example, the riding of his horse to the "riding" of his mistress. Other troubadour poems treat of feats of arms, others comment on contemporary political events, and a few even meditate on matters of religion. But whatever the subject matter, the best troubadour poems were always cleverly and innovatively expressed. The literary tradition originated by the southern French troubadours was continued by the *trouvères* in northern France and by the *minnesingers* in Germany. Thereafter many of their innovations were developed by later lyric poets in all Western languages. Some of their poetic devices were consciously revived in the twentieth century by such "modernists" as Ezra Pound.

An equally important twelfth-century French innovation was the composition of longer narrative poems known as romances. These were the first clear ancestors of the modern novel: they told engaging stories, they often excelled in portraying character, and their subject matter was usually love and adventure. Some romances elaborated on classical Greek themes, but the most famous and best were "Arthurian." These took their material from the legendary exploits of the Celtic hero King Arthur and his many chivalrous knights. The first great writer of Arthurian romances was the northern Frenchman Chrétien de Troyes, who was active between about 1165 and 1190. Chrétien did much to help create and shape the new form, and he also introduced innovations in subject matter and attitudes. Whereas the troubadours exalted unrequited, extramarital love, Chrétien was the first to hold forth the ideal of romantic love within marriage. He also described not only the deeds but the thoughts and emotions of his characters.

A generation later, Chrétien's work was continued by the great German poets Wolfram von Eschenbach and Gottfried von Strassburg. These are recognized as the greatest writers in the German language before the eighteenth century. Wolfram's *Parzival,* a story of love and the search for the Holy Grail, is more subtle, complex, and greater in scope than any other high-medieval literary work except Dante's *Divine Comedy.* Like Chrétien, Wolfram believed that true love could

Other troubadour poems

The Arthurian romances; Chrétien de Troyes

A Thirteenth-Century Miniature. From a Manuscript of Wolfram von Eschenbach's *Parzival.*

only be fulfilled in marriage, and in *Parzival,* for the first time in Western literature since the Greeks, one can see a full psychological development of the hero. Gottfried von Strassburg's *Tristan* is a more somber work, which tells of the hopeless adulterous love of Tristan and Isolde. Indeed, it might almost be regarded as the prototype of modern tragic romanticism. Gottfried was one of the first to develop fully the idea of individual suffering as a literary theme and to point out the indistinct line which separates pleasure from pain. For him, to love is to yearn, and suffering and unfulfilled gratification are integral chapters of the book of life. Unlike the troubadours, he could only see complete fulfillment of love in death. *Parzival* and *Tristan* have become most famous today in the form of their operatic reconceptions by the nineteenth-century German composer Richard Wagner.

Not all high-medieval narratives were so elevated as the romances in either form or substance. A very different new narrative form was the *fabliau,* or verse fable. Although *fabliaux* derived from the moral animal tales of Aesop, they quickly evolved into short stories that were written less to edify or instruct than to amuse. Often they were very coarse, and sometimes they dealt with sexual relations in a broadly humorous and thoroughly unromantic manner. Many were also strongly anticlerical, making monks and priests the butts of their jokes. Because the *fabliaux* are so "uncourtly" it used to be thought that they were written solely for the new urban classes. But there is now little doubt that they were addressed at least equally to the "refined" aristocracy who liked to have their laughs too. They are significant as expressions of growing worldliness and as the first manifestations of the robust realism which was later to be perfected by Boccaccio and Chaucer.

Completely different in form but similar as an illustration of growing worldliness was the sprawling *Romance of the Rose.* As its title indicates, this was begun as a romance, specifically around 1230 by the courtly Frenchman William of Lorris. But William left his rather flowery, romantic work unfinished, and it was completed around 1270 by another Frenchman, John of Meun. The latter changed its nature greatly. He inserted long, biting digressions in which he skewered religious hypocrisy, and made his major theme the need for procreation. Not love, but the service of "Dame Nature" in sexual fecundity is urged in numerous witty but extremely earthy images and metaphors. At the climax the originally dreamy hero seizes his mistress, who is allegorically depicted as a rose, and rapes her. Since the work became enormously popular, it seems fair to conclude that tastes, then as now, were very diverse.

In a class by itself as the greatest work of medieval literature is Dante's *Divine Comedy.* Not much is known about the life of Dante Alighieri (1265–1321), except that he was active during the early part of his career in the political affairs of his native city of Florence. Despite

Nature Perpetuates the Species. A miniature from a manuscript of the *Romance of the Rose.*

his engagement in politics and the fact that he was a layman, he managed to acquire an awesome mastery of the religious, philosophic, and literary knowledge of his time. He not only knew the Bible and the church fathers, but—most unusual for a layman—he also absorbed the most recent Scholastic theology. In addition, he was thoroughly familiar with Virgil, Cicero, Boethius, and numerous other classical writers, and was fully conversant with the poems of the troubadours and the Italian poetry of his own day. In 1302 he was expelled from Florence after a political upheaval and was forced to live the rest of his life in exile. The *Divine Comedy,* his major work, was written during this final period.

Dante's *Divine Comedy* is a monumental narrative in powerful rhyming Italian verse, which describes the poet's journey through hell, purgatory, and paradise. At the start Dante tells of how he once found himself in a "dark wood," his metaphor for a deep personal mid-life crisis. He is led out of this forest of despair by the Roman Virgil, who stands for the heights of classical reason and philosophy. Virgil guides Dante on a trip through hell and purgatory, and afterwards Dante's deceased beloved, Beatrice, who stands for Christian wisdom and blessedness, takes over and guides him through paradise. In the course of this progress Dante meets both historical beings and the poet's contemporaries, all of whom have already been assigned places in the afterlife, and he is instructed by them and his guides as to why they met their several fates. As the poem progresses the poet himself leaves the condition of despair to grow in wisdom and ultimately to reach assurance of his own salvation.

The Divine Comedy

Every reader finds a different combination of wonder and satisfaction in Dante's magnificent work. Some—especially those who know Italian—marvel at the vigor and inventiveness of Dante's language and images. Others are awed by his subtle complexity and poetic symmetry; others by his array of learning; others by the vitality of his characters and individual stories; and still others by his soaring imagination. The historian finds it particularly remarkable that Dante could sum up the best of medieval learning in such an artistically satisfying manner. Dante stressed the precedence of salvation, but he viewed the earth as existing for human benefit. He allowed humans free will to choose good and avoid evil, and accepted Greek philosophy as authoritative in its own sphere; for example, he called Aristotle "the master of them that know." Above all, his sense of hope and his ultimate faith in humanity—remarkable for a defeated exile—most powerfully expresses the dominant mood of the High Middle Ages and makes Dante one of the two or three most stirringly affirmative writers who ever lived.

Quarter Barrel Vaults, Typical of Romanesque Architecture. St. Etienne, Nevers.

The closest architectural equivalents of the *Divine Comedy* are the great high-medieval Gothic cathedrals, for they too have qualities of vast scope, balance of intricate detail with careful symmetry, soaring

Medieval architecture: (1) the Romanesque style

Worms Cathedral, Eleventh-Century Romanesque

Romanesque Sculpture. Shown here is Jesus with two of his Apostles. The elongation and distortion is typical. From a church in Spain.

height, and affirmative religious grandeur. But before we approach the Gothic style, it is best to introduce it by means of its high-medieval predecessor, the style of architecture and art known as the Romanesque. This style had its origins in the tenth century, but became fully formed in the eleventh and first half of the twelfth centuries, when the religious reform movement led to the building of many new monasteries and large churches. The Romanesque was primarily a building style: it aimed to manifest the glory of God in ecclesiastical construction by rigorously subordinating all architectural details to a uniform system. In this it was very severe: we may think of it as the architectural analogue of the unadorned hymn. Aside from its primary stress on systematic construction, the essential features of the Romanesque style were the rounded arch, massive stone walls, enormous piers, small windows, and the predominance of horizontal lines. The plainness of interiors was sometimes relieved by mosaics or frescoes in bright colors, and, a very important innovation for Christian art, the introduction of sculptural decoration, both within and without. For the first time, full-length human figures appeared on facades. These are usually grave and elongated far beyond natural dimensions, but they have much evocative power and represent the first manifestations of a revived interest in sculpting the human form.

In the course of the twelfth and thirteenth centuries the Romanesque style was supplanted throughout most of Europe by the Gothic. Although trained art historians can see how certain traits of the one style led to the development of the other, the actual appearance of the two styles is enormously different. In fact, the two seem as different as the epic is different from the romance, an appropriate analogy because the Gothic style emerged in France in the mid–twelfth century exactly when the romance did, and because it was far more sophisticated, graceful, and elegant than its predecessor, in the same way that the romance compared with the epic. The rapid development and acceptance of the Gothic shows for a last time—if any more proof be needed—that the twelfth century was experimental and dynamic, arguably at least as much as the twentieth. When the abbey church of St. Denis, venerated as the shrine of the French patron saint and burial place of French kings, was torn down in 1144 in order to make room for a much larger one in the strikingly new Gothic style, it was as if the president of the United States were to tear down the White House and replace it with a Mies van der Rohe or Frank Lloyd Wright edifice. Such an act today would be highly improbable, or at least would create an enormous uproar. But in the twelfth century the equivalent act actually happened and was taken in stride.

Gothic architecture was one of the most intricate of building styles. Its basic elements were the pointed arch, groined and ribbed vaulting, and the flying buttress. These devices made possible a much lighter and loftier construction than could ever have been achieved with the round arch and the engaged pier of the Romanesque. In fact, the

(2) the development of the Gothic style

Elements of the Gothic style

Left: *Rheims Cathedral.* Built between 1220 and 1299, this High Gothic cathedral places great stress on the vertical elements. The gabled portals, the windows above the doorways, the gallery of royal statues, and the multitude of pinnacles all accentuate the height of the structue. Right: *The High Chapel of La Sainte-Chapelle, Paris.* High Gothic is here carried to its logical extreme. Slender columns, tracery, and stained-glass windows take the place of walls.

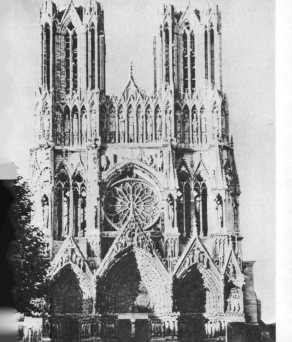

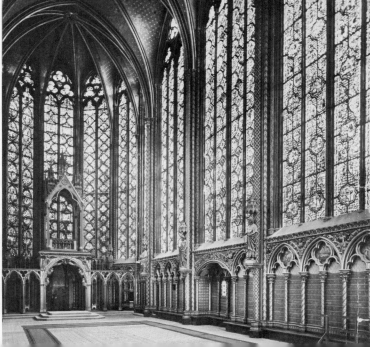

See color plates following page 384

The significance of Gothic architecture

Gothic cathedral could be described as a skeletal framework of stone enclosed by enormous windows. Other features included lofty spires, rose windows, delicate tracery in stone, elaborately sculptured facades, multiple columns, and the use of gargoyles, or representations of mythical monsters, as decorative devices. Ornamentation in the best of the cathedrals was generally concentrated on the exterior. Except for the stained glass windows and the intricate carving on woodwork and altars, interiors were kept rather simple and occasionally almost severe. But the inside of the Gothic cathedral was never somber or gloomy. The stained glass windows served not to exclude the light but to glorify it, to catch the rays of sunlight and suffuse them with a richness and warmth of color which nature itself could hardly duplicate even in its happiest moods.

Many people still think of the Gothic cathedral as the expression of purely ascetic otherworldliness, but this estimation is highly inaccurate. Certainly all churches are dedicated to the glory of God and hope for life everlasting, but Gothic ones sometimes included stained glass scenes of daily life that had no overt religious significance at all. More important, Gothic sculpture of religious figures such as Jesus, the Virgin, and the saints was becoming far more naturalistic than anything hitherto created in the medieval West. So also was the sculptural representation of plant and animal life, for interest in the human person and in the world of natural beauty was no longer considered sinful. Moreover, Gothic architecture was also an expression of the medieval intellectual genius. Each cathedral, with its mass of symbolic figures, was a kind of encyclopedia of medieval knowledge carved in stone for

Gothic Sculpture. The three kings bearing gifts, from the thirteenth-century cathedral of Amiens. Note the greater naturalism in comparison to the Romanesque sculpture shown on p. 476.

those who could not read. Finally, Gothic cathedrals were manifestations of urban pride. Always located in the growing medieval cities, they were meant to be both centers of community life and expressions of a town's greatness. When a new cathedral went up the people of the entire community participated in erecting it, and rightfully regarded it as almost their own property. Many of the Gothic cathedrals were the products of urban rivalries. Each city or town sought to overawe its neighbor with ever bigger or taller buildings, to the degree that ambitions sometimes got out of bounds and many of the cathedrals were left unfinished. But most of the finished ones are still vast enough. Built to last into eternity, they provide the most striking visual manifestation of the soaring exuberance of their age.

Surveys of high-medieval accomplishments often omit drama and music, but such oversights are unfortunate. Our own modern drama descends at least as much from the medieval form as from the classical one. Throughout the medieval period some Latin classical plays were known in manuscript but were never performed. Instead drama was born all over again within the Church. In the early Middle Ages certain passages in the liturgy began to be acted out. Then, in the twelfth century, primarily in Paris, these were superseded by short religious plays in Latin, performed inside the Church. Rapidly thereafter, and still in twelfth-century Paris, the Latin plays were supplemented or supplanted by ones in the vernacular so that the whole congregation could understand them. Then, around 1200, these started to be performed outside, in front of the Church, so that they would not take time away from the services. As soon as that happened, drama entered the everyday world: nonreligious stories were introduced, character portrayal was expanded, and the way was fully prepared for the Elizabethans and Shakespeare.

The revival of drama

As the drama grew out of developments within the liturgy and then moved far beyond them, so did characteristically Western music. Until the High Middle Ages Western music was *homophonic*, as is most non-Western music even today. That is, it developed only one melody at a time without any harmonic background. The great high-medieval invention was *polyphony*, or the playing of two or more harmonious melodies together. Some experiments along these lines may have been made in the West as early as the tenth century, but the most fundamental breakthrough was achieved in the cathedral of Paris around 1170, when the Mass was first sung by two voices weaving together two different melodies in "counterpoint." Roughly concurrently, systems of musical notation were invented and perfected so that performance no longer had to rely on memory and could become more complex. All the greatness of Western music followed from these first steps.

Medieval music: polyphony

It may have been noticed that many of the same people who made such important contributions to learning, thought, literature, architecture, drama, and music, must have intermingled with each other in the Paris of the High Middle Ages. Some of them no doubt prayed together in the cathedral of Notre Dame. The names of the leading scholars are remembered, but the names of most of the others are forgotten. Yet taken together they did as much for civilization and created as many enduring monuments as their counterparts in ancient Athens. If their names are forgotten, their achievements in many different ways live on still.

SELECTED READINGS

• *Items so designated are available in paperback editions.*

RELIGION AND THE CRUSADES

• Barraclough, G., *The Medieval Papacy,* New York, 1968. A forcefully argued analytical treatment. Noteworthy too for its illustrations.

Daniel-Rops, H., *Cathedral and Crusade,* 2 vols., New York, 1963. The best survey from a Roman Catholic perspective.

Erdmann, Carl, *The Origin of the Idea of Crusade,* Princeton, N.J., 1978. A brilliant advanced work on the background to the First Crusade.

Lambert, Malcolm, *Medieval Heresy,* London, 1977. A masterful synthesis.

Leclercq, Jean, *Bernard of Clairvaux and the Cistercian Spirit,* Kalamazoo, Mich., 1976.

• Mayer, Hans Eberhard, *The Crusades,* New York, 1972. The best one-volume survey.

Moorman, J. R. H., *A History of the Franciscan Order from its Origins to the Year 1517,* Oxford, 1968. Exhaustive.

Runciman, S., *A History of the Crusades,* 3 vols., Cambridge, 1951–54. Colorful and engrossing.

Southern, R. W., *Western Society and the Church in the Middle Ages,* Baltimore, 1970. An extremely insightful and well-written interpretation of the interplay between society and religion.

Tellenbach, G., *Church, State and Christian Society at the Time of the Investiture Contest,* Oxford, 1940. Stresses revolutionary aspects of Gregory VII's thought and career.

Ullmann, Walter, *A Short History of the Papacy in the Middle Ages,* 2nd ed., London, 1974.

THOUGHT, LETTERS, AND THE ARTS

• Baldwin, John W., *The Scholastic Culture of the Middle Ages,* Lexington, Mass., 1971. A fine introduction.

Bergin, T. G., *Dante,* New York, 1965.

Chenu, M. D., *Toward Understanding St. Thomas,* Chicago, 1964. An excellent approach to St. Thomas's work by a contemporary Dominican.

Cobban, Alan B., *The Medieval Universities,* London, 1975. The best shorter treatment in English.

• Crombie, A. C., *Medieval and Early Modern Science,* Vol. I, rev. ed., New York, 1959.

Curtius, E. R., *European Literature and the Latin Middle Ages,* New York, 1953. An exhaustive treatment of medieval Latin literature in terms of its classical background and influence on later times.

Frankl, P., *Gothic Architecture,* Baltimore, 1962.

Gilson, E., *Reason and Revelation in the Middle Ages,* New York, 1938. A brief but illuminating treatment by the greatest modern student of Scholasticism.

• Haskins, C. H., *The Renaissance of the Twelfth Century,* Cambridge, Mass., 1927. Treats Latin writings in many different genres.

• Henderson, George, *Gothic,* Baltimore, 1967.

Holmes, Urban T., *A History of Old French Literature,* 2nd ed., London, 1948.

Hoppin, Richard H., *Medieval Music,* New York, 1978.

• Knowles, David, *The Evolution of Medieval Thought,* New York, 1962. A very authoritative and well-written but often difficult survey.

Leclercq, Jean, *The Love of Learning and the Desire for God,* New York, 1961. About monastic culture, with special reference to St. Bernard.

Leff, G., *Paris and Oxford Universities in the Thirteenth and Fourteenth Centuries,* New York, 1968. Covers both thought and institutions of learning.

• Lewis, C. S., *The Discarded Image,* Cambridge, 1964.

• Mâle, E., *The Gothic Image,* New York, 1913.

• Morris, Colin, *The Discovery of the Individual,* London, 1972. A provocative interpretation which sees "individualism" as a twelfth-century discovery.

Reese, Gustave, *Music in the Middle Ages,* New York, 1940.

Southern, R. W., *Medieval Humanism,* New York, 1970. A collection of essays, almost all of which are exciting. Most exciting is the title piece.

• Ullmann, W., *Medieval Political Thought,* rev. ed., Baltimore, 1976. The best short survey.

Van Steenberghen, F., *Aristotle in the West,* New York, 1970. A short account of the recovery of Aristotelian thought in the High Middle Ages.

• Von Simson, O., *The Gothic Cathedral,* New York, 1956. A controversial argument that Gothic architecture was meant to be "scientific."

SOURCE MATERIALS

• *An Aquinas Reader,* ed. Mary T. Clark, New York, 1972.

• Chrétien de Troyes, *Arthurian Romances,* tr. W. W. Comfort, New York, 1914.

• Dante, *The Divine Comedy,* tr. J. Ciardi, New York, 1977.

• Goldin, F., ed., *Lyrics of the Troubadours and Trouvères,* New York, 1973.

• Gottfried von Strassburg, *Tristan,* tr. A. T. Hatto, Baltimore, 1960.

• Joinville and Villehardouin, *Chronicles of the Crusades,* tr. M. R. B. Shaw, Baltimore, 1963.

• *The Letters of Abelard and Heloise* (includes Abelard's *Story of My Calamities*), tr. B. Radice, Baltimore, 1974.

• Peters, Edward, ed., *The First Crusade: The Chronicle of Fulcher of Chartres and Other Source Materials,* Philadelphia, 1971.

The Romance of the Rose, tr. Harry W. Robbins, New York, 1962.
- *The Song of Roland,* tr. F. Goldin, New York, 1978.
- Thorndike, Lynn, ed., *University Records and Life in the Middle Ages,* New York, 1944.
- Tierney, Brian, ed., *The Crisis of Church and State, 1050–1300,* Englewood Cliffs, N.J., 1964. An excellent anthology of readings introduced and connected by masterful commentary.
- Wolfram von Eschenbach, *Parzival,* tr. H. M. Mustard and C. E. Passage, New York, 1961.

Chapter 16

THE LATER MIDDLE AGES
(1300–1500)

My lot has been to live amidst a storm
Of varying disturbing circumstances.
For you . . . a better age awaits.
Our descendants—the darkness once dispersed—
Can come again to the old radiance.

—The poet Petrarch,
writing in the 1340s

If the High Middle Ages were "times of feasts," then the late Middle Ages were "times of famine." From about 1300 until the middle or latter part of the fifteenth century calamities struck throughout western Europe with appalling severity and dismaying persistence. Famine first prevailed because agriculture was impeded by soil exhaustion, colder weather, and torrential rainfalls. Then, on top of those "acts of God," came the most terrible natural disaster of all: the dreadful plague known as the "Black Death," which cut broad swaths of mortality throughout western Europe. As if all that were not enough, incessant warfare continually brought hardship and desolation. Common people suffered most because they were most exposed to raping, stabbing, looting, and burning by soldiers and organized bands of freebooters. After an army passed through a region one might see miles of smoldering ruins littered with putrefying corpses; in many places the desolation was so great that wolves roamed the countryside and even entered the outskirts of the cities. In short, if the serene Virgin symbolized the High Middle Ages, the grinning death's-head symbolized the succeeding period. For these reasons we should not look to the later Middle Ages for the dramatic progress we saw transpiring earlier; but this is not to say that there was no progress at all. In the last two centuries of the Middle Ages Europeans dis-

The later Middle Ages: castastrophe and adaptation

played a tenacious perseverance in the face of adversity. Instead of abandoning themselves to apathy, they resolutely sought to adjust themselves to changed circumstances. Thus there was no collapse of civilization as there was with the fall of the Roman Empire, but rather a period of transition that resulted in preserving and building upon what was most solid in Europe's earlier legacy.

1. ECONOMIC DEPRESSION AND THE EMERGENCE OF A NEW EQUILIBRIUM

Economic crisis

By around 1300 the agricultural expansion of the High Middle Ages had reached its limits. Thereafter yields and areas under cultivation began to decline, causing a decline in the whole European economy that was accelerated by the disruptive effects of war. Accordingly, the first half of the fourteenth century was a time of growing economic depression. The coming of the Black Death in 1347 made this depression particularly acute because it completely disrupted the affairs of daily life. Subsequent recurrences of the plague and protracted warfare continued to depress most of the European economy until deep into the fifteenth century. But between roughly 1350–1450 Europeans learned how to adjust to the new economic circumstances and succeeded in placing their economy on a sounder basis. This became most evident after around 1450, when the tapering off of disease and warfare permitted a slow, but steady economic recovery. All told, therefore, despite a prolonged depression of roughly 150 years, Europe emerged in the later fifteenth century with a healthier economy than it had known earlier.

Agricultural adversity

The limits to agricultural expansion reached around 1300 were natural ones. There was a limit to the amount of land that could be cleared and a limit to the amount of crops that could be raised without the introduction of scientific farming. In fact, Europeans had gone further in clearing and cultivating than they should have: in the enthusiasm of the high-medieval colonization movement, marginal lands had been cleared that were not rich enough to sustain intense cultivation. In addition, even the best plots were becoming overworked. To make matters worse, after around 1300 the weather deteriorated. Whereas western Europe had been favored with a drying and warming trend in the eleventh and twelfth centuries, the fourteenth century saw the climate become colder and wetter. Although the average decline in temperature over the course of the century was only at most 1° Centigrade, this was sufficient to curtail viticulture in many northern areas such as England. Cereal farming too became increasingly impractical in far northern regions because the growing season became too short: in Greenland and parts of Scandinavia agricultural settlements were abandoned entirely. Increased rainfall also took its toll.

Terrible floods that deluged all of northwestern Europe in 1315 ruined crops and caused a prolonged, deathly famine. For three years peasants were so driven by hunger that they ate their seed grain, ruining their chances for a full recovery in the following season. In desperation they also ate cats, dogs, and rats. Many peasants were so exposed to unsanitary conditions and weakened by malnutrition that they became highly susceptible to disease. Thus there was an appalling death rate. In one Flemish city a tenth of the population was buried within a six-month period of 1316 alone. Relatively settled farming conditions returned after 1318, but in many parts of Europe heavy rains or other climatic disasters came again. In Italy floods swept away Florentine bridges in 1333 and a tidal wave destroyed the port of Amalfi in 1343. With nature so recurrently capricious economic life could only suffer.

*The pressure of
population*

Although ruinous wars combined with famine to kill off many, Europe remained overpopulated until the middle of the fourteenth century. The reason for this was that population growth was still outstripping food supply. Since people continued to multiply while cereal production declined, there was just not enough food to go around. Accordingly, grain prices soared and the poor throughout Europe paid the penalty in hunger. And then a disaster struck which was so appalling that it seemed to many to presage the end of the world.

The Black Death

This was the Black Death, a combined onslaught of bubonic and pneumonic plague which first swept through Europe from 1347 to 1350, and returned at periodic intervals for roughly the next hundred years. This calamity was fully comparable—in terms of the death, dislocation, and horror it wrought—to the two world wars of the twentieth century. The clinical effects of the plague were hideous. Once infected with bubonic plague by a flea-bite, the diseased person would develop enormous swellings in the groin or armpits; black spots might appear on the arms and legs, diarrhea would ensue, and the victim would die between the third and fifth day. If the infection came in the pneumonic form, i.e., caused by inhalation, there would be coughing of blood instead of swellings, and death would follow within three days. Some people went to bed healthy and were dead the next morning after a night of agony; ships with dead crews floated aimlessly on the seas. Although the successive epidemics left a few localities unscathed, the overall demographic effects of the plague were devastating. To take just a few examples: the population of Toulouse declined from roughly 30,000 in 1335, to 26,000 in 1385, to 8,000 in 1430; the total population of eastern Normandy fell by 30 percent between 1347 and 1357, and again by 30 percent before 1380; in the rural area around Pistoia a population depletion of about 60 percent occurred between 1340 and 1404. Altogether, the combined effects of famine, war, and, above all, plague reduced the total population of western Europe by at least one half and probably more like two-thirds between 1300 and 1450.

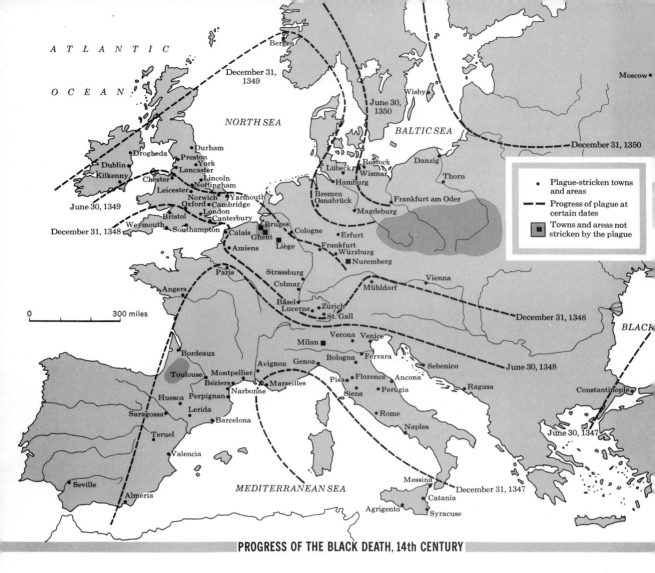

Map labels:

ATLANTIC OCEAN

NORTH SEA

BALTIC SEA

Moscow

Bergen — December 31, 1349

Wisby — June 30, 1350

December 31, 1350

Durham

Drogheda · Preston · York · Lancaster · Dublin · Lincoln · Kilkenny · Nottingham · Chester · Leicester · Norwich · Yarmouth · Oxford · Cambridge · London · Canterbury · Bristol · Weymouth · Southampton

June 30, 1349

December 31, 1348

Rostock · Lübeck · Wismar · Hamburg · Danzig · Thorn · Bremen · Osnabrück · Frankfurt am Oder · Magdeburg · Erfurt

Calais · Bruges · Ghent · Cologne · Amiens · Liège · Frankfurt · Würzburg · Nuremberg

Paris · Strassburg · Colmar · Vienna · Angers · Bâsel · Mühldorf · Lucerne · Zürich · St. Gall

December 31, 1348

June 30, 1348

BLACK

Bordeaux · Verona · Venice · Milan · Toulouse · Genoa · Bologna · Ferrara · Montpellier · Avignon · Sebenico · Béziers · Pisa · Florence · Ancona · Narbonne · Marseilles · Siena · Perugia · Ragusa · Huesca · Perpignan · Rome · Constantinople · Lerida · Saragossa · Barcelona · Naples · June 30, 1347 · Teruel · Valencia

Seville · Almeria

MEDITERRANEAN SEA

Messina · December 31, 1347 · Catania · Agrigento · Syracuse

0 ——— 300 miles

Legend:
- Plague-stricken towns and areas
- Progress of plague at certain dates
- Towns and areas not stricken by the plague

The Black Death disrupts society and economy

At first, the Black Death caused great hardships for most of the sur-vivors. Since panic-stricken people wished to avoid contagion, many fled from their jobs to seek isolation. Town-dwellers fled to the country and country-dwellers fled from each other. Even the pope re-treated to the interior of his palace and allowed no one entrance. With large numbers dead and others away from their posts, harvests were left rotting, manufacturing was disrupted, and conveyance systems were abandoned. Hence basic commodities became scarcer and prices rose. For these reasons the onslaught of the plague greatly intensified Europe's economic crisis.

But after around 1400 the new demographic realities began to turn prices around and alter basic economic patterns. Particularly, the prices of staple foodstuffs began to decline because production gradually returned to normal and there were fewer mouths to feed. Recurrent reappearances of the plague or natural disasters sometimes caused prices to fluctuate greatly in certain years, but overall prices of basic commodities throughout most of the fifteenth century went down or remained stable. This trend led to new agricultural specialization. Since cereals were cheaper, people could afford to spend a greater percentage of their income on comparative luxuries such as dairy products, meat, and wine. Hitherto farmers all over Europe had concentrated on cereals because bread was the staff of life, but now it was wisest, particularly in areas of poorer soil or unpropitious climate, to shift to specialized production. Depending upon whatever seemed most feasible, land might be used for the raising of livestock for milk, grapes for wine, or malt for beer. Specialized regional economies resulted: parts of England were given over to sheep-raising or beer production, parts of France concentrated on wine, and Sweden traded butter for cheap German grain. Most areas of Europe turned to what they could do best, and reciprocal trade of basic commodities over long distances created a sound new commercial equilibrium.

Another economic result of the Black Death was an increase in the relative importance of towns and cities. Urban manufacturers usually could respond more flexibly than landlords to drastically changed economic conditions because their production capabilities were more elastic. When markets shrank, manufacturers could cut back supply more easily to match demand; they could also raise production more easily when circumstances warranted. Thus urban entrepreneurs bounced back from disaster more quickly than landowners. Often

Economic consequences of the Black Death: (1) agricultural specialization

(2) the growth in importance of urban centers

The Four Horsemen of the Apocalypse. This woodcut, done by Albrecht Dürer at the end of the fifteenth century, well illustrates the mood of the later Middle Ages, when humans were overwhelmed by war, famine, and disease.

*The towns of northern
Germany and northern
Italy*

they took advantage of their greater strength to attract rural labor by means of higher salaries. Thereby the population balance between countryside and town was shifted slightly in favor of the latter.

Certain urban centers, especially those in northern Germany and northern Italy, profited the most from the new circumstances. In Germany a group of cities and towns under the leadership of Lübeck and Bremen allied in the so-called Hanseatic League to control long-distance trade in the Baltic and North Seas. Their fleets transported German grain to Scandinavia and brought back dairy products, fish, and furs. The enhanced European per capita ability to buy luxury goods brought new wealth to the northern Italian trading cities of Genoa and, especially, Venice because these cities controlled the importation of spices from the East. Greater expenditures on luxury also aided the economies of Florence, Venice, Milan, and other neighboring cities because those cities concentrated on the manufacture of silks and linens, light woolens, and other fine cloths. Milan, in addition, prospered from its armaments industry, which kept the warring European states supplied with armor and weapons. Because of varying local conditions, some cities and towns, above all those of Flanders, became economically depressed, but altogether European urban centers profited remarkably well from the new economic circumstances and emphasis on specialization.

*The growth of advanced
business and financial
techniques*

The changed circumstances also helped stimulate the development of sophisticated business, accounting, and banking techniques. Because sharp fluctuations in prices made investments precarious, new forms of partnerships were created to minimize risks. Insurance contracts were also invented to take some of the risk out of shipping. Europe's most useful accounting invention, double-entry bookkeeping, was first put into use in Italy in the mid–fourteenth century and spread rapidly thereafter north of the Alps. This allowed for quick dis-

A Late-Medieval Italian Town.
By Ambrogio Lorenzetti.

covery of computational errors and easy overview of profits and losses, credits and debits. Large-scale banking had already become common after the middle of the thirteenth century, but the economic crises of the later Middle Ages encouraged banks to alter some of their ways of doing business. Most important was the development of prudent branch-banking techniques, especially by the Florentine house of the Medici. Earlier banks had built branches, but the Medici bank, which flourished from 1397 to 1494, organized theirs along the lines of a modern holding company. The Medici branches, located in London, Bruges, and Avignon, as well as several Italian cities, were dominated by senior partners from the Medici family who followed common policies. Formally, however, each branch was a separate partnership which did not carry any other branch down with it if it collapsed. Other Italian banks experimented with advanced credit techniques. Some even allowed their clients to transfer funds between each other without any real money changing hands. Such "book transfers" were at first executed only by oral command, but around 1400 they started to be carried out by written orders. These were the earliest ancestors of the modern check.

In surveying the two centuries of late-medieval economic history, both the role of nature and that of human beings must be emphasized. The premodern history of all parts of the globe tends to show that whenever population becomes excessive natural controls manage to reduce it. Bad weather and disease may come at any time, but when humans are already suffering from hunger and conditions of overcrowding, the results of natural disasters will be particularly devastating. That certainly is what happened in the fourteenth century. Nature intervened cruelly in human affairs, but no matter how cruel the immediate effects were, the results were ultimately beneficial. By 1450 a far smaller population had a higher average standard of living than the population of 1300. In this result humans too played their part. Because people were determined to make the best of the new circumstances and avoid a recurrence of economic depression, they managed to reorganize their economic life and place it on a sounder footing. The gross European product of about 1450 was probably smaller than it was in 1300, but this is not surprising given the much smaller population. In fact, per capita output had risen with per capita income, and the European economy was ready to move on to new conquests.

2. SOCIAL AND EMOTIONAL DISLOCATION

Before the healthy new equilibrium was reached, the economic crises of the later Middle Ages contributed from about 1300 to 1450 to provoking a rash of lower-class rural and urban insurrections more numerous than Europe had ever known before or has ever known since.

The interaction of man and nature in late-medieval economic history

Social crisis: lower-class revolts

Rural insurrections: the
Jacquerie

It used to be thought that these were all caused by extreme deprivation, but as we will see, that was not always the case.

The one large-scale rural uprising that was most clearly caused by
extreme poverty was the northern French "Jacquerie" of 1358. This
took its name from the prototypical French peasant, "Jacques Bon-
homme," who had finally suffered more than he could endure. In
1348 and 1349 the Black Death had brought its terror and wreaked
havoc with the economy and with people's lives. Then a flare-up of
war between England and France had spread great desolation over the
countryside. The peasants, as usual in late-medieval warfare, suffered
most from the pillaging and burning carried out by the rapacious soldiers. To make matters even less endurable, after the English decisively defeated the French in 1356 at the Battle of Poitiers the French
king, John II, and numerous aristocrats had to be ransomed. As always
in such cases, the peasants were asked to bear the heaviest share of the
burden, but by 1358 they had had enough and rose up with astound-
ing ferocity. Without any clear program they burned down castles,
murdered their lords, and raped their lords' wives. Undoubtedly their
intense (and justified) economic resentments were the major cause for
the uprising, but it should be said too that 1358 was a year of deep political uncertainty for northern France, thus making an uprising of
peasants possible. While the king was in captivity in England, groups
of townsmen were trying to reform the governmental system by limiting monarchical powers, and certain aristocrats were plotting to
seize power. In the meantime, John II's son, Charles, was trying both to
raise a large ransom for his father and subdue the crown's enemies. Although we can never be certain, it seems unlikely that the peasants
would have revolted had they not sensed an opportunity to take advantage of France's political confusion. But in fact the opportunity
was not as great as they may have thought: within a month the privileged powers closed ranks, massacred the rebels, and quickly restored
order.

The English Peasants' Revolt of 1381—the most serious lower-class
rebellion in English history—is frequently bracketed with the Jacquerie, but its causes were very different. Instead of being a revolt of
abject desperation, it was one of frustrated rising expectations. By 1381
the effects of the Black Death should have been working in favor of
the peasants. Above all, a shortage of labor should have placed their
services in demand. In fact, the incidence of the plague did help to
increase manumissions (i.e., freeings) of serfs and raise salaries or
lower rents of free farm laborers. But aristocratic landlords fought
back to preserve their own incomes. They succeeded in having legislation passed that aimed to keep wages at pre-plague levels and force
landless laborers to work at the lower rates. Aristocrats furthermore
often tried to exact all their old dues and unpaid services. Because the
peasants were unwilling to be pushed down into their previous poverty and subservience, a collision was bound to take place.

*Background of the English
Peasants' Revolt*

The spark that ignited the great revolt of 1381 was an attempt to collect a national tax levied equally on every head instead of being made proportional to wealth. This was an unprecedented development in English tax-collecting that the peasants understandably found unfair. Two head-taxes were levied without resistance in 1377 and 1379, but when agents tried to collect a third in 1381 the peasantry rose up to resist and seek redress of all their grievances. First they burned local records and sacked the dwellings of those they considered their exploiters; then they marched on London, where they executed the lord chancellor and treasurer of England. Recognizing the gravity of the situation, the fifteen-year-old king, Richard II, went out to meet the peasants and won their confidence by promising to abolish serfdom and keep rents low; meanwhile, during negotiations, the peasant leader, Wat Tyler, was murdered in a squabble with the king's escort. Lacking leadership, the peasants, who mistakenly thought they had achieved their aims, rapidly dispersed. But once the boy-king was no longer in danger of his life he kept none of his promises. Instead, the scattered peasant forces were quickly hunted down and a few alleged trouble-makers were executed without any mass reprisals. The revolt itself therefore accomplished nothing, but within a few decades the natural play of economic forces caused serfdom to disappear and considerably improved the lot of the rural wage laborer.

The course of the revolt

Other rural revolts took place in other parts of Europe, but we may now look at some urban ones. Conventionally, the urban revolts of the later Middle Ages are viewed as uprisings of exploited proletarians who were more oppressed than ever because of the effects of economic depression. But this is probably too great a simplification because each case differed and complex forces were always at work. For example, an uprising in the north German town of Brunswick in 1374 was much less a movement of the poor against the rich than a political upheaval in which one political alliance replaced another. A different north German uprising, in Lübeck in 1408, has been aptly described as a "taxpayer's" revolt. This again was less a confrontation of the poor versus the rich than an attempt of a faction that was out of power to initiate less costly government.

The character of urban uprisings

The nearest thing to a real proletarian revolt was the uprising in 1378 of the Florentine *Ciompi* (pronounced "cheeompi"). The Ciompi were wool-combers who had the misfortune to be engaged in an industry that had become particularly depressed. Some of them had lost their jobs and others were frequently cheated or underpaid by the masters of the woolen industry. The latter wielded great political power in Florence, and thus could pass economic legislation in their own favor. This fact in itself meant that if there were to be economic reforms, they would have to go together with political changes. As events transpired it was a political crisis that called the Ciompi into direct action. In 1378 Florence had become exhausted by three years of war with the papacy. Certain patrician leaders overthrew the old

The Ciompi Revolt

regime to alter the war policy and gain their own political advantage. Circumstances led them to seek the support of the lower classes and, once stirred up, the Ciompi became emboldened after a few months to launch their own far more radical rebellion. This was inspired primarily by economic hardship and grievances, but personal hatreds also played a role. The Ciompi gained power for six weeks, during which they tried to institute tax relief, fuller employment, and representation of themselves and other proletarian groups in the Florentine government. But they could not maintain their hold on power and a new oligarchical government revoked all their reforms.

General observations on the nature of popular uprisings

If we try to draw any general conclusions about these various uprisings, we can certainly say that few if any of them would have occurred had there not been an economic crisis. But political considerations always had some influence, and the rebels in some uprisings were more prosperous than in others. It is noteworthy that all the genuinely lower-class uprisings of economically desperate groups quickly failed. This was certainly because the upper classes were more accustomed to wielding power and giving orders; even more important, they had access to the money and troops necessary to quell revolts. Sometimes elements within the lower classes might fight among themselves, whereas the privileged always managed to rally into a united front when faced by a lower-class threat to their domination. In addition, lower-class rebels were usually more intent on redressing immediate grievances than on developing fully coherent long-term governmental programs; inspiring ideals for cohesive action were generally lacking. The case of the Hussite Revolution in Bohemia—to be treated later—shows that religion in the later Middle Ages was a more effective rallying ground for large numbers of people than were political, economic, and social demands.

The crisis of the late-medieval aristocracy

Although the upper classes succeeded in overcoming popular uprisings, they perceived the economic and emotional insecurities of the later Middle Ages and the possibility of revolt as a constant threat, and became obsessed with maintaining their privileged social status. Late-medieval aristocrats were in a precarious economic position because they gained most of their income from land. In times when grain prices and rents were falling and wages rising, landowners were obviously in economic trouble. Some aristocrats probably also felt threatened by the rapid rise of merchants and financiers who could make quick killings because of sharp market fluctuations. In practice, really wealthy merchants bought land and were absorbed into the aristocracy. Moreover, most landowning aristocrats were able to stave off economic threats by expert estate management; in fact, many of them actually became richer than ever. But most still felt more exposed to social and economic insecurities than before. The result was that they tried to set up artificial barriers behind which they separated themselves from other classes.

A Party of Late Medieval Aristocrats. Notice the pointed shoes and the women's pointed hats, twice as high as their heads.

Two of the most striking examples of this separation were the aristocratic emphasis on luxury, and the formation of exclusive chivalric orders. The late Middle Ages was the period par excellence of aristocratic ostentation. While famine or disease raged, aristocrats regaled themselves with lavish banquets and magnificent pageants. At one feast in Flanders in 1468 a table decoration was forty-six feet high. Aristocratic clothing too was extremely ostentatious: men wore long, pointed shoes, and women ornately festooned headdresses. Throughout history rich people have always enjoyed dressing up, but the aristocrats of the later Middle Ages seem to have done so obsessively to comfort themselves and convey the message that they were entirely different from others. The insistence on maintaining a sharply defined social hierarchy also accounts for the late-medieval proliferation of chivalric orders, such as those of the Knights of the Garter or the Golden Fleece. By joining together in exclusive orders which prescribed special conduct and boasted special insignia of membership, aristocrats who felt threatened by social pressures again tried to set themselves off from others, in effect, by putting up a sign that read "for members only."

Another explanation for the exorbitant stress on luxury is that it was a form of escapism. Aristocrats who were continually exposed to the sight and smell of death must have found it emotionally comforting to retreat into a dream-world of elegant manners, splendid feasts, and multicolored clothes. In a parallel fashion, nonaristocrats who

Duke Philip the Good of Burgundy. The duke proudly wears the emblem of the Order of the Golden Fleece around his neck.

A Late-Medieval Crucifixion Scene. The Virgin has to be held up to keep from swooning, and the angels are weeping.

could not afford such luxuries often sought relief from the vision of death in crude public entertainments: for example, crowds would watch blind beggars try to catch a squealing pig but beat each other with clubs instead, or they would cheer on boys to clamber up greasy poles in order to win prizes of geese.

It must not be thought, however, that late-medieval people gave themselves over to riotous living without interruption. In fact, the very same people of all classes who sought elegant or boisterous diversions just as often went to the other emotional extreme when faced by the psychic stress caused by the troubles of the age, and abandoned themselves to sorrow. Throughout the period grown men and women shed tears in abundance. The queen mother of France wept in public when she first viewed her grandson; the great preacher Vincent Ferrer had to interrupt his sermons on Christ's Passion and the Last Judgment because he and his audience were sobbing too convulsively; and the English king, Edward II, supposedly wept so much when imprisoned that he gushed forth enough hot water for his own shave. The last story taxes the imagination, but it does illustrate well what contemporaries thought was possible. We know for certain that the Church encouraged crying because of the survival of moving statuettes of weeping St. Johns, which were obviously designed to call forth tears from their viewers.

People also were encouraged by preachers to brood on the Passion of Christ and on their own mortality. Fearsome crucifixes abounded,

A Dead Man Before His Judge. A late-medieval reminder of human mortality.

and the figure of the Virgin Mary was less a smiling madonna than a sorrowing mother: now she was most frequently depicted slumping with grief at the foot of the cross, or holding the dead Christ in her lap. The late-medieval obsession with mortality can also still be seen in sculptures, frescoes, and book illustrations that reminded viewers of the brevity of life and the torments of hell. The characteristic tombs of the High Middle Ages were mounted with sculptures that either showed the deceased in some action that had been typical of his or her accomplishments in life, or else in a state of repose that showed death to be nothing more than peaceful sleep. But in the late fourteenth century, tombs appeared that displayed the physical ravages of death in the most gruesome ways imaginable: emaciated corpses were displayed with protruding intestines or covered with snakes or toads. Some tombs bore inscriptions stating that the viewer would soon be "a fetid cadaver, food for worms"; some warned chillingly: "What you are, I was; what I am, you will be." Omnipresent illustrations displayed figures of grinning death, with his scythe, carrying off elegant and healthy men and women, or sadistic devils roasting pain-wracked humans in hell. Because people who painted or brooded on such pictures might the next day indulge in excessive revels, late-medieval culture often seems to border on the manic-depressive. But apparently such extreme reactions were necessary to help people cope with their fears.

The Prince of the World. A stone figure from the church of St. Sebald, Nuremberg, from about 1330. From the front the man is smiling and master of all he surveys; from the rear he is crawling with vermin.

3. TRIALS FOR THE CHURCH AND HUNGER FOR THE DIVINE

The intense concentration on the meaning of death was also a manifestation of a very deep and pervasive religiosity. The religious enthusiasm of the High Middle Ages by no means flagged after 1300; if anything, it became more intense. But religious enthusiasm took on new forms of expression because of the institutional difficulties of the Church and the turmoils of the age.

After the humiliation and death of Pope Boniface VIII in 1303, the Church experienced a period of institutional crisis that was as severe and prolonged as the contemporary economic crisis. We may distinguish three phases: the so-called Babylonian Captivity of the papacy, 1305–1378; the Great Schism, 1378–1417; and the period of the Italian territorial papacy, 1417–1517. During the Babylonian Captivity the papacy was located in Avignon instead of Rome and was generally subservient to the interests of the French crown. There were several reasons for this: the most obvious was that since the test of strength between Philip the Fair and Boniface VIII had resulted in a clear victory for the French king, subsequent popes were unwilling to risk French royal ire. In fact, once the popes recognized that they could not give orders to the French kings, they found that they had certain advantages to gain from currying their favor. One was a safe home in southern France, away from the tumult of Italy. Central Italy and the city of Rome in the fourteenth century had become so politically turbulent and rebellious that the pope could not even count on finding personal safety there, let alone sufficiently peaceful conditions to maintain orderly ecclesiastical administration. But no such danger existed in Avignon. Even though Avignon was not then part of the French kingdom—it was the major city of a small papal territory—French military might was close enough to guarantee the pope his much needed security. Another advantage of papal subservience to French power was help from the French in pursuing mutually advantageous policies in Germany and southern Italy. Perhaps most important was a working agreement whereby the French king would propose his own candidates to become bishops and the pope would then name them, thereby gaining sizable monetary payments. After 1305 the pro-French system became so entrenched that a majority of cardinals and all the popes until 1378 were themselves French.

At Avignon the popes were more successful than ever in pursuing their policy of centralizing the government of the Church. For the first time they worked out a really sound system of papal finance, based on the systematization of dues collected from the clergy throughout Europe. The papacy also succeeded in appointing more candidates to vacant benefices than before (in practice often naming candidates proposed by the French and English kings), and they proceeded against heresy with great determination, indeed with ruthlessness. But whatever the popes achieved in power they lost in respect and loyalty. The clergy became alienated as a result of being asked to pay so much money, and much of the laity was horrified by the corruption and unbridled luxury displayed at the papal court: there the cardinals lived more splendidly than lords, dining off peacocks, pheasants, grouse, and swans, and drinking from elaborately sculptured fountains that spouted the finest wines. Most of the Avignonese popes themselves were personally upright and abstemious, but one, Clement VI (1342–1352), was worse than his cardinals. Clement was ready to offer any spiritual benefit for money, boasted that he would appoint even a jackass as bishop if political circumstances warranted, and defended his incessant sexual transgressions by insisting that he fornicated on doctors' orders.

As time went on the pressures of informed public opinion forced the popes to promise that they would return to Rome. After one abortive attempt by Urban V in 1367, Pope Gregory XI finally did return to the Holy City in 1377. But he died a year later and then disaster struck. The college of cardinals, surrounded in Rome by clamoring Italians, yielded to local sentiment by naming an Italian as pope, who took the title of Urban VI. But most of the cardinals were Frenchmen and quickly regretted their decision, especially because Urban VI immediately began quarreling with them and revealing what were probably paranoid tendencies. Therefore, after only a few months, the French cardinals met again, declared the previous election void, and replaced Urban with one of their own number, who called himself Clement VII.

Unfortunately, however, Urban VI did not meekly resign. On the contrary, he named an entirely new Italian college of cardinals and remained entrenched in Rome. Clement VII quickly retreated with his own party to Avignon and the so-called Great Schism ensued. France and other countries in the French political orbit—such as Scotland, Castile, and Aragon—recognized Clement, while the rest of Europe recognized Urban as the true pope. For three decades Christians looked on helplessly while the rival pontiffs hurled curses at each other and the international monastic orders became divided into Roman and Avignonese camps. The death of one or the other pope did not end the schism; each camp had its own set of cardinals which promptly named either a French or Italian successor. The desperateness of the situation led a council of prelates from both camps to meet in Pisa in 1409 to depose both popes and name a new one instead. But neither the Italian nor the French pope accepted the council's decision and both had enough political support to retain some obedience. So after 1409 there were three rival claimants hurling curses instead of two.

The Great Schism

The Great Schism was finally ended in 1417 by the Council of Constance, the largest ecclesiastical gathering in medieval history. This time the assembled prelates made certain to gain the crucial support of secular powers and also to eliminate the prior claimants before naming a new pope. After the council's election of Martin V in 1417, European ecclesiastical unity was thus fully restored. But a struggle over the nature of Church government followed immediately. The members of the Council of Constance challenged the prevailing medieval theory of papal monarchy by calling for balanced, "conciliar," government. In two momentous decrees they stated that a general council of prelates was superior in authority to the pope, and that such councils should meet regularly to govern the Church. Not surprisingly, subsequent popes—who had now returned to Rome—sought to nullify these decrees. When a new council met in Basel in 1431, in accordance with the principles laid down at Constance, the reigning pope did all he could to sabotage its activities. Ultimately he was successful: after a protracted struggle the Council of Basel dissolved in 1449 in abject failure, and the attempt to institute constitutional government in the Church was completely defeated. But the papacy only won this victory over conciliarism by gaining the support of the rulers of the European states. In separate concordats with kings and princes, the popes granted the secular rulers much authority over the various local churches. The popes thus became assured of theoretical supremacy at the cost of surrendering much real power. To compensate for this they concentrated on consolidating their own direct rule in central Italy. Most of the fifteenth-century popes ruled very much like any other princes, leading

The end of the schism; conciliarism

The decline of clerical prestige

armies, jockeying for alliances, and building magnificent palaces. Hence, although they did succeed for the first time in creating a viable political state, their reputation for disinterested piety remained low.

While the papacy was undergoing these vicissitudes, the local clergy throughout Europe was undergoing a loss of prestige for several reasons. One was that the pope's greater financial demands forced the clergy to demand more from the laity, but such demands were bitterly resented, especially during times of prevailing economic crisis. Then too during outbreaks of plague the clergy sometimes fled their posts just like everyone else, but in so doing they lost whatever claim they had for being morally superior. Probably the single greatest reason for growing dissatisfaction with the clergy was the increase in lay literacy. The continued proliferation of schools and the decline in the cost of books—a subject we will treat later—made it possible for large numbers of lay people to learn how to read. Once that happened, the laity could start reading parts of the Bible, or, more frequently, popular religious primers. These made it clear that their local priests were not living according to the standards set by Jesus and the Apostles. In the meantime, the upheavals and horrors of the age drove people to seek religious solace more than ever. Finding the conventional channels of church attendance, confession, and submission to clerical authority insufficient, the laity sought supplementary or alternate routes to piety. These differed greatly from each other, but they all aimed to satisfy an immense hunger for the divine.

The most widely-traveled route was that of performing repeated acts of external devotion in the hope that they would gain the devotee divine favor on earth and salvation in the hereafter. People flocked to go on pilgrimages as never before and participated regularly in bare-

A German Flagellant Procession. These penitents hoped they could ward off the Black Death by their mutually inflicted tortures.

footed religious processions: the latter were often held twice a month and occasionally as often as once a week. Men and women also eagerly bought indulgences, i.e., papal grants, that were supposed to free them from time in purgatory, and they paid in advance for the reading of numerous requiem masses to save their souls after death. Obsession with repeating prayers reached a peak when some pious individuals tried to compute the number of drops of blood that Christ shed on the cross so that they could say the same number of Our Fathers. The most excessive and repugnant form of religious ritual in the later Middle Ages was flagellation. Some women who lived in communal houses beat themselves with the roughest animal hides, chains, and knotted thongs. A young girl who entered such a community in Poland in 1331 suffered extreme internal injuries and became completely disfigured within eleven months. Flailings were not usually performed in public, but during the first onslaught of the Black Death in 1348 and 1349, whole bands of lay people marched through northern Europe chanting and beating each other with metal-tipped scourges in the hope of appeasing the apparent divine wrath.

An opposite route to godliness was the inward path of mysticism. Throughout the European continent, but particularly in Germany and England, male and female mystics, both clerical and lay, sought union with God by means of "detachment," contemplation, or spiritual exercises. The most original and eloquent late-medieval mystical theorist was the German Dominican, Master Eckhart (c. 1260–1327), who taught that there was a power or "spark" deep within every human soul that was really the dwelling-place of God. By renouncing all sense of selfhood one could retreat into one's innermost recesses and there find divinity. Eckhart did not recommend ceasing attendance at church—he hardly could have because he preached in churches—but he made it clear that outward rituals were of comparatively little importance in reaching God. He also gave the impression to his lay audiences that they might attain godliness largely on their own volition. Thus he was charged by ecclesiastical authorities with inciting "ignorant and undisciplined people to wild and dangerous excesses." Although Eckhart pleaded his own doctrinal orthodoxy, some of his teachings were condemned by the papacy.

That Eckhart's critics were not entirely mistaken in their worries is shown by the fact that some lay people in Germany who were influenced by him did fall into the heresy of believing that they could become fully united with God on earth without any priestly intermediaries. But these so-called heretics of the Free Spirit were few in number. Much more numerous were later orthodox mystics, sometimes influenced by Eckhart and sometimes not, who placed greater emphasis on the divine initiative in the meeting of the soul with God and made certain to insist that the ministrations of the Church were a necessary contribution to the mystic way. Even they, however, believed that "churches make no man holy, but men make churches holy."

Most of the great teachers and practitioners of mysticism in the four-teenth century were clerics, nuns, or hermits, but in the fifteenth cen-tury a modified form of mysticism was spread among lay people. This "practical mysticism" did not aim for full ecstatic union with God, but rather for an ongoing sense of some divine presence during the conduct of daily life. The most popular manual that pointed the way to this goal was the Latin *Imitation of Christ,* written around 1427, probably by the north German canon Thomas à Kempis. Because this was written in a simple but forceful style and taught how to be a pious Christian while still living actively in the world, it was particularly at-tractive to lay readers. Thus it quickly became translated into the lead-ing European vernaculars. From then until today it has been more widely read by Christians than any other religious work outside of the Bible. The *Imitation* urges its readers to participate in one religious ceremony—the sacrament of the Eucharist—but otherwise it empha-sizes inward piety. According to its teachings, the individual Christian is best able to become the "partner" of Jesus Christ both by taking communion and also by engaging in Biblical meditation and leading a simple, moral life.

A third distinct form of late-medieval piety was outright religious protest or heresy. In England and Bohemia especially, heretical move-ments became serious threats to the Church. The founder of heresy in late-medieval England was an Oxford theologian named John Wyclif (c. 1330–1384). Wyclif's rigorous adherence to the theology of St. Augustine led him to believe that a certain number of humans were predestined to be saved while the rest were irrevocably damned. He thought the predestined would naturally live simply, according to the standards of the New Testament, but in fact he found most members of the Church hierarchy indulging in splendid extravagances. Hence he concluded that most Church officials were damned. For him the only solution was to have secular rulers appropriate ecclesiastical wealth and reform the Church by replacing corrupt priests and bishops with men who would live according to apostolic standards. This position was obviously attractive to the aristocracy of England, who may have looked forward to enriching themselves with Church spoils and at least saw nothing wrong with using Wyclif as a bulldog to frighten the pope and the local clergy. Thus, Wyclif at first received influential aristocratic support. But towards the end of his life he moved from merely calling for reform to attacking some of the most basic institutions of the Church, above all the sacrament of the Eu-charist. This radicalism frightened off his influential protectors, and Wyclif probably would have been formally condemned for heresy had he lived longer. His death brought no respite for the Church, how-ever, because he had attracted numerous lay followers—called Lol-lards—who zealously continued to propagate some of his most radical ideas. Above all, the Lollards taught that pious Christians should shun

(3) Heresy: John Wyclif and the Lollards

the corrupt Church and instead study the Bible and rely as far as possible on their individual consciences. Lollardy gained many adherents in the last two decades of the fourteenth century, but after the introduction in England of the death penalty for heresy in 1399 and the failure of a Lollard uprising in 1414 the heretical wave greatly receded. Nonetheless, a few Lollards did continue to survive underground, and their descendants helped contribute to the Protestant Revolution of the sixteenth century.

Much greater was the influence of Wyclifism in Bohemia. Around 1400, Czech students who had studied in Oxford brought back Wyclif's ideas to the Bohemian capital of Prague. There Wyclifism was enthusiastically received by an eloquent preacher named John Hus (c. 1373–1415), who had already been inveighing in well-attended sermons against "the world, the flesh, and the devil." Hus employed Wyclifite theories to back up his own calls for the end of ecclesiastical corruption, and rallied many Bohemians to the cause of reform in the years between 1408 and 1415. Never alienating anyone as Wyclif had done by criticizing the doctrine of the Eucharist, Hus gained support from many different directions. The politics of the Great Schism prompted the king of Bohemia to lend Hus his protection, and influential aristocrats supported Hus for motives similar to those of their English counterparts. Above all, Hus gained a mass following because of his eloquence and concern for social justice. Accordingly, most of Bohemia was behind him when Hus in 1415 agreed to travel to the Council of Constance to defend his views and try to convince the assembled prelates that only thoroughgoing reform could save the Church. But although Hus had been guaranteed his personal safety, this assurance was revoked as soon as he arrived at the Council: rather than being given a fair hearing, the betrayed idealist was tried for heresy and burned.

John Hus

Hus's supporters in Bohemia were justifiably outraged and quickly raised the banner of open revolt. The aristocracy took advantage of the situation to seize Church lands, and poorer priests, artisans, and peasants rallied together in the hope of achieving Hus's goals of religious reform and social justice. Between 1420 and 1424 armies of lower-class Hussites, led by a brilliant blind general, John Zizka, amazingly defeated several invading forces of well-armed "crusading" knights from Germany. In 1434 more conservative, aristocratically dominated Hussites overcame the radicals, thereby ending attempts to initiate a purified new religious and social dispensation. But even the conservatives refused to return to full orthodoxy. Thus Bohemia never came back to the Catholic fold until after the Catholic Reformation in the seventeenth century. The Hussite declaration of religious independence was both a foretaste of what was to come one hundred years later with Protestantism and the most successful late-medieval expression of dissatisfaction with the government of the Church.

The Hussite revolt

4. POLITICAL CRISIS AND RECOVERY

The story of late-medieval politics at first seems very dreary because throughout most of the period there was incessant strife. Almost everywhere neighbors fought neighbors and states fought states. But on closer inspection it becomes clear that despite the turmoil there was ultimate improvement in almost all the governments of Europe. In the course of the fifteenth century peace returned to most of the continent, the national monarchies in particular became stronger, and the period ended on a new note of strength just as it had from the point of view of economics.

Starting our survey with Italy, it must first be explained that the Kingdom of Naples in the extreme south of the Italian peninsula was sunk in endemic warfare or maladministration more or less without interruption throughout the fourteenth and fifteenth centuries. Otherwise, Italy emerged from the prevailing political turmoil of the late Middle Ages earlier than any other part of Europe. The fourteenth century was a time of troubles for the Papal States, comprising most of central Italy, because forces representing the absent or divided papacy were seldom able to overcome the resistance of refractory towns and rival leaders of marauding military bands. But after the end of the Great Schism in 1417 the popes concentrated more on consolidating their own Italian territories and gradually became the strong rulers of most of the middle part of the peninsula. Further north some of the leading city-states—such as Florence, Venice, Siena, and Genoa—had experienced at least occasional and most often prolonged social warfare in the fourteenth century because of the economic pressures of the age. But sooner or later the most powerful families or interest groups overcame internal resistance. By around 1400 the three leading cities of the north—Venice, Milan, Florence—had fixed definitively upon their own different forms of government: Venice was ruled by a merchant oligarchy, Milan by a dynastic despotism, and Florence by a complex, supposedly republican system that was actually controlled by the rich. (After 1434 the Florentine republic was in practice dominated by the banking family of the Medici.)

Having settled their internal problems, Venice, Milan, and Florence proceeded from about 1400 to 1454 to expand territorially and conquer almost all the other northern Italian cities and towns except Genoa, which remained prosperous and independent but gained no new territory. Thus, by the middle of the fifteenth century Italy was divided into five major parts: the states of Venice, Milan, and Florence in the north; the Papal States in the middle; and the backward Kingdom of Naples in the south. A treaty of 1454 initiated a half-century of peace between these states: whenever one threatened to upset the "balance of power," the others usually allied against it before serious warfare could break out. Accordingly, the last half of the fifteenth century was a fortunate age for Italy. But in 1494 a French invasion initiated a period of renewed warfare in which the French attempt at dominating Italy was successfully countered by Spain.

North of the Alps political turmoil prevailed throughout the fourteenth century and lasted longer into the fifteenth. Probably the worse instability was experienced in Germany. There the virtually independent princes continually warred with the greatly weakened emperors, or else they warred with each other. Between about 1350 and 1450 near-anarchy prevailed, because while the princes were warring and subdividing their inheritances into smaller states, petty powers such as free cities and knights who owned one or two castles were striving to shake off the rule of the princes. Throughout most of the German west these attempts met with enough success to fragment political authority more than ever, but in the east after about 1450 certain stronger German princes managed to assert their authority over divisive forces. After they did so they started to govern firmly over middle-sized states on the model of the larger national monarchies of England and France. The strongest princes were those who ruled in eastern territories such as Bavaria, Austria, and Brandenburg, because there towns were fewer and smaller and the princes had earlier been able to take advantage of imperial weakness to preside over the colonization of large tracts of land. Especially the Hapsburg princes of Austria and the Hohenzollern princes of Brandenburg—a territory joined in the sixteenth century with the easternmost lands of Prussia—would be the most influential powers in Germany's future.

Germany: the triumph of the princes

The great nation-states did not escape unscathed from the late-medieval turmoil either. France was strife-ridden for much of the period, primarily in the form of the Hundred Years' War between France and England. The Hundred Years' War was actually a series of conflicts that lasted for even more than one hundred years—from 1337 to 1453. There were several different causes for this prolonged struggle. The major one was the long-standing problem of French territory held by the English kings. At the beginning of the fourteenth century the English kings still ruled much of the rich southern French lands of Gascony and Aquitaine as vassals of the French crown. The French, who since the reign of Philip Augustus had been expanding and consolidating their rule, obviously hoped to expel the English, and war was therefore inevitable. Another cause for strife was that the English economic interests in the woolen trade with Flanders led them to support the frequent attempts of Flemish burghers to rebel against French rule. Finally, the fact that the direct Capetian line of succession to the French throne died out in 1328, to be replaced thereafter by the related Valois dynasty, meant that the English kings, who themselves descended from the Capetians as a result of intermarriage, laid claim to the French crown itself.

France: causes of the Hundred Years' War

France should have had no difficulty in defeating England at the start: it was the richest country in Europe and outnumbered England in population by some fifteen million to fewer than four million. Nonetheless, throughout most of the first three-quarters of the Hundred Years' War the English won most of the pitched battles. One reason for this was that the English had learned superior military tactics, using well-disciplined archers to fend off and scatter the heavily armored mounted French knights. In the three greatest battles of the long conflict—Crécy (1346), Poitiers (1356), and Agincourt (1415)—the outnumbered English relied on tight discipline and effective use of the longbow to inflict crushing defeats on the French. Another reason for English success was that the war was always fought on French soil. That being the case, English soldiers were eager to fight because they could look forward to rich plunder, while their own homeland suffered none of the disasters of war. Worst of all for the French was the fact that they often were badly divided. The French crown had always had to fear provincial attempts to assert autonomy: especially during the long period of warfare, when there were several highly inept kings and the English encouraged internal French dissensions, many aristocratic provincial leaders took advantage of the confusion to ally with the enemy and seek their own advantage. The most dramatic and fateful instance was the breaking away of Burgundy, whose dukes from 1419 to 1435 allied with the English, an act which called the very existence of an independent French crown into question.

It was in this dark period that the heroic figure of Joan of Arc came forth to rally the French. In 1429 Joan, an illiterate but extremely devout peasant girl, sought out the uncrowned French ruler, Charles VII, to announce that she had been divinely commissioned to drive the English out of France. Charles was persuaded to let her take command of his troops, and her piety and sincerity made such a favorable impression on the soldiers that their morale was raised immensely. In a few months Joan had liberated much of central France from English domination and had brought Charles to Rheims, where he was crowned king. But in May 1430 she was captured by the Burgundians and handed over to the English, who accused her of being a witch and tried her for heresy. Condemned in 1431 after a predetermined trial, she was publicly burned to death in the market square at Rouen. Nonetheless, the French, fired by their initial victories, continued to move on the offensive. When Burgundy withdrew from the English alliance in 1435, and the English king, Henry VI, proved to be totally incompetent, there followed an uninterrupted series of triumphs for the French side. In 1453 the capture of Bordeaux, the last of the English strongholds in the southwest, finally brought the long war to an end. The English now held no land in France except for the Channel port of Calais, which they ultimately lost in 1558.

More than merely expelling the English from French territory, the Hundred Years' War resulted in greatly strengthening the powers of the French crown. Although many of the French kings during the long war had been ineffective personalities—one, Charles VI, was even insane—the monarchy demonstrated remarkable staying power because it provided France with the strongest institutions it knew and therefore offered the only realistic hope for lasting stability and peace. Moreover, warfare emergencies allowed the kings to gather new powers, above all, the rights to collect national taxes and maintain a standing army. Hence after Charles VII succeeded in defeating the English, the crown was able to renew the high-medieval royal tradition of ruling the country assertively. In the reigns of Charles's successors, Louis XI (1461–1483) and Louis XII (1498–1515), the monarchy became ever stronger. Its greatest single achievement was the destruction of the power of Burgundy in 1477 when the Burgundian duke, Charles the Bold, fell in the battle of Nancy at the hands of the Swiss, whom Charles had been trying to dominate. Since Charles died without a male heir, Louis XI of France was able to march into Burgundy and reabsorb the breakaway duchy. Later, when Louis XII gained Brittany by marriage, the French kings ruled powerfully over almost all of what is today included in the borders of France.

Louis XI of France. A portrait by Fouquet.

Although the Hundred Years' War was fought on French instead of English soil, England also experienced great turmoil during the later Middle Ages because of internal instability. Indeed, England was a hotbed of insurrection: of the nine English kings who came to the throne between 1307 and 1485, five died violently because of revolts or conspiracies. Most of these slain kings had proven themselves to be incapable rulers, but there were other reasons for England's political troubles as well. One was that the crown had been too ambitious in trying both to hold on to its territories in France and also subdue Scotland. This policy often made it necessary to resort to heavy taxation and to grant major political concessions to the aristocracy. When English arms in France were successful, the crown rode the crest of popularity and the aristocracy prospered from military spoils and ransoms; but whenever the tides of battle turned to defeat, the crown became financially embarrassed and thrown on the political defensive. To make matters worse, the English aristocracy was particularly unruly throughout the period, not just because the aristocrats often had reason to distrust the inept kings, but because the economic pressures of the age made them seek to enlarge their agricultural estates at the expense of each other. This led to factionalism, and factionalism often led to civil war.

England: internal turmoil

After the English presence in France was virtually eradicated and the aristocracy could no longer hope to enrich itself on the spoils of foreign warfare, England's political situation became particularly desperate. As bad luck would have it, the reigning king, Henry VI (1422–1461), was one of the most incompetent that England has ever had. According to one recent authority, Henry "paralyzed and con-

The Wars of the Roses

fused the whole process of English government with a royal irresponsibility and inanity which had no precedent." Henry's willfulness helped provoke the Wars of the Roses that flared on and off from 1455 to 1485. These wars received their name from the emblems of the two competing factions: the red rose of Henry's family of Lancaster and the white rose of the rival house of York. The Yorkists for a time gained the kingship, under such monarchs as Richard III, but in 1485 they were replaced by a new dynasty, that of the Tudors, who began a new period in English history. The first Tudor king, Henry VII, steadily eliminated rival claimants to the throne, avoided expensive foreign wars, built up a financial surplus, and gradually reasserted royal power over the aristocracy. When he died in 1509 he was therefore able to pass on to his son, Henry VIII (1509–1547), a royal power that was as great as it had ever been before.

It is tempting to view the entire period of English history between 1307 and the accession of Henry VII in 1485 as one long, dreary interregnum which accomplished nothing positive. But that would not quite be doing justice to the time: in the first place, the fact that England did not entirely fall apart during the recurrent turbulence was an accomplishment in itself. Remarkably, the rebellious aristocrats of the later Middle Ages never tried to proclaim the independence of any of their regions; only once, in 1405, did they seek unsuccessfully to divide the country between them. Discounting that insignificant exception, aristocratic rebels always sought to control the central government rather than destroy or break away from it. Thus when Henry VII came to the throne, he did not have to win back any English territories as Louis XI of France had had to win back Burgundy. More than that, the antagonisms of the Hundred Years' War had the ultimately beneficial effect of enhancing an English sense of national identity. From the Norman Conquest until deep into the fourteenth century, French was the preferred language of the English crown and aristocracy, but mounting anti-French sentiment contributed to the complete triumph of English by around 1400. The loss of lands in France was also ultimately beneficial because thereafter the crown was freed from the inevitability of war with the French. This freedom gave England more diplomatic maneuverability in sixteenth-century continental politics and later helped strengthen England's ability to invest its energies in overseas expansion in America and elsewhere. Yet another positive development was the steady growth of effective governmental institutions; despite the shifting fortunes of kings, the central governmental administration expanded and became more sophisticated. Parliament too became stronger, largely because both the crown and the aristocracy believed that they could use it for their own ends. In 1307 Parliament had not yet become a regular part of the English governmental system, but by 1485 it definitely had. Later kings who tried to govern without it ran into severe difficulties.

Around the time when Louis XI of France and Henry VII of Eng-

land were reasserting royal power in their respective countries, the
Spanish monarchs, Ferdinand and Isabella, were doing the same on the
Iberian peninsula. In the latter area there had also been incessant strife
in the later Middle Ages; Aragon and Castile had often fought each
other, and aristocratic factions within those kingdoms had continually
fought the crown. But in 1496 Ferdinand, the heir of Aragon, married
Isabella, the heiress of Castile, and thereby created a union which laid
the basis for modern Spain.

Although Spain did not become a fully united nation until 1716
because Aragon and Castile retained their separate institutions, at least
warfare between the two previously independent kingdoms ended and
the new country was able to embark on united policies. Isabella and
Ferdinand, ruling respectively until 1504 and 1516, annexed Granada,
the last Muslim state in the peninsula, expelled the Jews, whom they
regarded as a divisive element in their society, and thoroughly subdued
their aristocracies. Having dealt with their major internal obstacles,
the Spanish rulers also started to embark on an ambitious foreign policy: not only did they turn to overseas expansion, as most famously
in their support of Christopher Columbus, but they also entered decisively into the arena of Italian politics. Enriched by the influx of
American gold and silver after the conquest of Mexico and Peru, and
nearly invincible on the battlefields, Spain quickly became Europe's
most powerful state in the sixteenth century.

Ultimately the clearest result of political developments throughout
Europe in the late Middle Ages was the preservation of basic high-
medieval patterns. The areas of Italy and Germany which had been
politically divided before 1300 remained politically divided thereafter.
The emergence of middle-sized states in both of these areas in the fifteenth century brought more stability than had existed before, but
events would show that Italy and Germany would still be the prey of
the Western powers. The latter were clearly much stronger because
they were consolidated around stronger national monarchies. The
trials of the later Middle Ages put the existence of these monarchies to
the test, but after 1450 they emerged stronger than ever. The clearest
illustration of their superiority is shown by the history of Italy in the
years immediately following 1494. Until then the Italian states appeared to the relatively well-governed and prosperous. They experimented with advanced techniques of administration and diplomacy.
But when France and Spain invaded the peninsula the Italian states fell
over like houses of cards. The Western monarchies could simply draw
on greater resources and thus inherited the future of Europe.

5. THOUGHT, LITERATURE, AND ART

Although it might be guessed that the extreme hardships of the later
Middle Ages should have led to the decline or stagnation of intellec-

tual and artistic endeavors, in fact the period was an extremely fruitful one in the realms of thought, literature, and art. In this section we will postpone treatment of certain developments most closely related to the early history of the Italian Renaissance, but will discuss some of western Europe's other important late-medieval intellectual and artistic accomplishments.

Theology and philosophy after about 1300 faced a crisis of doubt. This doubt did not concern the existence of God and His supernatural powers, but was rather doubt about human ability to comprehend the supernatural. Whereas St. Thomas Aquinas and other Scholastics in the High Middle Ages had serenely delimited the number of "mysteries of the faith" and believed that everything else, both in heaven and earth, could be thoroughly understood by humans, the floods, frosts, wars, and plagues of the fourteenth century helped undermine such confidence in the powers of human understanding. Once human beings experienced the universe as arbitrary and unpredictable, fourteenth-century thinkers began to wonder whether there was not far more in heaven and earth than could be understood by their philosophies. The result was a thoroughgoing reevaluation of the prior theological and philosophical outlook.

Crisis in theology and philosophy

The leading late-medieval abstract thinker was the English Franciscan William of Ockham, who was born around 1285 and died in 1349, apparently from the Black Death. Traditionally, Franciscans had always had greater doubts than Dominicans like St. Thomas concerning the abilities of human reason to comprehend the supernatural; Ockham, convinced by the events of his age, expressed these most formidably. He denied that the existence of God and numerous other theological matters could be demonstrated apart from scriptural revelation, and he emphasized God's freedom and absolute power to do anything He wished. In the realm of human knowledge per se Ockham's searching intellect drove him to look for absolute certainties instead of mere theories. In investigating earthly matters he developed the position, known as *nominalism*, that only individual things, but not collectivities, are real, and that one thing therefore cannot be understood by means of another: to know a chair one has to see and touch it rather than just know what several other chairs are like. Ockham also formulated a logic which was based on the assumption that words stood only for themselves rather than for real things. Such logic might not say much about the real world, but at least it could not be refuted, since it was as internally valid in its own terms as Euclidean geometry.

William of Ockham; nominalism

Ockham's outlook, which gained widespread adherence in the late-medieval universities, today oftens seems overly methodological and verging on the arid, but it had several important effects on the development of Western thought. Ockham's concern about what God *might* do led to the raising by his followers of some of the seemingly

The significance of Ockham's thought

absurd questions for which medieval theology has been mocked, for example, asking whether God can undo the past, or whether an infinite number of pure spirits can simultaneously inhabit the same place (the nearest medieval thinkers actually came to asking how many angels can dance on the head of a pin). Nonetheless, Ockham's emphasis on preserving God's autonomy led to a stress on divine omnipotence that became one of the basic presuppositions of sixteenth-century Protestantism. Further, Ockham's determination to find certainties in the realm of human knowledge ultimately helped make it possible to discuss human affairs and natural science without reference to supernatural explanations—one of the most important foundations of the modern scientific method. Finally, Ockham's opposition to studying collectivities and his refusal to apply logic to real things helped encourage *empiricism,* or the belief that knowledge of the world should rest on sense experience rather than abstract reason. This too is a presupposition for scientific progress: thus it is probably not coincidental that some of Ockham's fourteenth-century followers made significant advances in the study of physics.

Ockham's search for reliable truths finds certain parallels in the realm of late-medieval literature, although Ockham surely had no direct influence in that field. The major trait of the best late-medieval literature was *naturalism,* or the attempt to describe things the way they really are. This was more a development from high-medieval precedents—such as the explorations of human conduct pursued by Chrétien de Troyes, Wolfram von Eschenbach, and Dante—than a reaction against them. The steady growth of a lay reading public furthermore encouraged authors to avoid theological and philosophical abstractions and seek more to entertain by portraying people realistically with all their strengths and foibles. Another main characteristic of late-medieval literature, the predominance of composition in the European vernaculars instead of Latin, also developed out of high-medieval precedents but gained great momentum in the later Middle Ages for two different reasons. One was that international tensions and hostilities, including the numerous wars of the age and the trials of the universal papacy, led to need for security and a pride of self-identification reflected by the use of vernacular tongues. Probably more important was the fact that continued spread of education for the laity greatly increased a public that could read in a given vernacular language but not in Latin. Hence although much poetry was written during the High Middle Ages in the vernacular, in the later Middle Ages use of the vernacular was widely extended to prose. Moreover, countries such as Italy and England, which had just begun to cultivate their own vernacular literatures around 1300, subsequently began to employ their native tongues to the most impressive literary effect.

The greatest writer of vernacular prose fiction of the later Middle Ages was the Italian Giovanni Boccaccio (1313–1375). Although

The naturalism of late-medieval literature

Boccaccio

Boccaccio would have taken an honored place in literary history for some of his lesser works, which included courtly romances, pastoral poems, and learned treatises, by far the most impressive of his writings is the *Decameron,* written between 1348 and 1351. This is a collection of one hundred stories, mostly about love and sex, adventure, and clever trickery, supposedly told by a sophisticated party of seven young ladies and three men who are sojourning in a country villa outside Florence in order to escape the ravages of the Black Death. Boccaccio by no means invented all one hundred plots, but even when he borrowed the outlines of his tales from earlier sources he retold the stories in his own characteristically exuberant, masterful, and extremely witty fashion. There are many reasons why the *Decameron* must be counted as epoch-making from a historical point of view. The first is that it was the earliest ambitious and successful work of vernacular creative literature ever written in western Europe in narrative prose. Boccaccio's prose is "modern" in the sense that it is brisk, for unlike the medieval authors of flowery romances, Boccaccio purposely wrote in an unaffected, colloquial style. Simply stated, in the *Decameron* he was less interested in being "elevated" or elegant than in being unpretentiously entertaining. From the point of view of content, Boccaccio wished to portray men and women as they really are rather than as they ought to be. Thus when he wrote about the clergy he showed them to be as susceptible to human appetites and failings as other mortals. His women are not pallid playthings, distant goddesses, or steadfast virgins, but flesh-and-blood creatures with intellects, who interact more comfortably and naturally with men and with each other than any women in Western literature had ever done before. Boccaccio's treatment of sexual relations is often graphic, often witty, but never demeaning. In his world the natural desires of both women and men are not meant to be thwarted. For all these reasons the *Decameron* is a robust and delightful appreciation of all that is human.

Chaucer

Similar in many ways to Boccaccio as a creator of robust, naturalistic vernacular literature was the Englishman Geoffrey Chaucer (c. 1340–1400). Chaucer was the first major writer of an English that can still be read today with relatively little effort. Remarkably, he was both a founding father of England's mighty literary tradition and one of the four or five greatest contributors to it: most critics rank him just behind Shakespeare, and in a class with Milton, Wordsworth, and Dickens. Chaucer wrote several highly impressive works, but his masterpiece is unquestionably the unfinished *Canterbury Tales,* dating from the end of his career. Like the *Decameron,* this is a collection of stories held together by a frame, in Chaucer's case the device of having a group of people tell stories while on a pilgrimage from London to Canterbury. But there are also differences between the *Decameron* and the *Canterbury Tales.* Chaucer's stories are told in sparkling verse instead of prose and they are recounted by people of all different classes—from a chivalric knight to a dedicated university student to a thieving miller with a wart on his nose. Lively women are also represented, most memorably the gap-toothed, oft-married "Wife of Bath," who knows all "the remedies of love." Each character tells a story which is particularly illustrative of his or her own occupation and outlook on the world. By this device Chaucer is able to create a highly diverse "human comedy." His range is therefore greater than Boccaccio's and although he is as witty, frank, and lusty as the Italian, he is sometimes more profound.

Naturalism in late-medieval art

As naturalism was a dominant trait of late-medieval literature, so it was of late-medieval art. Already by the thirteenth century Gothic sculptors were paying far more attention than their Romanesque predecessors had done to the way plants, animals, and human beings really looked. Whereas medieval art had previously emphasized abstract design, the stress was now increasingly on realism: thirteenth-century carvings of leaves and flowers must have been done from direct observation and are the first to be clearly recognizable as distinct species. Statues of humans also gradually became more naturally proportioned and realistic in their portrayals of facial expressions. By around 1290 the concern for realism had become so great that a sculptor working on a tomb-portrait of the German Emperor Rudolf of Hapsburg allegedly made a hurried return trip to view Rudolf in person, because he had heard that a new wrinkle had appeared on the emperor's face.

Painting

In the next two centuries the trend toward naturalism continued in sculpture and was extended to manuscript illumination and painting. The latter was in certain basic respects a new art. Ever since the caveman, painting had been done on walls, but walls of course were not easily movable. The art of wall-painting continued to be cultivated in the Middle Ages and long afterwards, especially in the form of *frescoes,* or paintings done on wet plaster. But in addition to frescoes, Italian artists in the thirteenth century first started painting pictures on pieces of wood or canvas. These were first done in tempera (pigments mixed with water and natural gums or eggwhites), but around 1400 painting in oils was introduced in the European north. These new technical developments created new artistic opportunities. Artists were now able to paint religious scenes on altarpieces for churches and for private devotions practiced by the wealthier laity at home. Artists also painted the first Western portraits, which were meant to gratify the self-esteem of monarchs and aristocrats. The earliest surviving example of a naturalistic painted portrait is one of a French king, John the Good, executed around 1360. Others followed quickly, so that within a short time the art of portraiture done from life was highly developed. Visitors to art museums will notice that some of the most realistic and sensitive portraits of all time date from the fifteenth century.

The most pioneering and important painter of the later Middle Ages was the Florentine Giotto (c. 1267–1337). He did not engage in indi-

The Meeting of Joachim and Anna at the Golden Gate. A fresco by Giotto. Note how the haloes merge: this old and barren couple will soon miraculously have a child, none other than Mary, the mother of Jesus.

The naturalistic style of Giotto

See color plates following page 384

vidual portraiture, but he brought deep humanity to his religious images done on both walls and movable panels. Giotto was preeminently a naturalist, i.e., an imitator of nature. Not only do his human beings and animals look more natural than those of his predecessors, they seem to do more natural things. When Christ enters Jerusalem on Palm Sunday, boys climb trees to get a better view; when St. Francis is laid out in death, one onlooker takes the opportunity to see whether the saint had really received Christ's wounds; and when the Virgin's parents, Joachim and Anna, meet after a long separation, they actually embrace and kiss—perhaps the first deeply tender kiss in Western art. It was certainly not true, as one fanciful storyteller later reported, that an onlooker found a fly Giotto had painted so real that he attempted to brush it away with his hand, but Giotto in fact accomplished something more. Specifically, he was the first to conceive of the painted space in fully three-dimensional terms: as one art historian has put it, Giotto's frescoes were the first to "knock a hole into the wall." After Giotto's death a reaction in Italian painting set in. This was probably caused by a new reverence for the awesomely supernatural brought about by the horrors of the plague. Whatever the explanation, artists of the mid–fourteenth century briefly moved away from naturalism and painted stern, forbidding religious figures who seemed to float in space. But by around 1400 artists came back down to earth and started to build upon Giotto's influence in ways that led to the great Italian renaissance in painting.

In the north of Europe painting did not advance impressively beyond manuscript illumination until the early fifteenth century, but then it suddenly came very much into its own. The leading northern

European painters were Flemish, first and foremost the brothers Hubert and Jan van Eyck (c. 1366–1426; c. 1380–1441), Roger van der Weyden (c. 1400–1464), and Hans Memling (c. 1430–1494). The van Eycks used to be credited with the invention of oil painting; while that is now open to question, they certainly were its greatest early practitioners. The use of oils allowed them and the other fifteenth-century Flemish painters to engage in brilliant coloring and sharp-focused realism. The van Eycks and van der Weyden excelled most at two things: communicating a sense of deep religious piety and portraying minute details of familiar everyday experience. These may at first seem incompatible, but it should be remembered that contemporary manuals of practical mysticism such as *The Imitation of Christ* also sought to link deep piety with everyday existence. Thus it was by no means blasphemous when a Flemish painter would portray behind a tender Madonna and Child a vista of contemporary life with people going about their usual business and a man even urinating against a wall. This union between the sacred and profane tended to fall apart in the work of Memling, who excelled in either straightforward religious pictures or secular portraits, but it would return in the work of the greatest painters of the Low Countries, Brueghel and Rembrandt.

6. ADVANCES IN TECHNOLOGY

No account of enduring late-medieval accomplishments would be complete without mention of certain epoch-making technological advances. Sadly, but probably not unexpectedly, treatment of this subject has to begin with reference to the invention of artillery and firearms. The prevalence of warfare stimulated the development of new weaponry. Gunpowder itself was a Chinese invention, but it was first put to particularly devastating uses in the late-medieval West. Heavy cannons, which made terrible noises "as though all the dyvels of hell had been in the way," were first employed around 1330. The earliest cannons were so primitive that it often was more dangerous to stand behind than in front of them, but by the middle of the fifteenth century they were greatly improved and began to revolutionize the nature of warfare. In one year, 1453, heavy artillery played a leading role in determining the outcome of two crucial conflicts: the Ottoman Turks used German and Hungarian cannons to breach the defenses of Constantinople—hitherto the most impregnable in Europe—and the French used heavy artillery to take the city of Bordeaux, thereby ending the Hundred Years' War. Cannons thereafter made it difficult for rebellious aristocrats to hole up in their stone castles, and thus they aided in the consolidation of the national monarchies. Placed aboard ships, cannons enabled European vessels to dominate foreign waters in the subsequent age of overseas expansion. Guns were also invented in the fourteenth century, to be gradually perfected afterwards.

Late-medieval technological achievements: (1) the weapons of war

Cannons Being Used to Breach the Walls of a Castle. This scene depicts a late engagement of the Hundred Years' War.

Shortly after 1500 the most effective new variety of gun, the musket, allowed foot-soldiers to end once and for all the earlier military dominance of heavily armored mounted knights. Once lance-bearing cavalries became outmoded and fighting could more easily be carried on by all, the monarchical states that could turn out the largest armies completely subdued internal resistance and dominated the battlefields of Europe.

Other late-medieval technological developments were more life-enhancing. Eyeglasses, first invented in the 1280s, were perfected in the fourteenth century. These allowed older people to keep on reading when nearsightedness would otherwise have stopped them. For example, the great fourteenth-century scholar Petrarch, who boasted excellent sight in his youth, wore spectacles after his sixtieth year and was thus enabled to complete some of his most important works. Around 1300 the use of the magnetic compass helped ships to sail further away from land and venture out into the Atlantic. One immediate result was the opening of direct sea commerce between Italy and the North. Subsequently, numerous improvements in shipbuilding, map making, and navigational devices contributed to Europe's ability to start expanding overseas. In the early fourteenth century the Azores and Cape Verde Islands were reached; then, after a long pause caused by Europe's plagues and wars, the African Cape of Good Hope was rounded in 1488, the West Indies discovered in 1492, India reached by the sea route in 1498, and Brazil discovered in 1500. Partly as a result of technology the world was thus suddenly made much smaller.

Among the most familiar implements of our modern life that were invented by Europeans in the later Middle Ages were clocks and printed books. Mechanical clocks were invented shortly before 1300

(2) optical and navigational instruments

and proliferated in the years immediately thereafter. The earliest clocks were too expensive for private purchase, but towns quickly vied with each other to install the most elaborate clocks in their prominent public buildings. These clocks not only told the time but showed the courses of sun, moon, and planets, and performed mechanical tricks on the striking of the hours. The new invention ultimately had two profound effects. One was the further stimulation of European interest in complex machinery of all sorts. This interest had already been awakened by the high-medieval proliferation of mills, but clocks ultimately became even more omnipresent than mills because after about 1650 they became quite cheap and were brought into practically every European home. Household clocks served as models of marvelous machines. Equally if not more significant was the fact that clocks began to rationalize the course of European daily affairs. Until the advent of clocks in the late Middle Ages time was flexible. Men and women had only a rough idea of how late in the day it was and rose and retired more or less with the sun. Especially people who lived in the country performed different jobs at different rates according to the rhythm of the seasons. Even when hours were counted, they were measured at different lengths according to the amount of light in the different seasons of the year. In the fourteenth century, however, clocks first started relentlessly striking equal hours through the day and night. Thus they began to regulate work with new precision. People were expected to start and end work "on time" and many came to believe that "time is money." This emphasis on time-keeping brought new efficiencies but also new tensions: Lewis Carroll's white rabbit, who is always looking at his pocket watch and muttering, "how late it's getting," is a telling caricature of time-obsessed Western man.

The invention of printing with movable type was equally momentous. The major stimulus for this invention was the replacement of

(3) mechanical clocks

Horloge de Sapience. This miniature, from an early–fifteenth-century French manuscript, reflects the growing fascination with machines of all sorts and clocks in particular.

Left: *Paper-Making at a Paper Mill*. Right: *A Printing Press*. From a title page of a Parisian printer, 1520.

(4) the invention of printing

parchment by paper as Europe's primary writing material between 1200 and 1400. Parchment, made from the skins of valuable farm animals, was extremely expensive: since it was possible to get only about four good parchment leaves from one animal, it was necessary to slaughter between two to three hundred sheep or calves to gain enough parchment for a Bible! Paper, made from rags turned into pulp by mills, brought prices down dramatically. Late-medieval records show that paper sold at one-sixth the price of parchment. Accordingly, it became cheaper to learn how to read and write. With literacy becoming ever more widespread, there was a growing market for still cheaper books, and the invention of printing with movable type around 1450 fully met this demand. By greatly saving labor, the invention made printed books about one-fifth as expensive as handwritten ones within about two decades.

The effects of printing

As soon as books became easily accessible, literacy increased even more and book-culture became a basic part of the European way of life. After about 1500 Europeans could afford to read and buy books of all sorts—not just religious tracts, but instructional manuals, light entertainment, and, by the eighteenth century, newspapers. Printing insured that ideas would spread quickly and reliably; moreover, revolutionary ideas could no longer be easily extinguished once they were set down in hundreds of copies of books. Thus the greatest religious reformer of the sixteenth century, Martin Luther, gained an immediate following throughout Germany by employing the printing press to run off pamphlets: had printing not been available to him, Luther might have died like Hus. The spread of books also helped stimulate the growth of cultural nationalism. Before printing, regional dialects in most European countries were often so diverse that people who supposedly spoke the same language often could barely understand each other. Such a situation hindered governmental centralization because a royal servant might be entirely unable to communicate with inhabitants of the provinces. Shortly after the invention of printing, however, each European country began to develop its own linguistic standards which were disseminated uniformly by books. The "King's English" was what was printed in London and carried to Yorkshire or Wales. Thus communications were enhanced and governments were able to operate ever more efficiently.

In conclusion it may be said that clocks and books as much as guns and ocean-going ships helped Europe to dominate the globe after 1500. The habits inculcated by clocks encouraged Europeans to work efficiently and to plan precisely; the prevalence of books enhanced communications and the flow of progressive ideas. Once accustomed to reading books, Europeans communicated and experimented intellectually as no other peoples in the world. Thus it was not surprising that after 1500 Europeans could start to make the whole world their own.

Technological advancement a factor in Europe's subsequent global preeminence

SELECTED READINGS

• *Items so designated are available in paperback editions.*

Breisach, E., *Renaissance Europe, 1300–1517*, New York, 1973. The best college-level textbook on the period.

Bridbury, A. R., *Economic Growth: England in the Later Middle Ages*, 2nd ed., New York, 1975. A controversial argument against the dominant theory of economic depression.

• Brucker, G., *Renaissance Florence*, New York, 1969. An excellent introduction by one of America's foremost experts.

• Cipolla, C. M., *Clocks and Culture, 1300–1700*, London, 1967. Treats both technological developments and the importance of clocks as items of trade.

• Cole, Bruce, *Giotto and Florentine Painting, 1280–1375*, New York, 1976. A clear and stimulating introduction.

Dollinger, P., *The German Hansa*, Stanford, 1970.

Fourquin, G., *The Anatomy of Popular Rebellion in the Middle Ages*, New York, 1978.

Hale, John R., et al., *Europe in the Late Middle Ages*, Evanston, Ill., 1965. Specialized essays on numerous subjects.

Herlihy, David, *Medieval and Renaissance Pistoia: The Social History of an Italian Town*, New Haven, Conn., 1967. Important for its use of statistical evidence.

• Holmes, George, *The Later Middle Ages, 1272–1485*, New York, 1962.

• Huizinga, J., *The Waning of the Middle Ages*, London, 1924. A beautifully written classic on forms of thought and art in the Low Countries.

• Johnson, Jerah, and W. Percy, *The Age of Recovery: The Fifteenth Century*, Ithaca, N.Y., 1970.

Kaminsky, H., *A History of the Hussite Revolution*, Berkeley, Calif., 1967. Detailed and difficult but far and away the best treatment of the subject.

• Lerner, R., *The Age of Adversity: The Fourteenth Century*, Ithaca, N.Y., 1968.

Lewis, P. S., *Later Medieval France: The Polity*, London, 1968.

McFarlane, K. B., *The Nobility of Later Medieval England*, Oxford, 1973. An excellent collection of essays by a late master of the field.

• Meiss, M., *Painting in Florence and Siena After the Black Death*, Princeton, N.J., 1951. A stimulating attempt to relate art history to the spirit of an age.

• Miskimin, H. A., *The Economy of Early Renaissance Europe, 1300–1460*, Englewood Cliffs, N.J., 1969. The best short work on the subject.

Mollat, G., *The Popes at Avignon, 1305–1378*, London, 1963.

• Panofsky, E., *Early Netherlandish Painting*, 2 vols., Cambridge, Mass., 1953. A brilliant specialized history by a master art historian.

• Pernoud, R., *Joan of Arc*, New York, 1966. Joan viewed through the eyes of her contemporaries.

Perroy, E., *The Hundred Years War*, Bloomington, Ind., 1959. The standard account.

Scaglione, A., *Nature and Love in the Late Middle Ages*, Berkeley, Calif., 1963.

• Smart, Alastair, *The Dawn of Italian Painting, 1250–1400*, Ithaca, N.Y., 1978. More detailed than Cole.

Trinkaus, C., and H. A. Oberman, eds., *The Pursuit of Holiness in Late Medieval and Renaissance Religion*, Leiden, 1974. Essays that reveal the most recent trends in research.

Vaughan, Richard, *Valois Burgundy*, London, 1975.

• Waley, D., *Later Medieval Europe*, 2nd ed., London, 1975.

SOURCE MATERIALS

Allmand, C. T., ed., *Society at War: The Experience of England and France During the Hundred Years War*, Edinburgh, 1973. An outstanding collection of documents.

• Boccaccio, G., *The Decameron*, tr. M. Musa and P. E. Bondanella, New York, 1977.

• Chaucer, G., *The Canterbury Tales*. (Many editions.)

Colledge, E., ed., *The Mediaeval Mystics of England*, New York, 1961.

• Froissart, J., *Chronicles*, tr. G. Brereton, Baltimore, 1968. A selection from the most famous contemporary account of the Hundred Years' War. Reads more like a novel than like history.

The Imitation of Christ, tr. L. Sherley-Price, Baltimore, 1952.

John Hus at the Council of Constance, tr. M. Spinka, New York, 1965. The translation of a Czech chronicle with an expert introduction and appended collection of documents.

Meister Eckhart, tr. R. B. Blakney, New York, 1941.

Memoirs of a Renaissance Pope: The Commentaries of Pius II (abridged ed.), tr. F. A. Gragg, New York, 1959. A fascinating insight into the Renaissance papacy.

A Parisian Journal, 1405–1449, tr. J. Shirley, Oxford, 1968. A marvelous panorama of Parisian life recorded by an eyewitness.

• Pitti, B., and G. Dati, *Two Memoirs of Renaissance Florence*, tr. J. Martines, New York, 1967.

Chapter 17

INDIA, THE FAR EAST, AND AFRICA IN THE LATER MIDDLE AGES

Seldom [have] two civilizations, so vast and so strongly developed, yet so radically dissimilar as the Muhammadan and Hindu, [met and mingled] together. The very contrasts which existed between them, the wide divergences in their culture and their religions, make the history of their impact peculiarly instructive and lend an added interest to the art and above all to the architecture which their united genius called into being.

—Sir John Marshall, in *Cambridge History of India,* Vol. III

The centuries which are known in the West as the Middle Ages did not have quite the same importance for the civilizations of the Eastern lands as they did for the evolution of European civilization. The cultures of India and China were already highly advanced, while the western Europeans were only beginning to develop a stabilized society and to utilize their intellectual resources to a significant degree. In contrast to western Europe, which during the late medieval centuries was relatively free from external disturbances, both India and China experienced fresh invasions more sweeping in character than any they had known since the beginnings of their recorded history. They were able to survive the shock of these invasions with the essential features of their cultures intact, although permanent modifications took place in Indian society. Japan was unique among the principal Asian states in the fact that she was not subjected to foreign conquest. The tensions and conflicts within her own society, however, were tremendous, and they gradually produced a type of social and political organization which was remarkably similar to the feudal system of western Europe. The face of black Africa changed dramatically with the expansion of trade. Great kingdoms and empires encompassing diverse cultures, languages, and religious systems arose and urban centers of high civilization reflecting the convergence of Islamic and African cultures flourished.

Contrasts with the European Middle Ages

1. THE ESTABLISHMENT OF MUSLIM KINGDOMS IN INDIA (c. 1000–1500)

About the same time that the nations of western Europe were initiating the economic and intellectual progress which distinguished the later Middle Ages and which made possible the brilliant culture of the Renaissance, the peoples of India were harried by a series of marauding raids that devastated their society and sorely impaired their creative talents. The invaders of this period were devotees of Islam. They implanted the Muslim religion in India so firmly that it has ever since been the faith of a substantial minority of the population. But while the expansion of Islam in Africa, Spain, and the Middle East was associated with the quickening of cultural activities and with the attainment of relatively harmonious relations between the conquerors and their subject peoples, the Muslim conquests in India led to wanton destruction and created a deep and abiding cleavage between the opposing religious groups.

The first of the Muslim conquerors of India were Turks from Afghanistan. They did not come in numberless hordes, nor were they unresisted by native troops. The fact that they were able to sweep across the country and work such havoc is a commentary on the fateful political division of India and the lack of solidarity among her people. Ever since the decay of Harsha's empire in the seventh century, Hindustan had been disunited and subject to contention among various states. The strongest of the Hindu states were those inhabited by a group known as Rajputs. The origin of the Rajputs (the word means literally "sons of kings") is not known. It is probable that they were not Indians to begin with but the descendants of Huns and other invaders of the fifth and sixth centuries who had become assimilated into Hindu society. Generally they were regarded as belonging to the *kshatriya* (warrior) caste, and they prided themselves on their military traditions. The rulers and nobility of the Rajput kingdoms had developed a code of chivalrous conduct somewhat like the cult of chivalry of the medieval European knights. They were redoubtable horsemen, proud of their skill with the sword, and hypersensitive to insult. The Rajputs were the fiercest and bravest fighters in India, but they were unable to stem the Muslim advance.

Undoubtedly the helplessness of the Indian people during this time of invasion was intensified by the caste system, which was now exacting a heavy penalty. Each stratum of the population was hedged in by its own prescribed activities and loyalties—military defense was considered to be the function of the *kshatriyas* alone. The lower classes were impoverished and dispirited, and there was little incentive for concerted action in the common interest. By contrast, the Muslim invaders were a fresh and energetic people, excited by the prospect of rich spoils and inspired by an activist creed that promised certain

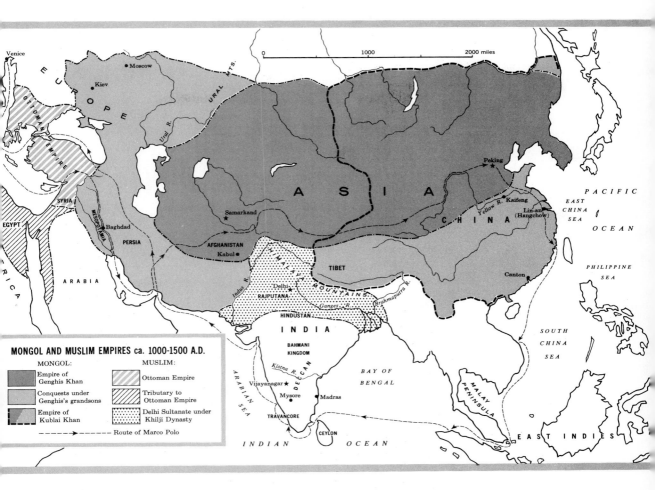

recompense for service in a holy war against idolators. The Hindus
were not prepared to cope with such fanatical zeal as their adversaries
displayed. Nevertheless, the Rajputs gave a good account of themselves in combat; and some of them, when they saw that opposition
was useless, removed with their retainers into the heart of the Indian
desert to rebuild their shattered communities in the region which
came to be called Rajputana.

After its initial impact the Muslim conquest of northern India
entered a new phase, characterized by the establishment of governmental centers and permanent residences on Indian soil. The most
important kingdom founded by the Turks, with Delhi as its capital,
gradually acquired control over all of Hindustan and even penetrated
into the Deccan. Between the thirteenth and the sixteenth centuries,
five successive dynasties of Turks or Afghans ruled from Delhi. The
fortunes of the kingdom and the character of the rulers during these

Extension of the Muslim conquests

Kutb Minar, near Delhi. This magnificent "pillar of victory," 238 feet high, was erected in the early thirteenth century by Kutb-uddin, the founder of a Muslim sultanate at Delhi.

300 years cannot be detailed here, but they varied tremendously. In one instance the sultan was a woman named Raziya, who demonstrated great energy and ability but was murdered with her husband—an Ethiopian—by jealous nobles (in 1240). Intrigues and assassinations were frequent because of the absence of an established rule of succession to the throne. By comparison with the Hindu caste-bound society, the Islamic community was democratic, and even an upstart who seized the throne by violence might be accepted as a legitimate sovereign if he proved capable. It was not uncommon for a slave who had been trained for administrative work to be entrusted with large responsibilities both civil and military and finally to usurp authority when a favorable opportunity arose. In fact, one line of Delhi rulers is known as the "Slave Kings" (1206–1290) because its founder had been a slave and viceroy of an early sultan.

Characteristics of Muslim rule

In spite of the fact that high positions were open to men of low birth, the administration was thoroughly autocratic in operation, and it derived its character from the personality, the ambitions, or the whims of the ruler. Cruelty, depravity, enlightened statesmanship, and humanitarian sensibilities were all exemplified in erratic sequence. For example, the founder of the Khilji Dynasty (1290–1318) was a benevolent and mild-tempered old gentleman who hated to shed the blood even of criminals. The nephew who assassinated and succeeded him was a monster of treachery and cruelty, and so extortionate that he reduced his Hindu subjects to poverty. The next sultan, although scholarly and abstinent by habit, was in some ways even worse than his predecessor. He compelled the entire population of Delhi to move to another site 600 miles distant, leaving the great city desolate. He disrupted commerce by debasing the currency, exacted such heavy taxes that whole villages were abandoned, hunted down men like wild beasts for sport, and dreamed of conquering Persia and China. But this dismal tyrant's successor (promoted to the throne by the army chiefs) during a long and peaceful reign of thirty-seven years adhered to principles of justice and benevolence considerably above the general standard of fourteenth-century states the world over. He reduced taxes, provided poor relief, granted loans to the peasants, and promoted prosperity by reclaiming wastelands and by building extensive irrigation works.

The five-century period of the Turkish invasions and the Delhi Sultanate witnessed many changes in India but few original or constructive cultural developments. The central fact, of course, was the introduction of the Muslim religion and its gradual accommodation to the conditions of the country. At the outset, reconciliation between Islam and Hinduism seemed impossible. Islam was strictly monotheistic, possessed a clear-cut and simple but dogmatic creed, regarded graven images as sinful, and emphasized the equality of believers. Hinduism was polytheistic (although tending toward monotheism or pantheism in its philosophy), taught that there are many equally valid approaches to an understanding of the divine being, delighted in symbols, pictorial forms, and architectural profusion, and carried the concept of human inequality to extremes. The Hindus were noncredal and disposed to tolerance; the Muslims considered it their sacred duty to spread the one true faith of Allah and his Prophet. Nevertheless, the two peoples gradually drew closer together. The Muslim sovereigns did not exterminate the Hindus whom they had subjected. They followed the shrewder policy of laying discriminatory assessments upon the "unbelievers"—a poll tax and a tax on Hindu religious festivals and pilgrimages. Naturally, a good many Hindus became converts to Islam, and those who did so were accepted on an equal basis by the dominant Muslim faction. Moreover, intermarriage took place between Hindus and Muslims in spite of religious scruples on both sides. As already indicated, some of the sultans and their officials were intelligent and progressive in outlook. The best of them tried to improve economic conditions; some were patrons of literature and the arts, encouraged scholarship, and erected splendid monuments.

It is apparent, however, that the general effects of the Turkish conquests were depressing. They were accompanied by orgies of slaughter and spoliation. They threw a pall over the creative spirit of the Hindus, bringing a marked decline in a tradition of intellectual and

General effects of the Turkish conquests

artistic enterprise that had once been vigorous. Turko-Afghan forces destroyed the major centers of Buddhism, including the great university at Nalanda, and almost completely wiped out the remnants of Buddhism in India. Mosques of excellent workmanship were constructed—often from the stones of demolished Hindu temples—and not all the existing Indian temples were destroyed; but the building of new Hindu religious edifices was prohibited under severe penalties. It is doubtful whether the equalitarian aspects of the teachings of Islam produced any ameliorative effects upon the Indian population. The immediate result, at least, was to create new divisions in an already too sharply divided society. One social effect of the Muslim impact was the subjection of women to a greater degree than ever before. The custom of *purdah* (the veiling and seclusion of women) dates from this era.

After the Turkish sultans had established themselves as sovereigns in Hindustan, they found their position threatened not only by potential Hindu rebellion and by intrigues among their own viceroys but also by new invasions from Central Asia, that inexhaustible reservoir of nomadic peoples. At this time the chief source of disturbance was the expansion of the Mongols, whose force was felt throughout the breadth of Asia and even in Europe. Early in the thirteenth century the famous Mongol chieftain and empire builder Genghis Khan made a brief foray into the Indus valley. His raid was only an incident, but the danger of a Mongol attack upon India persisted. Gradually groups of Mongols settled in northern India and adopted agricultural or industrial pursuits, most of them embracing the Muslim religion. So numerous were they in Delhi in the late thirteenth century that a section of the city was called "Mongol Town." Mongols were employed by the sultan as mercenary troops, in which capacity they were sometimes victimized by his suspicion of their loyalty, and tens of thousands of them were massacred.

The Great Mongol Conqueror Genghis Khan, Grandfather of the Founder of the Mongol (Yüan) Dynasty in China.

Mongol invaders: Timur

Near the end of the fourteenth century northern India was visited by the most devastating raid in all its history, led by Timur the Lame (Tamerlane). Timur, of Turkish descent, had started his career as the chieftain of a small tribal state in Turkestan. After misfortunes and amazing adventures he had welded together a powerful force of cavalry and embarked on a sensational career of conquest. Although he never assumed the title of Khan, he won recognition as overlord from most of the Mongols who had previously followed Genghis Khan. He overran Afghanistan, Persia, and Mesopotamia; then he invaded India with the avowed intention of converting infidels to Islam and procuring booty. He and his troops spent less than a year in India (1398–1399) but left a ruin behind them. The city of Delhi, sacked in a three-day orgy, was turned into a ghost town, so destitute that—to quote a contemporary—"for two whole months not a bird moved a wing in the city." Any place that offered resistance was destroyed and its inhabitants slaughtered or enslaved. Lord Timur carried off with him inestimable quantities of gold and precious stuffs, slaves for all his soldiers, and thousands of skilled craftsmen, including stonemasons to build a great mosque at his capital city of Samarkand in Turkestan. The Delhi Sultanate never fully recovered from the blow dealt to it and to its helpless Hindu subjects by Timur, the "Earth Shaker."

Throughout this period India embraced a number of states, both Muslim and Hindu, which were not included in the Delhi Sultanate. In the fourteenth century two large kingdoms came into existence in the Deccan. Ruled by Muslims, the Bahmani kingdom at its height included about half the Deccan, stretching from sea to sea, and was divided into four provinces. Some of the Bahmani sultans were well-educated and intelligent men, who built lavishly, encouraged trade, and maintained a cosmopolitan atmosphere at their court. In the late fifteenth century the administration deteriorated and the kingdom was broken up into five separate states.

The Bahmani kingdom

Turkish Prisoners before Timur. An Indian painting from the period of Akbar (1556–1605). The use of Arabic script as a decorative device in Indian painting reflects the Muslim influence.

*The empire of
Vijayanagar*

Even more splendid than the Bahmani kingdom was the Hindu empire of Vijayanagar, which at one time dominated the whole southern end of the peninsula as far north as the Kistna River (including, roughly, Madras, Travancore, and Mysore). The capital city, also named Vijayanagar ("City of Victory"), was strongly fortified, heavily populated, and probably—on the testimony of Italian, Portuguese, and Afghan visitors—one of the greatest cities in the world during the fifteenth century. The commerce of the kingdom was eagerly sought. Several kinds of precious stones, particularly large diamonds, were prominent among its exports. The court was sumptuous and the palaces magnificent. Architecture flourished on a grand scale and with an imaginative boldness reminiscent of the classical Sanskrit age. The foundations which underlay the brilliant culture of this last great Hindu empire, however, were not sound. In spite of an orderly government and in the midst of great wealth, the common people suffered from extreme privation and were fleeced by avaricious officials. Luxurious and profligate courts, the encouragement of prostitution in the temples, and the compulsory burning of widows (requiring the mass immolation of thousands of women on the death of a king) were hardly evidences of a healthy society. Unfortunately, a haughty and embittered rivalry between the Hindu and the Bahmani kingdoms weakened both states. In 1565 the almost impregnable city of Vijayanagar was taken and wantonly destroyed by troops from a league of neighboring Muslim powers, and the southern Hindu empire sank into a permanent decline.

2. CHINA UNDER THE SUNG, MONGOL, AND MING DYNASTIES (960–1644)

*Founding of the Sung
Dynasty*

For about fifty years following the collapse of the great T'ang Dynasty in the early tenth century, China was a divided country with power in the hands of military dictators. After this chaotic but relatively brief interregnum (known to Chinese tradition as the "Five Dynasties"), unity and a strong central government were re-established by an able general who assumed the imperial title and founded the Sung Dynasty. This dynasty, like its predecessor, the T'ang, endured for about three centuries (960–1279). Although the first Sung had been an army officer, he revived the ancient administrative system and restored the power of the civilian bureaucracy. In contrast to the T'ang, the Sung rulers did not adopt a policy of imperialism, and even relinquished control over portions of the empire. Territories in the north and the northwest were lost to seminomadic peoples who, while founding independent kingdoms, assimilated many aspects of Chinese culture. One of these northern groups, the Khitan, established a kingdom in southern Manchuria, annexed territory south of the Great Wall in the Peking area, and collected tribute from the Sung emperors. Although the Khitan were entirely separate from the Chinese in origin, a corruption of their name—"Cathay"—came to be a Western designation for China, a circumstance which indicates that the Khitan did not long retain their distinctive traits after coming into close contact with China's mature civilization.

Early in the twelfth century the Khitan state (Liao) was overthrown by a people of similar stock, the Juchên, who not only occupied Manchuria and Mongolia but also conquered the greater part of northern China. Thus, beginning about 1141, the Sung actually controlled only the Yangtze valley and regions to the south. They established their capital at Hangchow (then known as Lin-an), a magnificent port but far distant from the traditional centers of imperial administration. The later, or southern, Sung period was characterized by a less vigorous administration and by the familiar but depressing symptoms of dynastic decay. These disadvantages, however, were to some extent counterbalanced by the fact that southern China felt the influence of Chinese culture more fully than it had before. The peoples of the south and southwest not only became more completely incorporated into Chinese society but also began to contribute leadership to the state. The center of population was shifting to the south, and there was evidence also that originality and initiative were abundant in this area. During the Southern Sung period (1141–1279) northern China continued to be ruled by the Juchên from the old Sung capital at Kaifeng on the Yellow River. While the loss of so much territory to alien conquerors was humiliating to the Sung emperors, it produced no appreciable permanent changes in the north. The Juchên adapted themselves to Chinese ways as readily as had the Khitan. Both Buddhism and Confucianism obtained a strong hold upon them, and the rulers, following the established convention, adopted a Chinese dynastic title (*Chin* or *Kin,* meaning "Gold").

Peace, internal stability, and prolific cultural activity were characteristic of the Sung period, especially during the first century and a half. As earlier, a flourishing commerce contributed to an increase in wealth and promoted a knowledge of foreign lands. Overland trade declined, partly because the caravan routes were no longer controlled by the Chinese, but business was brisk in port cities of the southeastern coast. Foreign merchants, among whom the Arabs still predominated, were granted the right of residence in the trading centers, subject to the jurisdiction of an Inspector of Foreign Trade. At the same time the Chinese themselves were beginning to participate more extensively in oceanic commerce. The early Sung emperors undertook ambitious public works, including irrigation projects. Apparently society as a whole attained a fair level of prosperity, as evidenced by an increase in population.

The late eleventh century was significant for a reform movement

The Southern Sung period

Heavy Porcelain Vase with Simple Design. Sung Dynasty (960–1279).

The reforms of Wang An-shih (1021–1086)

launched by a scholar-official, Wang An-shih (1021–1086), who held the position of chief minister for a number of years. His proposals were the subject of acrimonious controversy and never were carried out in entirety, but they represented a realistic attempt to improve the administration, and they focused attention upon the plight of the common man. Wang promoted the establishment of public schools endowed with state lands, and he advocated revision of the civil-service examinations to encourage a knowledge of practical problems instead of proficiency in classical literary forms. His most determined efforts were directed toward a program of relief for the poor farmers by direct government assistance, by revision of the inequitable tax system and the abolition of forced labor, and by a redistribution of land. He wanted the government to control commerce, fix prices, buy up farm surpluses, and make loans to farmers at a low rate of interest on the security of their growing crops. Wang An-shih's proposals for agrarian relief anticipated some of the measures inaugurated by governments in recent times, and his overall program approximated ·a kind of state socialism. Although he insisted that he was merely adapting genuine Confucian principles to the needs of the time, his opponents branded him as a dangerous innovator. The contest between the Innovators (Wang's disciples) and the Conservatives continued into the next century, with the emperors favoring sometimes one and sometimes the other group; but the conservative faction ultimately prevailed. Wang's radical proposals, however, have been studied with interest by modern reformers in China and elsewhere.

The Mongol invaders of China: Genghis Khan and Kublai Khan

An invasion by the Mongols brought about the final collapse of the Sung Dynasty and subjected all China, for the first time in its history, to the rule of a foreign conqueror. The Mongol Asiatic empire, like so many of its predecessors, was established with almost incredible swiftness in a series of military campaigns, but it was for a brief period one of the largest ever known. In the early thirteenth century the great Mongol conqueror Genghis Khan overthrew the kingdoms adjacent to China on the north and then swept westward across all Asia. After making a brief foray into India he subdued Persia and Mesopotamia and occupied large stretches of Russian territory north and west of the Caspian Sea. Although the invasion of China was probably inevitable, the Sung emperor contributed to his own downfall by playing a double game with the Mongols. So eager was he to get rid of the Juchên rulers in north China that he sent troops to help the Mongols against them; then he rashly attacked the Mongol forces and exposed his own dominions to the fury of the ruthless and swift-riding horsemen. The conquest of southern China was completed by Genghis Khan's grandson, Kublai Khan, after many years of hard fighting, during which the Mongols not only had to occupy the coastal cities but also had to accustom themselves to naval warfare. In 1279 the last Chinese army was defeated (the commanding general is said to have jumped into the sea with the infant Sung prince in his arms), and Kublai became the master of China.

The huge Asiatic empire of the Mongols, which reached from the China Sea to eastern Europe, was too large to be administered effectively as a unit and did not long remain intact. Religious differences contributed to its dissolution. Before the end of the thirteenth century most of the western princes (khans) had become Muslims and repudiated the authority of Kublai's family, who favored a Tibetan form of Buddhism. Kublai's descendants, however, from their imperial capital of Peking, governed China for the better part of a century (1279–1368).

The dissolution of Kublai's empire

The accession of the Mongol (or Yüan) Dynasty seemed to threaten a serious interruption in the normal course of Chinese civilization. Mongol rule remained essentially a military occupation imposed upon traditional Chinese institutions. Fortunately the damage inflicted was only temporary, and there was actually some progress during this period of foreign domination. The Mongols were notoriously cruel conquerors, leaving ruined cities and mutilated corpses as monuments to the folly of those who resisted them. The bitterly contested occupation of southern China was accompanied by a decimation of the native population in some areas. Nevertheless, the Mongol rulers were wise enough to recognize the desirability of preserving such a great state as China and the advantage to be gained from taxing its people instead of exterminating them. The nomad warriors could not resist the influence of Chinese culture, and the traditional Chinese administrative system was not completely uprooted. The civil-service examinations were suspended for a time, and Chinese were excluded from most governmental posts, although the Mongol emperors employed foreigners of various nationalities in high positions at court. In the fourteenth century, when the dynasty showed signs of weakening and native unrest became ominous, the emperor reinstituted the examination system and admitted Chinese to office, chiefly at the lower level.

The rule of the Mongol emperors

While the Mongol emperors patronized Buddhism, they did not seriously interfere with other native cults and they permitted the introduction of Western religions, although Islam was the only one of these to retain a permanent place. The emperors' lavish endowment of temples and monasteries strained the economy by removing tracts of land from the tax registers and impoverished the peasants, whose holdings had been confiscated. Many peasants lost their lands when conscripted as laborers for the construction of palaces, irrigation works, and an improved transportation system. A notable undertaking was the rebuilding and extension of the Grand Canal linking the capital city of Peking to the Yangtze valley by an inland waterway.

Religious and economic policies

During the Mongol period China was by no means isolated from other regions. The area under the jurisdiction of Peking was consid-

The Imperial Post Road. This road, through a valley west of Chunking, is part of the old Imperial Post Road connecting Peking with the Tibetan capital, Lhasa.

Extension of foreign contacts

erably larger than the empire of the Sung, and the emperors attempted to increase it still further by schemes of conquest of dubious value. Kublai Khan made two attempts to invade Japan (in 1274 and 1281), employing both Chinese and Korean vessels, but a typhoon wrecked many of his ships and the Japanese annihilated the landing party. Fortunately, peaceful intercourse was continued with other nations, near and far. Overland commerce was facilitated by imperial highways which the Mongols built deep into Central Asia and even to Persia. That travel was comparatively safe is indicated by the large number of foreign visitors in China during this period. Foreign merchants enjoyed special privileges in the Mongol empire, while Chinese were discriminated against. Russians, Arabs, and Jews entered China for purposes of trade, as did Genoese and Venetians. The effects of this extensive commerce was to impair rather than strengthen the economy because it drained precious metals out of China and led to inflation of the currency. Marco Polo, the most famous of many European visitors, who lived and traveled widely in China for seventeen years (1275–1292), astonished his countrymen with his glowing report upon returning home (he described Hangchow, the Southern Sung capital, as "the finest and noblest city in the world"). But Marco Polo moved in privileged circles and failed to notice the condition of the common people. By the fourteenth century starvation was widespread and more Chinese had been reduced to slavery than at any other time in history.

In the fourteenth century, Mongol power was undermined by the decadence of the ruling house and by the growing discontent of the Chinese people, who never forgot that they had been subjugated by a barbarian conqueror. Rebellion was brought to a successful conclusion under the leadership of a dynamic, if somewhat grotesque, soldier of fortune, who captured Peking in 1368 and drove the last Mongol emperor into the wastes of Mongolia. This rebel leader was a man of low birth who had been orphaned at an early age and had exchanged the life of a Buddhist monk for that of a bandit. Nevertheless, he was accepted as having won the Mandate of Heaven and became the first emperor of the Ming ("Brilliant" or "Glorious") Dynasty, which lasted from 1368 to 1644. The dynasty proved to be extremely successful and gave renewed proof of the potency of Chinese institutions, although it added little that was new. The government adhered to the Sung patterns, or in some ways more closely to the T'ang, particularly in its emphasis upon the forceful expansion of territorial boundaries. Ming China was a large state, with its authority extending into Manchuria, Mongolia, Indochina, Burma, and the southwestern region facing Tibet. While the great Mongol empire of the thirteenth century had fallen to pieces, it gave promise of being resurrected by Timur (Tamerlane), the master of Turkestan and scourge of India. Although the Ming court regarded Timur's emissaries as tribute bearers, the "Earth Shaker" was actually setting forth on an expedition to conquer China when he died prematurely in 1405. In spite of this stroke of fortune, the Ming emperors made little effort to recover either Turkestan or Sinkiang.

A noteworthy aspect of the early Ming period was the development and rapid expansion of Chinese navigation. The mariner's compass had been in use perhaps since the eleventh century, and some large ships had been constructed; but now maritime enterprise was given tremendous impetus. Chinese sailing vessels, equipped with as many as four decks and comfortable living quarters, undertook voyages to the East Indies, the Malay Peninsula, Ceylon, India, and Arabia, returning with merchandise, tribute, and valuable geographical information. They may have ventured westward around Africa's Cape of Good Hope. In its heyday the Ming navy was more than equal to that of any contemporary European state, although when stationed in the home waters of the Yangtze region it was exposed to attacks from Japanese pirates. Overseas expeditions were discontinued after the demise of Timur and the decay of Mongol power in Central Asia reopened the caravan routes to the West. From about 1424 the government restricted Chinese shipping to coastal waters and the network of canals and discouraged foreign travel on the part of its subjects. The

The overthrow of the Mongols and establishment of the Ming Dynasty

Maritime achievements under the Ming Dynasty

Fall of the Ming Dynasty. The death of the last of the Ming emperors at the hands of the invading Manchus when they captured Peking in 1644.

result was not only a loss of revenue from commerce but also an unfortunate isolation of China at the very time when the Western peoples were beginning to emerge from their provincialism. Instead of retaining the initiative on the high seas, the later Ming rulers proved inefficient in defending their own coasts.

Decline of the Ming Dynasty

A decline in the vitality of the administration was apparent long before the Ming Dynasty came to a close. Officials became lazy and corrupt; power passed into the hands of court favorites and eunuchs; and exorbitant taxes oppressed the peasants to the point of ruin. While the costs of government mounted dizzily—in 1639 military expenditures alone were ten times greater than the entire revenue of the first Ming emperor—territories were being lost through incompetence and rebellion. Although the dynasty finally succumbed to another foreign invasion, internal dissension was the real cause of its collapse.

Cultural developments under the Sung and Ming: Neo-Confucianism

In turning from the political to the cultural developments that took place in China during the Sung, Mongol, and Ming dynasties, we may note that a renewal of interest in philosophical speculation occurred, reaching a climax in the latter half of the twelfth century. This revival represented a return to the fountainhead of Chinese thought—the sages of antiquity, particularly Confucius—but it introduced several new ideas and was not a mere repetition of ancient formulas. The most noted Chinese thinker of this period was Chu Hsi (1130–1200), who held a position at the Sung court and was an opponent of the so-called Innovators (disciples of Wang An-shih). Although Chu Hsi claimed to be interpreting Confucius' teachings in accordance with their original and uncorrupted meaning, he and his associates actually founded a Neo-Confucian school, with a metaphysics which incorporated elements of Taoism and Buddhism. They stressed the concept of the "Supreme Ultimate" or Absolute, a Final Cause which underlies the whole material universe and is antecedent to every rational or moral principle. Nevertheless, Chu Hsi, like his ancient master Confucius, was chiefly interested in human nature and its proper development in an ethical and social order. He reaffirmed Mencius' faith in man's natural capacity for good and upheld the traditional ethical system exemplified by the family and embodied in a paternalistic state administered by a bureaucracy of scholar-officials. The teachings of Chu Hsi, although stoutly contested by rival scholars in his day, eventually came to be regarded as the definitive commentary on the doctrines of the ancient sage. Venerated as orthodoxy, they discouraged creative thought among later scholars and administrators.

A prodigious output of literature has been characteristic of Chinese civilization during almost every period except the most ancient. Printing was very common from Sung times on. Books were printed from wooden blocks, from metal plates, and from movable type made of earthenware, tin, and wood. Poetry seldom equaled the best of the T'ang age in beauty or spontaneity, but lengthy histories, encyclopedias, dictionaries, geographies, and scientific treatises were produced. The most original literary developments were in the fields of the drama and the novel. The Chinese drama attained the level of a major art form during the Mongol Dynasty, partly because the suspension of the civil-service examinations, by cutting off opportunities for official careers, prompted men of talent to turn their attention to a medium of popular entertainment which they had previously considered unworthy of notice. The dramas of the Mongol period, of which more than a hundred have survived, combined lively action with vivid portrayal of character, and they were written in the common idiom of the people rather than in the classical language of scholars. The Chinese theater, like the English theater of Shakespeare's day, was largely devoid of scenery and properties, although the performers made use of elaborate costumes and heavy make-up. Ordinarily all the parts were filled by male actors. The plays were in verse, but, in contrast to the Elizabethan and modern Western drama, the speeches were sung rather than recited and the orchestra (placed directly on the stage) contributed an essential element to the production.

The Chinese novel, originating apparently in the tales of public storytellers, developed contemporaneously with the drama but matured a little later. Its growth was aided indirectly by the sterility of the academic atmosphere that pervaded the court and the bureaucracy of the Ming Dynasty. In the fifteenth century, veneration for Confucian

Fantastic Ceramic Figure of a Deity. Ming Dynasty (1368–1644).

Sung Printed Book. A page from the *Fa-yuan chu-lin* ("Forest of Pearls in the Garden of the Law"). The book was compiled by the Buddhist monk and scholar Tao-Shih in 688. It was printed in 1124, fully three centuries earlier than the Gutenberg Bible.

Development of the Chinese novel

Wooden Statue of Kuan-yin, "Goddess of Mercy." This popular deity, usually represented in female form, was actually derived from a legendary Indian bodhisattva. (In Mahayana Buddhism a bodhisattva was one who had attained enlightenment but chose to remain in the world to help others.)

orthodoxy, especially as embodied in the teachings of Chu Hsi, had become such a fetish among the official coterie of scholars that one of them declared: "The truth has been made manifest. . . . No more writing is needed.".[1] Some men of letters sought a creative outlet by composing narratives in the plain language of the people. In their hands the novel became a highly successful literary medium, skillfully contrived but purveying robust adventure, humor, warm feeling, and salty realism. Frequently historical themes were chosen for subject matter, but the tales also provided commentary—sometimes satirical—upon contemporary society and government.

Sung painting

A large proportion of the Chinese works of art still extant was produced during the period which is being reviewed here. Sculpture had declined in quality since T'ang times, but painting reached its highest peak of excellence under the Sung. The most beautiful and typical Sung paintings are landscapes, frequently executed in only one color but conveying the impression of an intimate understanding of nature in her various moods. Through economy of line, omission of nonessentials, and painstaking treatment of significant detail, the artists sought to bring to light the reality which lies hidden behind the world of appearances. Their dreamy creations were obviously influenced by the mystical teachings of Buddhism and Taoism. Landscape painting was at its ripest during the Southern Sung period, when the leading artists took full advantage of the natural beauty of the Hangchow region. They sometimes painted panoramic scenes on long strips of

[1]L. C. Goodrich, *A Short History of the Chinese People*, p. 196.

Spring Morning at the Palace of Han. Sung Dynasty. Chinese painting emphasized landscapes rather than people and the representation of poetic or philosophic ideas rather than facts.

silk. These were fastened to rollers and could be viewed leisurely by simply holding the rollers in one's hands and winding the painted scroll from one roller to the other.

Architecture attained particular pre-eminence under the Ming, a dynasty which delighted in glorifying and embellishing the visible aspects of Chinese culture. Ming architecture was by no means new in conception, but it was prolific and has left many impressive monuments. The popularity of elaborate gardens, summer residences, game preserves, and hunting lodges among the aristocracy provided opportunities for the designing of graceful pavilions and arched bridges. Fully developed by this period was the pagoda style of temple, distinguished by curving roofs which were usually of tile and frequently in brilliant colors.

China has only rarely been isolated from other parts of the world, and many of her cultural changes were the result of foreign contacts.

Ming architecture

Sage under a Pine Tree. Sung Dynasty. The gnarled and twisted tree exemplifies the Chinese interest in nature in both its pleasant and perverse moods.

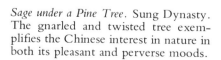

"War Spirit." A Ming Dynasty painting.

Achievements in agriculture and in the applied sciences

The Chinese were indebted to the Arabs for contributions in the field of mathematics and probably also in medicine, although the Chinese had themselves accumulated a considerable store of medical data. Inoculation against smallpox seems to have been practiced before the end of the Sung Dynasty. Eyeglasses came into use (from Italy) during the Ming period. New crops of Western origin began to be cultivated in China. Sorghum, introduced in the thirteenth century, and maize in the sixteenth have been raised extensively in northern China ever since. Cotton production, which also began in the thirteenth century, was greatly expanded under the Ming. One innovation which may have been of domestic rather than foreign inspiration was in the technique of warfare. The explosive properties of gunpowder had long been known, but not until the eleventh century were they utilized for the manufacture of lethal weapons. The Mongols, in the thirteenth and fourteenth centuries, employed bombs that perhaps were propelled by primitive cannons. Although these early artillery pieces were crude, they foreshadowed the increasingly destructive character of modern warfare.

3. THE RISE OF FEUDALISM AND MILITARY DICTATORS IN JAPAN (c. 900–1600)

Contrasts between Japan and China

Even though Chinese culture had been incorporated into the foundations of Japanese civilization and exerted a lasting influence, social and political trends in Japan during the medieval era were very different from those in the great mainland state. While China was frequently harassed by nomadic invaders and was temporarily subjugated by a foreign dynasty, her society and culture departed little from the ancient pattern. By contrast, Japan, enjoying the natural protection of her insular position, was not seriously affected by disturbances from without; yet her institutions were profoundly altered as the result of conflicts taking place within her own society. A theoretical unity and an arbitrary and artificial scheme of government had been imposed upon Japan by the reform of the mid-seventh century, which attempted to introduce the Chinese imperial system in its entirety. How completely the attempt had failed is illustrated by the events of the next thousand years. Only belatedly, and after indecisive and exhausting strife, was the basis discovered for a stable and unified society. And when stability was achieved, it was through improvised institutions which were inadequate to solve the problems certain to arise in the wake of economic and cultural change.

The political history of Japan during this period is characterized mainly by two factors: (1) the persistence of an indirect method of government, with the actual power shifting from one family to another but exercised in the name of an inviolate emperor, whose effective authority rarely extended beyond the environs of Kyoto; (2) the feudalization of society and the growth of extralegal military units which imposed their will upon territories under their control. To the end of the sixteenth century the technique of government was variable and uncertain, although the trend from civilian to military authority was unmistakable. At the opening of the seventeenth century a centralized administration was finally established which ended a long period of civil wars, enforced a coherent national policy, and endured almost unshaken until the middle of the nineteenth century. Even when it was overthrown, the habits which it had instilled in the Japanese people could not easily be uprooted.

In the ninth century the Fujiwara family, through intermarriage with the imperial family and through possession of the office of

Character of Japanese political history

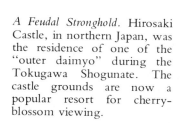

A Feudal Stronghold. Hirosaki Castle, in northern Japan, was the residence of one of the "outer daimyo" during the Tokugawa Shogunate. The castle grounds are now a popular resort for cherry-blossom viewing.

Feudalism

Swords of the Feudal Nobility.
This type of curved sword, of
fine steel, was worn suspended
from the girdle by great daimyo or court nobles during
Japan's early feudal age (twelfth
to fourteenth centuries). Note
the jewelel hilts, the ornately
decorated scabbards, and the
loops for hanging the swords.

regent, had acquired a dominant position in the government, reducing
the emperor to a figurehead. The Fujiwara retained their ascendancy
until the twelfth century, but their rule over the outlying sections
became more and more nominal as new lands were brought into production by reclamation or by conquest of the aborigines, and as
aggressive landowners succeeded in withdrawing their estates from
the jurisdiction of the imperial tax collectors. The men who possessed
estates in these frontier regions were not hampered by the elaborate
rules of etiquette or by the mania for classical Chinese studies that
absorbed the energies of the courtiers at Kyoto. They formulated their
own standards of conduct, largely dictated by the desire to preserve
and extend their holdings, and quarreled with one another over conflicting claims. Naturally, many small farmers relinquished their
property to powerful neighbors in return for protection and sank to a
position of serfdom. Gradually a manorial economy came into existence, showing some points of similarity to the manorial regime in
western Europe during the later Middle Ages.

By a remarkable coincidence of history Japanese society took on
aspects of feudalism at the very time when feudal institutions were
evolving in western Europe. Of course it would be a mistake to
assume that Japanese and Western feudalism were identical, but the
parallels between them are striking. In Japan and western Europe
alike, leadership was passing to a class of mounted warriors who
owned land, dominated the peasantry, and exercised governmental
power as a private right. In Japan the rising class of warrior-landlords
was derived partly from clan chieftains, partly from adventurers who
had established title purely by the sword, and partly from imperial
officials who had converted an administrative office into a family possession. The members of the landed class established hereditary claims
to their holdings and entered into binding agreements with one
another, creating a series of dependent relationships equivalent to a
system of lords and vassals. As in the case of European feudalism, the
system was extended partly through the voluntary surrender of property by small landowners who sought a noble's protection, and partly
through the granting of benefices or fiefs by great lords to lesser men
in order to secure their services as vassals. Another parallel to the
growth of European feudalism is seen in the fact that property belonging to religious foundations was frequently converted into fiefs. Some
Buddhist monasteries and temples became formidable military units,
but Japanese religious orders never attained an independence like that
of the higher clergy in medieval Europe. They remained generally
subservient to the aristocracy.

The Japanese warriors, who corresponded in status and in profession to the medieval knights, were known as samurai, or bushi. The
samurai developed a fraternal spirit and a code of conduct to which
they jealously clung as their special prerogative and which they called

"the way of the horse and the bow." (The term *bushido,* not used before the eighteenth century, denoted a romantic and artificial version of the old feudal code.) Like the European code of chivalry it stressed valor, loyalty, and the necessity of preferring death to dishonor. The samurai was bound above all else to protect, defend, or avenge his lord, to this end sacrificing his own life and, if need be, the lives of his family—a remarkable ideal in view of the sacredness of family ties in Japan. So sensitive was the samurai to any taint of dishonor that he was expected to commit suicide (by a ritual of falling on one's sword, known as hara-kiri) if there was no other way to wipe out the stain on his reputation.

In the twelfth century, feudal warfare culminated in a struggle between two powerful families, the Taira and the Minamoto. With the victory of the Minamoto, their leader reorganized the government on a basis which frankly recognized the paramount role of the landowning warrior-nobility. To avoid appearing as a usurper, the head of the Minamoto family assumed only a military title, becoming known as Shogun, and pretended to be acting as the agent of the emperor. In reality, for the next six and one-half centuries (1192–1867) Japan had a dual government: the civil authority at Kyoto headed by the emperor and embracing various ranks of court nobility whose functions were ornamental rather than essential, and the Bakufu ("Tent Government") headed by the Shogun and commanding the services of the powerful military leaders who owned most of the land. The creation of the Shogunate, as this military-feudal government came to be called, indicates how thoroughly feudalism had permeated Japanese society. The real governors of the country now were not the imperial bureaucracy but the vassals of the Shogun.

Although the Shogunate proved to be a durable institution, it did not remain perpetually in the hands of any one family. On the death of the first Shogun his widow's relatives seized control, with her connivance. This extremely capable woman became known as the "Nun Shogun," because she wielded political influence even after she had nominally retired into holy orders, and with her help the Hojo family came into power. For more than a century the Hojo appointed puppet Shoguns over whom they maintained a regency. Thus, by the early thirteenth century the government of Japan was a confusing series of subterfuges. The central authority (so far as any existed) was exercised by a regent in the name of a puppet general (the Shogun) who, in turn, was theoretically an underling of an emperor, who was himself controlled by a regent (or, in some cases, by an elder member of the imperial family living in retirement). Because the Hojo family had no inherent claim to superiority over other great feudal houses, its ascendancy created jealous dissatisfaction and led inevitably to further conflict. A remarkable incident occurred in 1333 when the Emperor Daigo II attempted to cut through the sham governmental fabric and

The Golden Pavilion (Kiukakuji). A residence built by Yoshimitsu, third Ashikaga Shogun in 1397.

assert his right to rule as well as reign. He mustered sufficient military forces to capture and burn the Shogun's headquarters at Kamakura and ended the Hojo regency. The sequel to this bold stroke, however, was simply a half century of civil war, with two rival emperors, each bidding for support. The schism in the imperial household was healed and order temporarily restored with the triumph of another great military family, the Ashikaga, who again reduced the emperor to a position of impotence.

The period of feudal warfare

The Ashikaga Shoguns (1392–1573) made the serious mistake of taking up residence in Kyoto, where they were exposed to the softening influence of court society and, by relaxing their vigilance, lost effective control over the turbulent lords of outlying districts. Feudal rivalry became increasingly unrestrained until, beginning in the late fifteenth century, Japan experienced 100 years of almost continual warfare. Robbery and pillage were rampant; almost all vestiges of a central government disappeared; even the private estates which the emperor had owned in various parts of the country were absorbed into the feudal domains. The imperial family as well as the Kyoto courtiers were subjected to humiliation by swaggering soldiers. Reduced to poverty, one emperor eked out a living by selling his autograph. In 1500 an imperial corpse lay unburied for six weeks because there was no money in the treasury. The Ashikaga Shogun was almost as impotent as the emperor and quite unable to stop the brigandage and slaughter carried on wantonly by feudal retainers and robber monks. Conditions in Japan seemed to be fast approaching anarchy when, at the close of the sixteenth century, the Shogunate was drastically and effectively reorganized by the Tokugawa family.

In spite of all the confusion and turmoil, however, there were constructive forces at work. The character of Japanese feudalism was changing in a significant direction. Large territorial units were taking shape under fairly competent administrative systems. This trend was the result partly of natural evolution and partly of the policy of the Shoguns. At the outset the Shogun had attempted to control the various fiefs by sending out officials responsible to him and appointed from the military capital at Kamakura; but these officials acquired hereditary status and merged into the hierarchy. The Constable in particular—an officer who was given administrative authority over a province—gradually became a great baron or magnate, absorbing into his own dominion the estates within his jurisdiction. The great lords grew in prestige and material resources at the expense of the lesser fiefholders. During the almost constant warfare of the fifteenth and sixteenth centuries, peasants were pressed into military service, and consequently the importance of the knights began to decline. The appearance of mass armies composed of commoners was comparable to the trend in European countries during this same period; but, while the European armies were recruited chiefly by the kings of national states, the Japanese forces were under the control of feudal lords.

Leadership was passing from the knightly (samurai) class as a whole to the great lords, who were known as daimyo ("Great Names"). The daimyo incorporated many small estates into their own possessions and employed the samurai as managers and as subordinate military commanders. The families which attained the status of daimyo came to be referred to as clans, but they were actually very different from the clans of early Japanese society. Their territories were feudal provinces, and the people under their rule were bound by vassalage or servitude rather than by blood relationship. The ascendancy of the daimyo, while it by no means eliminated feudal dissension, greatly reduced the number of rival units and also ensured a considerable measure of stability within each unit.

Economically and culturally, Japan's feudal age was a period, not of retrogression or stagnation, but of progress. That this was so may seem strange in view of the roughness of the times and the instability of political institutions, but the evidence is undeniable. The Japanese maintained commercial contacts with other Far Eastern countries and continued to receive stimulating influences from China. Foreign trade, increasing steadily from the twelfth century, led to the substitution of money for rice or cloth as a medium of exchange and promoted diversified economic activity. By the fifteenth century the Japanese were exporting not only raw materials, such as lumber, gold, and pearls, but also manufactured goods. Japanese folding fans and screens were in great demand in China, and steel swords were exported by the thousands to a large Far Eastern market. The curved swords forged by Japanese craftsmen in the thirteenth century are said to have been unsurpassed even by the famous blades of Toledo and Damascus.

*The samurai and Zen
Buddhism*

Society during Japan's feudal period was far from being purely agrarian. Commercial and industrial centers came into being, and a few developed into populous cities. Groups of merchants organized guilds for mutual protection and to promote the marketing of their wares. Moreover, in contrast to most of western Europe, the feudal classes participated in capitalistic enterprises. In addition to professional merchants, monastic orders, samurai, great nobles, and occasionally even the Shogun invested in trade.

As in earlier times, various schools of Buddhism contributed to cultural development, largely because they continued to serve as channels for intellectual and aesthetic currents from China. One of the most prominent sects, the Zen (from the Chinese *Ch'an*), was introduced at the close of the twelfth century and spread rapidly among the samurai. Zen Buddhism taught that enlightenment would come to the individual not through study or any intellectual process, but by a sudden flash of insight experienced when one was in tune with nature. Because it stressed physical discipline, self-control, and the practice of meditation in place of formal scholarship, the sect appealed to the warrior class, who felt that Zen teachings gave supernatural sanction to the attitudes which they had already come to regard as essential to their station. Though its doctrines were fundamentally anti-intellectual, its monks fostered both learning and art and injected several refinements into Japanese upper-class society. Among these were an unrivaled type of landscape architecture, the art of flower arrangement, and a delicate social ritual known as the tea ceremony—all of which were Chinese importations but elaborated with great sensitivity in Japan.

Religious developments in Japan during the medieval period were in many ways distinctive. New sects sprang up and caught the imagination of the common people. Some of them proposed the elimination of ceremony and the abolition of distinctions between clergy and laity. Others encouraged a fierce intolerance and a worship of national greatness. That the Japanese lower classes were aroused and encouraged by the new teachings is certain. During the tumultuous fifteenth and sixteenth centuries uprisings against the feudal nobles were instigated by religious congregations, and in a few instances the revolts were successful. These manifestations of popular intransigence, though, had little or no permanent effect upon Japanese society, which remained predominantly aristocratic in structure and tone.

Many other cultural changes resulted from the growth of a productive and diversified economy and from the mutual stimulation among competing religious sects. While sacred writings were being collected and translated in the monasteries, and while courtiers continued to write in the polished but lifeless classical manner, literature was enriched by the addition of tales of daring and high adventure conceived for the entertainment and edification of men of arms. These

Costume for the No *Dance
Drama* (seventeenth century).
Lavish and colorful pictorial
decoration was characteristic of
the costumes worn by *No* actors.

The No *Drama*. This art form is characterized by rhythmical recitation of texts, traditional music, and symbolic movement of players.

stories of knightly prowess, composed in a flowing poetical prose and sometimes sung to the accompaniment of a lute, are comparable to the heroic epics of medieval European chivalry. No counterpart of the European poems of romantic love, however, arose in fuedal Japan, where women had sunk to a position of abject subordination to male authority. All the arts were influenced by Chinese models, but the Japanese had long since demonstrated their originality in adapting styles to their own tastes. Particularly impressive were the paintings executed by monks of the Zen sect in the fifteenth and sixteenth centuries. These were chiefly landscapes and similar in style to those of the Chinese artists of the Ming Dynasty, but they possessed an individuality and freshness of their own.

The exacting aesthetic standards of the aristocratic patrons of the Zen sect are also evident in a specialized form of dramatic art, the *No,* which emerged during this period. The *No* "lyric-drama" or "dance-drama" was not a foreign importation but almost purely a native product. Its origins can be traced to ancient folk dances and also to ritualistic dances associated with both Shintoist and Buddhist modes of worship. In its perfected form, it became a unique vehicle of artistic expression and entertainment, which heightened the appeal of rhythm and graceful postures by relating them to dramatic incidents. The themes of the dance-dramas were traditional narratives, but they were presented with great restraint and by suggestive symbolism rather than by literal re-enactment, somewhat in the manner of a series of tableaux. The performers wore masks as well as rich costumes and

The No *drama*

chanted their lines to the accompaniment of drums and flutes. The *No* drama achieved great popularity among the samurai class and was at its height from the fourteenth to the sixteenth centuries. In spite of its extremely stylized character, it has never entirely disappeared from the artistic heritage of Japan.

4. THE EMERGENCE OF CIVILIZATIONS IN SUB-SAHARAN AFRICA

The period 1000 to 1500 A.D. represented a time of state formation in black Africa. Chieftaincies in many areas were consolidated under divine kings. Numerous kingdoms evolved into expansive territorial empires, embracing a rich diversity of cultures, languages, and religious systems. The process of empire-building was most pronounced in the savanna, or Sudanic zone of West Africa.

Dramatic growth in the trans-Saharan trade leads to state formation in the West African Sudan

Trans-Saharan trade expanded at a rapid rate after the eighth century, due in large measure to the initiative of Arabs and Berbers. Concurrently, growing demands from European and North African merchants for gold motivated West Africans to organize themselves on a larger, more efficient scale in order to meet these demands. Ghana's armies, under a black Soninke dynasty, captured the prosperous Berber trading center of Audoghast in the tenth century. Successive Ghanaian monarchs grew immensely rich by tightly controlling the flow of gold across their territory. A production tax was placed on gold exports and nuggets of a certain size were hoarded in order to keep the mineral rare. Ghana's hegemony extended to the upper Niger and Senegal rivers and to the burgeoning commercial centers of Timbuktu, Jenné, and Gao.

Ghana's wealth based mainly on gold exports

Ghana was not a Muslim empire, but its principal customers and those who controlled the strategic desert oases had become Muslims by the tenth century. Rulers in neighboring Takrur accepted Islam about 1000 A.D. and thus became West Africa's first kingdom to do so. Ghana itself had become dangerously dependent on Muslim financial advisers and merchants. Its pagan king was eventually forced to divide the capital city of Kumbi-Saleh into two parts, one for Muslims, the other for pagans.

The Almoravids overrun Ghana

Islam, the handmaiden of West African commerce, could not be contained. By 1054, large bands of nomadic Muslim Berbers had declared a holy war, or *jihad,* and succeeded in recapturing the vital Audoghast markets. Ghana, on the Saharan fringe, had already been weakened by environmental deterioration brought on by overgrazing of pastures and failure to rotate crops. Its capitulation to these puritanical Berber Muslims, called Almoravids, seemed almost inevitable. But the Almoravids brought insecurity to Ghanaian market places and fear along the caravan routes. This condition upset the delicate trade balance between the forest gold miners, the Ghanaian middlemen, and

The Almoravid movement

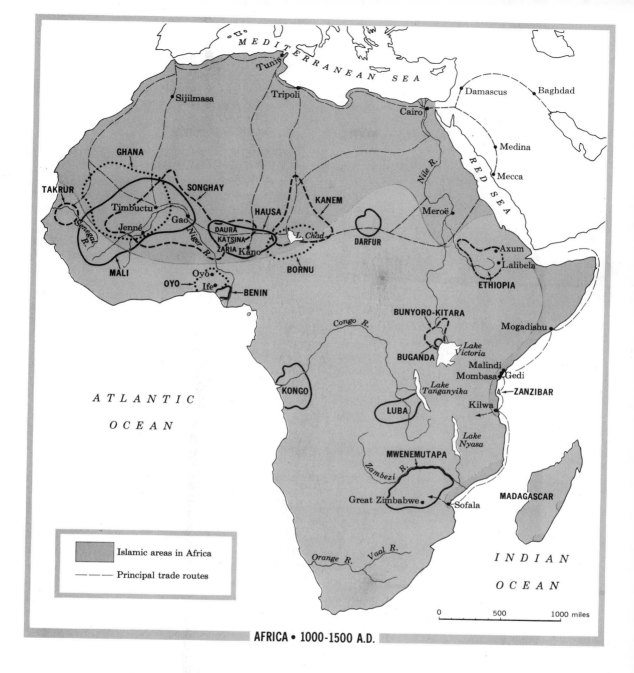

AFRICA · 1000–1500 A.D.

Islamic areas in Africa

Principal trade routes

the North African caravan operators. Indeed, Ghana emerged from the Almoravid movement in such a weakened condition that peripheral chieftaincies were able to secede. One of these vassal chieftaincies sacked the Ghanaian capital in 1224 and enslaved the ruling family. A decade later the victor himself succumbed to the superior magic of a Ghanaian royal hostage, named Sunjata.

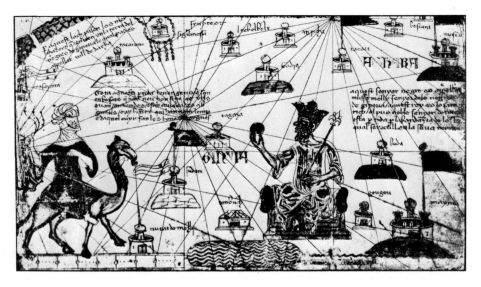

Mansa Musa of Mali Waiting to Receive a Muslim Trader. Detail of the Catalan Atlas, a map drawn on the island of Majorca in 1375.

The rise of Mali

Ghana was finished, but a new territorial empire called Mali was forged by the magician Sunjata, who is still regarded in Western Sudanic folk traditions as a god-hero and founding father. By gaining control of the gold-producing regions, Sunjata could attract the caravan traffic formerly monopolized by Ghana. The oral record also reveals that Sunjata expanded agriculture by introducing the cultivation and weaving of cotton.

Mansa Musa

Under Mansa Musa (1312–1337) Mali's authority reached into the middle Niger city-states of Timbuktu, Jenné, and Gao. He put Mali on the European world maps by performing a stunning gold-laden pilgrimage to Mecca, Islam's spiritual capital in the Middle East. Upon returning, Mansa Musa fostered the growth of Islam by constructing magnificent mosques in the major urban centers. With his seemingly inexhaustible supply of gold he commissioned Spanish and Middle Eastern scholars and architects to transform Malian cities into great seats of Islamic learning. Leading intellectuals were sent to Morocco and Egypt for higher studies, and at Timbuktu foundations were laid for a university at the famed Sankoré mosque. For decades after Musa, Mali enjoyed a reputation in the Muslim world for high standards of public morality and scholarship as well as for law, order, and security. People and goods flowed freely, enabling the cosmopolitan cities of Timbuktu, Jenné, and Gao to flower into major market centers. Through the leadership of Sunjata and Mansa Musa Islam became more deeply implanted among the elite and spread widely in the important towns.

Sunni Ali and the formation of Songhay

While Mansa Musa made great advances in establishing an efficient administrative bureaucracy, he neglected to develop a formula for succession. Court intrigue and factional disputes followed the death of each Mansa. Inevitably, central authority weakened. Gao seceded in 1375 and under Sunni Ali (1464–1492) it blossomed into an expansive territorial empire called Songhay.

As in Muslim India, it was not uncommon for slaves in Africa to assume considerable administrative and military responsibilities and on occasion to usurp authority. This happened in Songhay in 1493 when a high-ranking Muslim slave, named Muhammad Touré, staged a brilliant palace coup. Lacking traditional legitimacy rooted in a pagan past, he promoted Islamic practices and found Islam an invaluable instrument for political and cultural control. Using the praise-title of "Askia," Muhammad Touré (1493–1528) extended Songhay's frontiers deep into the strategic Saharan oases, across the middle Niger to include Mali, and eastward to the emporiums of Hausaland. He then created a labyrinthine bureaucracy with ministries for the army, navy, fisheries, forests, and taxation. Songhay itself was decentralized into provinces, each ruled by a governor chosen from among the Askia's family or royal followers. Muhammad Touré also established vast plantations, worked by slaves under conditions sometimes approaching those in the southern United States before the Civil War.

To facilitate commerce, Muhammad Touré introduced a unified system of weights and measures and appointed market inspectors to protect consumers. The Sankoré mosque at Timbuktu was transformed into an institution comparable to the great European universities of the later Middle Ages, with schools of theology, jurisprudence, mathematics, and medicine. On his pilgrimage to Mecca in 1497 he befriended world-famous Muslim scholars. A few

Askia Muhammad Touré and the growth of Islamic institutions

Songhay's cultural ascendancy

The Old Mosque at Timbuktu. Between the fourteenth and sixteenth centuries, Timbuktu was one of the leading Muslim centers of learning in the Western Sudan.

of them returned with him to Songhay as advisers on government and religion. And like the earlier Mali empire, Songhay established diplomatic relations with Morocco and Egypt, its major trading partners.

Islam a thin veneer

Islamic institutions of law, education, and taxation were deeply rooted in the major urban areas by the close of Askia Muhammad's rule in 1528. However, Islam was but a thin veneer elsewhere. Fully 95 percent of the population, consisting of rural peasants and petty chiefs, continued to follow traditional animistic beliefs and life styles. Nevertheless, in spite of serious internal divisions between Islam and the traditional ways. Songhay continued to prosper, reaching its zenith under Askia Daud (1549–1582). Stretching from the snow-capped Atlas Mountains of North Africa to the tropical Cameroon forests and embracing thousands of different cultures, it was clearly one of the world's most expansive empires.

*The Moroccan invasion
and Songhay's demise*

Songhay had overextended itself; and although its armies numbered more than 35,000, it could not keep the outlying regions in subjection. Its vital eastern markets were lost when several Hausa city-states reasserted their independence. In the northwest, Morocco, after defeating the Portuguese, sought direct control over Songhay's mines. Crack Songhay cavalry and archers were no match for Moroccan cannons and imported European arquebuses. After Songhay's defeat by the Moroccans in 1591, the empire—and indeed western Sudanic civilization—rapidly disintegrated. The Moroccans and their Portuguese mercenaries, unable to locate the gold mines or to maintain security on the roads and in the markets, abandoned Songhay altogether in 1612. Political anarchy filled the vacuum, the great cities declined, and trade and Muslim scholarship drifted eastward to the city-states of Hausaland in what is today northern Nigeria and the Niger Republic.

*The emergence of Hausa
kingdoms*

By the twelfth century, uncoordinated self-governing villages in Hausaland had coalesced into centralized kingdoms under semidivine dynasties. These kingdoms, though politically autonomous, shared a common Hausa language and cultural heritage. Daura, the founding kingdom, exercised a vague spiritual suzerainty over the others.

*Islamic penetration and
commercial expansion*

Islam had begun to penetrate Hausa aristocratic and trading circles in the fourteenth century. After 1452, the rural areas experienced a steady influx of red-skinned Fulani herdsmen, who for centuries had been migrating eastward from the Senegal River. The Fulani, who were fervent Muslims brought religious books and established new centers of Islamic learning. At this time, Hausaland was experiencing a commercial revolution with the opening of the kola trade with farmers of the southern forests. In Kano, Katsina, and Zaria, huge markets emerged as traders from disintegrating Songhay shifted their operations to the more secure walled towns of Hausaland.

Hausaland was exceptionally secure, thanks to the military protection offered by the wealthy and powerful kingdom of Kanem-Bornu, lying eastward near Lake Chad. Kanem-Bornu's geographical posi-

Gobirau Mosque, Katsina (northern Nigeria). This mosque was built in the fifteenth century, when the Hausa kingdoms shared strong cultural and economic ties with Songhay. It is constructed of mud mixed with a vegetable matter (katse) and oxen blood.

tion placed it at the gateway to the West African Sudan. Its stable dynasty gained power in 846 A.D. and embraced Islam in 1087. Under Mai Idris Alooma (1580–1617) Kanem-Bornu reached its peak. Alooma established diplomatic relations with Turkey, which had recently captured Tunis in North Africa from Spain. With Turkish advisers, Alooma bureaucratized his government and set it on firm Islamic foundations. A high court of law was organized and staffed by judges who dispensed only Muslim law. The army was equipped with Turkish muskets. The thirteenth-century hostel in Cairo for Bornuese pilgrims and scholars was greatly expanded. Hausaland, sandwiched between Songhay and Bornu, was commercially exploited by both neighbors, but it received considerable cultural enrichment from pilgrims passing through en route to Mecca.

Kanem-Bornu

After Songhay's collapse in 1591, trade shifted not only to Hausaland but also toward the southern forests. Between 1000 and 1500 A.D. the forest people of modern Nigeria experienced new infusions of grasslanders from the Sudanic zone. Leading lineages were transformed into ruling dynasties. They in turn fused scattered villages under priests and elders into small city-states. Ile Ife exercised the same kind of spiritual hegemony for the Yoruba settlers that Daura held for the Hausa in the north. Yoruba warriors from Ile Ife fanned out and established subordinate dynasties at Oyo, Benin, and elsewhere. Under Eware the Great (1440–1473) Benin city expanded into a territorial forest empire. Benin and Ife became centers of high civi-

The rise of forest civilizations

The Griot, Africa's Historian, Daura Emirate. The Praise Singer is the traditional oral historian of African societies. African history has been passed from generation to generation by griots.

lization. Their craft guilds produced naturalistic busts and plaques cast in bronze through the lost wax process. Eware encouraged ivory and wood carving and created a national orchestra. All these secular innovations were aimed at glorifying the ruling families. Art was no longer simply for life's adornment. It now upheld authority and graced the hallways of the sprawling Yoruba palaces.

The Akan forest states

In the hinterlands of modern Ghana, a similar though unrelated political process had begun not long before 1400. Mande traders from old Mali and Songhay pushed southward in a quest for more gold. Stronger demands from North Africa and Europe encouraged them to establish small centers of exchange at the forest's edge. These burgeoning communities represented a curious blend of pagan and Islamic, of forest and Sudanic cultures. The forest people, called the Akan, reacted to this commercial challenge by forging mini-kingdoms at the crossroads of trading activity. Thus, the southward movement of trade stimulated the rise of forest-based states, which in the sixteenth century reached their zenith as new commercial opportunities emanated from Europeans on the coast.

The emergence of Swahili civilization

In chapter 12 it was shown that after the ninth century A.D. the East African coast from Somalia southward received new arrivals. Some were Bantu from the interior, others were Shirazi Arabs from the Somali coast and Persian Gulf, and a few were from northwestern India. The non-African immigrants were sea-oriented merchants in search of African minerals, ivory, and slaves. The Bantu, with inland connections, were in an excellent position to supply their needs. By the twelfth century the Shirazi had founded a series of coastal Muslim city-states, extending southward to modern Mozambique. They married into local Bantu ruling families and initiated Islamic dynasties. Sofala and Kilwa became leading Afro-Asian towns and served as major outlets for gold and copper from the Rhodesian and Katangan plateaus of the interior. Between the twelfth and fifteenth centuries a distinctive Swahili coastal civilization emerged. Swahili civilization grew out of the convergence of Bantu, Arab, and Indian cultures and languages. Swahili mosques, though reminiscent of those gracing the southern Arabian shores, were unique in form and construction. The Swahili language, written in Arabic characters, was soft and melodic.

The Swahili city-states, like their Hausa counterparts, were Muslim, cosmopolitan, culturally homogeneous, yet politically independent of one another. They thrived on their middleman position between producers and consumers. Although Kilwa held commercial sway over Sofala intermittently from 1131 to 1333, it did not exhibit any expansionist tendencies. Rather, the various towns, like Mogadishu and Barawa (in modern Somalia), Gedi, Pate, Malindi, and Mombasa (Kenya), Zanzibar and Kilwa (Tanzania), and Sofala (Mozambique) engaged in vigorous competition with one another. Some towns even minted their own coins and maintained huge treasuries.

Indian Ocean trade, like that of the trans-Sahara, encouraged African rulers to centralize their societies in order to better meet foreign demands. Indeed, coastal requests for Katangan copper and Rhodesian gold led to a transition in leadership from ritual-bearing priests to secular kings commanding enormous military and economic power. Katanga in the thirteenth century was the first state to consolidate.

Middleman position of the Swahili city-states

The Mwenemutapa empire and Great Zimbabwe

Gedi. The ruins of this Afro-Arab town, founded in the early fourteenth century on the Kenya coast. This was the main entrance to the Sultan's palace.

*The Christian kingdoms
of Northeast Africa*

Ethiopian expansion

Within two hundred years Katangans had carried their ideas of divine kingship to other societies in the Zambezi valley. On the cool Rhodesian plateau a powerful Katangan kingdom arose, with its ruler assuming the praise name of "Mwenemutapa." His capital at Great Zimbabwe was fortified with massive elliptical walls of cut stone laid in place without mortar.

In the mid-fourth century A.D. the Axumite king Ezana converted to Christianity and made the faith the state religion in what then came to be called Ethiopia. Ethiopian clerics established churches and monasteries and received large tracts of land as gifts from the nobility and successive monarchs. Coptic Christianity, along with the institution of the monarchy, became powerful unifying forces. The monasteries emerged as centers of learning, and important religious texts were translated into Ge'ez, the language of the church hierarchy.

Shortly after Christianity became the state religion, Ethiopia conquered the neighboring empire of Kush, which was replaced by a number of smaller kingdoms collectively called Nubia. The seventh-century-A.D. Islamic expansion in North Africa led to the collapse of Christian Egypt and to Arab occupation of Persia and of Red Sea ports. In the same century, Beja nomads swept across the Eritrean plateau and cut Ethiopia off from Mediterranean and Middle Eastern trade and civilization. Ethiopia now expanded into the interior. In about 1100 A.D. its political center shifted southward from Axum to Lalibela in the almost inaccessible northwestern highlands. It became even more isolated from the Greco-Roman world after the conquest

Great Zimbabwe. This 34-foot-high conical tower was probably a shrine in the heart of the Mwenemutapa Empire (fifteenth century). The tower and adjacent wall were constructed by placing stone upon stone without mortar.

of the Nubian kingdoms by Arab rulers of Egypt in the late thirteenth and early fourteenth centuries. The early kingdom of Ethiopia reached its zenith in the fourteenth and fifteenth centuries with the conquest of non-Christian and non-Islamic states to the west. The church became a missionary agent for the monarchy by proselytizing and assimilating these conquered areas.

Islamic populations, both internal and foreign, continued to pressure the Christian regime. In the early fifteenth century centrifugal tendencies developed among local nobility. The neighboring state of Adal took advantage of this and proclaimed a jihad in 1529. It achieved a decisive victory over the Ethiopian emperor and brought much of his country under Muslim rule. Christian Ethiopia was saved from complete annihilation when Emperor Lebna Dengel, with the assistance of foreign Portuguese mercenaries, defeated the Muslims in 1541. With mixed success they also halted an invasion of pastoral Kushitic-speaking Galla peoples but were forced over subsequent centuries to share their lands with them. For the next three centuries, Ethiopia retreated into a sullen xenophobia, marked by civil strife, warlords, economic stagnation, and ultimately the disintegration of central authority.

The Muslim threat

Unrelated to these developments was the migration of Nilotic pastoralists into the fertile lands northwest of Lake Victoria in modern Uganda. Between the fourteenth and sixteenth centuries these immigrants, imbued with notions of divine kingship, married Bantu cultivators and established powerful kingdoms. These highly centralized polities, such as Bunyoro, Buganda, and Ankole, were non-Islamic, purely African creations.

SELECTED READINGS

• *Items so designated are available in paperback editions.*

INDIA—*See also Readings for Chapters 6 and 12*

Cambridge History of India, Vol. III, Cambridge, 1937.
Ikram, Mohamad, *Muslim Civilization in India,* ed. A. T. Embree, New York, 1964. Scholarly and readable.
Phillips, C. H., *India,* London, 1949. A useful survey, although devoting little space to the period before the coming of Europeans.
Sharma, S. R., *The Crescent in India,* Bombay, 1954.

CHINA—*See also Readings for Chapters 7 and 12*

Bruce, J. P., *Chu Hsi and His Masters,* London, 1923.
Fairbank, J. K., ed., *Chinese Thought and Institutions,* Chicago, 1957.

Fitzgerald, C. P., *The Southern Expansion of the Chinese People*, New York, 1972.

• Gernet, Jacques, *Daily Life in China (On the Eve of the Mongol Invasion 1250–1276)*, Stanford, 1970.

Hucker, C. O., *The Traditional Chinese State in Ming Times (1368–1644)*, Tucson, 1961. Brief but informative on political structure and operation.

———, *The Ming Dynasty: Its Origins and Evolving Institutions*, Ann Arbor, 1978. Readable and reliable.

• Hudson, G. F., *Europe and China: A Survey of Their Relations from the Earliest Times to 1800*, London, 1930. Interestingly presented.

Liu, James T. C., *Reform in Sung China: Wang An-shih (1021–1086) and His New Policies*, Cambridge, Mass., 1959. A good, brief interpretive study.

Parsons, J. B., *The Peasant Rebellions of the Late Ming Dynasty*, Tucson, 1970.

• Prawdin, Michael, *The Mongol Empire: Its Rise and Legacy*, tr. E. and C. Paul, London, 1940.

Shih Chung-wen, *The Golden Age of Chinese Drama: Yüan Tsa-chü*, Princeton, 1976.

Sowerby, A. deC., *Nature in Chinese Art*, New York, 1940.

Waley, Arthur, *An Introduction to the Study of Chinese Painting*, New York, 1958.

Williamson, H. R., *Wang An Shih, a Chinese Statesman and Educationalist of the Sung Dynasty*, 2 vols., London, 1935–1937.

Wright, Arthur F., ed., *Studies in Chinese Thought*, Chicago, 1953.

———, ed., *The Confucian Persuasion*, Stanford, 1960.

JAPAN—*See also Readings for Chapter 12*

• Duus, Peter, *Feudalism in Japan*, 2d ed., New York, 1975. Concise account of political developments from the sixth through the nineteenth century.

Sansom, George B., *A History of Japan, 1334–1615*, Stanford, 1961. A major contribution.

———, *The Western World and Japan*, New York, 1950.

Suzuki, D. T., *Zen and Japanese Culture*, New York, 1959.

• Waley, Arthur, *No Plays of Japan*, New York, 1922.

AFRICA

Ade Ajayi, J. F., and I. Espie, eds., *A Thousand Years of West African History*, Ibadan, 1967.

Boahen, Adu, *Topics in West African History*, London, 1968.

Davidson, Basil, *et al.*, *The Growth of African Civilization: A History of West Africa 1000–1800*, London, 1966.

Denyer, Susan, *African Traditional Architecture*, New York, 1978.

Gray, Richard, and David Birmingham, eds., *Pre-Colonial African Trade*, New York, 1970.

• Hull, Richard W., *African Cities and Towns before the European Conquest*, New York, 1976.

———, *Munyakare: African Civilization before the Batuuree*, New York, 1972.

Kilson, Martin, and Robert I. Rotberg, eds., *The African Diaspora*, Cambridge, 1977.

Mair, Lucy, *African Kingdoms,* Oxford, 1977.

Maquet, Jacques, *Civilizations of Black Africa,* New York, 1972.

Ogot, B. A., and J. A. Kieran, eds., *Zamani: A Survey of East African History,* Nairobi, 1968.

Oliver, Roland, ed., *The Middle Age of African History,* New York, 1967.

Ranger, T. O., ed., *Aspects of Central African History,* London, 1969.

SOURCE MATERIALS

Boxer, C. R., ed., *South China in the Sixteenth Century* (narratives of Portuguese and Spanish visitors, 1550–1575).

Chinese Novels and Short Stories: Buck, Pearl, tr., *All Men Are Brothers;* Howell, E. B., tr., *Inconstancy of Madam Chuang and Other Stories;* Waley, Arthur, tr., *The Monkey.*

• de Bary, W. T., ed., *Sources of Chinese Tradition,* "The Confucian Revival," New York, 1960.

• ———, ed., *Sources of Indian Tradition,* "Islam in Medieval India," New York, 1950.

• ———, ed., *Sources of Japanese Tradition,* "Medieval Japan," New York, 1958.

Gallagher, L. J., tr., *China in the Sixteenth Century: The Journals of Matthew Ricci. 1583–1610* (a Jesuit missionary), Milwaukee, 1942.

• Hall, J. W., and T. Toyoda, eds., *Japan in the Muromachi Age,* New Haven, Conn., 1974.

Hodgkin, Thomas, ed., *Nigerian Perspectives,* London, 1960.

• Hsiung, S. I., tr., *The Romance of the Western Chamber,* London, 1935.

• Keene, Donald, ed., *Twenty Plays of the No Theatre,* New York, 1970.

• Ma, Y. W., and J. S. M. Lau, *Traditional Chinese Stories: Themes and Variations,* New York, 1978.

McCullough, H. C., *The Taiheiki: A Chronicle of Medieval Japan,* New York, 1959.

McEwan, P. J. M., ed., *Africa from Early Times to 1800,* London, 1968.

Oliver, R., and G. Mathew, eds., *History of East Africa,* Vol. I, Oxford, 1968.

Reischauer, E. O., and Y. K. Yamagiwa, *Translations from Early Japanese Literature* (eleventh to thirteenth centuries), Cambridge, Mass., 1951.

Waley, Arthur, tr., *The Travels of an Alchemist, the Journeys of the Taoist Ch'ang Ch'un,* London, 1931.

Yule, Henry, tr., *The Book of Ser Marco Polo,* London, 1903.

Part Four

THE EARLY MODERN WORLD

Historians tend to agree that the European Middle Ages ended sometime roughly around 1500. As early as about 1350 in Italy a new movement, usually called the Renaissance, began to challenge and triumph over certain basic medieval assumptions. Around 1500, the Italian Renaissance spread to northern Europe and thereafter led to important achievements in science, which became basic foundations of modern European thought and civilization. Concurrently, in the sixteenth century a religious upheaval, known as the Protestant Revolution, began in Germany and spread to many other countries. This upheaval contributed to the beginnings of the modern era by ending the religious uniformity of the Middle Ages and fostering an upsurge of individualism and rational consciousness. In the economic realm, Europeans around 1500 sailed to distant continents and began to gain new sources of supply. Overseas discovery and colonization contributed to the Commercial Revolution, lasting from about 1450 to 1800, which established a dynamic regime of business for profit. From the point of view of politics, the period around 1500 ushered in an age of absolutism that lasted until about 1800: this was marked by the growth of absolute governments, headed in some instances by kings who equated themselves with the state and professed to rule by divine right. Finally, during the years from 1600 to 1789, there occurred an intellectual revolution, culminating in the "Enlightenment," or enthronement of reason. In Asia as in Europe, a rise in the level of civilization was accompanied by the establishment of autocratic centralized governments. The Mogul rulers of India and the Manchu Dynasty in China brought a large measure of stability and prosperity to those countries, but extravagance and a series of disastrous wars led the Mogul Dynasty to an early decline. In Japan, although feudalism remained intact, the rise of the Tokugawa Shoguns in 1603 provided the substance if not the form of absolute government. In contrast with western European varieties, both Chinese and Japanese despotism survived into the twentieth century. Meanwhile, the maritime supremacy and commercial initiative of western Europeans enabled them to exploit the riches of Africa. The widespread trade in African slaves, while swelling the coffers of European merchants, not only intensified conflict among and within African states but also hastened the decline of brilliant civilizations on that continent.

The Early Modern World

POLITICS	PHILOSOPHY AND SCIENCE	
	Civic humanism in Italy, c. 1380–c. 1450	
		1400
Renaissance popes, 1447–1521	Florentine Neoplatonism, c. 1450–c. 1600	
French invade Italy, 1494		
Henry VIII of England, 1509–1547	Machiavelli, 1469–1527	*1500*
Francis I of France, 1515–1547	Vesalius, 1514–1564	
Charles V, Holy Roman Emperor, 1519–1546	More's *Utopia*, 1516	
Troops of Charles V sack Rome, 1527	Index of Prohibited Books, 1559	
Spanish gain supremacy in Italy, 1529	Francis Bacon, 1561–1626	
	Galileo, 1564–1642	
Philip II of Spain, 1556–1598	Johann Kepler, 1571–1630	
Elizabeth I of England, 1558–1603	Hugo Grotius, 1583–1645	
Defeat of Spanish Armada, 1588	Thomas Hobbes, 1588–1679	
Henry IV of France, 1589–1610		
Edict of Nantes, 1598	René Descartes, 1596–1650	
Thirty Years' War, 1618–1648		
Supremacy of Richelieu in France, 1624–1642		
Louis XIV of France, 1643–1715		
	Bacon's *Novum Organum,* 1620	*1600*
	John Locke, 1632–1704	
English Civil War, 1642–1649	Descarte's *Discourse on Method,* 1637	
	Isaac Newton, 1642–1727	
Commonwealth and Protectorate in England, 1649–1660		
Age of Restoration in England, 1660–1688	Royal Society founded, 1662	
Peter the Great of Russia, 1682–1725		
Revocation of Edict of Nantes, 1685	Newton's *Mathematical Principles of Natural Philosophy,* 1687	
Glorious Revolution in England, 1688–1689		
War of the Spanish Succession, 1702–1714		
Frederick William I of Prussia, 1713–1740	Linnaeus, 1707–1778	*1700*
	Jean-Jacques Rousseau, 1712–1778	
Development of Cabinet system in England, 1714–1742		
Louis XV of France, 1715–1774		
Maria Theresa of Austria, 1740–1780		
Frederick the Great of Prussia, 1740–1786		
Seven Years' War, 1756–1763		
George III of England, 1760–1820		
Catherine the Great of Russia, 1762–1796		
Louis XVI of France, 1774–1792		
Joseph II of Austria, 1780–1790		
Outbreak of French Revolution, 1789		

	ECONOMICS	RELIGION	ARTS AND LETTERS
1400			Francis Petrarch, 1304–1374 Italian Renaissance, c. 1400– c. 1550

	Prosperity in Italy, c. 1450–
	  c. 1550
	Commercial Revolution,
	  c. 1450–c. 1800
	European voyages of discovery,
	  c. 1450–c. 1650
		Martin Luther, 1483–1546
		Ulrich Zwingli, 1484–1531
		Ignatius Loyola, 1491–1556
			Masaccio, 1401–1428
			Botticelli, 1444–1510
			Leonardo da Vinci, 1452–1519
			Erasmus, c. 1467–1536
			Albrecht Dürer, 1471–1528
			Ariosto, 1474–1533

1500		John Calvin, 1509–1564
		Luther attacks indulgences,
		  1517
		Henry VIII of England breaks
		  with Rome, 1527–1534
		Loyola founds Society of Jesus,
		  1534
		Anabaptists seize Münster, 1534
		Calvin's *Institutes,* 1536
		Calvin takes over Geneva, 1541
		Council of Trent, 1545–1563
		Peace of Augsburg divides Ger-
		  many into Lutheran and
		  Catholic areas, 1555
		Elizabethan religious compro-
		  mise in England, c. 1558–
		  c. 1570
		Revolt of the Netherlands,
		  1567–1609
			Raphael, 1483–1520
			Michelangelo, 1485–1564
			Rabelais, c. 1490–1553
			Northern Renaissance, c. 1500–
			  c. 1600
			Michelangelo's main work on
			  Sistine Chapel, 1508–1512
			Peter Brueghel, c. 1525–1569
			Palestrina, 1525–1594
			Montaigne, 1533–1592
			El Greco, c. 1541–c. 1614
			Cervantes, 1547–1616
			Edmund Spenser, c. 1552–1599
			Shakespeare, 1564–1616
			Claudio Monteverdi, 1567–1643
			Rubens, 1577–1640
			Bernini, 1598–1680
			Velásquez, 1599–1660
			Rembrandt, 1606–1669
			John Milton, 1608–1674
			Christopher Wren, 1632–1723

	Peasants' Revolt in Germany, 1524–1525 "Age of Silver" c. 1540–c. 1620		

1600	Economic decline of Italy,
	  c. 1600–c. 1800
	Height of mercantilism,
	  c. 1600–c. 1700		

		Spread of religious toleration,
		  c. 1650–c. 1800
			The Enlightenment, c. 1680–
			  c. 1800
			J. S. Bach, 1685–1750
			G. F. Handel, 1685–1759
			Voltaire, 1694–1778
			Rococo architecture, c. 1700–
			  c. 1800

1700	Spread of scientific farming,
	  c. 1700–c. 1800
	Height of enclosures in England,
	  c. 1710–c. 1810
	South Sea Bubble, 1720
		John Wesley, 1703–1789	Joseph Haydn, 1732–1809
			W. A. Mozart, 1756–1791

AFRICA AND THE AMERICAS	INDIA AND THE FAR EAST	

Height of West African forest civilizations,
1400–1472

Voyages of discovery and exploration, 1450–1600

1400

European maritime activity along African coasts,
1500–1800
Growth of African slave trade, 1500–1800
Portuguese dominance of East Coast city-states,
1505–1650

1500

Conquest of Mexico, 1522
Conquest of Peru, 1537

Arrival of Portuguese traders in China
and Japan, 1537–1542
Jesuit missionaries active in China and
Japan, 1550–1650
Akbar the Great Mogul, 1556–1605

British East India Co., chartered, 1600
Tokugawa Shogunate, 1603–1867

1600

Founding of Jamestown, 1607

Landing of Pilgrims, 1620

Taj Mahal, 1632–1647
Japanese isolation, 1637–1854

Downfall of kingdoms of Kongo and Ngola,
1665–1671

Manchu Dynasty in China, 1644–1912
Maratha Confederacy in India, 1650–1760

Rise of Asante empire, founded on Gold Coast
trade, 1700–1750

Decline of Mogul Empire in India, 1700
–1800

1700

Chapter 18

THE CIVILIZATION
OF THE RENAISSANCE
(c. 1350 – c. 1600)

What a piece of work is man, how noble in reason, how infinite in faculty, in form and moving, how express and admirable in action, how like
an angel in apprehension, how like a God: the beauty of the world, the
paragon of animals.

—Shakespeare,
Hamlet, II, 2.

Historians disagree about whether there was a fully defined period between medieval and modern times that should be called the "Renaissance." The reason for this is that it is doubtful whether there was any truly distinctive "Renaissance" politics or economics. Most recent scholars believe that there was not, and argue that the term "Renaissance" should be reserved for the exciting developments in thought, literature, and art that transpired between roughly 1350 and 1600. That is the approach that will be followed here. When we talk about a "Renaissance period" we mean to refer to a period in intellectual and cultural history. The following chapter will accordingly concentrate on intellectual and artistic trends.

The Renaissance as a period of distinct cultural developments

The term "Renaissance" is hardly accurate from the standpoint of historical research. It literally means rebirth, and is commonly taken to imply that in the fourteenth century there was a sudden revival of interest in the classical learning of Greece and Rome. But this implication is not strictly true because interest in the classics was by no means rare in the Middle Ages. Dante, for example, revered Vergil, and St. Thomas Aquinas considered Aristotle to be "the Philosopher."

The Renaissance no sudden development

What, then, was the Renaissance? While no two historians will ever agree on a single precise answer, certain major trends are clear. De-

The extension of classical learning beyond medieval accomplishments

Knowledge of the classics a foundation for new achievements

The Renaissance a new culture

spite what we have just said, a distinct feature of this period was the growth of classical learning; a growth which was not sudden but gradual and steady. Medieval scholars knew many Roman authors, such as Virgil, Ovid, and Cicero, but in the Renaissance the works of others such as Livy, Tacitus, and Lucretius were discovered and made familiar. Equally, if not more important was the Renaissance discovery of the literature of classical Greece. In the twelfth and thirteenth centuries Greek scientific and philosophical treatises were made available to westerners in Latin translations, but none of the great Greek literary masterpieces and practically none of the major works of Plato were yet known. Moreover, very few medieval westerners could read the Greek language. In the Renaissance, on the other hand, large numbers of Western scholars learned Greek and mastered almost the entire Greek literary heritage that is known today.

Ancient artistic monuments too were studied more carefully. Once Renaissance scholars, writers, and artists became thoroughly familiar with ancient accomplishments, they drew on them to reconsider and alter their own ideas and modes of expression. Thus greater knowledge of the classics contributed to important new accomplishments in the realms of thought, literature, and art.

Although the foundation of many Renaissance achievements was classical, the period can by no means be measured strictly in terms of Greek and Latin influences. The steady growth of urban society—particularly in the Italian city-states—led to the development of an urbane society, i.e., one which delighted in experimenting with new ideas and developing ever more sophisticated expressions of thought and art. This growth also helped create a culture that was increasingly nonecclesiastical, although the Church retained its power and influence to a large extent, and in fact adjusted to the spread of urbanity by becoming more urbane itself. Accordingly, the greatest accomplishments of the Renaissance were shared between the laity and the clergy, with the former achieving and maintaining an edge over the latter. The universities, dominated by the clergy in earlier times, now went into a temporary decline, with the concurrent rise of secular centers of learning—for example, academies and courts. An extremely important development which originated in this move toward secular intellectualism and urbanity was the spread of work in the vernacular as opposed to Latin, the language of the Church. This is not to say, however, that important work was not still written in Latin; on the contrary, we will see that humanism depended in large part on this ancient language. But Latin itself underwent important changes during the period.

It was once thought that Renaissance culture was fundamentally anti-Christian and almost "pagan" in its outlook because it was shaped so much by the ancient classics and by the laity. That interpretation, however, is now universally rejected. Many of the greatest

Renaissance thinkers and artists explicitly emphasized Christian beliefs in their work and most of the others took them for granted. Certainly no one before 1600 admitted to preferring Greek gods to Christ, let alone to espousing atheism. Aside from the common denominator of religious faith, it is difficult to speak of common Renaissance points of view because over the course of two and a half centuries writers and artists were bound to differ greatly in their opinions and outlooks. Some Renaissance figures continued to uphold the medieval tradition of emphasizing humanity's hope for otherworldly salvation and the precedence of the soul over the body, while others paid more "modern" attention to human life in this world. It does seem true, however, that there was a growth in the Renaissance period of optimism, naturalistic modes of expression, and individualism.

*The Renaissance
worldview*

One word above all comes closest to summing up the most common and basic Renaissance intellectual ideals, namely humanism. This word has two different meanings, one technical and one general, but both apply to the cultural goals and ideals of a large number of Renaissance thinkers. In its technical sense humanism was a program of studies which aimed to replace the medieval Scholastic emphasis on logic and metaphysics with the study of language, literature, history, and ethics. Ancient literature was always preferred: the study of the Latin classics was at the core of the curriculum, and, whenever possible, the student was expected to advance to Greek. Humanist teachers argued that Scholastic logic was too arid and irrelevant to the practical concerns of life; instead, they preferred the "humanities," which were meant to make their students virtuous and prepare them for contributing best to the public functions of the state. (Women, as usual, were generally ignored, but sometimes aristocratic women were given humanist training in order to make them appear more polished.) The broader sense of humanism lies in a stress on the "dignity of man" as the most excellent of all God's creatures below the angels. Some Renaissance thinkers argued that man was excellent because he alone of earthly creatures could obtain knowledge of God; others stressed man's ability to master his fate and live happily in the world. Either way Renaissance humanists had a firm belief in the nobility and possibilities of the human race.

Humanism

1. THE RENAISSANCE OF THOUGHT AND LITERATURE IN ITALY

The Renaissance had its beginnings in Italy for several reasons. One was that Italy had a stronger classical tradition than any other country of western Europe. Throughout the Middle Ages the Italians had managed to preserve the belief that they were descendants of the ancient Romans. In some Italian cities traces of the old Roman system of

*Why the Renaissance
began in Italy*

THE STATES OF ITALY DURING THE RENAISSANCE c. 1494

Lorenzo de' Medici. The leading patron of Florentine art and literature in the latter part of the fifteenth century.

education still survived in the municipal schools. It is likewise true that Italy had a more secular culture than most other regions of Latin Christendom. The Italian universities were founded primarily for the study of law or medicine rather than theology.

Italian economic developments also played a role in underwriting Renaissance cultural accomplishments. As we have seen, the Italian cities were the largest and richest of Europe; therefore they had the most funds to patronize the arts. At first urban governments and corporate organizations patronized artists who worked on churches and public monuments; public funds also helped support writers whose role was to glorify cities in letters and speeches. After about 1450 patronage was monopolized by the private sector: leading aristocratic families—for example, the Sforza in Milan, the Medici in Florence, the Este in Ferrara, and the Gonzaga in Mantua—became patrons of art and literature in order to glorify themselves. These families may not have been richer than their counterparts in northern Europe, but they turned to the patronage of Renaissance culture earlier. The main reason for this was that they had always lived in urban centers—as opposed to the northern aristocrats who customarily lived in country castles or on estates—and therefore became imbued with Renaissance ideals at an earlier date.

Patronage was not limited to the secular sphere: after about 1450, the papacy began to support scholarship and the arts in order to enhance the reputation of Rome and the Papal States. Nicholas V (1447–1455), called the "humanist pope," founded the Vatican Library. He was praised by a contemporary for "the high estimation he gained for books and writers everywhere." Later popes—including Alexander VI (1492–1503), Julius II (1503–1513; the "warrior pope"), and Leo X (1513–1521), the most worldly of the Renaissance popes—obtained the services of the greatest artists of their day, including Raphael and Michelangelo, and made Rome for a few decades the unrivaled artistic capital of the world.

We will return to art presently, but first let us survey the greatest accomplishments of Italian Renaissance scholars and writers. The history of Renaissance scholarship and literature must begin with Francis Petrarch (1304–1374), the earliest of the humanists in the technical sense of the word. Petrarch was a deeply committed Christian who believed that Scholastic theology and philosophy was entirely on the wrong track because it concentrated on abstract speculation rather than teaching people how to behave properly and attain salvation. Petrarch thought that the Christian writer must above all cultivate literary eloquence so that he could inspire people to do good. For him the only models of true eloquence were to be found in the ancient literary classics, which, in addition, were filled with ethical wisdom. So Petrarch dedicated himself to searching for undiscovered ancient Latin texts and writing his own moral treatises in which he imitated their style and quoted their phrases. Thereby he initiated a program of "humanist" studies that was to be influential for centuries. Petrarch also has a place in purely literary history because of his poetry. Although he prized his own Latin poetry over the poems he wrote in the Italian vernacular, only the latter have proved enduring. Above all, the Italian sonnets, later called Petrarchan sonnets, which he wrote for his beloved Laura in the chivalrous style of the troubadours, were widely imitated in form and content throughout the Renaissance period.

Because he was a committed Christian, Petrarch's ultimate ideal for human conduct was the solitary life of contemplation and asceticism. But in subsequent generations, from about 1400 to 1450, a number of Italian thinkers and scholars developed the alternative of what is customarily called "civic humanism." Two of the leading civic humanists were the Florentines, Leonardo Bruni (c. 1370–1444) and Leon Battista Alberti (1404–1472), but there were many others. The civic humanists agreed with Petrarch on the need for eloquence and the study of classical literature, but they also taught that man's nature equipped him for action, for usefulness to his family and society, and for serving the state. In their view ambition and the quest for glory were noble impulses which ought to be encouraged. They refused to condemn the

Pope Julius II. A portrait by Raphael.

Petrarch, the first humanist

Civic humanism

striving for material possessions, for they argued that the history of man's progress is inseparable from his success in gaining mastery over the earth and its resources. None of the civic humanists were anti-religious: most of them merely took Christianity for granted and were concerned primarily with worldly affairs. In addition to differing with Petrarch in their preference for the active over the solitary or contemplative life, the civic humanists went far beyond him in their study of the ancient literary heritage. Many of them discovered important new Latin texts, but far more important was their success in opening up the field of classical Greek studies. In this they were greatly aided by the cooperation of several Byzantine scholars who had migrated to Italy in the first half of the fifteenth century. These men gave instruction in the Greek language and taught about the achievements of their ancient forebears. In doing so they inspired Italian scholars to make trips to Constantinople and other cities in the Near East in search of Greek manuscripts. In 1423 one Italian humanist, Giovanni Aurispa, alone brought back 238 manuscript books, including works of Sophocles, Euripides, and Thucydides. In this way most of the Greek classics, particularly the writings of Plato, the dramatists, and the historians, were first made available to the modern world.

Renaissance Neoplatonism: Ficino and Pico

After about 1450 until about 1600 the dominance of the civic humanists in the world of Italian thought gave way to that of a school of Neoplatonists, who sought to blend the thought of Plato, Plotinus, and various strands of ancient mysticism with Christianity. Foremost among these were Marsilio Ficino (1433–1499) and Giovanni Pico della Mirandola (1463–1494), both of whom were members of the Platonic Academy founded by Cosimo de' Medici in Florence. The academy was a loosely organized society of scholars who met to hear readings and lectures. Their hero was unquestionably Plato: sometimes they celebrated Plato's birthday by holding a banquet in his honor, after which everybody gave speeches as if they were characters in a Platonic dialogue. Ficino's greatest achievement was the translation of Plato's works into Latin by 1469, thereby making them widely available to western Europeans for the first time. It is debatable whether Ficino's own philosophy may be called humanist, because he moved away from ethics to metaphysics and taught that the individual should look primarily to the other world. In Ficino's opinion "the immortal soul is always miserable in its mortal body." The same problem holds for Ficino's disciple Giovanni Pico della Mirandola, whose most famous work is the *Oration on the Dignity of Man*. Pico was certainly not a civic humanist because he saw little worth in mundane public affairs. But he did believe that there is "nothing more wonderful than man" because he believed that man is endowed with the capacity to achieve union with God if he so wills.

Hardly any of the Italian thinkers between Petrarch and Pico were really original: their greatness lay mostly in their manner of expression and in their popularization of different themes of ancient thought. The same, however, can no means be said of Renaissance Italy's greatest political philosopher, Niccolò Machiavelli (1469–1527). He belonged to no school but stood in a class by himself. No man did more than Machiavelli to overturn all earlier views of the ethical basis of politics or to pioneer in the dispassionate direct observation of political life. In his *Discourses on Livy* he praised the ancient Roman republic as a model for all time. He lauded constitutionalism, equality, liberty, in the sense of freedom from outside interference, and subordination of religion to the interests of the state. But Machiavelli also wrote *The Prince*, which reflects the unhappy condition of Italy in his time. At the end of the fifteenth century Italy had become the cockpit of international struggles. Both France and Spain had invaded the peninsula and were competing with each other for the allegiance of the Italian states. The latter, in many cases, were torn by internal dissension which made them an easy prey for foreign conquerors. In 1498 Machiavelli entered the service of the newly founded republic of Florence as second chancellor and secretary. His duties largely involved diplomatic missions to other states. While in Rome he became fascinated with the achievements of Cesare Borgia, son of Pope Alexander VI, in cementing a solidified state out of scattered elements. He noted with approval Cesare's combination of ruthlessness with shrewdness and his complete subordination of morality to political ends. In 1512 the Medici returned to overthrow the republic of Florence, and Machiavelli was deprived of his position. Disappointed and embittered, he spent the remainder of his life in exile, devoting his time primarily to writing. In his books, especially in *The Prince*, he described the policies and practices of government, not in accordance with some lofty ideal, but as they actually were. The supreme obligation of the ruler, he avowed, was to maintain the power and safety of the country over which he ruled. No consideration of justice or mercy or the sanctity of treaties should be allowed to stand in his way. Cynical in his views of human nature, Machiavelli maintained that all men are prompted exclusively by motives of self-interest, particularly by desires for personal power and material prosperity. The head of the state should therefore take nothing for granted as to the loyalty or affection of his subjects. The one ideal Machiavelli kept before him in his later years was the unification of Italy. But this he believed had no chance of accomplishment except by the methods of ruthlessness.

In addition to the work of Machiavelli, numerous other accomplishments were made in the realm of Italian literature in the years after 1500. One was *The Book of the Courtier*, published in 1516 by the diplomat and count Baldesar Castiglione. This vividly described Renaissance Italian court life with the aim of describing all the qualities necessary for becoming a "gentleman." More than any other book, it

The political thought of Machiavelli

Niccolò Machiavelli.

set forth and popularized the ideal of the typical "Renaissance man": one who is accomplished in many different pursuits and is also brave, witty, and "courteous," meaning civilized and learned. *The Courtier*'s popularity became so great that it was quickly translated into many other European languages and ran through more than a hundred editions. More deeply serious was the work of the historian Francesco Guicciardini (1483–1540). Having served many years as an ambassador of Florence and as a governor of papal territories, Guicciardini enjoyed a unique advantage in acquiring familiarity with the tortuous political life of his day. His special gifts as a historian were a capacity for minute and realistic analysis and an uncanny ability in disclosing the springs of human action. His masterpiece was his *History of Italy,* a detailed and dispassionate account of the varying fortunes of that country from 1492 to 1534.

Neither Castiglione nor Guicciardini were imaginative writers, but sixteenth-century Italians were accomplished in poetry as well, above all in the genre of vernacular epics. The most eminent of the writers of epics was Ludovico Ariosto (1474–1533), author of a lengthy poem entitled *Orlando Furioso (The Madness of Roland)*. Although woven largely of materials taken from the romances of adventure and the legends of the Charlemagne cycle, this work differed radically from any of the medieval epics. It incorporated much that was derived from classical sources; it lacked the impersonal quality of the medieval romances; and it was totally devoid of idealism. Ariosto, who was probably the greatest of Italian poets after Dante, wrote to make readers laugh and to charm them with felicitous descriptions of the quiet splendor of nature and the passionate beauty of love. His work represents the disillusionment of the late Renaissance, the loss of hope and faith, and the tendency to seek consolation in the pursuit of aesthetic pleasure.

2. THE ARTISTIC RENAISSANCE IN ITALY

Despite numerous intellectual and literary advances, the most long-lived achievements of the Italian Renaissance were made in the realm of art. Of all the arts, painting was undoubtedly supreme. We have already seen that around 1300 very impressive beginnings were made in the history of Italian painting by the artistic genius of Giotto, but it was not until the fifteenth century that Italian painting began to attain its majority. One reason for this was that in the early fifteenth century the laws of linear perspective were discovered and first employed to give the fullest sense of three dimensions. Fifteenth-century artists also experimented with effects of light and shade (*chiaroscuro*) and for the first time carefully studied the anatomy and proportions of the human body. By the fifteenth century, too, increase in private wealth and the partial triumph of the secular spirit had freed the domain of art to a large extent from the service of religion. As we have noted above, the Church was no longer the only patron of artists. While subject matter from biblical history was still commonly employed, it was frequently infused with nonreligious themes. The painting of portraits for the purpose of revealing the hidden mysteries of the soul now became popular. Paintings intended to appeal primarily to the intellect were paralleled by others whose main purpose was to delight the eye with gorgeous color and beauty of form. The fifteenth century was characterized also by the introduction of painting in oil, probably from Flanders. The use of the new technique doubtless had much to do with the artistic advance of this period. Since oil does not dry so quickly as fresco pigment, the painter could now work more leisurely, taking time with the more difficult parts of the picture and making corrections if necessary as he went along.

The majority of the painters of the fifteenth century were Florentines. First among them was the precocious Masaccio (1401–1428). Although he died at the age of twenty-seven, Masaccio inspired the work of Italian painters for a hundred years. Masaccio's greatness as a painter is based on his success in "imitating nature," which became a primary value in Renaissance painting. To achieve this effect he employed perspective, perhaps most dramatically in his fresco of the *Trinity;* he also used *chiaroscuro* with originality, leading to a dramatic and moving outcome. In the *Expulsion of Adam and Eve from the Garden,* he records the shame and guilt felt by the individuals in the biblical story.

The best known of the painters who directly followed the tradition begun by Masaccio was the Florentine Sandro Botticelli (1444–1510), who depicted both religious and classical themes. Botticelli's work excels in beautiful and accurate depiction of natural detail; he is a master, for example, at painting the female nude. But his major contribution to Renaissance painting derives from the philosophical basis of much of his work. In Florence he attracted the attention of the Medici, for whom he painted several portraits. Botticelli was also closely associated with the Florentine Neoplatonists. Two of his most famous paintings are *Primavera (Spring)* and *The Birth of Venus,* which illustrate Neoplatonic concepts regarding the classical goddess of love, Venus or Aphrodite. Later in his life Botticelli became a follower of the evangelical priest Savonarola, who came to Florence from Ferrara to preach fire-and-brimstone sermons against worldiness and paganism. Botticelli's *Mystic Nativity* was probably painted as a result of Savonarola's influence; it is a profoundly moving religious painting, in which he anticipates the apocalypse. The last years of Botticelli's life are shadowy; his popularity declined and it is believed he died in poverty.

Perhaps the greatest of the Florentine artists was Leonardo da Vinci

The Expulsion of Adam and Eve from the Garden. Masaccio's painting departed from the tradition of Giotto by introducing emotion and psychological study.

Botticelli

See color plates following page 384

Leonardo da Vinci

See color plates following page 384

The High Renaissance: Leonardo's naturalism

Studies of the Shoulder by Leonardo da Vinci

(1452–1519), one of the most talented and versatile people who ever lived. Leonardo was practically the personification of the "Renaissance man": he was a painter, musician, architect, writer, engineer, and inventor. The illegitimate son of a lawyer and a peasant woman, he was raised by his father and placed at an early age in the studio of Verrocchio, a Florentine artist of considerable repute. By the time he reached twenty-five, Leonardo set up his own artist's shop in Florence and gained the patronage of Lorenzo the Magnificent, the Medici ruler. But if Leonardo can be said to have had any weakness, it was his slowness in working and his difficulty in finishing anything. This displeased Lorenzo and other Florentine patrons, who thought an artist was little more than an artisan, commissioned to produce a certain piece of work for a certain price and on a certain date. Leonardo, however, strongly objected to this view—to him the artist was the equivalent of a philosopher. Therefore, in 1482 he left Florence for the Sforza court of Milan where he was given a freer rein in structuring his time and work. He remained there until the French invaded Milan in 1499; after that he wandered over the Italian peninsula, finally accepting the patronage of the French king, Francis I, under whose auspices Leonardo lived until his death.

The paintings of Leonardo da Vinci began what is known as the High Renaissance in Italy. His approach to painting was that it should be the most accurate possible imitation of nature. Leonardo was like a naturalist, basing his work on his own detailed observations of a blade of grass, the wing of a bird, a waterfall. He obtained human corpses for dissection—by which he was breaking the law—and reconstructed in drawing the minutest features of anatomy, which knowledge he carried over to his paintings. Leonardo worshiped nature, and was convinced of the essential divinity in all living things. It is not surprising, therefore, that he was a vegetarian, and that he went to the marketplace to buy caged birds which he released to their native habitat.

It is generally agreed that Leonardo's masterpieces are the *Virgin of the Rocks* (which exists in two versions), the *Last Supper,* and the *Mona Lisa.* The first represents not only his marvelous technical skill but also his passion for science and his belief in the universe as a well-ordered place. The figures are arranged in geometric composition with every rock and plant depicted in accurate detail. The *Last Supper,* painted on the walls of the refectory of Santa Maria delle Grazie in Milan, is a study of psychological reactions. A serene Christ, resigned to his terrible fate, has just announced to his disciples that one of them will betray him. The purpose of the artist is to portray the mingled emotions of surprise, horror, and guilt revealed in the faces of the disciples as they gradually perceive the meaning of their master's statement. The third of Leonardo's major triumphs, the *Mona Lisa,* reflects a similar interest in the varied moods of the human soul. Although it is true that the *Mona Lisa* is a portrait of an actual woman, the wife of

Francesco del Giocondo, a Neapolitan, it is more than a mere photographic likeness. The distinguished art critic Bernard Berenson has said of it, "Who like Leonardo has depicted . . . the inexhaustible fascination of the woman in her years of mastery? . . . Leonardo is the one artist of whom it may be said with perfect literalness: 'Nothing that he touched but turned into a thing of eternal beauty.' "

The beginning of the High Renaissance around 1490 was also marked by the rise of the so-called Venetian school. Its chief representatives included Giorgione (1478–1510), Titian (c. 1477–1576), and Tintoretto (1518–1594). The work of all these men reflected the luxurious life and the pleasure-loving interests of the thriving commercial city of Venice. Most Venetian painters had none of the preoccupation with philosophical and psychological themes that had characterized the Florentine school. Their aim was to appeal to the senses rather than to the mind. They delighted in painting idyllic landscapes and gorgeous symphonies of color. For their subject matter they chose not merely the opulent beauty of Venetian sunsets and the shimmering silver of lagoons in the moonlight but also the manmade splendor of sparkling jewels, richly colored satins and velvets, and gorgeous palaces. Their portraits were invariably likenesses of the rich and the powerful. In the subordination of form and meaning to color and elegance there were mirrored not only the sumptuous tastes of wealthy merchants, but also definite traces of Eastern influence which had filtered through from Byzantium during the late Middle Ages.

The Venetian painters

The remaining great painters of the High Renaissance all lived their active careers in the sixteenth century. It was in this period that the evolution of art reached its peak, and the first signs of decay began to appear. Rome was now almost the only artistic center of importance on the mainland of the Italian peninsula, although the traditions of the Florentine school still exerted a potent influence. Among the eminent painters of this period at least two must be given more than passing attention. One of the most noted was Raphael (1483–1520), a native of Urbino, and perhaps the most popular artist of the entire Renaissance. The lasting appeal of his style is due primarily to his intense humanism. He developed a conception of a spiritualized and ennobled humanity. He portrayed the members of the human species, not as dubious, tormented creatures, but as temperate, wise, and dignified beings. Although he was influenced by Leonardo da Vinci and copied many features of his work, he cultivated to a much greater extent than Leonardo a symbolical or allegorical approach. His *Disputà* symbolized the dialectical relationship between the Church in heaven and the Church on earth. In a wordly setting against a brilliant sky, doctors and theologians debate the meaning of the Eucharist, while in the clouds above, saints and the Trinity repose in the possession of a holy mystery. Raphael's *School of Athens* is an allegorical representation of the conflict between the Platonist and Aristotelian philosophies. Plato

The painters of the late Renaissance: Raphael

See color plates facing page 576

Michelangelo

See color plates following
page 576

(painted as a portrait of Leonardo) is shown pointing upward to emphasize the spiritual basis of his world of Ideas, while Aristotle gestures toward the earth to exemplify his belief that concepts or ideas are inseparably linked with their material embodiments. Raphael is noted also for his portraits and Madonnas. To the latter, especially, he gave a softness and warmth that seemed to endow them with a sweetness and piety quite different from the enigmatic and analytical Madonnas of Leonardo da Vinci.

The last towering figure of the High Renaissance was Michelangelo (1475–1564) of Florence. If Leonardo was a naturalist, Michelangelo was an idealist; where the former looked down to nature to record and reproduce natural phenomena, Michelangelo, who embraced Neoplatonism as a philosophy, was more concerned with metaphysical truths. But both were similar in their belief in the artist as more than an artisan. Michelangelo was a painter, sculptor, architect, and poet—and he expressed himself in all these with a similar power and in a similar manner. At the center of all of Michelangelo's paintings is the human figure, which is always powerful, colossal, magnificent. If man, and the potential of the individual, lay at the center of Italian Renaissance culture, then Michelangelo, who depicted the human, and particularly the male, figure without cease, is the supreme Renaissance artist. Michelangelo's greatest achievement in painting is the ceiling of the Sistine Chapel in Rome, which he worked on from 1508 to 1512 for Pope Julius II. The ceiling is a series of scenes which represent the history of humanity as portrayed in the Old Testament: among these are *God Dividing the Light from Darkness, God Creating the Earth, The Creation of Adam, The Creation of Eve, The Drunkenness of Noah.* Thirty years later Michelangelo finished the terrifying and monumental *Last Judgment,* also in the chapel, at the center of which is

The School of Athens by
Raphael

The Creation of Adam by Michelangelo. One of a series of frescoes on the ceiling of the Sistine Chapel in Rome. Suggesting philosophical inquiries into the meaning of life and the universe, it represents Renaissance realism at its height.

a figure of Christ who appears more like Hercules in his size and power.

In the realm of sculpture the Italian Renaissance took a great step forward by creating statues that were no longer carved as parts of columns or doorways on church buildings or as effigies on tombs. Instead, Italian sculptors for the first time since antiquity carved freestanding statues "in the round." These freed sculpture from its bondage to architecture and established its status as a separate art frequently devoted to secular purposes.

The first great master of Renaissance sculpture was Donatello (1386?–1466). He emancipated his art from Gothic mannerisms and introduced a more vigorous note of individualism than did any of his predecessors. His statute of David triumphant over the body of the slain Goliath, the first free-standing nude since antiquity, established a precedent of naturalism and of glorification of the nude which sculptors for many years afterward were destined to follow. Donatello also produced the first monumental equestrian statue in bronze since the time of the Romans, a commanding figure of the proud warrior, Gattamelata.

One of the greatest sculptors of the Italian Renaissance, and probably of all time, was Michelangelo. Sculpture, in fact, was the artistic field of Michelangelo's personal preference. Despite his success as a painter, he considered himself unfitted for that work. The dominant purpose which motivated all of his sculpture was the expression of thought in stone. His art was above mere naturalism, for he subordinated nature to the force and sweep of his ideas. (He wrote of releasing the "pure forms" which are trapped in the stone.) Other features of his work included the use of distortion for powerful effect, and a ten-

David by Donatello

Pietà by Michelangelo. This portrayal of tragedy was made by the sculptor for his own tomb. Note the distortion for effect exemplified by the elongated body and left arm of the figure of Christ. The figure in the rear is Nicodemus, but was probably intended to represent Michelangelo himself. Original in the cathedral of Florence.

dency to express his philosophical ideas in allegorical form. Most of his masterpieces were done for the embellishment of tombs, a fact significantly in harmony with his absorbing interest in death, especially in his later career. For the tomb of Pope Julius II, which was never finished, he carved his famous figures of the *Bound Slave* and *Moses*. The first, which is probably in some degree autobiographical, represents tremendous power and talent restrained by the bonds of fate. The statue of Moses is perhaps the leading example of Michelangelo's sculpture, showing his use of anatomical distortion to heighten the effect of emotional intensity. Its purpose was evidently to express the towering rage of the prophet on account of the disloyalty of the children of Israel to the faith of their fathers.

Some other examples of Michelangelo's work as a plastic artist create an even more striking impression. On the tombs of the Medici in Florence he produced a number of allegorical figures, two of which are known by the traditional titles of *Dawn* and *Sunset*. The first is that of a female figure, turning and raising her head like someone called from a dreamless sleep. *Sunset* is the figure of a powerful man who appears to sink under the load of human misery around him.

As Michelangelo's life drew toward its close, he tended to introduce into his sculpture a more exaggerated and spectacular emotional quality, and his figures tended to be more abstract. This was especially true of the *Pietà* intended for his own tomb. The *Pietà* is a statue of the Virgin Mary grieving over the body of the dead Christ. The figure standing behind the Virgin is probably a self-portrait. It is perhaps fitting that this profound but overwrought interpretation of human existence should have brought the Renaissance epoch in sculpture to a close.

To a much greater extent than either sculpture or painting, Renaissance architecture had its roots in the past. The new building style was eclectic, a compound of elements derived from the Middle Ages and from antiquity. It was not the Greek or the Gothic, however, but the Roman and the Romanesque which provided the inspiration for the architecture of the Italian Renaissance. Neither the Greek nor the Gothic had ever found a congenial soil in Italy. The Romanesque, by

The Villa Rotonda of Palladio. A highly influential Renaissance private dwelling near Vicenza. Note how Palladio drew for inspiration on the Roman Pantheon, pictured above, p. 254.

ove: *The Madonna of the Chair*, Raphael (1483–1520).
phael's art was distinguished by warmth and serenity, and
an uncritical acceptance of the traditions and conventions
his time. (Pitti Palace, Florence) Right: "Christ and
adonna." From *The Last Judgment*, Michelangelo
75–1564). This painting above the altar in the Sistine
apel, Rome, shows Christ as judge condemning sinners to
dition. Even the Madonna at His side seems to shrink from
s wrath. (Sistine Chapel)

Pope Paul III and His Nephews, Titian (1477–1576). This painting, with its rich harmony of color, is unusual in being both a
group portrait and a study of action. (National Museum,
Naples)

Charles V, Titian (1488–1576). (Alte
Pinakothek)

The Harvesters, Peter Breughel the Elder (1520–1569). Breughel chose to depict the life of humble people. (MMA)

The Virgin and Chancellor Rolin, Jan van Eyck (1390–1444). The early Flemish painters loved to present scenes of piety in the sumptuous surroundings of wealthy burghers. (Louvre)

Erasmus, Hans Holbein the Younger (1497–1543). This portrait is generally regarded as the best representation of the character and personality of the Prince of the Humanists. (Louvre)

St. Andrew and St. Francis, El Greco (1541–1614). (The Prado)

Burial of the Count of Orgaz, El Greco (1541–1614). El Greco's masterpiece immortalizes the character of the people among whom he dwelt. The elongated figures, gaunt faces, and bold and dramatic colors are typical of his work. (Iglesia S. Tomé, Toledo, Spain)

An Interior with a Woman Drinking, with Two Men and a Maidservant, Pieter de Hooch (1629–1677?). The subjects and setting contrast strongly with those of the Italian artists. (National Gallery, London) Below: *Crucifixion*, Matthias Grünewald (?–1528). This work is the central panel of the Isenheim Altarpiece, in the Unterlinden Museen, Colmar. (Scala)

Landscape with the Burial of Phocion, Nicolas Poussin (1594–1665). Many consider his paintings of the Roman hills to be models of French classicism. (Louvre)

The Calling of St. Matthew, Caravaggio (1573–1610). Painted for the altarpiece of the Church of San Luigi dei Francesci, Rome. (Scala)

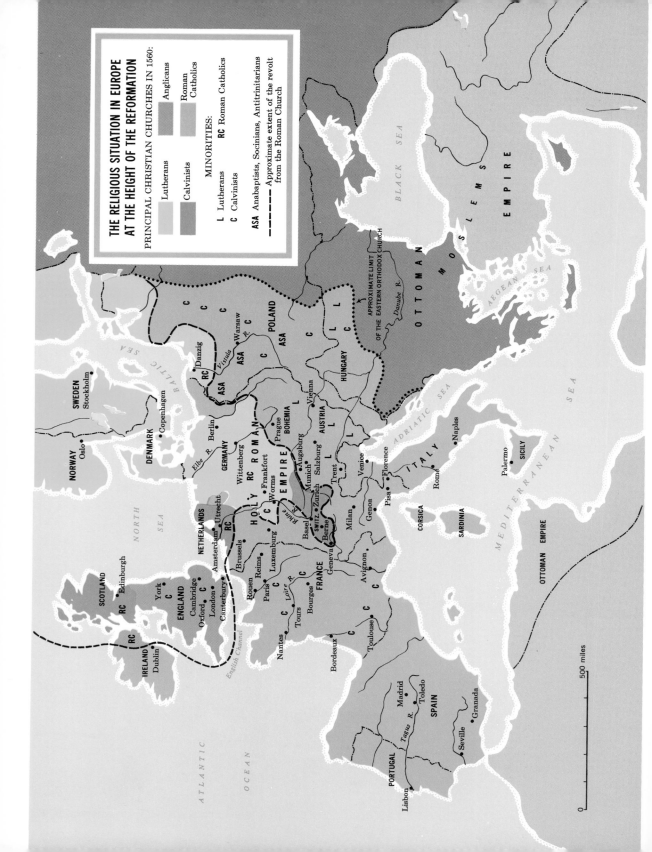

THE RELIGIOUS SITUATION IN EUROPE
AT THE HEIGHT OF THE REFORMATION

PRINCIPAL CHRISTIAN CHURCHES IN 1560:

Lutherans   Anglicans

Calvinists   Roman Catholics

MINORITIES:

L   Lutherans   RC   Roman Catholics

C   Calvinists

ASA   Anabaptists, Socinians, Antitrinitarians

– – –   Approximate extent of the revolt from the Roman Church

BLACK SEA

OTTOMAN   MOSLEMS   EMPIRE

AEGEAN SEA

APPROXIMATE LIMIT OF THE EASTERN ORTHODOX CHURCH

Danube R.

POLAND

ASA

Warsaw

Danzig

RC

Vistula R.

ASA

ASA

HUNGARY

L

L

C

L

SWEDEN

Stockholm

DENMARK

Copenhagen

BALTIC SEA

NORWAY

Oslo

Berlin

Elbe R.

GERMANY

Wittenberg

HOLY ROMAN EMPIRE

Frankfurt

Worms

Vienna

AUSTRIA

BOHEMIA

Prague

Augsburg

Munich

Salzburg

Trent

L

L

L

L

L

Venice

ADRIATIC SEA

ITALY

Florence

Pisa

Genoa

Milan

Naples

Rome

RC ROMAN

NORTH SEA

NETHERLANDS

Utrecht

RC

Amsterdam

Brussels

Rhine R.

SWITZ.

Basel

Zurich

Berne

Geneva

C

C

Luxemburg

Reims

Paris

Rouen

FRANCE

Loire R.

Bourges

Tours

Nantes

Bordeaux

Toulouse

Avignon

C

C

C

C

C

C

CORSICA

SARDINIA

MEDITERRANEAN SEA

OTTOMAN EMPIRE

SICILY

Palermo

SCOTLAND

Edinburgh

RC

York

C

ENGLAND

Cambridge

Oxford

C

London

Canterbury

IRELAND

Dublin

RC

English Channel

ATLANTIC OCEAN

SPAIN

Madrid

Toledo

Tagus R.

Granada

Seville

PORTUGAL

Lisbon

500 miles

0

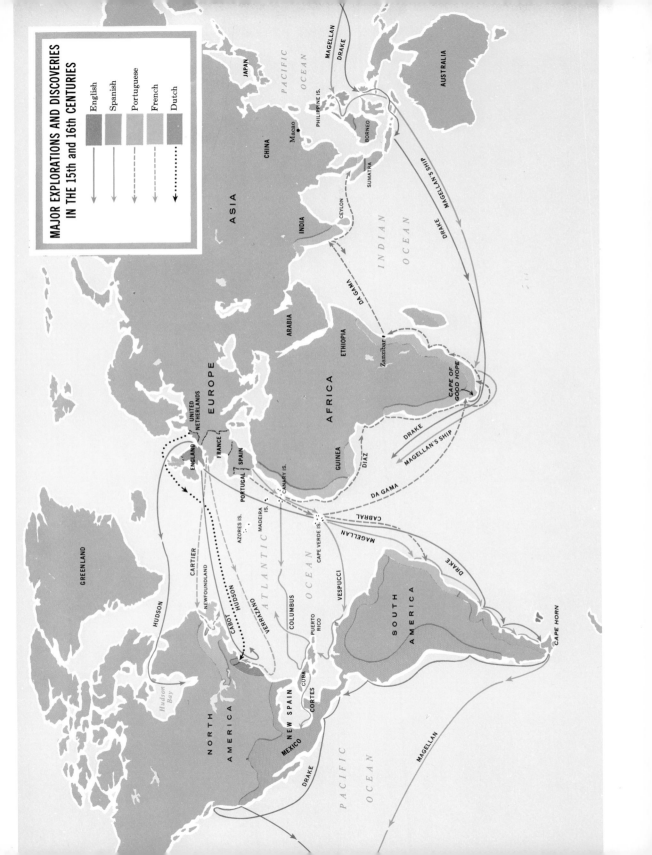

MAJOR EXPLORATIONS AND DISCOVERIES IN THE 15th and 16th CENTURIES

English
Spanish
Portuguese
French
Dutch

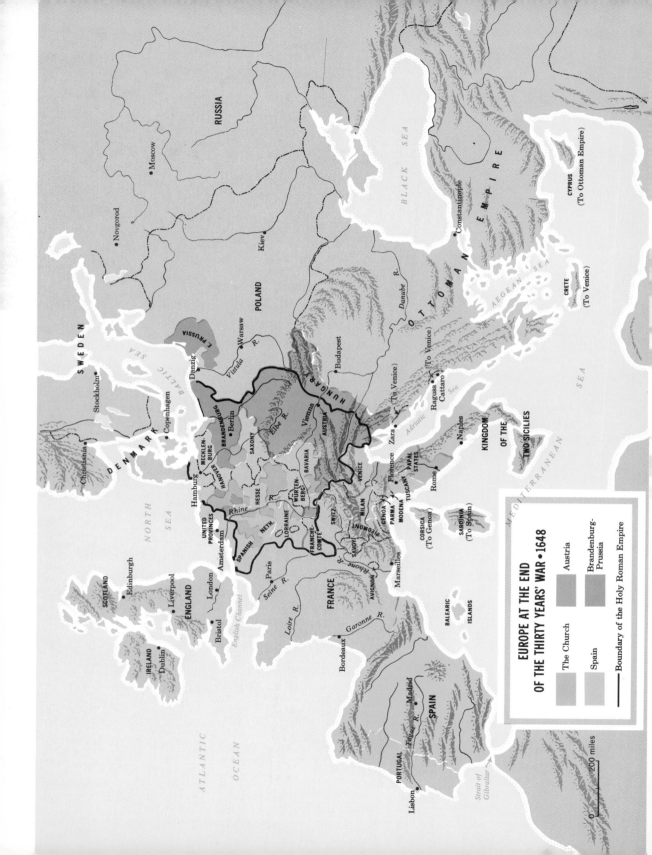

EUROPE AT THE END
OF THE THIRTY YEARS' WAR • 1648

The Church   Austria

Spain   Brandenburg-
Prussia

Boundary of the Holy Roman Empire

0   200 miles

RUSSIA

Moscow

Novgorod

Kiev

SWEDEN

Stockholm

Christiania

DENMARK

Copenhagen

BALTIC SEA

POLAND

Warsaw

E. PRUSSIA

Danzig

Vistula R.

BRANDENBURG

Berlin

MECKLEN-
BURG

HANOVER

Hamburg

SAXONY

Elbe R.

HESSE

WÜRTEN-
BERG

BAVARIA

Rhine R.

UNITED
PROVINCES

Amsterdam

SPANISH
NETH.

LORRAINE

FRANCHE-
COMTÉ

SWITZ.

AUSTRIA

Vienna

HUNGARY

Budapest

Danube R.

OTTOMAN EMPIRE

Constantinople

BLACK SEA

AEGEAN SEA

CYPRUS
(To Ottoman Empire)

CRETE
(To Venice)

VENICE

Zara
(To Venice)

Adriatic Sea

Ragusa
(To Venice)

Cattaro

(To Venice)

Florence

PAPAL
STATES

TUSCANY

Rome

MODENA

PARMA

GENOA

MILAN

PIEDMONT

SAVOY

Naples

KINGDOM

OF THE

TWO SICILIES

MEDITERRANEAN SEA

CORSICA
(To Genoa)

SARDINIA
(To Spain)

BALEARIC
ISLANDS

SCOTLAND

Edinburgh

IRELAND

Dublin

ENGLAND

Liverpool

London

Bristol

English Channel

NORTH SEA

Paris

Seine R.

Loire R.

FRANCE

Bordeaux

Garonne R.

Rhône R.

Marseilles

AVIGNON

ATLANTIC OCEAN

SPAIN

Madrid

Tagus R.

PORTUGAL

Lisbon

Strait of
Gibraltar

St. Peter's, Rome. Built to a square cross plan originally conceived by Bramante and revised by Michelangelo. Completed in 1626, the church rises to a total height of 450 feet.

contrast, was able to flourish there, since it was more in keeping with Italian traditions, while the persistence of a strong admiration for Latin culture made possible a revival of the Roman style. Accordingly, the great architects of the Renaissance generally adopted their building plans from the Romanesque churches and monasteries and copied their decorative devices from the ruins of ancient Rome. The result was an architecture based upon the cruciform floor plan of transept and nave and embodying the decorative features of the column and arch, or the column and lintel, the colonnade, and frequently the dome. Horizontal lines predominated; and, though many of the buildings were churches, the ideals they expressed were the purely secular ones of joy in this life and pride in human achievement. Renaissance architecture emphasized harmony and proportion to a much greater extent than did the Romanesque style. Under the influence of Neoplatonism, Italian architects concluded that perfect proportions in man reflect the harmony of the universe, and that, therefore, the parts of a building should be related to each other and to the whole in the same way as the parts of the human body. A fine example of Renaissance architecture is St. Peter's Church in Rome, built under the patronage of Popes Julius II and Leo X and designed by some of the most celebrated architects of the time, including Donato Bramante (c. 1444–1514) and Michelangelo.

The eclecticism of Renaissance architecture

3. THE WANING OF THE ITALIAN RENAISSANCE

Around 1550 the Renaissance in Italy came to an end after some two centuries of glorious history. The causes of its demise were varied. Possibly at the head of the list should be placed the French invasion of

The Entrance of Charles VIII into Florence. A painting by Francesco Granacci.

Political factors in the decline of the Italian Renaissance: the French invasion of 1494

1494 and the chaos that quickly ensued. The French monarch, Charles VIII, ruled over the richest and most powerful kingdom in Europe. Italy seemed an attractive prey for his grandiose ambitions. Accordingly, in 1494 he led an army of 30,000 well-trained troops across the Alps. The Medici of Florence fled before him, leaving their city to immediate capture. Halting only long enough to establish peace with a subservient new republican government, the French resumed their advance and conquered Naples. By so doing, however, they aroused the suspicions of the rulers of Spain, who feared an attack on their own possession of Sicily. An alliance of Spain, the Papal States, the Holy Roman Empire, Milan, and Venice finally forced Charles to abandon his project. Yet upon his death his successor, Louis XII, repeated the invasion of Italy, and from 1499 until 1529 warfare in Italy was virtually uninterrupted. Alliances and counteralliances followed each other in bewildering succession, but they only managed to prolong the warfare. The French won a great victory at Marignano in 1515, but they were decisively defeated by the Spanish at Pavia in 1525. The worst disaster came in 1527 when unruly Spanish and German troops, nominally under the command of the Spanish ruler Charles V but in fact entirely out of control, sacked the city of Rome, causing irreparable destruction. Only by 1529 did Charles finally manage to gain control over most of the Italian peninsula, putting the fighting to an end for a time. Once triumphant, Charles made a practice of restoring favorite princes as the rulers of Italian states. They continued to preside over their courts, to patronize the arts, and to adorn their cities with luxurious buildings, but in fact they were Spanish puppets and the greatest days of Italy were now clearly over.

To the political disorders was added a waning of Italian prosperity. This apparently brought no severe hardships until after 1600, but the shift of trade routes from the Mediterranean to the Atlantic region, following the discovery of America, was bound ultimately to have its effect. Italian cities gradually lost their supremacy as the centers of world trade. The prosperity they had enjoyed from a monopoly of commerce with the East had been one of the chief nourishing influences in the development of their brilliant culture. An important source of strength was now being drained away. (The effect of this "Commercial Revolution" is the subject of Chapter 16.)

A final cause of the decline of the Italian Renaissance was the Catholic Reformation. During the sixteenth century the Roman Church sought increasingly to exercise firm control over thought and art as part of a campaign to combat worldliness and the spread of Protestantism. In 1542 the Roman Inquisition was established; in 1559 Pope Paul IV issued the first Index of Prohibited Books. The effects of ecclesiastical interference in artistic life were devastating. Michelangelo's great *Last Judgment* in the Sistine Chapel—even though inspired by the thought of the Catholic Reformation—was criticized by some strait-laced fanatics for looking like a bordello because it showed too many naked bodies. Therefore, Paul IV ordered a second-rate artist to paint in clothing wherever possible. (The unfortunate artist was afterwards known as "the underwear-maker.") The most notorious example of inquisitorial censorship of free intellectual speculation was the disciplining of the great scientist Galileo, whose achievements we will discuss more carefully later on. In 1616 the Holy Office in Rome condemned the new astronomical theory that the earth moves around the sun as "foolish, absurd, philosophically false, and formally heretical." Accordingly, the Inquisition proceeded immediately against Galileo when he published a brilliant defense of the heliocentric system in 1632. In short order the Inquisition made Galileo recant his "errors" and sentenced him to house arrest for the duration of his life. Galileo was not willing to face death for his beliefs, but after he publicly retracted his view that the earth revolves around the sun he supposedly whispered, "despite everything, it still moves." Not surprisingly, Galileo was the last great Italian contributor to the development of modern astronomy and physics until modern times. It should not be thought that cultural and artistic achievement in Italy in the seventeenth century was completely extinguished. On the contrary, a great new style of architecture and sculpture known as the baroque was born and flourished in Rome under ecclesiastical auspices. Great advances were also made by Italian musicians without interruption from the sixteenth to the nineteenth century. But whatever seemed threatening to the Church could not be tolerated and the free spirit of Renaissance culture was found no more.

*The diffusion of the
Renaissance outside Italy*

4. THE RENAISSANCE IN THE NORTH

It was inevitable that after about 1500 the Renaissance which began in Italy should have spread to other European countries. Throughout the fifteenth century there had been a continuous procession of northern European students coming down into Italy to study in Italian universities such as Bologna or Padua, and there were also occasional Italians who traveled north of the Alps. Such interchanges helped spread ideas, but only after around 1500 did most of northern Europe become sufficiently prosperous and politically stable to provide a truly congenial environment for the widespread cultivation of art and literature. Intellectual interchanges, moreover, became much more extensive after 1494, when France and Spain started fighting on Italian battlefields. The result of this development was that more and more northern Europeans began to learn what the Italians had been accomplishing (Spain's forces came not just from Spain but also from Germany and the Low Countries). Then too leading Italian thinkers and artists, like Leonardo, began to enter the retinues of northern kings or aristocrats. Accordingly, the Renaissance became an international movement and continued to be vigorous in the north even after it started to wane on its native ground.

*The character of the
northern Renaissance*

It must not be supposed, however, that the Renaissance outside of Italy was the same in quality as the Renaissance within Italy. Above all, the northern European Renaissance was generally less secular. It is hard to account for this fully, but several reasons might be hazarded. One is that Italy had always had a more vigorous and independent urban society than the north. Even during the Middle Ages the Italian cities had patronized a more secular educational system in order to provide training for younger generations in business, law, and municipal public affairs. Since Italians could see Roman ruins all around them, they also developed greater familiarity at an earlier date with the classical tradition. That in turn allowed them to develop a more secular vocabulary and encouraged greater interest in depicting non-Christian themes in art. The north, on the other hand, had always focused on theological studies and had become more deeply imbued with religious mysticism. Northern Renaissance culture was never predominantly theological or mystical but it did emphasize religion to a greater degree than its Italian progenitor.

*The limited scope of the
German Renaissance*

One of the first countries to receive the full impact of the Italian humanist movement was Germany. This was a natural development, not only because of the proximity of the two countries, but also because of the steady migration of German students to the Italian universities. But the long-range influence of this humanism was not profound. What the results might have been if Germany had not been hurled so soon into the maelstrom of religious contention cannot be determined. The fact remains, however, that the Protestant Revolution stirred up extreme passions of intolerance which could not be other than inimical to the humanist ideal. A premium was now set upon faith, while anything resembling the worship of man or reverence for pagan antiquity was almost certain to be regarded as a work of the devil.

To fix a date for the beginning of the German Renaissance is practically impossible. In such prosperous cities of the south as Augsburg, Nuremberg, and Vienna there was a humanist movement, imported from Italy, as early as 1450. By the beginning of the sixteenth century it had spread elsewhere. Among its most notable representatives were Ulrich von Hutten (1488–1523) and Crotus Rubianus (1480–1523). Typical of the German humanist movement, both were less interested in the literary aspects of humanism than in its possibilities for the expression of religious and political protest. Hutten, especially, made use of his gifts as a writer to satirize the worldliness and greed of the clergy and to compose fiery defenses of the German people against foreigners. He was an embittered rebel against almost every institution of the established order.

German humanism

The chief claim to fame of Hutten and Rubianus is their joint authorship of the *Letters of Obscure Men* of 1515, one of the wittiest satires in the history of literature. This was written as a part of a propaganda war in favor of a humanist named Johann Reuchlin who wished to pursue his study of Hebrew writings, above all, the Talmud. When theologians from the University of Cologne and the German inquisitor general tried to have all Hebrew books in Germany destroyed, Reuchlin and his party strongly opposed the move. After a while it became apparent that direct argument was accomplishing nothing, so Reuchlin's supporters resorted to ridicule. Rubianus and Hutten published a series of letters, written in intentionally bad Latin, purportedly by some of Reuchlin's opponents from the University of Cologne. These were given such ridiculous names as Goatmilker, Goosepreacher, Baldpate, and Dungspreader, and shown to be learned fools who paraded forth examples of absurd religious literalism or grotesque erudition. Heinrich Sheep's-mouth, the supposed writer of one of the letters, professed to be worried that he had sinned grievously by eating on Friday an egg that contained the yolk of a chick. The author of another boasted of his "brilliant discovery" that Julius Caesar could not have written the *Commentaries on the Gallic Wars* because he was too busy with his military exploits ever to have learned Latin. Although immediately banned by the Church, the letters circulated nonetheless and were widely read. It is even possible that they helped prepare the way for the Protestant Revolution in Germany.

The Letters of Obscure Men

The German Renaissance in art was limited primarily to painting and engraving, represented chiefly by the work of Albrecht Dürer

Dürer's *Melancholy.* Ponderous "Melancholy" represents "theoretical insight which thinks but cannot act." Compare Dürer's more affirmative view of human potentialities shown on p. 584.

German painting: Dürer

(1471–1528) and Hans Holbein (1497–1543). Both of these artists were profoundly influenced by Italian traditions, though much of the Germanic spirit of somber realism is also expressed in their work. Dürer's best-known paintings are his *Adoration of the Magi, The Four Apostles,* and *The Crucified Christ.* The last is a study in tragic gloom. It shows the body of Jesus stretched on the cross against a bleak and sinister sky. The glimmer of light on the horizon merely adds to the somber effect of the scene. Some of Dürer's best-known engravings exhibit similar qualities. His *Melancholy* represents a female figure, a personification of the creative temperament, meditating on the limited nature of human creativity and knowledge, surrounded by the traditional instruments of learning, which seem useless.

Hans Holbein the Younger, the other great artist of the German Renaissance, derives his renown primarily from his portraits and drawings. His portraits of Erasmus and of Henry VIII of England are among the most famous in the world. An impressive example of his drawings is the one known as *Christ in the Tomb.* It depicts the body of Jesus, with staring eyes and mouth half-open, as neglected in death as the corpse of an ordinary criminal. The artist's purpose was to express the utter degradation which Christ had suffered for the redemption of humans. In his later career Holbein also drew many religious pictures satirizing the abuses in the Catholic Church which were believed to be

Erasmus

See color plates following page 576

the chief justification for the Protestant Revolution. He was one of the few prominent artists to devote his talents to the Protestant cause.

The history of Renaissance literature and philosophy in the Low Countries begins and ends with Desiderius Erasmus (1467?–1536), universally acclaimed as the prince of the humanists. The son of a priest and a servant girl, Erasmus was born near Rotterdam. For his early education he had the benefit of the excellent training given in a school of the Brethren of the Common Life. Later, after his father and mother were both dead, his guardians placed him in a monastery. Here the young Erasmus found little religion or formal instruction of any kind but plenty of freedom to read what he liked. He devoured all the classics he could get his hands on and the writings of many of the church fathers. When he was about thirty years of age, he obtained permission to leave the monastery and enroll in the University of Paris, where he completed the requirements for the degree of bachelor of divinity. But Erasmus subsequently revolted against what he considered to be the arid learning of Parisian Scholasticism. In one of his later writings he reported the following exchange: "Q. Where do you come from? A. The College of Montaigu. Q. Ah, then you must be bowed down with learning. A. No, with lice." Erasmus also never entered into the active duties of a priest, choosing rather to make his living by teaching and writing. By extensive reading of the classics he achieved a style of Latin expression so remarkable for its wit and urbanity that everything he wrote was widely read. But Erasmus's love of the classics was not born of pedantic interest. He admired the ancient authors because they gave voice to the very ideals of tolerance and humanitarianism which held so exalted a place in his own mind. He was wont to believe that Cicero and Socrates were far more deserving of the title of saint than many a Christian canonized by the pope. Erasmus died in Basel at the end of a long and unfaltering career in defense of scholarship, high standards of literary taste, and the life of moderation. He has been called the most civilized man of his age.

Erasmus. A woodcut by Hans Holbein the Younger.

As a philosopher of humanism Erasmus was the incarnation of the finest ideals of the northern Renaissance. Convinced of the inherent goodness of humanity, he believed that all misery and injustice would eventually disappear if only the pure sunlight of reason could be allowed to penetrate the noisome caverns of ignorance, superstition, and hate. With nothing of the fanatic about him, he stood for liberality of mind, for reasonableness and conciliation, rather than for fierce intolerance of evil. He shrank from the violence and passion of war, whether between systems, classes, or nations. Much of his teaching and writing was dedicated to the cause of religious reform. The ceremonial and superstitious extravagances in sixteenth-century Catholic life repelled him. But it was alien to his temper to lead any crusade against them. He sought rather by gentle irony, and occasionally by stinging satire, to expose irrationalism in all of its forms and to propa-

The tolerant thought of Erasmus

gate a humanist religion of simple piety and noble conduct based upon
what he called the "philosophy of Christ." Although his criticism of
the Catholic faith had some effect in hastening the Protestant Revolution, he recoiled in disgust from the intolerance of the Lutherans. Neither did he have much sympathy for the scientific revival of his time.
Like most of the humanists he believed that an emphasis upon science
would serve to promote a crude materialism and to distract men's interests from the ennobling influences of literature and moral philosophy. The best-known writings of Erasmus were his *Praise of Folly,* in
which he satirized pedantry, the dogmatism of theologians, and the
ignorance and credulity of the masses, and his *Colloquies* and *The
Handbook of the Christian Knight,* in which he condemned ecclesiastical
Christianity and argued for a return to the simple teachings of Jesus,
"who commanded us nothing save love for one another." In a less
noted, but nonetheless brilliant, work entitled *The Complaint of Peace,*
he expressed his abhorrence of war and his contempt for despotic
princes.

The art of the Low Countries during the Renaissance period found
its greatest practitioner in Peter Brueghel the Elder (c. 1525–1569).
Brueghel spent a few years in Italy studying the accomplishments of
the Italian Renaissance masters, but his own work remained distinctively Flemish in both subject matter and style. Brueghel continued
the tradition of earlier Flemish artists like the van Eycks in realistically
portraying scenes from everyday life, but he was one of the earliest
painters to pay particular attention to the life of the peasantry. Although he never idealized the roughness of peasants, his attitude to-

*Painting of the Low
Countries: Brueghel*

Knight, Death, and Devil by Dürer.
This engraving of 1513 illustrates the
ideal figure of Erasmus's *Handbook of a
Christian Knight.* The steadfast knight
is able to advance through the world
on his charger, his loyal dog at his
side, despite intimations of mortality
and the snares of the devil.

The Massacre of the Innocents. This painting by Brueghel shows how effectively art can be used as a means of social commentary.

ward them was definitely sympathetic. At first glance many of his paintings look like they are merely trying to recapture the world of nature and humanity without any comment, but closer inspection usually shows that initial appearances are deceptive. In fact, Brueghel was clearly a deeply moral and religious person. His *Land of Cockaigne,* which depicts fat people reclining in languid stupor after a great feast, is clearly meant to show that they are only living in a fool's paradise. His great *Massacre of the Innocents* is particularly moving in its quiet indictment of war and brutality. From a distance this looks like a simple scene of a wintry Flemish town buried in snow, but in fact heartless soldiers are methodically breaking into homes and slaughtering babies. The simple townspeople are helpless to stop them, and the artist seems to be saying: as it happened in the time of Christ, so it happens now.

See color plates following page 576

In France during the time of the Renaissance, there were outstanding achievements in literature and philosophy, illustrated especially by the writings of François Rabelais (1490?–1553) and Michel de Montaigne (1533–1592). Like Erasmus, Rabelais was educated as a monk, but soon after taking holy orders he left the monastery to study medicine at the University of Montpellier. He finished the course for the bachelor's degree in the short space of six weeks and obtained his doc-

The Renaissance in France: Rabelais

Rabelais

Montaigne

torate about five years later, in the meantime having served for a period as public physician in Lyon in addition to lecturing and editing medical writings. He seems from the start to have interspersed his professional activities with literary endeavors of one sort or another. He wrote almanacs for the common people, satires against quacks and astrologers, and burlesques of popular superstitions. In 1532 Rabelais published his first edition of *Gargantua,* which he later revised and combined with another book bearing the title of *Pantagruel.* Gargantua and Pantagruel were originally the names of legendary medieval giants noted for their prodigious strength and gross appetites. Rabelais's account of their adventures served as a vehicle for his robust, sprawling wit and for the expression of his philosophy of exuberant naturalism. In language far from delicate he satirized the practices of the Church, ridiculed Scholasticism, scoffed at superstitions, and pilloried every form of bigotry and repression. No man of the Renaissance was a more uncompromising individualist or exhibited more zeal in glorifying the human and the natural. For him every instinct of man was healthy, provided it was not directed toward tyranny over others. His celebrated description of the abbey of Thélème, built by Gargantua, was intended to show the contrast between his conception of freedom and the Christian ascetic ideal. At Thélème there were no clocks summoning to duties and no vows of celibacy or perpetual membership. The inmates could leave when they liked; but while they remained they dwelt together "according to their own free will and pleasure. They rose out of their beds when they thought good; they did eat, drink, labor, sleep, when they had a mind to it, and were disposed for it. None did awake them, none did offer to constrain them . . . for so Gargantua had established it. In all their Rule and strictest tie of their order there was but this one clause to be observed, *Do what thou wilt."*

A man of far different temperament and background was Michel de Montaigne (1533–1592). His father was a Catholic, his mother a Jew who had become a Protestant. Almost from the day of his birth their son was subjected to an elaborate system of training. Every morning he was awakened by soft music, and he was attended throughout the day by servants who were forbidden to speak any language but Latin. When he was six years old he was ready for the College of Guienne at Bordeaux and at the age of thirteen began the study of law. After practicing law for a time and serving in various public offices, he retired at thirty-seven to his ancestral estate to devote the remainder of his life to study, contemplation, and writing. Always in delicate health, Montaigne found it necessary now more than ever to conserve his strength. Besides, he was repelled by the bitterness and strife he saw all around him and was for that reason all the more anxious to find a refuge in a world of intellectual seclusion.

Montaigne's ideas are contained in his famous *Essays,* written during his years of retirement. The essence of his philosophy is skepticism in regard to all dogma and final truth. He knew too much about the diversity of beliefs, the welter of foreign customs revealed by geographic discoveries, and the disturbing conclusions of the new science ever to accept the idea that any one sect had exclusive possession of "the Truth delivered once for all to the saints." It seemed to him that religion and morality were as much the product of custom as styles of dress or habits of eating. He taught that God is unknowable, and that it is as foolish to "weep that we shall not exist a hundred years hence as it would be to weep that we had not lived a hundred years ago." Man should be encouraged to despise death and to live nobly and delicately in this life rather than to yearn piously for an afterlife. Montaigne was just as skeptical in regard to assumptions of final truth in philosophy or science. The conclusions of reason, he taught, are sometimes fallacious, and the senses often deceive us. The sooner men come to realize that there is no certainty anywhere, the better chance they will have to escape the tyranny which flows from superstition and bigotry. The road to salvation lies in doubt, not in faith.

A second element in Montaigne's worldview was tolerance. He could see no real difference between the morals of Christians and those of infidels. All sects, he pointed out, fight each other with equal ferocity, except that "there is no hatred so absolute as that which is Christian." Neither could he see any value in crusades or revolutions for the purpose of overthrowing one system and establishing another. All human institutions in his judgment were about equally futile, and he therefore considered it fatuous that man should take them so seriously as to wade through slaughter in order to substitute one for its opposite. No ideal, he maintained, is worth burning your neighbor for. In his attitude toward questions of ethics Montaigne was not so ribald a champion of carnality as Rabelais, yet he had no sympathy for asceticism. He believed it ridiculous that men should attempt to deny their physical natures and pretend that everything connected with sense is unworthy. "Sit we upon the highest throne in the world," he declared, "yet we do but sit upon our own behind." But in spite of his primarily negative attitude Montaigne did more good in the world than most of his contemporaries who founded new faiths or invented new excuses for absolute monarchs to enslave their subjects. Not only did his ridicule help to quench the flames of the cruel hysteria against witches, but the influence of his skeptical teachings had no small effect in combating fanaticism generally and in paving the way for a more generous tolerance in the future.

Despite the strong aesthetic interests of the French, as evidenced by their perfection of Gothic architecture during the Middle Ages, the achievements of their artists in the age of the Renaissance were of comparatively little importance. There was some minor progress in sculpture and a modest advancement in architecture. It was during this

*Reasons for the
backwardness of Spain in
the Renaissance*

*The character of Spanish
painting; El Greco*

See color plates following
page 576

Spanish drama

time that the Louvre was built, on the site of an earlier structure bearing the same name, while numerous châteaux erected throughout the country represented a more or less successful attempt to combine the grace and elegance of the Italian style with the solidity of the medieval castle. Nor was science entirely neglected, although the major accomplishments were few.

During the sixteenth and early seventeenth centuries Spain was at the height of its glory. Spanish conquests in the Western Hemisphere brought wealth to nobles and merchants and gave Spain a proud position in the front rank of European states. Notwithstanding these facts, the Spanish nation was not one of the leaders in Renaissance culture. The long war with the Moors had engendered a spirit of bigotry, the position of the Church was too strong, and the expulsion of the Jews at the end of the fifteenth century had deprived the country of talent it could ill afford to lose. For these reasons the Spanish Renaissance was limited to a few achievements in painting and literature, albeit some of these rank in brilliance with the best that other countries produced.

Spanish painting bore the deep impression of the bitter struggle between Christian and Moor. As a result it expressed an intense preoccupation with religion and with themes of anguish and tragedy. Its background was medieval; upon it were grafted influences from Flanders and from Italy. The most talented artist of the Spanish Renaissance was not a native of Spain at all, but an immigrant from the island of Crete. His real name was Domenico Theotocopuli, but he is commonly called El Greco (1541?–1614?). After studying for some time under Titian in Venice, El Greco settled in Toledo about 1575, to live there until his death. A stern individualist in temperament, he seems to have imbibed little of the warmth of color and sensuality of the Venetian school. Instead, nearly all of his art is characterized by emotionalism, stark tragedy, or enraptured flights into the supernatural and mystical. He often portrayed gaunt, ascetic-looking figures; his colors sometimes were cold and severe. His scenes of suffering and death seem deliberately contrived to produce an impression of horror. Among his famous works are *The Burial of the Count of Orgaz, Pentecost,* and *The Apocalyptic Vision.* Better than any other artist, El Greco expresses the fiery religious zeal of the Spanish people during the heyday of the Inquisition.

Literature in the Spanish Renaissance displayed tendencies not dissimilar to those in painting. This was notably true of drama, which frequently took the form of allegorical plays depicting the mystery of transubstantiation or appealing to some passion of religious fervor. Other dramatic productions dwelt upon themes of political pride or romance. The colossus among the Spanish dramatists was Lope de Vega (1562–1635), the most prolific author of plays the literary world has seen. He is supposed to have written no fewer than 1,500 comedies and more than 400 religious allegories. Of the total about 500 survive to this day. His secular dramas fall mainly into two classes: (1) the "cloak and sword plays," which depict the violent intrigues and exaggerated ideals of honor among the upper classes; and (2) the plays of national greatness, which celebrate the glories of Spain in its prime and represent the king as the protector of the people against a vicious and degenerate nobility.

Few would deny that the most gifted writer of the Spanish Renaissance was Miguel de Cervantes (1547–1616). His great masterpiece, *Don Quixote,* has even been described as "incomparably the best novel ever written." Composed in the best tradition of Spanish satirical prose, it recounts the adventures of a Spanish gentleman (Don Quixote) who has been slightly unbalanced by constant reading of chivalric romances. His mind filled with all kinds of fantastic adventures, he finally sets out at the age of fifty upon the slippery road of knight-errantry. He imagines windmills to be glowering giants and flocks of sheep to be armies of infidels, whom it is his duty to rout with his spear. In his disordered fancy he mistakes inns for castles and the serving-wenches within them for courtly ladies on fire with love of him. Set off in bold contrast to the ridiculous knight-errant is the figure of his faithful squire, Sancho Panza. The latter represents the ideal of the practical man, with his feet on the ground and content with the substantial pleasures of eating, drinking, and sleeping. The book as a whole is a pungent satire on chivalry, especially on the pretensions of the nobles as the champions of honor and right. Its enormous popularity was convincing proof that medieval civilization was approaching extinction even in Spain.

Cervantes

Don Quixote

In common with Spain, England also enjoyed a golden age in the sixteenth and early seventeenth centuries. Though its vast colonial empire had not yet been established, England was nevertheless reaping big profits from the production of wool and from trade with the Continent. The government, recently consolidated under the rule of the Tudors, was enhancing the prosperity of the merchants. Through the elimination of foreign traders, the granting of favors to English shipping, and the negotiation of reciprocal commercial treaties, the English merchant classes were given exceptional advantages over their rivals in other countries. The growth of a national consciousness, the awakening of pride in the power of the state, and the spread of humanism from Italy, France, and the Low Countries also contributed toward the flowering of a brilliant culture in England. Nevertheless, the English Renaissance was confined primarily to literature; the fine arts did not flourish.

The economic and political foundations of the Renaissance in England

The earliest writers of the English Renaissance may best be described as humanists. Although not unmindful of the value of classical studies, they were interested chiefly in the more practical aspects of humanism. Most of them desired a simpler and more rational Christianity and looked forward to an educational system freed from the

The early English humanists; Thomas More

Sir Thomas More. Portrait by Hans Holbein the Younger.

English Renaissance literature

The Elizabethan dramatists; Marlowe

dominance of Scholastic logic. Others were concerned primarily with individual freedom and the correction of social abuses. The greatest of these early thinkers was Sir Thomas More (1478–1535), esteemed by contemporary humanists as "excellent above all his nation." Following a successful career as a lawyer and as speaker of the House of Commons, More was appointed in 1529 lord chancellor of England. He was not long in this position, however, before he incurred the enmity of his royal master, Henry VIII. More was loyal to Catholic universalism and did not sympathize with the king's design to establish a national church under subjection to the state. When, in 1534, he refused to take the Oath of Supremacy acknowledging the king as the head of the Church of England, he was thrown into the Tower. A year later he was tried for treason on perjured evidence, convicted, and beheaded. More's philosophy is contained in his *Utopia,* which he published in 1516. Purporting to describe an ideal society on an imaginary island, the book is really an indictment of the glaring abuses of the time—of poverty undeserved and wealth unearned, of drastic punishments, religious persecution, and the senseless slaughter of war. The inhabitants of Utopia hold all their goods in common, work only six hours a day so that all may have leisure for intellectual pursuits, and practice the natural virtues of wisdom, moderation, fortitude, and justice. Iron is the precious metal "because it is useful," war and monasticism are abolished, and tolerance is granted to all who recognize the existence of God and the immortality of the soul. Despite criticism of the *Utopia* as conservative in many respects, the conclusion seems justified that the author's ideals of humanity and tolerance were considerably in advance of those of most other men of his time.

If there were any essential differences between the English literature of the Renaissance and that produced during the late Middle Ages, they would consist in a bolder individualism, a stronger sense of national pride, and a deeper interest in themes of philosophic import. The first great poet in England after the time of Chaucer was Edmund Spenser (1552?–1599). His immortal creation, *The Faerie Queene,* is a colorful epic of England's greatness in the days of Elizabeth I. Though written as a moral allegory to express the author's desire for a return to the virtues of chivalry, it celebrates also the joy in conquest and much of the gorgeous sensuousness typical of Renaissance culture.

But the most splendid achievements of the English in the Elizabethan Age were in the realm of drama. Not since the days of the Greeks had the writing of tragedies and comedies attained such heights as were reached in England during the sixteenth and early seventeenth centuries. Especially after 1580 a galaxy of playwrights appeared whose work outshone that of all their predecessors in two thousand years. Included in this galaxy were such luminaries as Christopher Marlowe (1564–1593), John Webster (c. 1580–c. 1625), Ben Jonson (1573?–1637), and William Shakespeare (1564–1616), of whom the first and the last are chiefly significant to the historian. Better than

A Map of Thomas More's Imaginary Island of Utopia. "Utopia's" fictional discoverer, Hythlodaeus, whose name means "dispenser of nonsense" in Greek, points to the island of Utopia, which means "no place." From an early edition.

anyone else in his time, Christopher Marlowe embodied the insatiable egoism of the Renaissance—the everlasting craving for the fullness of life, for unlimited knowledge and experience. His brief but stormy life was a succession of scandalous escapades and fiery revolts against the restraints of convention until it was terminated by his death in a tavern brawl before he was thirty years old. The best known of his plays, entitled *Doctor Faustus,* is based upon the legend of Faust, in which the hero sells his soul to the devil in return for the power to feel every possible sensation, experience every possible triumph, and know all the mysteries of the universe.

William Shakespeare, the most talented genius in the history of drama since Euripides, was born into the family of a petty tradesman in the provincial market town of Stratford-on-Avon. His life is enshrouded in more mists of obscurity than the careers of most other great men. It is known that he left his native village when he was about twenty years old, and that ultimately he drifted to London to find employment in the theater. Tradition relates that for a time he earned his living by holding the horses of the more prosperous patrons of the drama. How he eventually became an actor and still later a writer of plays is unknown, but there is evidence that by the time he was twenty-eight he had already acquired a reputation as an author sufficient to excite the jealousy of his rivals. Before he retired to his

The life and writings of William Shakespeare

native Stratford about 1610 to spend the rest of his days in ease, he had written or collaborated in writing nearly forty plays, to say nothing of 150 sonnets and two long narrative poems.

In paying homage to the universality of Shakespeare's genius, we must not lose sight of the fact that he was also a child of the Renaissance. His work bore the deep impression of most of the virtues and defects of Renaissance humanism. Almost as much as Boccaccio or Rabelais, he personified that intense love of things human and earthly which had characterized most of the great writers since the close of the Middle Ages. Moreover, like the majority of the humanists, he showed a limited concern with the problems of politics and scientific thought. Virtually the only political theory that interested him greatly was whether a nation had a better chance of prospering under a good king who was weak or under a bad king who was strong. His knowledge of science was limited primarily to alchemy, astrology, and medicine. But the force and range of Shakespeare's intellect were far from bounded by the narrow horizons of the age in which he lived. While few of the works of his contemporaries are now widely read, the plays of Shakespeare still hold their rank as a kind of secular Bible wherever the English language is spoken. The reason lies not only in the author's unrivaled gift of expression, but especially in his scintillating wit and primarily in his profound analysis of human character assailed by passion and tried by fate.

Shakespeare's dramas fall rather naturally into three main groups. Those written during his earlier years conformed to the traditions of existing plays and generally reflected his own confidence in personal

William Shakespeare. Portrait made for the First Folio edition of his works, 1623.

success. They include such comedies as *A Midsummer Night's Dream* and *The Merchant of Venice,* a number of historical plays, and the lyrical tragedy, *Romeo and Juliet.* Shortly before 1600 Shakespeare seems to have experienced a change of mood. The restrained optimism of his earlier plays was supplanted by some deep disillusion which led him to distrust human nature and to indict the whole scheme of the universe. The result was a group of dramas characterized by bitterness, overwhelming pathos, and a troubled searching into the mysteries of things. The series begins with the tragedy of intellectual idealism represented by *Hamlet,* goes on to the cynicism of *Measure for Measure* and *All's Well That Ends Well,* and culminates in the cosmic tragedies of *Macbeth* and *King Lear.* The final group of dramas includes those written during the closing years of Shakespeare's professional life. Among these are *The Winter's Tale* and *The Tempest.* All of them may be described as idyllic romances. Trouble and grief are now assumed to be only the shadows in a beautiful picture. Despite individual tragedy, the divine plan of the universe is somehow benevolent and just.

The main groups of Shakespeare's plays

5. RENAISSANCE DEVELOPMENTS IN MUSIC

Music in western Europe in the fifteenth and sixteenth centuries reached such a high point of development that it constitutes, together with painting and sculpture, one of the most brilliant aspects of Renaissance activity. While the visual arts were stimulated by the study of ancient models, music flowed naturally from an independent evolution which had long been in progress in medieval Christendom. As earlier, leadership was supplied by men trained in the service of the Church, but the value of secular music was now appreciated, and its principles were combined with those of sacred music to bring a decided gain in color and emotional appeal. The distinction between sacred and profane became less sharp; most composers did not restrict their activities to either field. Music was no longer regarded merely as a diversion or an adjunct to worship but as an independent art.

The evolution of music as an independent art

Different sections of Europe vied with one another for musical leadership. As with the other arts, advance was related to the increasingly generous patronage made possible by the expansion of commerce, and was centered in the prosperous towns. During the fourteenth century a pre- or early Renaissance musical movement called Ars Nova (new art) flourished in Italy and France. Its outstanding composers were Francesco Landini (c. 1325–1397) and Guillaume de Machaut (1300–1377). The madrigals, ballads, and other songs composed by the Ars Nova musicians testify to a rich secular art, but the greatest achievement of the period was a highly complicated yet delicate contrapuntal style adapted for motet and chanson. With Machaut we reach the first integral polyphonic setting of the Ordinary of the Mass.

Leadership provided by Italy and France

Renaissance Trumpeters and Singers. Reliefs by Luca della Robbia.

Synthesis of national elements

The fifteenth century was ushered in by a synthesis of English, French, Flemish, and Italian elements that took place in the Duchy of Burgundy. It produced a remarkable school of music inspired by the cathedral of Cambrai and the ducal court at Dijon. This music was gentle, melodious, and euphonious, but in the second half of the century it hardened a little as the northern Flemish element gained in importance. As the sixteenth century opened we find these Franco-Flemish composers in every important court and cathedral choir all over Europe, gradually establishing regional-national schools, usually in attractive combinations of Flemish with German, Spanish, and Italian musical cultures. The various genres thus created show a close affinity with Renaissance art and poetry. In the second half of the sixteenth century the leaders of the nationalized Franco-Flemish style were the Italian Palestrina (c. 1525–1594), who, by virtue of his position as papal composer and his devotion to a subtle and crystal-clear vocal style, became the venerated symbol of church music; the Flemish Roland de Lassus (1532–1594), the most versatile composer of the age; and Tomas Luis de Victoria (c. 1540–1611), the glowing mystic of Spanish music. Music also flourished in England, for the Tudor monarchs were active in patronizing the arts; several of them were accomplished musicians. It was inevitable that the reigning Franco-Flemish style should reach England, where it was superimposed upon an ancient and rich musical culture. The Italian madrigal, imported toward the end of the sixteenth century, found a remarkable second flourishing in England, but songs and instrumental music of an original cast anticipated future developments on the Continent. In William Byrd (1543–1623) English music produced a master fully the equal of the great Flemish, Roman, and Spanish composers of the Renaissance. The general level of music proficiency seems to have been higher in Queen Elizabeth's day than in ours: the singing of part-songs was a popular pastime in homes and at informal social gatherings, and the ability to read a part at sight was expected of the educated elite.

In conclusion, it may be observed that while counterpoint had matured, our modern harmonic system had been born, and thus a way was opened for fresh experimentation. At the same time one should realize that the music of the Renaissance constitutes not merely a stage in evolution but a magnificent achievement in itself, with masters who rank among the great of all time. The composers Palestrina and Lassus are as truly representative of the artistic triumph of the Renaissance as are the painters Raphael and Michelangelo. Their heritage, long neglected except at a few ecclesiastical centers, has within recent years begun to be appreciated, and is now gaining in popularity as interested groups of musicians devote themselves to its revival.

The greatness of the Renaissance musical achievement

6. THE SCIENTIFIC ACCOMPLISHMENTS OF THE RENAISSANCE PERIOD

Some extraordinarily important accomplishments were made in the history of science during the sixteenth and early seventeenth centuries, but these were not preeminently the achievements of Renaissance humanism. The educational program of the humanists placed a low value on science because it seemed irrelevant to their aim of making people more eloquent and moral. Science for humanists like Petrarch, Leonardo Bruni, or Erasmus was part and parcel of the "vain speculation" of the Scholastics which they attacked and held up to ridicule. Accordingly, none of the great scientists of the Renaissance age belonged to the humanist movement.

The nonscientific orientation of Renaissance humanism

Nonetheless, at least two intellectual trends of the period did prepare the way for great new scientific advances. One was the popularity of Neoplatonism. The importance of this philosophical system to science was that it proposed certain ideas, such as the central position of the sun and the supposed divinity of given geometrical shapes, that would help lead to crucial scientific breakthroughs. It is ironic that Neoplatonism seems very "unscientific" from the modern perspective because it emphasizes mysticism and intuition instead of empiricism or strictly rational thought. Yet it helped scientific thinkers to reconsider older notions which had impeded the progress of medieval science; in other words, it helped them to put on a new "thinking cap." Among

Renaissance foundations of modern science: (1) Neoplatonism

(2) a mechanistic view of the universe

A Cannon Foundry by Leonardo da Vinci

(3) the integration of theory and practice

the most important of the scientists who were influenced by Neoplatonism were Copernicus and Kepler.

A second trend that contributed to the advance of science was very different. This was the growth in popularity of a *mechanistic* interpretation of the universe. Renaissance mechanism owed its greatest impetus to the publication in 1543 of the works of the great Greek mathematician and physicist Archimedes. Not only were his concrete observations and discoveries among the most advanced and reliable in the entire body of Greek science, but Archimedes taught the view that the universe operates on the basis of mechanical forces, like a great machine. Because his view was diametrically opposed to the occult outlook of the Neoplatonists, who saw the world inhabited by spirits and driven by supernatural forces, it took some time to gather strength. Nonetheless, mechanism did gain some very important early adherents, foremost among whom was the Italian scientist Galileo. Ultimately mechanism played an enormous role in the development of modern science because it insisted upon finding observable and measurable causes and effects in the world of nature.

One other Renaissance development which helped lead to the rise of modern science was the breakdown of the medieval separation between the realms of theory and practice. In the Middle Ages the only "scientists" were Scholastically trained clerics who never for a moment thought of tinkering with machines, mixing chemicals, or dissecting corpses because this empirical approach to science lay outside the Scholastic framework. On the other hand, there were numerous technicians who had little formal education and knew little of abstract theories. But starting in the fifteenth century there was a growing integration of theory and practice. One reason for this was that the highly respected Renaissance artists bridged both areas of endeavor: not only were they marvelous craftsmen, but they studied and made advances in mathematics and science when they investigated the laws of perspective and optics, worked out geometric methods for supporting the weight of enormous architectural domes, and studied the dimensions and details of the human body. In general, they helped make science more empirical and practically oriented than it had been before. Other reasons for the integration were the decline in prestige of the overly theoretical universities and a growing interest in alchemy and astrology among the leisured classes. Here again we can see some irony: alchemy and astrology are today properly dismissed as unscientific superstitions, but in the sixteenth and seventeenth centuries their vogue led some wealthy amateurs to start building laboratories and measuring the courses of the stars. Thereby scientific practice was made eminently respectable. When that happened modern science was on the way to some of its greatest triumphs.

The actual scientific accomplishments of the Renaissance period were international in scope. The achievement par excellence in as-

Alchemists in Their Laboratory. This artist is clearly unsympathetic to the enterprise, but great early-modern scientists such as Kepler and Newton took alchemy very seriously.

tronomy—the formulation and proof of the heliocentric theory that the earth revolves around the sun—was primarily the work of the Pole Copernicus, the German Kepler, and the Italian Galileo. Until the sixteenth century the Ptolemaic theory that the earth stands still and is the center of the universe went virtually unchallenged in western Europe. Nicholas Copernicus (1473–1543), a Polish clergyman who had absorbed Neoplatonism while studying in Italy, was the first to posit an alternate system. Copernicus made no new observations, but he thoroughly reinterpreted the significance of the old astronomical evidence. Inspired by the Neoplatonic assumptions that the sphere is the most perfect shape, that motion is more nearly divine than rest, and that the sun sits "enthroned" in the midst of the universe, "ruling his children the planets which circle around him," Copernicus worked out a new heliocentric theory. Specifically, in his *On the Revolutions of the Heavenly Spheres*—which he completed around 1530 but did not publish until 1543—he argued that the earth and the planets move around the sun in concentric circles. Copernicus's system itself was still highly imperfect: by no means did it account without difficulties for all the known facts of planetary motion. Moreover, it asked people to reject their commonsense assumptions that the sun moves because it gives the illusion of moving across the sky and that the earth stands still because no movement can be detected. More serious, Copernicus contradicted passages in the Bible, such as the one wherein Joshua commands the sun to stand still. Accordingly, believers in Copernicus's heliocentric theory remained distinctly in the minority until the early seventeenth century.

It was Kepler and Galileo who ensured that Copernicus's revolution in astronomy would become triumphant. Johann Kepler (1571–1630), a mystical thinker who was in many ways more like a magician than a modern scientist, studied astronomy in order to probe the hidden

Progress in astronomy: Copernicus's heliocentric theory

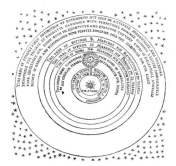

"A Perfect Description of the Celestial Orbes." A diagram by Copernicus, showing the relationship of stars, the planets, and the sun.

Kepler's laws of planetary motion

secrets of God. His basic conviction was that God had created the universe on the basis of mathematical laws. Relying on the new and impressively accurate astronomical observations of the Dane Tycho Brahe (1546–1601), Kepler was able to recognize that two assumptions about planetary motion that Copernicus had taken for granted were simply not in accord with the observable facts. Specifically, Kepler replaced Copernicus's belief in uniform planetary velocity with his own "First Law" that the speed of planets varies with their distance from the sun, and he replaced Copernicus's view that planetary orbits were circular with his "Second Law" that the earth and the other planets travel in *elliptical* paths around the sun. He also argued in favor of magnetic attractions between the sun and the planets which keep the planets in orbital motion. That approach was rejected by most seventeenth-century mechanistic scientists as being far too magical, but in fact it paved the way for the law of universal gravitation formulated by Isaac Newton at the end of the seventeenth century.

Galileo's confirmation of the Copernican revolution

As Kepler perfected Copernicus's heliocentric system from the point of view of mathematical theory, so Galileo Galilei (1564–1642) helped gain acceptance for it by gathering further astronomical evidence. With a telescope which he manufactured himself and raised to a magnifying power of thirty times, he discovered the moons of Jupiter, the rings of Saturn, and spots on the sun. He was able also to determine that the Milky Way is a collection of celestial bodies independent of our solar system and to form some idea of the enormous distances of the fixed stars. Though there were many who held out against them, these discoveries of Galileo gradually convinced the majority of scientists that the main conclusion of Copernicus was true. The final triumph of this idea is commonly called the Copernican Revolution. Few more significant events have occurred in the intellectual history of the world, for it overturned the medieval worldview and paved the way for modern conceptions of mechanism, skepticism, and the infinity of time and space. Some thinkers believe that it contributed also to the degradation of man, since it swept man out of his majestic position at the center of the universe and reduced him to a mere particle of dust in an endless cosmic machine.

In the front rank among the physicists of the Renaissance were Leonardo da Vinci and Galileo. If Leonardo da Vinci had failed completely as a painter, his contributions to science would entitle him to considerable fame. Not the least of these were his achievements in physics. Though he actually made few complete discoveries, his conclusion that "every weight tends to fall toward the center by the shortest way" contained the kernel of the law of gravity. In addition, he worked out the principles of an astonishing variety of inventions, including a diving boat, a steam engine, an armored tank, and a helicopter. Galileo is especially noted as a physicist for his law of falling bodies. Skeptical of the traditional theory that bodies fall with a speed

Galileo

directly proportional to their weight, he taught that bodies dropped from various heights would fall at a rate of speed which increases with the square of the time involved. Rejecting the Scholastic notions of absolute gravity and absolute levity, he taught that these are purely relative terms, that all bodies have weight, even those which, like the air, are invisible, and that in a vacuum all objects would fall with equal velocity. Galileo seems to have had a broader conception of a universal force of gravitation than Leonardo da Vinci, for he perceived that the power which holds the moon in the vicinity of the earth and causes the satellites of Jupiter to circulate around that planet is essentially the same as the force which enables the earth to draw bodies to its surface. He never formulated this principle as a law, however, nor did he realize all of its implications, as did Newton some fifty years later.

The record of Italian achievements in the various sciences related to medicine is also an impressive one. A number of Italian physicians contributed valuable information pertaining to the circulation of the blood. One of them described the valves of the heart, the pulmonary artery, and the aorta, while another located the valves in the veins. Equally significant was the work of certain foreigners who lived and taught in Italy. Andreas Vesalius (1514–1564), a native of Brussels, issued the first careful description of the human body based upon actual investigation. As a result of his extensive dissections he was able to correct many ancient errors. He is commonly considered the father of the modern science of anatomy.

Three other great Renaissance physicians were the German Paracelsus (1493–1547), the Spaniard Michael Servetus (1511–1553), and the Englishman William Harvey (1578–1657). Paracelsus resembled Copernicus and Kepler in believing that spiritual rather than material forces governed the workings of the universe. Hence he was a firm believer in alchemy and astrology. Nevertheless, Paracelsus relied on observation for his knowledge of diseases and their cures. Instead of following the teachings of ancient authorities, he traveled widely, studying cases of illness in different environments and experimenting with many drugs. Above all, his insistence on the close relationship of chemistry and medicine foreshadowed and sometimes directly influenced important modern achievements in pharmacology and healing. Michael Servetus, whose major interest was theology, but who practiced medicine for a living, discovered the lesser or pulmonary circulation of the blood, in an attempt to prove the veracity of the Virgin birth. He described how the blood leaves the right chambers of the heart, is carried to the lungs to be purified, then returns to the heart and is conveyed from that organ to all parts of the body. But Servetus had no idea of the return of the blood to the heart through the veins. It was left for William Harvey, who had studied under Italian physicians at Padua, to complete the discovery. This he did after his return to England about 1610. In his *Dissertation upon the Movement of the Heart* he

An Anatomical Demonstration. This Dutch engraving from 1610 combines a presentation of scientific inquiry with attitudes associated with late-medieval moralizing. The skeletons hold up signs which remind humans that they will return to dust.

described how an artery bound by a ligature would fill with blood in the section nearer the heart, while the portion away from the heart would empty, and how exactly the opposite results would occur when a ligature was placed on a vein. By such experiments he reached the conclusion that the blood is in constant process of circulation from the heart to all parts of the body and back again. Thus while thinkers and writers like Montaigne, Cervantes, and Shakespeare were probing into the mainsprings of human action, contemporary anatomists and physicians were literally taking humans apart and discovering their motive forces.

SELECTED READINGS

- *Items so designated are available in paperback editions.*
  Baker, Herschel, *The Image of Man: A Study of the Idea of Human Dignity in Classical Antiquity, the Middle Ages, and the Renaissance,* Cambridge, Mass., 1947. An outstanding and engagingly written survey from the perspective of a modern liberal.
- Baxandall, Michael, *Painting and Experience in Fifteenth Century Italy,* Oxford, 1972.
  Benesch, O., *The Art of the Renaissance in Northern Europe,* rev. ed., New York, 1965.
- Berenson, B., *The Italian Painters of the Renaissance,* New York, 1952.
- Burckhardt, J., *The Civilization of the Renaissance in Italy,* many eds. The nineteenth-century work that formulated the modern view of the Renaissance.

• Bush, D., *The Renaissance and English Humanism,* Toronto, 1939.

Butterfield, H., *The Origins of Modern Science,* London, 1949. Clear and wide ranging. Shows how science developed from major changes in intellectual orientations.

Chabod, F., *Machiavelli and the Renaissance,* London, 1958.

Chambers, R. W. *Thomas More,* London, 1936. A spirited defense of the view that More was a life-long committed Catholic.

• Chute, M., *Shakespeare of London,* New York, 1949. The best popular biography.

• Clark, Kenneth M., *Leonardo da Vinci,* 2nd ed., Cambridge, 1952.

• Dean, Leonard F., ed., *Shakespeare: Modern Essays in Criticism,* New York, 1957.

• Ferguson, W., ed., *The Renaissance: Six Essays,* rev. ed., New York, 1962.

• Ford, Boris, ed., *The Age of Shakespeare,* Baltimore, 1955. A good shorter handbook.

• Gilbert, Felix, *Machiavelli and Guicciardini,* Princeton, N.J., 1965. Examines the thought of these writers in terms of the political realities of their day.

• Gilmore, M., *The World of Humanism,* New York, 1952. A well-written survey.

Gould, Cecil, *An Introduction to Italian Renaissance Painting,* London, 1957.

Hale, J. R., *Machiavelli and Renaissance Italy,* New York, 1960.

———, *Renaissance Europe: The Individual and Society, 1480–1520,* London, 1971. A different kind of survey that does not treat the great events but examines the quality of life.

• Hay, D., ed., *The Renaissance Debate,* New York, 1965. A collection of readings on the question of how to define the Renaissance.

• Kearney, H., *Science and Change, 1500–1700,* New York, 1971. Supplements Butterfield in arguing that science progressed as the result of contributions made by three different "schools."

• Kristeller, P. O., *Renaissance Thought: The Classic, Scholastic, and Humanist Strains,* New York, 1961. Very helpful in defining main trends of Renaissance thought.

• ———, *Eight Philosophers of the Italian Renaissance,* Stanford, Calif., 1964. Admirably clear.

Lang, Paul H., *Music in Western Civilization,* New York, 1941.

• Levey, M., *Early Renaissance (Style and Civilization),* Baltimore, 1967. Art history.

• Panofsky, E., *Renaissance and Renascences in Western Art,* Stockholm, 1960. A difficult but rewarding attempt to distinguish the Italian Renaissance from its medieval predecessors.

Phillips, Margaret M., *Erasmus and the Northern Renaissance,* London, 1949.

• Ralph, Philip L., *The Renaissance in Perspective,* New York, 1973.

Reese, Gustave, *Music in the Renaissance,* rev. ed., New York, 1959. The leading work on the subject.

• Rice, E. F., Jr., *The Foundations of Early Modern Europe, 1460–1559,* New York, 1970.

• ———, *The Renaissance Idea of Wisdom,* Cambridge, Mass., 1958.

Seigel, J., *Rhetoric and Philosophy in Renaissance Humanism,* Princeton, N.J., 1968. Treats a basic tension in the thought of early Renaissance thinkers.

Simone, F., *The French Renaissance,* London, 1969.

Stechow, W., *Northern Renaissance Art: 1400–1600,* Englewood Cliffs, N.J., 1966.

Tolnay, C. de, *The Art and Thought of Michelangelo,* New York, 1964.

Tracy, James, *Erasmus: The Growth of a Mind,* Geneva, 1972. The best intellectual biography.

Whitfield, J. H., *A Short History of Italian Literature,* Baltimore, 1960.

• Wittkower, R., *Architectural Principles in the Age of Humanism,* rev. ed., New York, 1965. An art-historical classic.

SOURCE MATERIALS

Alberti, Leon Battista, *The Family in Renaissance Florence,* tr. R. N. Watkins, Columbia, S.C., 1969.

• Cassirer, E., et al., eds., *The Renaissance Philosophy of Man,* Chicago, 1948. Leading works of Petrarch, Pico, etc.

• Castiglione, B., *The Book of the Courtier,* tr. C. S. Singleton, New York, 1959.

• Erasmus, D., *The Praise of Folly,* tr. J. Wilson, Ann Arbor, Mich., 1958.

Kohl, B. G., and R. G. Witt, eds., *The Earthly Republic: Italian Humanists on Government and Society,* Philadelphia, 1978. New translations with excellent introductions.

• Machiavelli, N., *The Prince,* tr. R. M. Adams, New York, 1976. In addition to Machiavelli's text, this edition provides related documents and an excellent selection of scholarly interpretations.

• Montaigne, M. de, *Essays,* tr. J. M. Cohen, Baltimore, 1958.

• More, Sir Thomas, *Utopia,* tr. R. M. Adams, New York, 1975. In the same series as Adams's translation of Machiavelli's *Prince;* provides background materials and selected scholarly interpretations as well as the text.

• Rabelais, F., *Gargantua and Pantagruel,* tr. J. M. Cohen, Baltimore, 1955. A robust modern translation.

Chapter 19

THE AGE OF
THE REFORMATION
(1517–c. 1600)

For the word of God cannot be received and honored by any works, but by faith alone.

—Martin Luther, *On Christian Liberty*

In conformity to the clear doctrine of the Scripture, we assert that by an eternal and immutable counsel, God has once for all determined both whom He would admit to salvation and whom He would condemn to destruction. . . . In the elect, we consider calling as an evidence of election, and justification as another token of its manifestation, till they arrive in glory, which constitutes its completion.

—John Calvin, *Institutes* III.xxi

The preceding chapter has described the unfolding of a marvelous culture which marked the transition from the Middle Ages to the modern world. It became apparent that this culture, the Renaissance, was almost as peculiarly an echo of the past as a herald of the future. Much of its literature, art, and philosophy, and all of its superstitions, had roots that were deeply buried in classical antiquity or in the centuries of the Middle Ages. Even its humanism breathed veneration for the past. Only in science and political thought and in the vigorous assertion of the right of the individual to pursue his own quest for freedom and dignity was there much that was really new. But the Renaissance in its later stages was accompanied by the growth of another movement, the Reformation, which somewhat more accurately foreshadowed the modern age. This movement included two principal phases: the Protestant Revolution, which broke out in 1517 and resulted in the secession of most of northern Europe from the Roman faith; and the Catholic Reformation, which reached its height about 1560. Although the latter is not called a revolution, it really was

The later stages of the Renaissance accompanied by a religious revolution

such in nearly every sense of the term; for it effected a profound alteration of some of the notable features of late-medieval Catholicism.

In a number of ways the Renaissance and the Reformation were closely related. Both were products of the powerful current of individualism which gained momentum in the fourteenth and fifteenth centuries. Each had a similar background of economic causes in the growth of trade and in the rise of an urban society. Both partook of the character of a return to original sources: in the one case, to the literary and artistic achievements of the Greeks and Romans; in the other, to the Scriptures and the doctrines of the church fathers. But in spite of these important similarities, it is misleading to think of the Reformation as merely the religious aspect of the Renaissance. The guiding principles of the two movements had comparatively little in common. The essence of the Renaissance was devotion to the human and the natural, with religion relegated to a relatively subordinate place. The spirit of the Reformation was characterized by otherworldliness and contempt for the things of this life as inferior to the spiritual. In the mind of the humanist, man's nature was generally considered good; in the view of the Reformer it was unspeakably corrupt and depraved. The leaders of the Renaissance believed in urbanity and tolerance; the followers of Luther and Calvin emphasized faith and conformity. While both the Renaissance and the Reformation aimed at a recovery of the past, they were really oriented in different directions. The past the humanists strove to revive was Greek and Roman antiquity, though a few were concerned with the original Gospels as sources of an unspoiled religion. The Reformers, by contrast, were interested chiefly in a return to the teachings of St. Paul and St. Augustine. It goes without saying that the Renaissance, being an aristocratic movement, had less influence on the common man than did the Reformation.

For reasons such as these, it seems justifiable to conclude that the Reformation was not really a part of the Renaissance. In actual fact, it represented a much sharper break with the civilization of the Middle Ages than the movement led by the humanists ever did. The radical Reformers would have nothing to do with the basic theories and practices of thirteenth-century Christianity. Even the simple religion of love and selflessness for the betterment of the soul, as taught by St. Francis of Assisi, appeared to repel them almost as much as the mysteries of the sacramental dogma or the claims of Innocent III to spiritual and temporal power. In the main, the religious results of this clash with medieval Christianity have endured to this day. Moreover, the Reformation was intimately bound up with certain political trends which have persisted throughout the modern era. National consciousness, as we shall see, was one of the principal causes of the Protestant Revolution. While it is true that several of the humanists wrote under the influence of national pride, the majority were swayed by altogether different considerations. Many were scornful of politics, being interested solely in the individual; others, Erasmus among them, were thoroughly international in their outlook. But the Protestant Reformers could scarcely have gained much of a following if they had not associated their cause with the powerful groundswell of national resentment in northern Europe against an ecclesiastical system that had come to be recognized as largely Italian in character. For this reason, as well as for the reasons mentioned previously, it would seem warranted to regard the Reformation as one gateway to the modern world.

1. THE PROTESTANT REVOLUTION

The Protestant Revolution sprang from a multiplicity of causes, most of them closely related to the political and economic conditions of the age. Nothing could be more inaccurate than to think of the revolt against the Roman Church as exclusively a religious movement, though religious ideas occupied a prominent place in the minds of sixteenth-century Europeans. But without the basic political changes in northern Europe and the growth of new economic interests, Roman Catholicism would probably have undergone no more than a gradual evolution. Nevertheless, since religious causes were the most obvious ones, it will be appropriate to consider them first.

The multiplicity of causes of the Protestant Revolution

To the majority of Martin Luther's early followers the movement he launched was chiefly a rebellion against abuses in the Catholic Church. That such abuses existed no historian would deny. For example, many of the clergy at this time were poorly educated. Some, having obtained their positions through irregular means, were unable to understand the Latin of the Mass they were required to celebrate. Further, a considerable number of the clergy led extremely worldly lives. While some of the popes and bishops were living in princely magnificence, the lowly priests occasionally sought to eke out the incomes from their parishes by keeping taverns, gaming houses, or other establishments for profit. Not only did some monks habitually ignore their vows of chastity, but a few indifferent members of the secular clergy surmounted the hardships of the rule of celibacy by keeping mistresses. Pope Innocent VIII, who reigned about twenty-five years before the beginning of the Protestant Revolution, was known to have had eight illegitimate children, several born before his election to the papacy. There were numerous evils also in connection with the sale of religious offices and dispensations. As in the case of most civil positions, offices in the Church during the Renaissance period were commonly sold to the highest bidder. It is estimated that Pope Leo X enjoyed an income of more than a million dollars a year from the sale of more than two thousand ecclesiastical offices. This abuse was rendered more serious by the fact that the men who bought these positions were under a strong temptation to make

Religious causes: abuses in the Catholic Church

Pope Leo X. From an Italian miniature.

up for their investment by levying high fees for their services. The sale of dispensations was a second malodorous form of ecclesiastical graft. A dispensation may be defined as an exemption from a law of the Church or from some vow previously taken. On the eve of the Reformation the dispensations most commonly sold were exemptions from fasting and from the marriage laws of the Church. By way of illustration, first cousins would be permitted to marry for the payment of a fee of one ducat.

But the abuses which aroused the most outrage and brought pressure for reform were the sale of indulgences and the veneration of relics. An indulgence is a remission of all or of part of the temporal punishment due to sin—that is, of the punishment in this life and in purgatory. The theory upon which the indulgence rests is the famous doctrine of the Treasury of Merits developed by Scholastic theologians in the thirteenth century. According to this doctrine, Jesus and the saints, by reason of their "superfluous" virtues on earth, accumulated an excess of merit in heaven. This excess constitutes a treasure of grace upon which the pope can draw for the benefit of ordinary mortals. Originally, indulgences were not issued for payments of money, but only for works of charity, fasting, going on crusades, and the like. It was the Renaissance popes, with their insatiable desire for revenue, who first embarked upon the sale of indulgences as a profitable business. The methods they employed were far from scrupulous. The traffic in "pardons" was often turned over to bankers on a commission basis. As an example, the Fuggers in Augsburg had charge of the sale of indulgences for Leo X, with permission to pocket one-third of the proceeds. Naturally, only one motive dominated the business—to raise as much money as possible.

For centuries before the Reformation the veneration of sacred relics had been an important element in Catholic worship. It was believed that objects used by Christ or the Virgin, or the bodily remains of the saints possessed a miraculous healing and protective virtue for anyone who touched them or came into their presence. It was inevitable that this belief should open the way for innumerable frauds. Superstitious peasants could be easily convinced that almost any splinter of wood was a fragment of the true cross. And there was no dearth of relic-mongers quick to take advantage of such credulity. The results were fantastic. According to Erasmus, the churches of Europe contained enough wood of the true cross to build a ship. No fewer than five shinbones of the ass on which Jesus rode to Jerusalem were on exhibition in different places, to say nothing of twelve heads of John the Baptist. Martin Luther declared in a pamphlet lampooning his enemy, the archbishop of Mainz, that the latter claimed to possess "a whole pound of the wind that blew for Elijah in the cave on Mount Horeb and two feathers and an egg of the Holy Ghost."

Modern historians agree, however, that abuses in the Catholic

Church were not the primary religious cause of the Protestant Revolution. It was medieval Catholicism itself, not the abuses therein, to which the Reformers objected. Moreover, just before the revolt broke out, conditions had begun to improve. Many pious Catholics themselves had started an agitation for reform, which in time would probably have eliminated most of the glaring evils in the system. But as so often happens in the case of revolutions, the improvement came too late. Other forces more irresistible in character had been gradually gathering momentum. Conspicuous among these was the growing reaction against Scholastic theology, with its elaborate sacramental theory, its belief in the necessity of good works to supplement faith, and its doctrine of divine authority in the hands of the priests.

From preceding chapters the reader will recall that two different systems of theology had developed within the medieval Church. The first was formulated by St. Augustine around 400 A.D, on the basis of teachings in the Pauline Epistles. It was predicated on the assumption of an omnipotent God, who sees the whole drama of the universe in the twinkling of an eye. Not even a sparrow falls to the ground except in accordance with divine decree. Human nature is hopelessly depraved, and it is therefore as impossible for human beings to perform good works of their own volition as for thistles to bring forth figs. Only those mortals can be saved whom God for reasons of His own has predestined to inherit eternal life. Such in its barest outlines was the system of doctrine commonly known as Augustinianism. It was a theology well suited to the age of chaos which followed the breakup of the classical world. People in this time were prone to fatalism and otherworldliness, for they seemed to be at the mercy of forces beyond their control. But the doctrine continued to be taught throughout the Middle Ages, especially in parts of Germany, where the impact of high-medieval civilization was comparatively weak. To Luther and many of his followers it seemed the most logical interpretation of Christian belief.

The clash between two different systems of theology: the Augustinian system

With the growth of a more abundant life in southern and western Europe, it was natural that the pessimistic philosophy of Augustinianism should have been replaced by a system which would restore to humans some measure of pride in their own estate. The change was accelerated also by the growth of a dominant Church organization. The theology of Augustinianism, by placing human fate in the hands of God, had seemed to imply that the functions of an organized Church were comparatively unnecessary. Certainly no sinners could rely upon the ministrations of priests to improve their chances of salvation, since those who were to be saved had already been "elected" by God from all eternity. The new system of belief was finally crystallized in the Scholastic writings of Peter Lombard and St. Thomas Aquinas in the twelfth and thirteenth centuries. Its cardinal premise was the idea that humans had been endowed by God with freedom of

The late-medieval theology of Peter Lombard and St. Thomas Aquinas

will, with power to choose the good and avoid the evil. However, men could not make this choice entirely unaided, for without the support of heavenly grace they would be likely to fall into sin. It was therefore necessary for them to receive the sacraments, the indispensable means for communicating the grace of God to humanity. Of the seven sacraments of the Church, the three most important for the layperson were baptism, penance, and the Eucharist. The first wiped out the stain of previous sin; the second absolved the contrite sinner from guilt; the third was especially significant for its effect in renewing the saving grace of Christ's sacrifice on the cross. Except in emergencies, none of the sacraments could be administered by persons outside the ranks of the priesthood. The members of the clergy, having inherited this power from the Apostle Peter, alone had the authority to cooperate with God in forgiving sins and in performing the miracle of the Eucharist, whereby the bread and wine were transubstantiated into the body and blood of the Savior.

The Protestant Revolution a rebellion against the late-medieval system of theology

The Protestant Revolution was in large measure a rebellion against the second of these systems of theology. Although the doctrines of Peter Lombard and St. Thomas Aquinas had virtually become part of the theology of the Church, they had never been universally accepted. To some Christians who favored Augustinianism, they seemed to detract from the sovereignty of God and to contradict the plain teachings of Paul that human will is in bondage and human nature unspeakably vile. Worse still, in the opinion of these critics, was the fact that Scholastic theology greatly strengthened the authority of the priesthood. In sum, what the Reformers wanted was a return to a more primitive Christianity than that which had prevailed since the thirteenth century. Any doctrine or practice not expressly sanctioned in the Bible, especially in the Pauline Epistles, or not recognized by the fathers of the Church, they were strongly inclined to reject. It was for this reason that they condemned not only the theory of the priesthood and the sacramental system of the Church, but also such medieval additions to the faith as the veneration of the Virgin, the belief in purgatory, the invocation of saints, the cult of relics, and the rule of celibacy for the clergy. The Reformers were by no means rationalists: in fact, they were far more suspicious of reason than the Catholics. Their religious ideal rested upon the Augustinian dogmas of original sin, the total depravity of humanity, predestination, and the bondage of the will—all of which were far more difficult to justify by rationalism than the liberalized Scholastic teachings of St. Thomas Aquinas.

The political causes of the Protestant Revolution: the growth of national consciousness

As a political movement the Protestant Revolution was mainly the result of two developments: first, the growth of a national consciousness in northern Europe; and second, the rise of absolute monarchs. Ever since the late Middle Ages there had been a growing spirit of independence among many of the peoples outside of Italy. They had come to regard their own national life as unique and to resent interference from any external source. Although they were not nationalists in the modern sense, they tended to view the pope as a foreigner who had no right to meddle with local affairs in England, France, or Germany. This feeling was manifested in England as early as the middle of the fourteenth century, when the Statutes of Provisors and Praemunire were passed. The first prohibited appointments by the pope to Church offices in England; the second forbade the appeal of cases from the English courts to Rome. A law more extreme than either of these was issued by the king of France in 1438. The French law practically abolished all papal authority in the country, including the appointive authority and the right to raise revenue. To the civil magistrates was given the power to regulate religious affairs within their own districts. In Germany, despite the fact that there was no political unity, national feeling was by no means absent. It expressed itself in attacks upon the clergy by the Imperial Diet and in numerous decrees by the princes of separate states prohibiting ecclesiastical appointments and the sale of indulgences without their consent.

The growth of a national consciousness in all of these countries went hand in hand with the rise of absolute monarchs. Indeed, it would be difficult to say how much of the sense of nationality was spontaneous and how much of it was stimulated by ambitious rulers intent upon increasing their power. At any rate, it is certain that the claims of rulers to absolute authority were bound to result in defiance of Rome. No despot could be expected to tolerate long the exclusion of religion from his sphere of control. He could not *be* a despot so long as there was a double jurisdiction within his realm. The appetite of princes for control over the Church was whetted originally by the revival of the Roman law, with its doctrine that the people had delegated *all* of their power to the secular ruler. From this doctrine it was a comparatively easy step to the idea that all of the pope's authority could be properly assumed by the head of the state. But whatever the reasons for its growth, there can be no doubt that the ambition of secular princes to establish churches under their own control was a primary cause of the mounting antagonism toward Rome.

Historians disagree as to the importance of economic causation of the Protestant Revolution. Those who conceive of the movement as primarily a religious one think of the sixteenth century as a period of profound and agonized concern over spiritual problems. Such a condition may well have characterized the mass of the people. But it does not alter the fact that in the sixteenth century, as in all ages, there were ruling groups hungry for wealth and quite willing to use popular beliefs for their own advantage. Prominent among the economic objectives of such groups were acquisition of the wealth of the Church and elimination of papal taxation. In the course of its history the Church had grown into a vast economic empire. It was by far the largest landowner in western Europe, to say nothing of its enormous movable wealth in the form of rich furnishings, works of art, jewels, precious metals, and the like. Some of these possessions had been

The rise of absolute monarchs

Economic causes: the desire to confiscate the wealth of the Catholic Church

acquired by the Church through grants by kings, nobles, and other pious layfolk. Religious restrictions on taxation were also a galling grievance to secular rulers. Kings, eager for big armies and navies, had an urgent need for more revenue. But Catholic law prohibited the taxing of Church property. The exemption of episcopal and monastic property from taxation meant a heavier burden on the possessions of individual owners, especially on the property of merchants and bankers. Moreover, the lesser nobles in Germany were being threatened with extinction on account of the collapse of the manorial economy. Many of them looked with covetous eyes upon the lands of the Church. If only some excuse could be found for expropriating these, their difficult situation might be relieved.

Papal taxation, by the eve of the Protestant Revolution, had assumed a baffling variety of irritating forms. First came the *tithe,* which was supposed to be one-tenth of every Christian's income paid for the support of the parish church. Then there were innumerable fees paid into the papal treasury for indulgences, dispensations, appeals of judicial decisions, and so on. In a very real sense the moneys collected for the sale of Church offices and the *annates,* or commissions levied on the first year's income of every bishop and priest, were also forms of papal taxation, since the officials who paid them eventually reimbursed themselves through increased collections from the people. But the main objection to these taxes was not that they were so numerous and burdensome. The real basis of grievance against the papal levies was their effect in draining the northern countries of so much of their wealth for the enrichment of Italy. Economically, the situation was almost exactly the same as if the nations of northern Europe had been conquered by a foreign prince and tribute imposed upon them. Some Germans and Englishmen were scandalized also by the fact that most of the money collected was not being spent for religious purposes, but was being squandered by worldly popes to maintain luxurious courts. The reason for the resentment, however, was probably as much financial as moral.

Conflicts between merchant ambitions and the ascetic ideals of the Church

A third important economic cause of the Protestant Revolution was the conflict between the ambitions of the new merchant class and the ascetic ideals of medieval Christianity. Medieval Scholastic philosophers had argued that business for the sake of great profit is essentially immoral. No one has a right to any more than a reasonable wage for the service he renders to society. All wealth acquired in excess of this amount should be given to the Church to be distributed for the benefit of the needy. The merchant or craftsman who strives to get rich at the expense of the people is really no better than a common thief. To gain an advantage over a rival in business by cornering the market or beating down wages is contrary to all law and morality. Equally sinful is the practice of usury—the charging of interest on loans where no actual risk is involved. This is sheer robbery, the Scholastics argued, for it deprives the person who uses the money of earnings that are justly his; it is contrary to nature, for it enables the man who lends the money to live without labor.

While it is far from true that these doctrines were universally honored even by the Church itself, they nevertheless remained an integral part of the Catholic ideal, at least to the end of the Middle Ages. However, from the later Middle Ages onwards dynamic capitalism was beginning to supplant the old static economy of the medieval guilds. No longer were merchants and manufacturers content with a mere "wage" for the services they rendered to society. They demanded profits, and they could not see that it was any business of the Church to set limits on their earnings. Wages were fit only for hirelings, who had neither the wit nor the industry to go after the big rewards. In addition to all this, the growth of banking meant an even more violent conflict with the ascetic ideal of the Church. As long as the business of moneylending was in the hands of Jews and Muslims, it mattered little that usury should be branded as a sin. But now that Christians were piling up riches by financing the exploits of kings and merchants, the shoe was on another foot. The new crop of bankers resented being told that their lucrative trade in cash was contrary to the laws of God. This seemed to them an attempt of spokesmen for an outmoded past to dictate the standards for a new age of progress. But how was it that Italy did not break with the Catholic Church in view of the extensive development of banking and commerce in such cities as Florence, Genoa, Milan, and Venice? Perhaps one explanation is to be found in the fact that such business activities had taken earlier and deeper roots in Italy than in most parts of Germany. They had been established for so long a time that any possible conflict between them and religious ideals had been largely ignored. Besides, the religion of many Italians tended to approximate that of the ancient Romans; it was external and mechanical rather than profoundly spiritual. To many northern Europeans, by contrast, religion had a deeper significance. It was a system of dogmas and commandments to be observed literally under pain of the awful judgment of a wrathful God. They were, therefore, more likely to be disturbed by inconsistencies between worldly practices and the doctrines of the faith.

The full story of why the Protestant Revolution began in Germany is so complex that only a few of the possible reasons can be suggested as ideas for the student to consider. Was Germany relatively more backward than most other areas of western Europe? Had the Renaissance touched it so lightly that medieval religiosity remained quite pervasive? Or did economic factors operate more strongly in Germany than elsewhere? The Church in Germany held an enormous proportion of the best agricultural lands, and evidence exists that the country was seething with discontent on account of a too rapid transition from a static economy to an economy of profits and wages. It

Effects of the rise of competitive capitalism

Why the Protestant Revolution began in Germany

Martin Luther. A portrait by
Melchior Lorch.

*The doctrine of
justification by faith alone*

seems to be true, finally, that Germany was the victim of Catholic abuses to a greater extent than most other countries. How crucial was the shock resulting from these is impossible to say, but at least they provided the immediate impetus for the outbreak of the Lutheran revolt. Unlike England and France, Germany had no powerful king to defend its interests against the papacy. The country was weak and divided. At least partly for this reason, Pope Leo X selected German territory as the most likely field for the sale of indulgences.

I. THE LUTHERAN REVOLT IN GERMANY   By the dawn of the sixteenth century Germany was ripe for religious revolution. All that was necessary was to find a leader who could unite the dissatisfied elements and give a suitable theological gloss to their grievances. Such a leader was not long in appearing. His name was Martin Luther, and he was born in Thuringia in 1483. His parents were originally peasants, but his father had left the soil soon after his marriage to work in the mines of Mansfeld. Here he managed to become moderately prosperous and served in the village council. Nevertheless, young Martin's early environment was far from ideal. He was whipped at home for trivial offenses until he bled, and his mind was filled with hideous terrors of demons and witches. Some of these superstitions clung to him until the end of his life. His parents intended that he should become a lawyer, and with this end in view they placed him at the age of eighteen in the University of Erfurt. During his first four years at the university, Luther worked hard, gaining more than an ordinary reputation as a scholar. But in 1505, while returning from a visit to his home, he was overtaken by a violent storm and felled to the ground by a bolt of lightning. In terror lest an angry God strike him dead, he vowed to St. Anne to become a monk. Soon afterward he entered the Augustinian monastery at Erfurt.

Here he gave himself up to earnest reflection on the state of his soul. Obsessed with the idea that his sins were innumerable, he strove desperately to attain a goal of spiritual peace. He engaged in long vigils and went for days on end without a morsel of food. But the more he fasted and tortured himself, the more his anguish and depression increased. Told that the way of salvation lies in love of God, he was ready to give up in despair. How could he love a Being who is not even just, who saves only those whom it pleases Him to save? "Love Him?" he said to himself, "I do not love Him. I hate Him." But in time, as he pondered the Scriptures, especially the story of the Crucifixion, he gained a new insight into the mysteries of the Christian theology. He was profoundly impressed by the humiliation of the Savior's death on the cross. For the benefit of sinful humanity, the Christ, the God-man, had shared the fate of common criminals. Why had He done so except out of love for His creatures? The God of the storm whose chief attribute appeared to be anger had revealed Himself as a father who pities His children. Here was a miracle which no human

Luther Preaching. With one hand he points to popes, monks, and cardinals going into the mouth of hell. Hell is a beast with a snout, tusk, and eye. With the other hand Luther points to the crucifix. The Lord's Supper is being administered, both the bread and the wine, to the laity.

reason could understand. It must be taken on faith; and by faith alone, Luther concluded, can human beings be justified in the sight of God. This doctrine of justification by faith alone, as opposed to salvation by "good works," quickly became the central doctrine of the Lutheran theology.

But long before Luther had completed his theological system, he was called to lecture on Aristotle and the Bible at the University of Wittenberg, which had recently been founded by Frederick the Wise of Saxony. While serving in this capacity, he was confronted by an event which furnished the spark for the Protestant Revolution. In 1517 an unprincipled Dominican friar by the name of Tetzel appeared in Germany as a hawker of indulgences. Determined to raise as much money as possible for Pope Leo X and the archbishop of Mainz who had employed him, Tetzel deliberately represented the indulgences as tickets of admission to heaven. Though forbidden to enter Saxony, he came to the borders of that state, and many natives of Wittenberg rushed out to buy salvation at so attractive a price. Luther was appalled by such brazen deception of ignorant people. Accordingly, he drew up a set of ninety-five theses or statements attacking the sale of indulgences, and posted them, after the manner of the time, on the door of the castle church on October 31, 1517. Later he had them printed and sent to his friends in a number of cities. Soon it became evident that the Ninety-five Theses had voiced the sentiments of a nation. All over Germany, Luther was hailed as a leader whom God had raised to break the power of an arrogant and hypocritical clergy. A violent reaction against the sale of indulgences was soon in full swing. Tetzel was mobbed and driven from the country. The revolt against Rome had begun.

With the revenue from indulgences cut off, it was inevitable that the pope should take action. Early in 1518 he commanded the general of the Augustinian order to make the rebellious friar recant. Luther not

Luther's revolt against the sale of indulgences

only refused, but published a sermon stating his views more strongly than ever. Forced by his critics to answer questions on many points other than indulgences, he gradually came to realize that his own religion was utterly irreconcilable with that of the Roman Church. There was no alternative except to break with the Catholic faith entirely. In 1520 his teachings were formally condemned in a bull promulgated by Leo X, and he was ordered to recant within sixty days or be dealt with as a heretic. Luther replied by publicly burning the pope's proclamation. For this he was excommunicated and ordered to be turned over to the secular arm for punishment. Germany at this time was still technically under the rule of the Holy Roman Empire. Charles V, who had recently been elevated to the throne of this ramshackle government, was anxious to be rid of the insolent rebel at once, but he dared not act without the approval of the Imperial Diet. Accordingly, in 1521, Luther was summoned to appear before a meeting of this body at Worms. Since many of the princes who composed the Diet were themselves hostile toward the Church, nothing in particular was done, despite Luther's refusal to retract anything he had said. Finally, after a number of the members had gone home, the emperor forced through an edict branding the obstreperous friar as an outlaw. But Luther had already been hidden away in the castle of his friend, Frederick of Saxony. Here he remained until all danger of arrest by the emperor's soldiers had passed. Charles soon afterward withdrew to conduct his war with France, and the Edict of Worms was never enforced.

Thenceforth until his death in 1546 Luther was occupied with his work of building an independent German Church. Despite the fundamental conflict between his own beliefs and Catholic theology, he nevertheless retained a good many of the elements of the Roman system. With the passing of the years he became more conservative than many of his own followers. Though he had originally denounced transubstantiation, he eventually came around to adopting a doctrine which bore at least a superficial resemblance to the Catholic theory. He denied, however, that any change in the substance of the bread and wine occurs as the result of a priestly miracle. The function of the clergyman is simply to *reveal* the presence of God in the bread and wine. Still, the changes he made were drastic enough to preserve the revolutionary character of the new religion. He substituted German for Latin in the services of the Church. He rejected the entire ecclesiastical system of pope, archbishops, bishops, and priests as custodians of the keys to the kingdom of heaven. By abolishing monasticism and insisting upon the right of priests to marry, he went far toward destroying the barrier which had separated clergy from laity and given the former their special status as representatives of God on earth. He recognized only baptism and the Eucharist as sacraments, and he denied that even these had any supernatural effect in bringing down

The Pope as Antichrist. Belching forth toads and scorpions, the beast-man spreads fire and destruction. This drawing by Melchior Lorch is dedicated to Martin Luther and dated 1545.

grace from heaven. Since he continued to emphasize faith rather than good works as the road to salvation, he naturally discarded such formalized practices as fasts, pilgrimages, the veneration of relics, and the invocation of saints. On the other hand, the doctrines of predestination and the supreme authority of the Scriptures were given in the new religion a higher place than they had ever enjoyed in the old. Last of all, Luther abandoned the Catholic idea that the Church should be supreme over the state. Instead of having bishops subject to the pope as the Vicar of Christ, he organized his church under superintendents who were essentially agents of the government.

Of course, Luther was not alone responsible for the success of the Protestant Revolution. The overthrow of Catholicism in Germany was also abetted by the outbreak of social revolt. In 1522–1523 there occurred a ferocious rebellion of the knights. These petty nobles were being impoverished by competition from the great estates and by the change to a capitalist economy. They saw as the chief cause of their misery the concentration of landed wealth in the hands of more powerful princes and the Church. Obsessed with national sentiments, they dreamed of a united Germany free from the domination of powerful landlords and grasping priests. The leaders of the movement were Ulrich von Hutten, who had turned from a humanist into a fierce partisan of Luther, and Franz von Sickingen, a notorious robber baron and soldier of fortune. To these men the gospel of Luther seemed to provide an excellent program for a war on behalf of German liberty. Although their rebellion was speedily crushed by the armies of the archbishops and richer nobles, it had considerable effect in persuading the pillars of the old regime that too much resistance to the Lutheran movement would scarcely be wise.

The revolt of the knights was followed by a much more violent uprising of the lower classes in 1524–1525. Though most who took part were peasants, a great many poor workers from the cities were attracted to the movement also. The causes of this second rebellion were somewhat similar to those of the first: the rising cost of living, the concentration of holdings of land, and the religious radicalism inspired by Luther's teachings. But the peasants and urban workers were stirred to action by many other factors as well. The decay of the regime had eliminated the paternal relationship between noble and serf. In its place had grown up a mere cash nexus between employer and worker. The sole obligation now of the upper classes was to pay a wage. When sickness or unemployment struck, laborers had to make do with their slender resources as best they could. Furthermore, most of the old privileges which the serf had enjoyed on the manorial estate, of pasturing flocks on the common lands and gathering wood in the forest, were being rapidly abolished. To make matters worse, landlords were attempting to meet advancing prices by exacting higher rents from the peasants. Finally, the lower classes were angered by the

Founding the Lutheran church; Luther's doctrines

The outbreak of social revolution; the revolt of the knights

The uprising of the lower classes

Pages from a Bible Translated by Martin Luther, 1534. Left: The title page. Right: An illustration showing several episodes from the story of Jonah in a single composite picture.

fact that the revival of Roman law had the effect of bolstering property rights and of strengthening the power of the state to protect the interests of the rich.

Outcome of the Peasants' Revolt

The Peasants' Revolt of 1524–1525 began in southern Germany and spread rapidly to the north, until large parts of the country were involved. At first it was more like a strike than an insurrection. The rebels contented themselves with drafting petitions and attempting peaceably to persuade their masters to grant them relief from oppression. But before many months had passed the movement came under the influence of such radical leaders as Thomas Münzer (c. 1490–1525), who urged the use of fire and sword against the wicked nobles and clergy. In the spring of 1525 the peasants began plundering and burning cloisters and castles and even murdering some of their more hated opponents. The nobles now turned against them with fiendish fury, slaughtering indiscriminately both those who resisted and those who were helpless. In this they were encouraged by none other than Martin Luther himself. Because Luther had become a staunch ally of the German princes and was a thoroughgoing opponent of social reform, he wrote a violent pamphlet, *Against the Thievish, Murderous Hordes of Peasants,* in which he urged everyone who could to hunt the rebels down like mad dogs, to "strike, strangle, stab secretly or in public, and remember that nothing can be more poisonous, harmful, or devilish than a man in rebellion." The firm alliance of Lutheranism with the powers of the state thereafter helped insure social peace. In fact, after the bloody punishment of the peasant rebels there was never again to be a mass lower-class uprising in all of German history.

II. THE ANABAPTIST MOVEMENT   Shortly after the failure of the Peasants' Revolt a group of radical reformers who were dissatisfied with Luther's growing conservatism, but who did not wish to take up the sword, began to coalesce into the loosely organized movement called Anabaptism. The name means "re-baptism" and was derived from the fact that the Anabaptists held infant baptism to be ineffectual and insisted that the rite should be administered only when the individual had reached the age of reason. But a belief in adult baptism was not really their principal doctrine. The Anabaptists were extreme individualists in religion. Luther's teaching that all have a right to follow the dictates of their own conscience the Anabaptists took exactly as it stood. Not only did they reject the Catholic theory of the priesthood, but they denied the necessity of any clergy at all, maintaining that every individual should follow the guidance of the "inner light." They refused to agree that God's revelation to humanity had ceased with the writing of the last book of the New Testament, but insisted that He continues to speak directly to certain of His chosen followers. They attached much importance to literal interpretation of the Bible, even of its most occult portions. They believed that the Church should be a community of saints and required of their followers abstention from lying, profanity, gluttony, lewdness, and drinking intoxicating liquors. Many of the members looked forward to the early destruction of this world and the establishment of Christ's kingdom of justice and peace, in which they would have a prominent place. But the Anabaptists were not merely a group of religious extremists; they represented as well the most radical social tendencies of their time. Though it is certainly an exaggeration to call them communists, they did denounce the accumulation of wealth and taught that it was the duty of Christians to share their goods with one another. In addition, they declined to recognize any distinctions of rank or class, declaring everyone equal in the sight of God. Many also abominated the taking of oaths, condemned military service, and refused to pay taxes to governments that engaged in war. They abstained in general from political life and demanded the complete separation of Church and State. Their doc-

The nature of Anabaptism

The Siege of Münster in 1534

trines represented the extreme manifestation of the revolutionary fervor generated by the Protestant movement.

Unhappily for the fortunes of Anabaptism, a highly unrepresentative group of Anabaptist extremists managed to gain control of the city of Münster in northwestern Germany in 1534. Some of their fellow extremists from surrounding areas came pouring in, and Münster became a new Jerusalem where all of the vagaries of the lunatic fringe of the movement were put into practice. The property of unbelievers was confiscated and polygamy was introduced. A former tailor named John of Leyden assumed the title of king, proclaiming himself the successor of David, with a mission to conquer the world and destroy the heathen. But after a little more than a year Münster was recaptured by Catholic forces and the leaders of Zion were put to death by horrible tortures. As a result of this episode, Anabaptism was thoroughly discredited and all of its adherents were subjected to ruthless persecution throughout Germany and wherever else they could be found. Among the very few who survived were some who banded together in the Mennonite sect, named for its founder, the Dutchman Menno Simons (1492–1559). This sect, dedicated to the pacifism and simple "religion of the heart" of original Anabaptism has continued to exist until the present. Various Anabaptist tenets were also revived later by religious groups such as the Quakers and different Baptist and Pentecostal sects.

III. THE ZWINGLIAN AND CALVINIST REVOLTS IN SWITZERLAND The special form of Protestantism developed by Luther did not prove to be particularly popular beyond its native environment. Even in Germany it by no means triumphed everywhere (most of southern Germany remained Catholic), and outside of Germany Lutheranism became the official religion only in Denmark, Norway, and Sweden. But the force of the Protestant revolt made itself felt in a number of other lands. Such was especially the case in Switzerland, where national consciousness had been gathering strength for centuries. At the close of the Middle Ages the shepherds and peasants of the Swiss cantons had challenged the right of the Austrians to rule over them, and finally in 1499 had compelled the Emperor Maximilian to recognize their independence, not only of the house of Hapsburg but of the Holy Roman Empire as well. Having thrown off the yoke of a foreign emperor, the Swiss were not likely to submit indefinitely to an alien pope. Moreover, the cities of Zürich, Basel, Berne, and Geneva had grown into flourishing centers of trade. Their populations were dominated by prosperous merchants who were becoming increasingly contemptuous of the Catholic ideal of glorified poverty. Here also northern humanism had found acceptance in cultivated minds, with the effect of creating a healthy distrust of priestly superstitions. Erasmus had lived for a number of years in Basel. Lastly, Switzerland had been exploited by the indulgence peddlers to an extent only less grievous than that in Germany.

The father of the Protestant Revolution in Switzerland was Ulrich Zwingli (1484–1531). Only a few weeks younger than Luther, he was the son of a well-to-do magistrate, who was able to provide him with an excellent education. As a student he devoted nearly all of his time to philosophy and literature, with no interest in religion save in the practical reforms of the Christian humanists. Although he took holy orders at the age of twenty-two, his purpose in entering the priesthood was mainly the opportunity it would give him to cultivate his literary tastes. Ultimately, he turned his interest to religion and devoted his energies to reform of the Church. He accepted nearly all of the teachings of Luther except that he regarded the bread and wine as mere symbols of the body and blood, and he reduced the sacrament of Holy Communion to a simple memorial service. So ably did he marshal the anti-Catholic forces that by 1528 nearly all of northern Switzerland had deserted the ancient faith.

From the northern cantons the Protestant Revolution in Switzerland spread to Geneva. This city, located on a lake of the same name near the French border, had the doubtful advantage of a double government. The people owed allegiance to two suzerains, the local bishop and the count of Savoy. When these high-born chieftains conspired to make their power more absolute, the citizens rebelled against them. The result was their expulsion from the town about 1530 and the establishment of a free republic. But the movement could hardly have been successful without some aid from the northern cantons. Thus, it was not long until Protestant preachers from Zürich and Berne began arriving in Geneva.

Causes of the Protestant Revolution in Switzerland

Zwingli

Ulrich Zwingli. A sixteenth-century woodcut.

John Calvin. This woodcut shows the stern reformer in old age.

It was soon after these events that John Calvin (1509–1564) arrived in Geneva. Although destined to play so prominent a role in the history of Switzerland, he was not a native of that country but of France. He was born at Noyon in Picardy. His mother died when he was very young, and his father, who did not like children, turned him over to the care of an aristocratic friend. For his higher education Calvin was sent to the University of Paris, where, because of his bilious disposition and fault-finding manner, he was dubbed "the accusative case." Later, he shifted at his father's wish to study of law at Orléans. Here he came under the influence of disciples of Luther, evidently to a sufficient extent to cause him to be suspected of heresy. Consequently, in 1534 Calvin fled to Switzerland. He settled for a time in Basel and then moved on to Geneva, which was still in the throes of political revolution. He began preaching and organizing at once, and by 1541 both government and religion had fallen completely under his sway. Until his death in 1564 he ruled the city with a rod of iron. History contains few examples of men more dour in temperament and more stubbornly convinced of the rightness of their own ideas.

Calvin's rule at Geneva

Under Calvin's rule Geneva was transformed into a religious oligarchy. The supreme authority was vested in the Congregation of the Clergy, who prepared all legislation and submitted it to the Consistory to be ratified. The latter body, composed, in addition to the clergy, of twelve elders representing the people, had as its principal function the supervision of public and private morals. This function was carried out, not merely by the punishment of antisocial conduct but by a persistent snooping into the private life of every individual. The city was divided into districts, and a committee of the Consistory visited each household without warning to conduct an inquisition into the habits of its members. Even the mildest forms of self-indulgence were strictly prohibited. Dancing, card-playing, attending the theater, working or playing on the Sabbath—all were outlawed as works of the Devil. Innkeepers were forbidden to allow anyone to consume food or drink without first saying grace, or to permit any patron to sit up after nine o'clock unless he was spying on the conduct of others. Needless to say, penalties were severe. Not only were murder and treason classified as capital crimes, but also adultery, witchcraft, blasphemy, and heresy; and the last of these especially was susceptible to a broad interpretation. During the first four years after Calvin became ruler of Geneva, there were no fewer than 58 executions out of a total population of only 16,000.

Calvin's theology

The essentials of Calvin's theology are contained in his *Institutes of the Christian Religion,* which was originally published in 1536 and revised and enlarged several times thereafter. His ideas resemble those of St. Augustine more than any other theologian. He conceived of the universe as utterly dependent upon the will of an Almighty God, who created all things for his greater glory. Because of the original fall from grace all human beings are sinners by nature, bound hand and foot to an evil inheritance they cannot escape. Nevertheless, God for reasons of His own has predestined some for eternal salvation and damned all the rest to the torments of hell. Nothing that human beings may do can alter their fate; their souls are stamped with God's blessing or curse before they are born. But this did not mean, in Calvin's opinion, that Christians could be indifferent to their conduct on earth. If they were among the elect, God would have implanted in them the desire to live right. Upright conduct is a sign, though not an infallible one, that whoever practices it has been chosen to sit at the throne of glory. Public profession of faith and participation in the sacraments are also presumptive evidences of election to be saved. But most of all, the Calvinists required an active life of piety and good morality as a solemn obligation resting upon members of the Christian commonwealth. Like the ancient Hebrews, they conceived of themselves as chosen instruments of God with a mission to help in the fulfillment of His purposes on earth. Their duty was not to strive for their souls' salvation but for the glory of God. Thus it will be seen that the Calvinist system did not encourage its followers to sit with folded hands, serene in the knowledge that their fate was sealed. No religion has fostered a more abundant zeal in the conquest of nature, in missionary activity, or in the struggle against political tyranny. Doubtless the reason lies in the Calvinist's belief that as the chosen instrument of God he must play a part in the drama of the universe worthy of his exalted status. And with the Lord on his side he was not easily frightened by whatever lions lurked in his path.

The religion of Calvin differed from that of Luther in a number of ways. First, it was more legalistic. Whereas the Wittenberg Reformer had emphasized the guidance of individual conscience, the dictator of Geneva stressed the sovereignty of law. He thought of God as a mighty legislator who had handed down a body of rules in the Scriptures which must be followed to the letter. Secondly, the religion of Calvin was more nearly an Old Testament faith than that of Luther. This can be illustrated in the attitude of the two men toward Sabbath observance. Luther's conception of Sunday was similar to that which prevails in modern continental Europe. He insisted, of course, that his followers should attend church, but he did not demand that during the remainder of the day they should refrain from all pleasure or work. Calvin, on the other hand, revived the Jewish Sabbath with its strict taboos against anything faintly resembling worldliness. In the third place, the religion of Geneva was more closely associated with the ideals of the new capitalism. Luther's sympathies lay with the princes, and on at least one occasion he sharply censured the tycoons of finance for their greed. Calvin sanctified the ventures of the trader and the moneylender and gave an exalted place in his ethical system to the business virtues of thrift and diligence. Finally, Calvinism as com-

The religion of Calvin compared with that of Luther

pared to Lutheranism represented a more radical phase of the Protestant Revolution. As we have seen, the Wittenberg friar retained a good many features of Roman worship and even some Catholic dogmas. Calvin rejected everything he could think of that smacked of "popery." The organization of his church was constructed in such a way as to exclude all traces of the episcopal system. Congregations were to choose their own elders and preachers, while an association of ministers at the top would govern the entire church. Ritual, instrumental music, stained-glass windows, pictures, and images were ruthlessly eliminated, with the consequence that the religion was reduced to "four bare walls and a sermon." Even the observance of Christmas and Easter was sternly prohibited.

The spread of Calvinism

The popularity of Calvinism was not limited to Switzerland. It spread into most countries of western Europe where trade and finance had become leading pursuits. The Huguenots of France, the Puritans of England, the Presbyterians of Scotland, and the members of the Reformed Church in Holland were all Calvinists. It was preeminently the religion of city people; though, of course, it drew converts from other strata as well. Its influence in molding the ethics of modern times was enormous. Members of this faith had much to do with the initial revolts against despotism in England and France, as well as in overthrowing Spanish tyranny in the Netherlands.

IV. THE PROTESTANT REVOLUTION IN ENGLAND   The original blow against the Roman Church in England was not struck by a religious enthusiast like Luther or Calvin but by the head of the government. This does not mean, however, that the English Reformation was ex-

Contrast between Catholic and Protestant Churches. At the left is a Catholic church, showing the profusion of religious ceremonies, church adornments, and ecclesiastical vestments. At the right is a "reformed" Protestant church where most people are listening to a sermon in surroundings of stark simplicity.

clusively a political movement. Henry VIII could not have succeeded in establishing an independent English Church if such action had not had the endorsement of large numbers of his subjects. And there were plenty of reasons why this endorsement was readily given. Though the English had freed themselves in some measure from papal domination, national pride had reached such a point that any degree of subordination to Rome was resented. Besides, England had been the scene for some time of lively agitation for religious reform. The memory of Wyclif's scathing attacks upon the avarice of the priests, the temporal power of popes and bishops, and the sacramental system of the Church had lingered since the fourteenth century. The influence of the Christian humanists, notably Thomas More, in condemning the superstitions in Catholic worship, had also been a factor of considerable importance. Finally, soon after the outbreak of the Protestant Revolution in Germany, Lutheran ideas were brought into England by wandering preachers and through the circulation of printed tracts. As a result, the English monarch, in severing the ties with Rome, had no lack of sympathy from some of the most influential of his subjects.

The clash with the pope was precipitated by Henry VIII's domestic difficulties. For eighteen years he had been married to Catherine of Aragon and had only a sickly daughter, the future Queen Mary, to succeed him. The death of all the sons of this marriage in infancy was a grievous disappointment to the king, who desired a male heir to perpetuate the Tudor dynasty. But this was not all, for Henry had become deeply infatuated with the dark-eyed lady-in-waiting, Anne Boleyn, and was determined to make her his queen. He therefore appealed in 1527 to Pope Clement VII for an annulment of the marriage to Catherine. The law of the Church did not sanction divorce, but it did provide that a marriage could be annulled if proof could be presented that conditions existing at the time of the marriage made it unlawful. Queen Catherine had previously been married to Henry's older brother, Arthur, who had died a few months after the ceremony was performed. Recalling this fact, Henry's lawyers found a passage in the Book of Leviticus which pronounced a curse of childlessness upon the man who should marry his deceased brother's wife. The pope was in a difficult position. If he rejected the king's appeal, England would probably be lost to the Catholic faith, for Henry was apparently firmly convinced that the Scriptural curse had blighted his chances of perpetuating his dynasty. On the other hand, if the pope granted the annulment he would provoke the wrath of the Emperor Charles V, a nephew of Catherine. Charles had already invaded Italy and was threatening the pope with a loss of his temporal power. There seemed nothing for Clement to do but to procrastinate. At first he made a pretense of having the question settled in England, and empowered his own legate and Cardinal Wolsey to hold a court of inquiry to determine whether the marriage to Catherine had been legal.

Underlying causes of the Protestant Revolution in England

Henry VIII. Portrait by Hans Holbein.

Proclamation of the Anglican Church as an independent national unit

After long delay the case was suddenly transferred to Rome. Henry lost patience and resolved to take matters into his own hands. In 1531 he convoked an assembly of the clergy and, by threatening to punish them for violating the Statute of Praemunire in submitting to the papal legate, he induced them to recognize himself as the head of the English Church, "as far as the law of Christ allows." Next he persuaded Parliament to enact a series of laws abolishing all payments of revenue to the pope and proclaiming the Anglican Church an independent, national unit, subject to the exclusive authority of the king. By 1534 the last of the bonds uniting the English church to Rome had been cut.

Activities of the radical Protestants

But the enactments put through by Henry VIII did not really make England a Protestant country. Though the abolition of papal authority was followed by the dissolution of the monasteries and confiscation of their wealth, the Church remained Catholic in doctrine. The Six Articles, adopted by Parliament at the king's behest in 1539, left no room for doubt as to official orthodoxy. Auricular confession, Masses for the dead, and clerical celibacy were all confirmed; death by burning was made the penalty for denying the Catholic dogma of the Eucharist. Yet the influence of a minority of Protestants at this time cannot be ignored. Their numbers were steadily increasing, and during the reign of Henry's successor, Edward VI (1547–1553), they actually gained the ascendancy. Since the new king was only nine years old when he inherited the crown, it was inevitable that the policies of the government should be dictated by powers behind the throne. The men most active in this work were Thomas Cranmer, archbishop of Canterbury, and the dukes of Somerset and Northumberland, who successively dominated the council of regency. All three of these officials had strong Protestant leanings. As a result, the creeds and ceremonies of the Church of England were given some drastic revision. Priests were permitted to marry; English was substituted for Latin in the services; the use of images was abolished; and new articles of belief were drawn up repudiating all sacraments except baptism and communion and affirming the Lutheran dogma of justification by faith alone. When the youthful Edward died in 1553, it looked as if England had definitely entered the Protestant camp.

The Catholic reaction under Mary

Surface appearances, however, are frequently deceiving. They were never more so than in England at the end of Edward's reign. The majority of the people had refused to be weaned away from the usages of their ancient faith, and a reaction had set in against the high-handed methods of the radical Protestants. Moreover, the English during the time of the Tudors had grown accustomed to obeying the will of their sovereign. It was an attitude fostered by national pride and the desire for order and prosperity. The successor of Edward VI was Mary (1553–1558), the forlorn and pious daughter of Henry VIII and Catherine. It was inevitable that Mary should have been a Catholic, and that she should have abhorred the revolt against Rome, for the origin of the movement was painfully associated with her mother's sufferings. Consequently, it is not strange that upon coming to the throne she should have attempted to turn the clock back. Not only did she restore the celebration of the Mass and the rule of clerical celibacy, but she prevailed upon Parliament to vote the unconditional return of England to papal allegiance. But her policies ended in lamentable failure for several reasons. First of all, she fell into the same error as her predecessors in forcing through changes that were too radical for the temper of the times. The people of England were not ready for a Lutheran or Calvinist revolution, but neither were they in a mood to accept immediate subjection to Rome. Probably a more serious cause of her failure was her marriage to Philip, the ambitious heir to the Spanish throne. Her subjects feared that this union might lead to unfortunate foreign complications, if not actual annexation by Spain. When the queen allowed herself to be drawn into a war with France, in which England was compelled to surrender Calais, its last foothold on the Continent, the nation was almost ready for rebellion. Death ended Mary's inglorious reign in 1558.

The question whether England was to be Catholic or Protestant was left to be settled by Mary's successor, her half-sister Elizabeth (1558–1603), daughter of Anne Boleyn. Though reared as a Protestant, Elizabeth had no deep religious convictions. Her primary interest was statecraft, and she did not intend that her kingdom should be rent in twain by sectarian strife. Therefore, she decided upon a policy of moderation, refusing to ally herself with either the extreme Catholics or the fanatical Protestants. So carefully did she hew to this line that for some years she deceived the pope into thinking that she might turn Catholic. Nevertheless, she was enough of a nationalist to refuse even to consider a revival of allegiance to Rome. One of the first things she did after becoming queen was to order the passage of a new Act of Supremacy, declaring the English sovereign to be the "supreme governor" of the independent Anglican church. The final settlement, completed about 1570, was a typical English compromise. The church was made Protestant, but certain articles of the creed were left vague enough so that former Catholics might accept them without too much shock to their conscience. Moreover, the episcopal form of organization and much of the Catholic ritual was retained. Long after Elizabeth's death this settlement remained in effect. Indeed, most elements in it have survived to this day. And it is a significant fact that the modern Church of England is broad enough to include within its ranks such diverse factions as the Anglo–Catholics, who differ from Roman Catholics only in rejecting papal supremacy, and the "low-church" Anglicans, who are as radical in their Protestantism as the Lutherans.

The Elizabethan compromise

2. THE CATHOLIC REFORMATION

As noted at the beginning of this chapter, the Protestant Revolution was only one of the phases of the great movement known as the Reformation. The other was the Catholic Reformation, or the Counter-Reformation as it used to be called, on the assumption that the primary purpose of its leaders was to cleanse the Catholic Church in order to check the growth of Protestantism. Modern historians have shown, however, that the beginnings of the movement for Catholic reform were entirely independent of the Protestant revolt. In Spain, during the closing years of the fifteenth century, a religious revival inaugurated by Cardinal Ximenes, with the approval of the monarchy, stirred that country to the depths. Schools were established, abuses were eliminated from the monasteries, and priests were goaded into accepting their responsibilities as shepherds of their flocks. Though the movement was launched primarily for the purpose of strengthening the Church in the war against heretics, Jews, and Muslims, it nevertheless had considerable effect in regenerating the spiritual life of the nation. In Italy also, since the beginning of the sixteenth century, a number of earnest clerics had been laboring to make the priests of their Church more worthy of their calling. The task was a difficult one on account of the entrenchment of abuses and the example of profligacy set by the papal court. In spite of these obstacles the movement did lead to the founding of several religious orders dedicated to high ideals of piety and social service.

But the fires of Catholic reform burned rather low until after the Protestant Revolution began to make serious inroads. Not until it appeared that the whole German nation was likely to be swept into the Lutheran orbit did any of the popes become seriously concerned about the need for reform. The first to attempt a purification of the Church was Adrian VI, of Utrecht, the only non-Italian to be elected to the papal throne in nearly a century and a half, and the last until 1978. But his reign of only twenty months was too short to enable him to accomplish much, and in 1523 he was succeeded by a Medici (Clement VII), who ruled for eleven years. The campaign against abuses in the Church was not renewed until the reign of Paul III (1534–1549). He and three of his successors, Paul IV (1555–1559), Pius V (1566–1572), and Sixtus V (1585–1590), were the most zealous crusaders for reform who had presided over the Vatican since the days of Gregory VII. They reorganized the papal finances, filled the Church offices with priests renowned for austerity, and dealt drastically with those clerics who persisted in idleness and vice. It was under these popes that the Catholic Reformation reached its height.

These direct activities of the popes were supplemented by the decrees of a Church council convoked in 1545 by Paul III, which met in the Italian city of Trent at intervals between 1545 and 1563. This council was one of the most important in the history of the Church. The main purpose for which it had been summoned was to redefine the doctrines of the Catholic faith, and several of the steps in this direction were highly significant. Without exception, the dogmas challenged by the Protestant Reformers were reaffirmed. Good works were held to be as necessary for salvation as faith. The theory of the sacraments as indispensable means of grace was upheld. Likewise, transubstantiation, the apostolic succession of the priesthood, the belief in purgatory, the invocation of saints, and the rule of celibacy for the clergy were all confirmed as essential elements in the Catholic system. On the much-debated question as to the proper source of Christian belief, the Bible and the traditions of apostolic teaching were held to be of equal authority. Not only was papal supremacy over every bishop and priest expressly maintained, but there was more than a faint suggestion that the authority of the pope transcended that of the Church council itself. Thus the monarchical government of the Church was strongly reaffirmed. The Council of Trent also reaffirmed the doctrine of indulgences which had touched off the Lutheran revolt, although it did condemn the worst scandals connected with the selling of indulgences.

The legislation of Trent was not confined to matters of dogma, but also included provisions for the elimination of abuses and for reinforcing the discipline of the Church over its members. Bishops and priests were forbidden to hold more than one benefice, so that none could grow rich from a plurality of incomes. To eliminate the evil of an ignorant priesthood it was provided that a theological seminary must be established in every diocese. Toward the end of its deliberations the council decided upon a censorship of books to prevent heretical ideas from corrupting the minds of those who still remained in the faith. A commission was appointed to draw up an index or list of writings which ought not to be read. The publication of this list by the pope in 1564 resulted in the formal establishment of the Index of Prohibited Books as a part of the machinery of the Church. Later, a permanent agency known as the Congregation of the Index was set up to revise the list from time to time. Altogether more than forty such revisions have been made. The majority of the books condemned have been theological treatises, and probably the effect in retarding the progress of learning has been slight. Nonetheless, the establishment of the index must be taken as a symptom of the intolerance which had come to infect both Catholics and Protestants.

The Catholic Reformation would never have been as thorough or as successful as it was had it not been for the activities of the Jesuits, or members of the Society of Jesus. They did most of the rough political work in the Council of Trent, which enabled the popes to dominate that body in its later and more important sessions. The Jesuits also were largely responsible for winning areas that had fallen to Protestantism, such as Poland and parts of southern Germany, back into the

The Council of Trent

Reforms of the Council of Trent

Ignatius Loyola. Engraving by Lucas Vorstiman, 1621.

*The founding of the
Society of Jesus by
Loyola*

Catholic fold. The founder of the Society of Jesus was Ignatius Loyola (1491–1556), a Spanish nobleman from the Basque country. His early career seems not to have been particularly different from that of other Spaniards of his class—a life of philandering and marauding as a soldier of the king. But about the time the Protestant Revolution was getting well under way in Germany, he was painfully wounded in a battle with the French. While waiting for his injuries to heal, he read a pious biography of Jesus and some legends of the saints which profoundly changed his emotional nature. Overwhelmed by a consciousness of his wasted life, he determined to become a soldier of Christ. After a period of morbid self-tortures, in which he saw visions of Satan, Jesus, and the Trinity, he went to the University of Paris to learn more about the faith he intended to serve. Here he gathered around him a small group of devoted disciples, with whose aid in 1534 he founded the Society of Jesus. The members took monastic vows and pledged themselves to go on a pilgrimage to Jerusalem. In 1540 their organization was approved by Pope Paul III. From then on it grew rapidly. When Loyola died it already boasted no fewer than 1,500 members.

The Society of Jesus was by far the most militant of the religious orders fostered by the spiritual zeal of the sixteenth century. It was not merely a monastic society but a company of soldiers sworn to defend the faith. Their weapons were not to be bullets and spears but eloquence, persuasion, instruction in the right doctrines, and if necessary more worldly methods of exerting influence. The organization was patterned after that of a military company, with a general as commander-in-chief and an iron discipline enforced on the members. All individuality was suppressed, and a soldierlike obedience to the general was exacted of the rank and file. Only the highest of the four classes of members had any share in the government of the order. This little group, known as the Professed of the Four Vows, elected the general for life and consulted with him on important matters. They were also bound to implicit obedience.

As suggested already, the activities of the Jesuits were numerous and varied. First and foremost, they conceived of themselves as the defenders of true religion. For this object they obtained authority from the pope to hear confessions and grant absolution. Many of them became priests in order to gain access to the pulpit and expound the truth as the oracles of God. Still others served as agents of the Inquisition in the relentless war against heresy. In all of this work they followed the leadership of the Church as their infallible guide. They raised no questions and attempted to solve no mysteries. Loyola taught that if the Church ruled that white was black, it would be the duty of its followers to believe it. But the Jesuits were not satisfied merely to hold the field against the attacks of Protestants and heretics; they were anxious to propagate the faith in the farthest corners of the earth—to make Catholics out of Buddhists, Muslims, the Parsees of

India, and the indigenous peoples of the newly discovered continents. Long before the Reformation had ended, there were Jesuit missionaries in Africa, in Japan and China, and in North and South America. Yet another important activity of Loyola's soldiers was education. They founded colleges and seminaries by the hundreds in Europe and America and obtained positions in other institutions as well. Until the eighteenth century the society had a monopoly of education in Spain and a near-monopoly in France. That the Catholic Church recovered so much of its strength in spite of the Protestant secession was due in large measure to the manifold and aggressive activities of the Jesuits.

3. THE REFORMATION HERITAGE

The most immediate effects of the Reformation were a sharp rise in religious persecution and the onset of religious warfare throughout much of Europe. Both Catholics and Protestants took it for granted that diversity of religious belief within any country's boundaries simply could not be tolerated. Therefore religious dissenters were ruthlessly persecuted wherever they were found. In several instances the victims included leading intellects who let their religious speculations or researches carry them in new directions. The most eminent of the original thinkers put to death by the Catholics was Giordano Bruno, an early supporter of the Copernican heliocentric theory. Because Bruno taught the doctrine of a plurality of worlds, which offended biblical orthodoxy, he was haled before the Roman Inquisition (founded in 1542) and burned at the stake in 1600. One of the victims of Calvinist persecution at Geneva was Michael Servetus, the discoverer of the pulmonary circulation of the blood. In 1553 Servetus was condemned for rejecting the doctrine of the Trinity; after some discussion, John Calvin's own recommendation of "merciful" beheading was rejected by Servetus's other Calvinist judges and the daring thinker, whose ideas prefigured modern Unitarianism, was burned slowly at the stake, his major work tied around his arm.

Giordano Bruno

Michael Servetus

Not surprisingly, the prevalent attitudes of intolerance led to prolonged religious warfare between Catholics and Protestants. The first major religious struggle to break out was the Schmalkaldic War (1546–1547), waged by Charles V in an effort to restore the unity of the Holy Roman Empire under the Catholic faith. In a few months he succeeded in cowing the Protestant princes of Germany into submission, but he was unable to force their subjects back into the Roman religion. The strife was ultimately settled by a compromise treaty, the Religious Peace of Augsburg (1555), under which each German prince was to be free to choose either Lutheranism or Catholicism as the faith of his people. The religion of each state was thus made to depend upon the religion of its ruler. A much more prolonged and bloody struggle

Religious wars

took place in France between 1562 and 1593. Here the Protestants, or Huguenots as they were called, were decidedly in the minority, but they included some of the ablest and most influential members of the commercial and financial classes. Besides, they composed a political party involved in machinations against the Catholics for control of the government. In 1562, a faction of ultra-Catholics under the leadership of the duke of Guise forced its way into power and, by its threats of persecution of the Huguenots, plunged the country into civil war. The struggle culminated ten years later in the frightful massacre of St. Bartholomew's Day. The regent, Catherine de' Medici, in a desperate effort to put an end to the strife, plotted with the Guises to murder the Protestant leaders. The conspiracy unloosed the ugly passions of the Paris mob, with the result that in a single night 2,000 Huguenots were slain. The war dragged on until 1593 when Henry IV became a Catholic in order to please the majority of his subjects, but the religious issue did not approach a settlement until 1598 when Henry issued the Edict of Nantes guaranteeing freedom of conscience to Protestants.

The St. Bartholomew's Day Massacre. Thousands of Huguenots were killed in France in the continuing religious strife of the sixteenth century.

To a large extent the Revolt of the Netherlands was also an episode in the religious strife stirred up by the Reformation. Long after the Protestant Revolution began in Germany, the countries now known as Belgium and Holland were still being governed as dominions of the Spanish crown. Though Lutheranism and Calvinism had gained a foothold in the cities, the Protestants of the Netherlands were yet but a fraction of the total population. With the passage of time, however, the numbers of Calvinists increased until they included a majority of the townspeople, at least in the Dutch provinces of the north. Interference by the Spanish government with their freedom of religion led to a desperate revolt in 1565. Religious causes were, of course, not the only ones. Nationalist feeling was a leading factor also, particularly since the Spanish king, Philip II, persisted in treating the Netherlands as mere subject provinces. In addition, there were serious economic grievances—high taxation and the restriction of commerce for the benefit of Spanish merchants. On the other hand, it was religious hatred that was largely responsible for the bitterness of the struggle. Philip II regarded all Protestants as traitors, and he was determined to root them out of every territory over which he ruled. In 1567 he sent the violently anti-Protestant duke of Alva with 10,000 soldiers to quell the revolt in the Netherlands. For six years Alva terrorized the land, putting hundreds of the rebels to death and torturing or imprisoning thousands of others. The Protestants retaliated with almost equal savagery, and the war continued its barbarous course until 1609. It ended in victory for the Protestants, largely through the bravery and self-sacrifice of their original leader, William the Silent. The chief result of the war was the establishment of an independent Dutch Republic comprising the territories now included in Holland. The southern or Belgian provinces, where the majority of the people were Catholics, returned to Spanish rule.

The Revolt of the Netherlands

See color map following page 576

Severe religious warfare continued in the seventeenth century in the form of the Thirty Years' War and the English Civil War, both of which will be treated later on. By around 1650, however, men finally stopped slaughtering each other in the name of salvation, and a new age of toleration slowly began to dawn. The prolonged upheavals had left most of northern Germany and all of the Scandinavian countries Lutheran; Scotland, Holland, and parts of northern Germany and Switzerland Calvinist; England a compromise Protestant country; and the rest of Europe predominantly Catholic. These are roughly the religious divisions of Europe today. It would be a mistake to think that such diversity served to promote religious freedom: on the contrary, religious minorities were outlawed in almost all European countries until about 1800. After about 1650, however, countries at least stopped fighting each other on religious grounds.

End of religious warfare

Among the more clearly modernizing effects of the Reformation were the added momentum the movement gave to the rise of individualism and to the expansion of popular education. By simplifying rit-

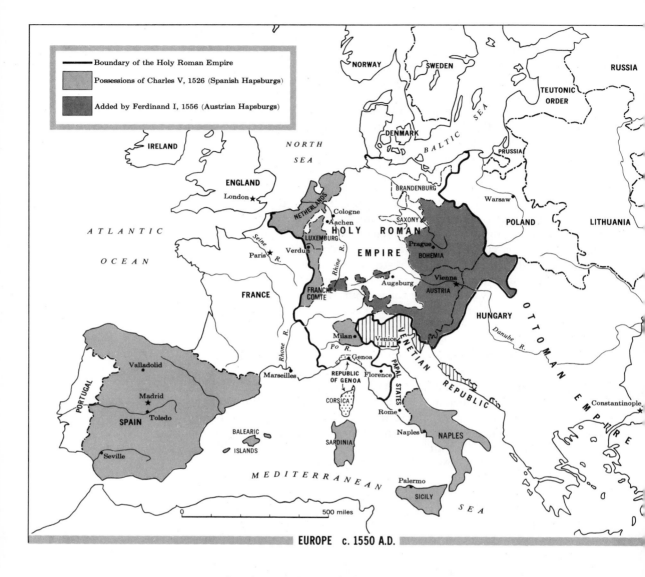

EUROPE c. 1550 A.D.

Increase in individualism

ual and organization the leaders of the Protestant Revolution liberated people from some of the collective constraints of the medieval Church. More importantly, Protestantism tended to assert the rights of private judgment. When Luther boldly resisted the claims of religious authority at the Diet of Worms by proclaiming, "Here I stand, I cannot do otherwise," he set a precedent for the autonomy of the individual conscience which would never be forgotten.

Growth in education

In addition, the Reformation had some effect in promoting the education of the masses. The Renaissance, with its absorbing interest in the classics, had had the unfortunate result of distorting the curricula of the schools into an exaggerated emphasis upon Greek and Latin and of restricting education to the aristocracy. The Lutherans, Calvinists, and Jesuits changed all of this. Ambitious to propagate their respective doctrines, they established schools for the masses, where even the son of the cobbler or peasant might learn to read the Bible and theological tracts in the vernacular. Practical subjects were often introduced in place of Greek and Latin, and it is a significant fact that some of these schools eventually opened their doors to the new science.

Certain tendencies of Reformation thought also helped ultimately to limit political absolutism. These tendencies were by no means to be found in Lutheranism. Quite to the contrary, Luther was a fervent adherent of St. Paul's doctrine that "the powers that be are ordained of God." Luther insisted that political disobedience was a greater sin than murder, unchastity, dishonesty, or theft, and held that the authority of kings and princes was never to be questioned by their subjects. Some observers indeed see in Luther's influence a powerful stimulus to the growth of authoritarian government in Germany. But Jesuit philosophers, on the other hand, attempted to revive the medieval idea of a higher "law of nature." This natural law embodied divinely shaped principles of right and justice which should be recognized as providing certain limitations upon the power of rulers. Certain Jesuits, moreover, taught that the authority of the secular ruler is derived from the people, and some even affirmed the right of the ordinary citizen to kill a tyrant in extraordinary circumstances. Going still further than the Jesuits, some Calvinists in France, England, and the Low Countries not only asserted the right of revolution but actively practiced it. In England too Protestant "Congregationalists" in the seventeenth century introduced the principle of democracy into their Church government and began to argue that such principles might be extended to the government of the state. Some went so far as to maintain that "the meanest man in England ought to have a voice in the election of the government he lives under." Such arguments were among the earliest expressions of truly democratic thought in modern times.

Religious controls on authoritarian governments

SELECTED READINGS

• *Items so designated are available in paperback editions.*
    Allen, J. W., *A History of Political Thought in the Sixteenth Century*, London, 1928. A very exhaustive older survey.
• Bainton, R. H., *Here I Stand: A Life of Martin Luther*, Nashville, Tenn., 1500. The best introductory biography in English: lively and authoritative. •
• ————, *Women of the Reformation*, Minneapolis, 1977.
    Brodrick, James, *The Origins of the Jesuits*, London, 1940.
• Dickens, A. G., *The Counter Reformation*, London, 1968.
• ————, *The English Reformation*, New York, 1964.
• ————, *Reformation and Society in Sixteenth-Century Europe*, London, 1966.
• Elliott, J. H., *Europe Divided: 1559–1598*, London, 1968. An excellent survey.

- Erikson, E. H., *Young Man Luther*, New York, 1958. A classic psychobiography that analyzes the young Luther's "identity crisis."

Geyl, P., *The Revolt of the Netherlands*, London, 1932.

Grimm, Harold J., *The Reformation Era: 1500–1650*, 2nd ed., New York, 1973. The best college-level text.

Gritsch, E. W., *Reformer without a Church: The Life and Thought of Thomas Muentzer*, Philadelphia, 1967.

- Harbison, E. H., *The Age of Reformation*, Ithaca, N.Y., 1955. An expert elementary introduction.

———, *The Christian Scholar in the Age of the Reformation*, New York, 1956. Treats the relation of scholarship to the Christian calling.

Hillerbrand, Hans J., *Men and Ideas in the Sixteenth Century*, Chicago, 1969.

- Hurstfield, Joel, ed., *The Reformation Crisis*, London, 1965. Stimulating essays.

Jones, Rufus M., *The Spiritual Reformers of the Sixteenth and Seventeenth Centuries*, New York, 1914. A lively account by a modern Quaker.

- McNeill, J. T., *The History and Character of Calvinism*, New York, 1954.

Monter, E. William, *Calvin's Geneva*, New York, 1967.

- O'Connell, M. R., *The Counter Reformation: 1560–1610*, New York, 1974.

Parker, G., *The Dutch Revolt*, Ithaca, N.Y., 1977.

- Spitz, Lewis W., *The Reformation: Basic Interpretations*, 2nd ed., Lexington, Mass., 1972. A collection of readings on points of scholarly dispute.

- Tawney, R. H., *Religion and the Rise of Capitalism*, New York, 1926. The most sophisticated and elegantly written defense of the "Weber thesis."

Trevor-Roper, H., *Religion, The Reformation and Social Change*, London, 1967.

- Troeltsch, E., *Protestantism and Progress*, New York, 1931. Argues the view that Protestants were not "modern."

- Weber, Max, *The Protestant Ethic and the Spirit of Capitalism*, London, 1930. Argues the thesis that Calvinism led to the triumph of the capitalist spirit.

Williams, George H., *The Radical Reformation*, Philadelphia, 1962. Detailed account of the "left-wing" Reformers.

SOURCE MATERIALS

Dillenberger, J., ed., *John Calvin: Selections from His Writings*, Garden City, N.Y., 1971.

———, *Martin Luther: Selections from His Writings*, Garden City, N.Y., 1961.

St. Ignatius Loyola, *The Spiritual Exercises*, tr. R. W. Gleason, Garden City, N.Y., 1964.

Ziegler, D. J., *Great Debates of the Reformation*, New York, 1969.

Chapter 20

THE COMMERCIAL REVOLUTION AND THE NEW SOCIETY (c. 1450–c. 1800)

Although a Kingdom may be enriched by gifts received, or by purchases taken from some other Nations, yet these are things uncertain and of small consideration when they happen. The ordinary means therefore to encrease our wealth and treasure is by *Forraign Trade,* wherein wee must ever observe this rule: to sell more to strangers yearly than wee consume of theirs in value.

—Thomas Mun, *England's Treasure by Forraign Trade*

I n the three and a half centuries between 1450 and 1800 enormous changes took place in European economic life which are often described as the Commercial Revolution. While there is much room for disagreement in detail about what these changes entailed, certain basic generalizations are commonly agreed upon. Above all, the Commercial Revolution encompassed a change from the semi-static, localized, and largely subsistence economy of the Middle Ages to the dynamic, worldwide, capitalist regime of modern times. Recovery from the fourteenth-century economic catastrophes was spurred by overseas discoveries, the influx of new articles of consumption and precious metals, the establishment of overseas markets, and advances in banking and trade. Larger numbers of people began to live off commerce and industry, and the profit motive became more pronounced than ever before. Also during the period of the Commercial Revolution, first Spain and Portugal, and then the north Atlantic states of England, France, and Holland replaced the northern Italian cities as the centers of European economic initiative and prosperity. Finally, in the eighteenth century revolutionary developments in European agriculture brought the European economy to the threshold of the Industrial Revolution. Taken together, all these changes meant unprecedented

Major changes in European economic life

new wealth for Europe and carried in their train important changes in social organization and material culture.

1. THE NATURE AND EFFECTS OF OVERSEAS EXPANSION

We have already seen in Chapter 13 that the European economy was beginning to expand around 1450 after about a century and a half of severe depression. No doubt expansion would have progressed steadily, but it was greatly accelerated in the sixteenth and subsequent centuries by the effects of overseas discoveries and conquests. The initial voyages of discovery were due primarily to Spanish and Portuguese ambitions for a share in the trade with the Orient. For some time this trade had been monopolized by the Italian cities of Venice and Genoa, with the result that the people of the Iberian peninsula had to pay high prices for the spices, silks, and drugs that were imported from the East. It was therefore quite natural that attempts should be made by sailors commissioned by Spanish and Portuguese monarchs to discover a new route to the Orient independent of Italian control. A second cause of the voyages of discovery was the missionary fervor of the Spaniards. The successful Spanish reconquest of the Iberian peninsula from the forces of Islam had generated a surplus of religious zeal, which spilled over into a desire to convert the overseas "heathen." To these causes should be added the fact that advances in geographical knowledge and technological expertise allowed mariners to venture more fearlessly into the open seas. It should be borne in mind, however, that these advances did not all transpire suddenly around 1490. The popular idea that all Europeans before Columbus believed that the earth was flat is simply not true: it would have been impossible after the twelfth century to have found an educated person who did not accept the fact that the earth is a sphere. Furthermore, technological aids like the compass and the astrolabe (a device used for measuring the position of heavenly bodies) were known long before Columbus's voyage. In fact, the Portuguese had already sailed boldly out into the Atlantic to reach the Azores Islands (one-third of the way to the New World) before 1350. Most likely, Europeans would have reached America and the Far East much earlier than they actually did had they not been held back by the depression and political upheavals of the later Middle Ages.

If we except the Norsemen, who discovered the North American continent about 1000 A.D., the pioneers in oceanic navigation were the Portuguese. By the middle of the fifteenth century they had explored the African coast as far south as Guinea. In 1497 their most successful navigator, Vasco da Gama, rounded the tip of Africa and sailed on the next year to India. In the meantime, the Genoese mariner, Christopher Columbus (1451–1506), became convinced of the feasibility of reaching India by sailing west. Rebuffed by the Portuguese, he turned to the Spanish sovereigns, Ferdinand and Isabella, and enlisted their support of his plan. The story of his epochal voyage and its result is a familiar one and need not be recounted here. Though he died ignorant of his real achievement, his discoveries laid the foundations for the Spanish claim to nearly all of the New World. Other discoverers representing the Spanish crown followed Columbus, and soon afterward the conquerors, Cortes and Pizarro. The result was the establishment of a vast colonial empire including what is now the southwestern portion of the United States, Florida, Mexico, and the West Indies, Central America, and all of South America with the exception of Brazil, which was taken by Portugal.

The English and the French were not slow in following the Spanish example. The voyages of John Cabot and his son Sebastian in 1497–1498 provided the basis for the English claim to North America, though there was nothing that could be called a British empire in the New World until after the settlement of Virginia in 1607. Early in the sixteenth century the French explorer Cartier sailed up the St. Lawrence, thereby furnishing his native land with some shadow of a title to eastern Canada. More than a hundred years later the explorations of Joliet, La Salle, and Father Marquette gave the French a foothold in the Mississippi valley and in the region of the Great Lakes. Following their victory in their war for independence in the early seventeenth century, the Dutch also took a hand in the struggle for colonial empire. The voyage of Henry Hudson up the river which bears his name enabled them to found New Netherland in 1623, which they were forced to surrender to the English some forty years later. But the most valuable possessions of the Dutch were Malacca, the Spice Islands, and the ports of India and Africa taken from Portugal in the early seventeenth century.

The results of these voyages of discovery and the founding of colonial empires were almost incalculable. To begin with, they expanded commerce from its narrow limits of Mediterranean trade into a world enterprise. For the first time in history the ships of the great maritime powers now sailed the seven seas. The tight little monopoly of Oriental trade maintained by the Italian cities was thoroughly punctured. Genoa and Venice gradually sank into relative obscurity, while the harbors of Lisbon, Bordeaux, Liverpool, Bristol, and Amsterdam were crowded with vessels and the shelves of their merchants piled high with goods. A second result was a tremendous increase in the volume of commerce and in the variety of articles of consumption. To the spices and textiles from the Orient were now added tobacco from North America; molasses and rum from the West Indies; cocoa, chocolate, quinine, and cochineal dye from South America; and ivory, slaves, and ostrich feathers from Africa. In addition to these commod-

Cortes

The British, French, and Dutch

The expansion of commerce into a world enterprise

Aden. A sixteenth-century woodcut of the seaport which was a base for merchants and travelers sailing to India.

ities hitherto unknown or obtainable only in limited quantities, the supply of certain older products was greatly increased. This was especially true of sugar, coffee, rice, and cotton, which were imported in such amounts from the Western Hemisphere that they ceased to be articles of luxury.

Another significant result of the discovery and conquest of lands overseas was an expansion of the supply of precious metals. When Columbus first sailed to America, the quantities of gold and silver in Europe were scarcely sufficient to support a dynamic economy. Indeed, it was nearly fifty years before the full impact of wealth from America made itself felt. For some time gold was the more abundant metal and was relatively cheap in relation to silver. About 1540 this relation was reversed. Massive imports of silver from the mines of Mexico, Bolivia, and Peru produced such a depreciation in the value of silver that quantities of gold had to be hoarded for critical transactions. Henceforth, for about eighty years, the European economy ran on silver. The result was a tremendous inflation. Prices and wages rose to fantastic heights in what may be considered an artificial prosperity. It did not affect all parts of Europe alike. The German silver-mining industry was ruined by the flood of silver from the Americas. As a consequence, the position of Germany declined, while England and the Netherlands rose to preeminence. For a brief period Spain shared this preeminence, but it was ill-fitted to continue it. Spanish industrial development was too feeble to supply the demand for manufactured products from the European settlers in the Western Hemisphere. Accordingly, they turned to the north of Europe for the textiles, cutlery, and similar products they urgently needed. By the end of the sixteenth century the Spanish economy, which had first seemed to be prospering greatly from the discoveries, lay almost completely in ruins.

The increase in the supply of precious metals

2. THE MAIN FEATURES OF THE COMMERCIAL REVOLUTION

The major traits of the Commercial Revolution have been partly suggested by the foregoing discussion of overseas expansion. The outstanding characteristic was the rise of capitalism. Reduced to its simplest terms, capitalism may be defined as a system of production, distribution, and exchange, in which accumulated wealth is invested by private owners for the sake of gain. Its essential features are private enterprise, competition for markets, and business for profit. Generally it involves also the wage system as a method of payment of workers; that is, a mode of payment based not upon the amount of wealth they create, but rather upon their ability to compete with one another for jobs. As indicated already, capitalism is the direct antithesis of the semi-static economy of the medieval guilds, in which production and trade were supposed to be conducted for the benefit of society and with only a reasonable charge for the service rendered, instead of unlimited profits. Although capitalism did not come to its full maturity until the nineteenth century, most of its cardinal features were developed during the Commercial Revolution.

A second important feature of the Commercial Revolution was the growth of banking. Because of the strong religious and moral disapproval of usury, banking had scarcely been a respectable business during the Middle Ages. For centuries the little that was carried on was

*Incidents of the
Commercial Revolution:
(1) the rise of capitalism*

(2) the growth of banking

Sixteenth-Century Mining. The greater complexity of new mining techniques called for greater sophistication of capitalistic organization.

Jacob Fugger

(3) the expansion of credit facilities

virtually monopolized by Jews. Nevertheless, exceptions did exist. As we have seen in Chapter 11, the Church did come to allow profit-making on commercial risks. The result was that several Italian families began to profit greatly from banking enterprises as early as the thirteenth century. The greatest Italian banks were ruined by the blows of the fourteenth-century depression, but afterwards newer and better managed Italian houses, like the bank of the Medici, took their place. By the fifteenth century the banking business had spread to southern Germany and France. The leading firm in the north was that of the Fuggers of Augsburg. The Fuggers lent money to kings and bishops, served as brokers for the pope in the sale of indulgences, and provided the funds that enabled Charles V to buy his election to the throne of the Holy Roman Empire. The rise of these private financial houses was followed by the establishment of government banks, intended to serve the monetary needs of the national states. The first in order of time was the Bank of Sweden (1657), but the one which was destined for the role of greatest importance in economic history was the Bank of England, founded in 1694. Although not technically under government control until 1946, it was the bank of issue for the government and the depositary of public funds.

The growth of banking was necessarily accompanied by the adoption of various aids to financial transactions on a large scale. Credit facilities were extended in such a way that a merchant in Amsterdam could purchase goods from a merchant in Venice by means of a bill of exchange issued by an Amsterdam bank. The Venetian merchant would obtain his money by depositing the bill of exchange in his local bank. Later, the two banks would settle their accounts by comparing balances. Among the other facilities for the expansion of credit were the adoption of a system of payment by check in local transactions and the issuance of bank notes as a substitute for gold and silver. Both of these devices were invented by the Italians and were gradually adopted

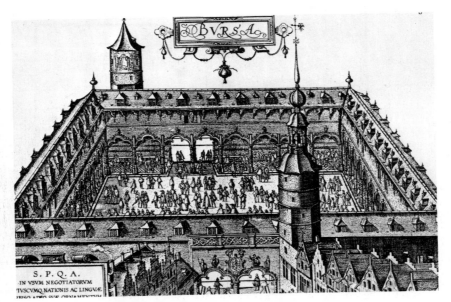

The Antwerp Bourse. Built in the sixteenth century, this was the place of exchange for merchants from all countries.

in northern Europe. The system of payment by check was particularly important in increasing the volume of trade, since the credit resources of the banks could now be expanded far beyond the actual amounts of cash in their vaults.

The Commercial Revolution was not confined, of course, to the growth of trade and banking. Included in it also were fundamental changes in methods of production. The system of manufacture developed by the craft guilds in the later Middle Ages was rapidly becoming defunct. The guilds themselves, dominated by the master craftsmen, had grown selfish and exclusive. Membership in them was commonly restricted to a few privileged families. Besides, they were so completely choked by tradition that they were unable to make adjustments to changing conditions. Moreover, new industries had sprung up entirely outside the guild system. Characteristic examples were mining and smelting and the woolen industry. The rapid development of these enterprises was stimulated by technological advances, such as the invention of the spinning wheel and the stocking frame and the discovery of a new method of making brass, which saved about half of the fuel previously used. In the mining and smelting industries a form of organization was adopted similar to that which has prevailed ever since. The tools and plant facilities belonged to capitalists, while the workers were mere wage-laborers subject to hazards of accident, unemployment, and occupational disease.

(4) the decline of the craft guilds and the rise of new industries

But the most typical form of industrial production in the period of the Commercial Revolution was the domestic system, developed first of all in the woolen industry. The domestic system derives its name from the fact that the work was done in the homes of individual artisans instead of in the shop of a master craftsman. Since the various jobs in the manufacture of a product were given out on contract, the system is also known as the putting-out system. Notwithstanding the petty scale of production, the organization was basically capitalist. The raw material was purchased by an entrepreneur (known as a clothier in the woolen industry) and assigned to individual workers, each of whom would complete his or her allotted task for a stipulated payment. In the case of the woolen industry the yarn would be given out first of all to the spinners, then to the weavers, fullers, and dyers in succession. When the cloth was finally finished, it would be taken by the clothier and sold in the open market for the highest price it would bring. The domestic system was, of course, not restricted to the manufacture of woolen cloth. As time went on, it was extended into many other fields of production. It tied in well with the new glorification of riches and with the conception of a dynamic economy. The capitalist could now thumb his nose at the old restrictions on profits. No association of his rivals could judge the quality of his product or the wages he paid to his workers. Perhaps best of all he could expand his business as he saw fit and introduce new techniques that would reduce costs or increase the volume of production.

(5) the domestic, or putting-out system

Merchants' Houses in Amsterdam, Seventeenth Century. Several of the principal thoroughfares of Amsterdam are canals.

Advantages and disadvantages of the domestic system

Undoubtedly, the domestic system had advantages for the workers themselves, especially as compared to its successor, the factory system. Though wages were low, there was no regular schedule of hours, and it was generally possible for the laborer to supplement the family income by cultivating a small plot of land and raising a few vegetables. Furthermore, conditions of work in the homes were more healthful than in factories, and the artisan had his family to assist him with the simpler tasks. Freedom from the supervision of a foreman and from the fear of discharge for petty reasons were also definite advantages. On the other hand, it must not be forgotten that the workers were too widely scattered to organize effectively for common action. As a consequence they had no means of protecting themselves from dishonest employers, who cheated them out of part of their wages or forced them to accept payment in goods. It is also true that toward the end of the Commercial Revolution the workers became more and more dependent upon the capitalists, who now furnished not only the raw materials but the tools and equipment as well. In some cases the laborers were herded into large central shops and compelled to work under a fixed routine. The difference between this and the high-pressure methods of the factory system was only a matter of degree.

That the Commercial Revolution would involve extensive changes in business organization was practically assured from the start. The prevailing unit of production and trade in the Middle Ages was the shop or store owned by an individual or a family. The partnership was

also quite common, in spite of its grave disadvantage of unlimited lia-
bility of each of its members for the debts of the entire firm. Obviously no one of these units was well adapted to business involving
heavy risks and a huge investment of capital. The first result of the attempt to devise a more suitable business organization was the formation of *regulated companies.* The regulated company was an association
of merchants banded together for a common venture. The members
did not pool their resources but agreed merely to cooperate for their
mutual advantage and to abide by certain definite regulations. Usually
the purpose of the combination was to maintain a monopoly of trade
in some part of the world. Assessments were often paid by the
members for the upkeep of docks and warehouses and especially for
protection against "interlopers," as those traders were called who attempted to break into the monopoly. A leading example of this type
of organization was an English company known as the Merchant Adventurers, established for the purpose of trade with the Netherlands
and Germany.

(6) *changes in business
organization; the growth
of regulated companies*

In the seventeenth century the regulated company was largely superseded by a new type of organization at once more compact and
broader in scope. This was the *joint-stock company,* formed through the
issuance of shares of capital to a considerable number of investors.
Those who purchased the shares might or might not take part in the
work of the company, but whether they did or not they were joint
owners of the business and therefore entitled to share in its profits in
accordance with the amount they had invested. The joint-stock company had numerous advantages over the partnership and the regulated
company. First, it was a permanent unit, not subject to reorganization
every time one of its members died or withdrew. And second, it made
possible a much larger accumulation of capital, through a wide distribution of shares. In short, it possessed nearly every advantage of the
modern corporation except that it was not a person in the eyes of the
law with the rights and privileges guaranteed to individuals. While
most of the early joint-stock companies were founded for commercial
ventures, some were organized later in industry. A number of the outstanding trading combinations were also *chartered companies.* This
means that they held charters from the government granting a monopoly of the trade in a certain locality and conferring extensive authority over the inhabitants. Through a charter of this kind the British
East India Company ruled over India as if it were a private estate until
1784, and even in a sense until 1858. Other famous chartered companies were the Dutch East India Company, the Hudson's Bay Company, the Plymouth Company, and the London Company. The last of
these founded the colony of Virginia and governed it for a time as
company property.

(7) *the joint-stock
company*

The remaining feature of the Commercial Revolution which needs
to be considered was the growth of a more efficient money economy.
Money, of course, had been widely in use ever since the revival of

*The Spanish Milled Dollar or
"Piece of Eight."* This was one of
the first coins to have its circumference scored or "milled."
It was cut into halves and quarters to make change.

trade in the eleventh century. Nevertheless, there were few coins with a value that was recognized other than locally. By 1300, the gold ducat of Venice and the gold florin of Florence had come to be accepted in Italy and also in the international markets of northern Europe. But no country could be said to have had a uniform monetary system. Nearly everywhere there was great confusion. Coins issued by kings circulated side by side with the money of foreign states. Moreover, the types of currency were modified frequently, and the coins themselves were often debased. A common method by which kings expanded their own personal revenues was to increase the proportion of cheaper metals in the coins they minted. But the growth of trade and industry in the Commercial Revolution accentuated the need for more stable and uniform monetary systems. The problem was solved by the adoption of a standard system of money by every important state to be used for all transactions within its borders. Much time elapsed, however, before the reform was complete. England began the construction of a uniform coinage during the reign of Queen Elizabeth, but the task was not finished until late in the seventeenth century. The French did not succeed in reducing their money to its modern standard of simplicity and convenience until the time of Napoleon. In spite of these long delays it appears safe to conclude that national currencies were really an achievement of the Commercial Revolution.

3. MERCANTILISM IN THEORY AND PRACTICE

*The meaning of
mercantilism*

The Commercial Revolution in its later stages was accompanied by the adoption of a new set of doctrines and practices known as mercantilism. In its broadest meaning, mercantilism may be defined as a system of government intervention to promote national prosperity and increase the power of the state. Though frequently considered as a program of economic policy exclusively, its objectives were quite largely political. The purpose of the intervention in economic affairs was not merely to expand the volume of manufacturing and trade, but also to bring more money into the treasury of the king, which would enable him to build fleets, equip armies, and make his government feared and respected throughout the world. Because of this close association with the ambitions of princes to increase their own power and the power of the states over which they ruled, mercantilism has sometimes been called *statism.* Certainly the system would never have come into existence had it not been for the growth of absolute monarchy in place of the weak, decentralized structure of feudalism. But kings alone did not create it. Naturally the new magnates of business lent support, since they would obviously derive great advantages from active encouragement of trade by the state. The heyday of mercantilism was the period between 1600 and 1700, but many of its features survived until the end of the eighteenth century.

If there was any one principle which held the central place in mercantilist theory, it was the doctrine of bullionism. This doctrine means that the prosperity of a nation is determined by the quantity of precious metals within its borders. The greater the amount of gold and silver a country contains, the more money the government can collect in taxes, and the richer and more powerful the state will become. But what of those countries that owned no bullion-producing colonies? How were *they* to achieve riches and power? For these questions the mercantilists had a ready answer. A nation without access to gold and silver directly should attempt to increase its trade with the rest of the world. If its government took steps to ensure that the value of exports would always exceed the value of imports, more gold and silver would come into the country than would have to be shipped out. This was called maintaining a "favorable balance of trade." To preserve this balance, three main devices would be necessary: first, high tariffs to reduce the general level of imports and to shut out some products entirely; second, bounties on exports; and third, extensive encouragement of manufactures in order that the nation might have as many goods to sell abroad as possible.

Bullionism and the favorable balance of trade

The theory of mercantilism also included certain elements of economic nationalism, paternalism, and imperialism. By the first is meant the ideal of a self-sufficient nation. The policy of fostering new industries was not intended merely as a device for increasing exports, but also as a means of making the nation independent of foreign supplies. In similar fashion, the mercantilists argued that the government should exercise the functions of a watchful guardian over the lives of its citizens. Relief should be provided for the poor, including free medical attention if they were unable to pay for it. These things were

Other elements of mercantilism: economic nationalism, paternalism, and imperialism

Coining Money in the Sixteenth Century. These coins were not "milled" and therefore were easily "clipped," a process of scraping portions of the valuable metal from the edges of the coin.

to be done, however, not with any view to charity or justice, but mainly in order that the state might rest upon a secure economic foundation and have the support of a numerous and healthy citizenry in case of war. Finally, the mercantilists advocated the acquisition of colonies. Again, the primary purpose was not to benefit individual citizens of the mother country, but to make the nation strong and independent. The types of possessions most ardently desired were those that would enlarge the nation's hoard of bullion. If these could not be obtained, then colonies providing tropical products, naval stores, or any other commodities which the mother country could not produce would be acceptable. The theory which underlay this imperialism was the notion that colonies existed for the benefit of the state that owned them. For this reason they were not allowed to engage in manufacturing or shipping. Their function was to produce raw materials and to consume as large a proportion of manufactured products as possible. In this way they would infuse lifeblood into the industries of the mother country and thus give it an advantage in the struggle for world trade.

The majority of those who wrote on mercantilist theory were philosophers and men of action in the world of business. Among the former were such advocates of political absolutism as the Frenchman Jean Bodin (1530–1596) and the Englishman Thomas Hobbes (1588–1679), who were naturally disposed to favor any policy that would increase the wealth and power of the ruler. While most of the apologists for mercantilism were interested in it mainly as a device for promoting a favorable balance of trade, others conceived it as a species of paternalism for increasing prosperity within the country. Some, for example, advocated a policy somewhat similar to contemporary ideas of government spending, by recommending that the state should appropriate a huge fund for the relief of the poor and for the construction of public works as a means of stimulating business.

Attempts to put various mercantilist doctrines into practice characterized the history of many of the nations of western Europe in the sixteenth and seventeenth centuries. The theories, however, were not universally applied. Spain, of course, had the initial advantage by reason of the flow of bullion from its American empire. And while the Spaniards did not need to resort to artificial devices in order to bring money into their country, their government nevertheless maintained a rigid control over commerce and industry. The policies of other nations were designed to make up for the lack of bullion-producing colonies by capturing a larger share of export trade. This naturally involved a program of bounties, tariffs, and extensive regulation of manufacturing and shipping. Mercantilist policies were largely adopted in England during the reign of Queen Elizabeth I and were continued by the Stuart monarchs and by Oliver Cromwell. Most of these rulers engaged in a furious scramble for colonies, bestowed monopolistic privileges upon trading companies, and sought in a wide variety of ways to control the economic activities of their citizens. The most interesting examples of mercantilist legislation in England were, first, the Elizabethan laws designed to eliminate idleness and stimulate production and, second, the Navigation Acts. By a series of laws enacted toward the end of the sixteenth century, Queen Elizabeth gave to the justices of the peace the authority to fix prices, regulate hours of labor, and compel every able-bodied citizen to work at some useful trade. The first of the Navigation Acts was passed in 1651 under Oliver Cromwell. With the aim of destroying Dutch predominance in the carrying trade, it required that all colonial exports to the mother country should be carried in English ships. A second Navigation Act was passed in 1660, which provided not merely that colonial exports should be shipped in British vessels but prohibited the sending of certain "enumerated articles," especially tobacco and sugar, directly to continental European ports. They were to be sent first of all to England, whence, after the payment of customs duties, they could be reshipped elsewhere. Both of these laws were based upon the principle that colonies should serve for the enrichment of the mother country.

*Mercantilism in
Germany: the cameralists*

The Germanic states during the Commercial Revolution were too completely occupied with internal problems to take an active part in the struggle for colonies and overseas trade. As a consequence, German mercantilism was concerned primarily with increasing the strength of the state from within. It partook of the dual character of economic nationalism and a program for a planned society. But, of course, the planning was done chiefly for the benefit of the government and only incidentally for that of the people as a whole. Because of their dominant purpose of increasing the revenues of the state, the German mercantilists are known as cameralists (from *Kammer,* a name given to the royal treasury). Most of them were lawyers and professors of finance. Cameralist ideas were put into practice by the Hohenzollern kings of Prussia, notably by Frederick William I (1713–1740) and Frederick the Great (1740–1786). The policies of these monarchs embraced a many-sided scheme of intervention and control in the economic sphere for the purpose of increasing taxable wealth and bolstering the power of the state. Marshes were drained, canals dug, new industries established with the aid of the government, and farmers instructed as to what crops they should plant. In order that the nation might become self-sufficient as soon as possible, exports of raw materials and imports of manufactured products were prohibited. The bulk of the revenues gained from these various policies went for military purposes. The standing army of Prussia was increased by Frederick the Great to 160,000 men.

The most thorough, if not the most deliberate, application of mercantilism was probably to be found in France during the reign of Louis XIV (1643–1715). This was due partly to the fact that the French

Jean Baptiste Colbert

*French mercantilism under
Colbert*

state was the fullest incarnation of absolutism and partly to the policies of Jean Baptiste Colbert, chief minister under Louis from 1661 until his death in 1683. Colbert was no theorist but rather a practical politician, ambitious for personal power and intent upon magnifying the opportunities for wealth of the middle class, to which he belonged. He accepted mercantilism, not as an end in itself, but simply as a convenient means for increasing the wealth and power of the state and thereby gaining the approval of his sovereign. He firmly believed that France must acquire as large an amount of the precious metals as possible. To this end he prohibited the export of money, levied high tariffs on foreign manufactures, and gave liberal bounties to encourage French shipping. It was largely for this purpose also that Colbert fostered imperialism, hoping to increase the favorable balance of trade through the sale of manufactured goods to the colonies. Accordingly, he purchased islands in the West Indies, encouraged settlements in Canada and Louisiana, and established trading posts in India and Africa. Furthermore, he was as devoted to the ideal of self-sufficiency as any of the cameralists in Prussia. He gave subsidies to new enterprises, established a number of state-owned industries, and even had the government purchase goods which were not really needed in order to keep struggling companies on their feet. But he was determined to keep the manufacturing industry under strict control, so as to make sure that companies would buy their raw materials only from French or colonial sources and produce the commodities necessary for national greatness. Consequently, he clamped upon industry an elaborate set of regulations prescribing nearly every detail of the manufacturing process. Finally, it should be mentioned that Colbert took a number of steps to augment the political strength of the nation directly. He provided France with a navy of nearly 300 ships, drafting citizens from the maritime provinces and even criminals to man them. He sought to promote a rapid growth of population by discouraging young people from becoming monks or nuns and by exempting families with ten or more children from taxation.

4. THE RESULTS OF THE COMMERCIAL REVOLUTION

*The foundation for
modern capitalism*

It goes without saying that the Commercial Revolution was one of the most significant developments in the history of the Western world. The whole pattern of modern economic life would have been impossible without it, for it changed the basis of commerce from the local and regional plane of the Middle Ages to the worldwide scale it has occupied ever since. Moreover, it exalted the power of money, inaugurated business for profit, sanctified the accumulation of wealth, and established competitive enterprise as the foundation of production and trade. In short, the Commercial Revolution was responsible for a large number of the elements that go to make up the capitalist regime.

But these were not the only results. The Commercial Revolution brought into being wide fluctuations of economic activity. What we now call booms and recessions alternated with startling rapidity. The inflow of precious metals, combined with a rise in population, led to rising prices and an unprecedented demand for goods. Businessmen were tempted to expand their enterprises too rapidly; bankers extended credit so liberally that their principal borrowers, especially nobles, often defaulted on loans. Spain and Italy were among the first to suffer setbacks. In both, failure of wages to keep pace with rising prices brought incredible hardships to the lower classes. Impoverishment was rife in the cities, and bandits flourished in the rural areas. In Spain, some ruined aristocrats were not too proud to join the throngs of vagrants who wandered from city to city. At the end of the fifteenth century the great Florentine bank of the Medici closed its doors. The middle of the century that followed saw numerous bankruptcies in Spain and the decline of the Fuggers in Germany. Meanwhile, England, Holland, and to some extent France, waxed prosperous. This prosperity was especially characteristic of the "age of silver," which lasted from about 1540 to 1620. In the seventeenth century decline set in once more after inflation had spent its force, and as a consequence of religious and international wars and civil strife.

The alternation of booms and recessions was followed by outbreaks of feverish speculation. These reached their climax early in the eighteenth century. The most notorious were the South Sea Bubble and the Mississippi Bubble. The former was the result of inflation of the stock of the South Sea Company in England. The promoters of this company agreed to take over a large part of the national debt and in return received from the English government an exclusive right to trade with South America and the Pacific islands. The prospects for profit seemed almost unlimited. The stock of the company rose rapidly in value until it was selling for more than ten times its original price. The higher it rose, the more gullible the public became. But gradually suspicion developed that the possibilities of the enterprise had been overrated. Buoyant hopes gave way to fears, and investors made frantic attempts to dispose of their shares for whatever they would bring. A crash which came in 1720 was the inevitable result.

During the years when the South Sea Bubble was being inflated in England, the French were going through a similar wave of speculative madness. In 1715 a Scotsman by the name of John Law, who had been compelled to flee from British soil for killing his rival in a love intrigue, settled in Paris, after various successful gambling adventures in other cities. He persuaded the regent of France to adopt his scheme for paying off the national debt through the issuance of paper money and to grant him the privilege of organizing the Mississippi Company for the colonization and exploitation of Louisiana. As the government loans were redeemed, the people who received the money were encouraged to buy stock in the company. Soon the shares began to soar, ultimately reaching a price forty times their original value. Nearly everyone who could scrape together a bit of surplus cash rushed forward to participate in the scramble for riches. Stories were told of butchers and tailors who were supposed to have become millionaires by buying a few shares and holding them for a rise in price. But as the realization grew that the company would never be able to pay more than a nominal dividend on the stock at its inflated value, the more cautious investors began selling their holdings. The alarm spread, and soon all were as anxious to sell as they had been to buy. In 1720 the Mississippi Bubble burst in a wild panic. Thousands of people who had sold good property to buy the shares at fantastic prices were ruined. The collapse of the South Sea and Mississippi companies gave a temporary chill to the public ardor for speculation. It was not long, however, until the appetite for speculative profits revived, and the stock-buying waves that followed in the wake of the Commercial Revolution were repeated many times over during the nineteenth and twentieth centuries.

*The rise of a new class
and the Europeanization
of the world*

Among other results of the Commercial Revolution were the rise of the middle class to economic power, the beginning of Europeanization of the world, and the revival of slavery. Each of these requires brief comment. By the end of the seventeenth century the middle class had become an influential group in nearly every country of western Europe. Its ranks included the merchants, the bankers, the shipowners, the principal investors, and the industrial entrepreneurs. Their rise to power was mainly the result of increasing wealth and their tendency to ally themselves with the king against the aristocracy. But as yet their power was purely economic. Not until the nineteenth century did middle-class supremacy in politics become a reality. By the Europeanization of the world is meant the transplanting of European manners and culture in other continents. As a result of the work of traders, missionaries, and colonists, North and South America were rapidly stamped with the character of appendages of Europe. No more than a beginning was made in the transformation of Asia, but enough was done to foreshadow the trend of later times when even Japanese and Chinese would adopt Western locomotives and shell-rimmed spectacles.

Slavery

The most tragic, and humanly reprehensible, result of the Commercial Revolution was the revival of slavery—i.e., the buying and selling of human beings for forced labor and profit. Slavery had practically disappeared from European civilization around the year 1000. But the development of mining and plantation farming in the English, Spanish, and Portuguese colonies led to a tremendous demand for unskilled labor. At first the colonizers attempted to enslave Native Americans, but they usually proved too susceptible to European infectious diseases. The need was filled in the sixteenth century, and another "commodity" added to the system of colonial trade, by the importation of Africans. From then until the nineteenth century, slavery was an integral part of the European colonial system, especially in those regions producing tropical agricultural products: e.g., sugar cane, tobacco, and, after about 1780, cotton.

Finally, the Commercial Revolution was exceedingly important in preparing the way for the Industrial Revolution. This was true for a number of reasons. First, the Commercial Revolution created a class of capitalists who were constantly seeking new opportunities to invest their surplus profits. Second, the mercantilist policy, with its emphasis upon protection for infant industries and production of goods for export, gave a powerful stimulus to the growth of manufactures. Third, the founding of colonial empires flooded Europe with new raw materials and greatly increased the supply of certain products which had hitherto been luxuries. Most of these required fabrication before they were available for consumption. As a consequence, new industries sprang up wholly independent of any guild regulations that still survived. The outstanding example was the manufacture of cotton textiles, which, significantly enough, was one of the first of the industries to become mechanized. Last of all, the Commercial Revolution was marked by a trend toward the adoption of factory methods in certain lines of production, together with technological improvements, such as the discovery of more efficient processes of refining ores. Thus the Commercial Revolution led inevitably to the Industrial Revolution, as we shall see.

Effects of the Commercial Revolution in preparing the way for the Industrial Revolution

5. REVOLUTIONARY DEVELOPMENTS IN AGRICULTURE

In the late seventeenth century and, above all, in the eighteenth century, sweeping changes occurred in European agriculture that may be regarded in part as effects of the Commercial Revolution. The rise in prices and increase in urban population brought about by commercial developments made agriculture an ever more profitable business and thus tended to stimulate agricultural improvements. In addition, one effect of overseas expansion was to familiarize Europeans with important new crops, above all, Indian corn and potatoes, which they could raise at home. But probably the most important influence of the Commercial Revolution on agricultural history was the triumph of the capitalist mentality. Landlords who had hitherto let peasants farm their lands inefficiently, now followed the model of businessmen in seeking a maximum of efficiency and profits. So long as these landlords were prepared to be ruthless, there were many revolutionary changes that they were able to bring about.

Relations between the Commercial Revolution and changes in agriculture

The countries that led the way in agricultural advance were Holland and England, no doubt largely because these countries had already participated to the fullest in the Commercial Revolution. Since England was able to advance rapidly beyond Holland, owing to its greater size and natural resources, we may limit our remarks here to English developments. It will be recalled from Chapter 11 that the typical medieval agricultural regime was one in which groups of peasants collectively cultivated long and narrow unfenced strips of land. Of those, one-third would lie fallow in any given year in order to restore fertility. Other neighboring lands would be given over to pastures and meadows for the grazing of collectively owned peasant herds. Most often, the actual ownership of all these lands was ill-defined or almost randomly parceled out; usually, however, there would be a prominent landlord in each area who could lay claim to owning a large percentage of the land even though peasants farmed it for him. The same individual might also claim legal title to the pastures and meadows. In England most of these landlords decided to "enclose" their lands in order to make them more profitable.

The earliest "enclosures" in England took place in the fifteenth and sixteenth centuries and entailed the conversion of lands into fenced-off sheep meadows. Because of the great profits to be accrued from wool, some landlords decided to convert common pastures that hitherto had supported peasant livestock into their own preserves for sheep-raising. Sometimes they also succeeded in converting grain fields into sheep pastures by evicting peasants whose leaseholds were none too secure. This caused grave hardships for the peasants concerned. As Thomas More wrote in his *Utopia* (1516) "sheep that used to be so meek and eat so little now are becoming so greedy and wild that they devour men themselves . . . for they leave no land free for the plough." The humanitarian More, however, was exaggerating somewhat. In fact, no more than about 3 percent of arable land had been enclosed before 1525 and part of that was not for sheep pasturage.

The really dramatic enclosure movement in England took place between 1710 and 1810 and aimed not to free land for sheep but to increase the efficiency of crop-raising. In this period landlords became convinced of the necessity for "scientific farming." Above all, they realized that by introducing new crops and farming methods they could reduce the amount of fallow lands and bring in higher yields. Some of the important new crops with which they experimented were clover, alfalfa, and related varieties of leguminous plants. These reduced fertility much less than cereal grains and actually helped to improve the quality of the soil by gathering nitrogen and making the ground more porous. Another new crop that had a similar effect was the turnip. The greatest propagandist for the planting of this unattractive vegetable was Viscount Charles Townshend (1674–1738), a prominent aristocrat and politician, who toward the end of his life left the royal court to experiment with agriculture. In this he became a model for subsequent aristocratic interest in scientific farming. Townshend gained the nickname of "Turnip" Townshend because he was so dedicated to converting people to the use of the turnip in new crop rotation systems.

Clover, alfalfa, and turnips not only helped in doing away with the fallow but they provided excellent winter food for animals, thereby aiding the production of more and better livestock. And more livestock also meant more manure. Accordingly, intensive manuring became another way in which scientific farmers could eliminate the need for letting land lie fallow. Other improvements in farming methods introduced in the period were more intensive hoeing and weeding, and the use of the seed drill for planting grain. The latter eliminated the old wasteful method of sowing grain broadcast by hand, most of it remaining on top to be eaten by birds.

Scientific farming dictated the necessity of enclosures because the "improving" landlord needed flexibility to experiment as he wished. He simply could not try to plant one narrow open strip with turnips while peasants were continuing to rotate all the contiguous areas on the basis of the age-old three-field system. Instead, it was necessary for him to have fenced-off compact plots to leave no doubt as to which territory was his own, to maximize efficiency in experimentation, and to keep away stray grazing animals. It must also be added that when the enclosure movement gathered momentum, landlords were not above using the principle of reorganizing and enclosing territories to gain new lands from the peasantry that hitherto had in no way belonged to them. In all this they had the government on their side. Parliament stopped trying to prohibit enclosures in 1640 and actually started directing them in 1710. Thereafter, throughout the eighteenth century, parliamentary "acts of enclosure" provided that all the lands of a given village be completely redistributed into compact, fenced parcels, with the leading landlords of an area gaining far and away the most land. (Parliament did this because it was dominated by the landowning aristocracy.) The result was that many peasants were driven off the land but also that productivity soared. In eighteenth-century England wheat production, for example, increased by one-third, and the average weight of livestock doubled. All told, the increased abundance and concentration of wealth brought about by the agricultural revolution and enclosure movement was a necessary prerequisite for the Industrial Revolution that began in England around 1780.

On the continent of Europe, aside from the minor exception of Holland, there was nothing comparable to the English advance in scientific farming. In most parts of the Continent agricultural change transpired more slowly and the real breakthrough in scientific methods came only in the nineteenth, or in some places the twentieth century. But the eighteenth century was nonetheless an important epoch in continental agriculture from the point of view of the introduction of new crops. Most important was the cultivation of maize

A Ball-and-Chain Pump. Men walking in the treadmill at the left powered this mid-sixteenth-century irrigation device.

Consolidation of holdings

New Crops

Interior of a French Peasant's Cottage, Seventeenth Century. Virtually all activities centered about the hearth, the only source of heat for the entire dwelling.

(Indian corn) and the potato, both introduced from the New World. Since maize can only be grown in areas with substantial periods of sunny and dry weather, it was not planted in north Atlantic regions of Europe, but in the seventeenth and eighteenth centuries its cultivation spread through Italy and the southeastern part of the Continent. Its enormous attraction was that whereas an average ear of grain would yield only about four seeds for every one planted, an ear of maize would yield about seventy or eighty. That made it a "miracle" crop, filling granaries where they had been almost empty before. The potato was an equally miraculous innovation for the European north. Its great advantages were numerous: one was that potatoes could be grown on the poorest, sandiest, or wettest of lands where nothing else could be raised; another was that they could be fitted into the smallest of patches. Raising potatoes even on small patches was profitable because the yield of potatoes was extraordinarily abundant. Finally, the potato was an excellent food for the human diet: it is rich in calories, has many vitamins and minerals, and contains some protein as well. At first northern European peasants resisted growing potatoes because the plant is not mentioned in the Bible, but in the course of the eighteenth century they became accustomed to it, sometimes after considerable governmental pressure. Frederick the Great of Prussia at first practically forced potatoes down his peasants' throats, but soon the crop became a staple there and in the rest of northern Germany. By about 1800 the average northern German peasant family would be eating potatoes as a main course at least once a day. In the same period the potato was also introduced into Ireland and England: as late as the 1960s an English playwright could entitle his play about the lower classes *Chips* [i.e., fried potatoes] *with Everything*.

Probably the single most noteworthy fact about the economic history of the European continent in the eighteenth century was that poor people gradually stopped dying from famine. Until about 1700 about half of all European peasants could expect to see someone in their immediate family die from starvation about once every ten years. Often when periodic famines came whole families would be decimated. But the introduction of new crops like maize and the potato helped change all this. The result was that population began to soar as never before and that labor was ultimately freed for industrialization. At last, people in Europe were literally learning that they did not have to live by bread alone.

End of famine

6. THE NEW SOCIETY

Profound changes in the texture of society inevitably accompany economic revolutions. The society which was brought into being by the Commercial Revolution, though retaining characteristics of the Middle Ages, was markedly different in certain features. For one thing the population of Europe was becoming considerably larger. All told, the European population in 1500 is estimated to have numbered about 80 million; by 1800 it had more than doubled, to reach about 190 million. In 1378 London had a population of about 50,000; by 1600 the total had reached more than 200,000; and by 1800 more than 1 million! The reasons for these increases are closely related to the religious and economic developments of the time. In northern Protestant countries the overthrow of clerical celibacy and the encouragement of marriage were factors partly responsible. But far more important was the increase in means of subsistence brought about by the Commercial Rev-

Population growth

A Peasants' Meal by Louis Le Nain. This French painting of 1642 shows that the chief item of consumption was still bread and that grown men were often so poor that they had to go barefoot.

olution and agricultural improvements. Not only were new products, such as potatoes, maize, and tomatoes added to the food supply, but older commodities, especially sugar and rice, were now made available to Europeans in larger quantities.

As the figures for London suggest, Europe was becoming not just more populous but also more heavily urbanized. In 1500 there were only three cities in Europe—excluding Turkish Istanbul—with populations of more than 100,000; in 1800 there were twenty-two. Certainly the growth of new opportunities for earning a living in commerce and industry enabled most countries to support a larger population; it is significant that the bulk of these increases occurred in cities and towns. Nonetheless, the extent of urbanization before 1800 should not be exaggerated. In the seventeenth century 70 to 80 percent of all laborers were still agricultural workers; and most industrial labor remained handicraft labor. As one historian, R. S. Dunn, has observed, *"manufacture* still retained its Latin meaning: to make by hand." Even as late as 1800 most industries were centered around small shops, not mechanized factories. Although cities and towns had grown in size, only 3 percent of the European population lived in large cities of over 100,000 people. In short, the Industrial Revolution was only just beginning and the triumph of modern urbanism was yet to come.

Just as urbanism had not yet fully triumphed, neither had the social status of the middle class. Historians used to talk of an ever "rising" middle class, but they now realize that this trend is too easily exaggerated. Without doubt, throughout most of the period there were great opportunities for ambitious and talented merchants to pile up fortunes and thereby climb some of the higher rungs of the social ladder. Yet merchants were never as respected as aristocrats: the French playwright Molière (1622–1673) for example, ridiculed "the bourgeois gentleman"—a rich merchant who clumsily tried to ape the ways of his "betters." Some of the professions, it is true, gained more wealth and dignity than they had enjoyed in the Middle Ages. Specifically, the artist, the writer, the lawyer, the university professor, and the physician emerged into positions of importance roughly comparable to what they now hold in modern society. But in general the age was by no means one of economic or social leveling. Indeed the aristocracy, which gained most of its livelihood from land, was as much economically and socially entrenched towards the end of the period as it was at the beginning.

The new egoism that characterized the middle and upper classes stood as a barrier to more generous treatment of the least fortunate human beings. Hearing a disturbance outside his quarters, the Emperor Charles V, in 1552, was reported to have asked who were causing the commotion. When told that they were poor soldiers, he said, "Let them die," and compared them to caterpillars, locusts, and june-

Slaves Being Ordered into the Hold of a Ship. Thousands of slaves died in the holds of ships during the long voyage to the Americas. Sympathetic but stylized illustrations such as this were designed to move the newspaper-reading public in the eighteenth century.

bugs that eat the good things of the earth. As a rule, the most pitiable fate was reserved for slaves and serfs. For the sake of big profits, blacks were hunted on the coast of Africa, captured and imprisoned in dungeons called "holding pens," and shipped to the American colonies. It may be of interest to note that one of the earliest Englishmen who engaged in this body-snatching business, Captain John Hawkins, called the ship in which he transported the victims the *Jesus.*

While black slaves were seldom employed in Europe proper, native Europeans were pitiably exploited as serfs. The institution of serfdom had died out in western Europe during the later Middle Ages, but after about 1600 it was revived and gained strength in those parts of Europe east of the Elbe river. There the desire for profit in agriculture and the collusion of the state with the aristocracy led to the growth of the "second serfdom"—a serf system much stronger than ever before. In East Prussia serfs often had to work from three to six days a week for their lord, and some had only late evening or night hours to cultivate their own lands. Worse, in Russia landlords had the power of life and death over their serfs and could sell them apart from the land and even apart from their families.

The second serfdom

Putting aside the plight of eastern European serfs, the eighteenth century did witness definite improvements in the living conditions of most Europeans. We have already seen that new items in the diet helped eliminate famine. Otherwise the poor stayed about as wretched as they had always been—the triumph over epidemic diseases like smallpox and malaria for the most part came about only in the nineteenth century—but there were improvements in the standard of living of the middle and upper classes. This is evidenced by the increasing per capita consumption of sugar, chocolate, coffee, and tea, which were not merely substituted for other foods and beverages but were additions to the average diet. The growing demand for linen and cot-

Changes in the standard of living

ton cloth, and for such articles of luxury as mahogany furniture designed by such masters as Chippendale, Hepplewhite, and Sheraton, may be taken as a further indication of rising prosperity.

The widespread adoption of the tobacco and coffee habits in the seventeenth and eighteenth centuries had interesting social and perhaps physiological effects. Although the tobacco plant was brought into Europe by the Spaniards about fifty years after the discovery of America, another half-century passed before many Europeans adopted the practice of smoking. At first the plant was believed to possess miraculous healing powers and was referred to as "divine tobacco" and "our holy herb nicotian." (The word nicotine is derived from Jean Nicot, the French ambassador to Portugal who brought the tobacco plant into France.) The habit of smoking was popularized by English explorers, especially by Sir Walter Raleigh, who had learned it from the Indians of Virginia. It spread rapidly through all classes of European society despite the condemnation of the clergy and the "counterblaste" of James I against it. The enormous popularity of coffee-drinking in the seventeenth century had even more important social effects. Coffee houses or "cafés" sprang up all over Europe and rapidly evolved into leading institutions. They provided not merely an escape for the majority of men from a cribbed and monotonous home life, but they took others away from the excesses of the tavern and the gambling den. In addition, they fostered a sharpening of wits and promoted more polished manners, especially inasmuch as they became favorite meeting places for the literary lions of the time. If we can believe the testimony of English historians, there was scarcely a social or political enterprise which did not have its intimate connections with the establishments where coffee was sold.

The coexistence of genteel coffee houses with the rise of slavery reflects the fact that the Commercial Revolution was founded on the pursuit of self-interest and maintained by indifference to intense human suffering. Nonetheless, the economic advances achieved by the Commercial Revolution did bring great benefits to many and would lead to still greater economic advances in subsequent ages.

SELECTED READINGS

• *Items so designated are available in paperback editions.*
• Braudel, F., *Capitalism and Material Life, 1400–1800,* London, 1973. A fascinating review of evidence pertaining to the entire world by one of the greatest of living historians.
• ————, *The Mediterranean and the Mediterranean World in the Age of Philip II,* New York, 1972. One of the most important and brilliant history

books of our age. Treats life in the Mediterranean regions in the second half of the sixteenth century with particular emphasis on how geography determines the course of human history.

• Burke, Peter, *Popular Culture in Early Modern Europe,* London, 1978. Synthesizes the most recent work on the period between 1500 and 1800. Fascinating.

Chambers, J. D., and G. E. Mingay, *The Agricultural Revolution, 1750–1880,* London, 1966. Now the standard work.

• Cipolla, C. M., *Before the Industrial Revolution: European Society and Economy, 1000–1700,* 2nd ed. New York, 1980. Wide-ranging and full of deft observations.

• Davis, Natalie Z., *Society and Culture in Early Modern France,* Stanford, Calif. 1975. Eight scintillating essays by a pioneer in the use of anthropological methods for the study of early modern European history.

• Goubert, P., *The Ancien Régime: French Society, 1600–1750,* London, 1973. Particularly strong in its descriptions of rural life. Includes selections from illuminating documents.

• Hale, J. R., *Renaissance Exploration,* New York, 1968. A magnificent short introduction.

Heckscher, E., *Mercantilism,* rev. ed., London, 1955. The most influential, but controversial, work on the subject.

• Hill, Christopher, *Reformation to Industrial Revolution* (The Pelican Economic History of Britain, vol. 2), rev. ed., Baltimore, 1969. Comprehensive.

Hufton, O. W., *The Poor of Eighteenth-Century France,* New York, 1974.

Kamen, Henry, *The Iron Century: Social Change in Europe, 1550–1660,* New York, 1971. Supports the recent view that there was an economic crisis in this period that interrupted preceding and succeeding periods of prosperity.

• Laslett, Peter, *The World We Have Lost: England Before the Industrial Age,* 2nd ed., New York, 1971. A very readable introduction to preindustrial social history, but controversial in parts.

• Mandrou, R., *Introduction to Modern France, 1500–1640: An Essay in Historical Psychology,* London, 1975. Assumes some prior knowledge of French history and culture, but full of fascinating information about daily life.

Minchinton, W. E., ed., *Mercantilism: System or Expediency?* Lexington, Mass., 1969. A collection of readings that provides a valuable corrective to Heckscher.

• Morison, S. E., *Christopher Columbus, Mariner,* New York, 1955. A good shorter version of this master storyteller's definitive *Admiral of the Ocean Sea* (1942).

• Parry, J. H., *The Age of Reconnaissance,* London, 1963. The best history of the discoveries that emphasizes the details of shipbuilding and navigation.

• Penrose, B., *Travel and Discovery in the Renaissance,* Cambridge, Mass., 1952. Engrossing.

• de Roover, R., *The Rise and Decline of the Medici Bank, 1397–1494,* Cambridge, Mass., 1963. Authoritative, often very technical.

Rudé, George, *Hanoverian London, 1714–1808,* Berkeley, Calif. 1971.

SOURCE MATERIALS

Barnett, G. E., ed., *Two Tracts by Gregory King,* Baltimore, 1936. An introduction to the work of the modern world's first real statistician.

Mun, Thomas, *England's Treasure by Foreign Trade,* Oxford, 1928. (Reprint of the original edition of 1664.) A vigorous early argument in favor of the balance of trade.

Parry, J. H., *The European Reconnaissance: Selected Documents,* New York, 1968.

Young, Arthur, *Travels in France During the Years 1787, 1788, 1789,* London, 1912. Vivid observations by an English traveler.

RULERS OF PRINCIPAL STATES SINCE 700 A.D.

The Carolingian Dynasty

Pepin, Mayor of the Palace, 714
Charles Martel, Mayor of the Palace, 715–741
Pepin I, Mayor of the Palace, 741; King, 751–768
Charlemagne, King, 768–814; Emperor, 800–814
Louis the Pious, Emperor, 814–840

MIDDLE KINGDOMS

Lothair, Emperor, 840–855
Louis (Italy), Emperor, 855–875
Charles (Provence), King, 855–863
Lothair II (Lorraine), King, 855–869

WEST FRANCIA

Charles the Bald, King, 840–877; Emperor, 875
Louis II, King, 877–879
Louis III, King, 879–882
Carloman, King, 879–884

EAST FRANCIA

Ludwig, King, 840–876
Carloman, King, 876–880
Ludwig, King, 876–882
Charles the Fat, Emperor, 876–887

Holy Roman Emperors

SAXON DYNASTY

Otto I, 962–973
Otto II, 973–983
Otto III, 983–1002
Henry II, 1002–1024

FRANCONIAN DYNASTY

Conrad II, 1024–1039
Henry III, 1039–1056
Henry IV, 1056–1106
Henry V, 1106–1125
Lothair II (of Saxony), King, 1125–1133; Emperor, 1133–1137

HOHENSTAUFEN DYNASTY

Conrad III, 1138–1152
Frederick I (Barbarossa), 1152–1190
Henry VI, 1190–1197
Philip of Swabia, 1198–1208 } Rivals
Otto IV (Welf), 1198–1215 }
Frederick II, 1220–1250
Conrad IV, 1250–1254

INTERREGNUM, 1254–1273

EMPERORS FROM VARIOUS DYNASTIES
Rudolf I (Hapsburg), 1273–1291

Adolf (Nassau), 1292–1298
Albert I (Hapsburg), 1298–1308
Henry VII (Luxemburg), 1308–1313
Ludwig IV (Wittelsbach), 1314–1347
Charles IV (Luxemburg), 1347–1378
Wenceslas (Luxemburg), 1378–1400
Rupert (Wittelsbach), 1400–1410
Sigismund (Luxemburg), 1410–1437

HAPSBURG DYNASTY

Albert II, 1438–1439
Frederick III, 1440–1493
Maximilian I, 1493–1519
Charles V, 1519–1556
Ferdinand I, 1556–1564
Maximilan II, 1564–1576
Rudolf II, 1576–1612
Matthias, 1612–1619
Ferdinand II, 1619–1637
Ferdinand III, 1637–1657
Leopold I, 1658–1705
Joseph I, 1705–1711
Charles VI, 1711–1740
Charles VII (not a Hapsburg), 1742–1745
Francis I, 1745–1765
Joseph II, 1765–1790
Leopold II, 1790–1792
Francis II, 1792–1806

Rulers of France from Hugh Capet

CAPETIAN KINGS

Hugh Capet, 987–996
Robert II, 996–1031
Henry I, 1031–1060
Philip I, 1060–1108
Louis VI, 1108–1137
Louis VII, 1137–1180
Philip II (Augustus), 1180–1223
Louis VIII, 1223–1226
Louis IX, 1226–1270
Philip III, 1270–1285
Philip IV, 1285–1314
Louis X, 1314–1316
Philip V, 1316–1322
Charles IV, 1322–1328

HOUSE OF VALOIS

Philip VI, 1328–1350
John, 1350–1364
Charles V, 1364–1380
Charles VI, 1380–1422
Charles VII, 1422–1461
Louis XI, 1461–1483
Charles VIII, 1483–1498
Louis XII, 1498–1515
Francis I, 1515–1547

Henry II, 1547–1559
Francis II, 1559–1560
Charles IX, 1560–1574
Henry III, 1574–1589

BOURBON DYNASTY

Henry IV, 1589–1610
Louis XIII, 1610–1643
Louis XIV, 1643–1715
Louis XV, 1715–1774
Louis XVI, 1774–1792

AFTER 1792

First Republic, 1792–1799
Napoleon Bonaparte, First Consul, 1799–1804
Napoleon I, Emperor, 1804–1814
Louis XVIII (Bourbon dynasty), 1814–1824
Charles X (Bourbon dynasty), 1824–1830
Louis Philippe, 1830–1848
Second Republic, 1848–1852
Napoleon III, Emperor, 1852–1870
Third Republic, 1870–1940
Pétain regime, 1940–1944
Provisional government, 1944–1946
Fourth Republic, 1946–1958
Fifth Republic, 1958–

Rulers of England

ANGLO-SAXON KINGS

Egbert, 802–839
Ethelwulf, 839–858
Ethelbald, 858–860
Ethelbert, 860–866
Ethelred, 866–871
Alfred the Great, 871–900
Edward the Elder, 900–924
Ethelstan, 924–940
Edmund I, 940–946
Edred, 946–955
Edwy, 955–959
Edgar, 959–975

Edward the Martyr, 975–978
Ethelred the Unready, 978–1016
Canute, 1016–1035 (Danish Nationality)
Harold I, 1035–1040
Hardicanute, 1040–1042
Edward the Confessor, 1042–1066
Harold II, 1066

ANGLO-NORMAN KINGS

William I (the Conqueror), 1066–1087
William II, 1087–1100
Henry I, 1100–1135
Stephen, 1135–1154

Angevin Kings

Henry II, 1154–1189
Richard I, 1189–1199
John, 1199–1216
Henry III, 1216–1272
Edward I, 1272–1307
Edward II, 1307–1327
Edward III, 1327–1377
Richard II, 1377–1399

House of Lancaster

Henry IV, 1399–1413
Henry V, 1413–1422
Henry VI, 1422–1461

House of York

Edward IV, 1461–1483
Edward V, 1483
Richard III, 1483–1485

Tudor Sovereigns

Henry VII, 1485–1509
Henry VIII, 1509–1547
Edward VI, 1547–1553
Mary, 1553–1558
Elizabeth I, 1558–1603

Stuart Kings

James I, 1603–1625
Charles I, 1625–1649

Commonwealth and Protectorate, 1649–1659

Later Stuart Monarchs

Charles II, 1660–1685
James II, 1685–1688
William III and Mary II, 1689–1694
William III alone, 1694–1702
Anne, 1702–1714

House of Hanover

George I, 1714–1727
George II, 1727–1760
George III, 1760–1820
George IV, 1820–1830
William IV, 1830–1837
Victoria, 1837–1901

House of Saxe-Coburg-Gotha

Edward VII, 1901–1910
George V, 1910–1917

House of Windsor

George V, 1917–1936
Edward VIII, 1936
George VI, 1936–1952
Elizabeth II, 1952–

Prominent Popes

Silvester I, 314–335
Leo I, 440–461
Gelasius I, 492–496
Gregory I, 590–604
Nicholas I, 858–867
Silvester II, 999–1003
Leo IX, 1049–1054
Nicholas II, 1058–1061
Gregory VII, 1073–1085
Urban II, 1088–1099
Paschal II, 1099–1118
Alexander III, 1159–1181

Innocent III, 1198–1216
Gregory IX, 1227–1241
Boniface VIII, 1294–1303
John XXII, 1316–1334
Nicholas V, 1447–1455
Pius II, 1458–1464
Alexander VI, 1492–1503
Julius II, 1503–1513
Leo X, 1513–1521
Adrian VI, 1522–1523
Clement VII, 1523–1534
Paul III, 1534–1549

Paul IV, 1555–1559
Gregory XIII, 1572–1585
Gregory XVI, 1831–1846
Pius IX, 1846–1878
Leo XIII, 1878–1903
Pius X, 1903–1914
Benedict XV, 1914–1922

Pius XI, 1922–1939
Pius XII, 1939–1958
John XXIII, 1958–1963
Paul VI, 1963–1978
John Paul I, 1978
John Paul II, 1978-

Rulers of Austria and Austria-Hungary

*Maximilian I (Archduke), 1493–1519
*Charles I (Charles V in the Holy Roman Empire), 1519–1556
*Ferdinand I, 1556–1564
*Maximilian II, 1564–1576
*Rudolph II, 1576–1612
*Matthias, 1612–1619
*Ferdinand II, 1619–1637
*Ferdinand III, 1637–1657
*Leopold I, 1658–1705
*Joseph I, 1705–1711
*Charles VI, 1711–1740
Maria Theresa, 1740–1780

*Joseph II, 1780–1790
*Leopold II, 1790–1792
*Francis II, 1792–1835 (Emperor of Austria as Francis I after 1804)
Ferdinand I, 1835–1848
Francis Joseph, 1848–1916 (after 1867 Emperor of Austria and King of Hungary)
Charles I, 1916–1918 (Emperor of Austria and King of Hungary)
Republic of Austria, 1918–1938 (dictatorship after 1934)
Republic restored, under Allied occupation, 1945–1956
Free Republic, 1956–

*Also bore title of Holy Roman Emperor.

Rulers of Prussia and Germany

*Frederick I, 1701–1713
*Frederick William I, 1713–1740
*Frederick II (the Great), 1740–1786
*Frederick William II, 1786–1797
*Frederick William III, 1797–1840
*Frederick William IV, 1840–1861
*William I, 1861–1888 (German Emperor after 1871)

Frederick III, 1888
William II, 1888–1918
Weimar Republic, 1918–1933
Third Reich (Nazi Dictatorship), 1933–1945
Allied occupation, 1945–1952
Division into Federal Republic of Germany in west and German Democratic Republic in east, 1949–

*Kings of Prussia.

Rulers of Russia

Ivan III, 1462–1505
Basil III, 1505–1533
Ivan IV, 1533–1584
Theodore I, 1584–1598
Boris Godunov, 1598–1605

Theodore II, 1605
Basil IV, 1606–1610
Michael, 1613–1645
Alexius, 1645–1676
Theodore III, 1676–1682

Ivan V and Peter I, 1682–1689
Peter I (the Great), 1689–1725
Catherine I, 1725–1727
Peter II, 1727–1730
Anna, 1730–1740
Ivan VI, 1740–1741
Elizabeth, 1741–1762
Peter III, 1762

Catherine II (the Great), 1762–1796
Paul, 1796–1801
Alexander I, 1801–1825
Nicholas I, 1825–1855
Alexander II, 1855–1881
Alexander III, 1881–1894
Nicholas II, 1894–1917
Soviet Republic, 1917–

Rulers of Italy

Victor Emmanuel II, 1861–1878
Humbert I, 1878–1900
Victor Emmanuel III, 1900–1946
Fascist Dictatorship, 1922–1943
  (maintained in northern Italy until 1945)

Humbert II, May 9–June 13, 1946
Republic, 1946–

Rulers of Spain

Ferdinand {
  and Isabella, 1479–1504
  and Philip I, 1504–1506
  and Charles I, 1506–1516
}
Charles I (Holy Roman Emperor Charles V),
  1516–1556
Philip II, 1556–1598
Philip III, 1598–1621
Philip IV, 1621–1665
Charles II, 1665–1700
Philip V, 1700–1746
Ferdinand VI, 1746–1759
Charles III, 1759–1788
Charles IV, 1788–1808

Ferdinand VII, 1808
Joseph Bonaparte, 1808–1813
Ferdinand VII (restored), 1814–1833
Isabella II, 1833–1868
Republic, 1868–1870
Amadeo, 1870–1873
Republic, 1873–1874
Alfonso XII, 1874–1885
Alfonso XIII, 1886–1931
Republic, 1931–1939
Fascist Dictatorship, 1939-1975
Juan Carlos I, 1975-

Principal Rulers of India

Chandragupta (Maurya Dynasty), c. 332–298 B.C.
Asoka (Maurya Dynasty), c. 273–232 B.C.
Vikramaditya (Gupta Dynasty), 375–413 A.D.
Harsha (Vardhana Dynasty), 606–648
Babur (Mogul Dynasty), 1526–1530
Akbar (Mogul Dynasty), 1556–1605
Jahangir (Mogul Dynasty), 1605–1627
Shah Jahan (Mogul Dynasty), 1627–1658

Aurangzeb (Mogul Dynasty), 1658–1707
Regime of British East India Company, 1757–1858
British *raj*, 1858–1947
Division into self-governing dominions of India
  and Pakistan, 1947
Republic of India, 1950–
Republic of Pakistan, 1956–
Republic of Bangladesh, 1971–

Dynasties of China

Hsia, c. 2205–1766 B.C. (?)
Shang (Yin), c. 1766 (?)–1100 B.C.
Chou, c. 1100–256 B.C.
Ch'in, 221–207 B.C.
Han (Former), 206 B.C.–8 A.D.
Interregnum (Wang Mang, usurper), 8–23 A.D.
Han (Later), 25–220
Wei, 220–265
Tsin (Chin), 265–420
Southern Dynasties: Sung (Liu Sung), Ch'i, Liang, Ch'eñ, 420–589

Northern Dynasties: Northern Wei, Western Wei, Eastern Wei, Northern Ch'i, Northern Chou, 386–581
Sui, 589–618
T'ang, 618–907
Five Dynasties: Later Liang, Later T'ang, Later Tsin, Later Han, Later Chou, 907–960
Sung, 960–1279
Yuän (Mongol), 1279–1368
Ming, 1368–1644
Ch'ing (Manchu) Dynasty, 1644–1912

Periods of Chinese Rule

Chinese Republic, 1912–1949

Communist Regime, 1949–

Periods of Japanese Rule

Legendary Period, c. 660 B.C.–530 A.D.
Foundation Period, 530–709 A.D.
Taika (Great Reform) Period, 645–654
Nara Period, 710–793
Heian Period, 794–1192
Kamakura Period, 1192–1333
Namboku-cho ("Northern and Southern Dynasties") Period, 1336–1392

Muromachi (Ashikaga) Period, 1392–1568
Sengoku ("Country at War") Period, c. 1500–1600
Sengoku Period, c. 1500–1600
Edo (Tokugawa) Period, 1603–1867
Meiji Period (Mutsuhito), 1868–1912
Taisho Period (Yoshihito), 1912–1926
Showa Period (Hirohito), 1926–

Rulers of Principal African States

Ewuare the Great, Oba of Benin, 1440–1473
Muhammad Runfa, King of Kano, 1463–1499
Afonso I, King of Kongo, 1506–1543
Ibrahim Maje, King of Katsina, 1549–1567
Idris Alooma, Mai of Bornu, 1569–ca. 1619
Osei Tutu, King of Asante, ca. 1670–1717
Agaja, King of Dahomey, 1708–1740
Sayyid Said, ruler of Zanzibar and Muscat, 1804–1856
Shaka, King of the Zulu, 1818–1828
Moshesh, King of Basutoland, 1824–1868
Menelik, King of Shoa, 1865–1889; Emperor of Ethiopia, 1889–1913
Haile Selassie, Emperor of Ethiopia, 1930–1974
H. F. Verwoerd, Prime Minister of South Africa, 1958–1966

Gamal Abdul Nasser, President of Egypt, 1956–1970
Leopold Sedar Senghor, President of Senegal, 1960–
Felix Houphouet-Boigny, President of the Ivory Coast, 1960–
Kwame Nkrumah, President of Ghana, 1960–1966
Julius K. Nyerere, President of Tanzania, 1962–
Jomo Kenyatta, President of Kenya, 1964–1978
Sese Seko Mobutu, President of Zaire, 1965–
Houari Boumedienne, head of Algeria, 1965–1978
Anwar el Sadat, President of Egypt, 1970–
Agostinho Neto, President of Angola, 1975–1979
Olusegun Obasanjo, head of Nigeria, 1975–1979
P. W. Botha, Prime Minister of South Africa, 1978–
Robert Mugabe, Prime Minister of Zimbabwe, 1980–

ILLUSTRATIONS IN COLOR

(Illustrations appear facing or following the pages indicated)

ILLUSTRATIONS IN THE TEXT

Index

Guide to Pronunciation

The sounds represented by the diacritical marks used in this Index are illustrated by the following common words:

āle	ēve	īce	ōld	ūse	bo͞ot
ăt	ĕnd	ĭll	ŏf	ŭs	fo͝ot
fătality	ēvent		ôbey	ûnite	
câre			fôrm	ûrn	
ärm					
ȧsk					

Vowels that have no diacritical marks are to be pronounced "neutral," for example: Aegean = ē-je'an, Basel = bäz'el, Basil = bă'zil, common = kŏm'on, Alcaeus = ăl-sē'us. The combinations ou and oi are pronounced as in "out" and "oil."

864, 865, 870, 900
Alexander II, tsar of Russia, 991
Alexander III, tsar of Russia, 991–92, 994
Alexander the Great, 45, 67, 73, 79, 106, 133, 213, 214, 217, 223, 229, 243, 266, 304
career of, 186–87
death of, 186, 211, 212
Alexandra, Tsarina, 1063, 1084
Alexandria, port of, 215, 216–17, 220, 223, 224, 225, 255, 283, 290, 307, 308, 944
Alexius Comnenus (à-lĕk′sĭ-ŭs kŏm-nē′nŭs), Emperor, 361, 365, 447
Al-Farabi (ăl-fär-äb′ē), 380
Alfred the Great, 392, 395, 425
algebra, 382
Algeria, 346, 881, 943
Algerian war, 1274–75, 1343
Ali (son-in-law of Muhammad), 375, 377
alienation, 859
Allah (ăl′ȧ), 371, 372, 523
see also Islam; Muslims
alliances, policy of, 865–66, 868, 1000–1, 1002, 1004, 1058
All-China People's Congress, 1296
Allende (ä-yĕn′dä), Salvador, 1168–69, 1170
Alliance for Progress, 1179
Alliance Society (China), 1023, 1024
All's Well That Ends Well (Shakespeare), 593
Alliance without Allies: The Mythology of Progress in Latin America (Alba), 1141
Allied Council for Japan, 1317
Almagest (Ptolemy of Alexandria), 224
Almoravids (Berber Muslims), 544–45
Alooma, Mai Idris, 549
alphabet, 106, 684, 1244
invention of, 36
Phoenician, 106
Alphonso XIII, king of Spain, 688
Alps, 239, 578, 580
Alsace (ăl′zás′), 687, 824, 910, 1003, 1066, 1070, 1071
altruism, 162
Alva, Duke of, 631
Álvarez, Juan, 1159
Alvarez, Luis Echeverría, 1164
Amazon River, 1165
Ambrose, St., 293–94, 387
Amenhotep IV, Pharaoh, 33
American Civil War, 547, 839, 915–16, 999, 1361, 1372
American colonies, 671, 778
American Indians, 14, 658, 1142
American Revolution, 672, 699, 776, 1041, 1196
Amin, Idi, 1282
Amnesty International, 1173
Amon-Re (a′mĕn-rā), 30, 32, 33
Amorites, 50–51
Amos (prophet), 82, 83, 85–86
Amritsar (ūm-rĭt′sȧr) massacre, 1216, 1217
Amsterdam, 637, 640
Amur River, 738, 1020
Anabaptist movement, 617–18

Anabasis of Alexander (Arrian), 211
Anagni, papal residence at, 446–47
Analects (Confucius), 158
anarchism, 190, 956, 960, 992
Anatolia, 1075, 1244, 1247
Anaxagoras (ăn′ăk-săg′ŏr-as), 207
Anaximander (ăn-ăk′sĭ-măn′der), 187, 194
Anaximenes (ăn′ăk-sĭm′en-éz), 187
ancestor worship, 339
Ancien régime (än-syĕn′ rā-zhĕm′), 787–93
Andaman Islands, 109
Andean Highland, 1141
Andean Pact, 1172
Angelus, The (Millet), 855
Angkor Wat (ăng′kôr wät) temple, 316
Anglican Church, 590, 624, 625, 664–65, 667, 668, 670, 671, 868, 885
Anglo-Catholics, 625
Anglo-Chinese War of 1839–1842, 1014, 1015
Anglo-Egyptian Treaty of Friendship and Alliance, 1248, 1249
Anglo-Japanese Alliance of 1902, 1039–40
Anglo-Persian Oil Company, 1261
Anglo-Saxons, 291, 387, 388, 389, 390, 391–92, 394, 395
Angola, 759, 946, 1341
independence, 1272
Angolan civil war, 1272
Animal Farm (Orwell), 1106
animals, domestication of, 12, 14
Ankara, Turkey, 1247
Ankole kingdom, 553
Anna Comnena, Princess, 365
Anna Karenina (Tolstoy), 972
Annam, 315
annates, 610
Anne, queen of England, 672, 673
Anne, St., 612
Antarctica, 1196
antibiotics, 1376
anticlericalism, 969, 985–86, 1158
Anti-Corn Law League, 874
Antigone (Sophocles), 198
Antigua, 1341
Antimonopoly Law (Japan), 1318
Antioch, 216, 283, 290, 362, 374
capture of (1098), 450, 451
Antiochus (ăn-tĭ′ŏ-kŭs) IV Epiphanes, 213
anti-Semitism, 450, 680, 985, 986, 1096, 1102, 1268
Antoninus Pius (ăn′tŏ-nī′nŭs pī′ŭs), Emperor, 249
Antonioni, Michelangelo, 1369
An-yang, 142
Apartheid (u-pärt′hĭt′) policy, 1269–70, 1271
Aphrodite (ăf′rŏ-dī′tĕ), 173, 236
Aphrodite of Melos (Venus de Milo), 223
Apocalyptic Vision, The (El Greco), 588
Apocrypha (a-pŏk′rĭ-fà), 85
Apollo, 313
Apology (Plato), 191
appeasement, policy of, 1120–21
Apuleius (ăp′ū-lē′yŭs), 252
Aqaba (ăk-à-bá′), port of, 1250

Aquinas (à-kwī′năs), St. Thomas, 459–60, 469–70, 508, 563, 607, 608
Aquitaine, province of, 503
Arabia, 76, 215, 258, 321, 359, 374, 531, 1044, 1244
Arabian-American Oil Company (Aramco), 1258, 1259
Arabian Desert, 76
Arabian Nights, 309, 377
Arabic language, 358, 379, 385, 453, 466
Arabian Sea, 308, 314–15
Arabic numerals, 308, 382, 385
Arab-Israeli War of 1956, 1249–50
Arab-Israeli War of 1967 (Six Day War), 1250
Arab-Israeli War of 1973 (Yom Kippur War), 1250, 1257
Arab League, 1264
Arab oil embargo (1973–1974), 1260, 1266
Arabs, 18, 46, 50, 301, 304, 308, 317, 324, 359, 370, 385, 388, 421, 527, 530, 544, 736, 741, 753
see also Islamic civilization
byzantine invasions, 359–60
conversion to Islam, 369–75
North Africa invasions, 345–46
slave trade, 1044
Aragon, 435, 445, 446, 453, 497, 507
Arbenz, Jacobo, 1175
Arcadians, 207
Archaeology of Ancient China, The (Chang), 146
Archaic period, 176
Archangel, port of, 681–82
archbishop, rank of, 282
archeologists, 4
Archimedes (är′kĭ-mē′dēz) of Syracuse, 225, 232, 596
architecture, see art and architecture
Arctic, 12, 13, 1196
Arctic Circle, 17
Argentina, 827, 1144, 1153, 1158, 1180
fascism, 1171–72
independence of, 1152
political history (twentieth century), 1170–73
population of, 1157, 1161
World War I, 1171
Argos, 176, 177
Arian Christians, 281, 282, 289, 292, 387
Ariosto, Ludovico, 570
Aristarchus (är′ĭs-tär′kŭs) of Samos, 223
aristocracy, 326, 338, 340–41, 493, 500, 501, 505, 506, 749, 1148, 1155, 1181
see also names of monarchs
Aristophanes (är′ĭs-tŏf′à-nēz), 198, 221
Aristotelianism, 296, 470, 471
Aristotle, 16, 171, 190, 207, 223, 244, 296, 365, 380, 381, 385, 466, 469, 475, 563, 613
philosophy of, 192–94
Ark of the Covenant, 81
Arkwright, Richard, 817, 821
Arameans (är′à-mē′anz), 60
Armenia, 1074, 1075, 1244
Armstrong, Neil, 1377
Arnold, Matthew, 970
Arouet, François Marie, see Voltaire

iv